For Margaret (For John)
With My Thanks for
many years of your help
and friendship
              Gage Mitchell

STATESMAN

STATESMAN

GEORGE MITCHELL AND THE ART OF THE POSSIBLE

Douglas Rooks

Camden, Maine

Published by Down East Books
An imprint of The Rowman & Littlefield Publishing Group, Inc.
4501 Forbes Boulevard, Suite 200, Lanham, Maryland 20706
www.rowman.com

Unit A, Whitacre Mews, 26-34 Stannary Street, London SE11 4AB, United Kingdom

Distributed by NATIONAL BOOK NETWORK

Interior photographs courtesy of the George J. Mitchell Dept. of Special Collections & Archives, Bowdoin College Library

MAINE ARTS COMMISSION This publication funded in part by a grant from the Maine Arts Commission, an independent state agency supported by the National Endowment for the Arts.

British Library Cataloguing in Publication Information Available

Library of Congress Cataloging-in-Publication Data
Names: Rooks, Douglas, 1953– author.
Title: Statesman : George Mitchell and the art of the possible / Douglas Rooks.
Description: Camden, Maine : Down East Books, 2016. | Includes index.
Identifiers: LCCN 2016006454 (print) | LCCN 2016012669 (ebook) | ISBN
     9781608933976 (cloth : alk. paper) | ISBN 9781608933983 (electronic)
Subjects: LCSH: Mitchell, George J. (George John), 1933– | Legislators—United
     States—Biography. | United States. Congress. Senate—Biography. | United
     States—Politics and government—1981–1989. | United States—Politics and
     government—1989–1993. | United States—Politics and government—1993–2001.
Classification: LCC E840.8.M545 R66 2016 (print) | LCC E840.8.M545 (ebook) |
     DDC 328.73/092—dc23
LC record available at http://lccn.loc.gov/2016006454

∞™ The paper used in this publication meets the minimum requirements of American National Standard for Information Sciences—Permanence of Paper for Printed Library Materials, ANSI/NISO Z39.48-1992.

Printed in the United States of America

For Janine,

who listens to all my stories

CONTENTS

INTRODUCTION *BY SENATOR ANGUS KING*   1

PROLOGUE   5

1   GROWING UP IN WATERVILLE   7

2   BRUNSWICK, BERLIN, AND WASHINGTON   24

3   A PARTY'S PROGRESS   34

4   A POLITICAL BAPTISM   51

5   INSIDE THE DEMOCRATIC PARTY   67

6   THE BIG TIME   80

7   A RARE OPPORTUNITY   104

8   FROM THE BAR TO THE BENCH   123

9   THE SENATE   142

10   REDEMPTION   158

11   OUTSIDE THE BELTWAY   185

12   THE SENATOR AND THE COLONEL   201

13   THE YEAR OF TWO ELECTIONS   220

14   TAKING IT TO THE TOP   238

CONTENTS

15   **THE BEDROCK OF GOVERNMENT**   265

16   **ENVIRONMENT IN THE BALANCE**   292

17   **WORLD VIEW**   322

18   **WHAT AILS THE PATIENT**   350

19   **SENATOR FROM MAINE**   375

20   **TWILIGHT**   404

21   **A PEACE THAT PASSES UNDERSTANDING**   429

22   **THE UNENDING CONFLICT**   451

23   **THE WORLD OF PROFIT**   474

24   **PASTIMES**   495

25   **LEGACY**   517

AFTERWORD   529

ACKNOWLEDGMENTS   533

BIBLIOGRAPHY   535

INDEX   545

INTRODUCTION

When I was a young committee staffer in the United States Senate more than forty years ago, I noticed an interesting thing: It mattered who showed up. The outcome of a committee session was almost completely determined by the passions, prejudices, perseverance, and personality of the individual members (and their staffers) who were in the room and engaged in the proceedings.

This may sound a little obvious, but my somewhat naive assumption going in was that public policy was largely predetermined by outside forces, and was like a big wheel, slowly grinding on its inevitable way, without much reference to the people involved. Outside forces—the issues which engaged public interest at the moment, the evolution of ideas, economic and cultural conditions, political realities—all played a major role in the discussion and debate, of course, but it was the flesh-and-blood protagonists at the table who made particular policies happen.

So if the people were important, what made them so? What were the qualities and characteristics which made some effective—and some less so—in imposing their will on the process? In short, what is leadership and how do we learn to practice it?

A lifetime of thinking about these questions (and ten years of trying to teach them at Bowdoin and Bates Colleges) has led me to several conclusions. The first is that leadership is not magic, not some mysterious elixir which, if drunk at birth, instills the ability to move people in one direction or another. It is, instead, a complicated series of personality and character traits which, when found in the right combination at the right time, can make a business successful, lead to victory on the battlefield, or even bend the arc of history.

The first question—what is leadership—is hard and has many answers, depending upon the demands of the times and the circumstances. But the second—how do we learn to practice it—is easier and brings me to this important book.

The best way to learn anything is by experience. The word "hot" didn't mean much to our son until he touched a light bulb; after doing so, he understood its meaning all too well. Of course, we can't directly experience all the challenges and circumstances which formed Lincoln, Churchill, or Bill Belichick, but we can study their personalities, their decisions, and the personal histories which formed them. History is, in reality, nothing more than condensed experience—and it is a powerful and indispensible teacher.

In the pages which follow, Doug Rooks is the ever-present observer who not only recounts the exceptional life of his subject, but also analyzes and interprets so that the book not only informs, but also teaches. In this sense, the book is as much leadership manual as biography; George Mitchell is not only subject, but becomes mentor as well.

Doug is that rare journalist who moves easily between reporter and columnist (both of which he has been over the years), the latter giving context and depth to people and events. I believe it also helps that Doug has his roots in Maine, for the story of George Mitchell is deeply intertwined with mid-twentieth-century Maine and the sense of the possible that imbued that era's politics.

The (hi)story of any leader begins at home, in the earliest days. And the first chapter of this book explains a lot about George Mitchell—his competitiveness, his intellect (which manifested itself in an early addiction to comic books, which I have noticed also in the early years of some of my brightest friends), his deep appreciation of the struggles of ordinary people, his pluck (there's no other word for someone who hitchhikes to his first—and only—college interview), his understanding of the importance of others in helping him along his journey, and his lifelong experience of the *opportunity* at the heart of the American idea.

I have found over the years that "self-made" success stories—people who rise to great heights from humble beginnings—seem to fall into two categories. The first are those who think they did it all by themselves and have little sympathy for anyone caught in their former circumstances. The government, which provided a free education, the infrastructure of daily life, and basic security through the system of laws and rules which allowed them to rise, is suddenly the enemy, especially as it tries to help the next generation of upward strivers.

The second group, however, are people like George Mitchell, who fondly recalls lessons from his immigrant(!) mother who worked the night shift in textile mills her whole life, the local businessman who steered him to college, and the mentor in Ed Muskie who taught him the power of politics to make real the promise of American life. It's no coincidence that when he decided to leave the Senate, George chose to devote his unspent campaign funds and a considerable share of his personal energy and commitment to providing scholarships to Maine kids who might not otherwise make it to college. Perfect.

George Mitchell is a leader by any definition; few of us will ever match his achievements. But by sharing in his experience, as we do through this extraordinary book, we can learn something important—not only about leadership, but perhaps just as importantly, about our country as well.

Senator Angus King
Brunswick, Maine

PROLOGUE

If you stand on the Two Cent Bridge across the Kennebec River today, looking north, you survey a vanished industrial past. On the east bank, the Winslow side, lie the brick and stone buildings of the Hollingsworth & Whitney mill, later Scott Paper Co., which shut down in 1997. On the west bank is downtown Waterville and the old Maine Central railroad yards, once a major rail hub. The bridge is quiet. On a winter day, it's rare to see anyone cross, but in 1933, the year George Mitchell was born, it was thronged every day with mill workers crossing to Winslow from the tenements built right down to the foul-smelling river, each paying the toll reflected in the name.

The old campus of Colby College extended north along the west bank, hemmed in between the river and the railroad yard. The Boys Club was there, too, and the skating pond next door that provided daily recreation for the Mitchell children each winter.

Colby moved two miles west, to Mayflower Hill, starting in 1937, leaving behind the railroad and the stench and the noise. The Lebanese community that lived among the tenements lining two narrow streets, Head of Falls and King Court, stayed longer—some of them until the buildings were torn down through Waterville's urban renewal federal grant program. Most of the college buildings disappeared, too, with only a handful remaining, contiguous to the downtown. In 1939, the growing Mitchell family moved uphill, to 94 Front Street, a house that still stands.

The mills are long silent, but the river has been reborn, in large part through the efforts of Mitchell's political mentor, Senator Ed Muskie, who wrote the original Clean Water and Clean Air acts, the nation's most important environmental laws. They were last renewed when Mitchell was Senate majority leader, yet still leave a large imprint.

The dams are still there, though smaller ones nearby have been removed, and alewives now swim up the Sebasticook River, a tributary stream. There's a faint hum at the power plant on the Winslow side, a reminder that hydroelectricity once formed the backbone of the power grid throughout the state.

The suspension bridge sways almost imperceptibly as a March breeze rises. The water creates a gentle din, and the current glints and shimmers in the sunlight. George Mitchell's mother, who emigrated from Lebanon when she was eighteen, worked at the mills on the Waterville side six days a week, joining the night shift in textile mills where the noise of the looms was deafening and the floors slippery from lubricating oil. She was seeking a better life for her children, and she found it.

1

GROWING UP IN WATERVILLE

Paul Mitchell's first memory of his brother George is of sledding down the steep hillside above the street they lived on, King Court. The tenements were built almost to the edge of the Kennebec River, which was frozen in winter but treacherous to traverse. There were fences and posts that prevented anyone from overshooting down the hill to the water, but it still wasn't easy navigating the sled on the icy hill.

George, four years old at the time, remembers egging on his older brother, who had a friend aboard and was reluctant to add another passenger. "I begged and begged," he recalls now, and continued even after Paul, then eleven, told him the sled was too small. Paul eventually let George climb on up front, while he sat behind his two passengers, steering with his feet. Down they went, but the overloaded sled veered out of control, striking a fence. George flew into a metal pole and broke his leg in several places, ending up in a hip-to-ankle cast that drew plenty of attention, and left him on "little baby crutches" the rest of the winter.

It is characteristic that both brothers still take responsibility for the accident—George, for his "cajoling," and Paul, for neglecting his duty as the older sibling. "I caught a lot of flak for it," he recalls, about his parents' reaction. Their sister Barbara remembers that their father forbade them from ever sledding there again, much to her chagrin.

George Mitchell Jr. was born at home on August 20, 1933, at a time when Waterville was a clangorous place. Though it was the pit of the Great Depression—Franklin Roosevelt had taken the oath as president just a few months earlier—the neighborhood included the rail yards of the Maine Central's maintenance sheds, with a constant shunting of trains. Both banks of the Kennebec were dotted with the great paper and textile mills. A Democrat had just been elected Maine's governor in the FDR landslide, an event that was not to be repeated for another two decades as Maine returned to its Republican "normalcy." Mitchell himself, a Democrat like all of his family, didn't display any interest in politics as a career until he was nearly thirty.

Mitchell was part of a large and growing family. His parents were George John Mitchell Sr., born to an Irish immigrant family in Boston, but adopted and raised by an older Lebanese couple in Waterville, and Mintaha Saad, born in Bkassine, a small Lebanese town, who emigrated at age eighteen and ended up living in a house next door to her future husband. Mintaha took the name Mary, although her grandchildren called her by the Arabic nickname for grandmother, Sittoo, while George Sr. was Jiddoo.

Mary and George had five children. Paul, the eldest, and John, later known as "Swisher" for his feats on the basketball court, were born in Westfield, Massachusetts, in 1926 and 1927. The family returned to Waterville, in part to take care of George Sr.'s aging parents, and after a gap in the birth order that may have included several miscarriages, had a son, Edward, who died shortly after birth. Robert, known as Robbie, was born in 1932, George Jr. a year later, and Barbara in 1935. The sons and daughter followed a similar pattern, moving away for college and employment, then returning to Waterville to marry and raise families. Even today, all the surviving Mitchells live in Waterville except for George, who left in 1950 to attend Bowdoin College and never returned, though he has been a constant visitor.

In January 2014, Mitchell, age eighty, who never served in state government, though, as he said, "not for the lack of trying," had his portrait installed at the State House. Addressing a joint session of the Legislature and surveying the packed balconies, filled mostly by the Mitchell clan, he extemporized by thanking "my *very* large, and supportive family."

The five children of Mary and George gave their parents seventeen grandchildren and thirty-nine great-grandchildren, most of whom have worked on at least one Mitchell campaign. Even more than most public figures, George Mitchell has relied on his family for his foundation and values. Robbie's widow, Janet, described the clan she married into as "large and loving and very chaotic," and said of George, "He's had a lot of support and he knows it. He does a lot for his family because his family did a lot for him."

The house where George Mitchell was born no longer exists. The two blocks of tenements were torn down and the site is now vacant, a product of the urban renewal grants from 1962 to 1973, of which Waterville was a major recipient. Today, the riverside location would be an attraction for sportsmen and condo dwellers alike, but not then. Like all the great rivers of Maine, the Kennebec was at the time a toxic stew of chemicals and organic compounds with a variety of distinctive odors, all of them foul. Veterans of the era of unchecked pollution said the pulp mills that produced the raw material for papermaking were worse than the paper mills themselves, but only by a matter of degree. Upriver in Skowhegan, the sulfurous compounds turned clapboarded buildings black.

"When you were on the water, that was the bottom in terms of housing," Mitchell recalls. "My grandfather, my father's adoptive father, had this little house really just within feet of the base of the Two Cent Bridge. You were right on the river, you could have jumped out and jumped in the water, and it smelled to high heaven. There were two distinct odors. One was the rotten egg smell, which was the dominant one. But there was also a very strong sulfur smell." Even in the 1970s, after the monumental legislation written by Mitchell's political mentor, Senator Ed Muskie—the Clean Water Act of 1972—had begun to take hold, the water still turned various colors after mill discharges, though the smell had largely abated. Muskie often told audiences one reason he went to Washington was to convince Congress to do what he, as governor, was unable to get the Legislature to tackle—cleaning up Maine's rivers.

At the time, most people thought pollution was a trade-off for the unprecedented prosperity Waterville enjoyed. As Janet Mitchell put it, people called it "the smell of money," and saw it as fair exchange for economic vitality. The annual spring log drives that lasted on the Kennebec until 1976 underlined the notion that this was an industrial river, not a natural resource.

As the Mitchell family grew, the house on King Court became increasingly crowded. After Barbara was born, five children were crammed into a single bedroom—Paul and John in one bed, Robbie and George in another, and Barbara in a crib. "When Barbara was old enough to get out of the crib, my father had no choice," George said. It can't have been easy, even with two parents working, but they found enough money to buy a house two hundred yards up the hill, just across Front Street; the house, in 1939, sold for $2,500, an "almost unimaginable sum," George said.

George Sr. created an upstairs apartment to help pay the mortgage, but with four bedrooms, it must have seemed palatial. Mitchell recalled it was "like going to the Garden of Eden." George and Robbie had one bedroom, Paul and John, another, while Barbara and their parents had their own rooms. The purchase was made through the Federal Home Loan Bank Board, a New Deal agency that spurred home ownership during a time when mortgage down payments were 25 percent, with repayment in five years.

George was six at the time, and though the house was well above the river, it was adjacent to an active rail line that was a primary reason for Colby College's move to Mayflower Hill, which began the same time as the Mitchells' move to Front Street. Freight trains ran close to Robbie and George's bedroom, and the noise was deafening, but the house remained in the family until George and Mary were elderly.

The family's improved circumstances mirrored the fortunes of Waterville, which reached its highest prosperity after World War II. Though Waterville's population never exceeded 25,000, it acquired a certain sophistication and urbanity out of proportion to its size. When Ed Muskie opened his law practice downtown, there were fashionable dress shops with a statewide clientele—one of which employed his future wife, Jane Gray.

Hathaway Shirt had its primary manufacturing plant downriver, below the main bridge to Winslow, housed with the corporate offices in an elegant brick building that became the first of the old mill structures to be reoccupied. Shirt manufacturing continued until 2002. When it closed, C. F. Hathaway was the last production shirt maker in the country. Muskie, and later, George Mitchell and Bill Cohen, who preceded him in office by two years, bought their shirts there when they were upgrading their wardrobes as US senators. Hathaway commissioned advertising featuring an eye-patched executive that became one of the best-known logos of the day. It was considered a model employer, with clean, well-lit sewing floors.

Responding to the National Recovery Act of 1933, Hathaway set a forty-hour work week at a minimum wage of $13 a week—an act hailed by the press and denounced by the economic professors of the day, as Mitchell relates in his book, *Not for America Alone*. The transformation of his hometown helped to make George Sr. a lifelong Democrat who venerated Franklin Delano Roosevelt. It was a faith his son was never to forsake.

Growing up, Barbara remembers Waterville as "a very vibrant place," the same phrase used by Janet, Robbie's widow, who added that Waterville "was very different from what it is today." In 1950, when George Mitchell graduated from Waterville High School, Colby freshmen still lived downtown; the move to Mayflower Hill was not completed until three years later. The old Foss Hall, a striking brick building, was one of the casualties of the move, as all but a handful of the old campus buildings were demolished. Not far from the Mitchell house was the Boys Club, which didn't admit girls until much later. It was not only the after-school gathering place for the neighborhood, but also offered Friday-night dances.

Waterville was then dominated by its ethnic neighborhoods, housing the mill workers who arrived early in the twentieth century. Head of Falls and Front

Street housed about two hundred Lebanese families, many having followed a man named William Abraham, who emigrated to Waterville from Jezzine in 1883. The more numerous Franco (or French-Canadian) clans lived farther south along the river. A sizable number of Jewish families also lived downtown. Young George mixed with all of them as soon as he left parochial school and entered junior high.

The most dramatic change to the downtown came through federal urban renewal grants administered by George's brother, Paul. Over a decade, the program removed dozens of buildings, the bulk of them to create a huge parking lot behind Main Street now known as the Concourse. The demolitions were thought necessary to compete with the burgeoning shopping malls. The Head of Falls tenements were also removed, right down to the lampposts. To this day, nothing except grass and a small parking lot occupies the site where three Mitchell children were born.

While the Lebanese families have since dispersed, the landmarks of the community, St. Joseph's Church and Joseph's Market, remain. Tony Jabar, who was close to both George and Robbie and had seven siblings, summed up his early years by saying, "For us, family was everything."

MARY MITCHELL WAS CONCERNED ABOUT GEORGE, her fourth child, almost from the beginning. He was noticeably smaller than the other boys, and seemed to grow more slowly, too. The young George Mitchell is sometimes described as "sickly," but Mitchell himself believes "frail" is closer to the truth, although still an exaggeration. He had no more childhood illnesses than the others, and attributes his parents' view of him to his early entrance to public school. He was just sixteen when he graduated from high school.

Mary decided on a remedy she knew from growing up in Lebanon: goat's milk. Nearly every Mitchell recalls a goat's milk story, and several wonder how the Mitchells, who didn't own a car, managed to find it. It appears they borrowed a car to go weekly to Clinton, where farmers kept goats. Once the milk was home, it occupied a separate place in the icebox, and George wasn't supposed to know it was special. Mary "would proceed to put the goat's milk into the regular glass bottles, thinking that he would not know the difference," Barbara said. "We were always told we could not touch those particular bottles. . . . George always knew he was drinking goat's milk and not cow's milk, but being such a good boy, he didn't want to upset her and let her think her little trick wasn't working."

Paul remembers their mother "was desperate to put some weight on George," and that "he wasn't a very good eater." John, who as "Swisher" was the high school athletic star, jokes that he wishes he had been offered the goat's milk, "so I could have brains like George Mitchell." As an adult, Mitchell rarely drinks milk of any kind.

The smells of cooking and baking pervaded the Mitchell house. Mary cooked Lebanese dishes for family, relatives, neighbors, and anyone else who came to visit. Jim Mitchell, Robbie and Janet's son, later a State House lobbyist, went to his grandmother's almost every day after school. Kibbeh, a ground-meat wrap, was a favorite, along with loubia, a bean dish, lots of lentils, and zatr, a spicy flat-bread. Tony Jabar prized her baklava. There were grape leaves in the garden to be dried for food wrapping. "I don't remember her opening too many cans," Barbara said. Everyone remembers the smell of bread after school, a food that, unlike milk, remains in George Mitchell's life today. "I still eat way too much of it," he said.

Mary's hospitality was legendary. An electrician once came to the house and she insisted he eat even though he had just had lunch. He later made sure he skipped a meal before arriving. "My mother grew up in a culture in which every guest had to be fed immediately," Mitchell said. "The meter reader, the plumber, the doctor, my mother would absolutely insist they have a meal. She would not take no for an answer." Said Janet of the family, "They were very hospitable to any guest that walked into the house. They enfolded you in their arms, and it's something I've passed down to all my children, nieces, and nephews."

Many children of first-generation Lebanese immigrants say they grew up without encountering "American" food until they were in their teens. Mary passed on her gifts to her daughters-in-law, who in turn taught their children, but not to her daughter, Barbara. "She didn't want me around when she was cooking," Barbara recalls. "She babied me. She'd say, 'You can learn to do these things another time.'"

Mintaha wasn't supposed to stay in America. Her sister, Marium, had immigrated to Waterville with her husband, leaving behind a young daughter. When the time came to be reunited, Mintaha, soon to become Mary, accompanied the young girl after an arranged marriage in Paris apparently fell through. She lived with her sister and brother-in-law in the Head of Falls neighborhood, and, after meeting George Mitchell Sr., decided to stay.

Mary earned her living in the textile mills of Waterville and towns upriver, before and after her marriage. She was a skilled weaver, and went from mill to mill. One was the nearby Wyandotte woolen mill, where she always worked the night shift, arriving home in time to feed her children breakfast and see them off to school.

Paul said his mother sometimes went farther afield for work, including Skow-hegan and Canaan. Closer to home were the American Woolen mill in North

Vassalboro and the Cascade mill in Oakland. The moves were often prompted by periodic shutdowns. "She always had work," George said, "because when one mill would go down, another would be running, and she'd just move to that one." Over the course of forty years, she worked at a dozen textile mills.

One summer Mitchell worked at a textile mill, and he said the floors were so slick with oil that workers had to shuffle from post to post. It was deafening. "You literally could not have a conversation even if you put your mouth right next to a person's ear and talked as loud as you could," he said. "And to think she did that at night for forty years, and raised five kids—she was a very strong and impressive person."

No one seems exactly sure when Mary slept. She must have had a few hours between when the children left for school and she began preparing dinner. Mitchell doesn't remember his father ever doing housework, although those from the neighborhood recall him doing yard work, wearing a broad-brimmed felt hat. "In the custom of the time, he never did anything at home," Mitchell said. "My mother did all the cooking, all the cleaning, all the washing, everything. In that era, husbands didn't help out."

Mary was intensely religious, attending Mass whenever she could; George Sr. was less observant, though he encouraged his children to attend. In a speech about Lebanon Mitchell gave just before leaving the Senate in 1994, he said, "My mother's values were simple and universal: God, family, country. My mother's faith was total and unquestioning, an integral part of her life. . . . Faith was so much a part of her and what she valued that she once described a local Republican candidate as a good man because she saw him often at daily Mass. That provoked my father, a lifelong Democrat, to say that it would take more than a few Masses to get him to vote for a Republican." Cyril Joly, the Republican, eventually became mayor.

GEORGE J. MITCHELL SR. WAS BORN IN BOSTON IN 1900, and placed in an orphanage. It wasn't until years later that the family discovered he was born Michael Joseph Kilroy, the youngest of six children, son of an Irish laborer and a mother who died while giving birth to him. The orphanage stood on the site of the present-day Symphony Hall.

At age four, the nuns accompanied him on one of the "Irish," or "orphan trains" that brought children without families to destinations around New England. In Maine, there were stops in Portland, Waterville, and Bangor, the latter being where Michael, soon to become George, was ushered to the altar rail at St. John's Church and claimed by an elderly couple named Mitchell. They soon moved to Waterville, where they later owned a store. The impromptu adoptions were a now largely forgotten feature of the day, and came to an end with the passage of adoption laws. "Any parishioner who wanted to adopt a child could just take the child and leave with him," Mitchell said. While most adoptees were treated well, some were put to work on farms, becoming more like indentured servants than family members.

Though raised in the Lebanese community, George Sr., who the Kilroys later knew as "Uncle Joe," stood out for his blue eyes and sandy brown hair. "He always knew he was different," said his daughter, Barbara, even though it was many years before the Kilroys initiated contact with him.

His adoptive parents, John and Mary Mitchell, their names anglicized, were Lebanese immigrants who lived in Alexandria, Egypt, before coming to the United States. George was their only child. Arabic was his first language, and he became fluent in English and in French, which he heard every day while working in a logging camp.

His schooling was minimal. It appears he did not attend beyond fourth grade, a circumstance that left him feeling insecure and even helpless through-out his working life. Along with his wife, Mary, he insisted on education as the focus of his children's lives. All five are college graduates, and several have graduate degrees. His facility with languages was often noted. "He spoke better Arabic than some of the Lebanese people living there," said Paul Maroon, Rob-bie's friend. Mary never learned to write English, and spoke it haltingly, though she wrote letters home in Arabic for others in the community.

George Mitchell Sr. was young and single when he spent at least one winter in the logging camp in western Maine. He rarely talked about himself, and his chil-dren didn't know this part of his past until after his death, when a lawyer called Mitchell and told him about his father's early life. The logging crew took the train to Farmington, walked miles into the woods, and stayed until spring. George Sr., as the youngest in camp, got the upper bunk next to the smoke hole in the ceiling.

"It was a cold and miserable winter," Mitchell said. "That was really a tough life." The elder Mitchell must have perfected his French that winter, since the other loggers spoke nothing else.

While the children grew up, their father was a laborer at the gas plant owned by Central Maine Power (CMP), the state's largest utility. Gas for lighting was produced from coal, dirty and unpleasant work, but all that was available to a man with his limited schooling. Ultimately, CMP was required to divest its ownership, and the successor company struggled, eventually shutting down the plant. It was the darkest period of his father's life, as Mitchell recalls it. His brothers were off at college, and he was often alone with his father. They argued. "He became very depressed, silent," Mitchell recalls. "For many people like that, their entire self-esteem is bound up in their work, and to be unemployed for a year after having worked since he was a small boy was very hard for him."

Finally, George Sr. found work as a janitor at Colby College, and "You'd think he'd become president of the college. He loved it," his son recalls. He became head custodian, but Mitchell believes that for most of his life, his father earned less than his mother. He enjoyed seven years of retirement before he died of a heart attack in 1972, before his son's first campaign.

In a commencement speech at Colby, Mitchell recalled the summer he worked on the grounds crew after graduating from Bowdoin College and awaiting US Army induction. "I am especially fond of the lawn in front of Foss Hall, on which I labored so hard," he said. His father, who "loved Colby with an intensity to match that of the most dedicated alumnus," liked to joke about finding a job for his son. "This led my father to suggest that this institution had advanced to the point where you needed a Bowdoin degree to mow the lawns at Colby."

George Sr. had a lifelong respect for education. Barbara remembers his admiration for Donaldson Koons, geology department chairman, who later inspired her to study geology at the University of Maine. "Oftentimes the doors were open, and my father would stand and listen to his lectures time and time again." He would go home to tell his children what he'd learned.

ALL OF THE MITCHELL CHILDREN ATTENDED St. Joseph Maronite School for the primary grades, a two-room school, after which they attended Waterville Junior High and then Waterville High School. The separate parochial schools for the French and Lebanese families created a sense of rivalry, though a relatively mild one. Barbara remembers that during Saturday-afternoon double features at the Opera House, "We all sat on one side, and the French kids on the other." But the two communities merged in the public school system, and differences never extended much beyond name-calling, she said.

George did not stand out with his teachers. His childhood friend, Tony Jabar, remembers him as "a very placid student; he was never outspoken or aggressive." While another friend said he was "very scholarly," few agreed. Mitchell himself said he was an "indifferent student," despite early signs of a keen intelligence. His brother John remembers that George loved to read, but mostly comic books, or funny books, as they were then known. "I think he must have read every single comic book that was ever published," John said. Captain Marvel was a favorite.

That preference lasted until high school, when an English teacher, Elvira Whitten, asked him to stay after class one day. She asked him what he read, and when he said, "Not much," she gave him a book, John Steinbeck's *The Moon Is*

Down, and asked him to read it and provide a report. He stayed up all evening reading. She then gave him another book, *Parnassus on Wheels*, by Christopher Morley. This went on through a dozen or so books until one day, she said, "You can choose your own books now." It began a lifelong habit, which Mitchell said "changed my life." In all the years since, except when he was Senate majority leader, he's always had a book in progress.

Janet Mitchell said Elvira Whitten inspired many students. She recalls writing an autobiography in her sophomore year after being assured, "You could really write what you felt in your heart." Whitten was dying of cancer by Janet's senior year, yet "she corrected every paper, answered any question."

After school, the Boys Club was the place where the neighborhood gathered. All the Mitchells were there except Barbara. She did play pickup baseball, often being chosen in the same round as George. By that time, his older brothers, particularly Paul and John, were "famous athletes," but George was not.

"I developed a real massive inferiority complex for a long time, not being as good in athletics as my brothers," Mitchell said. "I was younger and smaller than most of the kids, because I was born in August and entered school in September, and then skipped a grade." Paul said that he hoped George wouldn't skip any more grades, "because then he'd never make the team." Mitchell did play varsity basketball at Waterville High and at Bowdoin, though in a supporting role.

Unable to match his brothers in athletics, George took up cribbage, which ultimately featured evening-long tournaments among the four boys. Cribbage was George's passion, according to Janet. Barbara remembers games lasting until midnight that kept her from getting any sleep upstairs. "They fought, they screamed, they yelled," she said, "but they always ended up shaking hands as they left."

ROBBIE WAS CLOSEST IN AGE TO GEORGE, and his constant companion. His future wife, Janet, met him in high school when they were both fifteen, Robbie displaying the same smile all the Mitchell boys were noted for. "I remember he was at the bottom of the stairs and I was coming down the stairs and he was a very handsome young man with a wonderful smile, and I thought, 'That's the one for me.'"

From an early age, Robbie was the family entrepreneur, a tireless promoter who made even the most unlikely scheme seem like enormous fun. School friend Paul Orloff remembers cutting down fir and spruce Christmas trees and bringing them to town to distribute to downtown merchants. The trees sold for $5, and brought $2 each to the young entrepreneurs. Robbie rented a cotton candy machine and convinced Paul Orloff to haul it to the Bangor State

Fair. Soon, summer fairs became a regular circuit, with his brother George and friends providing the labor.

George remembers his brother somehow arranging to bring Emmett Kelly, the famous clown, to Waterville. Later ventures attracted semipro basketball teams and even canine TV star Rin Tin Tin. In the backyard of the Waterville home Robbie bought for his growing family, which eventually included seven children, he built an in-ground swimming pool with family labor. One morning he announced to Janet, "We're going to build a tennis court," and they did.

Mitchell left behind an autobiographical fragment called "My Childhood," apparently written in high school, which is among the few available documents from his youth. In it, he recalls the after-school exploits of himself, Robbie, and Tony Jabar, along with, occasionally, Tony's brother Paul. In one instance, he and Tony, playing "cops and robbers," decided to ambush Paul from a porch where George, then five years old, and Tony were hiding. "As Paulie and Robbie rounded the corner, Tony grabbed a milk bottle and smashed it over Paulie's head. We couldn't understand why Paulie didn't get up. Fifteen minutes before that we had seen the same thing happen to Gene Autry at the Opera House; he hadn't even fallen down." After "a few minutes and about three buckets of water," Paul revived.

The next year, after the move to Front Street, the gang built a makeshift ball field on a nearby vacant lot, including a wire fence Mitchell remembers as "twenty feet high." The boys created a betting pool, contributing a nickel apiece, with the prize going to whoever could drive a ball over the center-field fence. "Paulie Jabar and my brother Robbie were the only boys ever to receive it," he writes.

The gang spent many hours in a vacant, cutover lot, dotted by tree stumps and thickets, that they called "Big Chief," which Mitchell says lay between the Waterville Iron Works and the Kennebec River. In one episode, in shooting at bottles with BB guns along the bank, Paulie lost his balance and went tumbling into the foul water. Another time, playing around the log booms that fueled the Hollingsworth & Whitney paper mill across the river, all of the boys ended up in the river after trying to keep Robbie from sliding in. "Four successive splashes resounded against the swirling current of the Kennebec," Mitchell writes. "Another spanking!"

Other afternoons were spent with Peter, Paul, and Louis Maroon, from another Lebanese family, who lived a block away. Mitchell and Louis, Paul remembers, were the youngest and last to be picked for teams. A later "This Is Your Life" event in 1992 at the chamber of commerce featured Paul reminiscing about "the old Front Street gang."

Paul Orloff, Mitchell's age, but a year behind him in school, says of George, "He was a smart little kid and he was pretty sharp, but he didn't seem to have all the athletic abilities the older boys did, and sometimes the boys would make fun of him."

George and Robbie, just twenty months and a year apart in school, remained close throughout their lives. Mitchell admired his brother's business acumen. After taking time off for military service, Robbie began searching for a job with more regular hours than those he had as a New York Life insurance salesman. He was hired by the Federal Deposit Insurance Corporation in 1957, eventually rising to several senior posts. Toward the end of his career, amid the upheaval of the savings and loan crisis, he became an interim bank president at Pepperell Trust in Biddeford and Olympic Bank in Boston.

By that time, he had been diagnosed with a form of leukemia, myelofibrosis, a rare bone marrow disorder. He kept his sense of humor to the end, dying in 1996, at age sixty-four, while his brother was chairing peace talks in Northern Ireland.

In *Making Peace*, Mitchell's memoir about the talks, he recalls that Robbie, as a high school senior, had been most valuable player when Waterville won another state championship, while the following year George didn't make the varsity team. Over years of public speaking, Mitchell honed and refined these tales until they became staples of his speeches, campaign appearances, and books, often with an appropriate moral or lesson. In *Making Peace*, he chose the moment of his brother's death to relate one of his favorites.

The Boys Club where they both spent countless afternoons closed at nine p.m., and Robbie told George he had obtained "the concession" to clean the place after hours. Robbie was willing to share the profits if George helped clean. As Mitchell tells it, what was initially a ninety-minute shift usually consisted of him sweeping the floors and cleaning the bathrooms while Robbie chatted on the phone with Janet. George got $2.50, and another "concession" at the Maine Employment Commission office next door soon opened up. With the two cleaning jobs, delivering newspapers, and washing cars, he earned $10 a week, "an incredible amount of money for me at the time."

Mitchell later learned, by chance, that Robbie was being paid $15 a week for each of the "concessions," so "he was paying me $5 a week while keeping $25." When he worked up the courage to confront his brother, Robbie told him that he'd taken the initiative, and George would otherwise be earning nothing. Robbie said he promised to split the proceeds, but not fifty-fifty. He said, "I'm management and you're labor, and management always gets paid more." Mitchell remembers thinking, "When I grow up I want to be in management." And while Mitchell always maintained impeccable relations with labor groups, he sought out executive and management positions in government, law, and business.

When Robbie joined the FDIC, he had to hitchhike or take the train to Burlington, Vermont, not having his own vehicle. When George, who was also returning from the military, "saw that Robbie didn't have a car, he *gave* him a car," a green Ford, Janet recalls. George paid $1,700 for the car in Fort Lee, New Jersey. Janet remembers it as "a beautiful, generous act."

JOHN MITCHELL WAS AMONG THE BEST BASKETBALL players Maine has ever produced. The nickname "Swisher," or "Swish," described his elegant shots, and stuck with him all his life; even his grandchildren use it. Although Paul and Robbie also starred on the Waterville High team, Swisher was in a class of his own.

Thomas Nale, a second cousin from Waterville, recalls when Swisher starred in the New England tournament. In the 1944 title game, the underdog Waterville team pulled off a memorable upset. Coach Wally Donovan pioneered a pressing, man-to-man defense, and "a fast-break offense which people never saw. . . . Waterville was all speed." His exploits continued, with Paul, at the University of Rhode Island. Swisher "was a tremendous ball handler," Nale said. "He was the only player in college history to hold Bob Cousy"—the future Boston Celtics star—"under double figures." Cousy and Swisher later became friends. He became the assistant basketball coach at Colby College under the legendary coach Dick Whitmore, a post he held for forty-four years.

From an early age, Swisher and Paul set their sights on sports. Swisher recalls that, when the Ursuline nuns who taught at St. Joseph's put George in a higher grade, the older brothers were concerned, thinking, "Don't move him up any more. . . . He won't be able to play when he gets to high school." George did make the team, but on the varsity he lagged far behind the records of his three brothers. George grew up as Swisher's brother—that was the inevitable introduction wherever they went.

As the oldest, Paul had George's respect from an early age. By the time Paul and John were in high school, they were distant figures; both had graduated from college and served in the military by the time George finished high school. For those who knew him growing up, George was already set apart. Thomas Nale said, "I saw him having something that the others didn't have, but they were getting the write-ups with the basketball and football and everything else. Even though George wasn't getting the headlines, there was something inside of me, that I just felt, 'This was the special one.'"

After serving in the US Naval Air Force, Paul completed his undergraduate work at the University of Maine and earned a master's from Columbia University in 1950. He was interested in teaching in Waterville, but was told getting the graduate degree was a mistake because the school department wouldn't hire anyone at the top of the salary scale. He went to work for Liberty Mutual in New York for five years before transferring to Boston. Paul's wife, Yvette, wanted to return to Waterville, and he took over a small insurance agency there, which became locally prominent as GHM Insurance.

By 1962, Paul was serving on the board of aldermen while Waterville was pursuing federal urban renewal grants. His familiarity with the program in Boston was sufficient for the chairman of the Waterville Urban Renewal Authority to name Paul executive director. Charles Street, later known as the Concourse, ran through downtown and contained many of the "blighted" buildings. Demolition was the technique urban renewal used to remove "blight," and eighty-four buildings were torn down, most to make way for the six-hundred-car parking lot behind Main Street.

The Model Cities program, championed by Ed Muskie and enacted in 1966 as part of Lyndon Johnson's Great Society initiatives, was conceived in part because of what congressional Democrats perceived as the excesses of urban renewal. Model Cities, scrapped by the Nixon administration, emphasized community involvement and restoration, not removal. Portland obtained a Model Cities grant, while Waterville and Bangor demolished much of their downtowns under the older program. Model Cities became the template for saving existing buildings. The first version of the federal Historic Tax Credit program, now a staple of downtown redevelopment, came from Model Cities.

Today, Paul Mitchell acknowledges the controversies created by urban renewal, but says the program was worthwhile for Waterville because federal grants allowed the city to substantially rebuild its downtown infrastructure. George Mitchell says he doesn't feel qualified to comment, since he left Waterville after high school and hasn't lived there since.

BARBARA WAS THE YOUNGEST OF THE FIVE CHILDREN and the only female at a time when women's prospects were limited. There were compensations, though. Her parents thought her no less capable than her brothers. She became a teacher, a career Paul and George also considered. As a child, her older brothers insisted she be included in the informal games denied her at the Boys Club, and she held her own alongside George.

She married relatively late in life, choosing Eddie Atkins, a friend of Muskie's and owner of a downtown print shop that became a vital cog in the Muskie and Mitchell political operations. She, too, remembers George's generosity. He once presented her with an Omega watch at a time when his income was decidedly modest. Years later, at a formal dinner in London recognizing Mitchell's diplomatic achievements, she found herself wondering whether her brother might have forgotten it was her birthday. After a number of toasts and standing ovations, Mitchell called for silence—and then made a toast to honor Barbara. About the only place his competitive instincts took over was on the tennis court, where, playing doubles with Barbara, they would often defeat their brothers. George wasn't good about sharing, though. She said, "Every ball was his."

Barbara became the family historian, and her brothers, including George, rely on her for her knowledge and memory. She was chosen in 1964 to go with her mother for Mintaha's only visit to Lebanon since her departure in 1922. Bkassine, her home village, is in the mountains near the city of Jezzine, a Maronite Christian enclave. Barbara remembers it as austere but beautiful, with the surrounding desert dominating the landscape. She met her aunts and other relatives, as George did much later after becoming a senator.

WHILE GEORGE MITCHELL HAS FREQUENTLY SAID his mother was the most important person in his life, his father also was a powerful influence. Though he regretted his own lack of schooling, George Sr. was passionate about his children's education. Something of an autodidact, he had two major interests on which he quizzed them relentlessly: railroads and geography. The railroad interest remained primarily his father's, but George Jr. also acquired a lifelong fascination with places and maps. His father subscribed to *National Geographic*, which at the time included a map in every issue. In the evenings after school, the father found endless ways of testing the knowledge of his children, and George was the one he called on most often. After years of enduring endless quizzes, Mitchell tried to catch his father out, but never did.

One day in 1972, not long before his father died, he asked him about the country with the most cities with one million inhabitants, which his father knew was China, and the number, fourteen—and was able to rank them in exact order. "I told him I'd stump him next time," Mitchell said. His father replied, "You never have, and you never will." In *Not for America Alone*, he ends the story with, "We both laughed. I never saw him again." For his first thirty-eight years, George Mitchell always signed his name with "Jr." added. After his father died, he became just "George Mitchell."

George was an altar boy at St. Joseph's Church, and his father insisted he not only attend the priest, but be audible to the congregation. Barbara, excluded from this role, remembers the practice sessions on Saturdays, with father and son at opposite ends of the house, from the dining room to a hallway behind the kitchen. "George would have to read it and read it and read it until my father was happy," she said. Barbara also stood behind her father, making faces and sticking her tongue out at her brother, but rarely disrupted his concentration.

"He read that Epistle every Sunday when we were kids," she said. George took pride in his preparation, "because everybody in the church could hear every word I said."

If there was a choice to be made between academics and athletics, George Sr. chose academics. Although his boys earned schoolboy athletic glory—Paul was almost as big a star in baseball as Swisher was in basketball—he seemed indifferent to their achievements, and rarely attended a game. Instead, it fell to Mary, who could barely understand the games, to attend and cheer for her sons. Although he didn't favor George, this attitude might have caused him to value his achievements more. Mitchell remembers his father saying, about his lack of athletic prowess, "Don't worry about it; it doesn't amount to anything. You study and work hard and things will work out fine."

His father was always the one to sign his grade reports. In his senior year, George earned mostly As and Bs, but received Cs in chemistry and trigonometry. His yearbook entry notes he was a college-track student, and includes the motto, "Don't be a wise guy." Mitchell wasn't involved in student government except for one curious incident. The senior class staged a mock election campaign that featured the liberal Reds and the conservative Blues, which, the yearbook reports, "raged through the next week until election day, Friday, October 7. When all the shouting had quieted, election tallies gave the Reds a sweeping victory, as they had captured every office except one senate position." The one Blue senator was George Mitchell.

Mitchell remembers his father crying only rarely, but it happened once when he was twelve. "I shared my father's grief" after Franklin Roosevelt died. The father's lifelong devotion to Roosevelt and the New Deal also became the guiding political philosophy of his son.

GEORGE WAS COMPLETING HIS SENIOR YEAR of high school when his father lost his job. Although his father struggled to find work, at least one CMP executive found a way to take an interest in the Mitchell family. Hervey Fogg, who had known the elder Mitchell at the gas plant, had heard about George Jr.'s potential, and suggested he could arrange an interview at Bowdoin. "It was a foot in the door," said Barbara.

Mitchell soon had the appointment, and in those days, a successful interview often led directly to admission. The day Mitchell was due on the Brunswick campus, he walked to the bridge to Winslow at 8:30 a.m., where the morning traffic was at its peak. With neither a car nor public transportation, he was hoping to find a ride before the interview time, after lunch. The very first car that came along stopped, and Mitchell was on his way. He arrived before ten a.m., and had several hours to wait.

"He was so nervous," Swisher remembers. "It was a place he'd never been before." Mitchell passed the time by walking around campus and taking note of the buildings. By the appointed time, he had memorized the name of every structure on the Bowdoin campus—a feat that foreshadowed a talent he made use of throughout his professional life.

At the interview, Mitchell made a favorable impression. The only question was whether he could afford to attend. Even with tuition at modest levels, it was a stretch. The college could offer work on campus, but he would have to find other jobs as well. Throughout his four years at Bowdoin, Mitchell would need the equivalent of a full-time job in addition to his studies. Yet by the end of the day, he began to realize that the answer could be yes.

2

BRUNSWICK, BERLIN, AND WASHINGTON

When George Mitchell arrived on the Bowdoin College campus in September 1950, he was just seventeen years old. His admission had been unexpected, and he wasn't fully ready for the experience. About his freshman year, he said, "It wasn't a particularly good situation. I was immature, and a bit overwhelmed by the independence I had."

At the time, Bowdoin had fewer than one thousand students, all undergraduates, and it was all male—then, as now, occupying a central place in the life of Brunswick, a large town for Maine, but still with just over twenty thousand residents. Women weren't admitted until 1971. Nearly all Bowdoin freshmen joined a fraternity, and Mitchell was no exception. He pledged to Sigma Nu house, which also served as a dining and residence hall. Mitchell said his fraternity brothers were "good guys and fun to be around," but he did not make any lasting friendships—though he did use the opportunity to further hone his cribbage game. He eventually became the fraternity's chapter steward, which provided free room and board, and in his senior year moved to a dormitory as a freshman proctor.

Mitchell's intelligence remained mostly under wraps. He can be quite critical of his collegiate self, saying, "I was never highly organized. I didn't have good study habits or good discipline." While there were no formal class ranks, he believes he would have been in the top half but could have done better. Bowdoin has long been a leading Maine college, and many graduates "appear marked for success in life," he said. "Very few would have said that about me."

Only a few of his professors made a lasting impression, even though, as an alumnus, Mitchell has appeared on campus dozens of times, and later chose

Bowdoin's Hawthorne-Longfellow Library as the repository for his papers. Economics courses with Albert Abramson remain with him, as do several taught by LeRoy Greason, later college president. Mitchell majored in European history, and graduated in June 1954. Despite tuition assistance, Mitchell worked the equivalent of a full-time job through all four years at Bowdoin, which may account for some academic shortcomings. The job he most often recalls was making deliveries for Brunswick Oil & Lumber.

Basketball was another important focus, despite Mitchell's doubts about his abilities. As part of his work on campus, he was given the concession for the basketball team, by himself this time, selling advertising for the programs at home games. He arranged the printing and kept the balance, providing another modest source of income.

Paul Brountas, a classmate, remembers him as a "very, very good player" on the court, but Mitchell demurs. "I might have had a good game or two, but I was far from being a star," he said. Bowdoin's varsity was less competitive in its division than Waterville High had been in the schoolboy leagues. "We usually had one or two good players, but that was about it," he said.

Brountas and Mitchell do not remember meeting on campus; much of the socializing involved fraternities or academic majors. Brountas, whose parents were Greek immigrants, became active in Democratic politics in his native Massachusetts, and was an early friend and supporter of Michael Dukakis in his runs for governor and president. After watching the televised mayhem surrounding the 1968 Democratic National Convention, Brountas was inspired to volunteer for Ed Muskie's vice presidential campaign. On Mitchell's recommendation, he was hired to do advance work on the campaign plane.

Basketball, along with cribbage, was a means of social entrée. Robert "Hap" Hazzard, another classmate from Gardiner, Maine, lived next door to Mitchell and remembers him as "just one of the guys. He was not someone you'd say, 'Hey this guy's going to be something,' he was not that way." But Mitchell "was someone that, if you ever needed help, you'd feel very comfortable going to him." He added, "Fortunately, I never needed to." One night, Hazzard heard a knock on the door and found Mitchell saying, "Hap, time to stop studying; let's go over and shoot some hoops" at the old gymnasium. "And that's the way I remember him," he said.

The years at Bowdoin were when Mitchell first fell in love. At the time, there was a lot of weekend travel between Bowdoin and the other liberal arts schools, including Colby, in Mitchell's hometown. A childhood friend, Germaine Orloff, was attending Colby and introduced Mitchell to one of her friends, Beryl Wellersdieck, from Rockville Center on Long Island, New York. Soon, they were dating seriously, and their relationship lasted more than two years. Mitchell gave her his fraternity pin—a gesture then considered an engagement. Orloff called Beryl "a gorgeous, lovely girl," and Mitchell agreed. "She was a wonderful, wonderful girl," he said recently. She was the same age as Mitchell but a year behind him in school, something that figured in the end of their relationship. Mitchell had enrolled in the ROTC and expected to join the US Army after graduation, when Beryl would be entering her senior year. "I didn't want to get married," Mitchell recalls, "knowing I'd be leaving for at least two years." While Mitchell was in Berlin, Beryl met another student, from California, married him, and moved to the West Coast.

Mitchell's shyness about dating parallels that of his political mentor, Ed Muskie. Though Muskie was a far more prominent figure in his high school class in Rumford, being named valedictorian, he had few dates. He told an interviewer, "I was very shy and I suspect I was not a very hot date. I was rather in awe of girls, truth be known." Germaine Orloff said of Mitchell in high school, "He didn't seem to be terribly involved with a lot of people. I don't remember him with a girlfriend, but I remember thinking, 'Gosh, he's cute.' . . . I thought, 'Gee, I wish he'd ask me for a date,' but he never did."

THE BOWDOIN ROTC PROGRAM WAS DESIGNED to funnel graduates into the Army Transportation Corps, but it appeared there would be a surplus, and cadets were asked to consider alternatives. Mitchell, who had already attended summer training at Fort Eustis, near Williamsburg, Virginia, was interested in serving in the Intelligence Corps. There was a disadvantage, however: no guarantee about call-ups, which for the Transportation Corps would have occurred right after graduation. Mitchell decided to take the chance, saying, "I didn't have any real plans for the future. I was twenty years old." And there was another attraction— the opportunity to go abroad. "I hadn't been anywhere or seen anything," he said.

The wait seemed interminable. That was the summer the Bowdoin graduate worked on the Colby grounds crew. Just as Mitchell did with the story about his brother Robbie at the Boys Club, his father "loved telling that story" about his overqualified son. "He told it over and over again," and, as Mitchell admits, "It was very funny." When his reporting date finally arrived, it was far from convenient—the day after Christmas, 1954. He was enrolled in the Army Intelligence School at Fort Holabird in Baltimore for an eighteen-week course.

It was Mitchell's first taste of academic success. "I did quite well at the school, and it really made a difference in my life and my outlook on things," he said. He was asked by one of the student commanders to be his deputy, and his first reaction was to say, "Me, a deputy commander? You've got to be kidding."

But the offer was serious, and he accepted. It contributed to Mitchell's feeling, as he expressed it later, that he "grew up" in the army.

Mitchell was commissioned a second lieutenant, and the Intelligence assignment was to Berlin. The flight from McGuire Air Force Base in New Jersey aboard a military transport was the first time Mitchell had been in the air. He arrived in Frankfurt and took an overnight sleeper to Berlin—another first—with a fellow officer from Texas. He arrived in West Berlin early on Sunday morning.

The city was not yet divided by the Berlin Wall, and was relatively open. Buses ran between the two sides, and crossings on foot were rarely restricted until the wall was built in 1961, in an effort to stem a tide of refugees from East to West. West Berlin was then entirely surrounded by the Soviet zone—East Germany.

Mitchell and the Texas officer reported for duty, and an annoyed personnel director, called away from a golf game, barked out orders. Mitchell suggested the other officer go first, and he became supply officer, spending two years handing out uniforms and equipment. Mitchell was assigned to "C2," one of the counterintelligence teams doing interrogations. He initially spent some time on a protective detail for German rocket scientists, part of a group once headed by Wernher von Braun, who led the Nazi program that produced the V-2 missile and was later the top designer for the US Army and NASA. But Mitchell soon concentrated on his basic work, evaluating the asylum-seekers who crossed the border at military checkpoints.

The screening center was in the Marienfelde district, and Mitchell's team had a seemingly simple task that was in practice highly complex. Most asylum-seekers were trying to reunite with family in what was now a divided Germany, but some were plants—"sleeper" agents sent by the East German government to infiltrate the West. The team was also in charge of identifying a third group—those sympathetic to the West who might have the willingness and ability to go back east and become spies themselves.

Mitchell, who wasn't yet old enough to vote, was for the first time confronted with making life-or-death decisions about others. A legitimate asylum-seeker sent back to the East might well face imprisonment or execution. Mitchell supervised two dozen interrogators, half native German-speakers, and half army enlisted men who spoke German. In practice, Mitchell said, most cases were quickly resolved. Based on answers to questions about work, family, and geography, it was usually easy to determine whether someone was telling the truth. Yet there were more difficult cases, and when the interrogators couldn't agree, it was up to Mitchell to make the call. While most refugees were processed at the central facility, the army maintained safe houses, where there were lengthy interrogations and hard decisions to be made. Mitchell sometimes stayed overnight, at one address in particular.

There was a steady flow of refugees, thousands of them. "They were primarily from East Germany, but also from Czechoslovakia, Poland, and from what were then the westernmost parts of Russia," Mitchell said. "We tried to ferret out anyone who was being sent over on behalf of a Communist government . . . and there were many, many of them, and also to tried to recruit some people to go back to the East."

The operation naturally produced reams of paperwork. "We accumulated this database," he said. Gradually, through interviews and reports from their own spies, the counterintelligence teams built a picture of the East's security structure. "We tried to prevent people from coming in," he said. "We did make some arrests, and we also recruited people to go back." Asked whether his judgments were correct, he said, "There was no way for us ever to know that."

Sleeper agents did manage to enter West Berlin by one means or another. The most notorious case was that of Günter Guillaume—a top aide to former Berlin mayor and West German chancellor Willy Brandt—who was revealed as an East German spy in May 1974, forcing Brandt's resignation.

Mitchell traveled as part of his duties, visiting London, Amsterdam, and Paris during twenty months abroad. He was stationed in Berlin at a moment, following the airlift of 1948, when Americans were still seen as liberators. "Americans were very popular and the Germans were very gracious and hospitable, and there were relatively small numbers of Americans there at the time," he said. While the built-up areas of Berlin were densely populated, there was also a forested area known as the Grunvald ("green woods"), and a lake called the Wannsee where Mitchell and his friends liked to sail, and which reminded him in some ways of Maine. "I loved Berlin," he said. "I liked the people. I liked the place. It was just a wonderful experience."

During the second year, he begin to think about what he'd do back home, since his enlistment would end in November 1956. His first thought was to apply to graduate school. With the help of a history professor at Bowdoin, Ernst Helmreich, he applied to and was accepted at Northwestern University. To the extent he envisioned a career, Mitchell thought that he might become a history professor.

His brother Paul disagreed. He said he found it "almost impossible" to imagine George as a history professor, and said law school would be a much more suitable choice. As it happened, one of Mitchell's closest friends in Berlin was Charles "Smooth" McKelvey, from the Scranton, Pennsylvania, area. The nickname, Mitchell said, was because McKelvey "was the opposite of smooth."

The larger-than-life McKelvey, later active in state politics, had recently graduated from the Georgetown University Law School. Addressing Mitchell's doubts, he said, "Georgetown has a very good night school. You could go in the evening and work full-time during the day." Mitchell applied, was accepted, and informed Northwestern he wouldn't be attending. Mitchell made friends in Berlin with other lawyers-to-be. One, George Padgett, from New Jersey, also attended Georgetown, later becoming general counsel for the Lionel Corporation, maker of the famed model trains.

As the year progressed, Mitchell began to think about staying in the army. He enjoyed the work, and his superiors urged him to reenlist. He was tempted. He checked with Georgetown, and was told he could defer his admission one year. After that, he'd have to reapply. The minimum reenlistment was two years. Mitchell decided he didn't want to forfeit law school admission, and resigned his commission.

His discharge papers record his promotion to first lieutenant on June 27, 1956; that he was honorably discharged; and that he left the army on November 27, with one year, eleven months, and one day of active service, plus credit for six months' ROTC training. The identification line shows he had black hair, brown eyes, was five feet, ten inches tall, and weighed 170 pounds. He received the National Defense Service Medal, and suffered no wounds.

In later life, Mitchell gave evidence that his military service was important to him. When he was appointed to the US Senate in 1980, he joined the Veterans' Affairs Committee, and remained there even after giving up other committee assignments. During his campaigns, he noted that at times he was the only member of the Maine congressional delegation with military service. He often spoke to military groups, and rarely missed the state American Legion chapter's annual convention. There's little doubt Mitchell's participation in what was then still a citizen army contributed to the powerful, but subtly expressed, patriotism that inflects many of his best speeches.

Mitchell went back to Berlin as Senate majority leader in 1989, just after the fall of the Berlin Wall, which stood for twenty-eight years. As he surveyed the rubble of the wall where so many lives had been lost, he noticed some teenage boys who were offering to rent a hammer and a chisel to anyone seeking souvenirs.

"I gave them my 50 pfennig and took the hammer and chisel and knocked out a couple of pieces of rock from the Wall," he said. Mitchell decided "It was a great example of how entrepreneurs are everywhere. These young German boys made a lot of money, because there was a lot of business at the time." The Senate leader had to wait in line. He took the pieces home and kept them on the dresser in his Washington apartment until he left the Senate five years later. When he was packing up and winnowing his belongings, he threw them away.

Mitchell also journeyed to the safe house where he had supervised interrogations some three decades earlier. The homeowner was there, he spoke

English, and they chatted. Mitchell said that he'd stayed there, but did not say why. "It brought back a flood of memories about when I'd worked there and made some very difficult decisions on what to do with people," he said. "I then learned, probably for the first time, the awesome responsibility when you control someone else's life. Many of these people were vulnerable, and I had the authority to cause their arrest, to cause them to be sent back, to cause them to be held, and it weighed heavily on me, trying to make what I thought was a right and fair decision, especially being a young kid who didn't really have a lot of experience." It wasn't until he became a federal judge, years later, that he felt a similar responsibility.

IT WAS NOVEMBER 1956 WHEN MITCHELL was discharged from the army, and it was already the second semester at Georgetown Law when he arrived in Washington. He found the adjustment difficult. "[I felt I was] in over my head right away," Mitchell recalls. Bowdoin, then as now, emphasized its small classes and individual attention from professors. His first law school class, held in a large lecture hall, was overwhelming. "I thought the whole school was attending," he said. The case-study method of instruction was also unfamiliar.

Though he'd chosen Georgetown because it allowed him to hold a full-time job, this proved even more challenging than it had been at Bowdoin. He worked five days a week as a claims adjuster for Travelers Insurance, then had two hours of classes each evening. "After that, I was not inclined to do a lot of studying," he recalls. It took four years of classes, year-round, for Mitchell to earn his law degree, but partly from necessity he became more organized and began to excel. By his final year, he placed third in his class.

The greatest gain "was a vast improvement in my writing skills," Mitchell recalls, which enabled him to present cases "lucidly and cogently, and in an organized fashion." Later, in the Senate, he found that "there are a lot of very able, smart people who don't have good communications skills, and write poorly. It held them back."

Mitchell found it difficult, between work and study, to make friends, but he looked back on his Georgetown years with gratitude. Georgetown had been founded by a Catholic, Bishop John Carroll, and Mitchell found it still had "a diverse and pluralistic student body" without the elitism of more prominent schools. In a speech he gave at Georgetown's bicentennial in 1989, he said the nation's educational institutions had been criticized for a lack of discipline and rigor, but said Georgetown was "an institution whose standards have never fallen, whose students receive full education value for the time and energy they devote to their studies, and which has given so much more than mere factual knowledge." He added, "It was here at Georgetown that we learned the meaning of the idea of 'learning,' not as a matter of cramming unrelated facts into our minds, but as a matter of becoming aware of that universe of knowledge on whose threshold we stand. We learned law, not only as a matter of precedents and statutory construction, but as a matter of justice."

WHILE HE WAS STILL IN LAW SCHOOL, Mitchell married Sally Heath of Concord, New Hampshire, in 1959. She had caught his eye when he attended services at a Catholic church near where they both lived. In his memoir, *The Negotiator*, Mitchell writes, "I noticed a tall, slender, attractive woman walking just ahead of or behind me, to a townhouse just two doors away. I very much wanted to meet her but couldn't figure out an appropriate opening line." He thought of his brother, Robbie, an expert in these situations, but still couldn't find the words.

Finally, she spoke to him one morning as they descended the church steps, saying, "Hello, neighbor." Mitchell recalls, "It wasn't much, but it was enough." She was almost exactly one year younger than Mitchell. After graduating from Concord High School, she had gone to work in the office of Governor Hugh Gregg, and then moved to Washington to work for Senator Styles Bridges; both were Republicans. By the time they met, she was working in the Federal Aviation Administration, a civil service position.

Because she had worked in two political offices, Mitchell's friends assumed that Sally would be pleased when her husband began to form political aspirations of his own. Instead, "Her years of working in political offices had bred in her an intense dislike of politics," he wrote. When they made plans together, it involved moving to Maine—Portland, not far from where Sally grew up—and Mitchell had yet to even consider politics as a career. Friends saw the couple as well matched, and there's little evidence of strain in their personal lives together. The trouble always seemed to center on politics.

Many years later, when there were early suggestions Mitchell might someday run for president, a friend, Nancy Chandler, reported that Sally was "horrified" by the idea. Chandler, who with her husband Bruce, later a Superior Court judge, had rented an apartment from Swisher Mitchell in Waterville, was close to both George and Sally, and served on the Democratic National Committee with him. When Mitchell lost the 1974 race for governor, Chandler said Sally was "relieved," adding, "She never wanted to live in the Blaine House," the official governor's residence. Janet Mitchell remembers Sally as "an incredibly intelligent and incredibly shy" person who was reserved at family gatherings, when she attended.

One of George Mitchell's closest friends, Harold Pachios, a Portland attorney who worked in the Johnson administration as Bill Moyers's deputy press secretary, got to know Sally well over the years, and agrees with these descriptions. "She was very quiet and introspective. She hated being in the public eye, or having any involvement in politics. She just didn't enjoy public engagement of any kind."

When the Mitchells moved to Maine in 1965, it was shortly before the birth of their daughter, Andrea. They bought a modest house on Falmouth Road in Falmouth, about three-quarters of a mile from the nearest village. Pachios said of Sally, "She was very tall and attractive, and they were a striking couple. I liked her, but she was a loner."

As HIS LAW SCHOOL GRADUATION APPROACHED in 1960, Mitchell explored job prospects. His first priority was getting back to Maine, and he wanted to work for a law firm. "I wrote more than a dozen letters and sent out résumés," he said. "I was only interviewed by two or three firms, and I wasn't offered a job." Maine's law firms at the time were small, patrician, Republican, and Protestant. According to Tony Buxton, later Mitchell's campaign manager in the 1974 governor's race, the first question in one interview was, "What religion are you?" Buxton said, "At that point, he got up and left." Others say the firm was Verrill Dana, one of the state's largest.

Mitchell's next thought was to seek a transfer to Maine from Travelers, where he'd worked for four years, but was told the Portland office was out because "everybody wants to go to Maine." Then, "out of the blue," a letter arrived from the US Department of Justice, informing him about the Honors Law Graduate Program, which guaranteed employment for top graduates of large law schools like Georgetown. Mitchell accepted, and was assigned to the Antitrust Division, but still focused on returning to Maine.

The work was perhaps not what the new law school graduate had envisioned for the start of his legal career. The Antitrust Division was considered a backwater, with few high-profile cases; it would be easier to make a mark in the Criminal Division. Mitchell eventually gained experience as a prosecutor, but he pursued antitrust cases with diligence and thoroughness.

In briefs and memos, he displayed not only a clear writing style, but also shrewd analysis of a case's strengths and weaknesses. One investigation involved a Kentucky bank merger the Antitrust Division was vetting for possible anticompetitive effects. The government was considering filing against First National and Security Trust in Lexington, and Mitchell was evaluating possible witnesses.

Of one he wrote, "He is extremely knowledgeable about Lexington and the banking situation there and made a good impression. He is, however, extremely cynical, and I would not recommend calling him to testify unless he expresses a willingness to do so. It is my impression that he might repudiate or deny statements made to us privately."

Of another, Mitchell wrote, "He would not be an effective witness on our behalf for several reasons. He is quite elderly and is extremely talkative; it is my feeling that he would be almost completely unmanageable as a witness." Mitchell also analyzed the position of a thirty-five-year-old executive at the competing Second National, who was officially neutral. "I feel he is probably opposed to the merger but is either afraid or refuses to express that opposition. In short, he is a wealthy young man who is vice president of the bank only because his family owns it."

Mitchell left notes for five cases during less than two years at Justice. There are glimpses of wider terrain. Asked to comment on fledgling satellite communications, he offered, under the title, "Administrative and Regulatory Problems Relating to the Authorization of Commercially Operable Space Communication," the following conclusion: "Satellite communication will by its very nature play an important part in international relations. The United States is presently engaged in a worldwide struggle to demonstrate that our economic system of free competitive enterprise can itself compete favorably with the Communist system of controlled monopoly. The satellite communication system can well be a prime example of the effective operation of the free enterprise system, and it is, therefore, of vital importance to the national interest that no single private concern dominate."

Mitchell was also involved, tangentially, in filings for the AT&T antitrust case that had included a 1956 consent order, and was, years later, one of the division's most celebrated cases, leading to the breakup of the Bell System.

He resigned his position on March 26, 1962. He'd received an inquiry from the office of Senator Edmund S. Muskie of Maine. Muskie, who had then served in the Senate a little over three years, had a vacancy for the office's number-two position, serving under Administrative Assistant Don Nicoll. Nicoll had asked John Jabar, who worked for Muskie and was the brother of Mitchell's childhood pal Tony, if he knew of any promising young Mainers, and Mitchell's name came up, partly because he was already working in Washington. Nicoll called Mitchell.

"I didn't know who he was, and I'd never met Senator Muskie," said Mitchell. Nicoll explained there was a family connection, and that he'd been recommended. An interview later, Mitchell was offered the job of executive assistant, equivalent to what later was called legislative director. Mitchell was twenty-eight, and, until then, had never considered a career in politics.

3

A PARTY'S PROGRESS

Had Ed Muskie not been elected governor in 1954, it's doubtful that George Mitchell's political career would have unfolded as it did. Mitchell learned politics, and became a candidate himself, entirely within the structure of what was then a nearly new political organization. Mitchell never forgot the party-building lessons he learned from Maine Democrats, and he has been more loyal to the party's candidates, and devoted to its platform, than almost any of his peers. Without 1954 and all that followed, a life in politics would have seemed as unlikely to Mitchell as his becoming a professor had been to his brother, Paul. Muskie's candidacy created a template for Democratic success, though it took nearly thirty years to fully achieve.

Before 1954, the Maine Democratic Party barely existed as a statewide organization. Democrats had not elected a governor since 1934, and had never elected a US senator. They had few legislators. What strength Democrats did have lay in mill towns where generations of French Canadians from Quebec had migrated to work in the then-thriving textile mills and shoe shops. Biddeford, Lewiston, and Waterville sent Democrats to the Legislature, but Portland was solidly Republican. Nor were the party's leaders particularly interested in expanding their electoral reach. The major authority they wielded came in the form of federal patronage—a traditional form of political influence substantially expanded by Franklin Roosevelt's New Deal.

It's often said that Edmund S. Muskie revived the Maine Democratic Party, in partnership with Frank M. Coffin—now a lesser-known political figure who nonetheless was elected to Congress, ran for governor, and became chief judge of the federal First Circuit Court of Appeals, serving for forty-one years. It would be more accurate, though, to say that Coffin and Muskie invented the state Democratic Party in its contemporary form. They provided it with ideas, an agenda, and a credibility that it had utterly lacked, putting it on course to become Maine's majority party.

After the Civil War and its reorientation of Maine as one of the most Republican states in the Union, Maine Democrats were elected in numbers only when Democrats had national success in landslide proportions. Democratic governors were elected in 1910 and 1914 at the height of the Progressive era, but not again until Louis Brann in 1932, the Roosevelt landslide. Yet Roosevelt himself never carried Maine. Brann attempted to gain a US Senate seat in 1936 and lost narrowly; that was the end of his political career. After the 1952 election that brought in Dwight Eisenhower as president, with a Republican Congress, Maine Republicans appeared as dominant as they had ever been.

One of Coffin's first acts after being elected chairman of the state Democratic Party in 1954 was to hire Don Nicoll, a twenty-six-year-old reporter for a Lewiston radio station, as the party's first full-time employee, with the title of executive secretary. Years later, Nicoll recalled that his mother could never understand why he, with a wife and two children, would give up a perfectly good job in broadcast journalism to undertake the unpredictable life of a hired political hand. But the move turned out to be central to the careers of Coffin, Muskie, and Nicoll. Nicoll went to Washington to work as Coffin's administrative assistant—the position now called chief of staff—when Coffin was elected to Congress. When Coffin lost his bid for governor in 1960, Nicoll moved to Muskie's office as AA, where he met George Mitchell a little over a year later.

One reason Democrats were open to new leadership was that their power structure had disappeared with Eisenhower's election. Before that, Nicoll said, "Many of the fights over leadership positions revolved around the power that went with it to control patronage. In 1952, that was wiped out, and a number of the Democratic leaders . . . tended to withdraw, leaving only your rank-and-file Democrats plus some of the new leaders who emerged following the end of World War II."

Republicans suddenly had a new tool of influence, but it was a double-edged sword. Squabbling over their newfound spoils divided the seemingly monolithic party, and there were other disputes. A scandal involving the state liquor contract didn't hurt Republicans in 1952, when they faced weak opposition, but it still resonated with some voters. There was also an increasingly bitter split between the party's two wings, with the moderates led by US Senator Margaret Chase Smith, then serving the first of four six-year terms. The conservative wing was dominated by followers of Senator Joseph McCarthy, then holding his first public hearings to root out those who he alleged were Communists in the US State Department.

Smith's "Declaration of Conscience" in 1950, the first major challenge to McCarthy, reads differently in a Maine context. Her Maine Senate colleague was Ralph Owen Brewster, a veteran Republican who was governor in the 1920s, when he had a dalliance with the Ku Klux Klan, won three US House terms in the 1930s, and was elected to the Senate in 1940. He had come under the sway of McCarthy as Cold War battle lines hardened with the Soviet Union and China. When Brewster sought a third term in 1952, moderate Republicans challenged him. Their candidate was Governor Frederick Payne, and in a battle that brought 134,000 Republicans to the primary, a record, Payne narrowly ousted Brewster.

In 1954 Smith faced a primary challenge from Robert Jones, a young Bates College graduate who openly backed McCarthy. Smith won overwhelmingly, but Republican divisions festered. Don Nicoll, the new Democratic Party professional, saw the Republicans as "full of dry rot," and said, "I had come to the conclusion that the state was ripe for a Democratic victory."

Muskie saw it differently. At the outset of 1954, he said his party's fortunes were "not at the bottom of the barrel, but under the barrel."

ED MUSKIE, WHO GRADUATED FROM Bates College and Cornell Law, returned from his World War II navy service to a one-person law practice in Waterville that was barely functioning. He began taking divorce cases and some criminal defense work, but decided that politics might be a quicker route to establishing himself. He decided to stand for the Legislature in 1946. Waterville was one of the few cities where a Democrat stood a chance, and Muskie received the blessing of Harold Dubord, a Democratic National Committee member who decided Muskie, as a wartime veteran, would be an asset. Asked why he ran, Muskie told Theo Lippman and Donald Hansen, authors of a 1971 biography, "If I lived down South, I'd probably be a Republican. Somebody's got to do it."

There was more to it than that. Muskie's father was a tailor who left Poland in 1903 to escape Tsarist conscription, settled in Buffalo, New York, and then moved with his wife to Rumford, a growing paper-mill town. He was described by his son as "a closet Democrat." He voted in the Republican primary, the only contested races, then favored Democrats in November. The Republican businessmen who frequented his shop listened to his political commentary while being fitted for custom suits, whether they liked it or not.

Muskie was close to his father in a way that parallels George Mitchell's relationship with his mother—an almost reverential regard time never dimmed. There's evidence Stephen Muskie had high hopes for his firstborn son. He invented the apparently unique surname, "Muskie," for him, having become a citizen earlier under his original Polish name, Stefan Marciszewski.

In the legislative session of 1947, Muskie was one of 24 Democrats in a 151-seat chamber. Republicans excluded Democrats from important committees, and Muskie was consigned to Federal Relations and Military Affairs. The big issue of his first session involved a veterans' bonus—highly popular in both parties. Muskie favored a version relying on horse-racing revenues. Governor Horace Hildreth proposed a sales or income tax in a special session. Muskie didn't bite, saying, "We soldiers that fought the war, by God, we're not going to be blamed for a sales tax." A plan using "sin taxes" went to voters in a referendum and was defeated. Adoption of a sales tax was still four years off.

Muskie generally got along well with Republican leaders, and became popular enough with fellow Democrats to be chosen minority leader in 1948 and 1950. His political instincts were not unerring. He ran for mayor in 1947, but lost to a Republican, a bank president, in part because he refused to disavow his friendship with an unpopular Franco party boss.

His legislative career was cut short when he resigned in 1951 to become state director of the Office of Price Stabilization. The Truman-era program was intended as a transition from the price controls and rationing of the war years to free-market pricing. Inflation had soared, and President Truman announced a wage-price freeze. In Maine, Muskie emphasized voluntary compliance, saying, "It is going to be my effort to make the OPS in Maine a public agency, not a police agency," adding, "We hope you will look upon us as people to whom you can come for advice and assistance."

For Muskie the job offered a federal salary and unrivaled opportunity to meet people. He traveled all over the state and shook far more hands than he ever could have as a legislator. The OPS effort worked—inflation dropped sharply—but Muskie objected to congressional efforts to weaken the program, and resigned in 1952. He spent the next year as a lobbyist. Despite some successes, the experience, he said, showed him "how little influence the Democratic Party had in the legislative work of the state."

In 1948, he had married Jane Gray, whom he'd met shortly after returning to Waterville. Ed was thirty-four, Jane, twenty-one. They'd waited because of family concerns that she was too young to marry. A son, Stephen, named after his father, was born in 1949, the first of five children. The Muskies bought a small house in Waterville for $8,000. In April 1953 Muskie suffered a fall that almost ended his life. He was wallpapering the upstairs hallway when he leaned back against a temporary railing. It gave way and he tumbled backward down the stairs.

Muskie broke his back, and was in a coma for two weeks. His doctors thought he might not live, but, under the care of devoted nuns at Sisters' Hospital (later Seton Hospital), Muskie made a slow, painful recovery. All that summer he stayed at the cottage on China Lake—Mainers called them "camps"—that he'd bought as a bachelor. He crawled down to the lake to swim, gradually recuperating, though back pain was a lifelong problem, according to Don Nicoll.

Later in the summer, Muskie, who had joined the Democratic National Committee, invited Frank and Ruth Coffin to the cottage for a picnic. He'd heard about Coffin's speeches calling for a new focus in the Democratic Party, and decided it was time to get acquainted.

MUSKIE HAD MADE AN EARLIER OVERTURE, offering the position of general counsel for the Maine OPS office to Coffin, who declined, though he later said, "I always valued that early and completely unresearched vote of confidence." Coffin was corporation counsel for the city of Lewiston, which paid $6,000 for part-time work. Muskie earned $8,000 for the full-time OPS position.

Like Muskie, Coffin had Democratic politics in his background—or half of it. His father was a staunch Republican, but his mother came from a long line of Democrats. His grandfather, Frank Morey, had served as Maine House speaker during the Progressive Era. Although the judicial aura Coffin acquired later in life cast him as being remote from politics, this was not true earlier.

Bob Dunfey, whose family owned a hotel chain and was a major financial backer of Democratic candidates, remembers an early campaign event attended by Muskie, Coffin, and numerous Democrats from New Hampshire and Maine. Coffin was short, and when it came his turn to speak, Dunfey said, "He got up on a chair and stood on the table to give his speech. He wanted to get some life into the party."

Margaret McGaughey, who later worked for George Mitchell in the US Attorney's office, was a law clerk for Coffin, and said he "had an impish sense of humor combined with a very powerful intellect. He had a very strong sense of where he wanted to go."

Nicoll first heard "the speech" from Coffin at a Jefferson–Jackson Day dinner in 1953. "He called on the party to mount the ramparts and change the state of Maine," Nicoll recalled. Nicoll's report impressed his station manager, who then suggested he interview Coffin on-air. After the session, Nicoll said, "I asked him when he was going to stop making speeches and start doing something for the party." Nicoll wanted Coffin to run for the Second District congressional seat. Coffin declined, but that turned out not to be the end of the matter.

Muskie could be a shrewd judge of talent, and decided Coffin, five years his junior, needed a push. In March, Coffin opened his morning paper to discover he'd been picked to head the platform committee for the state convention in Lewiston. Coffin didn't know that Muskie was behind the offer. He decided to give it a try, asking Jim Oliver, a former Republican congressman turned Democrat, to help. Don Nicoll also assisted.

Coffin had read about another minority Democratic Party, in Kansas, creating voter interest by sending out a questionnaire. At the time, party platforms were constructed by party regulars, often just before the convention opened. The idea of consulting with voters was new, and caught the interest of reporters who covered politics. Maine then had three evening editions as well as the morning dailies, so that amounted to a lot of news space.

Coffin sent out two thousand questionnaires and got an astonishing number back. The results were announced at news conferences around the state, creating a pre-convention buzz the Democrats had never before had. One recipient was Dr. Dean Fisher, commissioner of health and welfare for incumbent governor Burton Cross. Nicoll, who describes Fisher as "a very profane man," interviewed him and Cross at WLAM. "He was waving the document around and asking reporters, 'Have you seen what these silly Democrats are doing now? Sending out questionnaires even to the governor and state commissioners.'" Nicoll added, "They thought this was a great joke. In a way, it was the beginning of the downfall of that administration."

The Democrats gathered in Lewiston for the March convention with new energy. The program cover cheekily featured a donkey in a pith helmet, saying, "Time I shot me an elephant." They secured a notable keynote speaker, Harry Truman's Commerce secretary, Averell Harriman, then running for governor of New York. After Muskie won the governorship in September, due to Maine's then-unique system of separating state from national elections, Harriman called on Muskie to campaign for him in New York, where he won.

The convention quickly adopted Coffin's platform, but there was a problem. "We still had no candidates," Muskie said. Muskie wasn't anxious to put his name forward. And not everyone was happy with Muskie's convention role. Nicoll remembers Louis Jalbert, who saw himself as Lewiston's Democratic kingmaker, jabbing at Muskie outside the hall, saying, "You're all through, Muskie. You're all through." No one remembers what the disagreement was about.

After the convention, Coffin was elected party chair. With the filing date looming, Coffin and Muskie set out to fill a ticket that needed candidates for governor, US Senate, and three congressional seats. Coffin hired Nicoll even though no one knew where the money would come from. The party occupied a second-floor office, rent-free, through the generosity of Henry Benoit, a department store owner. It was cozy. There was one desk, and one chair. The desk, Nicoll said, "was probably sixty or seventy years old and breaking down." A local union painter etched MAINE DEMOCRATIC PARTY on the door. When Nicoll planned strategy with Muskie and his campaign manager, Dick McMahon, "Ed got the chair and Dick and I sat on newspaper piles."

As the new chairman, Coffin was at pains to maintain ties to older Democrats who'd supported the party for years, and without whom there'd be no chance of winning. Coffin was particularly fond of George Ramsdell, a retired Bates professor who "became a Democrat under the influence of William Jennings Bryan. We had people who went back a long, long ways." Coffin got two dozen old-timers together for a photo that played on front pages, and included Benoit and Kenneth Sills, former president of Bowdoin College. "The names brought respect from Republicans," Muskie said, "and so we had become respectable."

The candidate search wasn't going well, however. A Colby College history professor, Paul Fullam, was interested in the Senate race, though no one thought he could defeat Margaret Chase Smith, whose popularity in Maine soared after her chastisement of Joe McCarthy. To Coffin's way of thinking, 1954 represented a dry run for a more substantial slate in 1956. He targeted Democrats from past campaigns still known to voters. Even though "there was very little prospect for success," the rapidity with which potential candidates said no was discouraging. Harold Dubord, Muskie's mentor, ruled out running for governor, as did five or six others. "They really would turn us down out of hand," Coffin said. "They didn't even sleep on it overnight."

Muskie, who made appeals himself, eventually got tired of hearing, "If this is so important, why don't you do it?" Dick McMahon, his manager, called Muskie "really a reluctant candidate," and Muskie explained his reasoning. "It was important to get the governorship [filled] because otherwise there was no chance of getting people for the other spots. We didn't have enough candidates for the Legislature to elect a majority even if they all won," he said. "I was not one of the first names that came to mind. I wasn't interested, really."

Just before the April deadline, Muskie agreed to run. Coffin had always believed Muskie would prefer the governor's race, and said, "He was willing to run for Congress, but I think he was very happy to run for governor." The Democrats fielded a full slate. Fullam, who almost pulled out because of a heart ailment that would kill him only a year later, stayed in. Jim Oliver, from the platform committee, ran for the First District seat. Tom Delahanty, later a Superior Court judge and Coffin's close friend, ran in the Second District, and Ken Colbath in the Third District.

Fullam said he decided to run because, on an evening walk with his young son near their home, they looked up in the sky at the night plane to Boston, and the son said, "Is that the plane that's carrying the bomb?" Coffin said Fullam "was shaken by his son's attitude of hopelessness. And he decided that, come hell or high water, he was going to run."

MUSKIE MADE HIS ANNOUNCEMENT on April 8, 1954. In his brief statement, he said, "Maine desperately needs two-party competition at the polls and in the development of sound programs for the benefit of our people. We of the Democratic Party believe this. Independent, thinking people in increasing numbers share that belief." Muskie also said, "Maine people are asking for young, progressive, constructive leadership—men who place the cause of good government above partisan politics." And he concluded, "I will do my best to discuss the issues and conduct my campaign in such a way as to contribute something substantial to the cause of better government, whatever the results of the election. I am willing to do my part. . . . The rest will be up to the voters."

The appeal for two-party government was something Muskie, and Coffin, in his later congressional races, would stress in almost every speech. It was credible, in large part, due to the feuds, public and private, among the Republicans. And the reference to "thinking people" was an allusion to Adlai Stevenson, who while losing to a war-hero president in 1952, also inspired a generation of young, idealistic Democrats.

Muskie immediately began traveling around the state with Dick McMahon, staying in supporters' homes. At first the audiences were small, "maybe eight to ten people, maybe fewer," Coffin said. Gradually, the gatherings grew. Economic issues were prominent, and so were fisheries—a big deal at the time. Muskie spoke with feeling about an issue featured in almost every campaign for governor since then, even today: the loss of Maine's young people to emigration to other states. A group of elderly Republican women in Castine, home to the Maine Maritime Academy, were moved to tears. McMahon also felt himself tearing up. "I had to leave, I couldn't stand it," he said. "This guy was hot and had the women going for him. . . . They were all Republicans, but they loved him that night."

It was in Rangeley, a fabled fishing resort in northwestern Maine, that Muskie hit his stride. His topic was catch-and-release fishing, but something about his audience caused him to put his prepared speech aside and begin talking about his father, and growing up in Rumford. His lowly beginnings and drive to succeed struck a chord.

"We're sitting in the back of the room and you could hear a pin drop," McMahon said. "They came expecting to hear about why he ought to be governor, and instead, he's telling them about fishing with his father. It was wonderful." Reporter Peter Damborg was there, and his account helped to spread the word about a new approach to politics. Muskie, almost by accident, had discovered how to connect with audiences. "They were enraptured," Coffin said of the performance. "He found his voice and became the superb stump orator he was well reputed to be."

Muskie wasn't always scintillating. Don Nicoll, often present, remembers some "dreadfully dull, repetitive speeches," but said, "Ed felt very strongly that the role of a political leader was to provide education on the issues." One who responded was Ken Curtis, who was elected governor in 1966, and said in the early days that Muskie was "almost like a teacher. He could explain the political process in a way that was very inspiring, at least to me and to young people."

At the start, Muskie wasn't even the best Democratic candidate. Paul Fullam attracted more attention in his Senate race. His style was likened to Stevenson's, and, said Nicoll, "He was the only person I ever heard who could talk to rank-and-file Democrats about Aristotle and get them excited." Muskie said, "He added class to the ticket. You couldn't conceivably think of him as someone who was running for selfish reasons."

There was a unified Democrat ticket in 1954, and the candidates often appeared together, especially on television for the first election where there were significant numbers of viewers—as much by necessity as design. The party raised a whopping $18,000 for the five candidates, which wasn't quite as little as it seemed. On fledgling stations in Portland and Bangor, $100 would buy a fifteen-minute broadcast slot, enough time to introduce all five candidates.

Newspapers were still the dominant political medium, and as Muskie began to warm up audiences, coverage grew. Newspapers assigned a reporter to each major candidate, so even if editorial pages remained hostile, as they did, the Democrats became familiar to voters. Muskie later said news stories were instrumental in making people believe he had a chance to win.

Radio may have played a greater part than television, Nicoll believes, even though people remembered TV ads more often. Radio got voters to focus, he said; television clinched the sale. Muskie had an unexpected talent for the new medium. He almost always spoke to the precise length of the take. "He was physically always very impressive," Coffin said, "and unlike appearances outside of television, he was very disciplined and could stop very gracefully with a completed thought." The long takes were another bonus. "It was television without the vices of television today," Coffin said. "It wasn't a sound bite. At fifteen minutes, you couldn't fake it."

For their first campaign appearance, Coffin introduced the five candidates, and the broadcast finished with Muskie. "The whole object," Coffin said, "was to introduce the issues and to let the voters of Maine know that Democratic candidates did not have horns."

Muskie could see the effect. The day after a TV appearance, the candidates were politicking at Eastern Fine Paper in Brewer; at paper mills, though fertile ground for Democrats, it was often hard to get anyone's attention. Not that day. Muskie said, "I would have spent the whole budget for television after that one experience."

Muskie was helped by the contrasting appearance of his opponent, Governor Burton Cross. On the final night, Republicans and Democrats booked thirty-minute appearances. All five Democrats appeared, while Cross went on only with other state officials. The Republicans went first, and, Nicoll said, "appeared very stiff and accusatory." Cross, said Coffin, looked "remote and strait-laced, and . . . the contrast was telling."

Political upsets usually occur when a candidate is fortunate in his opponent. Cross had bested two Republican opponents in the 1952 primary, both less conservative. Leon Hussey owned an Augusta hardware store, while Neil Bishop was a farmer. Bishop proved the greater problem. In 1954, he launched a "Republicans for Muskie" effort. In an odd turnabout, Bishop returned to the GOP fold, running against Coffin in 1958, when he was reelected to a second term in Congress, and ending up as Muskie's Republican opponent in 1970, when Muskie won his third Senate term.

Cross made several missteps. Oblivious to his opponent's growing appeal, he may have increased it by telling reporters, "Muskie isn't the strongest candidate they could have picked." Near the end, the two candidates appeared, by coincidence, at a fair in Rockland, and Cross, egged on by reporters, said he'd debate Muskie, then said he'd "talk" to him, then declined to do anything. It was clear to reporters that Muskie's criticisms were getting under his skin.

Then in September, just before the election, Hurricane Edna hit the Northeast, following Hurricane Carol by just ten days. Many lost their homes. But Cross, after an overflight, pronounced the damage "not half as bad" as he'd expected.

IN JULY, LIONEL LEMIEUX, A LEWISTON REPORTER and political columnist, told an audience the meager primary vote for Muskie, in comparison to Cross's, meant "the much-heralded Democratic resurgence is only a ripple on the political lake." Later, he pronounced Democrats had "peaked too soon." Governor Cross told friends he'd win by 45,000 votes—the margin he'd enjoyed over Jim Oliver in 1952.

When returns came in, small towns that regularly showed no votes for Democrats recorded a respectable number for Muskie. He carried Castine, where he'd impressed the Republican women, even though Republicans outnumbered Democrats four to one. By mid-evening, it was clear Muskie would be elected, and he won by 20,000 votes, taking 54 percent.

The other Democrats lost, though Paul Fullam cut Margaret Chase Smith's majority in half, and Jim Oliver came within 4,000 votes in the First District. In the Legislature, Democrats picked up just ten House seats. But Muskie's victory was so unexpected it made news around the country: The September election had created the slogan, "As Maine goes, so goes the nation." And, whatever its predictive power, in November Democrats took back both houses of Congress, holding uninterrupted sway until Republicans reclaimed the Senate in 1980.

By six a.m., reporters from national wire services were at Muskie's door in Waterville, trying to find out more about the man who'd pulled off such an astonishing upset. Muskie was in demand instantly as a campaigner, visiting not only New York, but half a dozen other states. As for Lionel Lemieux, author of Muskie's "Dewey Beats Truman" moment, he was known forever after as "Ripples."

Muskie's victory was, first and foremost, an extraordinary personal achievement. Not only was the Republican Party dominant, but many traditional sources of support for Democrats were lacking. The head of the Maine AFL-CIO at the time was a Republican. Labor support was considered such a liability that when Muskie ran for reelection in 1956, the *Boston Herald* published a photo of Muskie, who had mediated a strike in Lewiston, standing between the union leader and the factory manager—and cropped out the manager, to show Muskie favoring labor. Muskie ran the original photo in his ads.

A more intriguing question is why Muskie's Catholic and immigrant background didn't damage his chances. Muskie's Catholicism wasn't a problem in Waterville, but it could have hurt him statewide. Republicans did not make an issue of it. Burton Cross was so confident that he simply ignored Muskie's challenge. The only places Muskie remembers the issue coming up were in the "Bible Belt" towns of Newport and Houlton. Muskie saw a post-election newspaper story that cataloged his "firsts": "The first Democrat in twenty years. The first son of a Democrat. The first Catholic ever." A supporter responded by saying, "If the election were held tomorrow, you'd lose." By winning, Muskie paved the way for other Catholics, including George Mitchell, to run.

THE 1954 VICTORY WAS WON BY A NEW POLITICAL TEAM. Frank Coffin and Ed Muskie weren't personally close, but their similarities and contrasts made them unusually compatible partners. They went in different directions after 1960,

Coffin's last political campaign. Muskie held political office for twenty-six consecutive years, while Coffin had an even longer stay on the federal bench. Yet a biographer's judgment—"There was a closeness of thought between the two that approached the uncanny"—seems apt.

Don Nicoll offered a nuanced portrait, looking back after they passed from the scene; Muskie died in 1996, Coffin in 2009. "Coffin and Muskie had a similar approach to life," he said. "Neither of them had a career plan, but they were both highly disciplined and dedicated to doing the best possible job, always pushing for perfection." They shared "a commitment to the general public welfare, as the phrase was used by James Madison. In that respect, they were two peas in a pod."

"They were both brilliant in their own way," Nicoll said. "Ed was the one with the antennae, the physical presence and charisma. Frank was more of an inside player. He was shorter"—Muskie, at six feet, four inches, was nearly a foot taller—"and he quickly understood what people were thinking and feeling. He also learned the nuts and bolts of building an organization. Frank was the one who cheerfully took on all the tasks." Nicoll recalls Muskie saying of the partnership, "As the grasshopper said to the ant, I just lay down policy around here."

Coffin had a strong regard for Muskie. "I just liked him immensely," he said of their first meeting at China Lake. "We had fun together. We each had a weird sense of humor, and we loved to play with words, only he was pretty bad—he was awful with some of his puns." More substantively, Coffin said, "I don't know any public man who has such a consistently good record. I don't think I could find any area or any big issue on which I thought he was wrong."

Muskie recognized that his own success had a great deal to do with Coffin's coordinated strategy for the five-member ticket. "They were willing to be part of the team, to pool our resources," he said. "Everybody emphasized the governorship as the important race, and none of them had any problem with that."

AFTER THE SHOCK OF MUSKIE'S WIN, expectations for the forty-year-old Democratic governor were modest. The Republicans expected to win in 1956, and, with few Democratic legislators, it was difficult to see how Muskie could enact his program. He later crafted an alliance with the most powerful Republican. Robert Haskell was Senate president, and president of Bangor Hydro-Electric, the state's second-largest utility. The combination of business and politics was typical at the time, ensuring that lawmakers didn't stray from the needs of manufacturers, banks, railroads, and private utilities.

Haskell was an able legislator, but the two clashed over Muskie's campaign promise to establish a state industrial development authority. Haskell saw it as a bureaucratic boondoggle. As the session dragged on, Muskie told Haskell he planned to take his case to the public via television. Haskell reconsidered, cleared the bill, and the two worked surprisingly closely together. Muskie demonstrated political artistry. Late in his second term, after he'd been elected to the US Senate, he wanted to have his friend Tom Delahanty confirmed to the Superior Court. Muskie left the governorship early so Haskell could be governor for a week, and Delahanty got his judgeship.

Muskie knew he needed Republican votes, and avoided vetoing bills. "If a bill came to my desk, and I found some good in it," he said, he would invite in Republican leaders and suggest changes that were often accepted. He appointed Maurice Williams, a State House veteran, as his finance chief, and strategized with him about ways to get Republicans interested in new programs. What he hit on was a supplemental budget, a new device that would showcase the most popular initiatives. The Legislature would first fund current services, then debate the supplemental budget. To enact it, they'd also have to find the money to pay for it.

Muskie knew he was getting somewhere when he traveled to a coastal town to find a trainer for his new collie, a gift from a constituent. At the end of a dirt road, he came across the trainer, also a farmer. "The minute you saw him and his environment, you knew he had to be a Republican, and an old one at that," Muskie said. They struck a deal, and the farmer said, "Governor, I want you to know I've been following what you've been saying to the Legislature. You've been asking them for more money and, goddamn it, they ought to give it to you." Muskie called it "my first vote of confidence."

After winning reelection comfortably in 1956, Muskie had the Republicans' respect, and proposed a more ambitious program. He wanted better roads, repairs to decrepit state facilities, and a major financial commitment to schools. He got most of it. One long-lasting achievement was the Sinclair Act, creating regional school districts that replaced many small high schools. The new districts allowed the increased funding to be spent much more efficiently—a hallmark of his career in Augusta and in Washington. Muskie got lawmakers to approve a highway bond that was by far the largest borrowing package ever put to voters, who approved it three to one. Lawmakers also agreed to invest in state hospitals and university buildings, and approved a one-cent sales tax increase.

Muskie also managed to charm the all-Republican Executive Council that had to approve his appointments. Though Muskie wanted to abolish the council, it would be nearly twenty years before Democrats had the votes to do it. The council had been blocking the Delahanty appointment before Haskell intervened. Muskie tried everything. On a boat trip along the coast with the councilors, Muskie stripped naked and got the councilors to follow him into the frigid water for a brief skinny-dip.

One problem where Muskie made no headway was the pollution overwhelming Maine's rivers. No more than token legislation was passed while he was governor, though it included a classification system for water quality that would later cause him, and George Mitchell, some embarrassment. The pollution problem had to wait for his days in Washington.

IN 1958, AS HE'D DONE FOUR YEARS EARLIER, Muskie affected reluctance to take the next step. He'd made a gentleman's agreement with Republican leaders. They supported his proposed constitutional amendments to create a four-year term for governor and to move state elections to November. In return, Muskie agreed not to seek reelection in 1958. The Senate race was the obvious choice, yet he delayed.

"I did not leap at the opportunity," he said. "Normally these announcements are made about January first. Well, January first came and went. . . . I didn't make the decision to run for the Senate until April first." Muskie claimed Democrats couldn't find anyone who could win against Frederick Payne, who'd defeated Owen Brewster in the 1952 primary and was seeking a second term. Muskie worried about losing ground. Though Frank Coffin was in Congress, there had been little progress at the Legislature. Muskie was by far the Democrats' best vote-getter, and returned to his original theme: "I made the decision to run because if I didn't, that would largely be the end of the effort to make Maine a two-party state."

It was no contest. Muskie won by more than 60,000 votes, taking 61 percent and carrying all sixteen counties, as he'd done in the 1956 governor's race. And 1958 was a banner year for Democrats nationally. The Senate freshman class included not only Muskie, but a cross section of liberal Democrats. Overall, Democrats gained thirteen seats, converting a narrow majority into an overwhelming sixty-four seats. Among those joining Muskie as freshmen were Thomas Dodd of Connecticut, Phil Hart of Michigan, Eugene McCarthy of Minnesota, Frank Moss of Utah, and Gale McGee of Wyoming. The "wave" off-year election was undoubtedly a factor in Muskie shedding the caution he had learned so well as governor, and setting his sights on the path-breaking environmental legislation that became his most important accomplishment. He became close to Hart and McCarthy, and years later said he missed the relaxed evenings where senators formed real bonds.

When he arrived in Washington, Muskie got off on the wrong foot. His initial meeting with Lyndon Johnson, Senate majority leader, was a disaster. Johnson wasn't subtle in his exercise of power, and he exiled Muskie to forbidding committee assignments Mitchell would later inherit.

The story of what happened has been told many times, with accounts reasonably consistent. Muskie told David Nevin, author of a 1972 biography, that he'd thought he and Johnson could get along, saying Johnson "was a practical fellow who understood you had to give and take in politics to get things done, and that's the way I had learned to work in Maine." Muskie didn't understand that politics is practiced differently in other parts of the country.

Johnson opened by telling the forty-four-year-old freshman that deciding how to vote on the myriad motions, amendments, and procedures the Senate considers would be difficult. "There'll be times, Ed," Johnson said, "when you won't know how you're going to vote until they start calling the M's."

Johnson then began a spiel about the upcoming vote on amending Rule 22, which governed the filibusters that were, and still are, a unique feature of the Senate. Armed with a huge, two-thirds, partisan majority, liberal Democrats were eager to break the filibusters—often conducted by members of their own party—that had blocked civil rights legislation for years, and had led Johnson to accept a watered-down version in 1958. They believed they had enough liberal Republican support to have a chance.

Johnson was reputed to have two lists. One was his head count on Rule 22. The other covered freshman committee assignments—then under the majority leader's sole control. Rule 22 specified that to end debate, two-thirds of the entire Senate had to agree. Johnson's plan would alter it to two-thirds of those present. Muskie preferred the reformers' version—three-fifths, or sixty votes. It wasn't until after Watergate, in 1974, that Democrats pushed through that change. Muskie had been listening to Johnson about why he shouldn't commit himself too soon. Johnson then asked, "Ed, you haven't had much to say on Rule 22." Muskie retorted, "Well, Lyndon, we haven't gotten to the M's yet."

Muskie wanted to serve on Foreign Relations, Interstate and Foreign Commerce, and Judiciary. He knew Foreign Relations was off limits to freshmen, but was hopeful about the other two. Johnson gave him none. He was assigned to Banking, which was on his list, and two obscure committees that weren't: Public Works and Government Operations. The question is whether it was his zinger to Johnson that prompted his exile. The later-disgraced Bobby Baker, the Senate secretary who carried out Johnson's orders, told other senators the Maine freshman was "chickenshit." Equally likely, Muskie's unwillingness to go along with Johnson's first vote request caused this demonstration of the leader's legendary power. The frosty relations between the two were long in thawing.

Later leadership changes favored Muskie's ambitions. By 1961, Johnson was gone, surprising many by agreeing to serve as John Kennedy's vice president. Mike Mansfield, a second-term liberal from Montana, became leader, and Hubert Humphrey from Minnesota, who'd proposed a civil rights plank at the 1948 National Convention, became whip. The Senate and national careers of Muskie and Humphrey would soon become intertwined.

Muskie worked to improve his lot on committees. He helped to create or enhance subcommittees on two of them. Inter-Government Relations and Housing became part of Government Operations, allowing him to play a key role on revenue sharing and federal housing, including the Model Cities Act. On Public Works, he chaired a special subcommittee on Environmental Pollution that became permanent. Today, it's the Environment and Public Works Committee, and it became Muskie's most prominent Senate role—and later, George Mitchell's.

His alliance with liberals didn't change Muskie's style. Later accused by Democratic activists of being too cautious, and described as "a man who by nature avoided conflict and unfavorable odds," Muskie knew this was the only way to get things done in the Senate. What a biographer referred to as "Muskie's essentially conservative nature, as opposed to his essentially liberal views on issues of the day," presented both pitfalls and opportunities. It took twelve years to achieve his first major success with environmental legislation, but when he did, the triumph proved lasting.

FRANK COFFIN'S POLITICAL CAREER WAS MUCH SHORTER than Muskie's. In 1956, he was elected to an open seat in Congress. Coffin defeated James Reid, a moderate Republican close to Senator Payne, in what Coffin called "a real fight, and a fair one. It's the kind of campaign you seldom see these days"—as close to a contest of ideas as politics ever comes. Coffin was reelected by a wide margin over Neil Bishop, the unpredictable Republican who'd been a thorn in Burton Cross's side.

The 1958 election favored Democrats in Maine, too, and Clinton Clauson, a Waterville chiropractor, upset former Governor Horace Hildreth, who served from 1944 to 1948. Hildreth was considered a sure thing by Republicans, who believed they could easily reclaim the governorship with Muskie gone. Clauson, one of the half-dozen Democrats Coffin and Muskie tried to get to run in 1954, was not their first choice; they preferred Maynard Dolloff, Muskie's Agriculture commissioner, who later ran and lost in 1962.

"Doc" Clauson "became a very eager candidate a few years later," Muskie recalled. But Clauson died at age sixty-four, after less than a year in office. Republican Senate President John Reed, a potato farmer from Fort Fairfield, succeeded him, and faced a special election in 1960 for the final two years of what would have been the first four-year governor's term.

Coffin finally saw his chance to become governor, and entered the race confidently. If Democratic candidates were so highly regarded that Clauson—whom Coffin called "just a good, down-to-earth, ordinary fellow"—could be elected, he figured he'd have an easy time against an "accidental" governor like Reed. Coffin ended up losing by 20,000 votes. Explanations differ. Coffin decided he'd underestimated Reed's abilities. Ken Curtis, who ousted Reed six years later, scoffed, saying Reed "was a fun person to run against. You could find a lot of holes there."

The decisive factor was likely the anti-Catholic backlash that delivered Maine to Richard Nixon over John Kennedy. Jim Oliver, the former Republican who had finally made it back to Congress as a Democrat, lost his First District seat. Democratic legislative gains were reversed. The tide was nearly as strong as four years later, when Barry Goldwater's run against Lyndon Johnson produced the first Democratic Legislature in Maine since the Civil War. It proved the last hurrah for anti-Catholic, anti-immigrant sentiment in Maine. By 1994, when Angus King became the first nonnative Mainer elected governor, the issue hardly came up.

Coffin received condolences from Kennedy. The new president told him, "Well, Frank, we really got out the vote, didn't we?" Kennedy found a place for Coffin, appointing him deputy administrator of AID, the Agency for International Development, where he oversaw reorganization of foreign aid programs, including the Alliance for Progress Kennedy hoped would improve relations with Latin America. Just before he was assassinated, Kennedy moved to appoint Coffin ambassador to Panama. Coffin then, like Muskie, ran afoul of Lyndon Johnson. Coffin knew Johnson slightly from his four years in Congress, and once told Johnson he was in error—*wrong* was the word he used—and that was enough. Though he faithfully followed most Kennedy decisions, Johnson scuttled the nomination.

It was only after Johnson's landslide win in 1964 that Muskie began working on Johnson about Coffin filling a vacancy on the First Circuit Court of Appeals. After months of prodding, Johnson relented. He told Muskie, "You just hold my feet to the fire a little bit longer, Ed, and this will work out." Coffin took his seat in 1965, and remained there for the rest of his professional career.

As a judge, Coffin was more reflective than Muskie. His partner's contribution, Coffin said, was that by establishing two-party competition, "He gave Maine people a sense of participation. . . . They had a say, and it's been a very refreshing thing." Muskie's legacy "changed the whole cast of Maine politics, and improved both the Democrats and the Republicans." Looking further ahead, Coffin said, "We've had a George Mitchell because of Muskie. It's a very deep thing that he brought about."

4

A POLITICAL BAPTISM

George Mitchell went to work for Ed Muskie in the spring of 1962, beginning an association that would take many forms over the next three and a half decades. Aside from brief periods on Muskie's campaign in 1968 and 1972, however, Mitchell worked for Muskie for less than three years. He was clear about his ultimate objective. "I told Senator Muskie and Don Nicoll at the time that I really didn't have any interest in politics, that the objective was to get a job with a law firm back in Maine," he said. "Senator Muskie himself had practiced law in Maine; he said he understood. He asked me for a commitment to stay through the election of 1964, when he would be seeking reelection."

The story of Mitchell's hiring evoked a point of pride in the new executive assistant. When Muskie was introducing his aide, he often mentioned that Mitchell had come to him looking for a job. Mitchell said, however, that he was asked to join the office, and hadn't applied. After several attempts, he said, "I decided to stop correcting him."

Don Nicoll, who made the initial call to Mitchell, can see both points of view. Muskie, he said, was never attentive to staffing details, and probably assumed Mitchell, as a young lawyer, was eager to get experience on Capitol Hill. It had been John Jabar, who knew the Mitchell family well, who'd made the initial recommendation. Jabar, Tony's brother, was one of Muskie's three-member field staff in Maine. Mitchell also got the approval of Marjorie Hutchinson, manager of the Waterville office, who had been with Muskie since she kept his law practice afloat during his military service.

Nicoll remembers that Mitchell "was a very attractive candidate" during his interview, and that he was anxious to move on from the Justice Department.

"He was a bright young lawyer from Waterville with good family connections," he said. "He was affable, highly competent, and would fit in and work well with staff." On Nicoll's recommendation, Muskie agreed to hire him. Nicoll called it "serendipity."

John Jabar, however, later left under a cloud at the beginning of Muskie's 1968 campaign. While on Muskie's staff, he had arranged federal loans for two corporations that were building nursing homes, and had Paul Mitchell as a partner. A congressman and a senator called attention to the arrangement, which was not illegal at the time, and Muskie ordered Jabar to divest. When he did not, he was fired—a rare instance for anyone on Muskie's staff.

While it may seem hard to believe that Mitchell, who grew up in Waterville while Muskie had his law practice there, had never crossed paths with him, that appears to be the case. Mitchell remembers hearing Muskie's name in connection with a 1954 campaign event while he was a senior at Bowdoin, but he didn't attend. He was abroad for most of Muskie's service as governor, and was home only briefly after that. Had Muskie's offer not come his way, Mitchell reflected later, "I probably would still be a career Justice Department lawyer in Washington."

If Mitchell had no specific interest in politics, he did have one notable example in his own family's past. A Kilroy sister of his father's birth family had a remarkable political career in Portland. Jane Callan, who married Francis Kilroy, George Sr.'s older brother, decided to run for the Legislature, and was elected as a Democrat in 1934. Though Portland was then a solidly Republican city, Jane Callan Kilroy was elected several times to the House, and also served many years on the Democratic National Committee, said her grandson, Brian Kilroy. She was president of the Order of Women Legislators and was an early supporter of John Kennedy's presidential bid. Mitchell's aunt was far from shy, often belting out the National Anthem at party events. She apparently irritated Muskie, who at one point, Kilroy said, complained to Mitchell about her, and got the reply, "That's my aunt you're talking about."

Mitchell had barely settled into the Senate office when there was a visit from Albert "Jim" Abrahamson, a Bowdoin economics professor who knew Mitchell from his time on campus. They chatted, and when Mitchell told him about his ambition to return to Maine, Abrahamson said, "I know a law firm in Maine that's looking for a lawyer." The firm was Jensen Baird, and the partner Abrahamson knew was Merton Henry, a Republican who'd worked for Senator Frederick Payne until he lost to Muskie. Ken Baird, another partner, came to Washington, interviewed Mitchell, and made him an offer. When Mitchell explained he'd joined Muskie's office just two weeks earlier, and had made a commitment through the 1964 election, Baird said they'd still be interested. Mitchell recalls him saying, "From time to time I'll come down and talk to you and we'll see how this thing works out." After nearly two years of searching, Mitchell had found two jobs in just a few weeks.

Mert Henry, who later became prominent in the Maine Republican Party, remembers Mitchell asking his advice. On a trip back to Maine, Mitchell went to see Henry, who said, "We were very impressed by his résumé and by what he had done." Jensen Baird had been formed in 1961, the first new law firm in Portland in years, and was looking to expand. Henry spoke from experience in advising Mitchell. "I told him he ought to take the job with Senator Muskie for a couple of years, but not to make it a career in Washington, because working on Senate staffs can be a very tenuous sort of situation. If the senator loses, you have to start all over again."

Senate staffs at the time were much smaller than today; the major expansions, both in personal office and committee staffs, came in the 1970s. Nicoll and Mitchell acted as the main policy advisers to Muskie, and they divided the workload. Nicoll recalls that Mitchell covered the Banking and Currency Committee, except for the Housing and Urban Affairs subcommittee, where Nicoll had a strong interest. Later, he would assist Muskie in one of his greatest legislative feats: passage of the Model Cities Act against seemingly insuperable odds.

Mitchell was also assigned to Defense and Veterans' Affairs, where he worked on military base closings proposed by the Pentagon, and the sugar beet project in Maine that was designed as a cover crop to replenish soil depleted by potato growing, the state's biggest agricultural product. Mitchell was also involved in transportation at Public Works, while Nicoll covered the special environmental subcommittee. Mitchell oversaw constituent service and coordination with the field office staff. On international affairs, Nicoll said, "I'm a little vague about that, but we were both involved," and Mitchell fielded queries on treaty questions and legal jurisdictions, such as border issues with Canada. Mitchell also accompanied Muskie when he went back to Maine, while Nicoll stayed in Washington.

Nicoll remembers clearly that when Mitchell arrived, "He was the only person I knew who wrote sentences that were a page long." Nicoll, with his early training in journalism, worked with Mitchell on a style more appropriate to the short memos and letters Muskie wanted. "I spent time editing his material so we had more than one sentence on a page, and getting him to move away from legalese," Nicoll said. While Muskie rarely acknowledged staff work, crafting most of his own speeches, he always wanted a text to work from. "George and I would spend a fair amount of time on speeches, trimming and clarifying as we went," Nicoll said. Of the young executive assistant, Nicoll said, "He had a clear desire to be liked, and he never wanted to ruffle feathers." Mitchell's relationship with Muskie began to grow, and Muskie relied on him explicitly during his 1964 campaign, the first time he faced reelection.

Mitchell remembers much humdrum routine, such as appointing postmasters. Before Congress created a separate postal corporation, each postmaster—and Maine had hundreds—was appointed by the president, with advice from his party's senator, in this case, Muskie for John Kennedy, then Lyndon Johnson. Reviewing applicants, many with party or family connections, was time-consuming. "As Senator Muskie once said, for every appointment he made, he made one friend and ten enemies," Mitchell said.

GEORGE MITCHELL GOT TO KNOW HIS NEW BOSS during trips to Maine. It's geographically the largest state in New England, and its population centers are dispersed throughout the nearly four hundred miles from "Kittery to Fort Kent," the traditional phrase depicting its range from south to north. Driving Ed Muskie was a challenge for his staff, Mitchell included. Muskie often used cars and driving as a metaphor for his own experiences, including his favorite story, told so many times his staff could barely resist blurting out the ending.

It went like this, according to the 1972 Muskie biography: A Mainer is standing along the roadside of his farm when a Texan pulls up in a brand-new car. "The Texan had shiny boots and a big hat and whipcord breeches. 'How big is your place?' he asked. 'Oh,' the farmer said, 'a couple hundred acres.' 'Well,' said the Texan, 'I'll tell you: When I get up in the morning I get in my car and I drive hard all day and maybe I'll get to the end of my place, and maybe I won't.' There was a long pause, and then the Mainer says, 'I had a car like that once.'"

The story was popular during Muskie's 1968 vice presidential campaign, and reflects his inherent distaste—shared by Mitchell—for boasting or any public display. It also suggests a wry appreciation for the rural Maine method of survival, with its old cars and barely functioning agricultural machinery. It seems no accident that one of Muskie's friends and most loyal campaign supporters was a car dealer from southern Maine, Shep Lee.

Don Nicoll had good reason to turn down the assignment of driving Muskie around Washington. He took over as AA from John Donovan in 1961, and got a warning about the dangers. Annoyances with his travel schedule were legion, and Muskie thought the problem was never slow traffic, but that the driver had taken the wrong route. "He complained bitterly about this all the time," Nicoll said Donovan told him. His response was, "Why do you do this? He's perfectly capable of driving himself." And from then on, none of the AAs drove Muskie, except, occasionally, Leon Billings, a key environmental aide who became Muskie's last Senate chief of staff in 1978.

In Maine, a variety of campaign workers and staffers drove Muskie. Tom Allen, who represented the First Congressional District from 1997 to 2009, remembers picking up Muskie and Mitchell at an airstrip in the wilds of Washington County. He drove Muskie to Narraguagas High School in Cherryfield for a speech, and then to Bangor, after dark. Allen didn't know the narrow, winding road and his driving speed didn't suit Muskie. "I knew they wanted me to hightail it along," he said, "but to be honest, I was afraid I was going to kill the senator."

Kermit Lipez, now a senior judge on the First Circuit Court of Appeals, worked at the Senate office during the 1972 campaign, and drew the unenviable task of driving Muskie to Washington National Airport when no one else could be found. "I had been told he was a notorious backseat driver," Lipez said. "He always insisted he knew the best way to get wherever you were taking him. And taking him to the airport was a particularly grueling experience because he was always afraid he was going to miss the plane." The route Lipez knew was blocked by construction, but somehow they made it in time, "and he was actually quite gracious once he knew he was going to make the plane."

Mitchell's driving experiences with Muskie reflected their eventual closeness, and the criticisms were more nuanced. Once, while they were driving north on the Merritt Parkway in Connecticut, Muskie objected to the number of times Mitchell pulled out to pass other cars and return to the right-hand lane. "Have you ever thought about how much longer it takes you, how many miles you add to the trip, by changing lanes?" he said. Mitchell admitted, "I never, never have thought of that, and I don't see how you could possibly calculate it." Muskie's response: "Well, you should think about it."

A more colorful story, also beginning on the Merritt Parkway, this time southbound, figures in the 1972 biography. Mitchell was driving separately behind the Muskies' Valiant station wagon, with Muskie driving, along with Jane and the kids. Muskie didn't make much money as a senator, and maintaining a house in Maine and Washington was a stretch, so Jane bought school clothing in Waterville each summer. There wasn't enough room in the car, so Muskie had tied boxes to the roof under a tarp.

Mitchell said, "I saw the tarp beginning to come off, so I drove alongside his car and tapped my horn and pointed up at the tarp. He stopped, madder than hell, saying, 'Damn it all, what's wrong with you?' I showed him the loose tarp and he tied it down quickly and drove off and I fell in behind." This happened twice more, with Muskie "getting madder and madder." When they reached the New Jersey Turnpike, Muskie ignored Mitchell's summons, and "pretty soon the tarp came clear off and those boxes rose up in the air like an airplane taking off and flew back and crashed against my windshield and clothes went flying everywhere." Muskie was all for leaving the clothes behind, but Jane said, "That's the whole winter wardrobe for the kids; we can't leave them." Mitchell ended by saying, "We set off down the Jersey Turnpike picking up clothes, the senator muttering and cursing."

As Dick McMahon and Muskie had during the 1954 campaign, Mitchell often ended up sharing a motel room with Muskie. "It's kind of unthinkable now, but there would be twin beds and Senator Muskie and I would share a room. And he talked a lot to me, and I listened, and I observed him going about the task of being a senator."

It was on a trip to Muskie's hometown of Rumford that Mitchell first wrote a speech for him, for delivery to the Sons of Italy. "I must have read a half-dozen books and got the Library of Congress to do research. I later joked to Italian Americans who are friends of mine that I knew ten times more about Italian-American history than they did, which I really did. I was very nervous, and I did a lot of work on it." The master was not impressed. "The senator immediately found every flaw and pointed them out to me in what I might call rather clear, direct terms." Mitchell went back to work. "He brought out the best in you, and in the end was quite pleased with his speech and it went over well."

At times, the drives engaged them at a deeper level. Mitchell has often told the story of his nighttime drive with Muskie along "The Airline," Route 9 west from Calais, at the time a winding, treacherous stretch of road through unorganized territory and no towns or villages. Among the best versions is one he included in the 2014 speech to the Legislature. It was at the end of the six-night trip that had begun with the speech to the Sons of Italy. Mitchell was driving through rain and fog, "with none of the friendly banter of the earlier part of the week."

Breaking the silence, Muskie said, "What did you think of my speeches?" Mitchell hesitated. "I had seen his temper firsthand, and was a little afraid of him." During the tour, "I had seen how everyone he met complimented him, often lavishly. I had yet to hear anyone offer a critical comment." Mitchell, however, sensed that Muskie "expected the truth from me, so I decided to give it to him. I was generally positive about the week, but added that I thought there was one major problem with all the speeches: They were just too long and repetitious." Mitchell continued, "After a long and ominous silence, he said, 'You're a smart young man. I think it's likely that someday you'll be in elected office, giving speeches like I have this week. When you do, you'll find that there's nothing in the world like the sound of your own voice.'"

Omitted in the speech, but present in an earlier account was what Mitchell was thinking during the "several minutes" Muskie kept silent amid "the sound of the windshield wipers, thump, thump, thump." As Mitchell recalled, it was, "Have I lost my job? Is he going to throw me out of the car?" And he recorded that, after Muskie delivered the line, "there's nothing in the world like the sound of your own voice," he laughed heartily.

In the 2014 speech, Mitchell added a reflection. "Since then, when I've gone on too long in a speech, when I've struggled to bring it to a close, I've thought of Ed Muskie. Even the smartest man I've ever known succumbed to the temptation of talking too much." It may have been at that moment that Mitchell began acquiring, as he termed it in the title of a recent political retrospective, "The Art of Listening."

Not everyone was as understanding of the great man's foibles, and few of Muskie's staff members achieved anything like Mitchell's closeness to the boss. Don Nicoll believes there was a mismatch in Muskie's impulses concerning hiring. "One of his flaws, if you will, presents an intriguing conundrum," Nicoll said. "Muskie liked to draw on a wide range of people who were extraordinarily well-qualified, but he didn't really want to deal with more than one or two people. He was almost oblivious to a large number of his staff members." Anita Jensen, later Mitchell's speechwriter, worked ten years for Muskie, and remembered she started in a cramped room where the desks almost touched. An aisle had to be kept clear so Muskie could go out the back way, though he almost never did, and sightings were rare.

Muskie was demanding. Leon Billings's wife told Nicoll she hated Muskie because he kept her husband from getting home at night, "but that was exactly what he wanted," Nicoll said. "He wasn't unapproachable, but he felt no need to cultivate his staff members." When he did display an interest, it came as a surprise. Jensen said she was stunned when, after she had suffered a miscarriage, Muskie gave her a hug. With Mitchell, it was different. "George, from the beginning, did see a lot of Ed," Nicoll said.

Muskie took some getting used to. Nicoll remembers one of Mitchell's first days at the office when he presented a memo he'd written and got a gruff response. "He was so taken aback by the heated response that he started to back out of the office," Nicoll said, who then made it clear to Mitchell this was normal behavior.

It wasn't long before Muskie began to show a real fondness for the new executive assistant. "George is one of those individuals who really wants to be liked," Nicoll said. "That came through loud and clear from the first time you met him." And Muskie responded. "He cultivated a very warm relationship with Ed. Once he got by the initial shock and established that relationship, he was very comfortable with Ed, and Ed was very comfortable with George," Nicoll said, adding, "It was clear that Ed regarded him as his protégé." Nicoll had a different kind of relationship with Muskie. "There was a complete division between our personal and professional lives. I was somebody he depended on in the office, where I enjoyed his absolute confidence."

By the time of his national campaigns, for vice president in 1968 and for president in 1972, Muskie was relying even more heavily on Nicoll, and the relationship showed signs of strain. One longtime associate observed that, "Over the years, with all that pressure, they just wore each other out." That didn't happen with Mitchell. For both campaigns, Muskie asked Mitchell to leave his law firm to join him, and he did. Their trust and fondness for each other were undiminished.

One reason why Muskie had few intimate friends is that he had lost several early on. Dick Dubord, Harold's son from Waterville, was particularly close, and was described as "friend in residence" aboard the *Downeast Yankee*, the name Muskie applied to the plane assigned to him by Hubert Humphrey's campaign. Dubord's sparkling wit amused Muskie no end, but he died of a heart attack in 1970 at age forty-eight, and no one took his place.

Even later, Mitchell was sometimes taken aback by the level of conflict Muskie managed to tolerate. As a biographer put it, "Muskie sometimes provokes savage arguments with his close aides in order to test his ideas, thrusting the aide into the position he is himself considering taking, and then attacking relentlessly in order to expose the position's flaws."

Mitchell was forced into an awkward position when he and Nicoll negotiated debates with staff for Clifford McIntire, the six-term Republican congressman who left his seat to contest Muskie's reelection in 1964. One of McIntire's negotiators was Mert Henry, Mitchell's future law partner. Mitchell reached an agreement only to have Muskie reject it. This happened twice more, until Mitchell had finally had enough. As Nicoll remembers it, Mitchell told Muskie, "This is it. I'm not going to go back again." And after a long "dead silence," Muskie said, "All right."

The debates about the debates continued. Muskie was incensed about a charge McIntire had made in one of their earlier meetings—that Muskie's vote on a trade bill had prompted the closing of the Worumbo Mill, one of Maine's largest textile plants. The issue involved the "peril point" governing tariffs for industries that might be harmed by foreign competition. It was later repealed and superseded by the 1962 legislation Muskie voted for.

To Mitchell's amazement, Muskie decided that the next debate should focus entirely on McIntire's charge, and the question, "Did the enactment of the Peril Point legislation cause the closing of the Worumbo Mill?" Mitchell said, "By modern standards it was a rather mild charge . . . but it really made Senator Muskie mad." Nicoll thought the proposal ridiculous, but Mitchell responded, "Don, I'm inclined to agree with you, but Senator Muskie insists on it." And Mitchell was even more amazed when the McIntire camp agreed.

In the debate, Muskie demolished McIntire's position, in part because, as Mitchell observed, "there really wasn't direct cause and effect." It wasn't the first nor the last time he had occasion to admire Muskie's debating skills, which he'd acquired at Bates College after joining the debate team run by Professor Brooks Quimby—a deliberate effort to overcome his shyness. "He had all the elements for a good debater: a complete mastery of the details of the issues, and a great facility with language, good rhetorical skills," Mitchell said. "And in those debate contexts was one example of how he could be concise and precise when he needed to be."

Nicoll thought Muskie was ill at ease in the 1964 campaign because it was soon evident it would be a Democratic sweep led by Lyndon Johnson. Muskie "was much less comfortable with campaigning than when it was a close contest. He almost seemed to get more irritable and uneasy. Of all the campaigns, except for the difficulties of the '72 campaign, that was the one where he was least happy." Whatever Muskie's view, he defeated McIntire with 253,511 votes to his opponent's 127,040. The 67 percent Muskie won was his best showing, and the first campaign George Mitchell helped run was a smashing success.

MITCHELL WAS AWARE OF HIS MENTOR'S FLAWS. Muskie's limited income in the early days, which lasted until his national prominence increased his speaking fees, produced some less than endearing habits. Mitchell told an interviewer in 1971 that, "The last two or three times I've eaten with him he's surprised me by paying the bill." Not offering to pay the bill was a habit Mitchell never emulated; his family experience encouraged him always to be the host, and he picked up tabs even when no one expected him to.

Something he did share with Muskie was an aversion to excessive praise, both on the providing and the receiving end. When Muskie's campaign was testing ads for his 1970 reelection campaign, the voiceover included an announcer intoning reverently, "Edmund Muskie is a great man." Muskie had barely been able to sit still, and said immediately, "Why can't we just say, 'Ed Muskie is a good senator.' That's the truth, I am a good senator. And let's say Ed, not Edmund; Edmund is an odd name, [and] it's hard to say. I like plain Ed." No scriptwriter tried to use Muskie's middle name, Sixtus, which his father had chosen for his saint's name, after an obscure medieval pope.

Mitchell was frank about the effect Muskie had on him. In a 2002 interview, Mitchell said, "He was the greatest public figure in Maine's history, and he was extremely impressive, physically imposing at six-foot-four and [with] a lanky frame, with a powerful intellect. He could be tough on staff at times, very demanding, but it brought out what I think is the best in everyone around him." Mitchell said, "I was in awe of him at the time, really still am."

In a speech for Muskie's eightieth birthday celebration in 1994, which Mitchell wrote but couldn't deliver due to Senate business, he focused on the details of environmental legislation with which, by that time, he was intimately familiar himself, describing how it captured the sweep of Muskie's ambition: "Before the Clean Air Act of 1970 became law, the federal government was prohibited from regulating air quality. We could collect data. We could analyze that data and tell people that they were slowly being poisoned. But we could do nothing to stop it. Ed Muskie changed that. He spent countless hours studying, drafting, arguing, convincing. The resulting legislation . . . allowed us to take control of the air we breathe."

NO ONE DOUBTS THAT GEORGE MITCHELL has a temper, but it was nothing like Ed Muskie's; in fact, it's what often came to mind whenever people were asked about their impressions of Ed Muskie. At a symposium hosted by Don Nicoll in 2010, there were so many comments and recollections of Muskie's legendary temper that Nicoll decided to compile contributions from all Muskie's living chiefs of staff. The results were printed as "Temper and Temperament in an Admirable Man: A Tempered Conversation" in 2013. While Nicoll believes Muskie's bouts of temper were only a sidelight to his towering achievements, a reader of the conversations could be forgiven for thinking otherwise. And there's no doubt that the episode in Manchester, New Hampshire, in the winter of 1972 that signaled the end of Muskie's presidential campaign—not yet captured in any biography— forms an enduring impression of Muskie's place in political history.

It started early. His older sister Irene remembered his "terrible temper" from their childhood games of casino, whist, and rummy. "Ed just couldn't bear to lose a game. If he lost he'd throw the cards, yell, and stamp off." He even chased her into the pantry once, where she screamed because she was afraid he would hit her. As governor, during a heated discussion with an aide, he hurled a heavy book, just missing the aide. Angus King, who served as governor from 1995 to 2003, and began his political career as an aide to Second District congressman Bill Hathaway, remembers Mitchell displaying a telephone during a Muskie "roast" at the Eastland Hotel in Portland. "He pulled out from under the podium a disconnected telephone, with the wires loose, that he claimed Muskie had thrown at him at one point when he was working for him in Washington."

Joking aside, there's little doubt that Mitchell, like all those close to Muskie, was at times the object of his outbursts. During a tense moment in the 1968 vice presidential campaign, Muskie obliquely admitted, without exactly apologizing, his fault. After giving Mitchell a dressing-down, he said, "George, how does it feel to give up your law practice and work without pay and spend months away from your family so you can get this kind of crap?"

Ed Bonney, whom Mitchell hired as the state Democratic Party's executive secretary during his term as chairman, said of Muskie, "It could be the smallest things" that set him off. "I know George felt the wrath of that more than once, because he shared that with me." Muskie also exercised his temper more strategically, on the Senate floor. He once gave J. William Fulbright of Arkansas, one of the chamber's most cerebral members, a fearsome tongue-lashing, which earned a rave review from another southerner, Ernest Hollings. He told Muskie, "Ed, you were great out there—I wish you'd get mad and stay mad right through 1972." But that was not Muskie's way.

Jane Muskie, who during the presidential campaign was subjected to vicious rumors by the opposition, was quite open about the battles with her husband, in which she gave as good as she got. "We say a lot a cruel things to each other and sometimes we hurt each other a lot," she told a biographer. "And then we make up."

One failing of several US senators at the time, excessive use of alcohol, wasn't one of Muskie's vices. His favorite campaign restaurant stop in Maine involved a steak and a vodka martini, but not several. Mitchell was clear on this point. "I've never seen the senator anywhere remotely near intoxicated. He's careful about his drinking. If he had, I would have known about it because I saw him late in the evenings and early in the mornings."

Don Nicoll's compilation, "Temper and Temperament," discloses some more likely theories. Nicoll believed that Muskie's bouts with back pain contributed to his irritability. Although Muskie rarely mentioned it, and it wasn't evident when Nicoll went to work for him, pain "became a very serious issue" during his national and 1970 Senate reelection campaigns, Nicoll said. A rough ride in a jeep with an Air Force driver shook up Muskie severely, and may have damaged nerves in his leg. "Pain was a constant problem, but it wasn't evident all the time," Nicoll said.

Muskie's reliance on pain medication become enough of a concern that Nicoll urged him to consult with Dr. Paul Pfeiffer in Waterville, who Nicoll said was "very concerned about overmedication" during the 1968–1969 period. But Nicoll points out that "Muskie's so-called temper never interfered with the performance of his serious responsibilities. He vented at those closest to him. In dealing with his colleagues, it was far more calculated, far more strategic."

Another possibility Nicoll raised about Muskie's temper is that it was behavior modeled by his own father. Muskie often spoke of his father's impulsiveness, and how when he decided to buy the tailor shop in Rumford, he neglected to tell his new bride, who'd expected to continue living near her family in Buffalo. "Why did he feel it was all right to impose his pain on others, particularly those close to him?" Nicoll asked. "My best guess is that it reflects a pattern he learned from his father. He loved and admired his father . . . but he also noted his father's argumentative style and intensity of feeling."

Ed felt the lash of his father's belt more often than his siblings. One day, the enraged Stephen inadvertently used the wrong end, and gave him a painful wallop with the buckle. It was the last time he used the belt on any of the children. There was intense affection between them. Near the end of Stephen's life, Lucia Cormier, a state representative from Rumford, was picking up Muskie and saw him and his father standing on the sidewalk together. Muskie kissed his father good-bye as she watched. "There was great warmth there, between father and son," she said. Stephen Muskie died at age seventy-two, the same age as George Mitchell Sr. when he suffered a fatal heart attack.

John McEvoy, who succeeded Nicoll as AA in the Senate office when Nicoll left to work on the presidential campaign, thought Muskie suffered from depression, and felt it prompted mood swings, from long periods of silence to intense bursts of anger. He said, "The senator's temper and his outbursts were not so much a lack of self-control, but a symptom and a result of the deep depression which seemed almost always to envelop him." McEvoy also speculated the antidepressants that came into use after Muskie retired would have helped him. "I have often wondered what Senator Muskie would have been like, had he [had] the advantage of a moderate dose of Prozac every day." Nicoll isn't persuaded by the depression theory. It's possible, he said, "but I never saw evidence of it, and he never had that diagnosis."

Muskie himself seemed to have viewed his temper as the obverse of his shyness. He was successful in breaking through his natural reserve in a long and successful public career, but there was a price. He told a biographer, "I don't think my family ever understood the agony I went through in overcoming shyness."

Muskie's silences were almost as frequent as his outbursts. On long, transcontinental plane trips, he would sit gazing out the window, in an almost trancelike state. A biographer observed, "He looks without seeing in silences that last for hours, and the assumption is that he is revolving in his mind the things that other men discuss and analyze and ponder aloud as a matter of course."

Another antidote for shyness is attention, especially the public attention that Muskie, like most politicians, came to crave. An unnamed "Republican friend from Waterville" told a biographer, "All of us need a sense of public acceptance, and Muskie needs it more than most. He needs the cheering crowds, and what's more, he needs to earn it. That's part of the addiction to politics . . . [and] it's not just the crowds and the tinsel, but the basic knowledge that you are important and that you are doing something that is significant and worthwhile."

Evaluating the example Muskie set, and what it meant for Mitchell, is necessarily speculative, but certain broad themes are common to both men. In an address to Maine Democrats during the 1968 campaign, at a moment when the crisis of Vietnam was peaking and the vision of the Great Society was eroding, Muskie reminded his audience of their collective responsibilities. "The easy answer is to protect what we have, and let the others look out for themselves. That won't work. It simply won't work." He left them with a challenge: "The question is whether the affluent are ready to share, at a time when the affluent have never had more and the poor have never had less, by comparison."

He took on the theme even more pointedly in a speech to a Polish-American convention in Ohio. Alluding to the Declaration of Independence's "pursuit of happiness," Muskie said, "When we say 'the happiness of the people,' we mean all of them—without exception, without distinction." Later, he said, "Others do not share that belief. Where there is poverty, they sow hate. Where there is love, they sow distrust. Where there is comfort, they sow fear. Where there is common interest, they sow division. You and I know that hate, distrust, fear, and division can only lead to anarchy and tyranny, the twin offspring of the enemies of freedom."

Two years earlier, he evoked his experience as governor as well as his work in the Senate in a letter to constituents. "This is a good time to remember what our national experience so well demonstrates—that a society built upon the potential for enlightenment, self-improvement, and self-discipline of the individual citizen will work in the best interests of all. We can disagree [about] a problem and still deal with it effectively. We can criticize each other vigorously and still work together constructively. We know we can make our democratic system work, because we have done so. In this spirit, may all look forward to the [new year] as another opportunity to demonstrate the ability of a free and enlightened people to govern themselves."

Ed Muskie was a liberal in his day, and more so in retrospect. The rating of his Senate votes by Americans for Democratic Action, the benchmark, was 94 percent—similar to Hubert Humphrey, Phil Hart, and other liberals. His concerns shifted in the later 1970s after he became chairman of the brand-new Senate

Budget Committee, but he always maintained that government must regulate the private sector vigorously in pursuit of the public interest.

Perhaps the most important lesson he left for Mitchell was his skill, bordering on genius, for managing legislation, both in committee and on the floor. While the Clean Air and Clean Water acts were his most important achievements, he overcame even greater odds, whether defending the Senate budget agreement against powerful committee chairmen, or shepherding an innovative bill for recession relief through a skeptical Senate. The Model Cities Act, however, stands out in his twenty-two-year Senate career because it seemed dead before Muskie revived it.

Amid a background of racial strife and inner-city decay, Lyndon Johnson decided a new approach to urban redevelopment was needed. The Demonstration Cities program became part of his Great Society initiatives, yet it was still languishing when Johnson asked Muskie to work on it in the spring of 1966. It wasn't because their personal relations had necessarily improved, but because Muskie had made himself the Senate expert on urban issues through his work on the housing subcommittee. Because he had no vested interest—Portland, the largest city in Maine, had barely 60,000 people—Muskie was seen as an honest broker more than senators from larger states.

Muskie didn't like the bill drafted by Joseph Califano, Johnson's domestic policy adviser. It began with the name—at the time, "demonstration" evoked street protests more than infrastructure improvements—and extended through the legislation's text. He thought the language strident and confrontational, and that it reduced rather than increased the bill's chances for passage. Muskie agreed to be the floor manager, but insisted on a free hand in rewriting the bill. Instead of the top-down urban renewal approach emphasizing demolition and rebuilding, it required community boards to shape the final plans. Historic buildings would be rescued through tax credits for developers. Grants would be awarded on merit, not just the political strength of mayors and congressmen.

Johnson dispatched Califano and Larry O'Brien, the postmaster general and Johnson's congressional liaison, to Kennebunk, where Muskie now summered, to work out the details. Jane Muskie served a mammoth pot of lobster stew, and after five hours the deal was made. Don Nicoll conducted research all summer and redrafted the bill. The new approach worked wonders. An unappreciative committee chairman decided not to block it and, as it went to the floor, Califano agreed to drop the "Demonstration Cities" title.

The sticking point was the bill's price tag—at $2.3 billion over five years, a substantial new commitment. When it appeared it might doom the bill, Muskie retreated. Tom McIntyre of New Hampshire, a conservative Democrat no one suspected of being a big spender, was delegated to propose an amendment to reduce the cost to $900 million over two years. That was almost the same outlay per year, but it did the trick.

Even so, vote counters saw the bill losing as the Senate began debate. Rural senators had little interest in a program that did little for their constituents. John Tower of Texas proposed an amendment to convert Model Cities to a study. It was a passionate speech by Muskie—not recorded because of a malfunction—that turned the tide. Majority Leader Mike Mansfield later said, "It's the only instance I know of . . . where votes were changed on the floor by the way the bill was managed and presented. That's when Ed Muskie made himself in the Senate." Robert Kennedy called it the best speech he'd ever heard. The initial tally sheet showed nearly two-to-one opposition, and it passed by nearly the same margin. Johnson was, in his way, grateful, telling Muskie, "What you and I did, Ed, we both married above ourselves." The Johnsons and Muskies occasionally socialized after that.

The Model Cities program didn't last long; Richard Nixon's opposition killed it. But it did create a new template for redevelopment efforts that has endured, ensuring residents and local communities have a say when federal economic development funds are used in their name.

AFTER MUSKIE'S REELECTION IN 1964, Mitchell began preparing his return to Maine. The partnership agreement at Jensen Baird was complete. But Muskie had one more assignment for his protégé. As part of the Johnson landslide, the Democrats had suddenly become the majority party at the Legislature for the first time in more than a century. At the time, Maine had a "big box" at the top of the ballot that allowed voters to choose all candidates from a particular party, and many of them used it. A "split ticket" in Maine required a conscious choice to stray.

In 1964, the results were astonishing. The Democrats won a solid majority in the House. In the thirty-four-member Senate, they had held only five seats to the Republicans' twenty-nine. For the 1965 session, the totals were nearly reversed. In 1966, things flipped back, despite the election of another Democratic governor, and it would be ten years before Democrats again enjoyed a majority in either House or Senate. The Class of 1964 included many Democrats who carved out notable careers, including Joe Brennan, who served in Congress and as governor from 1979 to 1987, John Martin, who was House speaker for nineteen years, and Gerry Conley, Brennan's mentor who later became Senate president.

Legislative Democrats were at least as shocked by their good fortune as the public was when Muskie was elected governor. A friend of Muskie's, and Mitchell's, Ed Stern, a perennial "placeholder" candidate in a Republican district, responded to his election by saying, "I demand a recount." Not only had Democrats not expected to command a majority, but they also had no idea how to run the Legislature, after being excluded from key committees. Muskie, de facto head of the party, knew the dangers of lawmakers falling on their collective faces, and dispatched Mitchell to assist.

Floyd Harding was born in the farming town of Albion in 1923 and moved to Presque Isle to become counsel for the Maine Potato Growers, opening his own law practice in 1954. He and his wife had nine children. He served three terms in the Senate and, after the election of 1964, was elected majority leader. Harding said Mitchell wouldn't like to be described as someone Muskie sent to Maine on a political mission. "He was just trying to be helpful, that's what he was trying to do," he said. "And he was very helpful. George Mitchell had a gentle way about him, so he and I became friends, and when he ran for governor, he lost."

Harding thinks he helped Mitchell to build a special relationship with Aroostook County, where he was soon to spend time as an attorney representing Freddie Vahlsing, who built a mammoth sugar beet plant in nearby Easton. Harding was quick to share his opinion of Muskie. He had drawn the task of setting up a campaign schedule for him the previous year, and Muskie would stay too long at one stop and then blame "the faceless bastards who set up this schedule." Harding stood up to Muskie, saying, "They're not faceless. Maybe they're bastards, but I'm the person who set up this schedule, and I'm a very humble person." Muskie shot back, "You should be humble, because you have a hell of a lot to be humble about."

Harding says of Mitchell, "He helped me and he helped other people with a lot of problems, and we were grateful for his help. . . . He'd draft bills and draft motions, and he was very skilled at that, and he was polite. . . . Of Ed Muskie, we used to say he didn't suffer fools gladly, but George Mitchell was very sympathetic with us fools, and he suffered us fools gladly."

Mitchell was popular in Aroostook County, even during the 1974 governor's race, because he never came on strong, Harding said. "They always remember George as the guy that did the right thing, at no matter what expense. . . . He didn't wear his Democratic affiliation on his sleeve; he didn't even talk about being a Democrat. He talked about the people, trying to help the people with the problems they had, and that was his byword."

5

INSIDE THE
DEMOCRATIC PARTY

By returning to Maine, George Mitchell achieved a goal he and his wife had set six years earlier, during a vacation on Cape Cod shortly before their marriage. Mitchell had changed, however. His indifference to politics had vanished. As he writes in his memoir, "I had gotten a taste of politics, and I liked it." From the beginning of his law practice, he looked for ways to gain experience among Maine Democrats, just as his partner, Mert Henry, did with the Republicans.

Early in 1965, Mitchell became the sixth lawyer to join Jensen Baird, now a four-year-old firm in downtown Portland. He learned the ropes from Mert Henry, Ray Jensen, Ken Baird, and Bob Donovan, becoming a partner a year later, and remained with the firm, with several leaves of absence for campaigning, until 1977, when he was appointed US attorney for Maine. When another partner was added, the official name became Jensen, Baird, Gardner and Henry. Like most Maine law firms, it was a general practice, though each partner had a legal specialty.

Mitchell started in real estate; at the time, most lenders contracted with law firms for mortgage closings. "When you first started at Jensen Baird you had to learn to search titles in the registry of deeds," said Henry, "because that was the bread and butter of doing all the mortgage work for the savings and loan associations. And he learned it." Henry knew that Mitchell had trial experience at the US Department of Justice, and encouraged him to seek out cases. Some initial clients, however, were unexpected.

A prominent lawyer from Waterville, Julius Levine, was seeking a divorce, and asked Mitchell to represent him. Mitchell tried to decline, telling Levine he had never tried a divorce case. Levine's wife was represented by Bruce Chandler, "a very good friend of mine, and a terrific lawyer," Mitchell said, and he recommended Severin Beliveau of Rumford, later a close political associate. Levine was insistent, however.

A few days later, Mitchell got a call from his mother, who asked, "Why are you being so mean to Julius Levine?" Mitchell tried to explain, but realized she had no patience for the rules of the legal system. "A long time ago your father had some problems and Louis Lester Levine helped him," she told her son. "And now Louis Lester's son wants your help, and I want you to help him." Seeing no alternative—"What am I going to say to my mother?"—he took the case. After several days of trial, Levine negotiated a settlement, and told Mitchell he was pleased with the result. Word of mouth is a powerful form of advertising in Maine, and Mitchell soon began getting more calls. "I ended up trying a whole bunch of divorce cases, and it happened really just completely by accident," he said.

Some years later, in 1970, Mitchell ran into Joe Brennan at the Portland courthouse. Brennan had left the Legislature to run for county attorney, the only elected prosecutor position in Maine, now called district attorney. Brennan knew Mitchell only slightly, but his reputation was solid. "He was very involved in party politics," Brennan said. "I wasn't." Brennan had four or five appointments to make, and asked Mitchell if he'd be interested in becoming an assistant county attorney, a part-time position paying $6,000 for two days a week. Brennan made him an offer, but said, "I was just sort of kidding. I didn't think he'd have any interest whatsoever."

A few days later, Mitchell accepted the job; he wanted courtroom experience, and this was a fast way to get it. One of Brennan's favorite stories about the man he was ultimately to appoint to the US Senate involves two political writers for the *Portland Press Herald*, who razzed Mitchell and congratulated him on his "promotion to obscurity." As Brennan said with satisfaction, "They didn't mean any harm, but it was not a promotion to obscurity. It turned out to be just the opposite."

Brennan was impressed by Mitchell's courtroom skills. One high-profile case they tried together involved two Portland police officers alleged to have beaten up a man and taken his wallet. His offense, in their eyes, was to have sold a watch to one of their girlfriends, who pronounced it "junk." Maine's legal system seemed like an even smaller place in the 1970s. The officers were represented by Dan Lilley, later a renowned defense attorney, who had been Brennan's Republican opponent in the county attorney race, and Dana Childs, who from 1964 to 1966 had been House speaker during Brennan's first term in the House. The prosecution won convictions, though by the time the verdicts came in, Mitchell had departed to help run Ed Muskie's 1972 campaign. "I was not popular with a lot of police then," Brennan recalled, and it came up during later campaigns, where he and Mitchell were sometimes accused "of prosecuting cops, not criminals."

Mitchell was dogged in putting together a complicated embezzlement case against a town official who was skimming cash from the daily receipts. Most small towns had no more than rudimentary accounting systems. "George took the case when no one else would," Brennan said. Although they worked together for only ten months, Brennan got to know Mitchell well. "He was thorough, he worked hard, he'd take a file home if it was a complicated case, he'd go out into the little courts and try a drunk-driving case. He did anything he was asked to do, and he did it all well, and he never, never made enemies."

Mert Henry said Mitchell "was very meticulous in his preparation and won cases that nobody thought he could possibly win." He went up against Herb Sawyer, a debate partner of Henry's at Bowdoin, who represented an insurance company and was convinced there was no way he could lose, but he did. Sawyer told Henry, "Boy, I've got to be better prepared if I'm going to have him on the other side." Mitchell's courtroom success, Henry said, started with his personality. "He was a warm and friendly person, without being ingratiating, and that had a good influence on juries."

MITCHELL TOOK ON ONE CLIENT IN A DECISION he may later have regretted. Ed Muskie, who'd encouraged Freddie Vahlsing to take over the Aroostook sugar beet project that appeared to be failing, suggested Mitchell represent Vahlsing, and he agreed. Vahlsing was a larger-than-life character who tended to bewilder Mainers with his loud, brash charm, even while making his development schemes sound persuasive. He flew his plane in and out of Maine from New Jersey, and wore cowboy boots, not often seen in Maine's farm country.

Unlike corn and soybeans that get federal subsidies, or even Idaho potatoes, which get subsidized water, Maine's potato crop was at a disadvantage, and about to lose top rank in national production. After thirty years of intensive, one-crop cultivation, the soil was depleted, and required an adequate rotation crop. Muskie had been advised sugar beets might fill the bill. The US embargo against Cuba had cut off a major source of raw sugar, and sugar beets were a good alternative. While not directly subsidized, sugar beet acreage was controlled by the US Department of Agriculture; sugar beet producers were given six allotments of 33,000 acres each. Since potato growing had expanded to over 100,000 acres in Maine, one allotment seemed a good fit. But there was a catch: Without a refinery in place, or at least under construction, Maine would lose out.

A committee led by a bank president and the head of the Bangor & Aroostook Railroad convinced the Great Western Sugar Company of Denver, the nation's largest processor, to come aboard. The congressional delegation—three Republicans and Muskie—Republican governor John Reed, all signaled enthusiastic support. After the allotment was granted in 1964, Great Western planted test plots. The yields were disappointing. The company decided sugar beets were stunted by Aroostook County's shallower topsoil. Mainers, naturally, thought there was something wrong with the company's agricultural techniques.

Freddie Vahlsing then entered as the white knight. His father thrived in the food-processing business, and the Vahlsings had shipped potatoes from Aroostook County since 1928. In 1961, Vahlsing had obtained a loan guaranteed by the Area Redevelopment Administration (ARA), a Kennedy administration initiative, to build a frozen french fry plant in Easton, at the headwaters of the Prestile Stream, prized by trout fishermen. Potato starch plants, which then discharged plenty of scrap, were polluting streams, and the state responded by requiring sewage-treatment plants in towns like Mars Hill. In the pioneering system of water classification, where enforcement was often waived, the state had rated Prestile Stream "B," the next grade below drinkable water, as a lever to encourage cleanup, and not reflecting its current condition.

Vahlsing was asked to build the sugar beet refinery next to his french fry plant. He liked the idea, with the apparent guarantee of a healthy supply. But a new problem arose. The potato plant was already compromising Prestile Stream's water quality, and the ARA wouldn't guarantee the loan unless something changed. The Legislature, in special session, downgraded the classification to "D," the lowest designation. It passed 110–30 in the House, 25–2 in the Senate, and was signed by Reed. The legislation limited the reclassification to nine months, a provision forgotten in the ensuing controversy.

The sugar beet plant was built in record time, and the potato market also started to improve. Maine farmers, government allotment or no, weren't anxious to try a new crop they knew nothing about. The first year, 1966, only 3,300 acres were planted, and the crop was processed in a few days. While that improved to 10,000 acres and 26,000 acres during the next two years, the soil was often marginal and yields were low. The best production came from the Kennebec and Androscoggin river drainages—far from the Aroostook County farms sugar beets were supposed to revive.

Vahlsing, described as "an exuberant man, a backslapper who seems to love attention and often is found around the fringes of politics," was in danger of defaulting on his loans. He decided, in 1968, to retrieve his fortunes by purchasing a bumper potato crop other processors thought should go to the cull pile. It was an environmental disaster. The Prestile Stream stank to such a degree that Canadians on the St. John River, to which the Prestile flows, tried to dam it. The irony was that the sugar beet plant never produced enough sugar to pollute anything.

Vahlsing began to make himself scarce. He had agreed to pay for a party at the 1968 Democratic National Convention in Chicago. The party attracted eight hundred people, but not Vahlsing. It took the intervention of Governor Ken Curtis, who had succeeded Reed, to get Vahlsing to pay the $2,000 tab. By the end of the year, the sugar beet plant was silent and never processed another beet. Ultimately, Aroostook found better rotation crops, such as broccoli. Said Harold Pachios, "We had the right idea. We just had the wrong crop."

The political fallout was intense. Legislators were outraged that the state was on the hook for $3 million of the $30 million construction cost, and they were different lawmakers—the Legislature had switched back to overwhelming Republican control in 1966. Muskie and, to a lesser extent, Mitchell, were tarred by the brush of Vahlsing's failure, and even more so by Muskie's support for temporarily lowering Prestile Stream's classification. In the eyes of some environmentalists, it forever tarnished Muskie's image as "Mr. Clean." Many years later, it was common to hear someone say, in discussing Muskie's legacy, "But what about the Prestile Stream?"

Mitchell, too, was tagged with the charge during his 1974 run for governor, and even during his 1982 Senate campaign. When John Day, political reporter for the *Bangor Daily News*, pressed him during the Senate race, Mitchell responded notably more tersely than to other questions. He said, about his appearance representing Vahlsing before a legislative committee, "I was asked to go up there, not to testify, but just to be available to answer questions. One or two came up. I was asked to respond. I did. I didn't think of myself as a lobbyist, but I was registered as one. I practiced law. His company asked me to represent them. I did. Everything I did was entirely appropriate. I resigned after a period of four years. His firm was just one of many clients I had." Mitchell pointed out that, as part of his 1979 confirmation as a federal judge, he had undergone more elaborate ethical scrutiny than anything asked of US Senate candidates.

Mitchell's own concerns were more about his client's odd behavior. "He'd call you up at nine o'clock at night and ask you to be somewhere at ten the next morning, as though you had nothing else to do in your life, and be very unhappy if I'd say, 'I can't because I've got a trial starting tomorrow morning. Give me a little more notice.'"

Dan Wathen, a state judge who served twenty years on the Supreme Court, including ten years as chief justice, was an attorney for Vahlsing alongside Mitchell. "I got the dirty side," he said—he took the potato plant, while Mitchell covered the sugar beet operation. Both of Wathen's parents worked for the Vahlsing Potato Company, where his father was a buyer and his mother was the forewoman of the processing crew—nearly all of them women. Wathen had met Mitchell while he was still an aide to Muskie, and welcomed his involvement. Despite the difficult circumstances, Wathen, and his mother, were charmed by Mitchell. "He has a real twinkle in his eye, and a sort of a sly smile, I mean a subtle smile, which is really engaging," Wathen said. "When you meet him, I can understand why my mother thinks he's the best thing since wrapped candy." When they divided the work, "George, with a big smile, said I deserved to represent Vahlsing, Inc.," the existing company. "Even then," Wathen said, "it showed you he knew what he was doing."

And despite the hue and cry over Vahlsing's bankruptcy and hasty exit, Wathen points out that the potato plant was bought by McCain's and expanded, while the sugar beet refinery was converted by the Huber Corporation for wood processing. "They still pay most of the taxes in town," he said.

While Mitchell had left Muskie's office behind, politics was still a priority, as it was for Mert Henry. They were close personally, even if sometimes on opposite sides. Looking back on twelve years together, Henry said, "Our offices were right next door to each other, and when you lunch together almost every day, you get to know somebody very well. . . . We talked politics a great deal. George was always supportive of my activities as a Republican, and I was supportive of his activities in the Democratic Party." Henry and the other partners approved Mitchell's leaves. "We always encouraged George to pursue those things. He had a great interest in politics, and it was good for the firm to have the publicity."

The next step was with the Maine Democratic Party. In 1966, Peter Kyros stepped down as chairman to run for what would be the first of four terms representing the Congressional First District, and there was no obvious successor. Ed Muskie called to find out if Mitchell would be interested. He began campaigning in the usual way, by visiting state committee members from all sixteen counties. "Since there was little or no competition," Mitchell said, "I was elected unanimously at the state convention in May."

Muskie wanted a loyalist in the key state party position. His national ambitions were beginning to bear fruit. He'd been mentioned as a running mate for Lyndon Johnson in 1964 before Hubert Humphrey got the call. By all appearances, Muskie made little effort to act as party boss, even though, as the contemporary party's co-creator, he could have. A biographer said flatly, "Muskie exercises no authority over the party." But influence is another matter, and in Mitchell, Muskie had a trusted lieutenant for what proved an eventful two years.

Today, nurturing ambitions entirely within the framework of a party organization isn't something a rising candidate would consider. But in the Maine Democratic Party of the 1960s, it made perfect sense. Both of Mitchell's immediate predecessors, Bill Hathaway and Kyros, had used the position as a springboard to successful runs for Congress. Hathaway won the Second District House seat in 1964, while Kyros won in the First District two years later. Hathaway ran while still serving as party chair, which raised a few eyebrows. The downsizing of the House delegation from three members to two in 1962 benefited the newcomer, Hathaway, who challenged Clifford McIntire, then won the open seat two years later when McIntire stepped down to take on Muskie.

After Frank Coffin's three-year tenure as party chair, the job had passed to other Lewiston and southern Maine officials little known today. But from 1962 to 1988, almost every chair ran for Congress or for governor, including Hathaway, Kyros, Mitchell, Beliveau, David Bustin, Pachios, Barry Hobbins, and Rick Barton.

A month after the 1966 convention, Ken Curtis emerged from a three-way primary having easily bested both the House speaker and Senate president from the 1965–1966 legislative session, Dana Childs and Carlton Reed. Curtis, just thirty-five, was about to become the youngest man ever elected governor, and represented a political force every bit as powerful as Muskie twelve years earlier. Mitchell worked closely with him from day one.

"It was an exciting time," recalled Charlie Micoleau, later Muskie's Senate chief of staff, who was hired by Mitchell in 1967 as the state party's first research director. "There were fresh ideas for modernizing state government, and while the Republicans regained control of the Legislature, there were enough Democrats to be a legislative force to be reckoned with." Kermit Lipez, Muskie's one-time driver who became a key aide to Curtis, remembers the campaign as "boldly progressive on everything but government spending." Curtis thought, perhaps naively, that his ambitious plans wouldn't require a tax increase.

It was Curtis's personal qualities, though, that struck Mitchell most forcibly. Curtis had grown up in a tiny hamlet in the small town of Leeds, called Curtis Corners—five generations of Curtises had farmed there—and couldn't wait to get away, first to Maine Maritime Academy and law school, then into politics. Curtis, Mitchell said, "was a really natural politician, just a wonderful, warm, generous, open personality that people tended to like right away." They bonded. "I was very deeply involved in the campaign in every respect," he said. Lipez could see the affinity, saying of Mitchell, "He is also a very warm, upbeat person, very funny, interested in people, naturally curious."

Perhaps Mitchell's greatest service was helping Curtis construct his Maine Action Plan, a blueprint for his administration, filled with concrete proposals. It read like the party platforms of the day, but was far more detailed and specific. Curtis's desire for the plan was pragmatic. After working for Jim Oliver during his one term in Congress, he had been Maine director of the Area Redevelopment Authority, which provided contacts similar to those Muskie gained through the Office of Price Stabilization. He ran for Congress himself in 1964, and amid the Johnson landslide came within a few hundred votes of unseating Stan Tupper, a liberal Republican. Since Democrats controlled the Legislature, Curtis became secretary of state, which he found preferable to attorney general—too many unpopular decisions.

Curtis knew he'd still be seen as unseasoned. "Part of my problem was I was young, and people doubted whether I had the experience to be governor," he said recently. Mitchell was one of several Democrats Curtis enlisted, and he chose Mitchell to write the crucial section on state government—the last of the plan's ten "points," each of which Curtis introduced in speeches around the state. Curtis said of Mitchell, "I respected his ability for getting things done. I would often ask him to help me in drafting things. I didn't know anyone who was any better."

In the introduction to Point 10, Mitchell quoted Joshua Chamberlain, the Civil War hero who came home and was elected governor in 1866, serving four one-year terms, on the role of state government: "A government has something more to do than to govern, and to levy taxes to pay the governor. It is something more than a police to arrest evil and punish wrong. It must also encourage good, point out improvements, open roads of prosperity, and infuse life into all right enterprises. It should combine the best minds of the state for all the high ends for which society is established and to which man aspires. That gives us much to do." Mitchell then noted that Chamberlain was a Republican, but, "Were he alive today, he would be a stranger in his party, for the Republicans have long ceased to practice what Chamberlain preached."

Point 10 was a virtual catalog of the reforms Curtis would pursue during eight years in office. Many of the specific changes were accomplished, including abolition of the Executive Council, instituting annual legislative sessions, professionalizing the State Retirement System, creating a state corrections system, and reorganizing the Executive Branch. Curtis combined more than 150 separate agencies into a Cabinet-style administration with, initially, sixteen commissioners. He also established the University of Maine System and State Planning Office.

Some proposals, including having the governor appoint the secretary of state, treasurer, and attorney general rather than having the Legislature choose them, and creating a lieutenant governor, were never accomplished. The lieutenant governor section, envisioning the position to include ceremonial work, featured a sharp jab at the incumbent, saying, "For seven years, John Reed has devoted more time to personal image-building than to the hard work of running the State of Maine. Any governor must engage in a certain amount of ceremony, though none in history have quite carried ribbon-cutting to the extreme that Governor Reed has." As with Muskie's television appearances and frequent chats with reporters in 1954, Curtis's statewide presentations of the Maine Action Plan provided a contrast between what he saw as the stand-pat Reed and his own vigorous reform plan.

Curtis's campaign attracted considerable interest. Bobby Kennedy came to Maine twice to campaign with Curtis, and it was after a street rally in Lewiston that Kennedy told Curtis he thought he was going to win. Curtis still wasn't sure, but couldn't help but be encouraged. In November, Curtis ousted Reed by a 21,000-vote margin. To this day, Reed and Muskie's opponent in 1954, Burton Cross, are the only Maine governors in a century to be defeated in re-election bids.

In a message to Democratic supporters, Mitchell took pride in his accomplishments after just a few months as party chairman. "I want to extend to you my heartfelt congratulations for a job well done," he wrote. "I am sure that Ken Curtis, Bill Hathaway, and Peter Kyros would be among the first to say that they couldn't have won without the help of hundreds of dedicated Democrats like you throughout Maine. With the election of a governor and US Representatives from the First and Second Congressional Districts, we have turned an important corner in the history of the Democratic Party of Maine."

The top-of-the-ticket success didn't carry down to legislative races, however. Republicans were firmly installed, with majorities in both House and Senate that they maintained until the Watergate year of 1974, as Curtis was leaving office. Charlie Micoleau, who assessed the situation for Mitchell, figured it out quickly. "It only took a few weeks into that legislative session before it became obvious to me that Ken Curtis's problem was not a lack of articulate members of the Legislature or a lack of speechwriters or policy wonks. The missing ingredient was that he lacked votes."

Micoleau and Mitchell worked on candidate recruitment. "George had a very, in classic George J. Mitchell fashion, meticulous plan to go about this."

At his law firm—party chairman was an unpaid position—Mitchell produced a list of potential candidates, then dispatched Micoleau to meet them and speak at local party functions. "You could see George's law training in this, and how he really focused on details," he said. "If you were going to present a plan or an idea or concept, then it had to be carefully thought through in terms of how it was going to work, who was going to do it, when it was going to get done." It foreshadowed Mitchell's later work when he was picked by US Senate Democratic Leader Robert Byrd to head the Democratic Senatorial Campaign Committee in 1984.

The 1968 election produced sufficient Democratic gains for Curtis to push through a personal and corporate income tax the following year, with the assistance of moderate and liberal Republicans. He had butted heads with Republican leaders in the previous session over their plan to raise the sales tax rather than his preferred option, the income tax. Mitchell and Curtis continued to grow closer. By 1967, they addressed each other in letters as "Ken" and "Georgie."

The state 1968 convention unfolded for Mitchell with a sense of foreboding. Lyndon Johnson had announced he wouldn't seek reelection on March 31, bowing to outrage among Democrats over his Vietnam policies, and Mitchell fully expected an "end the war" plank to be introduced. Mitchell, like Muskie, was struggling as the war threatened to engulf not only Johnson, but the entire party. Mitchell saw his role as party chairman as supporting the president. Curtis, who eventually broke with Johnson over the war, along with Joe Brennan, captured their reluctance to do so. "Johnson worked on me continually about the war," Curtis said. "We still believed in the old way, as with World War II and Korea, you support the president."

Johnson also got Maine support from an unexpected quarter during the initial troop buildup. Governor Reed was chosen to chair the National Governors Association in a compromise after a fight between two other contestants. He was seen as someone who wouldn't rock the boat, and gave Johnson his full support.

Mitchell had been given an advance copy of a speech Larry O'Brien was due to deliver before the Wisconsin primary, which was preempted when Johnson announced he would not seek reelection. The next day, Mitchell wrote to Johnson. "Your address last night was a magnificent demonstration of your deep and abiding desire for peace. I hope—as do all Americans—that this effort will lead to a just peace in Southeast Asia. Some five weeks ago I sat in the White House with several other state chairmen and listened to you discuss the war in Vietnam. The enormity of the burden you are carrying struck me then with unforgettable force. Thus for you and your family I am glad and relieved by your decision. But for America I am sad. No president has ever demonstrated so much concern and compassion for the poor and oppressed. No person has ever done more for them." Mitchell added, "The controversy over the war can never obscure your progressive accomplishments in the domestic field"—though for years afterward, that is exactly what happened.

Speaking to the Hancock County Democratic Committee on March 25, Mitchell had warned, "Important as Vietnam is, it is not the only issue facing us today. And those Democrats who are trying to turn this into a one-issue election are paving the way for a Republican victory in November."

Mitchell did give advice that diverged from full support, however. After Johnson's State of the Union address in January, he wrote to special assistant Marvin Watson, reporting that, in Maine, "press reaction has been restrained and moderate—neither particularly effusive in support nor negative in criticism." After his report, he added a personal note concerning Johnson's longstanding offer to halt the bombing of North Vietnam if Hanoi would agree to peace talks. "It seems to me that, despite the obvious risks involved, a bombing pause—accompanied by careful documentation if they take advantage of our restraint—is in the overall national interest at this time." Coincidentally or not, Johnson took that step in the speech announcing his withdrawal.

Despite his trepidation, Mitchell helped convince the state convention on May 18 to adopt a Vietnam plank the regulars had written. It promoted peace talks but not withdrawal. He had a knottier problem, however, when it came to discussion of who Maine Democrats would support for president. Before the convention, Hubert Humphrey, the convention speaker, had let Muskie know he'd consider him as his running mate, and at the convention wore a Muskie button. Ken Curtis was already supporting Bobby Kennedy, as was Bill Hathaway. County chairs and state committee members were, in the meantime, asked to support Muskie as a "favorite son" candidate, which would give Muskie leverage at the Democratic National Convention in Chicago.

"George was in an awkward position, needless to say," said Micoleau. "He was state chair, but was absolutely committed to Ed Muskie." At the critical meeting, attended by some thirty party leaders, Mitchell got all but two votes for Muskie. "There was a popular governor on a different side of the fence, so there was a risk involved," Micoleau said. "It demonstrated to me that here is a fellow who planned ahead, knew how to count his votes, and once he set a goal was very persistent in achieving it." At the Chicago convention itself, however, Hathaway gave a speech supporting Kennedy and attacking the favorite-son plan. Muskie said the plan wasn't his, and Hathaway backed down, but it wasn't the last time the two were at loggerheads.

The favorite-son plan was not quite what it seemed; Muskie wasn't being selected by the delegation—Humphrey was. As Mitchell recalls it, "I was caught in the middle, but it was rather clear in my mind that Maine, and the Maine Democratic Party, specifically, would be best served by support for Vice President Humphrey's campaign. Both on its own, that he had the best chance to win, despite the problems involved in the Vietnam War, and secondly, because it offered the best opportunity for Senator Muskie." Mitchell said it was highly unlikely Kennedy would consider Muskie. A month later, Robert Kennedy was assassinated on the night of the California primary, less than five years after his brother had been slain in Dallas.

Mitchell also had to finesse another issue—why Humphrey, who by that time was running for president, was the only candidate invited to the state convention. He played it straight. "The invitation to Mr. Humphrey was extended several months ago, long before anyone knew he would be a candidate for the presidency. In view of the change in circumstances since the invitation was first extended, I have invited Senators Kennedy and McCarthy to address the convention." Neither accepted. While agreeing to support Mitchell's decisions at the convention, Curtis couldn't resist a little ribbing. In an April 23 letter accepting the favorite-son plan, he wrote Mitchell, "Please pardon my delay in answering, but I have been busy campaigning for Senator Kennedy. All kidding aside."

Not long after the state convention, Muskie decided that, with Humphrey closing in on the nomination, he was likely to be picked as vice president. He needed Mitchell on the Democratic National Committee, so Mitchell wound up his party chairmanship in preparation for joining the DNC. Unlike most past chairs, who just resigned, Mitchell wanted to create a transition. He chose Severin Beliveau, who chaired the Oxford County Committee and was a Franco-American, still an important asset. Beliveau and Harold Pachios later made their careers in Maine as partners in Preti, Flaherty, Beliveau & Pachios, one of the state's largest law firms.

Mitchell had also hired Ed Bonney as the party's executive director while he was serving as Cumberland County chairman. Bonney was happy to come aboard when he discovered he'd get a pay raise from what he was earning at the W. T. Grant department store. Bonney was impressed with Mitchell's fund-raising abilities, often working with Bob Dunfey of the hotel chain family. "He and George raised a lot of money—a lot of money, for Ken Curtis," Bonney said. Beliveau and Bonney ended up serving through the end of the Curtis administration, by far the longest partnership of a party chair and executive secretary.

Beliveau credits Mitchell with capitalizing on the early successes of Ed Muskie and Frank Coffin to move to the next stage, building the Democratic Party into the dominant position in state politics it occupied for the next four decades. "He developed the party as an effective political operation in Maine," Beliveau said. By making it a full-time, year-round enterprise, Mitchell "elevated it . . . to an operation that was really relevant and contributed significantly to control the Legislature and help the congressional candidates at every level. He's the one who introduced a professional approach to politics in Maine."

When Beliveau succeeded Mitchell, he moved the party office from Lewiston, the traditional Democratic stronghold, to Augusta, where for a time the party owned its own building, at 66 State Street, not far from the State House, emphasizing its statewide focus. There was a full-time staff of five, including an executive director, printer, and marketing director. It wasn't until the 1970s that the Maine Republican Party felt the need to hire a part-time executive director.

The professional staff effort was necessary, Beliveau said, "because we were still the minority party at the time. We had to work harder." Despite successes statewide, Democrats did not win a lasting majority in the House of Representatives until 1974, with a Senate majority established in 1982. Beliveau said party support was critical to both developments. The party chair was not only chief recruiter of candidates for Congress and the Legislature, sometimes choosing themselves, but also provided much of the financial support and training for first-time candidates. The state office was the hub of Democratic political operations.

Once Democrats became established at the State House, however, the center of gravity shifted. Political recruitment was centralized in the majority offices under longtime House Speaker John Martin and his close political associate, Senate President Charles Pray. With the rise of political action committees as fund-raising conduits, congressional candidates began working on their own, and the Maine Democratic Party's role withered. After the 1980s, the state party chair position returned to the near obscurity it had occupied before Frank Coffin's political lightning bolt in 1954.

6

THE BIG TIME

From his new seat on the Democratic National Committee, George Mitchell was in a prime position to observe the process that put Ed Muskie on the 1968 national ticket. The Democratic National Convention in Chicago was the first many young Maine Democrats had attended, and there was a strong sense of anticipation about Muskie, even though Humphrey also considered thirty-seven-year-old Senator Fred Harris of Oklahoma for vice president until almost the last minute. Humphrey later said, "When it came to making a choice between Harris and Muskie, I went for the quiet man. I know I talk too much, and I wanted someone who makes for a contrast in style. Two Hubert Humphreys might be one too many."

Mitchell was inside the convention hall when Humphrey and Muskie were nominated, and knew nothing of the mayhem outside, as police clubbed antiwar protesters in bloody confrontations that to some recalled the civil rights marches in the South. Only later, on television, did they see what was going on, and it led to a sense of unreality. "We thought we were involved in the center of action in the convention," Mitchell said, "but in fact, the center of action was elsewhere, and we're kind of bystanders to the whole process."

Mitchell had taken what Ed Bonney considered a big risk in celebrating Muskie's impending nomination. The Mainers were staying at the Holiday Inn on Lakeshore Drive, and Mitchell told Bonney and Beliveau, "We've got to be ready for a big party." Beliveau expressed his doubts. "If we hired musicians and $10,000 worth of food and stuff, and Humphrey doesn't choose him, what are we going to do?" But Mitchell was sure, saying, "I know he's going to choose him, so let's get ready." Beliveau had made his own gesture toward the big time, chartering a United Airlines jet to take the entire delegation to Chicago.

But Bonney also saw what was about to happen on the streets. At the Field Museum, a staging area for the Illinois National Guard, his wife pointed out that the jeeps were being equipped with frames of barbed wire. "It made you feel like you were in a different country," he said.

A vice presidential campaign is far more abbreviated than a presidential bid, so there was little time to get organized. Muskie ended up relying on a troika of advisers. Don Nicoll, his chief of staff, was someone he considered essential, even though Nicoll's strength was policy and Senate business, not politics. As early as 1964 Muskie had come to rely more on Mitchell for political advice. The third player was Berl Bernhard, a Washington attorney who'd served on the staff of John Kennedy's Civil Rights Commission. Muskie knew Bernhard from his days chairing the Democratic Senatorial Campaign Committee, where Bernhard served as counsel, and was impressed both by his legal skills and political instincts. The three worked reasonably well together during the brief vice presidential campaign, but it was a different story three years later, when Muskie launched his 1972 presidential bid.

The scenes from Chicago haunted the early days of the Humphrey-Muskie ticket, which sank in the polls after starting even with Richard Nixon and Spiro Agnew. Muskie had another, and more familiar, problem for vice presidential nominees—he got little attention in the early going. Then, at a campaign stop at the courthouse in Washington County, Pennsylvania, that all changed.

Both Humphrey and Muskie were relentlessly heckled at campaign stops, and Muskie had thought of a way to turn the no-win situation to advantage. He shared it with Humphrey, who liked it, but didn't use it. It was September 25, and draft-age students were there, along with a contingent of union members at the opposite end of the fight over the future of the Democratic Party. In television footage that aired on all three network news shows that evening, Muskie arrives onstage after wading through a mass of protesters. He starts to speak, but can't be heard. After the crowd begins to quiet, a student can be heard saying, "Say something." Muskie responds, "Well, that's not a bad idea. If you give me the chance I will try." Another student says, "You have a chance; we don't." A union supporter of Muskie shouts, "Give 'em hell, Senator," to which Muskie replies, "I am not going to outshout anybody. I have never made a campaign a shouting match, and don't intend to start now."

Muskie then invited the students to send up one of their number, promising ten minutes of uninterrupted comment, as long as he got the chance to be heard afterward. Rick Brody, a twenty-one-year-old senior English major from Massapequa, Long Island, came onstage. He began haltingly, but then found his voice. "You guys say we are dirty and unwashed—we are the true Americans." At that point, Brody was booed, and Muskie interjected, "I said I was willing to listen to him, and I hope that all the rest of you will, too." Brody then added, "We love the flag just as much as anyone else. We want America to stand for what the Constitution stands for, which is, everyone is equal under the law, which is not true in this country." He then suggested that the only truly antiwar candidate, Gene McCarthy, "wasn't listened to," and said, "Wallace is no answer, Nixon is no answer, Humphrey is no answer. . . . Sit out this election. Don't vote for president."

Muskie had discarded his prepared remarks, which focused on increased federal aid to education under the Johnson administration. Instead, he addressed some of Brody's charges directly and others obliquely. Muskie told the story of his father, who had fled to America in the early years of the century, without a dime to his name, and lived just long enough to see his son elected governor. "Now, that may not justify the American system to you, but it sure did to him," he said. He condemned the idea of boycotting elections, and said that "staying away from elections" only perpetuates the power of elites. He said, "This is a country and a system that will work only if we trust our people, only if our people trust our leaders." And he condemned "this business of building walls between different segments of our society in the mistaken belief that by so doing, we can build safety and security for the privileged."

Brody himself wasn't much impressed. He told a reporter that Muskie's invitation was "a good political move," but said, "He's still a hawk." That wasn't the verdict of his peers, however. Muskie won over the students. A front-page *Washington Post* story was headlined, "From Jeers to Cheers, Muskie Turns Unruly Crowd into Cheering Admirers," and referred to it as "one of the spectacular performances of the 1968 political campaign." At Syracuse University, after more heckling, he said, "It isn't for the young to be always right or always fair. It is for the young to protest and be the motivating force for change—to prod their elders, to prod our institutions." Muskie had become a national political star. Five days later, Hubert Humphrey broke with Johnson on the war, endorsing an unconditional bombing halt. Humphrey began his climb back from oblivion to a photo finish for the Democratic ticket.

Mitchell had spent the first month of the campaign in Washington, organizing the staff and attending to the multitudinous details of creating a campaign from scratch. Then he joined Muskie on the road. One of his coups was convincing Harold Pachios, an advance man for Lyndon Johnson's 1964 campaign, to leave his new job at the US Department of Transportation to work for Muskie. Pachios had first declined, but Mitchell reasoned with him, saying, "If the Republicans win, you're out, because you're a Democrat." On the other hand, "If you won't help us and we win, you're out." Pachios saw the logic. Mitchell also hired Shep Lee, the car dealer, to work in California.

There were personal benefits, too. On a trip to Maine, Humphrey campaigned in Waterville, and then went to the Mitchell house on Front Street. It was, said Mary Mitchell Friedman, Robbie and Janet's daughter, "one of the greatest things that ever happened to my grandmother." Mary "was just overwhelmed by that." A clear vinyl pillow with the initials "HHH" had pride of place on her sofa for years afterward. The family went to work, too. "We spent countless days and nights at Atkins print shop stuffing envelopes and addressing envelopes and just doing the whole campaign," Mitchell Friedman said. "So by the time my uncle started running for office, we were a force to be reckoned with."

Muskie, while buoyed by the acclaim, was not nearly as comfortable on the national campaign trail as he had been in Maine. Muskie toured extensively in the Midwest and Mid-Atlantic states, where his ethnic Catholic roots appealed to disaffected blue-collar Democrats. After another long day in Pennsylvania, he arrived at a hotel in Harrisburg for dinner, only to be informed by Mitchell that there was another speech. Muskie blasted him. "One more speech, and oh, I got angry," he told a biographer. "I had poured it out all day, speech after speech. . . . And after you've done that all day, you are exhausted and drained."

Mitchell saw Muskie's development as a candidate, and Humphrey's "growing sense of confidence" in his running mate. Mitchell said all presidential campaigns "begin with the presidential campaign staff wanting to exert total control over the campaign, including the vice presidential candidate and his staff." Over time, "As Senator Muskie's performance demonstrated what a good candidate he was . . . there was a gradual emancipation and sense of independence."

Berl Bernhard saw some troubling signs, though. "One time we were flying to Seattle, and in mid-flight Hubert said, 'Cancel Seattle and go to San Antonio,' and I thought, Jesus, we're not ready for that," Bernhard said. He came to see that Muskie had similar tendencies: "There was not a clear line; there were never clear lines. Ed didn't like clear lines." Bernhard recalls a night in Cleveland when dissident Democrats held an anti-Humphrey rally. He tried to convince Muskie to address the crowd. "It was the first real screamer I had with Ed." It got so loud that Jane Muskie emerged from the bedroom to ask what was wrong. But Muskie never went down, and Bernhard's own remarks were, he said, "not effective." Bernhard said of Muskie, "He was a loyal citizen, and he was a hell of a campaigner. But he showed the signs, as in 1971 and 1972, of that tiredness. He didn't have Hubert's energy, or Bob Kennedy's energy."

The Humphrey-Muskie ticket came within 700,000 votes of Nixon-Agnew in November, but with George Wallace taking the Deep South, Nixon won a comfortable majority in the electoral college.

Muskie was seen as a winner, though, the candidate who, had he been at the top of the ticket, "would have won," according to Majority Leader Mike Mansfield, who knew both senators well. A famous cartoon depicted Muskie taking Humphrey on his back and carrying him toward the finish line. Richard Goodwin, John Kennedy's speechwriter, also had a house in Maine. He said, "Muskie was the only guy who didn't sound like a political hack. He was the only one talking to the people who didn't sound like a holdover from the 1930s."

Mitchell addressed the next race in a long letter to Don Nicoll on August 7, 1969. It begins, "I saw the Senator last weekend and discussed briefly with him the situation with respect to 1972. Since our conversation was relatively brief, and not very private, I didn't get a chance to get into much detail. So I am taking this opportunity to tell you what I feel, with the request that if you think my suggestions have any merit, you pass them along to the Senator for his consideration." He struck a characteristic note of deference. "If at any time either you or he feel that I'm sticking my nose in where it doesn't belong or isn't wanted, I hope you'll let me know." He recognized Nicoll's proficiency with policy, and said, "I have no doubt that you would do your usual excellent job (especially if I can occasionally add some of my BS to your facts)."

Mitchell said the campaign should start no later than January 1971, and to make even that date possible, Muskie should add staff to his 1970 reelection team specifically devoted to creating a national campaign. Seven full-time employees would be needed, he said—three for issues, two for politics, a press spokesman, and a secretary. One of his suggestions was Charlie Micoleau, who was indeed one of the first hired. The staffing would cost $200,000 annually, Mitchell said, added to $100,000 for the Senate reelection. "Under present circumstances I believe it can be done. If it cannot, then maybe we'd all better stop thinking about 1972 anyway." He concluded: "I have discussed the above suggestions and in general terms on the phone with Dick Dubord and Hal Pachios, and they both concur."

The 1970 reelection campaign began with a concern that was to become more acute for the 1976 Senate race, Muskie's last—that his national campaigns required him to take positions, and to be absent from Maine for so long, that voters would feel he was neglecting them. Muskie wouldn't have been the first senator defeated for reelection by the perception he'd become too close to Washington. It happened to Margaret Chase Smith in 1972.

Mitchell, who covered Maine while Nicoll stayed in Washington, advised Muskie to locate the reelection team primarily in Maine, and hired a talented group. They included Micoleau; John Martin, who'd been elected in 1964 and had already moved up to House minority leader; and Tom Allen, the future congressman just returned from England, where he'd been a Rhodes Scholar along with Bill Clinton.

Micoleau recalls the "upstairs, unventilated stuffy office" just across Main Street in Waterville from Muskie's old law office. "George would come in two or three days a week and then he'd be on the phone every day." Micoleau said, "Ed Muskie did carry Maine overwhelmingly in 1970," which allowed him "the political freedom to then run for president." He added, "A lot of the credit for the running, the details of that campaign, went to George, and should go to George because he really worked terribly hard, traveled all over the state, and had a strong sense of how to organize the senator's support." Mitchell was the campaign chair, and unpaid. Mitchell, Micoleau said, was easy to work for. "He was just a good-humored person. He didn't yell at people, and some of his jokes were actually funny at the time—and he didn't repeat them as often as he subsequently did."

Mitchell also showed he would have done well as a pollster. He several times challenged Don Nicoll and Mert Henry to predict statewide outcomes. In 1966, all three guessed the winners in races for governor and Congress, but Mitchell came closest to the actual numbers. In 1970, when Ken Curtis won by just eight hundred votes over Jim Erwin when the income tax was the big issue—Mitchell headed Curtis's legal team for the recount—he correctly forecast the nail-biting result; Nicoll thought Curtis would get 53 percent, while Henry predicted an Erwin win.

Charlie Micoleau also earned his stripes in the 1970 Muskie campaign. As early as a February 2, 1969, memo to Don Nicoll while he was still on the state party staff, he outlined a strategy for "winning by the greatest possible margin," which included coordinated support for Kyros, Hathaway, and Curtis, all up for reelection, and assisting in key legislative races. The presence of four prominent Democrats made it vital to coordinate, since the $250,000 he estimated they'd raise themselves was a far cry from the $15,000 Muskie had shared with four candidates sixteen years earlier. Micoleau said precinct work would also be vital.

Muskie was fortunate in his opponent. Neil Bishop had a certain cantankerous charm, but he had been in politics a long time, and had lost several more races since he'd organized "Republicans for Muskie" in 1954. Muskie coasted to victory, winning 62 percent and nearly 200,000 votes in the off-year election.

The biggest political event for Muskie that year occurred not in Maine, but on national television, on the evening before Election Day.

Richard Nixon and Spiro Agnew had been active campaigners, further developing the "law and order" theme that had proven effective against Humphrey in 1968. There was real concern among Democrats that the message would unseat a number of prominent Senate liberals from Muskie's 1958 class. The possibility that Republicans might take the Senate could not be dismissed.

Nixon bought fifteen minutes of network television time the evening before the election. The Democrats chose Muskie for their own fifteen-minute slot. Muskie took the lead largely because of Ted Kennedy's accident on July 16, 1969, at Chappaquiddick Island, when Mary Jo Kopechne died in his submerged car after he drove off a pier. Up to that point, Kennedy had been the presumed front-runner, bearing the standard of his two murdered brothers.

Democrats pulled together an organization called the Committee for National Unity, and Averell Harriman, who'd campaigned with Muskie in 1954, signed a $100,000 note to guarantee airtime. The idea apparently came from Geoffrey Cowan, a young Washington attorney and 1968 Gene McCarthy backer, who said Muskie "was the only guy with enough stature to oppose the president." Richard Goodwin produced drafts on his manual typewriter up in Kingfield, where he lived off the grid, and drove them to Waterville, where Muskie reviewed them. The footage was filmed at a supporter's house in Cape Elizabeth, not far from Kennebunk, where ocean waves crashed in the background, setting a tone that contrasted with the Nixon spot. The president used a recording of a Phoenix campaign stop with a roaring crowd. On television, however, as a Muskie biographer related, "It had a raucous tone of intemperance that was exacerbated by the poor quality of the television tape."

Muskie spoke quietly, and looked straight at the camera during most of his talk. He appealed for calm. "In the heat of our campaigns, we have all become accustomed to a little anger and exaggeration. Yet—on the whole—our political process has served us well. . . . It has worked for almost two hundred years, longer than any other political system in the world. And it still works." Muskie moved quickly to his theme. "But in these elections of 1970, something has gone wrong. There has been name-calling and deception of almost unprecedented volume. Honorable men have been slandered. Faithful servants of the country have had their motives questioned and their patriotism doubted. The attack is not simply the overzealousness of a few local leaders. It has been led, inspired, and guided from the highest offices in the land."

Muskie tried to make his appeal nonpartisan. "The danger from this assault is not that a few more Democrats might be defeated—the country can survive that. The true danger is that the American people will have been deprived of that public debate, that opportunity for fair judgment, which is the heartbeat of the democratic process." He insisted that there was no "issue" of law and order, "only a problem," and pointed out that under Ronald Reagan as governor, "there is no more law and order in California today than when he took office."

The rhetorical peak of the address came after Muskie paused, looked even more intently into the camera, and said the message from the president was that Democratic candidates "favor violence and champion the wrongdoer." He paused again, then said, "That is a lie. And the American people know it is a lie." For most viewers, about thirty million, that was his most memorable line.

Muskie also provided historical context, recalling Joe McCarthy's attacks on General George Marshall as secretary of state. "It is the same technique," he said. The historical record, he went on, shows that progress occurs "under the leadership of the Democratic Party." It's "not that we are smarter or more expert, but we respect the people. We believe in the people."

He concluded by drawing a contrast between "the politics of fear and the politics of trust. One says: 'You are encircled by monstrous dangers. Give us power over your freedom so we may protect you.' The other says: 'The world is a baffling and hazardous place, but it can be shaped to the will of men.' Ordinarily, that division is not between parties, but between men and ideas. But this year the leaders of the Republican Party have intentionally made that line a party line. They have confronted you with exactly that choice." On November 17, Representative Peter Kyros entered the speech into the *Congressional Record*.

It was a sensation. Phone calls and mail poured into Muskie's Senate office. On Election Day, Nixon's hopes of a Republican tide were dashed. Only one of the Senate liberals, Al Gore Sr. of Tennessee, was defeated, and several won by slim margins. Democrats gained nine House seats. The results are more impressive in that several liberals, including Frank Moss and Gale McGee, were later defeated in 1976 despite Jimmy Carter's presidential win. Richard Goodwin had no doubt about the speech. At the Fenway Motel in Waterville, where Muskie and his circle watched the returns, Goodwin mightily annoyed the campaign staff by saying, "Well, I made another president last night."

Muskie was thrust into the front-runner role he retained for the next year. But there was a downside. Muskie's staff was utterly unprepared for the volume of the response. Letters went unanswered; requests to help, offers of support, simply went by the wayside. Muskie hadn't heeded Mitchell's recommendation that he "staff up" during the 1970 reelection campaign. As Berl Bernhard recalls it, "People were writing and calling, and we had no way to respond. . . . People got angry and thought, 'Well, he's not capable.'" Bernhard said, "It was both a wonderful and disastrous event."

GEORGE MITCHELL SPENT THE EARLY PART OF 1971 crisscrossing New England by car to nail down Democratic support. The New Hampshire primary was nearing the peak of its political influence—it was Johnson's near loss to McCarthy in 1968 that had triggered his decision to withdraw—and while the primary vote was a long way off, Muskie needed to shore up support in his own region. Governor John Dempsey of Connecticut was an early supporter, and Mitchell met with numerous Democrats in Massachusetts, Vermont, New Hampshire, and Rhode Island. He said, "I have a clear recollection that the response was overwhelmingly favorable. There was a lot of support for Senator Muskie, not just because of his person and his policies, but [because] he was from New England and there was obviously a sense of affiliation. . . . It was a pleasant task." But Mitchell didn't join the campaign payroll until October.

Muskie had grown from Maine senator to a truly national figure. His speeches were notable events, and didn't necessarily fit the expected patterns. He addressed the National Governors Association in San Juan, Puerto Rico, in September. Mark Shields, who later went into journalism, was then on Muskie's staff, and wrote in a memo, "Senator Muskie is the only legitimate candidate for the presidency who has served as a governor. He should forge this bond with incumbent governors early in his address." Another staffer reported the result: "The speech to the governors' conference went very well. He didn't start delivering it until 11:53 p.m., after everyone had consumed their fair share of alcohol. He managed to keep the undivided attention of the audience at that late hour."

Muskie had intended a conventional address. He gave a quick summary of what would "win the kind of visible approval that might look good in tomorrow's *New York Times.*" He said, "I wanted to speak as an American, to congratulate most of the governors in the South for their courage in defending the rule of law through a difficult and troubled month." He abandoned the text when, the previous day, thirty-eight inmates and nine guards held as hostages died at Attica State Prison after Governor Nelson Rockefeller ordered an armed assault.

He said, "The events at Attica Prison are another stark proof that something is terribly wrong in America. How many of us are really ready to face that truth? So many of us still turn our heads and pretend that we just don't see." Four decades later, Muskie's words are haunting. "We mourn today's victims, but because we did so little about yesterday's, it will all happen again tomorrow."

Muskie was a liberal, and called for a return to the approach of Lyndon Johnson's Great Society. "The only decent course now is a single, clarifying decision—at long last, a genuine commitment of Washington's vast resources to the human needs of people." He called for prison reform, "not more years of papering over the plain fact that our jails are monstrous, inhuman dungeons, schools for crime and centers of sexual abuse." Muskie did not claim to have found a solution, but he warned, "We cannot join the half of our fellow citizens who already believe that this nation is headed for a final breakdown. . . . At least we can restore the hope of so many who are so close to giving up."

An even more unusual speech came in October when he addressed the Liberal Party of New York. It was titled, "The Challenge of Liberal Consensus." Its first words must have given listeners a jolt. "We meet tonight in a time of failure for American liberalism. You can see the failure everywhere in this city and across the country. For too long, the sound of liberal alarm has been answered by little more than the echo of our own voices." He then cataloged the ways that liberals had "sounded the alarm" about the expanding war in Indochina, the consequences of segregation and racism, a defense budget that continued to expand. Nor did Muskie offer his audience an out. "The blunt truth is that liberals have achieved virtually no fundamental change in our society since the end of the New Deal."

Muskie faulted the liberal response to the dispute over "law and order." Even though some politicians "pandered to people's fears with swift and easy answers, most liberals responded first by ignoring the issue of crime, and then by denouncing those who pointed to the problem. We said that it was wrong to do battle with the Bill of Rights—and it is. But what we did not say frequently enough or persuasively enough was that repression is not only wrong, it will not work." He said liberals had offered no real solutions, and "let others create the impression that law and order was a black vs. white issue, even though black women are five times as likely as white women to become the victims of a violent crime."

Challenging audiences was part of what Muskie conceived of as his duty as a presidential candidate. After some excesses of truth-telling, Bernhard would say, "That's what happens when you have an honest candidate." Saying what people wanted to hear wasn't why Muskie was campaigning.

There was plenty of talent. Speechwriter Bob Shrum joined the staff, as did media guru Bob Squier, who choreographed the Election Eve speech. Tony Podesta and Tony Lake also came aboard. For many of them, it was their first national campaign in careers that continued for decades afterward. Eliot Cutler, who, after a long career in business, ran for Maine governor in 2010 and 2014, was an early addition, and became chief scheduler. Muskie's "brain trust" was equally impressive. It included Averell Harriman, former Secretary of Defense

Clark Clifford, Harry McPherson, Johnson's White House counsel, former Deputy Defense Secretary Paul Warnke, and future Secretary of State Cyrus Vance, whom Muskie would succeed in 1980.

In the end, it did not quite add up. A key problem, which often plagues candidates from small states, was money. Muskie's campaign never reached its fund-raising goals. Berl Bernhard provided testimony to the Senate select committee investigating the Watergate-related machinations of the Committee to Reelect the President, which also reviewed the other campaigns. He said, "We raised approximately $2.2 million in 1971 and expended virtually all of it. We raised just under $3 million from January 1, 1972, to . . . April 7, 1972"—shortly before Muskie suspended his campaign—"and expended virtually all of that."

These are startlingly low numbers, even in the era before public financing of presidential campaigns, and well before the explosion of campaign cash. Bernhard was in charge of fund-raising, but he had numerous other responsibilities, too. Muskie did have one solid financier in Arnold Picker, chairman of the board of United Artists. Bernhard said Picker "could well have been the most decent wealthy man in the United States." But Picker was virtually unique. Clark Clifford and Averell Harriman provided prestige, but didn't help pay the bills.

Bernhard told the select committee, "Except for the initial few months of the campaign we were always in the hole. We never had enough money to pay our obligations." By mid-1971, "I was forced to lay off ten of our staff people and impose salary cuts on between ten to fifteen others." When the campaign finally "staffed up" by February 1972, to 125 employees, it almost immediately started cutting back, with forty staff positions gone by March 15. "On March 31, we simply did not pay most of the people, except for thirty-three of the lower-paid staff," Bernard said.

While it is natural to fault the staff or the fund-raisers, the basic problem lay with the candidate himself. Because Muskie had chaired the Democratic Senatorial Campaign Committee from 1966 to 1968, the same position George Mitchell held from 1984 to 1986, it could be assumed he had already demonstrated aptitude. But Muskie's appointment had come about almost solely because of the scandals surrounding Senator Thomas Dodd of Connecticut, who'd previously held the post. Dodd's alcoholism and erratic behavior had become so severe that his own staff provided the evidence that led to his censure by the Senate—the same penalty imposed on Senator Joseph McCarthy a decade earlier. It was Muskie's reputation for rectitude and integrity that got him the job. In fact, Muskie often expressed contempt for those whose jobs focused on money-raising, and seems to have considered himself above it. Bernhard said when he gave Muskie a list of twenty potential donors, "I'd be lucky if, a week later, he'd called one of them."

Mitchell saw it all at firsthand, and learned a painful lesson, one that he heeded in all of his own campaigns. "George was a wonderful candidate," Charlie Micoleau said, "because you'd say, 'Here are ten people you should call,' and he'd call every one of them. . . . George was always very willing in that regard."

Bernhard's desperation to find places where Muskie could quickly raise money, despite his aversion, reached almost comical proportions. A fund-raiser with Governor Milton Shapp of Pennsylvania went reasonably well—except that the expenses made a huge dent in the proceeds. With difficulty, Bernhard convinced Muskie to appear at the home of oil magnate Marvin Davis. "The place was jammed," Bernhard said, "and I expected Mr. Davis to stand up, because he wanted to be part of our finance committee, to announce his intention to support Ed. Not a word." Bernhard queried Davis on how much had been raised. It was just $12,000. The event had been Davis's anniversary party.

Without money or serious organizing efforts, the campaign relied by necessity on endorsements. Muskie's Senate colleagues, and many Democratic governors, were more than willing. Their priority was defeating Richard Nixon, and they didn't see anyone else likely to do the job. By January 1972, Muskie had been endorsed by eight present or former senators, nine present or former governors, and seventeen House members. In March, Senator Birch Bayh of Indiana endorsed Muskie, and delivered the entire Democratic House delegation. But it was not translating into enthusiasm from rank-and-file Democrats.

There was one endorsement Bernhard tried hard to get, but could not. Lyndon Johnson had been driven from office by Vietnam, but Bernhard thought his blessing would still be valuable. "He was very troubled by the war," Bernhard said. "His public statements didn't reflect the way he really felt." Bernhard visited the LBJ ranch and "rattled around in a jeep." Johnson, who was ill and died in January 1973, didn't respond warmly. Johnson said of Muskie, "He really hasn't supported the efforts I've made," despite his steadfast public solidarity on Vietnam. Bernhard believes "the early estrangement" between the two was still there. There was no endorsement.

Bernhard's meeting with Hubert Humphrey went better. He remembers a cordial breakfast session in which Humphrey's esteem for Muskie was on display. "Let's get this whole thing settled," Humphrey announced, and said he and Muskie both represented "the left side of the middle," and that only one should run in 1972. "I've had my turn," Humphrey said. "Now it's Ed's turn. I'm not going to undermine him."

Traditional Democratic groups were wary of Muskie, and it was clear early on that they would need special treatment. Labor never warmed to him; Muskie came from a small state where unions were generally weak. The bigger problem, though, was Vietnam. Muskie, like all Democratic leaders, had been obliged to stick with Johnson, and Humphrey had been willing to make only a tactical break late in the 1968 campaign. Mike Mansfield began sponsoring amendments to defund the war early in the Nixon administration, and Muskie, too, began shifting from hawk to dove. The pace of his change didn't impress some party activists, but by the time he started seriously campaigning, in 1971, it would have been hard to fault his positions. On Moratorium Day on college campuses, October 15, 1969, Muskie, at his alma mater, Bates College, called for a fixed date for troop withdrawal. Yet young draft-age Democrats continued to view Muskie with suspicion.

Bernhard said he never understood the intensity of the war issue for Democrats. "It was crazy, because Vietnam was basically over," he said. President Nixon was drawing down American troops rapidly, and his "Vietnamization" policy to continue the war seemed to have at least a chance of success. Nixon faced only token opposition in the primaries from Pete McCloskey, yet young Democrats seemed unsatisfied with a candidate who didn't denounce the war at every campaign stop, or make it the centerpiece of his campaign. George McGovern, who had barely registered in the polls in mid-1971, filled that role. More to the point, immediate withdrawal became a prerequisite for most of the party's biggest fund-raisers.

The external problems were mirrored by internal struggles. Mitchell didn't work full-time until October 1971, and by that time the Muskie campaign's problems ran deep. Muskie started with same trio—Nicoll, Bernhard, and Mitchell—as in 1968. Nicoll took charge, while Bernhard worked from his Washington law firm, Verner & Liipfert, and Mitchell remained in Maine. Nicoll, however, hadn't divorced himself entirely from Senate business. Years later, Nicoll said he shouldn't have moved to the 1972 campaign staff at all, or at least should have focused solely on issues. After ten years with Muskie, and many campaigns, "I was just burnt out," he said. Nicoll never returned to Muskie's Senate office, and in 1973 left for Maine, where he became a vice president for Maine Medical Center in Portland.

Bernhard pressed Muskie to decide who was in charge, but Muskie appeared in no hurry to sort things out. Nicoll proposed a kind of co-directorship, which Bernhard thought wouldn't work. Finally, Muskie demoted Nicoll and replaced him with Bernhard. When he arrived, Mitchell was designated deputy campaign manager, though Muskie looked first to Mitchell, and paid him more,

$36,000, while Bernhard received $32,000. The decade-long relationship with Mitchell, and their evident ease with each other, also buttressed Muskie's trust.

By all accounts, Mitchell and Bernhard got along well, and are law partners to this day. When Mitchell left the Senate in 1994, it was to join Verner & Liipfert rather than any of the Maine firms that would have welcomed him. The prognosis for the 1972 campaign, however, remained grim. In December 1971, a memo criticizing Bernhard's management—though not Mitchell's—went to Muskie from John McEvoy, the new Senate AA, Bob Shrum, Bob Squier, and Nicoll. It faulted Bernhard's "current preoccupation with fund-raising," and "a lack of administrative support, and some confusion as to lines of responsibility." It recommended an increased role for Mitchell, and also assigning Nicoll to the candidate's plane.

By that time, it was probably too late. On December 23, Tony Podesta wrote to Mitchell, "I have spent several hours today trying to determine whether or not we plan to do newspaper advertisements to increase the listenership on January 4"—the date of Muskie's formal announcement. "After having talked with some twenty people at the office, the best conclusion I can make is that you are the only one who knows what's going on."

Muskie hadn't had a good fall. One ominous note came at a Democratic National Committee meeting on October 13. Mitchell was a delegate to the McGovern Commission that was rewriting delegate selection rules after the 1968 convention debacle. McGovern got the job in part because it seemed unlikely he'd run for president. Mitchell, on Muskie's behalf, gave the nominating speech for Senator Harold Hughes of Iowa to chair the credentials committee. Instead, the DNC picked a novice, black attorney Patricia Harris, later a McGovern supporter. The balance was already shifting.

Party pros had been dismayed by one of Muskie's early trips to delegate- and donor-rich California, which featured what a biographer called the "ludicrous spectacle" of Muskie repudiating a staff-written speech after it had already been released to the press. Washington columnists Evans and Novak, who had a particular animus toward Muskie, faulted Muskie's "irrational scheduling, uncoordinated speechwriting, and tardy organization."

Perhaps more seriously, Muskie made an unnecessary blunder while on a tour of the Watts section of Los Angeles. A black student asked Muskie whether a black candidate could be elected in 1972, and whether Muskie would consider one for his ticket. Muskie said he would not. He said the country should be able to accept a black vice presidential candidate, but that voters weren't ready. It was a classic "honest" Muskie answer, and alienated potential supporters. Denunciations in the black press were nearly unanimous.

As 1972 dawned, Muskie still led all prospective Democratic candidates, and he remained viable against Nixon. Just as a primary candidate should have been peaking, however, his support was softening. The endorsements had created no bandwagon effect. The first sign of trouble was the withdrawal in December of Senator Henry Jackson of Washington, Muskie's rival for primacy in environmental legislation. Jackson was the first choice of labor, and the only plausible candidate clearly to Muskie's right. His failure to gather any steam showed the weakness of union leaders and the strength of student demonstrators.

THE IOWA CAUCUSES DIDN'T ACHIEVE THEIR primacy until after Jimmy Carter's surprise victory there in 1976, and Muskie won there and in Arizona, with McGovern second. The first big primary was New Hampshire, near Muskie's home turf. Muskie was expected to carry New Hampshire by a big margin, a theme that became incessant in the weeks before the primary. Reporters suspected that Muskie's support was soft even though few had uncovered any real evidence. They kept pressing Muskie to say how he expected to do, but he resisted, saying only that he expected to win. The press, nonetheless, created the notion that Muskie needed to get at least 50 percent.

The biggest story, however, was not the vote itself but Muskie's appearance March 4 in front of the Manchester *Union Leader* building on a flatbed trailer, three days before the primary. Muskie had been subjected to inflammatory editorials by William Loeb, publisher of the *Union Leader*, who ran them on the front page. Muskie, like nearly all Democrats and many Republicans, was "soft on communism," according to Loeb. References to the "shifty-eyed" candidate, and "Moscow Muskie" were regular occurrences, and galling, given his father's narrow escape from Tsarist oppression. But it was two Loeb editorials, shortly before the primary, that drove Muskie over the edge.

The first concerned the "Canuck letter," later exposed as a Nixon forgery, which Loeb printed without verifying its authenticity, and continued to claim was genuine even though the writer was never found. It was the leading edge of the "dirty tricks" campaign financed by the Committee to Reelect the President, or CREP—often pronounced "creep"—and run by Donald Segretti, who was convicted in the Watergate trials and served time.

Not all of the Nixon "dirty tricks" were nasty; some were merely mischievous, albeit disruptive. Mitchell, who arranged the campaign's logistical details, found his name used in curious ways. At a stop in Milwaukee, he was awakened by a phone call at four a.m. from the hotel lobby saying a dozen limousines were parked out front, and when would the senator and his party be down to use them? Another wakeup call informed him that fifty pizzas were ready downstairs. On still another occasion, Mitchell found his signature had been forged on an $1,800 restaurant and bar bill, and he spent considerable time and energy contesting the charges. In an even stranger incident, a number of African ambassadors and their families showed up at a Muskie fund-raiser and had to be accommodated; they were under the impression it was an American embassy function. "We ended up paying a lot of bills we really weren't responsible for," Mitchell said. "It was a diversion of energy and resources," he said, and, collectively, "had a hugely negative effect."

The "Canuck letter" was much more consequential. The author was likely Ken Clawson, a former *Washington Post* reporter who had moved to the CREP payroll. Clawson bragged about his authorship, then denied it in an October 10 *Post* story by Bob Woodward and Carl Bernstein, while admitting he'd met "briefly" with the *Union Leader*'s managing editor, Joseph McQuaid. McQuaid said Clawson had been "helpful."

The letter is certainly crude, undoubtedly by design, with misspellings and strange syntax. It was addressed to "Mr. Loeb" at the "Manchester Guardian," the name of the British newspaper. It described meeting Muskie during a Florida campaign stop, where a man "asked him what did he know about blacks and the problems with them—he didn't have any in Maine, a man with the senator said. No blacks, but we have Cannocks [*sic*]." When the writer asked what this meant, "Mr. Muskie laughed and said come to New England and see." It was signed "Paul Morrison" from "Deerfield Beach, Florida." No such person was ever found. Loeb nonetheless used it in another editorial attack on Muskie, accusing him of hypocrisy about race and ethnicity.

Copies of the letter circulated widely in the Franco-American wards of Manchester, all rich with Democratic voters. It was followed by strange middle-of-the-night phone calls from people identifying themselves as from the Muskie campaign and talking crazily about blacks and "Canucks." Muskie, of course, had nothing to do with them.

The second editorial used a gossip item from *Newsweek* which claimed Jane Muskie had been drinking excessively and had used foul language in a public place. Loeb reprinted the piece and headlined it, "Big Daddy's Jane." It was this editorial that led to Muskie's passionate defense of his wife in the speech given from the flatbed trailer, including the charge that Loeb was a "gutless coward."

What happened next, however, remains fixed in controversy. David Broder of the *Washington Post*, the most respected political reporter of his day, wrote that Muskie broke down and cried, and used those words in the lead of his front-page story. The full effect wasn't immediate, but after Muskie defeated McGovern, 46 percent to 37 percent, three days later, the incident was incorporated into the storyline that Muskie had failed. Bernhard said Broder later admitted he might have been wrong about the tears, that Muskie's version—it was melting snow on his face—could have been correct.

Woodward and Bernstein were among those who misremembered the events. In their later "Canuck letter" story, they wrote, "Immediately following his 'crying speech,' Muskie's standing in the New Hampshire primary polls began to slip." There were no polls taken between the speech and the vote. For his part, Mitchell thinks it's possible that Muskie did cry. "I've always felt that, though he denied it, it was clear that tears did come to his eyes."

Muskie's performance followed a rapid trip to Manchester from Florida, where he'd just appeared at a drug treatment center. Muskie's visit was meant to dramatize his conviction that treatment, rather than imprisonment, was the best way to deal with drug addiction. The event was moving, and both Muskie and teens at the rehab center had tears in their eyes. The temperature was in the 80s in Florida and in the 30s in Manchester. The combination of defending his wife and the emotional experience at the treatment center, Mitchell said, might have caused Muskie to break down.

Bernhard, who stayed behind in Florida, liked Muskie's plan to rent the flatbed trailer and to confront the blank wall of the *Union Leader* building. "I remember approving this stuff and saying it sounded great to me," he said. Mitchell was there, as was Severin Beliveau, who remembers that Muskie "was all fired up, almost beside himself." Mitchell said, "It was a cold, snowy day, he was tired, he had made a long trip, and, as he said many times, he wasn't as effective when he was tired." No staff member raised an objection. Yet the spectacle of a presidential candidate shaking his fist at an unseen writer of scurrilous editorials was a curious campaign tactic. In a sense, Muskie had appeared naked in public, and paid a price. Whether myth or fact, the "crying" incident damaged Muskie. It would be years before politicians could cry in public and have it interpreted as compassion rather than weakness.

It didn't look like a debacle at first. At a subsequent appearance in Hartford, Connecticut, Mitchell said, response was positive. "The first reaction of the Democrats in Hartford was that it was a good thing, that it showed that he's human and he had emotion." Averell Harriman, however, called it "a disaster," and suggested it would end the campaign.

Muskie soon began experiencing actual defeats rather than just failing to meet expectations. Things got much worse in Florida. A week after New Hampshire, Muskie finished fourth in a primary won by segregationist George Wallace. Some advisers had suggested pulling out of Florida, where the odds appeared hopeless, but Muskie never considered that option. He felt wounded earlier by the entry of his old ticket-mate Hubert Humphrey, who got into the race, Bernhard said, proclaiming "My sails are full," despite his earlier pledge to stay out. With unions preferring Jackson, traditional liberals gravitating back toward Humphrey, and McGovern buoyed by antiwar voters, Muskie's support rapidly crumbled.

The Florida defeat was agonizing to Muskie. He was confronted again with dirty tricks almost certainly orchestrated by CREP, including, at a rally with Jewish voters, banners that were jarringly anti-Semitic. At a whistle-stop in Jacksonville, he sought to counter Wallace's "white power" campaign. "The day is going to come when blacks as well as whites can be president," Muskie said. "It's going to come because we're going to make it so." He said, "I don't believe the people of Florida are going to vote for a regional candidate simply to make a protest." But that is what they did. The balloting split 41 percent for Wallace, 19 percent for Humphrey, 14 percent for Jackson (despite his withdrawal), and 9 percent for Muskie. Exit polls, however, still showed voters thought Muskie had the best chance to beat Nixon.

Bernhard vividly remembers the last night in Florida as Muskie remained upstairs at the Dupont Plaza hotel in Miami while the volunteers and get-out-the-vote team gathered in the lobby. Bernhard went upstairs to ask Muskie to come down and "fire up the volunteers." Muskie was reading a book, and ignored the plea. Hearing about the crowd, Hubert Humphrey showed up and began to shake the hands of Muskie volunteers. Distraught, Bernhard told Muskie about Humphrey's arrival. Muskie continued to read, saying, "It's time for you to leave. I'm not going down there."

In his concession speech, Muskie made no effort to hide his bitterness. "Some of the worst instincts of which human beings are capable have too strong an influence in our elections. The George Wallace victory here in Florida is a threat to the unity of this country. . . . George Wallace believes that the way to advance himself is to exploit the fears of those he appeals to. He is a demagogue of the worst possible kind." Mitchell believes the speech was a mistake, that it made Muskie come off as a sore loser, and that if he wanted to denounce Wallace, he should have done so before the vote, not after.

On March 21, Muskie won the Illinois primary, but the downward slide resumed, and Muskie never won another primary. The "brain trust" gathered one more time, along with campaign staff, to discuss the situation. Only Washington attorney Edward Bennett Williams was in favor of continuing. The campaign was suspended, and all offices closed. The California office was auctioned to the highest bidder, which turned out to be the Humphrey campaign, paying $5,000.

Though Mitchell agreed with the decision to withdraw, in later years Muskie occasionally reproached him with the thought that, had he stayed in, he somehow could have won the nomination despite his performance in the primaries. "I don't think he would have," Mitchell said, "but it was a subject that weighed heavily on him for a long time afterward."

Don Nicoll believes the Muskie campaign was "doomed from the start," that he was a centrist candidate in a year in which the Democratic voting base turned increasingly radical, choosing a candidate, George McGovern, who was sure to fail in November, much as the Republicans had suffered a landslide defeat eight years earlier when the convention nominated Barry Goldwater in a tidal wave of enthusiasm. McGovern's slogan, "Come Home, America," simply didn't resonate with voters who were far more concerned with domestic issues.

Others argue that Muskie, who had never faced primary opposition before, was visibly ill at ease in criticizing any of his opponents. Eliot Cutler observed that "He'd spent his whole career in Maine politics building a big tent." Until he laced into Wallace, he'd rarely criticized anyone, including McGovern. Muskie's poor fund-raising also came back to haunt him. Other Democratic front-runners have stumbled and righted their campaigns, including Walter Mondale and John Kerry. But without money, Muskie had no chance to turn things around.

THERE'S ANOTHER EXPLANATION FOR MUSKIE'S DEFEAT. It begins with the question, "When did Watergate begin?" The conventional timeline starts with the Watergate break-in on June 17, 1972, when five burglars were arrested by Capitol Police and were ultimately traced back to the Committee to Reelect the President, which used $350,000 in cash, laundered through a local bank, to finance the operation. But the "dirty tricks" campaign's target all along had been Muskie. Nixon's team strongly believed he was the biggest threat, and in April 1971 Muskie led Nixon in several polls. Pat Buchanan wrote to Nixon on March 24, 1971, that "If Mr. Muskie is not cut and bleeding before he goes into New Hampshire, he will very likely do massively well there, building up irresistible momentum. . . . Muskie today is a figure ideally situated to unite the warring factions of his party, and if they are united, that is bad news for us."

When did Watergate begin? In December 1970, barely a month after Muskie's riveting Election Eve speech, there was a burglary at Berl Bernhard's law office. Nothing appeared to be missing, but campaign documents Bernhard had prepared for Muskie were disarranged, and the photocopier had logged an extensive amount of copying. Bernhard reported the burglary to Capitol Police, but the case was never solved. It had virtually the same pattern, however, as the

Watergate break-in. And it was soon clear that the effort to disrupt Muskie's campaign was about far more than "dirty tricks."

The campaign began having serious problems with leaks to the press. Bernhard was startled to see references in the Evans and Novak column to memos he'd just sent to Muskie at his Senate office. Once, Muskie called him to find out what the columnists were talking about; he hadn't read the memo himself yet. Bernhard said, "We started asking ourselves who on the staff was doing it?" Bernhard later suspected Jackson campaigners, or even McGovern forces. He never imagined that a Republican president would interfere with a Democratic primary campaign. Such things weren't done.

The effect was pernicious. Bernhard began limiting the number of staffers with access to key memos and polling data, and thus the responses and ideas he could receive in return. The office became highly centralized, with fewer and fewer people in the loop. Bernhard said the most insidious effect may have been the way staff members viewed each other. "Trust is vital to any political campaign," he said. "There are so many decisions, so many risks, that you have to have absolute loyalty. And if you don't have it, don't run for president."

The Watergate hearings the next year revealed that the courier between Bernhard's law office and Muskie's Senate office, "Fat Jack" Buckley, was on the payroll of CREP. The copies were passed to Evans and Novak in—the columnists said—"plain brown envelopes." Other sabotage included a fictitious Harris poll, printed on Muskie stationery and distributed to Congress, headlined, "51 Percent Say Ted [Kennedy] Unfit for White House." The disruptions caused by the Nixon campaign's deceptions and infiltration were hardly the only problem the Muskie forces were having, but Bernhard believes that they had "measurable and powerful negative effects" on the campaign's formative stages.

There's also evidence that CREP efforts influenced actual voting, especially in the critical New Hampshire primary. In his select committee testimony, Bernhard analyzed voting results in the Franco-American wards of Manchester and Nashua.

In 1968, the Lyndon Johnson slate of "uncommitted" delegates trounced Eugene McCarthy in Manchester, even though McCarthy came close to defeating Johnson statewide. Bernard said he expected even better results in Manchester, yet Muskie got only 38 percent there, against 58 percent in Nashua. Had Manchester Franco voters cast their ballots as their counterparts in Nashua did, Muskie would have won better than 50 percent statewide, the threshold the press had set. Then, Bernhard said, "New Hampshire would have represented a major win rather than what was written off as a marginal victory."

Nixon's obsession with Muskie still seems hard to explain. Mark Shields offered a theory when he said in an interview following a centennial observance of Muskie's birth, that Nixon's curiously fragile personality played a part. "There's nothing worse than losing an office that you've been elected to in the past," he said. "It's like a man getting thrown out of the house by his wife." For Nixon, "Not losing became the dominant motive."

THERE WAS ONE MORE POLITICAL CONTEST in 1972, for which George Mitchell was front and center. The McGovern debacle in November, when Nixon took 60 percent and all but seventeen electoral votes, was the biggest defeat ever sustained by a Democratic nominee. McGovern had installed Jean Westwood, a grandmother of nine from Utah, and a Mormon, as Democratic National Committee chair, for what would normally have been a four-year term. But the outrage of party leaders at the magnitude of McGovern's loss made it certain there would be a move to unseat her at the December DNC meeting.

Westwood was not a typical party chairman—usually older males with a lifetime of political experience. She was a political neophyte with an unusual way of expressing herself. In a speech to the National Press Club on September 8, 1972, with the election outcome still in some doubt, she said, "I wouldn't give $114,000, or $10 million, for that matter, for a plastic administration, wrapped up in cellophane, served neat and tidy by Disneyland. They peddle their candidate like soap. And let me tell you one thing: They *don't* have the whitest wash in town." She was prescient, however, about the Watergate break-in, characterizing the Nixon response as, "First, deny everything, then, when that doesn't work, cover up and order more shredding machines."

The leading DNC candidate was Robert Strauss, a Texan who was already committee treasurer. Strauss had been angling for the job for months, and in other times might have been easily accepted. There was a downside, however. Strauss was a friend of Richard Nixon's, and close to John Connally, his college roommate. Connally, the former Texas governor wounded while riding with John Kennedy in Dallas, had become a Republican and was serving as Nixon's Treasury secretary—one of the first fruits of the "Southern strategy." Texas Secretary of State Bob Bullock said choosing Strauss would be "tantamount to handing over the Democratic Party to Republican John Connally."

Liberal committee members searched for a candidate, and found George Mitchell, who was already on the executive committee. As a member of the McGovern Commission, Mitchell had maintained friendly ties with that now-defeated campaign, and was acceptable to the "regulars," too, because of his association with Muskie.

A *CBS Evening News* report on November 22, with Roger Mudd substituting for Walter Cronkite, gave the flavor in Mudd's introduction, where he referred to "a quadrennial political game called Let's Find a Scapegoat." Strauss and Mitchell were guests. Strauss made it clear Jean Westwood had to go, saying she "will find it impossible to bring the party together. That just isn't my opinion. This is a historical fact." Mitchell was more circumspect. "There is not now a vacancy, and unless and until there is, I'm not a candidate. However, should Jean Westwood decide to step down . . . I would seriously consider seeking the office."

Westwood resisted calls for her resignation, and went into the climactic December 9 DNC meeting telling supporters she wouldn't step down. It wasn't until after the committee considered a no-confidence motion, which she survived, that she agreed to resign. Mitchell had to campaign for the job without actually seeming to, unlike Strauss, who mounted an all-out effort. Mitchell wrote to a supporter on November 29 that he still hadn't decided whether or not to run. His low-key effort, budgeted at $5,000, was led by Nancy Chandler, the Mitchell family friend who'd joined the DNC earlier that year.

"I was happy to go and help him out," Chandler recalled, "but I didn't know anybody on the committee. I was brand-new, just elected, and I went down and stayed in a hotel, and he gave me a list of people and phone numbers, and I started calling, and we mounted a campaign and there was a lot of support for George." She knew what she was up against. The Strauss forces "delivered roses and chocolate candy to people's doors, and we had no such budget." The cautious brochure supporting Mitchell was signed by eight committee members, including Hugh Gallen, a future governor of New Hampshire. It warned that "The Democratic Party faces the possibility of a damaging confrontation. At the very time we need to reunite all elements of the party, we are disturbed to see the appearance of factionalism and divisiveness." The brochure concluded, "Should a vacancy occur, George Mitchell of Maine possesses the experience and independence which make him ideally suited to assume the leadership."

After Westwood resigned, balloting began. There was a third candidate, Charles Manatt from California, also a liberal, who insisted on staying in; he later served as DNC chair from 1981 to 1985. On the first ballot, Strauss led by a comfortable margin, though Mitchell had broad support. Manatt got votes almost solely from California, and was eliminated. On the second ballot, Mitchell picked up most Manatt supporters, but, crucially, two West Virginia members switched from Mitchell to Strauss, who was elected by one and a half votes; under party rules, some delegations split votes.

Jim Sasser, a fellow member who missed the vote when his flight was canceled, and later served with Mitchell in the US Senate, commiserated by letter. Sasser said he had "heard you were a splendid candidate and covered yourself and your supporters in glory, even in defeat. Apparently, the '70s aren't going to be my decade—first Albert Gore, then Ed Muskie, and now George Mitchell!" He also said, "I am convinced that had you started earlier you could have won." And he noted he still had twenty thousand Muskie buttons in his basement. They eventually made their way to Maine and were used in the 1976 Senate campaign. Charlie Micoleau also struck a lighthearted note, writing, "It was fun—call us again the next time you run for office!"

Mitchell wasn't unduly bothered by the defeat. He and Strauss got along, and he continued to serve on the executive committee. Not everyone was so forbearing. Strauss represented the Chrysler Corporation while serving as chairman, which his detractors claimed was a conflict of interest. Strauss contended he had to continue, since he was willing to serve the DNC without pay. Soon, Mitchell was able to save Strauss from a serious tactical error that would certainly have inflamed opposition to the new chairman.

Strauss was deciding what to do about a lawsuit, filed by former interim chairman Larry O'Brien, against the Republican National Committee over the Watergate break-in, which had invaded the DNC suite at the Watergate Hotel. It was also the headquarters of the Association of State Democratic Chairmen, then chaired by Severin Beliveau. On April 20, 1973, R. Spencer Oliver, the state chairs' executive director, wrote voicing discontent with Strauss. "I have been concerned by Mr. Strauss' strange, prolonged, and almost total silence on the Watergate case since he became Democratic National Chairman. I have also been puzzled by his effort to have me removed. . . . It is absolutely necessary that an independent prosecutor be appointed immediately to pursue the criminal aspects of the Watergate case. Larry O'Brien stated repeatedly from the time the burglars were caught that an independent prosecutor should be appointed. The conduct of the criminal trial last January proved that he was right."

Strauss, instead, was proposing to settle for $500,000, claiming that legal expenses had already amounted to $200,000, and that the party was broke. Mitchell wrote to Strauss on April 17 to dissuade him. In a letter marked "Personal," he elaborated his reasoning. He first said the public was having difficulty distinguishing the various strands of the already-complex Watergate investigation, including the January trial before Judge John Sirica, who drew attention to the cover-up, the Senate Committee investigation, and the civil suits. "In the eyes of most people I talk with, these all blur into one big mess," he wrote. More distressingly, "Most people think the Watergate affair is sordid, but they think the Democrats would be just as capable of doing something like it as are the Republicans." Putting these observations together, "If the DNC now accepts a large sum of money to settle the civil suit, the average citizen will think we've sold Republican silence for money. . . . I think it could reduce the already low esteem in which all political organizations and politicians are now held by the American public." Strauss decided not to settle.

Mitchell served on the DNC until he was appointed US Attorney for Maine in 1977, when he also gave up his law practice. Pursuing the chairmanship and losing seems not to have bothered him much; he had already set his sights on another target.

Berl Bernhard perceived a significant difference in Mitchell and Muskie's campaign styles. "Ed really, at the core, did not like campaigning. Period. . . . George was different. Even though he would probably deny it, he enjoyed the fray, in his own way, which was professional, very disciplined, and always . . . articulate and precise." Even Muskie's devastating loss in 1972 could be seen in another context. Muskie had come closer to the presidency than any Mainer since James G. Blaine narrowly lost to Grover Cleveland in 1884. Ken Curtis said of Muskie, "I don't see him as a failure. I see him as a finalist. He earned tremendous acclaim for a senator from a small state."

7

A RARE OPPORTUNITY

After the grueling political battles of 1972, George Mitchell returned to Maine and his law practice. He, Sally, and Andrea had moved to a new house in South Portland, on Channel Road, a long stone's throw from Danford Cove on Casco Bay, and near the city line with neighboring Cape Elizabeth, which was becoming Portland's wealthiest suburb. The brick house was eclectic in style, and larger than the one on Falmouth Road. Sally had a light-filled studio where she pursued her avocation of painting watercolors. Andrea was eight, and attending a local public school.

As 1973 began, Mitchell was beginning to focus on a run for governor the following year. He had learned many lessons while working on four of Ed Muskie's campaigns, and was ready to put them to use on his own behalf. Seeking the governorship, however, would be a bold move. Mitchell hadn't served in the Legislature, in a county office, and had in fact never won an election—usual prerequisites for seeking the top job, which had become an increasingly powerful office, thanks to the Muskie and Curtis reforms. But he was greatly admired in Democratic Party circles, both in Maine and nationally, and had made valuable connections—not least among donors who could support his campaign. He had hired campaign staff, devised budgets, and performed the support tasks any candidate needs for a statewide run.

As Mitchell surveyed the scene, it was important to consider his stance on issues still convulsing the party. As it turned out, Vietnam would rapidly fade in 1974, to be replaced by Watergate and fallout from a president caught in a web of deception and criminal acts. Mitchell had already made his peace on Vietnam. In 1972, he responded to Thomas Maynard, who had mounted an "independent

Democrat" campaign for Congress to oppose the war in 1966. "Now, your own senator is in favor of withdrawal from Southeast Asia," Maynard wrote, and challenged Mitchell about his statements when he was state party chairman. Mitchell replied, "My explanation for my change in attitude regarding US policy in Vietnam is simple: I was wrong, as were many other Americans. I have no hesitancy about acknowledging that you and others were right on this issue."

Recent changes in Maine election laws would also have a significant effect on the next governor's race. The traditional ballot had a "big box" in which voters, still using paper ballots, could mark for all Democratic or Republican candidates. There was a lot of straight-ticket voting, which may have cost Frank Coffin the governorship in 1960, even as it swept in a Democratic legislature in 1964. An ambitious young Republican named Robert A. G. Monks, a liberal within the party, and in later life a corporate shareholder advocate, set out to change that. Monks wanted to run in 1972, and was mulling a primary bid against Margaret Chase Smith, rumored to be considering retirement. Many Smith supporters believe she would have stepped down had Monks not challenged her. Her campaign in 1972 was noticeably weaker than previous efforts, though she beat Monks by nearly two to one.

Earlier, Monks had decided he'd have a better shot in November if the big box were eliminated, and he financed a petition drive to bring the issue to the ballot. The question passed easily, confronting Governor Curtis with a dilemma: When should the big box be removed? He ultimately decided the new law required it be gone in November, enraging fellow Democrat William Hathaway, who was giving up his congressional seat to challenge Smith.

Monks, the initiative's author, had already lost, but the big box was of intense interest to Hathaway. He initially believed it would help him enormously, with Muskie at the top of the ticket. Instead, it was George McGovern, who, Hathaway later admitted, would have dragged him down to defeat. Hathaway beat Smith despite Maine's overwhelming 1972 vote for Richard Nixon, and later told Curtis it was the biggest favor he'd ever done him. In the 1974 governor's race, though, the new ballot made it easier to vote a split ticket, or even consider an independent outside the party system.

The most talked-about gubernatorial candidate for 1974 was Congressman Peter Kyros, who'd been elected with Curtis in 1966 and was just starting his fourth two-year term. He'd been reelected comfortably, but his stock was already falling. Sandy Maisel, a Colby College government professor who later ran for Congress, said of Kyros, "He became one of the most reviled people in the state of Maine." A former career navy officer, Kyros was brilliant but extraordinarily brusque with staff, and even constituents. Harold Pachios's theory about Kyros was that "After four elections for Congress, he had met a majority of people in the First District, and they didn't like him."

Severin Beliveau, who worked with him as state party chair, called Kyros "arrogant and patronizing," and wasn't surprised he regularly faced primary opposition. Ed Muskie had welcomed Kyros warmly in 1966, saying, "Peter is a bright and able young lawyer, and in my judgment, conducting a very good campaign." By 1972, however, Curtis declined to endorse Kyros for reelection, and Muskie followed suit. Nonetheless, Kyros was touted as the likely front-runner.

Portland newspaper columnist Jim Brunelle interpreted Mitchell's defeat in the DNC chairman contest as boosting Kyros. Had Mitchell won, Brunelle theorized, he would have been in a better position to run in Maine; it seemed certain Mitchell would be running for something. Kyros took his soundings and, on October 28, 1973, bowed out. The way was open for Mitchell, and others, to stake their claims.

Initial reviews for the soon-to-be-candidate were positive. Tom Quinn, an old political hand, wrote to Beliveau about a November 20 fund-raiser, "Very good reception for George. He handled himself very well with over 100 enthusiastic people showing up. I think he will be a much better candidate than people originally thought, very relaxed with a good sense of humor."

Mitchell formally announced on January 4, 1974. Reflecting the political atmosphere of the moment, he said, "The depth of public disillusion with politics only measures the potential for our renewal." He called for public financing of state elections, and for a $50 limit on all campaign contributions. He attempted to balance the need for progress both in protecting the environment and creating new jobs, dubbed "pickerel or payroll." Mitchell proposed creating new Heavy Industrial Zones to attract employers, and "to increase state purchases of land to maintain open spaces for public use." He then invoked what became his campaign theme, "the two Maines," which he saw not as a geographical division between urban and rural, as it has become since, but between economic classes, justifying his push for new industry. He said, "Open space and natural beauty are small consolation to Maine's poor."

In a speech a day earlier, Mitchell elaborated his thoughts. "Each of us has freely chosen to live in Maine. It's an attractive and appealing way of life to us and the increasing number of people who want to come here to live. But beneath the pleasant surface lies the grim reality of a second Maine. Where one out of five families lives in a home without plumbing. Where one out of six families has an income below the poverty level. Where unemployment is well above the national average. . . . The challenge facing us is to make the two Maines one—to improve the lives of the people of the second Maine without destroying the things that make the first Maine such an attractive place to live."

In a follow-up newspaper story on January 5, Mitchell acknowledged that he wasn't as well-known as some other candidates, and tried to make a virtue of it. "It is not [name] recognition pure and simple which elects someone. It is favorable recognition. . . . Becoming known is only half the problem. Becoming known favorably is the other half."

Mitchell's palm card—a small laminated bookmark—features a photo of the candidate with his striped tie loosened, and the slogan, "The more you care about Maine, the more you should know about George Mitchell." There's a family photo, complete with dog, on the reverse, a list of achievements, and this capsule biography: "George Mitchell was born and raised in Waterville. His father, the son of immigrants, and his mother, herself an immigrant, worked in local mills to support their five children. Their four sons achieved recognition as the Mitchell basketball brothers."

The open seat, and the opportunity to succeed a popular and successful governor like Curtis, attracted several able Democrats in what became a six-way primary, with three other serious contenders. Lloyd LaFountain of Biddeford, who had served two terms as York County attorney and as US Attorney, was the southernmost candidate. From the north came state senator Peter Kelley of Caribou, who'd made his name backing a Maine Public Power Authority to oversee the Dickey-Lincoln hydroelectric project planned for the St. John River. There was another state senator: Joe Brennan from Portland, elected Senate minority leader in his first term, returning to the Legislature after his stint as Cumberland County prosecutor.

One of Mitchell's first tasks was to hire a staff. First was Mike Aube from Biddeford, a twenty-three-year-old graduate of Boston College who'd run for the Legislature in 1972, the summer he graduated. He then became president of Maine Young Democrats, a group thriving in the Vietnam protest years. Aube said, "I was impressed with George Mitchell's intellect, and his thought process, and how he felt about certain issues." He and a fellow Young Democrat, Debbie Bedard, kept after Mitchell to give them a try. In September 1973 they were his first hires, at $55 a week. They staffed the Portland office on Congress Street, a few blocks from Mitchell's law office. Aube later worked for Ed Muskie on the then-new Senate Budget Committee, upon Mitchell's recommendation.

Mitchell expected staffers to be prompt, well-organized, and diligent, and Aube contrasted him with Muskie. "He had learned from his days working with Ed Muskie that screaming and shouting were probably not something that was his style," he said. "He had been screamed and shouted at too many times." Aube also worked for Mitchell briefly after his US Senate appointment, and said, "Ed Muskie was the boss you feared when you were called to the chamber, as opposed to George Mitchell, who would actually come around and sit in the chair next to you and talk."

The campaign manager was twenty-seven-year-old Tony Buxton, who'd grown up in Readfield, graduated from Bowdoin, and served in the army. Buxton is now a partner with Preti Flaherty. He felt that Muskie favored Mitchell, though, as usual, Muskie stayed out of the primary race. Ken Curtis, he believed, would have preferred Brennan as a fellow "Bobby Kennedy man," but Curtis claims he never really thought about a successor, and had no preference. Buxton said, "We had a campaign staff of about ten people, several paid the great sum of $25 a week, and all of whom have stayed in touch ever since."

Mitchell countered his lack of visibility, Buxton said, by effectively using the "two Maines" theme. It played well both in the cities, where many poor families lived, and in the rural mill towns, where fears of job loss were perennial. Buxton also noticed Mitchell's diligence with individual voters. "George would see a lot of people on a good day, and we'd get their names and addresses, or their names, and we would find their addresses in the phone book." After that, each got "a very nice personal letter, and they in fact were individually typed, and they had an incredible impact."

Mitchell was intent on getting a well-qualified campaign treasurer, and he found one in Scott Hutchinson, then vice president and later president of Canal Bank in Portland. Hutchinson was that rarest of birds—a banker enrolled as a Democrat. He did so after becoming friendly with Ken Curtis through a town baseball league. Curtis then asked Hutchinson if he'd be treasurer for his 1966 race. When he inquired at the bank about changing parties, he was expecting a no, but the bank president thought it might be a good idea to have someone on the other side.

When Hutchinson went to change his registration in Cumberland, he said, "I guess I was probably the first Democrat they ever had up there." Hutchinson continued his fund-raising for Mitchell through his 1988 Senate campaign. He provided a credibility with donors that most Democrats lacked. Mitchell ended up spending $100,571 through the June primary, far more than his opponents. He even surpassed his eventual Republican opponent, Jim Erwin, who spent $80,274. Erwin's primary opponent, Harry Richardson, spent $153,218, mostly his own money. There was subsequently a brief controversy about whether Mitchell had violated a state law capping advertising expenses at $35,000. The election commission ruled he hadn't; the punctilious attorney general, Jon Lund, had counted campaign buttons and bumper stickers as advertising.

The vast spaces of rural Maine are difficult for statewide candidates to cover, and Mitchell was fortunate to find someone proud to be called a "political operative," Clyde MacDonald of Hampden. For $20 a week, MacDonald represented Mitchell around northern Maine from the Bangor office, and the two logged a lot of miles together.

MacDonald didn't seem Mitchell's type. He was a student radical at the University of Maine, and was active in Moratorium Day and many other protests. He'd heard of Mitchell while serving in 1973 on the Mikulski Commission, named for Barbara Mikulski, which was sorting out national delegate-selection procedures still snarled following the end of the McGovern commission. MacDonald came up with a way to break a deadlock on proportional representation of women and minorities without using rigid quotas.

When Mitchell called to seek his support, MacDonald proposed a deal involving Mitchell's DNC vote, and said, "If you'll support me on proportional representation, I'll support you for governor." Mitchell agreed. MacDonald brought with him an organization of antiwar Democrats, which were still numerous, but was also adept at attracting Old Guard supporters. After the 1974 campaign, Mitchell convinced Muskie to open a Bangor Senate office, and MacDonald was hired to staff it.

His three major primary opponents presented different challenges for Mitchell. Brennan was presumed the toughest. He was known throughout Cumberland County, with 20 percent of the state's population, and Brennan had fashioned a blue-collar, working-class appeal in the ethnic enclaves that still dominated Democratic politics. Brennan grew up, and has lived almost all his life, on Munjoy Hill in Portland, an East End neighborhood with narrow streets lined with tenements and large families. Brennan had seven siblings, and his father, an immigrant from Ireland, was a longshoreman. After Brennan graduated from law school and began practicing, he noticed how differently juveniles were treated by the court system. "Those from the fancy neighborhoods, the Falmouths, the Cape Elizabeths, they get in a jam, they get a psychologist," he said. "The kids from housing projects in Bayside Park in Portland, they [go] to jail." These legal disparities helped drive Brennan's political ambition.

Peter Kelley overcame the obstacle of hailing from far northern Maine by involving himself in the public power movement. After the Legislature failed to act, Kelley helped get the measure on the 1973 referendum ballot, knowing that a successful campaign might well serve as a springboard to a statewide race. After polling well in the early going, however, support wilted as Central Maine Power and Bangor Hydro-Electric spent heavily and defeated the measure. Kelley led the early polls for the nomination, but he entered late and didn't raise much money.

The weakest of the top four turned out to be Lloyd LaFountain. From far southern Maine, he was flanked by two strong Portland candidates, and it's never been easy to build a statewide base from York County, which has no major city. As Joe Brennan liked to observe, prosecutors don't make many friends pursuing their work, and Maine was, and remains, a low-crime state, limiting that issue's appeal. At one point, Mike Aube expressed concern that LaFountain might be gaining traction, but Mitchell, who maintained his Waterville base, told him, "That's fine. Every vote that goes to Lloyd LaFountain doesn't go to Joe Brennan."

As Mitchell began campaigning in earnest, in early 1974, he was "spectacularly organized," Tony Buxton remembers. He also recalled that, though he had the title, "I don't think there was any doubt that George Mitchell was his own campaign manager"—something he acknowledged later was a mixed blessing. Mitchell himself was more skeptical, telling a reporter, "We're really talking about who is the least disorganized. All campaigns are disorganized. Success obliterates all the errors." And he began to strike a distinctive note, saying on August 28, "At most political functions, politicians do the talking and the people do the listening. I think we ought to reverse that occasionally." He made a pledge to, as governor, hold monthly town meeting–style gatherings.

Mitchell was an early and consistent supporter of campaign finance reform. The previous fall, he'd convinced Curtis to introduce legislation, enacted in 1974, that limited personal and family contributions to candidates for governor and the US Senate to $35,000, and limited spending to 50 cents per voter in the November election. It took effect in July, and thus had no impact on that year's primaries. Mitchell also promised to "publish a full financial statement each year . . . whether or not the law requires that." He released his statement early on. For tax year 1973, he was paid $46,048 by Jensen Baird and earned $300 on savings bonds. He paid $10,387 in federal income tax and $1,097 in state tax. He listed $91,145 in assets—a $65,000 house, an $1,800 Plymouth sedan, and a mortgage of $23,467, for a net worth of $64,178. Mitchell challenged other candidates to report voluntarily, but few did.

Though he was now settled in Portland—one newspaper profile referred to him as a "country club lawyer"—his Waterville support was still valuable. Jim Mitchell, his nephew, then in the eighth grade, said he "was just starting to understand politics," but was pressed into service. "Most of us nieces and nephews were recruited, some willingly, some unwillingly, to work on his 1974 campaign," he said.

The hub was the Atkins Print Shop owned by Barbara Mitchell's husband, Eddie Atkins, which mounted what was, at the time, a sophisticated media operation manned by, as Jim Mitchell put it, "a little army of envelope lickers and stamp lickers." Buxton remembers their work. "During the '74 primary, all the Mitchell kids from age eleven to seventeen would show up every Saturday in some city and leaflet the city, and they were good, boy, they didn't stop for anything." The house on Front Street hosted the candidate and whoever was with him. Mike Aube met Mary Mitchell, whom he describes as "absolutely wonderful," but "small and frail," and who still presided. "Whenever we'd go there, the brothers and the sister would show up, it was like, I don't know if a whistle went off, but they'd all come and have lunch."

Campaigning often brings friends, staff, and the candidate into unusual proximity, and Mitchell's quirks and foibles tended to be noticed, and remembered. Bruce and Nancy Chandler had moved from Waterville to an old farmhouse in China near the main road, and Mitchell complained of a sleepless night. Bruce said, "We couldn't figure out what the noise was he was talking about; we were out in the middle of nowhere. Must have been mice in the walls." The problem, according to Aube, who was traveling with Mitchell, was the traffic. "If there were six cars that went by between ten p.m. and six a.m., I'd be shocked. That's when I learned that he needs the back bedroom. He really is a light sleeper."

Mitchell's clothes came in for comment. Nancy Chandler remembers that, "We had a lot of work getting George ready for that campaign." Bruce said, "His pants used to come up above his ankle bone, and he wore ties that were just as dull as they could possibly be." On primary night, they held a "necktie party" for Mitchell that featured vivid, Hawaiian-style ties. Mitchell responded, "I'm taking them up to the attic. They'll light it up."

Sandy Maisel, the Colby professor, organized students for Mitchell, and had similar observations. "I tried to convince him that you don't go to a country fair with a coat and tie on, and to loosen up, and it was very, very difficult for him to do that." Clyde MacDonald tried to get Mitchell to trade in his black plastic eyeglass frames. On a drive through Aroostook County, he told Mitchell his complexion and the glasses didn't help his television image. MacDonald advocated light-colored frames more like his own. After several miles Mitchell reminded him, "I'm working day and night and wearing myself to a frazzle." When MacDonald agreed, Mitchell added, "I don't want to be governor enough to get glasses like yours." It wasn't until years later that Mitchell changed them.

A more serious concern was the state of Mitchell's marriage. Scott Hutchinson remembers a meeting before the official campaign announcement. "He was having some marital problems, and wanted to know what we thought, what effect" a separation or divorce might have, Hutchinson said. The group of advisers assured him it would have minimal impact; he and Sally stayed together. She was far from happy, though, according to Nancy Chandler. Asked about

Sally's reaction to the campaign, Chandler said, "They were trying hard to have another child, and that was where her focus was. Sally was never into politics."

Mitchell arrived at the state convention in May with uncertain prospects. He'd campaigned almost nonstop for five months, but had started the race as the least-known of the four major candidates. His slogan about the two Maines was striking a responsive chord, however, and Mitchell planned to lobby delegates well before the speechmaking. By this time, state conventions were noisy three-day events, with well over a thousand delegates. Buxton said, "We had a card system with the biographies of every delegate, we had people assigned to that delegate, so that by the end of the first night we had a head count of which delegates were for Mitchell, which were neutral and could be swayed, and which ones were gone to somebody else." The count showed delegates trending toward Mitchell, and no other candidate had similar tools. The final count showed 1,017 of 1,700 delegates supported him—a positive, but not necessarily conclusive, result for the June primary. The choice between Brennan and Mitchell was tough for many. Severin Beliveau, though he'd worked closely with Mitchell for years, supported Brennan.

Brennan hadn't raised nearly as much money as Mitchell, and made this a focus of his convention speech, pointing in particular to Mitchell's use of a Boston ad agency. "I didn't have to go down to the Boston advertising firm of Hill, Holliday, Connors and Cosmopulos to package an image and come back to the Maine voters," Brennan recalls saying. "I was in the ring, fighting for all these causes." And he repeated "Hill, Holliday, Connors and Cosmopulos" to make sure delegates got the point. Brennan said Mitchell came back with the perfect response, saying, "Some people can only build themselves up by tearing other people down." The audience cheered.

Mitchell's speech was serious but relatively brief, and the conclusion focused on John Kennedy, not so much for his specific achievements as for his leadership qualities. "He brought to this nation a spirit that was missing then, the traditional American spirit of idealism, of pride in our nation, trust in our government, faith in ourselves, and optimism about our future. That spirit is gone now," Mitchell said. "In its place we have cynicism, shame, mistrust, and pessimism. But the American spirit can be restored. Indeed, it must be restored. And we can do so by again heeding three ancient truths which represent John Kennedy's legacy: That what most people want out of life is pride, self-respect, and dignity. That we get them by doing something meaningful with our lives. And that the most meaningful form of human activity is helping others. Those three sentences sum up the meaning of the Democratic Party to me."

Some observers saw the Brennan–Mitchell contest striking sparks. They were virtually the same age, both lawyers from Portland, and occupied the same political space. Peter Kelley seemed the obvious alternative, but he never recaptured his early appeal.

After the convention, Mitchell had to decide whether to support two controversial platform planks delegates had adopted—one calling for amnesty for Vietnam draft resisters, the other supporting civil rights for gays and lesbians. Mitchell wasn't comfortable with either plank, and other candidates either distanced themselves from the provisions or disavowed them. Mitchell had objected to the civil rights plank, as worded, because it seemed to designate a separate class of citizens. But he also felt an obligation to defend the convention votes.

The day after the convention Mitchell was campaigning at a Bangor truck stop. Barry Valentine, his driver, was with him, and can recall Mitchell telling him, "Only my wife knows me better than you do." At the truck stop, three drivers "with their John Deere hats on and sitting in a booth" shook hands with Mitchell; then one pointed to the front page of the *Bangor Daily News* and the headline about the controversial planks. He said, "Is it true you support cowards and queers?" Mitchell took a seat, and began explaining. Valentine wishes he could have captured the fifteen-minute discussion on film.

"There were these really tough truck driver guys sitting there, nodding their heads up and down when he explained his position," and "the transition from these guys scowling with the accusatory finger, and then they're just mild and they're nodding, following everything he said." Valentine was awed by Mitchell's ability to persuade. "I always told people that 'No matter how smart you think you are, spend about fifteen minutes with George Mitchell, and you won't feel quite so smart.'"

On primary night, the early returns from small towns favored Kelley. As the larger municipalities, including mill towns, came in, Mitchell took a small and then decisive lead. The outcome wasn't as close as expected. Mitchell won by nearly 10,000 votes, tallying 33,312—more than Curtis had received four years earlier in a two-way primary. Brennan was second, with 23,443 votes, Kelley third, with 21,358, and LaFountain fourth, with 7,954. Another notable shift was that, for the first time, there were nearly as many votes cast by Democrats as Republicans—96,794 in the Republican primary, against 88,777 for Democrats.

Mitchell quickly reached out to his rivals. He managed to convince Brennan to attend a post-election press conference, and even drove with him to Augusta. Each primary opponent signed on as co-chairmen of the forthcoming Mitchell campaign, something a reporter said "is believed to be unprecedented." Brennan's staff wasn't pleased with the decision, but the relationship that began in the Cumberland County attorney's office continued to evolve.

Mitchell emerged from the primary with name recognition, a serious fund-raising effort, and a Republican opponent with troubles all his own. After nearly beating Ken Curtis in 1970 on the state income tax issue, Jim Erwin won the nomination by only 1,300 votes over Harrison Richardson, who'd taken a crucial stand for the income tax. Richardson, having paid for his own campaign, asked for a recount, which delayed the start of Erwin's fall campaign by several weeks. Erwin sought a recount against Curtis in 1970, but said that if he'd lost by a similar margin to Richardson, he wouldn't have contested the result. It was Erwin's third try; he'd also challenged Governor Reed in the 1966 primary.

Erwin struck the expected note of confidence at the state convention in April, saying, "The Republican Party is going to elect the next governor of this state." And he was certainly no radical. Just before the primary, he told a Lewiston reporter, "If I had to name one activity that has the highest priority for me as governor, I would candidly say it will be creating opportunities by which the working men and women can attain a higher standard of living and keep young people in the state." On the other hand, he could also be tone-deaf. In a televised May 31 debate, he said, "My own observation is that women are not as downtrodden as they would have us believe."

Curtis, despite nearly losing to Erwin, didn't think highly of his political skills, calling him "a good Republican soldier." In 1972, Erwin had agreed to serve as state chairman for the Committee to Reelect the President, accompanied by an official release stating, "With Mr. Erwin's leadership, we feel completely confident that Maine will continue to be a leader in the Nixon column." Nixon carried Maine in 1972 as he had in 1960, though losing it in 1968 with Ed Muskie on the ticket. As Watergate unfolded, the Nixon connection became a decided liability.

Although independents had qualified for the ballot before—a relatively easy procedure in Maine—one who made the race in 1974, Jim Longley, began attracting attention early. Not since the days of the Progressive, Prohibition, and Socialist parties had there been a serious third-party candidate. In some years, the Democratic nominee hadn't been all that serious.

Longley was different. An insurance agency owner from Lewiston, the traditional Democratic stronghold, he had a drive and passion for politics, and ended up campaigning seventeen hours a day. Until 1974, he had been a loyal Democrat, though definitely conservative. He had volunteered and been an advance man for Muskie, and had worked for Curtis. The friendly ties are conveyed in a notice from Citizens for Curtis coordinator Neil Rolde, dated August 7, 1970. "On August 17, there will be an informal meeting of Friends of Governor Curtis to discuss his election campaign. The meeting will be held at

Jim Longley's camp at Tacoma Lake and will start at 7 p.m. However, Jim has invited anyone who can come early for a swim and/or a game of tennis."

Late in his second term, with a burst of inflation nationally, Curtis felt pressure from those who believed state government's costs were rising too rapidly. He appointed Longley, a self-proclaimed efficiency expert, to undertake what became known as the Maine Management and Cost Survey, a review of everything state government did. Curtis told Longley, "You're the person who can do this best," but before making the appointment, tried to ensure that Longley had no political ambitions. Longley replied, "There's no way I'm going to run for governor." Curtis now considers appointing Longley "the biggest mistake I ever made as governor."

Longley pursued his task with almost demonic intensity. Those whose offices he arrived at, often unannounced, remember him checking everything down to the paper clips. Those who helped with the survey soon found out they were supposed to produce big savings; Longley never questioned their size. Like Jim Erwin during the 1970 campaign, who claimed he could cut 20 percent from state agencies without reducing services, Longley produced markedly exaggerated savings. He then insisted the Legislature, still dominated by Republicans, take up or down votes on each provision. Predictably, most were voted down, yet Longley had tapped into a potent source of votes—and insisted he could cut the budget by 25 percent. Even Mitchell, during the 1974 campaign, said the Legislature should take a detailed look at each survey provision. Tony Buxton said Longley "seldom slept, he was tireless, and he also had insured thousands of Maine people." And now Longley had a platform. As Charlie Micoleau put it, he was "running for efficiency, against waste, and against both Democratic and Republican parties. Longley was going to represent 'the people.'"

In the early going, Longley barely registered in the polls. Just after the primary, under the headline, "Independent Can't Capture the Blaine House," the Democratic State chair, Violet Pease, asserted, "In Maine our political system has never witnessed an independent win any major election, and I don't expect there'll be much change this year. I have very little patience with independents, and I think it's unfortunate they couldn't get into the mainstream." Longley was still in single digits in mid-August. Yet the race had begun to shift. Erwin wasn't doing well. Supporters of Harry Richardson felt that Erwin had had his turn. And as Watergate neared its climax, Erwin's numbers sank. Mitchell, who started even with Erwin, opened up a significant lead.

It was Sunday morning, September 8, and Bob Lenna was alone in the Mitchell campaign office in Portland. A relatively new staffer, he happened to be on hand when Mitchell called, looking for Tony Buxton. After hearing that Buxton wasn't there, Mitchell asked Lenna, "What do you think?"

Gerald Ford had just issued a full and unconditional pardon to Richard Nixon, who had resigned exactly one month earlier. The timing on Sunday, with most of the nation in church, was designed to minimize news coverage. Lenna said, "As much as I would have been happy to see Richard Nixon spend the rest of his natural life in jail, it was a bad thing for the country; it just wasn't the thing to do." Lenna, later director of the Maine Bond Bank, said he doesn't know if his advice influenced Mitchell, but the candidate was thinking along similar lines.

A few hours later, shortly before Ford went on national TV to explain his decision, Mitchell issued this statement: "There are, of course, arguments both for and against President Ford's decision to pardon Mr. Nixon. While it is true that others have been prosecuted for crimes similar to those which Mr. Nixon may have committed, it is also true that no one else has suffered the degree of disgrace and humiliation he has. President Ford's decision was one of compassion, and I think it was appropriate under all these circumstances. However, this decision renders completely inappropriate Mr. Ford's earlier request to Congress to give Mr. Nixon hundreds of thousands of public dollars over and above his pension. Since Mr. Nixon no longer faces the threat of prosecution, President Ford should withdraw that request."

The Nixon pardon, coming just as the post–Labor Day campaign season began, had a dramatic but variable effect around the country. Many were outraged by Ford's decision, which was instrumental in the Democrats' gain of forty-eight US House seats, and played a role in Ford's own defeat by Jimmy Carter two years later. Many voters were relieved that Watergate was over, and the subject received little press attention in Maine. Democratic candidates were quick to condemn the pardon, while most Republicans defended it. Erwin's support for Ford was predictable, but Mitchell's was highly unusual. His lawyerly response didn't reach out to those in his own party who despised Nixon for his role in continuing the Vietnam War, followed by the Watergate cover-up.

There was outrage among Mitchell's own campaign staff. They insisted on a meeting, to which Lenna wasn't invited, and vented for nearly an hour, according to Buxton. He opposed Mitchell's statement, but Woody Jones, the press secretary, was the most heated. Buxton said Mitchell listened for a long time, then finally moved the conversation back to the campaign's next steps. "He emphasized that it was time for the nation to heal, and if the pardon could help that along, then it wasn't a bad idea." Buxton believes the statement was typical of Mitchell's actions throughout the campaign. "He wasn't going to change from who he was to score a political point. He wasn't going to be a candidate who plays on emotion, even though he knew that Nixon was anathema to most Democrats." There may have been some staff members who entered the meeting ready to resign, but none did.

The pardon statement was consistent with what Mitchell had been saying all along. In a speech to Maine Young Democrats more than a year earlier, on May 26, 1973, he had said getting angry about Watergate wouldn't solve anything, but that fixing the campaign system "will require drastic action, of the sort which the Congress and the President have been unable or unwilling to take in the past." He identified "money and excessive secrecy" as the problem, and outlined his own plan. "The present system for financing campaigns is demeaning and disgraceful. Candidates become beggars in their attempts to raise money, and in so doing many of them compromise themselves." Public financing of presidential campaigns, then extending it to congressional races, was the best answer, he said—a position he maintained throughout his public career.

One candidate not shy about condemning the pardon was Longley, and, as September rolled along, he ascended in the polls, stoking anti-politician sentiment that was a force everyone could feel. When Mitchell's campaign mistakes were analyzed, his decision to ignore Longley comes to the fore. He recognized it himself. The candidates held a late debate in Presque Isle, carried on a Bangor television station. By this time, Mitchell said, "It was clear that Longley was a charismatic, eloquent person who was a serious contender," but "It was not at all clear until the very end that he had a reasonable chance to win. And he made a lot of statements that should have been challenged, and could have been challenged, but nobody wanted to take it on."

Longley advocated closing branches of the fledgling University of Maine System in Aroostook County, which would have been highly unpopular with viewers. On camera, Erwin passed a note to Mitchell that read, "How long are you going to let this guy get away with this?" Mitchell returned a note saying, "I think you're the perfect guy to respond." The debate went on and, Mitchell said, "The result was neither of us responded, and of course in the end Erwin's campaign collapsed." Erwin's voters gravitated toward Longley. Mitchell was now campaigning against the wrong opponent.

Tom Allen, the future congressman, volunteered in Mitchell's campaign, and saw what was happening. He said Mitchell "didn't want to challenge Longley . . . so Longley was able to get out there and run for governor without having the kind of pushback that anyone would get today." Allen's own campaigns taught him "there has to be some back-and-forth, some argument, and it can be done at a high level or it can be done at a low level, but it needs to be done, and I don't think George really did it."

Negative assessments of losing campaigns are legion, and there's no shortage of them for Mitchell's 1974 run. The dominant one, however, was expressed by Floyd Harding, the former state senator, who said Mitchell "was too goddamn serious." Mitchell, drawing on his experience with Muskie, had researched every state and national issue and had position papers on them all. A college professor, Frederick Sontag, had clipped and analyzed pieces from magazines, newspapers, and trade publications, and his folders fill two entire boxes in the Mitchell archives. Charlie Micoleau said Mitchell "was much more comfortable planning a campaign than he was being the candidate, which was odd, particularly when you look at him subsequently." Ken Curtis's assessment was that Mitchell "was almost too articulate. He hadn't evolved. He was still developing his real abilities." Kermit Lipez said, "His very human, warm, funny side did not come through in the campaign, and for a lot of folks he appeared to be more distant and cerebral and formal than he really was."

Some criticism was harsher. Orlando Delogu, professor at the University of Maine School of Law, and self-described "professional gadfly," wrote to the candidate on October 8 with "one or two offhand suggestions." The first: "Your television spots strike many of the people I speak to and myself as sterile in the extreme. There is seldom any humor, you are seldom smiling. Though these TV spots are no doubt accurate, they come out canned. You appear much more lifeless than you, in fact, are." The letter doesn't mention Longley, and suggests Mitchell take up various issues, but returns to the original theme. "I would also suggest you devote some time to door-to-door or downtown street walking. You simply are not projecting an image of closeness to the people, humanness and personal warmth." On October 19, Mitchell replied, saying, "I appreciate the fact that you obviously have given a great deal of time and thought to the progress of my campaign, and you may be assured that I will carefully consider your suggestions."

One of the campaign's disappointments was that there was so little interest in the environmental issues on which Ed Muskie had built his Senate career, and which had played a major role in state politics since the 1960s. Watergate and skyrocketing oil prices loomed much larger with voters. *Maine Times* writer Phyllis Austin assessed the campaign's problems on November 1, just before the election. "George Mitchell has barnstormed the issues. He has a Plan for the Economy, a Plan for the Elderly, a Plan for the Environment, a Plan for the Indians, a Plan for Handling Gripes. Mitchell's various campaign headquarters have his position papers in neat stacks, labeled according to topic. . . . But sometimes it seems that Mitchell's plans are a protective, insulating device that hides the Real George Mitchell from having to grope for what he really believes."

Longley, meanwhile, had managed to strong-arm television station managers into providing airtime for last-minute ads after the regular schedules, including Mitchell's, had run out. Longley's ads featured the candidate, sitting on a stool, giving a then-novel anti-politics message and repeating his slogan, "Think about it." Bob Lenna, who later asserted that Longley was "among the worst governors we've had since World War II," nonetheless admired his chutzpah, and said Longley's "extraordinarily effective three-word campaign phrase . . . took on a life of its own and clearly created a brand identity."

When the break for Longley began is hard to pin down. Mitchell staffers believe their candidate sensed it two or three weeks before Election Day, but final polls still showed Mitchell ahead. One clue, however, was that the *Bangor Daily News* poll showed undecided voters increasing—always trouble for the frontrunner. Buxton said there was an effort by Republican legislative leaders to steer voters toward Longley after it was clear Erwin was fading, with Joe Sewall, soon to be Senate president, particularly active.

Yet the biggest boost to the Longley campaign came from an editorial endorsement in the *Bangor Daily News*. The newspaper had always endorsed Republicans, so backing an independent was stunning. The *Maine Sunday Telegram* in Portland, with the largest circulation, had made no endorsement in 1964 to avoid backing Lyndon Johnson, and applied a similar technique in 1974, even though the editors detested Longley and failed to mention him. The message was to "vote your party," and the editorial concluded, "Frankly, while the major candidates are far from carbon copies of each other, we are not sufficiently impressed or turned off by one or the other to justify choosing between them for the purpose of influencing our readers."

The Longley phenomenon seemed hard to believe for many veteran campaigners. Clyde MacDonald said the Bangor endorsement transformed Longley "overnight from a joke candidate into a serious candidate." Muskie traveled to Maine to survey the scene, and told Mitchell he was in danger of losing. Ken Curtis campaigned for the Democratic ticket in Lewiston, and felt the tide going out. "We're not responsible for Richard Nixon, Spiro Agnew, and that whole crowd in Washington," he told his audience. "God knows we tried to tell the people what they were like." Bruce Chandler, Mitchell's driver during the final weeks, said, "The last two or three days, you could just feel the momentum going the other way. It was uncanny; it was weird." When they arrived at a plant gate, a traditional draw for Democrats, the union workers, heads down, ignored Mitchell. The next-to-last day, referring to Longley, Mitchell said to Chandler, "He's going to win." An exit poll showed 27 percent of Longley voters decided to back him in the last week, and 8 percent on Election Day.

THE DEMOCRATS GATHERED AT THE EASTLAND HOTEL in Portland. Early returns were mixed, but by mid-evening Longley led. Before midnight, it was clear Mitchell had lost. Longley won by a small but decisive margin, just under 10,000 votes. He took 39.1 percent to Mitchell's 36.4 percent. Erwin got just 23.1 percent. Longley essentially won the election on his home turf, carrying Lewiston by two to one, and the twin city of Auburn by nearly three to one. The two cities together gave Longley a margin of 8,346 votes, nearly equal to his advantage statewide. This led to the mistaken impression that Longley had carried Androscoggin County, and Mitchell, the rest of the state. In fact, voting was otherwise consistent across the state, with Democrats strongest in cities and Republicans—and in this case, Longley—favored in rural areas. Mitchell won only four of the sixteen counties: Cumberland, York, Oxford, and Washington, his southern turf and the paper mill towns. Another erroneous memory was that Mitchell lost his hometown. He won in Waterville, 3,154 to 2,468, and in Augusta, yet lost Kennebec County.

Mitchell wasn't the only Democrat to lose. Peter Kyros's congressional seat went to Republican David Emery, a twenty-six-year-old legislator who got the assignment because no one expected anyone to beat a four-term incumbent in a Democratic year. Democrats did take the majority in the state House of Representatives, an edge they maintained until 2010. But party members who'd lost patience with Kyros believed he learned nothing from a vigorous primary challenge from Jadine O'Brien, director of Portland's Model Cities program. Sandy Maisel said of Kyros, "He beat himself." Even Emery agreed that Kyros effectively lost the seat. "Every place I went people would say, 'Well, I've always voted for Peter, but I don't really like him,'" Emery said. "The result is as much Peter's failure to take the race seriously . . . as it was to any great insights I had in campaign strategy." Emery's winning margin was 432 votes, and, like the Curtis–Erwin and Erwin–Richardson contests, a recount confirmed the result. Though no one could have imagined it at the time, the political paths of George Mitchell and David Emery were to intersect eight years later.

John Mitchell, who as Swisher had led Waterville High to sixty-six consecutive wins and the New England basketball championship, was devastated. "I had never taken a loss that hard," he said. "It was a heartbreaking thing. We all thought it was the end of his political career." Mitchell's law partner, Mert Henry, described the scene that night. "It was clear, about 10:30 p.m., that George was losing. So I got dressed—I was watching TV in bed—and went into the Eastland, and George was in his suite upstairs, and when I knocked on the door, Sally, his wife, looked at me with a sort of a smile. . . . Bill Hathaway was there, and Peter Kyros, and a couple of other people with George. But Sally sort of smiled, and I went in." When Mitchell took him to a corner to talk, he said,

"Well, what am I going to do now?" And Henry said, "You get your butt into the office tomorrow morning at eight." Mitchell showed up promptly, impressing the staff, and then left for vacation with Sally to the Virgin Islands.

The 1974 governor's race still perplexes many who thought they knew Maine politics. Longley became the first governor since the four-year term was instituted not to seek reelection, though he had a brief flirtation with the New Hampshire presidential primary in 1976. He died of a heart attack two years after leaving office. Don Nicoll said independent governors like Longley are "ego party" candidates who thrive in years when voters are resentful, comparing his win to Angus King's in 1994, and Eliot Cutler's near-miss in 2010. All of them were former Democrats.

Notes and telegrams to Mitchell poured in. Bill Cohen, reelected to a second term in Congress, said, "You and your fine staff have won the respect of the state of Maine for the campaign you waged and the positive spirit in which you addressed the issues." Faye Broderick, who'd earlier served with Mitchell on the DNC, said, "I've been sick for two days, just thinking of this nightmare. I could not believe it, and neither did anyone else." Another supporter wrote, "I listened to Jim Longley speak during the campaign, and came away feeling thankful that he had no chance of winning." And Jimmy Carter, governor of Georgia, who knew Mitchell through the DNC, wrote, "You ran a good race and should have won. I'll be available to help you next time."

Mitchell himself wrote to Maynard Dolloff, the 1962 Democratic nominee who'd lost to John Reed. "The first political campaign in which I was involved on a full-time basis was your campaign for Governor. . . . I learned much from the campaign itself. But I learned more from observing you after the election, which you narrowly lost. I admired the manner in which you accepted the decision, and your commitment to continue in public service. At a time when bitterness and quitting would have been very human and understandable reactions, you displayed grace and a renewed determination. At the time I had no idea that I would some day be in a similar situation. But I am. And I only hope that I can respond in the same spirit that you did."

Mitchell had been prepared to win. He had asked Kermit Lipez to organize a transition team, which also included Andy Nixon, a business owner, and Peter Bradford, chairman of the state Public Utilities Commission. They met twice, but got only as far as possible Cabinet appointments. Mitchell also heard from Pat Sherlock, an Associated Press reporter transferring to New York. Sherlock enclosed a story he'd written in the event of a Mitchell victory. It began, "Governor-elect George J. Mitchell has been preparing for the Maine governorship since his boyhood days in the mill district of Waterville. His eight comprehensive position papers, which deal largely with unmet human needs, clearly reflect attitudes developed during those early years when his Irish-American father was struggling to raise five Depression-era children by working as a laborer and janitor." Sherlock's cover letter said, "I like to plan ahead, and this was the only election story I wrote in advance. I'm sorry it never ran."

Perhaps the most meaningful gesture was a letter from Frank Coffin, who lived near Mitchell in South Portland. It reads:

> I write to you as one of the very, very few who can thoroughly appreciate how you and Sally must be feeling in these acrid days following the election.
>
> Notice that I did not say "your defeat." One suffers a defeat when one enters a fight and is bested by the superior capabilities of a competitor. But when other factors enter the ring, the fight is not one between man and man, or even a choice of substantive issues, but a contest between man and man-plus-people's aspirations or fancy. When Ed Muskie ran in 1954, he was the beneficiary of the quest for novelty. So was I in 1956. It is ironic that for quite a while the responsive chord was struck by an appeal to bring back a two-party system. Well, that was accomplished superbly, only to find that two parties are not adequate to the task in the minds of many. In any event, there was an undercurrent of highly charged thought running against party leaders, just because they represented the system.
>
> So, the first thing I have to say is—don't waste even a minute blaming yourself. If you had been lazy, arrogant, complacent, or even just plain inefficient, you might well indulge in some self-criticism. But you were none of these. I think you ran a superb campaign—intelligent, communicative, decent, and well organized. There is always the temptation to ask—If I had done thus-and-so differently, would that have made the difference? Well, if you had reacted differently, you wouldn't have been George Mitchell—and who knows how many of your supporters would have been turned off? I can think of a few things I would have done differently in my campaign, but I have finally concluded that they would not have made a net difference. So—you did not, by any stretch of the imagination, "let the party down." Indeed, you gave it as good and fine a candidate as it ever had.
>
> The second thing I want to say is something my mother always told me, and now I most generally, and certainly in matters like this, believe: This will somehow, in the inscrutable course of time, turn out for the best. It did for me, and I know it will for you. How, no one can predict—but politics, law, and who knows what else are open to you. At a young age you have had a rare opportunity and have lived up to it to the best of your very large abilities. Such an experience is one through which you can only gain.

8

FROM THE BAR
TO THE BENCH

In time, George Mitchell came to terms with the outcome of his campaign for governor, but it was a process not of days or months, but years. He returned to his law practice and continued his service on the Democratic National Committee, but for a long time he had every intention of running for governor again in 1978. Though he can seem cautious and deliberate in speech and action, Mitchell has never shied away from long odds. To his friend Harold Pachios, Mitchell is a risk-taker, someone who's willing to take chances that other politicians aren't. Instead of the sure thing, or at least the likely thing, he is willing to try something he's never attempted before, and sometimes things that hardly anyone else is willing to try.

After the 1974 election, Mitchell didn't initially agree with criticisms that he'd been too serious, too stiff, that his campaign appearances, particularly on television, were not reflective of the private self those close to him knew well. Kermit Lipez observed, "In that first campaign, for some reason, his public personality did not accurately reflect that private personality—the cerebral side of him seemed to be more on display than this very warm, personal side. What's fascinating is that the next time that had dramatically changed. There was a merger between the private man and the public man." But it occurred slowly.

"At first, I didn't think I had to dramatically change my style," Mitchell said years later. "To me, the result of the campaign didn't stem from an inability to present myself well, and accurately. But after a while, when you hear the same thing over and over, well, you begin to think that maybe you're wrong, and they're right."

Lipez believes that over the next couple of years, Mitchell went through "a period of self-examination, talking with people about how he could be a better campaigner. And he got some advice to lighten up, to let people see his true nature. He took that to heart and worked at changing his public persona to be more consistent with the person he actually was. For any politician, likeability is an important quality—it's much harder to succeed without it. George was enormously likeable and publicly became so."

Tony Buxton thinks Mitchell began his "years in the wilderness" with a period of study and reading, concentrating on the works of the founders and writers of the Constitution, and on British and American history. Mitchell doesn't remember anything so systematic, though he said, "I've always had a book going, throughout my life." And while he moved on from the one campaign he lost, he never forgot it. Buxton was meeting Bill Clinton for the first time, when Mitchell was Senate majority leader and making the introduction, and he remembers Mitchell saying, "Mr. President, this is Tony Buxton, who ran my first and only losing campaign." Buxton was quick to add, "Mr. President, if you know George Mitchell, I think you know exactly who ran that campaign." Buxton said, "It has been a point of contention ever since."

There was a more immediate decision following the 1974 election. Democrats had won the Maine House of Representatives and thus were in the position, for the first time since 1964, to elect the attorney general, treasurer, and secretary of state. Many thought Mitchell would embrace the opportunity to become attorney general; during the 1972 campaign, Maine reporters often speculated that, in a Muskie administration, Mitchell would be a shoo-in for US Attorney General. But Mitchell declined, instead throwing his support to Joe Brennan. Had Mitchell made the race, it might have been close, but with his backing, Brennan was the overwhelming choice—the second important state office he'd held, while Mitchell was still without one.

Some supporters urged Mitchell to run for Congress in 1976; first-term Republican David Emery had won in a stunning upset, and the betting was he would be vulnerable to a challenge. Mitchell wasn't interested. On October 22, 1975, he wrote to Eliot Cutler—who would become involved in national politics again, on Walter Mondale's vice presidential campaign—saying, "I am not going to run for Congress. My present intention is simply to wait and run for governor again in 1978." He added, "Be careful, or you are going to be making so much money in New York you won't be able to come back to Maine." As late as December 3, 1976, Mitchell wrote to another correspondent, "I definitely intend to run for governor again."

One of the rewards of settling back into a law practice where he'd enjoyed substantial success was cultivating and enjoying an extensive network of friends. Unlike Muskie, who had few confidants—one explanation of his continued closeness to Mitchell, despite the trials they endured—George Mitchell enjoyed a variety of friends, from fellow attorneys to pizza shop owners and car dealers.

The leading contender for "first friend" was Hal Pachios. There were many similarities, and some differences, in their backgrounds. Pachios is three years younger than Mitchell; his grandparents had been immigrants from Greece, and his father had a successful career with Prudential Insurance in Portland. He attended the Kent School in Connecticut, and then Princeton, before serving in the US Navy. He, too, took night law classes at Georgetown and was hired by Bill Moyers, who was helping to organize the fledgling Peace Corps. Pachios was congressional liaison for the new program, which is how he met Mitchell in Muskie's office in 1962. They soon became fast friends. Pachios did advance work for Lyndon Johnson's 1964 campaign, then became Moyers's deputy in the White House press office. After the 1968 campaign he returned to Maine, where Mitchell helped him land a job with Preti Flaherty. Both he and Severin Beliveau became partners, and the firm was renamed Preti, Flaherty, Beliveau, and Pachios.

One of Pachios's services to Mitchell was introducing him to tennis, which they both started playing after the 1972 Muskie campaign. After some casual rounds of pool and workouts at the batting cage—Pachios said Mitchell was "a pretty good hitter"—they tried golf, Muskie's game, "but George didn't like it very much." Tennis was the sport Mitchell warmed to. Pachios said it "was a good game for George because he is a focused guy, and he's a very steady and consistent guy, and his tennis game reflected that, and he got better and better, much too good for me." For most of the 1970s, a group of friends from the Portland area, including Mitchell and Pachios, would meet for singles and doubles matches, eventually including informal tournaments. At least one of the participants sees tennis as illustrating fundamental aspects of Mitchell's character.

Walter Corey, an attorney with Bernstein Shur, worked for Ken Curtis as his federal coordinator, where he met Mitchell, then state party chair. Mitchell "was very outgoing and genial," Corey said, "and had a razor-quick mind, and he and I spent a lot of time talking about policy." Together, they edited political speeches they prepared. "George intellectually was head and shoulders above virtually all of his contemporaries," Corey said. "It was very insightful, because if you were attentive and you watched the way a person behaved on the tennis court, you could learn a lot about him."

What Corey observed about Mitchell was that "his most outstanding and extraordinary quality in tennis, as in the rest of his life, is his mental toughness." On the tennis court, "George was a relentless player. There was never a ball he wouldn't go for, and most often get and return." The other notable quality was Mitchell's decisiveness. "A lot of players get tangled up and lose their bearings" in deciding which way to go, but "George always had a great instinct for knowing what to do, and doing it. . . . He's a guy who could live with his mistakes."

Mitchell was not an outdoorsman, but he did go sailing with Pachios on his boat, ranging along the Maine coast in summer. Once, in the fog off Port Clyde, they were trying to find a bell buoy, which Mitchell heard. Pachios left the wheel to look at the chart, telling Mitchell to steer toward the buoy. He was kneeling on the deck when the boat struck an object with a bang. It was the buoy, and Mitchell said, "You told me to steer toward the buoy." Pachios tells the story to tease Mitchell, but, inevitably, Mitchell reveals the sequel, which is that Pachios was seasick on the return run. "He always wins that one," said Pachios.

Another close friend was Joe Angelone, who ran a pizza parlor in Portland, a relatively new food in Maine at the time. It became a political gathering place, similar to haunts in Providence, Rhode Island, where Angelone grew up. Mitchell could relax with him, and was also impressed by his political insights. The attraction crossed political boundaries. Bill Cohen, after being elected to the Senate in 1978, stopped by frequently. Shep Lee—the car dealer who sold Mitchell a car when he began working for Muskie, "the cheapest he could find"—also became close. Lee said that although Mitchell was in Maine less often after the 1970s, he "maintained his old friendships, and he never forgot his old loyal friends. Most people who rise . . . probably leave some of the old friendships behind; they no longer fit. He never did that. He always respected and regarded old friends as important."

THOUGH MITCHELL HAD SETTLED BACK INTO LIFE at Jensen Baird, he was restless. He was less involved in Muskie's 1976 reelection campaign, in part because a tough potential opponent, Cohen, decided to take a pass, and waited to challenge Bill Hathaway two years later. Muskie's race against Robert Monks wasn't especially challenging. Because Mitchell was still serving on the DNC, politics was presumed to be part of his future. But what part?

Mitchell recalls that near the end of 1976, he had dinner with Joe Brennan at the old Roma restaurant in Portland. By that time, Mitchell said, "I had accepted as accurate the criticisms of me, that I probably couldn't get elected. I can't pinpoint a moment when the conviction settled in." As they talked, Brennan told Mitchell he planned to run for governor in 1978. That prompted

Mitchell to begin considering his own decision. "I came to the conclusion that, while I had beaten him in a primary in '74, I lost in the general election. He was a very good candidate, and a good guy, and I probably couldn't get elected even if I might win a primary. So, I kind of thought, 'I'll do the legal stuff.'"

The "legal stuff" turned out to include an offer from Muskie for US Attorney for Maine. It was one of the few patronage positions left, and was prestigious in the legal community. Mitchell's immediate predecessor, Peter Mills, a Republican, liked the job so much that, after serving eight years under Dwight Eisenhower, he came back after the Kennedy and Johnson administrations to serve another eight years under Nixon and Ford. With a Democratic president and Democratic Senate, there wasn't much question Mitchell would be easily confirmed, and he had previous ties to Jimmy Carter. Mitchell accepted early in 1977. He had shelved his ambition to be governor, and that opportunity never arose again.

Before resuming federal service, his first since the Justice Department's Antitrust Division, Mitchell resigned from his law firm and the DNC. He wrapped up his partnership, and tried his last case opposite Dan Wathen, who had helped represent Freddie Vahlsing during the ill-fated sugar beet venture. Wathen remembers the case well. It was a personal injury suit, and reminds one how small a state Maine really is.

Mitchell's client was the son of Frederick Payne, the former Republican US senator, while Wathen represented Paul MacDonald, a District Court judge, a Republican who'd previously been secretary of state. MacDonald had rear-ended Payne's car, so there was little question about liability, but the two sides disagreed about damages, so the case went to trial. MacDonald had limited eyesight, so Wathen kept him out of the courtroom. Mitchell "insinuated, without ever making a claim," Wathen said, that Payne's injuries were so severe that they required having a testicle removed.

Wathen decided to put the matter to rest by calling his own witness, a doctor, who had asserted in a letter that the surgery wasn't connected to the accident. It was a classic example, Wathen said, of how "you [should] never ask a question on cross-examination you don't know the answer to." When he asked the doctor to reiterate his statement, the witness said, "I said that, but now I'm not so sure." Wathen decided Mitchell had led him on. When Wathen told the insurance company what had happened, they settled. Wathen and Mitchell then went to lunch, and Wathen asked how this case would count against his partnership. When Mitchell told him he'd share receipts only until a certain date, Wathen called the insurance adjuster to speed up the check. "George did genuinely appreciate that," Wathen said. "We were adversaries, but we were friendly adversaries."

After swift confirmation, Mitchell was sworn in as US Attorney for Maine on May 2, 1977, at the federal courthouse in Portland. In his remarks, he said, "I have been asked many times why I accepted this position, by friends in private and by reporters in public. A variety of motives have been ascribed to me. And so, I thought I would take this opportunity of a captive audience held here by the Court to explain."

Mitchell described the naturalization ceremony that day, where seventy-seven people "became citizens of their own free will," and added, "For most Americans citizenship is an accident of birth, and as a result too few of us give any thought to the meaning of American citizenship, especially to the duties and responsibilities that go with it. We are truly blessed to live in the most free, most open, most prosperous society in all of human history. This is partly by chance, but it is also at least in part the result of human choice and human endeavor."

He was stating some of the enduring themes of his public career, especially the balance between the rights and responsibilities of citizenship, with similar duties for those who represent citizens in government. He said, "Confidence in our institutions, public and private, is eroding. In no area of our society is this more evident than in the administration of justice." As a public servant, Mitchell said, "I hope to contribute in some small way to the restoration of public confidence in our system of government and the administration of justice. I hope to help roll back the tide of cynicism and distrust that at times seems to be the inevitable wave of the future."

One of his first tasks was to hire a staff; the US Attorney appoints the lawyers in the office. One assistant attorney was Jim Brannigan, a career prosecutor who covered the Bangor office. Mitchell tried many of his own cases and said of Brannigan, "I learned a lot from him; he was extremely helpful to me. He really knew how to run an office, how to try a case." His selections for his two assistants in Portland were unusual. The first was Paula Silsby, daughter of a prominent Hancock County Republican whose grandfather had been a Superior Court judge. The other, when a position was added, was Margaret McGaughey.

The US Attorney's office in Maine had never had a female assistant; now it had two. While women were beginning to graduate from law schools in greater numbers, Tony Buxton doesn't believe Mitchell's choices reflected any conscious intent to promote women. "I've never perceived George Mitchell as having any bias whatsoever," he said. "It just isn't part of his brain. He does try to lift people up; he truly believes in a meritocracy, and he always chose to align himself with intelligent people." Nonetheless, the National Organization for Women gave Mitchell an award.

Silsby, a young Superior Court law clerk, had asked Mitchell if she could observe a juvenile hearing involving a case where he represented, pro bono, a young man named Donald Ruby. Ruby had shot and killed a father and son who were out hunting. He was tried as an adult, but the charge was reduced from second- to fourth-degree manslaughter. Afterward, Mitchell and Silsby talked, and he asked if she might be interested in working for him. She was hired on June 1, 1977, and soon found that Mitchell was not a micromanager. "George was very hands-off. I could always go to him, but . . . I had an enormous amount of discretion and authority by virtue of my position . . . and managed to get through, at age twenty-six, without any disasters." He was also demanding. "He can be intimidating," Silsby said. "He's not a man to tell you that you had done something well, but he certainly told you if you erred." Yet Silsby saw another side. "He's a raconteur, a wonderful storyteller, with this sort of giggle that is delightfully boyish, and so at odds with the austerity of the persona I knew he wanted to cultivate and present to the world."

The next year, Mitchell hired McGaughey, who had practiced in Boston for four years after law school, but was "desperate to get back to Maine." She became a law clerk for Frank Coffin, whose office was also in the Portland courthouse. McGaughey said, "I remember very clearly George Mitchell coming upstairs to talk to Judge Coffin about me, and thought, 'Oh my gosh, my life hangs in the balance.'"

The young assistants soon had plenty of work, for, as McGaughey put it, "Maine pretty much came on the map in terms of the criminal element. Up until then, federal crime in Maine had been fairly small-scale, stealing Social Security checks, or odometer fixing, or bait fish." After Mitchell took office, "the big marijuana boats started coming into Maine, and those cases would tie up all four of us for months at a time." She was also struck by Mitchell's active role. "He was the people person; he was the one who argued the motions, who examined the witnesses at trial, who negotiated the pleas. He was not especially fond of the purely academic side of practicing law, which is what I loved. So his management style was to let me do what I liked, and he would do what he liked. . . . We were given enormous responsibility for lawyers fresh out of law school."

Another task for Mitchell was mending relations with Judge Edward Gignoux, the sole trial judge, who had frequently clashed with Peter Mills. The root of their disagreements stemmed from Gignoux's appointment in 1957. Mills had been one of the top two candidates, along with James Reid, a state judge, and each had a Republican senator's backing. Margaret Chase Smith favored Mills, while Frederick Payne preferred Reid. Gignoux, then an attorney at Verrill Dana, emerged as the compromise candidate. Gignoux was taken aback by

Mills's freewheeling style. When Mills's public comments led to a rebuke from the bench, Mills termed it a "gag order," with Gignoux later warning Mills that his comments to the press came "at your own peril." On at least one occasion, the First Circuit Court of Appeals overturned a conviction after Mills had asserted on television that the court was coddling white-collar criminals. Mitchell's style was lower-key, and the judge and prosecutor were on the same page from the beginning.

Patrick Hunt, a native of Island Falls in northern Maine, was a Drug Enforcement Agency investigator working out of Boston. He was impressed by Mitchell's professionalism in his first visit to the Portland office to confer on a case with Mitchell and Jim Brannigan. "I noticed how unusually bright these two men were, what great listeners, and how they asked questions that no one else had ever asked before," he said. Hunt also noticed that the office "had been freshly carpeted, the walls were painted, the furniture was organized, files could be located, and the tone had changed dramatically." Hunt saw that for Steve Ridge, the court administrator "who had never been treated properly," life had also improved. Mitchell, Hunt said, went out of his way to speak to special agents in Boston, their superiors, and agency directors in Washington. "He reached out to them and made it a point to develop a greater sense of collegiality." The improved relations with Judge Gignoux also paid dividends. "Convictions went up, indictments went up. . . . The US Attorney's office stopped losing cases and started winning cases."

Hunt said that he was "astounded" that Mitchell answered his own phone, and said he had "an uncanny ability to memorize names and faces." Mitchell's memory is a persistent theme. It was enormously useful in the courtroom. Paula Silsby, on meeting Mitchell for the double homicide hearing, was amazed that he recalled her from a campaign stop at the Hilltop Campground in Ellsworth, where she had listened as Mitchell talked to her father. "You can imagine how extraordinarily flattering that is, to have somebody even recognize your name, let alone remember every fact and circumstance as to where you met."

George Isaacson, who clerked at Jensen Baird after Mitchell hired him—and who married Margaret McGaughey in 1981, with Mitchell in attendance—remembers Mitchell's case preparation. He could be discussing a client, or an opposing counsel, and call them without ever looking up a phone number. Many years later, when Mitchell was Middle East envoy for President Obama, Silsby heard a seemingly incredible story about the filming of a documentary on Palestine. Mitchell was well into the take, which the filmmaker described as "just extraordinary, because he was able to articulate and organize his thoughts without one 'er' or 'uh,' and had given this incredibly succinct, pithy analysis."

There was a problem with the microphone; every time a "p" sound was spoken, it over-resonated. The film crew was about to postpone the recording, but Mitchell, after a short break, repeated the take—without using a single "p."

Mitchell's habit of answering his own phone came in handy while he was preparing one of his first major cases, involving a large antiques theft ring. "One day I got a call from a staff member from US Senator John Chafee's office telling me that the family home in Sorrento had been broken into and valuable antiques had been stolen," he said. Chafee had heard about Mitchell's investigation and, as it happened, Mitchell had just broken the case. A woman from western Maine who wintered in Virginia went to an auction in Petersburg and discovered an antique chest stolen from the Maine family home. By tracing the chest back to Maine, investigators arrested and Mitchell convicted a Lewiston man who had in turn sold it to a Boston auction house.

The burglary ring, with the Boston auction house a major buyer, was sophisticated and bold. "They got so brazen about it, they started breaking into antiques stores up and down the coast of Maine," Mitchell said. Sorrento, a summer community on an isolated peninsula, was an ideal site. "There was one antiques store in Rockport that was emptied out," Mitchell said. "They literally backed the truck up to it on a Sunday night, [then] drove it to Boston." Of the cases taken to trial, Mitchell won four convictions, and another defendant pleaded guilty. Chafee got his antiques back. The resulting prosecutions also included the only jury acquittal in the sixteen cases Mitchell tried during two and a half years as US Attorney. In all, by November 1979, twenty-five defendants were charged, twenty convicted at trial, one acquitted, and one case dismissed. Three suspects remained fugitives from justice.

Mitchell and Chafee didn't meet during the antiques trials, though they spoke by phone. When Mitchell was sworn into the Senate in 1980, the first senator he met was Chafee, "and we became friends instantly," Mitchell said. Chafee, a moderate Republican from Rhode Island, worked closely with Mitchell on environmental legislation, and, for a time, on health care as well.

The "drug boat" trials that consumed so much time during Mitchell's tenure represented the leading edge of the "war on drugs" proclaimed by Richard Nixon. Margaret McGaughey got to observe Mitchell during the trials, and remembers him as "very charismatic. These big marijuana cases were quite glamorous," she said. "There would be boatloads with fifteen or twenty tons of marijuana and twenty to twenty-five defendants, each of whom would have their high-paid, out-of-state lawyers. And then there would be the three of us. So it was organized seat-of-the-pants; we were all learning." The scope of the marijuana cases was so new to Maine that they spawned further criminal acts.

At one point, a group of thieves attempted to steal a truck holding a one-and-a-half-ton marijuana shipment held as evidence by attempting to bribe the Coast Guard officers who were guarding it.

Gerry Petruccelli, who had worked with Mitchell on campaigns, joined Preti Flaherty and did occasional criminal defense work. He was opposing counsel in one of the marijuana cases, and appreciated Mitchell's sense of theater. "George had brought into the courtroom and piled around the well of the court, the gate, the bar, all of these bales of marijuana," Petruccelli said. "It looked like New Orleans and Katrina; it looked like the sandbags had been piled up. And I'm trying a case sitting in front of a wall of bales of marijuana."

Petruccelli thought his best chance of winning was a motion to suppress evidence. He said, "George, to his great credit, recognized that the search had some problems. . . . The DEA guys, and some state law enforcement people, had really done a lot of searching before they thought, 'Maybe we ought to go get a warrant.' And even Judge Gignoux thought that was a fifty-fifty call." But, "He decided against my client [and] in favor of the government, and the rest is history."

Mitchell extended legal courtesy. When he was trying to pin down evidence with an elusive sheriff, Mitchell called the sheriff, spoke to him, and told Petruccelli, "I'll stipulate to the fact; don't worry about the sheriff." In other pretrial maneuvering, Petruccelli tried to convince the judge that the jury might be prejudiced because of Mitchell's run for governor. Under questioning by Gignoux, "One of them after another is saying, 'Oh no, never heard of him.'" It was an issue that would return in Mitchell's 1982 Senate race.

Mitchell's successes in the drug war did gain favorable notice. On November 1, 1979, he was awarded the DEA Medal of Honor. Mitchell's citation reads, "In his two and a half years as US Attorney, his trials resulted in convictions in federal court of some eighty defendants, seizures of more than 100,000 pounds of controlled substances, and the forfeiture to the government of more than $2 million in cash, seized boats, trucks, and court fines."

One of the more unusual cases Mitchell handled was a charge of distributing obscene films, involving child pornography, for which Kevin Menard went on trial. Obscenity laws had undergone a century-long oscillation since the Comstock laws of the 1870s, which made it a crime to distribute obscene literature through the mail. Standards were relaxed in the 1920s, then tightened following World War II. A 1973 US Supreme Court decision created a three-part test. Prosecutors, juries, and judges were still struggling with the new standards when Mitchell prosecuted *U.S. v. Menard*, with the defendant convicted after a three-day trial on April 4, 1978. Postal inspectors had intercepted films that

Menard, who lived in Rhode Island, had shipped to Maine. They depicted boys ages eight to fourteen in homosexual acts, and the only legal question, since Menard admitted shipping them, was, Mitchell wrote, "whether the films were in fact obscene, and, if so, whether he knew they were obscene when he shipped them."

The case, which raised concerns among some civil liberties advocates, occasioned a fourteen-page rebuttal by Mitchell to a letter written to *Maine Times* by David Chute, and headlined, "Dissent on the Kiddie Porn Trial." Mitchell submitted the essay as an example of legal writing for his confirmation as a federal judge. Mitchell had little trouble demolishing Chute's basic argument—that the First Amendment provided unlimited protection for speech or expression. Courts have consistently found that free speech rights are not absolute, Mitchell said. What seemed to bother him was the claim that criminal prosecutions would have a chilling effect, what he called Chute's "constant equating of child pornography films with freedom of speech, the repeated suggestion that unless we permit their distribution the death of democracy is at hand." Since then, the law has continued to evolve, and federal obscenity trials are rare.

While Mitchell was able to hire two more attorneys by the time he left the office, the major expansion of federal prosecutions occurred in the 1980s and '90s. Tom Delahanty II, son of a judge and political associate of Ed Muskie, initially turned down Mitchell's offer of an assistant attorney position, but then succeeded him when Mitchell was elevated to the federal bench. He held the job only briefly, to the end of the Carter administration, but then returned in 2010 as an Obama appointee.

Looking back, Delahanty said, "When we wanted to have a staff meeting, we just went out to lunch together." The US Attorney staff for Maine is now six times larger, with some thirty assistant attorneys at work. Paula Silsby and Margaret McGaughey became career employees, both serving more than thirty years, "unlike George, who can't keep a job," as Silsby put it. She became US Attorney herself in the George W. Bush administration, though Bush never nominated her. Recommended by Senator Olympia Snowe, she was installed through an unusual administrative procedure.

It was during his service as US Attorney that Mitchell began to develop and explore the distinctive principles that guided his public career. One was an instinctive, and nearly absolute, intolerance of any form of legal discrimination. He had walked away from a possible first job when a law firm partner asked about his religion. George Isaacson, who is Jewish, was touched when Mitchell asked him after he'd joined Jensen Baird whether he'd feel comfortable joining meetings at the Cumberland Club, which had ended its ban on Catholics and, only recently, on Jews. "It struck me as quite remarkable," Isaacson said, "when you had a senior partner who was talking to the most junior associate, and was sensitive enough to ask."

Ken Cole, an attorney who joined Jensen Baird and was later a state Republican Party chair, said Mitchell "was truly a Democrat in a philosophical sense, in terms of his beliefs and how he saw the law. . . . He was somebody who did not just parrot what he said to be elected but actually believed it." Ralph Lancaster, a Mitchell contemporary who served three years as Judge Gignoux's clerk, saw it as a period when trust was assumed. "With one exception in fifty years of practice, I have never had a lawyer in Maine go back on his word," he said.

Mitchell also developed a strong distaste for self-promotion, and any instance where a public figure made exaggerated claims for himself. Eliot Cutler, who he'd warned about moneymaking a few years earlier, finally exceeded his tolerance. Cutler, after his work on the Mondale campaign, had landed a position at the Office of Management and Budget in the Carter administration, supervising energy policy. In correspondence, Mitchell is usually reserved, but he let loose in an August 16, 1979, letter to "Dear Eliot":

> Last week I was in Boston. I opened up the *Boston Globe* to read about the Red Sox and there, instead of a picture of Yaz, I saw a picture of you, accompanied by a lengthy story in which you described to the reporter how important you are. This week I was in Bangor. I picked up the *Bangor Daily News* to find out what has been going on in northern Maine, and there, on the front page, I saw a familiar face and a now familiar story in which you told the people of Maine how important you are. No more is necessary! You have finally achieved that for which you have striven these many years: you are now more important than Senator Muskie.

Tony Buxton liked to tell an anecdote about a visit to Mitchell's Portland office when he was in law school, with Mitchell's encouragement. He was about to take the bar exam, and was none too sure of his future. Mitchell invited him to lunch, and when they went out, confronted the dilemma posed by a man panhandling: Should street people get handouts? Mitchell solved the problem. He'd seen a waitress he knew heading toward a restaurant and took the man by the arm, called to the waitress, and gave her a $5 bill, telling her, "Would you please see that this man gets lunch?" Buxton remembers thinking, "If I had $5, I might have given him $5."

Buxton had waited in the office while Mitchell called the opposing counsel on a case, an appeal to the First Circuit. Mitchell told the attorney, "I'm going to quote a case that's not in my brief, and I want you to know what the case is, and I'll drive somebody up to you with a copy, because it's a new case." Buxton took in what Mitchell was doing, then asked, "Why didn't you just give it to him when you got there, or why didn't you surprise him?" Mitchell looked at him a moment, then said, "My job is not to win. My job is to see that justice is done."

IN THE FALL OF 1978, ED MUSKIE'S LONG CAMPAIGN to create a second judgeship in the Maine District Court bore fruit, with a Democratic president and a favorable Judiciary Committee alignment. There were a large number of potential candidates—Dan Wathen, though a Republican, applied—but little doubt about whom Muskie favored. Giving up his US Attorney's post would, for Mitchell, be leaving politics behind. He would enter a different world, one where campaigning and horse-trading were forbidden, and where practitioners were expected to keep even friends and former associates at a distance.

Frank Coffin, who had already been on the Appeals Court bench more than a decade, became an admired legal scholar and writer, and summed up his tenure in a passage from his book, *The Ways of a Judge*, published in 1980. Appellate judges, he wrote, "are often no more visible or comprehensible to the citizen than the vapor-inhaling priestesses at the Oracle of Delphi. The judges sit in a phalanx behind their elevated bench, listen to argument, ask a few questions, and, weeks or months later, issue an opinion. Exactly what goes on, if anything, between argument and decision is veiled in mystery." There would be the attraction of more concentrated legal writing, which was important to Mitchell. As Coffin put it, "A remarkably effective device for detecting fissures in accuracy and logic is the reduction to writing of the results of one's thought processes."

Mitchell's colleagues didn't see him as an obvious candidate. Charlie Micoleau served on Muskie's review panel and said Mitchell was "superbly qualified." Yet he wondered, "Did he really want to withdraw from politics so thoroughly? There were those like myself who felt he had so much to offer as an elected official that it would be a shame to put himself in a position where he couldn't run or be active in politics." Margaret McGaughey was surprised a judgeship appealed to Mitchell, because "he was such a social person, and being a judge is a rather reclusive profession."

Mitchell told Micoleau, "If you're a lawyer, one of the heights of ambition—if you're a good lawyer, and you respect and admire the law and enjoy its practice—is to be in a judgeship where you're a trier of fact, as well as law." On a less elevated level, a clue to Mitchell's thinking came in a lunchtime conversation with Gerry Petruccelli. The talk was casual until Mitchell leaned forward and said, "It looks like I'm going to have to take that judgeship up at Bangor that Muskie's after me to take." He said, "I don't want to go back to the law firm, and my political career is over." Petruccelli often used the story in his University of Maine Law School classes, telling students, "Don't be planning your career too precisely, because you don't really know where you're going to end up."

The world Mitchell seemed to be leaving behind in 1979 was the subject of a skit Ed Bonney wrote for a dinner that fall to celebrate the twenty-fifth anniversary of the Maine Democratic Party's revival by Muskie and Coffin. The skit featured five former party chairs, with Bonney playing the part of Frank Coffin. It featured a mock meeting led by Harold Pachios, who was stepping down to run, unsuccessfully, against David Emery, and some razzing of Bill Hathaway for not stepping down in a similar situation. The meeting reflected the early, lean years, with Coffin fretting about a campaign debt from a vanished Bangor hotel, and Severin Beliveau, who'd presided over the party's peak years in the 1970s, advocating a vast celebration: "We'll have fireworks, skyrockets, jet planes overhead, Democrats marching four abreast down the Maine Turnpike on their way to the largest free lobster bake in the history of Maine." In a cover note to Mitchell, Bonney wrote, "We thought it not wise to write a part for you because of your pending elevation to the judiciary."

Becoming a judge required a more extensive disclosure statement than he'd filed for the US Attorney post. Mitchell earned $51,417 for 1976 as a Jensen Baird partner, his last full year. He was paid $42,834 as US Attorney in 1978, and received $19,284 as a payout for his partnership. His largest political contribution was $550 to Bill Hathaway in 1978; he made annual donations to the Democratic State Committee, ranging from $150 to $337.

Some of the most challenging confirmation questions came from the Republican minority on the Senate Judiciary Committee, where Strom Thurmond was ranking member. Mitchell was asked about the "original intent" theory of the Constitution, which contends that the intentions of the Framers should be faithfully followed. Chief Justice John Marshall was quoted as saying the Constitution shouldn't be extended to "objects not contemplated by the Framers." Mitchell replied, "The fundamental principles of the Constitution are permanent and must remain unchanged." He then diverged from "original intent" in observing that "those principles must be applied in a society far different from the society in which the Framers lived and worked." Not even Thomas Jefferson, "whose intellect and vision remain unsurpassed," could have foreseen a nation of "215 million Americans, some of whom walked on the moon." He concluded, "Our capacity to apply unchanging principles to changing circumstances is a major reason for the longevity and continued vitality of our Constitution."

When Mitchell was asked about "judicial activism," at that time involving judges ordering desegregation of schools, prison reform, and improving mental hospitals, Mitchell first drafted an answer that stated, "I do not believe in judicial activism. I feel the judiciary should adhere to its traditional function of resolving irreconcilable differences between parties with an immediate interest." In his submitted response, however, he took a different tack, noting the absence of concrete examples of "activism" in the question. If legal questions of jurisdiction, standing, and ripeness are met, Mitchell wrote, "A federal judge cannot shrink from deciding a case merely because his or her decision may affect persons or interests other than the immediate parties, or because it may impose a duty on government." He cited the "exclusionary rule," which holds that a judge must disallow evidence from an illegal search, as an example.

In remarks made elsewhere, Mitchell expressed skepticism about whether judges were really exceeding their authority. He quoted with approval a *New York Times* editorial that cited Alabama governor George Wallace's complaint that the courts were trying to create "a hotel atmosphere" in jails, and federal judge Frank Johnson's reply: "The elimination of conditions that will permit maggots in a patient's wound for over a month before his death does not constitute a hotel atmosphere."

Mitchell received a letter of support from Governor Joe Brennan dated September 19, addressed to Judiciary Committee Chairman Ted Kennedy. Brennan praised Mitchell's "extremely high intelligence, with an excellent command of the law." He added, "George possesses that sensitivity and concern that would assure that those without wealth and influence in the community would be treated with the same dignity and concern that the wealthy and influential receive as a matter of course. I believe that George would conduct himself as a judge in a manner so that 'equal protection of the law' would not be a meaningless, high-sounding phrase."

Mitchell's nomination again faced no significant obstacles. He was confirmed on October 14, and sworn in by Frank Coffin on November 2, 1979. During the ceremony, Mitchell thanked his law partners, saying, "They took me in as a young, inexperienced lawyer, taught me how to practice law, and graciously tolerated my comings and goings." From his staff, he singled out administrator Steve Ridge. "Many of you may not realize that for over twenty-five years, Steve has been the real US Attorney," Mitchell said, "while a succession of front men—I being but the latest—have pretended to run the show."

He also thanked Ed Muskie, but added, a little mischievously, "I cannot help but note that this is the first time . . . we have both attended a public function at which I spoke and he didn't. And I must say, Senator, that I'm enjoying it very much." He noted that his successor, Tom Delahanty, was not only the son but the grandson of a judge—John Clifford, who had preceded Gignoux—who was also a former US Attorney. Finally, he asked "for patience and tolerance from you lawyers, especially those unlucky men and women who will be trying cases before me for the next year or so, as I become accustomed to being on the other side of the bench."

A few days later, Mitchell wrote to Gignoux, thanking him for his welcome. "Since this is a new experience for me, I hope you will feel at complete liberty to tell me when I am doing something that shouldn't be done, or when I am not doing something that should be done. I expect to have to rely on you to a considerable degree during this early period, but will try not to make a nuisance of myself."

When Gignoux was appointed in 1957, his caseload was modest, to the point where he had to be assured he would get other assignments. One was the "Chicago Seven" trial of antiwar protesters from 1969–1970, stemming from events at the 1968 Democratic Convention. The trial judge, Julius Hoffman, lost control of his courtroom. He was removed from the case and replaced by Gignoux, who proved equal to the task, and the trial concluded with considerably less fireworks.

In 1988, after a renovation and expansion, the federal courthouse in Portland was named in Gignoux's honor, and Mitchell, about to be reelected to the Senate, offered a tribute. He quoted a Gignoux speech where the judge said, "Probably the least of the errors a trial judge can commit is to be wrong. . . . There is always a court of appeals to correct him. But if the trial judge is unfair, if he is impatient, if he is peremptory, if he conducts the trial without full consideration of the rights of the parties, he has failed in his ultimate obligation." Mitchell shared this approach, and admired Gignoux without qualification. "Shortly after I entered the Senate, I was asked how it felt to try to fill Ed Muskie's big shoes," he said. "I answered, Believe me, after you've tried to fill Judge Gignoux's shoes, everything else is easy."

Joe Brennan had a different take on Gignoux, after appearing before him in the Indian Land Claims case. Brennan felt Gignoux favored Tom Tureen, lead attorney for the tribes, because Tureen had a Princeton education. Brennan said of Gignoux, "He was very articulate, right out of the movies, perfect enunciation of every word, and he kind of looked down on me." Ralph Lancaster, who clerked for Gignoux, identified aspects of the judge that appealed to Mitchell, "his intellect, his fairness, his judgment . . . and his compassionate nature. He was a strict adherent to the law, but he had a large heart."

Mitchell heard only a few cases during his brief tenure. One was argued by Harold Friedman, who'd also appeared opposite Mitchell when he was US Attorney. Friedman had sought a trial lawyer position and went to see Mert Henry, who referred him to Mitchell. There were no openings at Jensen Baird, but Mitchell recommended Friedman to Harold Pachios at Preti Flaherty, who hired him. "When he became a federal judge, I argued the first case before him and I lost," Friedman said. "And I went up to the Court of Appeals in Boston, and they affirmed Judge Mitchell's decision. I was then at a loss; I had to try to figure out a way to get even with him. Here was this wonderful person who got me my first job, and then he ruled against me. So what could I do to get even? I married his niece"—who was Mary Mitchell Friedman, Janet and Robbie's daughter.

Mitchell swore in a number of attorneys to the bar, and his remarks on one occasion provide a succinct version of his legal philosophy. He specified three factors in a successful practice—preparation, experience, and integrity. He emphasized that passing the bar exam was just the beginning. "I know what many of you are thinking, because some years ago I sat where you now sit, heard similar words, and thought, 'This business about preparation is ridiculous. Sure, I'll prepare every case carefully, but so will the attorney on the other side.' . . . The hard and unfortunate fact is that not all lawyers prepare all cases. . . . I ask you—I urge you—don't get complacent; don't ever reduce the thoroughness of your preparation." Experience, he said, comes only with time. Integrity, though, may be the great challenge. "You will soon discover that the practice of law is intensely competitive, particularly in litigation. The more pitched a courtroom battle becomes, the more inevitably the temptation arises to use against your opponent the same type of improper tactic you feel he or she has used against you. The drive to win can create an irresistible urge to fight fire with fire. Resist that temptation. . . . One tactical decision executed honorably works better than a dozen dirty tricks. Judges recognize and reward integrity. Juries do. And your peers do."

Lawyers generally returned the favor. Steve Murray, in a letter of February 11, 1980, pointed out that Mitchell had been involved as US Attorney in a spruce budworm spraying case—a controversial program that involved state funding of an effort to contain an insect doing widespread damage to the forest. "We do want to note," Murray said, "that neither our clients nor we have any objection to your hearing the case, and in fact, would request you to do so."

In an interview with a federal court newsletter, *The Third Branch*, Mitchell expressed concern about the growing backlog of civil cases that had been created in part by passage of the Speedy Trial Act, requiring preferential treatment for criminal cases. He also recognized a pitfall faced by trial lawyers becoming judges "who have a tendency to be active trial lawyers when they are in fact judges," he said. "I must say that I can understand why some judges have succumbed to that temptation, because I do feel it myself. When I see an important point overlooked or an objection that should be made, my immediate reaction is to jump in."

Another judicial duty that made a lasting impression involved naturalization ceremonies Mitchell conducted at the Bangor courthouse, on November 5, 1979, just after he was seated, and on May 2, 1980, just before he resigned. He welcomed twenty-eight new citizens on November 5 from Korea, Britain, Canada, the Philippines, Vietnam, Lebanon, Poland, China, Portugal, Colombia, and Ecuador. There were thirty-eight on May 2. On both occasions, he made remarks similar to when he was sworn in as US Attorney. But his reflections on citizenship deepened with time, and became the basis for a story he often tells, summing up his beliefs about the meaning of being an American.

In 2014, he put it this way: "A group of people, who'd come from all over the world and who'd gone through the required procedures, gathered before me in a federal courtroom. There I administered to them the Oath of Allegiance to the United States, and I made them Americans. It was always very emotional for me because my mother was an immigrant, my father, the orphan son of immigrants. They had no education. My mother couldn't read or write English. She worked the night shift at a textile mill. My father was a janitor. But because of their efforts, and because of the openness of American society, I, their son, got the education they never had and was able to become the majority leader of the US Senate. After every ceremony I made it a point to speak personally with each new American, individually or in a family group. I asked them how they came, why they came. I asked about their hopes and dreams, their fears. They were as different as their countries of origin, but there were common themes, best summarized by a young Asian man. When I asked him why he came, he replied, in slow and halting English, 'I came because here in America everybody has a chance.' Think about the fact that a young man who'd been an American for just a few minutes, who could barely speak English, was able to sum up the meaning of America in a single sentence."

In later years, Mitchell's service as a federal judge was frequently noted, as was his "judicial temperament," and he used it to good advantage. Dan Wathen demurred, saying, "In my mind, he's more of a peacemaker. Yes, he's got an attitude that would serve him well as a judge, but . . . it's more than that. It's really that he's thoughtful, careful, and deliberate—very deliberate." Ralph Lancaster was not surprised by his resignation. "George was a politician at heart, and the judiciary role is confining," he said. "Your circle of friends narrows. If you're on a multi-judge panel, you better like them, because they're the people you're going to be dealing with all the time. . . . So I think George would have, if he'd stayed, found it very, very confining."

Paula Silsby said she thought the judgeship might have been a consolation prize after the 1974 governor's race. "One is a life of law and research and contemplation . . . a very insulated life," she said. "And then there's the political side, which is so tactical and so people-oriented. . . . Politics was his real love, so I wasn't surprised at all. In fact, I was thrilled, because what are the chances that anybody would have this happen to them, when it's their real love, and which they for all intents and purposes had seen as over."

Mitchell was scheduled to sit with the First Circuit Court of Appeals on June 5–6, 1980. A few months earlier, Coffin had written to Mitchell about a remanded case, saying, "You will probably get a case on which I took some initial action, or, to be precise, inaction." Coffin may have looked to Mitchell as a possible successor on the appeals court, with perhaps a promotion beyond that. Don Nicoll said his conversations with Coffin suggested "he was highly critical of someone who'd give up a judgeship." Of Mitchell, Nicoll said that, unlike Coffin and Muskie, "He has been someone who has constantly moved on."

Mitchell did not keep his appointment with the First Circuit Court of Appeals. Though he'd received a lifetime appointment, his tenure on the federal bench lasted only a little more than six months.

9

THE SENATE

It was late in 1979, and Ed Muskie was getting restless. He had returned to the Senate after his presidential run in 1972, and, after a time, regained his footing. His 1976 reelection bid went more smoothly than many of his staff had anticipated, and his popularity in Maine seemed undiminished. But the liberal mood that had fueled his triumphs in environmental legislation in the early 1970s was fading. His environmental subcommittee had been tasked with coming up with revisions of the Clean Air Act, in large part because Detroit was finding it impossible to meet one of the three pollution standards, for nitrogen oxide (NOx), contained in the 1970 law. But after nearly two years of work, the bill failed enactment in 1976, due to, ironically, the intransigence of the automobile industry. It had to be revived the following year with a more sympathetic president in the White House.

Despite his reelection, Muskie was wary of hanging on too long. He had seen what happened to Margaret Chase Smith, with whom he'd served for his first fourteen years in the Senate. She was defeated in 1972 by Bill Hathaway in a race some of her supporters believed she shouldn't have made. Muskie's chief of staff, Leon Billings, earlier his principal adviser on the Environment and Public Works Committee, recalls attending a fund-raiser for Washington's Senator Warren Magnuson, where the candidate, who went on to lose his Senate seat in 1980, was plainly drunk. "Don't you ever let me run for reelection if I'm in that condition," Muskie told Billings. Magnuson had been in the Senate for thirty-six years. If he ran for another term in 1982, Muskie would serve thirty.

Not long after, Billings and Muskie were discussing ways to make a graceful exit. Billings mentioned the possibility of a presidential appointment, to which

Muskie replied, "Oh, Jimmy Carter would want to make me goddamn director of OMB." Billings mentioned Treasury secretary as a possibility, which Muskie found more appealing. When he said "secretary of state," Muskie responded, "That I would really like to do." Though he had given up his Foreign Relations seat to become Budget Committee chairman, Muskie's international travels as a presidential candidate had whetted his appetite. Billings then discussed the possibility with Frank Moore, Carter's congressional liaison, and heard back that the president might be interested if Secretary of State Cyrus Vance decided not to stay for a second term.

Vance actually left sooner. After the failure of the Iranian hostage-rescue mission and other policy differences, he formally resigned on April 28, 1980. The obvious replacement was Vance's deputy, Warren Christopher, but Carter decided he preferred someone like Muskie, who could win quick Senate confirmation—as he did, on May 8, less than two weeks later. And so it was that Christopher remained available to become Bill Clinton's first secretary of state in 1993.

Muskie knew Governor Joe Brennan would appoint his successor, but before saying yes to the White House, he wanted to talk to him. So, before Vance's formal resignation, he got the White House to send a plane from Andrews Air Force Base to Brunswick Naval Air Station, for what was as close to a secret political meeting as Maine has ever seen. Muskie asked Brennan to come alone, except for his driver, but he himself brought along two advisers—Billings, and Berl Bernhard, who he continued to trust implicitly despite the two losing national campaigns. Bernhard had scant interest in the intricacies of Maine politics, and played only a minor role. Billings, however, was a participant as well as an observer.

The military plane landed, and was greeted on the runway by the base commandant, who accompanied them to his office, where Brennan was waiting. Muskie outlined the reasons for his decision, and asked Brennan to convey the wish that his successor keep his staff on for a transitional period—as Brennan recalls, six months to a year. Then the talk turned to who Brennan might consider. The obvious candidate was Ken Curtis. Since completing his second term as governor, Curtis served as DNC chair under Carter, a decision he later came to regret, and then moved to the more congenial post of ambassador to Canada. But when Muskie mentioned Curtis, Brennan said, "I could never do that. I could never pick him after what happened to me."

There were three irritants between Curtis and the man who had, after four years of Jim Longley, become governor himself. Kermit Lipez, who remained close to Curtis, attended a meeting at the Blaine House where a dozen Curtis adherents tried to convince Brennan the former governor was the man for the job. Brennan, already known for keeping his own counsel, wasn't likely to be swayed by such an approach, but Lipez found the meeting illuminating.

The first difficulty was that Curtis, who had been neutral in the 1974 primary, was perceived as favoring Phil Merrill, Brennan's main party rival, in 1978. It wasn't a formal endorsement, but Curtis attended a Merrill fund-raiser—"My wife warned me I shouldn't do it," he said recently—which politically amounted to the same thing.

The second issue was conflict over the Indian Land Claims case, then being litigated, which wasn't settled until late 1980, when Congress enacted a bill to compensate the Penobscot and Passamaquoddy tribes and allow them to buy land in northern and eastern Maine. Muskie and Hathaway were sympathetic to the Indians' claims, as was Curtis, but Brennan, as state attorney general, had taken a hard line against any legal liability. As a Portland liberal, this enhanced his appeal statewide. Lipez found Brennan relatively untroubled by the policy differences, and didn't seem concerned about the 1978 race. But he said Brennan "became really heated" when the third issue was raised.

In Maine, judges at all levels are appointed to seven-year terms, and, if they desire, are usually reappointed. Brennan decided not to reappoint Maurice Pilot, a Bangor District Court judge who Brennan believed hadn't been performing his duties. Curtis, then in Canada, got a call from John Day, *Bangor Daily News* political reporter, who asked about his policy on reappointing judges, and Curtis said that, as a rule, he did so when asked. Curtis thinks it's likely Day didn't make the context clear, and when his response was headlined, it appeared Curtis was faulting Brennan. Lipez believes "It was all a misunderstanding," but it was one that—on the basis of Brennan's reaction—he wouldn't forgive.

The next name that came up, "almost casually," Billings said, was Hathaway's. Bernhard, who knew Hathaway from his years in Washington, said the former senator "made no bones about the fact that he should be appointed," and Hathaway called Brennan to lobby him. Neither Muskie nor Brennan showed much interest. Brennan had few dealings with him, and Hathaway had sided with the tribes much more openly than Muskie. Muskie's own relations with Hathaway were strained, and Billings believed Hathaway "gave away his seat" by being less than diligent in his Senate work. It was less than two years since Hathaway's defeat by Bill Cohen. Appointing a recently rejected candidate would have been problematic for Democrats trying to retain the seat in 1982.

Billings then mentioned Mitchell. Muskie quickly said, "He'll never take the job. I just got him a judgeship." But Brennan must have indicated interest, because they discussed the thorny problem of approaching a sitting federal judge about a plainly political matter. Billings proposed calling Gayle Cory, practically a member of the Muskie family in addition to her office duties, who had also remained close to Mitchell. Cory would call Mitchell, ask him about the Senate seat, and was instructed to say, "Nobody's asked me to make this call. I just wanted to know." When she did, Billings said she reported that "George darn near came down the telephone wire with enthusiasm." The question of Mitchell's availability had been answered.

After the meeting, the wait began. Even when Vance's resignation was announced, Brennan made no move. He decided it would be inappropriate to announce Muskie's successor until he had been confirmed as secretary of state, and so everyone endured an interminable ten days. While Brennan took his time, he said later that once he knew Mitchell would take the job, that was his sole focus.

Mitchell was far from the obvious choice. There were many besides Hathaway who thought they had a better claim, and weren't shy about telling Brennan's aides, the press, and anyone else who would listen. John Martin, House speaker since 1974, thought he'd be an ideal choice. He told an interviewer in 2009 that he was in contention for the Senate appointment, and that "I was probably friendlier with Joe Brennan than George Mitchell was." Gerry Conley, a state Senate colleague, spoke with Brennan. Conley had given up his leadership position to allow Brennan to serve as Democratic leader before the 1974 gubernatorial primary, but Brennan made it clear he wouldn't return the favor. Severin Beliveau thought he would be considered, though not picked.

Another possibility, though a fainter one, was Elmer Violette, a Muskie favorite. Violette came from Van Buren, in northern Maine, and had been a party leader since Muskie's first campaigns. He'd run against Margaret Chase Smith in 1966, then accepted a Maine Superior Court judgeship in 1973 from Ken Curtis. There was an ironic twist to Muskie and Violette's relationship. Muskie may have been leaning Violette's way when the second federal judgeship opened up. Muskie had been mightily annoyed, according to Billings, when a group of Mitchell's friends, including Beliveau and Harold Pachios, lobbied him about Violette's lack of "judicial temperament," suggesting he was unqualified. Muskie then asked Billings to do an assessment of Mitchell's and Violette's strengths and weaknesses. Billings decided Violette had plenty of judicial temperament, but nonetheless found Mitchell a superior candidate. Violette was more than a decade older, and Billings said, "It was the sense that George was a very thoughtful, smart, young attorney and that he would be better suited for the job." It was Billings's impression that Muskie accepted this conclusion reluctantly. Brennan did, however, appoint Violette to the Maine Supreme Court the following year.

Because the Senate appointment became such an important turning point not only in the careers of Mitchell and Brennan, but also in Maine politics, it's become encrusted with folklore and curious beliefs. One is the contention, made by several reporters and repeated long afterward, that Brennan considered appointing himself. There's no reason to believe he did. Being governor was the job Brennan loved, and he'd been in the post less than two years. When he was term-limited in 1986, he did move to a US House seat, but was so eager to come back that he challenged an incumbent governor in 1990 and ran again in 1994, losing both times. The reporters' theory neglected another crucial political fact. Since Brennan's successor as governor would have been Senate President Joe Sewall—the Republican many Democrats believed had helped to defeat Mitchell in 1974—the move was practically unthinkable.

Mitchell professed to be unaware he was being considered. In his memoir, *The Negotiator*, he said that the first he knew of it was when Shep Lee, his friend and Muskie's, called on the first weekend in May, not long before Brennan would announce his choice. Lee said, "I'm calling about the Senate seat." Mitchell figured Lee knew who the candidate was, but Lee said, "Joe hasn't made up his mind yet. He wants to know if you've thought about it." Mitchell says he had dismissed the notion: "I'd been appointed a federal judge just six months earlier, and I was widely considered to be a political loser." Lee said Curtis wouldn't be picked, and urged Mitchell to say he'd consider an offer. The ruse Billings had put together with Gayle Cory apparently worked. He later defended the gambit by saying, "We lied because we had to."

Mitchell, after telling Lee he'd think about it, received two calls the next day, one friendly, the other from a caller who claimed Muskie was "forcing" Mitchell on Brennan. This has been a sensitive subject ever since. There's no evidence Muskie pressured Brennan on Mitchell's behalf, or that it would have worked if he had. Mitchell believes Muskie actually wanted Brennan to pick Curtis, on the grounds of electability. Still, it's rare any politician has been as dependent on another for advancement as Mitchell was with Muskie. He not only worked for him and directed his campaigns, but his candidacy for DNC chair and appointments as US Attorney for Maine and federal judge wouldn't have happened without Muskie's support. This time was different. It was not Muskie's call.

There were reasons Brennan and Muskie weren't close. Brennan saw much of the Maine Democratic establishment Muskie had created as distinct, by class and political leanings, from his own crowd. Billings says Muskie's office staff favored Merrill in the 1978 primary—he himself was a rare Brennan supporter—though in deference to Muskie's iron-clad neutrality, those sentiments stayed within the office.

Some who knew Mitchell well were stunned that Brennan would consider him. Clyde MacDonald called it "the most astounding thing that happened in my whole political career," and said, "I didn't think there was a prayer that Brennan would appoint his old enemy Mitchell," based on enmity from the 1974 campaign. But much had happened since then. One gesture, as Brennan liked to remind Mitchell, was that Paul Mitchell hosted one of the first fund-raisers for Brennan in 1978. Brennan, for whom politics was intensely personal, said, "Nobody else would. Waterville was just Mitchell territory." And he was pleased to hear, in later years, Paul saying to his brother, "I had more to do with your appointment than Brennan."

Mitchell himself hadn't been idle. He encouraged Brennan to run for attorney general, and when he heard of Brennan's plans for 1978, he decided to exit the race. He spent that May weekend pondering. Sally, despite their pact to stay in Maine, said, as she had when he ran for governor, that she'd accept his decision, but under no circumstances would she return to Washington. He agreed to her condition.

Mitchell also called Mert Henry, his former law partner, who recalls spending hours on the phone with his friend. Henry pointed out the advantages of staying on the bench, though he did say it seemed unlikely Mitchell would be promoted to the First Circuit Court of Appeals, since each state had only one judge, and Frank Coffin was "obviously ensconced for the foreseeable future." They discussed prospects for 1982, including possible Republican candidates. Henry said he couldn't tell what Mitchell would decide, but that "George has always had in the back of his mind the dream of succeeding Ed Muskie."

Brennan was also taking advice. His top aide, Gordon Weil, had advocated for a placeholder candidate—Russell Wiggins, publisher of the *Ellsworth American* and a former *Washington Post* editor—but when Brennan asked him about Mitchell, Weil said, "I think he'd be perfect." Weil also dismissed the idea that Muskie would lobby for Mitchell. As it had the suitors for Ken Curtis, Weil said such an approach would have backfired.

When Brennan called, Mitchell said yes. Brennan told him, "You can do the best job for the people of Maine," and Mitchell readily agreed to retain Muskie's staff. When Brennan said he had one thing to ask, Mitchell held his breath. He's reported Brennan's next words differently at times, but the most concise version is: "I ask only that you do the best you can for the people of Maine and the nation based on your conscience and your best judgement. I will never ask you for anything else." To which Mitchell always adds, "And he never did." Mitchell tells the story frequently, and always when he and Brennan appear together. His staffers sometimes think they've heard the story too often, but not Brennan.

Mitchell says his appointment created "an enormous political risk" for Brennan, since they would run together in two years, and this created "a deep determination to succeed, for him as well as for myself."

Many have wondered why Mitchell did take the Senate appointment, knowing the odds were against winning election in his own right. Very few federal judges ever resign to engage in politics. The process almost always works the other way. In the Senate, Mitchell's status as a former judge was an immediate calling card. Mitchell knew the risks, but said going through life without taking risks is inherently unrewarding. Hal Pachios called him "a risk-taker," and the Senate appointment is the most prominent example.

As was his wont in later years, Mitchell liked to present his major decisions in a humorous, even self-deprecating light. In 1990, he reprised his Senate appointment in a rollicking speech to the AFL-CIO's Building and Construction Unions, given when he was Senate majority leader and also had become the Democrats' top fund-raiser and after-dinner speaker. "My friends would ask me, especially my lawyer friends, why would anybody in his right mind leave a federal judgeship to go to the Senate?" He said that, on a February day in Bangor with the temperature twenty-two below, he'd been reading the newspaper before presiding in court, and discovered that ten US senators were inspecting American defense installations in Barbados. Unaware of any such bases, when he reached the Senate, "I asked a couple of senators who'd been on that trip, and they said, 'Well, we spend two weeks down there looking for one.'" He added the punch line, "So when the governor called me up and offered to appoint me to this job, I thought, 'Why not.'" Mitchell went on to describe why the Senate—with its filibusters, endless delays, all-night sessions—was not what the founders anticipated, but here, as elsewhere, he managed not to take himself too seriously.

When he appeared at the Democratic State Convention on May 16, as he was taking up his Senate duties, Mitchell played it straight. He told the delegates, "I have known Joe Brennan well for fifteen years. Through those years we have been good friends. I like and respect Joe Brennan today as much as I did in 1971, when I served as one of his assistants in the Cumberland County attorney's office, or in 1974, when we were both candidates for governor." He added, "It will be a great pleasure to run on the same ticket with him in 1982."

He detoured to a favorite anecdote about Winston Churchill being told a political opponent was at least a humble man, and Churchill retorting, "He has much to be humble about." Mitchell said, "I, too, have much to be humble about. More than anyone else, I am aware of my shortcomings. But that awareness is matched by a determination . . . to reach the standard of excellence set by

Ed Muskie." He then tied the three leaders together: "It says something about America and the Democratic Party when a governor who is the son of an Irish immigrant longshoreman from Portland appoints the son of a Lebanese immigrant factory worker from Waterville to replace the son of a Polish immigrant tailor from Rumford in the United States Senate."

George Mitchell later made much of the "asterisk" beside his name, and the failure of most appointed senators to win election. But in truth he had a priceless gift—time. Maine is among the few states that has no provision for a special election to fill a vacant US Senate seat. Since the filing deadline was in April, Mitchell's appointment in May came too late for that year's ballot. He would have two and a half years—longer than a US House term—to prepare, and he intended to make the most of it.

The transition from Muskie to Mitchell in the Senate marked the end of their long professional association; by the end of the year, Muskie had entered private life. He was fond of saying, when asked about his protégé's prospects, that "George can do anything he wants to do." Mitchell, while always praising Muskie's intelligence, his brilliance in debate, and his ability to create path-breaking legislation, can at times appear ambivalent about being too much in his shadow. To Kermit Lipez, this is natural. He said, "Every successful politician values his or her own independence, and will insist upon that independence."

ESTABLISHING HIMSELF IN THE MIDDLE of a hectic Senate session was no easy feat. Mitchell was sworn in on May 19, and found himself thrown into a key environmental debate. The Senate was considering a bill to switch electric power plants from petroleum to coal following the second 1970s energy crisis, but with only meager environmental protections. Charlene Sturbitts, an environmental aide for Muskie who then joined Mitchell, said, "Muskie was going to lead that fight, and he was gone." When she told Mitchell what was at stake, "He jumped in, and led the floor fight," along with his Republican committee counterpart, Robert Stafford of Vermont. They didn't win, but it was Mitchell's introduction to the issue of acid rain—a cause that would become a distinctive focus during his first decade in the Senate.

Mitchell's self-effacing nature—and the reality that, while senators may caucus frequently, they are independent operators—led to some amusing episodes. Like Muskie, Mitchell's office was in the Russell Building, but because of minimal seniority, he got a cramped third-floor office rather than Muskie's palatial first-floor space. For weeks, Mitchell went through the bag-check line because the security guard didn't recognize him. One of his aides saw this and accosted the guard with, "This is Senator Mitchell," and it never happened again.

Tom Gallagher, who had worked for the Budget Committee, recounted that Mitchell was turned away from Delta Airlines' VIP lounge at Logan Airport in Boston. "He was not the kind of guy to say, 'But I'm a US senator,'" Gallagher said, but when someone else pointed this out, Delta paged him, to no effect. "So they called our office and said, 'Do you know where your senator is? We just kicked him out of our lounge.'" Later, when Mitchell joined the Finance Committee, a Delta lobbyist presented him with a lifetime pass to all the airline's lounges.

For Hal Pachios, these incidents capture a side of Mitchell rarely matched by his colleagues. "One of the things that happens to people in Washington, over a period of time, people are opening the car door, and saying, 'Senator, let me get that door, Senator, let me do this.'" Mitchell, Pachios said, "never fell for that stuff, never got taken in by it. He was the exact same person after being Senate majority leader that he was when he was a lawyer in Portland, or even working for Muskie." Not everyone saw Mitchell in those terms. Hoddie Hildreth, son of the 1940s governor, a Republican state senator and noted conservationist, knew Mitchell at Bowdoin, and took a more patrician view, while mixing up the details of his parentage. Mitchell, he said, "is a lot more of a 1930s liberal than I am. And to be honest, I think he's never gotten over the fact that his mother was a cleaning lady, and that's colored his thinking."

MITCHELL BEGAN EVALUATING THE STAFF he'd inherited from Muskie, figuring out who could help him as the Senate's most junior member. With his Budget Committee chairmanship and the impressive staff it commanded, more than fifty employees, Muskie, by the end of his tenure, had at least one hundred people working for him. Mitchell's staff numbered less than twenty. The problem worsened after November 1980 when Democrats lost the Senate, and former majority staff, like Tom Gallagher, had to find new postings.

Mitchell's first chief of staff, Jim Case, a committee counsel who took on the AA role after Leon Billings moved with Muskie to the State Department, set about finding him a permanent chief. He recommended David Johnson, a soft-spoken Kansan who had joined Muskie's campaign in 1971, worked for the Government Operations Committee, then shifted to the Carter administration. When Carter lost in November, he job-hunted. While Johnson and Mitchell built an enduring professional relationship that continues to this day, the beginning was not auspicious.

Case had convinced Johnson he was the logical choice for Mitchell, but when he flew to Portland in December, no one came to the airport to pick him up. "Finally, in walks George Mitchell," Johnson said, "who I knew by having seen a photograph, but I'd never met him. And he was wearing a white tennis sweater, and it was in the middle of winter, and he was on his way to go play tennis. And he literally looked at his watch and said, 'Let's go sit in the coffee shop and get this over with.'" They sat down and people came over to chat. "Here's a brand-new United States senator, attracting quite a lot of attention, simply because of who he was and because he was wearing a white tennis sweater," Johnson said. "It was hard to stay focused." After a few minutes of Johnson's presentation, "He looked at his watch again and said, 'Do you want this job or not?'" A startled, but elated, Johnson said yes, and figured his reputation preceded him: "I guess on that day I was looking pretty good to him." Later, Johnson decided the scheduling must have gone awry, but he never asked about it.

When he arrived in Washington the next Monday, he got a similar reception. When he introduced himself as the new AA, the woman behind the desk said, "No, you're not." It wasn't until Jim Case vouched for Johnson that he convinced them, "and I'm not even sure he knew it had all been decided." Gayle Cory showed him the ropes, and told him, "You'll be the fifth AA I've taken to raise, and you look to me like you need some raising." She was perhaps Mitchell's most trusted aide, "and we worked together very, very closely," Johnson said. "I've worked in offices where there is a lot of tension and infighting . . . and there was absolutely none of that around George."

It did take time to develop a rapport. Johnson recalls early on that Mitchell seemed to be checking his every move. He finally told his boss, "You have a hundred things to do every day, and ten of them only you can do. . . . The other ninety I can do in your name." Yet the tension continued. The two often worked late together, and Mitchell usually drove Johnson home. When they stopped one evening Johnson didn't get out, and when Mitchell asked why, he said, "I have something I have to say to you." With his "heart in his throat," Johnson then said, "Every time you ask me to do something, before I can do it you've asked me if I've done it. It happens every day." He continued, "I know it's your way of letting me know how important these things are . . . but if you don't get off my back, it just isn't going to work." Johnson's announcement was met with "utter silence," and he got out, telling his wife he didn't know what would happen. Mitchell accepted the criticism, though, and Johnson observed, "One of his great strengths is to be able to change and adapt and to look at a situation and know how he needs to come at it to bring the kind of solutions he's looking for."

Charlie Jacobs, who worked for Muskie and joined Mitchell as his executive assistant, Johnson's deputy, said their chiefs of staff reflected the two senators' contrasting personalities. "David is very pleasant to deal with, he wasn't loud, and not surprisingly, he mirrored Mitchell in many ways. Mitchell is a soft-spoken person who doesn't lose his temper or visibly get angry, and David was similar." Jacobs said that Leon Billings, the AA he worked with most, "was similar to Muskie in that he would occasionally lose his temper and was more—what's the word?—louder."

A formidable personality already in the office was Anita Jensen. Her parents were Latvian, and she was born in what was later East Germany amid the chaos of the end of World II. She never knew her father, who was presumed killed, and immigrated to the United States where she ended up in Ed Muskie's Senate office. Jensen recalls that "I was supposed to be Eliot Cutler's secretary, but he didn't really need a secretary," and she instead made her mark sorting out the mailroom, which she described as knee-deep with unanswered mail.

Mitchell immediately recognized her abilities, and "from day one," as she recalled it, she became his speechwriter, producing an astonishing amount of material over the next fourteen years. Mitchell wrote a great deal himself, and was meticulous about revising drafts from Jensen, but came to rely on her encyclopedic knowledge and ability to ferret out obscure facts. Mitchell's reliance on Jensen continued after the Senate years, and until a few months before her death in January 2015, she continued to check references for his speeches and public appearances. It wasn't difficult to learn Mitchell's voice, she said—his preference for plain, unadorned prose was very much her own style. "It was very easy to write," she said, "and more like talking." Mitchell "was not a fan of histrionic speeches, not a lot of throwing your weight around." The speeches Richard Goodwin wrote for Muskie, she said, were not among her favorites.

Even casual visitors to Mitchell's office came away with vivid recollections of Jensen. She was a furiously fast, and accurate, typist—she once skewered Maynard Toll, a Muskie AA, as "hopeless with a typewriter." Kermit Lipez served with her briefly, and said, "Nobody has ever been able to type as fast as Anita . . . and she could talk almost as fast as she could type. She was an absolute whirlwind, and also had this biting wit." She seemed in constant motion. Mike Hastings, who moved from Bill Cohen's Senate office to Mitchell's, remembers her taking memos and turning them around in short order. She thought nothing of writing a short speech in half an hour. "She would wear tall, spike heels, and when she finished one of these floor statements, she would whip it out of her IBM Selectric typewriter and take off down the corridors," Hastings said. "You could hear her coming; people all around knew when Anita was headed to the Senate floor, because you could hear those heels."

Jensen's temperament seems poles apart from Mitchell's, and it was a rocky start, from her point of view. She felt Muskie "deserted me" when he left for the State Department, and Mitchell was not a commanding presence. Muskie's departure, she told an interviewer, "set me up for fourteen glorious years with

George Mitchell," then added, "Sorry, cheap sarcasm." She often drove Mitchell to work, and fussed over his propensity for buying navy blue blazers with brass buttons at Brooks Brothers. She had blunt opinions about his wonderment that the Senate couldn't function more like the orderly federal courts. She found his attitude "rather naive and silly. How can you possibly expect a group of adults to do whatever you want?" The Senate's seemingly impossible calendar did frustrate Mitchell, and one staffer wondered whether this was a motivation to run for majority leader. Beneath the gruffness, though, Jensen formed a bond. Her loyalty to Mitchell continued long after he left Washington.

Mitchell's relationship with staff was different than Muskie's. Except for top aides, people who worked for Muskie might not see him for months at a time, and he channeled information through his chief of staff and legislative director. Mitchell's preference, when working on legislation, was to meet with the relevant aide along with the chief of staff, who coordinated any follow-up. Eliot Cutler thought the two acquired information differently. Muskie, he said, was "an extraordinary strategist and tactician, and a prodigious worker, but worked alone, worked by reading." Mitchell's approach "was much warmer, much more inclusive, much more collegial. . . . I presume he still takes in a lot more information through his ears than Muskie did." The two were similar, though, Cutler said, when it came to negotiating. Muskie "knew the facts better than anybody else," and "had an ability to forge compromise, to figure out what the other person needed, and a way to give it to him or her without dramatically compromising his own objectives. And I think George learned a lot of that."

The work of Congress is done largely through committees, and Mitchell's first three assignments were Environment and Public Works, Banking, and Veterans' Affairs, the first two inherited from Muskie. He remained on EPW and Veterans throughout his tenure; his army service remained part of him, and Mitchell rarely missed an opportunity to address a veterans' convention. Dennis DeConcini, an Arizona Democrat who served with him on Veterans, perceived its importance to Mitchell, though he never heard him talk about his military service. Mitchell also wanted to serve on Judiciary, but Jim Case advised against it. "I didn't think that was a good committee for him, simply because of the terrible issues he'd have to face," Case said. "It wasn't about judges; it was more about abortion battles and those kinds of issues [when] he was in an election cycle right away."

Although the Democrats lost their majority in November, it did create new opportunities for Mitchell. He credits David Johnson with convincing him to try for the Finance Committee, which, unlike the Budget Committee, has widespread powers, overseeing the entire tax code while playing a key role in health care legislation, and often producing significant campaign donations. Lloyd Bentsen, in particular, was a master at exploiting these connections. Mitchell made his pitch to the Democratic Steering Committee, though Minority Leader Robert Byrd made the final call. He followed another senator who had never lost an election, and was eminently qualified. During a break, several senators advised Mitchell he didn't have a chance, because "You don't have much of a future."

Mitchell took the opposite tack. "I have never won an election," he said. "Of all the senators who have appeared before you asking for help, I'm the one most in need. And so, if in your deliberations you factor in trying to assist people who are trying to work their way up, I ought to be assigned to the Finance Committee." The reverse psychology worked.

The job description for US senators includes a large measure of self-absorption, so Mitchell's arrival—as an unheralded, out-of-sequence freshman from a small state—didn't register with many colleagues, but the reviews from those who did notice were favorable. Bill Cohen, who barely knew Mitchell at this point, issued a welcoming floor speech—written by Mike Hastings, who would join Mitchell's staff five months later. As a freshman in 1978, Cohen joined the Armed Services Committee, his lasting interest, rather than Foreign Relations, as Hastings had hoped. Hastings admits to being "very intrigued by this new senator from Maine." Alan Simpson, for ten years assistant Republican leader to Bob Dole, remembers Cohen mentioning that Mitchell was a fellow Bowdoin graduate, and saying, "Here comes another one. He's of the other faith, but he's a good egg, and I think you'll like him."

For a few, no introduction was needed. John Chafee had the antiques case and a Maine connection; Carl Levin, a Michigan Democrat elected in 1978, had a brother in Congress who'd run the 1972 Muskie campaign in Michigan. "I heard great things about him from my brother," Levin said, "and anyone who supported Ed Muskie was good enough for me." Levin was also impressed Mitchell had given up a judgeship, calling it "pretty startling."

Bob Packwood from Oregon, a Republican who became chair of the Finance Committee just as Mitchell was joining it, thought the new senator handled himself well. "When a new senator's elected," he said, "there's always a period of judging. Some people make a mistake and think they're a firecracker, and they are judged accordingly. George was very good. . . . He understood he was coming into an elite organization, and he was coming in not having earned his spurs in the sense of being elected, and therefore he'd better observe the traditions and the niceties. . . . He was all of that, and he knew exactly why he was doing it."

Bill Bradley, a fellow Democrat on Finance who made tax reform his signature issue, also had come on in 1978, directly following his retirement from the

NBA, after winning two titles with the New York Knicks—and without the support of New Jersey's political establishment. Bradley immediately recognized Mitchell's potential—"a very likeable person, and extremely competent, bright, methodical, a true judge, infinite patience, clear strategic sense, and he liked basketball." That was the first link. "I didn't talk to anybody about basketball, but George had a brother who was a great basketball player, Swisher, I think his name was." Bradley had also known Hal Pachios when they were interning in Washington together, "and there were these little connections." Bradley said, "George played the basketball card well, and so we developed a relationship sitting next to each other. We saw what each of us did, we saw how prepared each of us was, we saw what was ours and what was the staff's, and we got a sense of each other's competence level."

In time, Senate floor staff also got to know Mitchell. Charles Kinney, first appointed in 1974, stayed on when Mitchell became majority leader, and said he "was quiet, studious, focused, learning everything he could about the place." Mitchell's experience on Muskie's staff was helpful, Kinney said. "He did not need to learn the floor plan, he knew a lot about how the place worked and operated." Patrick Griffin was already a Senate veteran when Mitchell arrived, serving on the Budget Committee staff before becoming a key aide to Robert Byrd; he later started a lobbying firm with Mitchell's chief of staff, David Johnson. Griffin saw more of the freshman in Mitchell. "He was just like a new kid on the block," Griffin said, and "was a very congenial, funny, down-to-earth fellow, so we took good care of him, or at least we tried to." Griffin noticed an affinity with Byrd. "Senator Byrd took a liking to him early on; he thought he was a very bright, very impressive guy. He thought maybe he had leadership capabilities, and said so on several occasions."

DURING HIS FIRST YEAR IN THE SENATE, Mitchell worked on issues of particular significance to Maine. One was the Dickey-Lincoln project on the St. John River, authorized by Congress in 1965, but which had never proceeded beyond preliminary designs despite the efforts of Muskie and Hathaway. As a new senator, Mitchell was unlikely to do better, but he tried. His advocacy set up an unusual floor debate with Bill Cohen, who, like most Republican colleagues, opposed Dickey-Lincoln as an unwise use of federal tax dollars. The issue had been raised in the 1974 governor's race, with opponents arguing that it was a boondoggle, unlikely to reduce electric rates, and that it would cause serious environmental degradation of the St. John and Allagash rivers.

Advocates like Mitchell thought Republicans were hypocritical in raising environmental concerns. During their brief control of the Legislature from 1964 to 1966, it was Democrats who sponsored the bond issue creating the Allagash Wilderness Waterway, and protected most of the main river and its tributaries. Muskie had wanted the Allagash to be federally protected under the Wild and Scenic Rivers Act of 1968, but resistance from the Republican Legislature thwarted his bid; ultimately, the state agreed to co-management under federal law, but with state rules.

Mitchell presented an elaborate rationale for Dickey-Lincoln, saying it was justified in the wake of spiraling petroleum prices, and that the environmental impacts were manageable. He tried to get the Senate to agree to build a small impoundment, the Lincoln School dam, separate from the main dam in Dickey township. But the public power authority to manage the project failed in the Legislature and at referendum, and once-abundant streams of federal funding were drying up. Like the east-west highway and the Passamaquoddy Bay tidal project that had so intrigued Franklin Roosevelt, Dickey-Lincoln would never leave the drawing board.

There were better prospects for the Indian Land Claims Act. Resistance to the tribal claims had worked well in the 1978 election for Cohen in defeating Hathaway, and for Joe Brennan in becoming governor. It was clear legal proceedings could drag on for years, since there was so little precedent to deal with the tribes' claim to nearly two-thirds of the state. Since he had spoken so clearly about the issue during his campaign, Brennan was unlikely to make any concessions. He often used his brother, who ran a parking concession in Portland, as an example of the unfairness of current generations being forced to pay. "My brother, he works like hell," Brennan said, "and he pays taxes to help anybody that needs help nowadays, but I don't think he had any responsibility for what might have been done to someone's great-great-great-great-great grandfather two hundred years before that." In a report he presented to the Legislature as attorney general, Brennan concluded, "I firmly believe that it would be wrong for the State of Maine to give in to the pressures of the litigation and give state lands or monies to the tribes to settle these suits. I believe the legal issues should be settled in a court of law."

During Brennan's tenure as attorney general, he had enthusiastic support on the issue from Governor Jim Longley. David Flanagan, Brennan's legal counsel, said both were "adamantly opposed to any kind of settlement. . . . I wouldn't call them allies, I'd call them co-belligerents." While Brennan, as governor, continued to oppose a settlement, he shifted toward the position that, as long as there was no state liability, he'd consider it. The new stance, Flanagan said, was that "any funds anybody else wanted to contribute—i.e., the federal government—that was fine. There was never any antipathy toward the tribes. If you could get federal money that would make them better off, hence the state was better off . . . it was fine."

The settlement, signed by President Carter in October 1980, provided $81.5 million to the tribes to buy land and to provide trust funds for tribal members. The deal was beginning to gel when Mitchell arrived, but he pushed hard to conclude it, according to Flanagan, who said, "I can remember being so impressed by Senator Mitchell's command of the facts and the law and the case. Even though it was extremely complex, he has that trial lawyer's gift for being able to succinctly state the positions of the sides and discuss the merits. . . . There have been other issues where I had the same feeling, but none more so than on that case."

As a newly prominent public figure, Mitchell's personal habits occasioned increasing comment. For Anita Jensen, his taste in clothes still left much to be desired. The women in the office, she said, were appalled by a striped belt he insisted on wearing because it was a family gift. "But he became more sartorially acceptable as time passed," she said. "He looked like the sort of guy who might have been born wearing a shirt and tie and carrying a briefcase. *Casual* is not a word I associate with Mitchell."

But it was Mitchell's abstemiousness with food and drink that got the most attention. Harold Pachios tells the story of a dinner at the Palm restaurant, then one of Washington's trendy locales, where Mitchell met his brother, Robbie, and Pachios. They arrived at his office, but Mitchell said, "I've got one more appointment. You guys go down to the Palm, order me a steak and french fries and a tossed salad, and I'll be there about fifteen minutes after you get there. Order after you've been there five minutes." They did, and "the food arrived maybe a minute or two after he arrived, he ate and left, that was it. The whole thing took twenty-five minutes. . . . George and food—food's no big deal to him."

When Mitchell arrived at a reception and took a glass of wine, his companions noticed that, half an hour later, the level in the glass hadn't declined. Some friends and associates found it frustrating. Berl Bernhard, his law partner, said, "The only problem is one, he doesn't drink, and secondly, his eating habits are absolutely, excruciatingly boring. What does he eat for lunch if you go? It'll be a little sandwich with lettuce and cucumbers and tomatoes or something. . . . He doesn't have too many bad habits, unfortunately."

Well before the end of the first year, even before hiring David Johnson, Mitchell knew he wouldn't be elected in 1982 without campaigning virtually nonstop. When he and Jim Case were discussing his prospects at the Bangor courthouse—he was wrapping up his judgeship—Mitchell said he wanted to return to Maine frequently, a departure from Muskie, who went back half a dozen times a year. Case recalls him saying, "I'm going to take this job, but I'm coming back to Maine every single weekend." Case's response was, "That's doable, but you're going to be tired."

10

REDEMPTION

There was never any doubt in George Mitchell's mind that he would seek a full six-year Senate term. He'd come a long way since he said, before going to work for Ed Muskie, "I really didn't have any interest in politics." He wouldn't have given up a lifetime judicial appointment without a renewed commitment to politics. He wanted not only to validate Joe Brennan's trust, but also to vindicate Ed Muskie's judgment that he could do whatever he set his mind to.

The prospects were far from encouraging, however. Being chosen by a governor and not the voters, while not exactly a curse, was far from an unmixed blessing. Mitchell's assessment seems apt. "Having been appointed was a hindrance, being an incumbent was a help. The appointed part was like having an asterisk . . . and I was constantly referred to as the appointed senator," he said. "I was acutely aware of it, and I felt that other senators were as well, that they treated me differently. . . . I hadn't earned my way there."

Since his appointment, the skies had darkened considerably. The lightning bolt had been the election of Ronald Reagan, and, especially, the Democrats' loss of the Senate majority they had held for twenty-six years. Democrats were used to working with Republican presidents. They weren't used to being the minority. While Jimmy Carter's defeat by Reagan seemed likely, the Senate landslide was unexpected, at least within the Senate. As the newly empowered GOP surveyed the landscape for 1982, the Maine Senate seat was at the top of their list.

Democrats were particularly concerned about the National Conservative Political Action Committee, one of the first big independent spending operations created, ironically, by post-Watergate reform legislation that also authorized public funding for presidential elections. NCPAC (pronounced "Nickpac") is today just another fund-raiser, but in 1980 it was a giant killer. It had targeted five Democrats, calling them "five of the most liberal senators in the history of the country"—George McGovern of South Dakota, Birch Bayh of Indiana, Alan Cranston of California, John Culver of Iowa, and Frank Church of Idaho. Of the five, all were Senate veterans except Culver. Most PAC money in 1980 went to support Reagan, $12.3 million of the $16 million raised. But NCPAC was unique in targeting Senate races, spending $1.4 million against the five Democrats. The totals ranged from $181,000 to defeat Bayh to $339,000 aimed at ousting Church, who led investigations of the CIA and NSA. All except Cranston were defeated.

Mitchell was so concerned about NCPAC targeting him that he dispatched an emissary to gauge TV station managers' attitudes about running what were then unusually aggressive ads. Gerry Petruccelli, the law professor and Mitchell backer, met with CBS, NBC, and ABC affiliates to try to convince them not to run NCPAC ads. One must have been a Mitchell supporter. "He kind of had a little twinkle as he was listening to me, like, 'You're preaching to the choir.'" The second manager veered into a discussion of air dates, but said, "There's only so many minutes in a day, and we do have to make choices." The third manager "gave this sophomoric first-draft Fourth of July speech about the First Amendment." Had NCPAC entered the race, Petruccelli figures at least one station would have run the ads.

The first serious campaign activity came in March 1981 when Congressman David Emery formed an exploratory committee. The committee, he wrote, "will be taking a professional poll to find out our standing vs. George Mitchell. We will not go forward until we are certain that the Emery candidacy is viable and that the Senate seat is winnable." The poll results, which became part of Maine political lore, astonished everyone. The pollster, V. Lance Tarrance & Associates, reported on April 29 to Emery: "If the election were held today, you would badly defeat George Mitchell. Your lead is both verifiable and substantial—61-25 percent, with 15 percent undecided." It's less often remembered that the poll included a question adding Second District Congresswoman Olympia Snowe and Ken Curtis; there, 38 percent preferred Emery, 30 percent Snowe, 17 percent Curtis—and just 7 percent wanted Mitchell.

Emery had no intention of announcing this early, but the poll results were too amazing to keep quiet, so he leaked them. John Day, by now the *Bangor Daily News* Washington correspondent, got the call. As Day recalls it, Snowe had also completed a poll, and, having heard about the Emery gambit, shared results. "I went over to George's office and said, 'I'm doing a polling story and I just need your reaction to these numbers." When Mitchell heard them, "His jaw kind of dropped. . . . I'm sure he assumed he was behind, but I'm pretty sure he had no idea the numbers were that bad." Mitchell was thirty-six points behind.

It wasn't a surprise that Emery entered eagerly. He was still young—when elected in 1974, he'd been one year past the twenty-five required by the Constitution. But after eight years in Congress, he was ready to move on. Emery said, "The world was out there, grabbing me by the lapels and saying, 'OK, you're going to be the next senator.' It was everyone's expectation. . . . The whole universe was out there pulling me in this direction." Unlike Mitchell, the constant travel was beginning to wear on Emery. "One of the reasons I ran for the Senate," he said, "was I was just sick of going home weekends to campaign for election every two years, and the constant pressure of raising money."

Mitchell thinks his first bit of luck was when Snowe decided not to run on June 8, with one news story headlined "It's Too Cold for Snowe." He assumes she would have been a stronger candidate than Emery, but this may be retrospective reasoning. Snowe won Cohen's seat in 1978, and had served just two years. She also passed on running against Mitchell in 1988, and only made her bid in 1994, when he retired.

Of greater concern to Mitchell were persistent rumors that Curtis would enter the race. Mitchell believed he stood to lose to Curtis in a primary, and the prospect of such a race was unsettling. "Ken and I were very close friends," he said. "I was Democratic state chairman when he was elected governor, and I helped draft both of his inaugural addresses. I think he's a great guy, and it would have been a very difficult thing for me to run against him. I think he had the same feeling." In September, Curtis announced an exploratory committee. "I braced for a rush away from me and toward Curtis," Mitchell said. "To my surprise, it didn't happen. . . . It may have been faint, but I still had a political pulse."

In the Mitchell archives, there's a draft statement, never used, that outlines the case against a Curtis candidacy and includes editing in Mitchell's hand. "Curtis says that Senator Mitchell is doing a good job and he claims to have great respect for Mitchell," it reads. "But he also says that since his polls show Senator Mitchell to be behind his expected opponent, Congressman Emery, then Curtis will have a better chance to win. To ask an incumbent Democratic officeholder, who virtually everyone agrees is doing a good job, to step aside just because he is behind in a poll taken over a year before the election is most unfair." It concludes: "It's lucky for Ken Curtis himself that Democrats didn't apply that standard to him when he ran for reelection. As everyone will recall, he was far behind in the polls, much further behind than Mitchell is now."

Curtis suffered a mild heart attack and exited the race. Most expected him to run, but he more recently told an interviewer, "My personality is such that I would not have made a good senator. I liked the governorship because it was more activist oriented. And certainly George was far more articulate than I ever thought about being. . . . And he had political ambition, and that's the perfect background for a United States senator."

Things were not quite as bleak as they appeared. Bob Lenna, who'd been in the campaign office when Ford pardoned Nixon, said, "I never believed those numbers"—that they reflected mostly name recognition. Frustrating as it must have been for Mitchell, despite a year in office he hadn't advanced much beyond the point when Gerry Petruccelli asked Judge Gignoux to poll the jury, and found few had ever heard of Mitchell. "George who?" was a frequent line in newspapers. In 1981, Emery was riding a wave of acclaim for Reagan, who'd just convinced the Democratic House to approve his mammoth income tax cut—25 percent over three years—and the developing recession hadn't yet raised unemployment.

After the shock from his opponents' early polls, Mitchell redoubled his efforts to not only return to Maine weekly, but also to attend as many football games, bean suppers, parades, and club meetings as he could. Mike Hastings said Cohen worked hard before an election, "but usually that election period was only a year long." Mitchell, by contrast, "worked around the clock. I have never seen anybody work that hard." During two and a half years as appointed senator, he said, "Senator Mitchell worked as if it was the last week of the election." The schedule meant he had even less time at home than he and Sally anticipated when they made their pact that allowed him to go to Washington, while she stayed in Maine.

The transition back to Maine wasn't always easy. David Johnson contrasted Muskie's Washington routine with Mitchell's constant travel, and said, "It was hard to keep it all sorted out, and there were plenty of times that it was a big honking mess. Often he'd get to Boston and couldn't fly to Portland because of weather, and we'd hear from him that he was in a car with a bunch of guys he met at the airport, and they were all driving to Portland together." He'd sometimes get a hint of the strain his boss was under. It wasn't unusual then for the Washington staff to order beer on Fridays and relax at the office before heading home. "I remember him standing by my desk one time, looking at the beer and looking at me, and looking at the suitcases in his hands, and he said, 'You know, you have a much better job than I do.'"

Sometimes, though, it seemed worth it. The Waterville Rotary Club was known as a haven for Republicans. Jack Frost, a businessman, told a reporter that Mitchell "made a very good impression. I was pretty much in favor of what Reagan is doing and has done, but what Mitchell says makes a lot of sense. He's a brilliant fellow." Dwight French kidded with Mitchell afterward, saying, "Georgie, you keep talking like that and there won't be any Republicans left to vote for Emery," to which Mitchell responded, "You won't get struck by lightning if you vote for me." After Mitchell left, French said, "I'm afraid he's going to win."

THOSE WHO KNEW MITCHELL SAW HOW DIFFERENT he was from the forty-year-old who'd run for governor. Walter Corey, the lawyer and frequent tennis partner, said, "I saw George with renewed vigor, with new wind in his sails. He had tasted those few years of being senator, and he liked it immensely; he knew he was good at it. Having had the experience of seeing the Senate through Muskie's eyes . . . gave him insight that few other people would have. And he capitalized on that." Janet Mitchell said, "He had learned from what happened in 1974. He learned how to campaign with Mainers. He was funny, down-to-earth, and he knew how to laugh at himself in a way that was very engaging." Charlie Jacobs remembers hearing that Joe Sewall, still state Senate president, after hearing Mitchell speak, said, "the Republicans better not underestimate George Mitchell."

The changing style was matched by changes in strategy. Mitchell knew he couldn't let dubious statements go unanswered, as he'd done with Longley. Though he didn't necessarily agree that he was "too bookish, too issue-oriented, and not emotional and personal enough," he did acknowledge that, in the governor's race, "We put out almost every day a press statement that related to an issue." In the 1982 campaign, "I limited the number of issues we tried to deal with. There are hundreds of issues, but you can't tackle them all; you've got to pick priorities."

Mitchell hosted a "kitchen cabinet" at his home in South Portland almost weekly. It included Tony Buxton, Woody Jones, and Scott Hutchinson from the 1974 campaign, as well as friends like Joe Angelone and, once Curtis dropped out, Kermit Lipez. Buxton said, "It was an interesting process because it was very thoughtful, very thorough, and not terribly political." Bob Tyrer, Bill Cohen's young press secretary, had studied Mitchell up close, and said, "He was a very transformed person, who clearly had come to understand that being the smartest guy in the room didn't necessarily translate into votes, or take into account that voting is an emotional type of behavior. People want to feel connected to the candidate. Most people after they're fully formed adults have difficulty making changes like that, but he became a very good candidate."

How important this was is suggested in a November 12, 1980, strategy memo. Concerning "the human side of GJM," it says, "The general observation is that 'to know George Mitchell is to like him.' However, although the consensus was that GJM has 'loosened up' since 1974, he still remains 'not human enough' and 'too perfect.'"

One important change was Mitchell's ability to employ storytelling and humor. Johnson saw him working at it. Mitchell already possessed "a well-developed sense of humor with people he was close to," Johnson said. What he lacked was the ability to use it with voters. Johnson is convinced that Mitchell's ability to hone a small but effective repertoire of funny, pointed stories was "one of the definers of his ability to learn, and grow, and to change."

Charlie Jacobs remembers Mitchell sometimes pressed his staff on the subject. "I've got to have some jokes," he said. "When I give speeches, I need to have jokes." Jacobs, who knew Ed Muskie well, said, "Muskie was a natural politician, somehow he was born with those genes. I don't think Mitchell was; he learned it all. But he's so disciplined and smart and verbal that he could do it. He learned how to be funny."

The most famous example came to be known as "the cow joke," but like most anecdotes, people remembered the punch line more than the setup, which was vital to the effect. During the campaign, the "cow joke" became so familiar that staff could lip-sync it. "At parties, we recited the story, word for word," Johnson said. Floyd Harding, who also worried about Mitchell's formality, tried to give him a cow joke to warm up farm audiences. Harding's joke involved milking: "When you took a cow's udder in your hand, and she'd turn around and smile, and she'd say, 'Thanks for the warm hand.'" Harding says "it went over good."

By 1982, Mitchell had a much better cow story, involving his early experiences as an appointed senator. He included it in a speech to the Rockland Rotary Club in December 1980, before it became a staple item. He set it up by contrasting his arrival in the Senate with the dignity of a federal courtroom. "When I was a judge I had a robe and I sat in an elevated position in the courtroom and everybody was polite to me," he said. Even when he made an adverse ruling, the lawyers "would stand up and say, 'Thank you, Your Honor.'" In the Senate, "When I vote against someone's interests (and I find that every vote I cast is against someone's interests), they call me a lot of names, but 'Your Honor' is not among them."

The scene shifts to a North Vassalboro dairy farm, where, after a farmer says, "Would you mind coming out back and having your picture taken with two of my cows?," Mitchell hesitates, then realizes "you do a lot of funny things in public office," and says yes. "I'd be glad to have my picture taken with the cows, but do you mind telling me why?" The farmer explained that Saudi Arabia, then trying to establish a dairy herd, had selected ninety milk cows, including these prize heifers. "It will only take a couple of minutes," the farmer said. "You might get your picture in the paper, news being what it is."

The cows were uncooperative. "When I looked to the left, the heifers looked to the right, and by the time the photographer got around, the heifers went the other way." Finally the photo was taken and did, in fact, appear in the Waterville *Morning Sentinel* the next day. A few days later, he was in Sidney, across the Kennebec River, and his knock was answered by an elderly Maine farmer. Before he could introduce himself, the farmer said, "I know who you are." Mitchell, who was rarely recognized outside Waterville and Portland, asked how the man knew him. He said, "I seen your picture in the paper with them cows." Mitchell ventured, "What did you think?" The farmer, Mitchell said, "looked me right in the eye and said, 'I think we ought to keep the cows and send you to Saudi Arabia.'"

The story never failed to win laughter and applause, and its appeal drew on the long tradition of politicians doing silly things for votes. But it was the self-deprecating punch line that won over Mainers, and helped banish the owlish "country club lawyer" image that had dogged Mitchell. By making himself the butt of the joke, he disarmed suspicion and won a hearing for his more serious proposals.

Another campaign story that became a minor classic involved the first Senate filibuster Mitchell endured. At the time, a filibuster meant shutting down all Senate business until the votes to end debate were rounded up, or the bill withdrawn. Rule changes since then have allowed other bills to go forward, and a debate-limiting device has become a de facto block on legislation. Robert Byrd, majority leader during Mitchell's first months, and his successor, Bob Dole, disliked the filibuster and kept the Senate in session overnight to discourage them.

In the version Mitchell elaborated in later years, he began, "The Senate was in session until midnight each of the first four nights I was here, and I began to think I'd made an error in judgment in accepting this appointment, and I knew the next week I'd made the biggest mistake of my life. Because the following Monday, I'd been a senator less than seven days when a filibuster occurred, and the result is round-the-clock session without stop." Mitchell, "new and naive," stayed in his seat until "I looked around, and to my surprise, I was the only person in the room." Two senators eventually returned to continue speaking for hours. Finally, a procedural vote occurred, and "the back door opened; into the Senate poured about ninety-five senators , cast their votes, and they all left, including the guys who were arguing." They were replaced by two more, and

Mitchell continued to sit, "tired and hungry," until he finally asked the Senate clerk where everyone was going—and was shown a room off the Senate chamber with dozens of army cots lined up.

"And there, lying in their clothes, were the members of the United States Senate—one of the great disillusioning moments of my life," he said. The clerk pointed to an empty cot. "It was the closest I'd ever been to such famous people. I climbed right over Howard Baker, and that wasn't easy. I next encountered Ted Kennedy, and that was very difficult, because it was before he went on a diet." Finally, he made it, and said, "I wished I could go back to being a federal judge, but knew that I couldn't. And so I did what we all tend to do in such circumstances: I started feeling sorry for myself. And I was lying there, wallowing in self-pity, when I rolled over and looked on the next cot, and saw just a few inches away Senator John Warner of Virginia. At that time he was married to Elizabeth Taylor." Following the laughter that always came, he said, "Here's a guy who could be home, legally in bed with Elizabeth Taylor, and he's spending the night with me."

Mitchell drew various morals to the story, noting that there's always someone whose troubles are worse than our own. In earlier, earthier versions, he added, "As I lay there thinking, I had a powerful urge to ask him how I stacked up to Liz." And he vowed, during the next filibuster, "to seek out the cot next to him, and about five in the morning, I'm going to pop the question."

In the ways of oral history, John Warner has a different, more decorous version. In his, Mitchell imagines he sees "a young senator next to me with a big smile on his face, sound asleep." Mitchell, who is having difficulty falling asleep, finds "The scene calmed me—I drifted off into my own sleep, as I realized that husband was dreaming he was home with his wife, Elizabeth Taylor."

The "cot story" worked equally well with Maine and national audiences alike, puncturing the absurdity of Senate rules and traditions, while equalizing the roles between the famous and the backbenchers. Senators often borrowed the story, sometimes with Mitchell's permission.

Mitchell even ventured into the tricky topic of religion. In a story much less well known, he described a meeting involving Joe Brennan and the congressional delegation about a dismal state budget, which he enlivened with his recent Sunday appearance "at a fundamentalist Bible church in a very small town way up in western Maine." The minister, Mitchell said, "was one of these fire-and-brimstone preachers, and he gave a very, very lengthy introduction—about half an hour," which Mitchell found "very accurate and factual." The minister "concluded by bringing me up to the front of the church and saying to the audience that I had been placed in the United States Senate by the hand of God."

To the delegation, Mitchell then said, "I have heard Joe Brennan called a lot of names in the last year, but I have never heard him called God before." And, to Dave Emery and Olympia Snowe, both mulling over Senate bids, he offered a Bible passage that said, "What the Lord hath wrought, let no man put asunder," adding, "Olympia got the message; Dave didn't." In outmaneuvering potential opponents, it has rarely been done better.

Mitchell still retained his seriousness. His campaign brochure slogan was, "A responsible leader for Maine and the nation." By emphasizing the dual role, he invited comparison with Emery that would work to his advantage. His announcement speech on January 7, 1982 was also devoid of jokes. It laid out concerns about the Reagan recession, and called for an end to "the ruinous tight-money, high-interest policies that have crippled our economy"—but were also taming inflation. And he identified the three issues that he would pursue doggedly: Reagan's proposal to reduce Social Security benefits, the specter of nuclear war Reagan's defense buildup evoked for many, and the acid rain that was decimating forest growth and killing freshwater fish throughout the Northeast.

MITCHELL OFTEN SAID HIS BEST CAMPAIGN MOVE was hiring Larry Benoit to manage it. Benoit, who grew up in Cape Elizabeth when it was still rural, had his first taste of politics when he organized for Muskie in northern New Hampshire in 1972, then went to work for Peter Kyros, who'd won reelection for the last time. Benoit, given to succinct political judgments, said, "Peter lived on the edge, and he paid the price." After Kyros's defeat in 1974, Benoit became a field representative for Muskie. He was still there when Mitchell inherited the Muskie operation, and, as with Anita Jensen, Mitchell recognized Benoit's potential. Benoit had a clear view of the whole operation while also excelling with technical details. His first move was to urge Mitchell to launch a television ad campaign to cut into the numbers of Mainers who didn't know him well enough to have an opinion.

Mitchell was skeptical. It was more than a year before the election and conventional wisdom held that advertising so far in advance was money wasted. But Mitchell scraped up $25,000 to launch the effort, and chose an unconventional firm to prepare the spots. Lee Bobker of Vision Associates wrote and produced documentary films; political work was a sideline. Most political ads were still formal and stilted. Bobker's idea was to feature Mitchell's biography and use informal settings. When he interviewed Mitchell to get him talking, he was struck by how clearly Mitchell expressed himself; most of his subjects hemmed and hawed.

A transcript shows that when he tested Mitchell on the Reagan economic program, Mitchell spoke of the need "to introduce fairness into our tax and economic policies." He was interrupted by a mosquito, but when he resumed, Mitchell said, "I don't think there's a person in this state, I don't think there's a person in this country, who would be unwilling to share in the burden of improving our national economy if they felt that all Americans were sharing in the burden. The problem now is that all Americans are not being asked to share in the burden. The sacrifices are being imposed on those least able to bear them, while those most able to bear them are not making a fair share of the sacrifice." The lines appeared almost verbatim in the ads.

Other scripts featured Mitchell talking about growing up in Waterville and the opportunities provided through his parents' hard work and sacrifices. No one decision got the Mitchell campaign on track, but the ad campaign helped Mainers to see Mitchell not as a has-been, but as senatorial.

Mitchell's attention to detail extended to his campaign chairs, usually a respected political elder who took the title while others did the work. Mitchell named four co-chairs, and two were women. Libby Mitchell, later Maine House Speaker and Senate President, was one. The other was Barbara Trafton, a young legislator who served on the DNC. She said, "This is the first time any statewide candidate had been thoughtful enough to look at not only geographic diversity, but demographic diversity and gender diversity. So we had this little balanced team, and I was the young woman [who] got to get on the ark."

The campaign treasurer was Barbara Keefe. She had started the Maine Women's Political Caucus in 1974, predecessor of the Maine Women's Lobby, which had endorsed Mitchell for governor. Keefe considered herself a rebel and dissenter. They kept in touch and, when Mitchell asked her to be treasurer, he had one condition—"If you get mad at me in the middle of the campaign, that you don't resign." She remembers working with Najeeb Lotfey, Mitchell's accountant, who told her that the treasurer was legally responsible for everything that goes on. After Watergate, this was no small reminder. "If anything is wrong with these books," Lotfey told her, "the senator does not go to jail, the lawyers don't go to jail, you go to jail." Keefe served the same role in 1988, and found that Mitchell "was always squeaky clean, and it's like a stamp of approval of the way a campaign should be handled."

Mitchell also decided to cultivate newspapers, something Muskie had never done. Muskie assumed, probably correctly, that newspapers would never endorse his candidacies, but his assumption carried over to reporters, and Muskie regularly battled with the *Bangor Daily News*. Mitchell said, "It was unfair to him, he felt, in ways that were just wrong, so the only way to deal with it was to go around and denounce it, and try to undermine its influence." Though none of the major dailies had endorsed him for governor, Mitchell took a different tack. "Every newspaper when I entered the Senate was Republican, but I also felt they were open to argument, open to persuasion," he said. "Particularly in the early years . . . I went to every paper over and over again. I made myself available for questions, I answered every question a reporter ever had, or editorial board, and I think that ultimately helped me."

Introducing the candidate via television and newspapers would only go so far. He needed to connect with voters individually. Larry Benoit said the state's voter lists were outdated and inaccurate. Each town or city followed its own policies. Though he knew it wouldn't be cheap, with Mitchell's approval Benoit set out to create new lists, town by town. He hired David Lemoine, later state treasurer, to travel to each town or city and photocopy their lists with a copier he brought in a station wagon. The voter project cost about $80,000, nearly 10 percent of the campaign budget, but it was money well spent. A fledgling computer software company in Falmouth processed the data. Lemoine found most town clerks cooperative. "The vast majority of folks were not a problem, although it depended on the part of the state I was calling as to how much of my Maine accent I let go," he said. One clerk threatened to bill the campaign for electricity, but still let them use the office.

"Essentially, we created the state's first electronic political database," Benoit said. The system was primitive by comparison to what came later, but it got the job done, beginning what Benoit called "my love affairs with computers." The system cranked out targeted appeals in a way that has since become familiar. Older voters heard about Reagan's proposal to cut Social Security benefits, while environmental and nuclear arms letters went to different groups. The countless individuals Mitchell met while campaigning all got "personalized, highly professional letters" within a few days, Benoit said. More than fifty thousand individual letters were sent.

Mary McAleney, who started with Mitchell in 1982 and was later a Washington chief of staff, thought Benoit worked every bit as hard as Mitchell. "If you look at pictures of Larry during the '82 campaign, you can see how much weight he lost," she said. "Larry was running that campaign, managing it, making sure the money was there, that the connections were made, that no phone call went unanswered."

David Emery's equally considerable investment in computer programs was far less productive. When he ran out of money, he blamed his staff's excessive spending on a malfunctioning system.

At first, Mitchell's campaign made little progress on fund-raising. He was so focused on learning the Senate and making contact with voters that finding money was a lower priority. Like most politicians, Mitchell disliked asking for money. He decided to call Paul Ziffren, a DNC member from California he knew slightly from the 1972 Muskie campaign, as he relates in his memoir. Ziffren was a skilled fund-raiser and often hosted events. When Mitchell asked, though, Ziffren turned him down, saying he didn't know him well—that a junior senator from Maine would have little appeal on the West Coast, and there were already too many events that month, October 1981. Mitchell persisted, though, and Ziffren finally agreed to mail out invitations for a Sunday brunch in Beverly Hills.

Mitchell flew to Los Angeles, but when Ziffren met him at his hotel, he told him the brunch was off—there had been no response. As Mitchell learned, mailings were a poor way of attracting attendance, but the bigger problem was that Senator Henry "Scoop" Jackson was also holding a fund-raiser. As consolation, Ziffren said he could introduce Jackson, but Mitchell declined. He said, "As I looked at Ziffren I saw the face of my high school basketball coach telling me I didn't make the tournament team. I choked back my hurt, my anger, my welling feeling of despair, and said simply, 'Thanks, Paul. I appreciate your effort.'"

In an interview, Mitchell says he did attend the Jackson fund-raiser and spoke with Jackson, who took a liking to him. Jackson had repeatedly clashed with Muskie, and his welcome to Mitchell may have been relief at the end of their rivalry. Unlike Muskie, Jackson ran again for president in 1976 and did no better. As for his fund-raising drought, Mitchell said, "It was another in a series of painful lessons. If I really wanted to be elected to the Senate, I had to shed my reluctance about fund-raising. Right or wrong, it was how the system worked. I had wanted the honor of the Senate without having to do all the unpleasant but necessary work to get there."

Personal contact by the candidate was essential. Surrogates were useful only for follow-ups and for organizing "asks." Scott Hutchinson, again his finance chair, said the Dunfey family connection was a big help, because their hotel chain provided contacts all over the country. "George could go to Chicago for breakfast, and come back with $10,000, $15,000, $20,000, or New York or Boston," he said. His incumbency provided dividends, at least when he overcame the perception that he was certain to lose. His position on the Finance Committee also became an asset. Though Mitchell didn't know it yet, David Emery was having an even harder time raising money, and by March 1982 was begging contributors, writing, "We have spent all the money raised to date. Now, the campaign cupboard is bare. We're grinding to a halt, just when our opponent is stepping up his campaign." By February 1982, Mitchell had raised $272,200, with $87,600 from Maine donors. He was on his way to solvency.

The budget of $892,000 held up well, and Mitchell ended up raising just short of $1 million—a respectable total for a small state's Senate race at the time. The biggest items were advertising buys, about 40 percent of the total, followed by staffing, direct mail, polling, phones, and television ad production. By August 15, Mitchell had $220,000 on hand, including $52,000 from the Democratic Senatorial Campaign Committee, and was ready for his stretch run.

DAVID EMERY APPEARED TO HAVE ALL THE ADVANTAGES. He had been easily re-elected three times, and did not suffer from Peter Kyros's streak of arrogance. He overawed Olympia Snowe, and with the adoption of the Reagan budget, tax cut, and defense buildup, had firmly attached himself to the president's coattails. Yet there were skeptics, not only in the Mitchell camp, but in the Republican Party as well.

Scott Hutchinson had done a favor for Emery when, just after his first race for Congress, he was $10,000 in debt and the Maine National Bank, which had handled Emery's financial affairs for years, refused to grant a loan. Hutchinson approved the loan, later became a friend, and even attended Emery's wedding. But he believed the Republican hierarchy had more influence on Emery's decision to run than the candidate's own desires. "I don't think he had the fire in his belly he should have had," Hutchinson said. "He had great polls when he was a congressman, but he didn't do a heck of a lot either. He didn't have a big record to go out there and pound on and show."

Ken Cole at Jensen Baird, later a Maine Republican Party chair, was more critical. "David became too much of a Washington pol," he said, "gained too much weight, was too white, just looked like a southern Democrat almost in the old sense." Barbara Trafton, Mitchell's campaign co-chair, had met with Emery on a volunteer lobbying trip that included visits with Cohen and Muskie. Emery's office, she said, "was very ill equipped, and I remember seeing a stack of about six books holding up one side of his desk. And I thought, 'Here I am for the Maine Library Association, and you're holding up your desk with books.'" Compared with Mitchell, she said, "There was a real difference in demeanor, in intellect." David Johnson thought Emery listened too carefully to handlers. He remembers him "in a formal three-piece suit with a pin-striped vest. It just didn't fit him. His strength was as a guy who was pretty close to the ground, politically."

Hal Pachios remembers visiting Mitchell in Washington when he was "way behind Emery in the polls." They stopped by the Senate TV studio, available to members for weekly reports and other productions. He watched as Mitchell gave a dramatically improved performance, and was struck once again by "the power of incumbency." He decided, even then, "that it would take an atomic bomb to get George Mitchell out of this office."

Mitchell's field staff got to see him far from Washington or Portland, and noticed differences from the 1974 campaign. John Diamond, a state legislator who was hired to work in northern counties, remembers an early event in Belfast with an embarrassingly small turnout. Mitchell was dressed formally, but midway through, "He took his jacket off, and it's the first time I remember seeing him at an event where he actually took his jacket off," Diamond said. "He was very loose, he was smiling, he was funny. And I remember saying 'Whoa, where did this come from?'" After that, the "sans jacket" look became part of the routine.

Clyde MacDonald noticed the contrast right away. After an appearance in Machias, in far eastern Washington County, a janitor came up after Mitchell spoke, and told MacDonald, "I love to listen to him. He explains things so even people like me can understand." And MacDonald admired Mitchell's ability to handle different audiences—including his own radical antiwar friends. "He never said anything that made people think he was a bleeding-heart liberal, but his actions were just the opposite."

John Baldacci, a future governor and Mitchell cousin once removed, won a state Senate seat that November, and his most vivid impression from campaign stops was Mitchell's joint appearances with Joe Brennan. "I remember what a powerful, dynamic ticket that was. That was a huge year in 1982, when George and Joe were on the ticket together. We had never won as many [Senate] seats, and we owe all of that to . . . Joe Brennan and George Mitchell, because we just had a powerful one-two punch."

The 1982 Fourth of July parade in Bangor included five thousand helium balloons for Mitchell, and John Diamond heard "this wave of applause coming, as soon as he starts coming down the hill, everybody is applauding for him," he said. "Not your typical greeting for a politician, but almost like welcoming a hero." David Emery received "a smattering of applause."

THE THREE ISSUES MITCHELL CHOSE TO EMPHASIZE were acid rain, the nuclear freeze, and Social Security, which appealed to strikingly different audiences. Despite the path-breaking legislation championed by Muskie, environmental issues hadn't worked in 1974. This time, Mitchell singled out acid rain, and made the issue his own. The science showing that acid deposition from coal-burning power plants was destroying lakes and stunting tree growth was relatively recent, but overwhelming, and Mitchell studied it carefully and spoke pointedly about it. Clyde MacDonald said it helped him connect with rural audiences. "They love to hunt and fish, and the average sportsman never had that much interest in environmental issues before. But this caught their attention."

Emery was also working on acid rain, but he was handicapped by the Reagan administration's hostility to environmental causes. Emery sponsored a bill that was quickly dismissed by the National Clean Air Coalition. "Coal washing would be woefully inadequate as the centerpiece of an acid rain program," the group said in a letter to Emery. "Our fear is that such a proposal from a member of the New England delegation could undermine efforts to achieve passage of an effective acid rain control program." In May 1982, Emery endorsed the House version of Mitchell's bill which, the coalition said, "has more support than any of the four competing clean air bills in the House."

Perhaps Mitchell's biggest victory of his Senate career to date came in July after Majority Leader Howard Baker, GOP veteran of the Environment and Public Works Committee, where Mitchell also served, supported a compromise version of Mitchell's acid rain bill. Shortly thereafter, even reluctant Republicans came on board, resulting in 15–0 approval from the full committee. While it didn't receive a floor vote that year, or in any Congress until Mitchell became majority leader, it was a signal victory for an unelected senator, and put him on the map as an environmental legislator.

The nuclear freeze movement also peaked that year, with voters alarmed by aggressive rhetoric from Reagan's Defense Department about nuclear superiority, and annual defense budget increases nearing 15 percent. Mitchell endorsed the freeze wholeheartedly. In a speech to the League of Women Voters and World Affairs Council on February 19, 1982, Mitchell began by observing, "The head of the International Atomic Energy Agency . . . warned two days ago that the agency cannot prevent proliferation. It can only sound the alarm when it suspects misuse of nuclear energy plants for weapons production." He said the administration's plan to use plutonium in spent fuel from electricity-generating reactors would reverse "one of the most basic elements of our nuclear policy— to maintain the distinction between civilian nuclear power production and the production of weapons for war."

Mitchell argued that not only was the Reagan proposal faulty, but it would also end arms control negotiations with the Soviet Union. "Arms control agreements are not needed between nations which are allies," he said. "Arms control agreements are not a reward for good behavior. They are a vital safeguard for ourselves."

One answer, he said, was a verifiable and equitable freeze on nuclear forces. While Emery, and others, attempted to deride the "freeze" movement as appeasement of Soviet aggression in Afghanistan, it struck a chord among

Mainers. Mitchell's campaign ads featured his stand, and he discussed it with editorial boards. He had again put Emery on the opposite side of an issue that started working in his favor.

Mitchell noticed that Reagan's early proposals to revamp Social Security, including elimination of the minimum benefit, were causing unease on Capitol Hill, and he began hearing from voters. "Social Security was a huge issue," Mitchell said. "I identified with it, and learned from the lack of establishing priorities among issues in the '74 campaign." When Emery tried to tag Mitchell with a lack of fiscal discipline, citing the need to reduce Social Security, he had a ready comeback. The staff had a list of all his votes on spending issues, which showed that Mitchell had voted to cut defense spending by $44 billion while voting to increase domestic programs by $42 billion. During a debate in which Emery accused him of being a "tax-and-spend Democrat," Mitchell pulled out an index card and cited chapter and verse of his votes, noting that Emery's votes in Congress showed the opposite spending priorities. "It was fortunate," David Johnson said, "that he voted to cut more than he had voted to increase."

An issue that wasn't prominent in the campaign, but troubled Mitchell, was abortion. It was less than a decade since *Roe v. Wade*, and for Catholics like Mitchell, the issue was particularly difficult. He accepted the church's teaching, and emphasized that he was personally opposed to abortion. He consistently voted against federal funding for abortion. After Republicans took the majority, legislative activity increased. There were a variety of "human life" bills and constitutional amendments. Mitchell voted against the bills, emphasizing that they were attempts to overturn *Roe* without amending the Constitution.

He attempted to occupy the middle ground against Emery, who took a blanket anti-abortion position. Mitchell said, "I am opposed to abortion. I have a deep personal and religious conviction against it. While there are members of all faiths on both sides of the issue, the Catholic Church has taken a leading role in favor of a constitutional amendment prohibiting abortion. As a Catholic I am very much aware of the Church's position. But as a public official, my obligation is to the Constitution and all of the American people." He said there were more than fifty "human life" bills and amendments before Congress, and he criticized Emery for co-sponsoring one of the more extreme versions that would have prohibited abortion except to save the life of the mother. Mitchell cited pragmatic grounds. "As much as I am opposed to abortion, I cannot support such an extreme proposal," he said. "It would be unenforceable and unworkable." He said an estimated 1.5 million abortions were performed annually under the *Roe* decision, but that nearly a million a year had occurred before it. "The law wasn't enforced," Mitchell said. "It simply drove the practice underground."

Mitchell was sensitive to the right-to-life criticism that now came with the job. He issued a densely reasoned, six-page reply to an invective-filled letter by University of Maine professor Terrence Hughes, which had appeared in the *Church World*. Mitchell provided a detailed review of his votes on various bills and floor amendments sponsored by Senator Jesse Helms. In the end, Mitchell's position probably didn't cost him many votes. In the First District race to replace Emery, the pro-choice candidate, Republican John McKernan, prevailed over Democrat John Kerry. When Emery attempted a comeback in 1990, he also reversed his anti-abortion position.

MITCHELL WAS STARTLED, AT A CAMPAIGN APPEARANCE in June, to hear a member of the audience stand up and say, loudly, "Why are you against veterans?" When Mitchell assured him he was not, the man replied, "Yes, you are. I've got the proof right here," waving a document he then handed to Mitchell. It was headlined "Special Report to Maine Veterans," and had been sent to every veteran the Emery campaign could find. It cited a survey of congressional votes from the Veterans of Foreign Wars and proclaimed that Emery had voted the right way for veterans 92 percent of the time, while Mitchell had compiled a zero percent rating. "It can't be," was Mitchell's first thought. He had served in the army and on the Veterans' Affairs Committee, while Emery had done neither. How could he have a zero rating? He placed an urgent call to Larry Benoit, who couldn't figure it out either. Mitchell had a sleepless night, and worried until Benoit called him back the next afternoon.

"You're not going to believe this," were Benoit's first words. The explanation of the unbelievable charge was simple. The VFW's political action committee had rated congressional votes in the House and Senate, but concluded its survey before Mitchell had joined the Senate. Mitchell didn't have a zero rating; he simply hadn't voted on any of the bills—something the VFW explained in a footnote. It was what the Emery campaign did next that turned a simple mistake into a cause célèbre.

Emery never publicly commented on the snafu. He delegated it to his campaign manager, George Smith. Smith was as young as Emery, and had managed his first campaign almost on a lark; no one expected a twenty-six-year-old to win a seat in Congress. Looking back, both Emery and Smith often said that the Senate campaign was "run from Washington," and, in fact, when the campaign was floundering, Smith was replaced. But the VFW survey was all theirs. Emery had already taken criticism—and not just from Democrats—for his characterization of Mitchell, in his speech to the Republican State Convention, as a "political chameleon." The response on the VFW mailing was a classic example of how not to handle a political blunder.

Smith first told reporters a lower-level staffer had compiled the information used in the campaign broadside. The *Portland Press Herald* reported, "Emery's campaign manager, George Smith, at first insisted that the material was accurate and that no retraction would be made. Later, he said it was all a matter of 'honest misinterpretation.'" When the questions kept coming, Smith finally conceded, and the campaign responded to the Mitchell camp's complaints by agreeing to send a corrective mailing—which didn't happen until October. As Mitchell observed, by then it didn't matter. Emery took a pounding from every editorial page in the state.

The *Press Herald* dismissed the idea that it was an honest mistake. "Even the most enthusiastic campaign operative might be moved to wonder how Mitchell, an Army veteran and a member of the Senate Veterans' Affairs Committee, could rank so poorly on veterans' issues." The *Morning Sentinel* suggested that "The Emery campaign's distortion of Mitchell's voting record suggests a worried challenge, not a confident candidacy."

When Emery took no action, the *Press Herald* ran another editorial, saying, "A direct disavowal is needed: first, because it is obviously the fair and right thing for Emery to do; and second, because only public word from Emery himself can lay to rest any suggestion the newsletter's misinterpretation of Mitchell's record was not a deliberate ploy." Sensing opportunity, Mitchell took out a full-page ad in the *Maine Sunday Telegram* on July 11 detailing his record and reminding voters he was "the only veteran in the Maine Congressional delegation."

National publications took note. The Germond-Witcover Report said, "As a political atrocity, this falls a little short of Watergate, but it was clearly enough to turn the momentum of the campaign sharply and put Emery on the defensive. Moreover, although the whole thing happened a month ago, the issue still is percolating—among other reasons because the Emery campaign has not yet delivered on a promise to send a corrective mailing." On July 30, Benoit wrote to Smith, saying, "I am sure you realize the more time that elapses between the original false mailing and the corrective mailing, the less meaningful the corrective mailing will be." There was still no action.

EVERYONE CLAIMED LATER TO HAVE SENSED exactly when the tide turned in the Mitchell–Emery race, but clearly it was sometime that summer. Mitchell's favorite moment came during a Senate Democratic caucus lunch, when Daniel Patrick Moynihan, noting improving poll numbers, proclaimed, "Why, one of the polls shows that even George Mitchell is only twenty points behind," which raised a laugh, and, Mitchell said, "made me feel about two inches tall." Another Mitchell recollection of Moynihan has him saying, "I saw a poll that shows even George Mitchell has a chance to win. It may be remote."

Even earlier Mitchell showed skill in rallying his party. His speech at the Democratic State Convention in May was widely praised. In *Maine Times*, whose coverage was still skeptical, Dennis Bailey provided a qualified endorsement. "There were some hopeful signs, and surprisingly George Mitchell was one of them. While his Friday night speech was not the most stirring ever heard, for Mitchell it was something of a watershed event. It was as if Mitchell had finally crossed the threshold and earned his party's total affection. His speech was well-written, intelligent, and delivered with a bit more gusto than he is usually credited with." Emery's lead had shrunk significantly. In late spring, he registered 46 percent to Mitchell's 42 percent, with 12 percent undecided.

A symbolic test of campaign strategy came during Augusta's "Whatever Race," a colorful collection of homemade rafts that floated by the State House each Fourth of July weekend. It was meant to celebrate the "rebirth" of the Kennebec River, and dramatic improvements in water quality that followed enforcement of the Clean Water Act. The Republican Party entered a raft, with Emery as skipper.

John Day reprised the event, beginning, "The classic July omen took place two weeks ago," when "Mitchell and Emery campaign workers floated downstream on competing rafts in a race with obvious symbolic overtones. Emery placed so much stock in the affair that he captained his own raft, wife Carol at his side. By all accounts it was a disaster. The float took on water and stalled in the middle of the river. Fearing he would lose the crowd, Emery called for a motorized tow, disqualifying his craft from winning any trophies. But the boost didn't stop the raft from nearly sinking, forcing Emery and his wife to desert ship in full view of thousands of potential voters." Day quoted an unnamed Republican saying, "It was the most pitiful sight you ever saw. I felt embarrassed for David." Emery, Day said, was "enraged," and, "Two days later the congressman fired his press secretary and accepted the resignation of his deputy campaign director. Campaign manager George Smith, Emery's closest political adviser, was told to devote more attention to fund-raising."

Mitchell did not set foot on the Democrats' raft, which stayed afloat. Mary McAleney said the campaign rules were: "No rafts. No funny vehicles. No funny hats." About Emery's Whatever Race debacle, she said, "We figured it was a sign."

Press skepticism of Emery continued. Tom Delahanty sent Mitchell the front page of the *Fort Fairfield Review*, which included an item headlined "David

Emery Speaks to Issues." After the introduction, noting that Emery had visited Aroostook County and made stops in Fort Fairfield, Houlton, and Caribou, it said, "Following is the complete text of everything that Emery said of importance while in Fort Fairfield, according to one observer:————." The rest of the space is blank.

Dissension in Republican ranks was growing. As usual, John Day was alert to signs of trouble. He quoted a Cohen aide claiming Emery was "tailgating" on such issues as Bath Iron Works construction contracts for navy destroyers, a term Day defined as "jumping on an issue at the last minute to take credit for work done by another politician." Day said Cohen was annoyed by Emery brochures displaying his photo alongside Cohen's, with the inscription, "Senator to Be." And Olympia Snowe expressed annoyance over Emery's claim that he had aided House budget negotiations between her Republican moderate "gypsy moths" and Democratic "boll weevils." Said Snowe, "The hard work was done before Emery ever got involved." An unnamed Snowe aide said, "We've had it with Emery. The guy has absolutely no class."

On Mitchell's behalf, David Johnson pounced on Emery's comments that his campaign was broke because of overspending on computers. "Emery has done a great job of spending $600,000 to become the underdog," Johnson told a reporter. "It's ironic that the guy who's supposed to be a careful budgeter can't even manage to keep a campaign in the black." August campaign reports showed Emery $100,000 in debt and Mitchell with $85,000 in reserve.

In Maine's Senate race, Ronald Reagan turned from an asset into a liability. A case in point was Emery's stance on the federal budget. Since Republicans were still in the minority in the House, they needed every vote they could get. On a critical vote in May 1981, a Republican bid for a single budget vote, without any floor amendments, Emery helped defeat the Democrats' "rule" to govern debate. He then voted for the Gramm-Latta substitute, with some Democrats also in favor, and said of the budget, "I have absolutely no questions or reservations about it." By the time the 1982 Reagan budget was released, he had shifted, saying "It's nearly impossible for me to support any of the budget."

Mitchell got support from unexpected quarters. He received a letter from the noted poet, Philip Booth, who lived along the coast and, like his neighbors, usually voted Republican. He wrote in March, "I've been part of Castine since something like 1797; my wife has been part of the town since 1946. You might think that we were rock-ribbed and granite-headed Republicans. No, we only know that we know a good United States senator when we see one, and that you, on very many counts, have in the Senate represented our sense of what makes sense for both Maine in the small and America in the large." He enclosed a contribution, and concluded, "We hope this small amount may encourage you . . . to continue to speak out for all of us who value substance more than image, who believe that America in general and Maine in particular is made of people who would rather come to terms with reality than sit around the White House projecting home movies of themselves."

National Republicans went to bat for Emery, though in a limited way. Vice President George H. W. Bush said the Maine race, and Congressman Paul Trible's Senate bid in Virginia, were "the most important in the nation." Trible won, but served only one term. There was speculation Reagan would visit Maine. He did agree to head a Washington fund-raiser on September 21, a $500-a-plate affair that raised $100,000 at a time when Emery badly needed it. In his remarks, Reagan said, "It makes no sense for Maine to have sent Bill Cohen to the Senate and then elect somebody else to cancel out his vote."

Mitchell had national support, too. Alan Cranston, who survived the NCPAC ads in 1980 to serve two more terms, campaigned with Mitchell in Augusta, and said, "California has produced three presidents—Herbert Hoover, Richard Nixon, and Ronald Reagan. I think we can do better." But Bob Dole, appearing with Emery in Portland, said Republicans would pick up "three to four Senate seats," including Mitchell's.

Some Mitchell colleagues went out of their way to praise him, even such notorious non-campaigners as taxpayer watchdog William Proxmire of Wisconsin, who never raised any money. Proxmire, who chaired the Banking Committee, where Mitchell served before moving to Finance, said of him, "He's already distinguished himself as one of the ablest, most perceptive, and effective interrogators I've seen since I've been in the Senate. Senator Mitchell's cross-examination of one witness after another was the most competent, relevant, probing, and revealing that I've seen in a long, long time."

By late summer, things were going so well that Lee Bobker, the television producer, warned against overconfidence. He wrote, "I am concerned that we are coasting on our success much like an athletic team that 'sits on a lead,' and it worries me. I think we need to be more aggressive in exploiting our advantage and the seeming disarray of our opponent."

Emery had much earlier challenged Mitchell to debate, and Mitchell quickly accepted. They agreed to an initial meeting in June, and Mitchell suggested three more. In the end, they did two. Both candidates handled themselves well, supporters agreed, and Mitchell developed a sharper, more streamlined style. At the final debate in Portland on October 21, he said of Emery, "He'll say no to the elderly, he'll say no to the poor. He'll say no to the blind. But he'll never say no to the Pentagon."

By October, Emery was trailing, and decided to put Mitchell on the defensive during debates. He chose his opponent's votes on defense spending. Emery criticized Mitchell's vote for Nancy Kassebaum's amendment. The Kansas Republican moderate had proposed real annual growth of 7 percent instead of the president's proposed 10 percent. Kassebaum said the amendment "would not cause the demobilization of a single military unit, would not cancel any weapons program, and would not reduce the size of [the] US defense structure." The amendment failed, but Mitchell easily parried the thrust.

Emery tried again on the Pentagon's proposal to overhaul the aging battleship *Iowa*. He claimed that, by opposing the request, Mitchell had taken away possible work from Bath Iron Works. Mitchell had done his homework, and said, "BIW has built one battleship in its history, and that was in 1904." He said BIW had no interest in the *Iowa* contract, and told reporters to "call the president of Bath Iron Works. Ask him. He's a Republican. He does not know I'm making this request." When they did, a surprised Bill Haggett said Mitchell gave "an absolutely honest answer," and that he had "fought as hard as anyone" to get work for the shipyard.

David Johnson, who had stayed in Washington, took his vacation weeks in Maine during the final stretch and vividly remembers the Portland debate, less than two weeks before the election. "George was in command of so many facts and their analysis and how they fit together. The audience had equal numbers of Mitchell and Emery supporters. Here was a debate at a pivotal moment in the campaign, one of the most important in the country, and here we were, stuck in this little hot room with stadium seating, and it was so civilized. . . . And, as far as I know, nobody was packing heat, and there were no character-related accusations. I thought, 'Wow, what a great country this is, and what a great state this state is.'"

Mitchell also made numerous joint appearances with Emery. They were inundated with requests. Through the summer months, Mitchell's confidence grew with the favorable reaction of crowds and positive notices in the press. The opposite was true for Emery. His once-commanding lead had disappeared, and his campaign was broke. He demoted George Smith in August. The campaign professionals he brought in were quite a surprise.

In his memoir, Mitchell, discussing what eventually became a warm and lasting professional friendship with Bill Cohen, mentions that in 1982, "Cohen supported my opponent, sending two of his most trusted aides to Maine to take charge of David Emery's campaign," as if this were normal campaign procedure. It was not. Senators of the opposite party traditionally support their party's nominee in campaign appearances and fund-raising. They don't dispatch their closest political advisers to rescue a floundering campaign, as Cohen did. Reaction among the Mitchell camp was a combination of disbelief and outrage.

David Johnson said "it was shocking," and that while Cohen helping Emery was expected, this move was not. "It was unusual, and we were surprised and disheartened by it." When he later went to work for Mitchell at the Democratic Senatorial Campaign Committee, Johnson said Cohen's aid to Emery was one of the first things reporters asked about.

The two aides were Tom Daffron, a Cohen veteran who'd been hired as his first chief of staff, and Bob Tyrer, his young press secretary. Daffron had been a speechwriter for Senator Charles Percy, an Illinois Republican, and, after two stints with Cohen, was chief of staff for Fred Thompson of Tennessee and Lisa Murkowski of Alaska. Tyrer, who succeeded Daffron as chief of staff, was looking to make his mark and, according to Daffron, was more enthusiastic about the Maine assignment. Tyrer, he said, "was a young, exuberant fellow, and thought we had a chance to pull this thing off."

The Boston press took to the Cohen vs. Mitchell story, and Daffron was frequently quoted on the state of the Emery campaign. Their start date was August 28, and David Broder, now dean of national political writers, devoted a column to the upheaval in Emery's campaign. "We have to raise money and hire good staff," Daffron told him. "Mitchell has run a good campaign. They have a new TV ad buy starting September 7. We have nothing. . . . If we can stay competitive, then maybe we can get the campaign back on the issues, and we have a shot. But if the trend can't be stopped, we could be blown away." Broder then observed, "The saga of Emery's self-inflicted wounds is almost unbelievable." Daffron told a *Boston Globe* reporter, "This campaign cannot afford another serious mistake. . . . It's like sitting on a time bomb: One mistake, and it all blows up in your face."

Daffron later betrayed something of a guilty conscience, suggesting he was there primarily for the money. "I told a national newspaper reporter, and this was not necessarily a good reason, that I had a child that wanted to go to college, and it was fairly difficult to do on a federal wage."

In a recent interview, Cohen said he didn't think the Emery campaign affected his relationship with Mitchell. David Johnson disagrees. "I had strong feelings about it then, and I still do. I talked about it the last time I saw Tom Daffron." Johnson believes it did have an effect on Mitchell—that "he was hurt, both professionally and personally," and, for a time, it changed the way the two worked together. "You could say it was just politics, but it did have a chilling effect."

November arrived with Mitchell holding a firm, and in some polls, a substantial lead. John Day, who had dropped several bombs on the Emery camp, switched to the horse race, and in his last column suggested tracking polls showed a close race, within 1 percent. That was not the general mood. When Bob Packwood, chairman of the Republican Senatorial Campaign Committee, was asked about Maine prospects, he said, "No comment."

The *Bangor Daily News*, after its fling with Jim Longley, returned to endorsing Republicans, and, somewhat dutifully, praised Emery for understanding "the fundamentals of good government—less interference in the private sector, less spending and lower taxes." The Portland papers had resumed endorsements, and favored Democrats Mitchell and Brennan in the statewide races, and Republicans McKernan and Snowe for Congress; all four won.

Commentary in smaller newspapers focused on Mitchell's ability to do more than create sound bites, and his respect for the voters. The Biddeford *Journal Tribune* cited Mitchell's evenhanded statements on the economy. Peter Cox, writing the *Maine Times* endorsement, said, "What we like most about George Mitchell is that even when we disagree with his conclusion, we find that his logic is sound. As an example, Mitchell personally opposes abortion. We do not. . . . On the other hand, Mitchell opposes a constitutional amendment on abortion, and he thinks to outlaw something the majority believes should be legal breeds disrespect for the law. His argument is much more complex and convincing than we can portray in this space." Cox also observed that Emery "did excellent constituent work, and his voting record was unusually responsive to the mood of Maine. But when he decided to run for the US Senate, he stepped out of his league." The *Camden Herald* was less flattering, saying Emery's campaign "sets a putrid record for mud-slinging and general vindictiveness."

ON ELECTION DAY, THE MITCHELL STAFF WORKED on new ways to get the message out. Mike Hastings, in Portland, led a group to Tukey's Bridge, which spans Back Cove next to the B&M Baked Beans plant, and carries Interstate 295 traffic into downtown. Their sign-waving with Mitchell slogans created a "staged spontaneous demonstration," as Hastings put it, "and we got a lot of publicity for it."

That evening, Mitchell and his wife were on their way to a campaign party in Lewiston when the polls closed at eight p.m. Just afterward, they heard Tom Brokaw on NBC radio projecting Mitchell the winner. By the time they got to the Eastland Hotel in Portland, the celebration had begun.

On the top floor, Ed Muskie was waiting in his suite. Hastings had the unenviable task of guiding him to the ballroom where Muskie would appear without detracting from Mitchell's entrance. They used a circuitous route through the Eastland kitchen, and by the time they got there, Hastings said, Muskie was furious, and said, "I feel like Bobby Kennedy down in the kitchen." He added,

"Muskie wanted to be up in the lobby where he could see all his buddies and make a very impressive entrance."

Upstairs, the crowd waited for Mitchell, and when he, Sally, and Andrea made their way onto the podium, dozens of supporters tried to take up positions around the winner. Swisher was trying to get particularly close to his brother. As Mitchell's political career ascended, his brother no doubt recalled the glow of his own athletic glory. Now, Mitchell had won his first electoral victory, and his patron, Ed Muskie, was sidelined, while the brother who'd always gotten the headlines and applause was bidding for the photographers' attention. At that moment, Mitchell said, "Gone were my high school basketball coach, those Portland law firms that wouldn't even talk to me, the pollster who said I had no chance to win, the Beverly Hills non-crowd." And, in a story Mitchell tells over and over, when the *Portland Evening Express* the next day ran a photo of Mitchell with Swisher leaping into the frame, the caption identified "Senator George Mitchell celebrating his upset victory with an unidentified supporter."

Mitchell won with 279,819 votes to Emery's 179,882, or 61 percent. It was a margin fully in keeping with Muskie's dominance in four previous Senate elections, and marked a complete reversal of Emery's first poll, where he'd been favored by 61 percent. Mitchell carried fifteen of Maine's sixteen counties, falling short only in Knox, by 106 votes. Joe Brennan compiled a nearly identical margin over his challenger, Charlie Cragin. Overall, Mitchell's win wasn't typical of that year's US Senate races. Though the Democrats increased their House majority by twenty-six seats, Republicans actually gained one in the Senate, and the moderate New England Republicans, including several Mitchell was close to—John Chafee and Robert Stafford, along with Connecticut's Lowell Weicker—narrowly survived.

Perhaps the most surprising result was Maine Democrats' sweep of the state Senate. They won twenty-three races and lost only ten, a better than two-thirds majority that equaled their 1964 showing—and this time, the result was lasting. Democrats controlled the Senate for all but one term during the next twenty-eight years. Freshmen like John Baldacci won open seats, while other challengers defeated three Republican incumbents, including Senate President Joe Sewall. The winning Democrat, Mike Pearson, was a young House member, and one of many candidates to use Mitchell's voter lists. The strains of a long campaign are reflected in a note Pearson wrote to Mitchell's office, saying, "I am sorry if I was difficult on the phone, but it has been a real struggle for me for nearly two months, and when one is in politics one gets frustrated sometimes. Again, my apology and thanks. I really think it is going to happen this time."

The 1982 election was also the last time Sally and George Mitchell appeared together on a campaign stage. Mary McAleney said, "I know how hard she worked on that campaign," even though she found public appearances difficult. Mitchell says that despite Sally's aversion to politics, she wanted him to win, and supported him whenever he felt he needed her.

Mert Henry had a succinct explanation for Emery's loss. "He and his staff did a lot of stupid things in 1981 and '82, and he made himself very vulnerable, and George ran probably the best campaign I have ever seen anyone run in Maine." George Smith, who despite his demotion remained close to Emery, rejects the notion that Emery sabotaged his chances. "The way George Mitchell ran that campaign validated himself, and Olympia Snowe wouldn't have beat him that year," Smith said. "He won it. Dave Emery remained popular."

Sandy Maisel, the Colby government professor, saw Emery as an "everyman," who fit the mold of the "moderate, not flag-waving Republican who is one of us." But Emery, he said, wasn't seen as a potential national leader, the way Muskie, Margaret Chase Smith, and Cohen were. "There was nothing bad about David Emery, but once you get an incumbent in, if they do pretty good constituent services, it's very hard to beat them."

David Johnson said, "There was a steady path toward the election victory, in ways that I didn't appreciate . . . that George had planned and had foreseen and had a notion that drove his actions in a way that was well conceived and extremely well executed. It didn't happen by accident." A month later, Johnson was traveling with Mitchell, and said, "I'm really looking forward now to working for a senator who's not up for reelection." Mitchell responded, "You still are. It's just a little further away."

Mitchell learned how to raise money, and even came to excel at it, but was never comfortable with the process. Three days after the election, he held a news conference at the State House to announce an advisory panel to recommend campaign finance reform proposals. "American political campaigns are too long and too expensive," he said. "The recent Senate campaign here in Maine was no exception. It lasted more than a year and, when all the bills are paid by both campaigns, will have cost about $2 million." He cited the *Buckley v. Valeo* decision, striking down spending limits as an obstacle, but said there were other ways to rein in spending. It was not until 1996, after Mitchell left office, that Maine voters by referendum approved the Clean Elections Act, which made Maine the first state to provide public financing for legislative and governor's races.

Mitchell asked Ken Curtis to serve, and he responded with a letter on December 23. "After careful reflection," Curtis wrote, "I must ask to be excused from your Task Force on Campaign Finance Reform. There is nothing at all personal attached to the decision. The time has come when it is obvious to me that I should wean myself from Maine politics. It is difficult to be a former officeholder. I lightly equate this to being an ex-con. It is extremely difficult to go straight." But Mitchell made another appeal, and Curtis joined the group.

Perhaps the most gratifying letter came from Frank Coffin, who said, "What a joy it is to write this letter of congratulations! Much better than the letter I wrote after your gubernatorial campaign. But one thing I said in that more somber letter proved true: Things *do* work out for the best. Ruth and I rejoice with you, Sally, and Andrea, not only for the victory and for the amazing margin, but for the style and content of your campaign. You are exactly what state and nation need in the United States Senate. May you have a long and satisfying career there."

11

OUTSIDE THE BELTWAY

With his come-from-behind victory in the 1982 Senate race, and a ringing endorsement from Maine voters, George Mitchell could afford to enjoy a moment of satisfaction with few second thoughts. The six-year term granted US senators is unique in American politics. No comparable federal or state office carries more than four years. The Senate was designed as a deliberative body by the founders, and Mitchell's thoughtful, careful style would seem to be what the designers had in mind. Yet as early as the Christmas recess that year, he says in his memoir, his thoughts were elsewhere. He was considering "how totally the Senate consumes its members. For two and a half years, I had worked long hours, seven days a week. Getting elected to a full term became the overwhelming focus of my life. Fund-raising took more and more of my time. During the 1982 campaign I had become more aggressive and adept at asking for money. But the better I got, the more I disliked it. And I was dismayed to learn that it required a permanent, ongoing effort."

Mitchell didn't attribute these thoughts to Sally's concerns about his deepening involvement in politics—"That wasn't new." His own doubts, he said, began at this moment. "I knew that at some point I would term-limit myself," he said. Mitchell may retrospectively portray the decision with greater clarity than he felt at the time, but doubts remained with him over the next twelve years.

The option of simply slowing down wasn't seriously considered. Mitchell had announced his initiative for campaign finance reform just after the election. By January, when the Senate reconvened, he was already planning an extensive series of hearings in Maine, as a Finance Committee member, about Social Security. The meetings established Mitchell as someone who would be constantly attentive to needs and opinions in his home state, and set the pattern for public forums on a variety of issues, including many where Mitchell would be a target of citizen ire as well as a conveyor of public concerns. None of Maine's previous senators, including Ed Muskie and Margaret Chase Smith, had done anything comparable. Mitchell set a new standard for senatorial listening and outreach.

Mary McAleney, assigned to the Lewiston office, remembers the hearings well. The pattern for Social Security had been set earlier, when he was first making his rounds as an appointed senator. "He went around the state everywhere, and talked to everyone," she said. Her first encounter with Mitchell as a senator was in South Portland. "It was a hot summer night, and the Boys and Girls Club was filled. And the way he could explain the whole thing—the challenge of what was at stake, and how he handled the crowd that was overflowing the room— was extremely impressive. People all over the state felt that way."

Estelle Lavoie, who'd also worked for Muskie, was impressed by how Mitchell immediately threw himself into his work. She noticed that Howard Metzenbaum, a liberal Democrat from Ohio whose Senate office was across the hall, took a month off after the election. Mitchell, however, wanted Social Security meetings around the state; there were forty-six in all. "It was unbelievable," she said. "Not just Biddeford-Saco, there was one in Biddeford, one in Saco, one in Lewiston, one in Auburn, one in Bangor, one in Brewer. It was like that, everywhere." She said Mitchell told audiences that "It was going to involve a series of tax increases over the course of the next ten to twenty years to make the program solvent."

MITCHELL COULD NOW BE MORE ASSERTIVE in shaping his staff—offering six years of employment, an eternity on Capitol Hill, rather than a short-time stint. Some Muskie veterans, such as Bob Rose, the communications director, had already departed. Other holdovers, such as Charlie Jacobs, could see that Mitchell related to his staff differently than Muskie. "Mitchell was more constant, always sort of pleasant and easygoing," Jacobs said. "Once, something had gone wrong, and he had every right to be angry about it, and the worst thing he ever said was, 'This really distresses me.' . . . He was just very even-keeled. I don't think I ever heard him utter a swear word. I'm sure he does, but I never heard it."

Although no one doubted Mitchell's credentials as a Democrat, he was remarkably nonpartisan in selecting staff. Paula Silsby, one of his successors as US Attorney in Maine, was the first he'd chosen from a prominent Republican family, but there were others. Mike Hastings had worked for Bill Cohen first, though it was mostly because of his opposition to the Vietnam War.

Susan Longley, daughter of Jim Longley, also went to work for Mitchell. She'd gone to Washington seeking a job, and been turned down. "I returned to Maine, and Senator Mitchell heard that Governor Longley's daughter had been by," she said. He consulted Gayle Cory, his unerring guide to Maine, and decided they should make an offer. "I was hired because I was Governor Longley's daughter, child, offspring, the person who had beat him," she said. "He was generous enough to say, we'll go out of our way to include her." She remembers discussion of a federal grant to Maine that another staffer had heard about and wanted to announce. During the Reagan years grants were scarcer, and there was competition with the three Republican delegation members to assume credit. But when Mitchell was asked, he said, "We don't like it when they do that to us, and we're not going to do that to them. Give the others a call, and we're going forward together." Longley, later a Democrat, was also pleased by the support Mitchell gave her when she ran for the state Senate in 1994.

Another important selection was Sarah Sewall, daughter of Loyall Sewall, who served as Maine Republican Party chairman. She is also related to Joe Sewall, the Maine Senate president. Sarah Sewall succeeded Mike Hastings and became Mitchell's chief foreign policy aide, a role that expanded substantially when he became majority leader. Sewall had already interned with Olympia Snowe, been a Rhodes Scholar, and worked for a dovish defense think tank at the time of Ronald Reagan's "Star Wars" address, when she was interviewed for the new foreign affairs position. It was her father's role in Maine, however, that captured everyone's attention. "It was awkward for his staff," she said. "I was on my knees, saying, you can offend Republicans around me, you can say mean things. I won't take it personally, I won't rat, I won't tape-record you. It was awkward."

Hastings encountered similar issues. His primary motivation for moving to Mitchell's staff was that Cohen had decided to stick with defense, rather than foreign policy issues, the latter more in line with Hastings's interests, and he left Mitchell's office in 1984 to do charitable work in Africa. After coming on in October 1980, he was initially on the Budget Committee staff, in a slot Mitchell had inherited from Muskie, and kept his head down, hoping no one would notice: "You don't usually go from one senator to the other senator, particularly when they're from different parties."

When the Portland papers' Washington correspondent saw him in Mitchell's office, the game was up. It was just after the Republican landslide in November, and the story was headlined "Hastings Jumps, Frying Pan to Fire." He managed to serve consecutively on the minority staffs of both parties. "It's very difficult to switch teams," Hastings said. "You're never trusted by the team you left, and you're never completely trusted by the team you join."

Where Mitchell departed most radically from Senate conventions was in hiring women. When Charlene Sturbitts, environmental aide for both Muskie and Mitchell, was hired in 1972, women were at the bottom of the staff chart. "In those days there was so much sexism," she said. "There were very few women on the Hill who were not secretaries. And I had decided . . . that I would say I couldn't type, because I knew that I would end up as a secretary if I could." She and one colleague were the only women on the Public Works Committee staff, as it was then called. "We were treated fine by everyone on the committee, but the lobbyists treated us terribly, and would sometimes refuse to talk to us and say things like, 'If I can't talk to Leon [Billings], then I don't want to talk to anyone.' . . . I had just never experienced that kind of treatment, and it really upset me." Her initial experiences convinced Sturbitts to buttress her résumé by going to law school. She found Ed Muskie "gender-neutral," though that meant that "he would treat anyone equally well or badly, without respect to their gender." She does give Muskie credit, however, that in staffing the new Budget Committee, he picked Karen Williams as chief counsel, the first woman to hold such a post.

There were various reasons for hiring women. Diane Dewhirst, who headed communications for Mitchell at the Democratic Senatorial Campaign Committee, and later moved to the Senate office, said, "The idea that I was a woman and I was inexpensive was a selling point for me, because they had lots of white guys." Mary McAleney was offered what was announced as a policy post in Washington, and remembers her first conversation with Gayle Cory, who functioned as deputy chief of staff. Cory invited her to her house, "as only Gayle could, you know, with the bourbon and the cigarettes." After some office conversation, Cory said, "Now, just what do you think George Mitchell needs the most help on—figuring out where to go in Maine, who to talk to, and taking care of Maine, or being told how to vote on a housing issue?" Although McAleney continued to work on housing, before long she was a full-time scheduler and, four years later, chief of staff in the Senate office.

Cory was another talent Mitchell recognized and refined. She had volunteered for Muskie's first Senate campaign in 1958, then joined the office staff as a receptionist. Her brother, attorney Buzz Fitzgerald, was later Bath Iron Works president and a Mitchell confidant. Sister and brother were both uncanny judges of character, and had a way of defusing tension, whether dealing with impatient lobbyists or feisty union shipbuilders. She had grown up a committed Democrat in a Republican household. Her daughter, Carole, said, "They had pretty storied discussions around the kitchen table, and Mom was always on her own, against the rest of them." Cory often had heated political arguments with her father—good training for the Muskie office. Yet with Muskie, personal business was most prominent.

Carole said, "Cory represented a liaison between the family and the office." She became close to both Ed and Jane Muskie, "and she was very close to those kids, almost like a second mother." Her relationship with Mitchell was more professional, yet she retained a nurturing role. "She socialized with staff, and was very much like a mother hen," Carole said. "She definitely mothered many of the younger staff." Carole also has "a vivid memory of that office, lots of noise, lots of chatter, people were always very happy, but busy, and smoke—everyone, everywhere, everyone smoked back then."

Bob Carolla, who took over Mike Hastings's domestic portfolio when he arrived in 1984, was quick to notice Cory's role with Mitchell. He said, "She was one of his anchors in terms of keeping him grounded, both in the reality of Maine and in terms of someone he could trust. . . . If he ever needed being pulled into line, she was the one who could say, 'George.'" Carolla found she always had a good sense of how far to go with case work for a constituent, and "what's the decent thing to do, the right thing to do, even if it violates some regulation someplace."

There were many women with authority. Donna Beck, the office manager, kept track of everything in the Senate office and, later, the majority office as well. As an enforcer, she was legendary, and the boss was not exempt. "I only heard Senator Mitchell yell once," she said—over a disclosure issue involving a book advance. Beck insisted the advance fell under the definition of "future employment," and needed to be disclosed. This was not long after House Speaker Jim Wright had been forced to resign because of ethics issues surrounding a book deal, so there was heightened scrutiny. Beck says Mitchell "hemmed and hawed," then told her to write to the Senate Ethics Committee to determine whether it should be disclosed—something few senators were doing.

When the answer was yes, Beck remembers Mitchell "slammed his fist on the desk and said, 'All of the other members are going to be mad at me, because now they're going to have to redo their financial disclosure statements.'" But in Beck's experience, "It's little things that get members in trouble; sometimes it's the silliest of things." Usually, "he was very easygoing," she said. "He'd get angry, but he wasn't a screamer, and expressed his points very well."

Then there was Anita Jensen. At times, it took another female staffer to keep her within bounds. Kelly Horwitz, who started in the mailroom—"I was extra good with the autopen," the device used for Mitchell's facsimile signature—was one assigned to keep up with Jensen's extraordinary production, and eventually wrote speeches herself. "I joke that my career has been one in which I've always worked with amazing, highly talented, demanding women that no one else can work with," she said. Susan Longley detected another strain in Jensen's personality, however. "Beneath that occasional gruffness, there was a very dear soul who was sensitive. . . . She could tell from a distance" if something was wrong. On one particularly difficult day, Longley sought refuge in the Senate cafeteria, where Jensen approached her and said, "I'm here. What's the matter?"

There were more traditional opportunities, too. Almost on a lark, Horwitz decided to compete for the title of Cherry Blossom Princess for the Maine State Society in Washington. "This is about the furthest thing removed from what I normally do," she said. "I don't know what possessed me." She was selected, attended a week of "fashion shows and lunches" with the other state contestants, and then—when a "wheel of fortune" was spun, found herself the national designee for cherry blossom festivals in Japan. She ran into Mitchell, then majority leader, at the Russell Office Building after a parade, and he paused in an interview to say to the reporter, "I think Kelly got more press than I did this week."

Jeff Porter, who was frequently Mitchell's driver in Maine, married a Mitchell staffer he met while in Washington, and says that in many Mitchell offices, women were a distinct majority. He joked that "They needed a male around somewhere; I was the token. Among his most senior staffers, there were always more women than men, and that's unusual."

MITCHELL WAS FAR MORE ATTENTIVE TO STAFF than Muskie, but never welcomed the familiarity that had staff calling Bill Cohen by his first name. Bob Carolla saw that Gayle Cory called him George "when she was really mad at him," but otherwise, "She kept the distance from and respect of the senator. We never called him George; it was always 'Senator.'" Steve Hart, a legislative assistant hired in 1983, noticed that in Maine, people often used Mitchell's first name, and—after working on 1982 campaigns for Phil Merrill and John Kerry—carried the practice to Washington. Charlene Sturbitts took him aside and said, "We don't refer to him as George."

Some staff members were in awe of Mitchell's abilities to quickly analyze memos, documents, and floor statements, and his uncanny recall of people and events. Jeff Porter said, "The only reason he needed staff is because he didn't have enough time in the day . . . because if it was driving the car to working the front desk or cutting clips, he'd do it better than anybody else." Carolla said Mitchell was patient with staff who provided memos that failed to get to the heart of an issue. "The problem is," Mitchell would say, "you're assuming a level of understanding that I do not have." Carolla said this actually meant, "You're being too complex; don't make this so complicated, just tell me the essence."

Steve Hart worked for Mitchell until he left the Senate, and saw how the staff resembled their boss. "Mitchell had a staff that did not have a real flair for the dramatic or the flamboyant—neither did he." They were "generally lower-key, had the ability to function under pressure, and I don't view our staff as hyper-partisan." Even during campaigns, Porter remembers that disagreements were kept in bounds. "What I miss about Mitchell's office is there was a core," he said. "We could fight like cats and dogs, we could be mad at each other, and at the end of the day, you're going out and having a beer. . . . Almost every night we'd end up going out together."

One prevailing opinion among those who knew Mitchell only in Washington is that he could be tight with a dollar. Salaries were, and still are, lower in Maine than in most Northeastern states, and Mitchell was well aware of how federal salaries compared. He also liked to have money left over, and it became a point of pride to turn back money to the Treasury. Unlike Muskie, at least until he became majority leader, Mitchell did not have the committee posts to allow him to shift payroll out of his personal office.

Lula Johnson, who worked on the floor staff and as an aide to Russell Long, was imbued with Senate traditions, including largesse. "I always called him cheap, he was always tight about money, and I was always asking him about it," she said. She told Mitchell, "I need a raise because I don't live in Maine. The cost of living may be less in Maine, but I live here." Yet she also admired him because "he was always surrounded with women who are very strong, and very sharp."

Anita Jensen thought Mitchell was not always as respectful as his reputation suggested. "He had a tendency sometimes to treat the staff as not being perhaps the brightest bulbs on the tree, and some of us took umbrage with that. . . . I don't think it crossed his mind that some of us felt moderately insulted. I certainly never told him that." Steve Hart, who'd grown up in Washington before moving to New England to work on political races, doesn't agree with the contention Mitchell was tightfisted. "I got what I thought were very fair increases in my salary," he said. When he looked at comparable jobs, "I didn't find a whole lot of people willing to pay me what he was paying me."

Mitchell's generosity was evident in other ways. When the staff took Donna Beck out to lunch to mark her retirement, Lauren Higgins, who grew up in Waterville and served on the personal staff, first assumed Mitchell would be too busy, but phoned anyway and was assured he would attend. When he arrived, people were considering how to cover the guest of honor's tab. When Higgins told him everyone was chipping in, he told her, "I just paid the whole bill."

There were exceptions to the salary scale. Jane O'Connor, who came from an Augusta political family, was in her twenties when she joined the Washington staff, and got closer to Mitchell than many. She had decided, amid the late 1980s real estate boom, to buy a condo instead of renting, then found the loan payments, along with student loan debt, more than she could handle, so she took a part-time job at a video store. One day, she noticed that a well-dressed woman renting videos had presented Mitchell's card. On Monday, Mitchell himself returned the videos and was stunned to find O'Connor behind the counter. "What are you doing here?" he asked. "Don't I pay enough?" After she said she was embarrassed, he dropped the subject, but later asked her, "How can I get you out of the movie business?" During a staff review of salaries, he intervened, and told her, "It's not what you asked for, but it's more than the staff was proposing." She quit "the movie business."

At times, the inevitable foul-ups of political life did get to Mitchell. Jeff Porter's future wife, Mary Federle, worked on scheduling and often made flight reservations. Though it was farther away than National Airport, Mitchell sometimes flew out of Dulles because the schedule was more convenient. One Friday afternoon, she booked a flight that regularly departed at 5:40, but had been shifted to 5:10. Mitchell missed the plane, and had to wait three hours. When Porter met him at the Portland Jetport, "He was still mad; he was mumbling under his breath. Of course, he had no idea that we were dating." Mitchell called Federle two days later, and she said, "If that's the only mistake I ever made, I would have been in good shape. He was very kind about it, but it was awful." Porter said, "Had it been the senator arranging that schedule, he would have triple-checked."

DURING THE EARLY YEARS, MITCHELL BEGAN developing what would become an important relationship with Democratic Leader Robert Byrd. Byrd succeeded Mike Mansfield as majority leader in 1977, and remained leader when Democrats were relegated to the minority in 1980. Elected to the House in 1952, Byrd was part of Muskie's Senate class of 1958. He served continuously in public office from 1947, when he joined the West Virginia House of Delegates at age thirty, until his death in 2010. Unlike Mitchell, the Senate was his entire life, and his fifty-one years there is a record, exceeding even Strom Thurmond, who died in office in 2003 at the age of one hundred. Byrd was the last senator to have joined the Ku Klux Klan, something he often said he regretted.

Mitchell and Byrd came from strikingly different political traditions, but had points in common. When Mitchell was appointed in 1980, Byrd had already served ten years in leadership. He had defeated Ted Kennedy for majority whip in 1970, after Kennedy's unimpressive performance in his first two years. Byrd became known as the best whip the Democrats ever had, but his performance as leader received less glowing reviews. A senator of the old school, he had little feel for the increasing public scrutiny of Congress after Watergate, and he long resisted televising sessions and hearings; the Senate finally did so only in 1986.

One common interest was history. Byrd's two-volume history of the Senate, published in 1989 to mark the two hundredth anniversary of Congress, began in 1980 as a lengthy series of lectures delivered on the floor. Mitchell, though he never pursued his graduate degree, has been attentive to historical writing throughout his career. Historical analyses, some quite detailed, have played a part in all of his five books. Anita Jensen says Mitchell asked her about Byrd's orations, some two hours or more, which, like most Senate speeches, were often delivered to a nearly empty chamber. She suggested he write Byrd an appreciative note. While Mitchell at first demurred, when he did so he received a gratifying response.

Byrd kept his own counsel, but other senators noticed a growing regard for the junior senator from Maine. It undoubtedly played a part in Mitchell's appointment to the Finance Committee, and his designation as the ranking minority member on the environmental subcommittee of EPW—a decision that would have fateful consequences when Mitchell succeeded Byrd.

Patrick Griffin, who'd served on the Senate Budget Committee staff, joined Byrd's leadership office in 1981, and saw the relationship developing. "Senator Byrd took a liking to him early on," he said. "He thought he was a very bright, very impressive guy. He thought maybe he had leadership capabilities, and said so on several occasions to me. Byrd wanted that relationship." Griffin was less impressed initially. Mitchell, he said, "was very cautious, and I didn't see what Byrd saw. I just thought he was a pretty cool guy, funny, laughed easily."

There's no doubt Mitchell learned what not to do with the leader, following Ed Muskie's disastrous introduction to Lyndon Johnson. Mitchell was respectful, deferential, and spent time listening to Byrd and getting to know him before offering opinions. He also noted the Senate's tradition of strict seniority, which favored Southern senators who often served longer than anyone else. Jim Case, Mitchell's first chief of staff, said, "The Southern Democratic senators still held a lot of power, the old guard in the Senate, which has now been forgotten, but they were there then—Senator Stennis, Senator McClellan of Mississippi and Alabama."

Along with Byrd, committee chairmen held a weekly prayer breakfast, "and Senator Mitchell quickly decided that he wanted to attend," Case said. "I was a little surprised, but then this was a way for him to share values with people, let them know what his values were, and to develop relationships on a personal level." The Protestants were willing to welcome a Catholic. The prayer breakfasts were unusual because there was no agenda, no staff attended, and no one interrupted. Ten years later, Harris Wofford of Pennsylvania, another appointed Democratic senator who then won election, discovered the prayer breakfast was a good way to meet Republicans; by that time, the partisan shift in the South that Lyndon Johnson predicted had come to pass. "Cocktail parties you just buzz and it isn't a real conversation," Wofford said. "You don't really get to know people, and at committee meetings you're on opposite sides and arguing against each other." Mike Mansfield attended the prayer breakfast until shortly before he died. By that time, Mitchell was majority leader and made only occasional appearances, but kept it on his calendar.

DAVID JOHNSON HAD DECIDED IT WAS TIME for a new job. By 1984 he had been Mitchell's chief of staff for more than three years—a long time by Senate standards—and wanted something a little less hectic. He went to work for the Pharmaceutical Manufacturing Association, then just a sliver of what became the "Big Pharma" colossus.

The new chief was Rich Arenberg, who started on Paul Tsongas's 1974 congressional campaign in Massachusetts when Tsongas beat an incumbent, and joined his staff. Tsongas then defeated incumbent Republican senator Edward Brooke in 1978, the first black senator elected since Reconstruction. In late 1983, Tsongas was diagnosed with cancer and decided not to seek reelection—though after a 1986 bone marrow transplant, he returned to politics and won the 1992 New Hampshire presidential primary. Arenberg was available, and as an experienced chief of staff was a sound choice for a senator with leadership aspirations.

"I knew these jobs open and close very quickly," Arenberg said, and asked Tsongas to approach Mitchell, which he did. That Tsongas was a staunch liberal and fellow New Englander may have influenced Mitchell's decision, but he took his time. The first discussions were in February 1984, but Arenberg wasn't hired until October. "It was quite a considerable process, and I hadn't anticipated it would be like that," Arenberg said. "But it really foreshadowed something I really respect about Senator Mitchell, the very careful, thoughtful way he approaches problem-solving and decision-making."

Arenberg, later Senator Carl Levin's legislative director, said all three senators were different. Tsongas "was visceral, he was more candid than not only any political person, but any person I've known." Tsongas changed his mind frequently, "and he was very comfortable with that," Arenberg said. Mitchell was more measured. "I'm not a lawyer, but they refer to it as *stare decisis*—the idea that decisions are built on prior decisions, and you don't . . . like to turn the ship around once it was headed in a given direction. For that reason, he was very careful about what direction he wanted to go in."

The first decision Arenberg brought to Mitchell involved a memo where he'd outlined options and made a recommendation. He was taken aback when Mitchell said, "Why do I have to decide this now?" Tsongas, who "shot from the hip," never would have done that, Arenberg said. "I never forgot that first lesson," he said. "It was the more judicial notion that decisions ripen . . . and I came to value that, to take your time making a decision and to carefully weigh the factors and gather the facts. . . . It's clearly served George Mitchell well. . . . Even after he'd left the Senate, he's been able to bring that process to bear on very difficult questions and arrive at solutions in situations that are very trying."

SHORTLY AFTER ARENBERG CAME ABOARD IN 1984, Ronald Reagan was reelected easily, but his coattails were short. Democrats lost sixteen seats in the House but picked up two in the Senate, leaving Bob Dole only a 53–47 margin. On the Democratic side, Byrd was deciding who would chair the Democratic Senatorial Campaign Committee (DSCC), a bigger and more important job than in Muskie's day. After six years with Wendell Ford, Lloyd Bentsen of Texas had taken over in 1982 and demonstrated his fund-raising prowess by dramatically increasing totals invested in key races, raising $11 million. As Finance Committee chairman, he was well placed to approach large donors. While on the House side, Jim Wright and his lieutenant, Tony Coelho, were both soon to be forced out by ethics violations, Bentsen kept the lines clearer. His achievement in beating back the Reagan tide did not go unnoticed, but he wasn't interested in serving longer.

Bennett Johnston of Louisiana, who'd held the DSCC post from 1976–1977, thought the job should be his, and expected Byrd, a fellow Southerner, to appoint him. Byrd had other notions. Johnston, while a capable legislator, had clashed with Byrd on relatively minor issues, and for someone like Byrd, even small slights could add up. Mitchell, in his first years on Finance, had impressed Bentsen, and since Bentsen had compiled a sterling record at the DSCC, his opinion had weight. Byrd also saw that Mitchell gave a good account of himself on television. For someone who'd be responsible for campaigning in every state where a Democrat was on the ballot, this was another plus. Shortly after the election, Byrd announced Mitchell was his choice. Jim Sasser, who'd known Mitchell since they'd served on the DNC, and became a Senate ally, said he was surprised, "and I was a little alarmed about it, or maybe apprehensive. I knew that Bennett Johnston had prodigious fund-raising capabilities, and I worried that George Mitchell, coming from a rather sparsely populated state like Maine, I worried about his ability to raise the necessary funds."

Mitchell's first decision was hiring an executive director for the thirty-member staff, and he had only one candidate in mind. David Johnson, who'd worked only a few months for the Pharmaceutical Manufacturers, remembers that Mitchell got right to the point. Johnson said he was interested, but needed time to consider. Mitchell told him to take his time, "But when you give me your answer, I want it to be yes." It was.

For the first time in his Senate career, Mitchell wasn't able to get back to Maine every weekend. He traveled the country, first recruiting candidates, then campaigning for those who volunteered or whom he managed to convince. Mitchell, Johnson said, was "driven by his sense of responsibility to his colleagues," and he pushed himself as hard as during the 1982 race. For someone claiming to intensely dislike fund-raising, the results were remarkable. He managed to surpass Bentsen's record, taking in nearly $13 million. Mitchell typically notes that this was "far less than the Republicans." This was true, but beside the point. With the decline of unions and the rise of business lobbying, Republicans regularly surpassed Democrats by a huge margin. Mitchell didn't catch up to the Republicans, but he narrowed the gap. And with their get-out-the-vote strengths, Senate Democrats were positioned to campaign on better terms.

Audrey Sheppard, the DSCC political director, had been hired after the 1980 debacle and stayed on to work for Mitchell. She credited Alan Cranston for realizing the fund-raising budget could be far more ambitious than in the late 1970s, when post-Watergate restrictions limited party contributions. For the DSCC, that was just $17,540 per candidate, but Cranston, she said, "knew there was this other part of the law that we could give up to four cents per eligible voter, and that came to something like $87,500 in the tiniest states, and $1 million plus in the largest states." Though Cranston never chaired the DSCC, he became the principal fund-raiser for Wendell Ford's Leadership Circle, seeking donations starting at $15,000. Cranston, Sheppard said, "receded" after Bentsen took over. Mitchell made sure Bentsen became Leadership Circle chair.

Sheppard appreciated Mitchell's skills. "We've all worked for people who really want to micromanage the staff, and others who just knew that you knew what you were doing . . . and he really let us lead this effort, and didn't make deals where we would find out a lot of money was going to somebody for the wrong reasons." Mitchell kept most of the existing staff, though with Johnson firmly in charge.

Diane Dewhirst was traveling in Europe when she heard that Johnson wanted to talk to her; she'd been recommended by Sheppard. Mitchell had noticed that Tony Coelho, on the House side, had hired a full spectrum of staff, including technology managers and communications people, and Dewhirst seemed to have the right attitude, even though she'd never been a communications director. Reagan was at the peak of his popularity and, Dewhirst said, "We were in dire straits." But Mitchell analyzed the races to determine which ones were worth investment, while she made up a list of the most influential reporters. "We'd have Jules Witcover come in and have a tuna sandwich with the Senator," she said. "And the three of us would sit at this little table in his office, and he'd talk some middle-class tax-cut stuff that was going on in the Finance Committee, but he'd also just kind of talk. And sometimes we'd get an article and sometimes we wouldn't, but it was a down payment. And we did that with twenty-five reporters."

Jim Sasser worked on candidate recruitment along with Bill Bradley and Max Baucus, but said, "We were sort of spear carriers; he was the person who really did the work and got the job done." Mitchell's confidential memo to Byrd on December 17 listed his choices for various DSCC jobs. He urged that Bentsen stay on, and recommended new members, including Bradley, Johnston, and Baucus. The others were a mix of regional and philosophical shades, and included Lawton Chiles of Florida, Gary Hart of Colorado, Sam Nunn of Georgia, Don Riegle of Michigan, and Paul Simon of Illinois. He had specific slots in mind—the Leadership Circle for Bentsen, Johnston for business, and Riegle for labor.

Without exactly giving up on any of the thirty-four races at stake, Mitchell looked for markers on where to invest. "In some states, where there was a strong and entrenched Republican, or the state had a history of voting Republican, we often didn't have many candidates and it was an aggressive search effort," Mitchell said. "In other states, where Democrats had a good chance, there were many, many candidates, and it was trying to figure out who might be the strongest and how could we appropriately help them. And then a third category, places where good candidates may be thinking about running, but aren't certain how much help they'll get, and spending time with them, describing what we could or would try to do, encouraging them and reassuring them there would be help in a variety of ways, not just financial support."

Despite the towering political figure of Ronald Reagan, there were advantages for Democrats not immediately apparent. Many Republicans up for reelection were first-termers who'd been swept in with Reagan in 1980, and were now facing voters without the president on the ballot. There was also the history that the party of two-term presidents loses seats in the second midterm election. Some Democratic Senate candidates were obvious. Tom Daschle of South Dakota, a popular congressman elected statewide, ran against James Abdnor, a Republican farmer without previous experience when he ousted George McGovern in 1980.

Mitchell was also happy to convince Governor Bob Graham, who was term-limited, to enter the race in Florida, where he was matched against Republican Paula Hawkins. It was a dinner conversation with, of all people, former Senate Majority Leader Howard Baker, a Republican who'd retired in 1984, that prompted Graham to run. Graham had told Baker he felt Congress was dysfunctional, but Baker responded that, "There were some new people who had come into the Senate, and George Mitchell was one, who were going to begin to change the culture of the institution, and that it would be an exciting place to serve." After Graham won by a comfortable margin, he recalls that Baker was "a little bit reticent" in acknowledging his advice, particularly with Republicans.

Where there were multiple Democrats, the DSCC had to hold back, since it couldn't favor one candidate over another, and investing in all of them wasn't feasible. That was the case in Maryland, where seven Democrats jumped in to succeed retiring Republican Charles Mathias. Barbara Mikulski, years after her work for the DNC, had served ten years in Congress but was considered a long shot against Governor Howard Hughes and Congressman Michael Barnes. Barnes warned that if Mikulski won the primary, she'd be easy pickings for Linda Chavez, the telegenic Republican. *People* magazine described Mikulski as "frumpy, loud and sometimes rude," while calling Chavez "well tailored, well spoken and well connected." Mikulski won the September primary, but found she was out of cash. "It was the first woman-on-woman race, and I needed a breather to add money," she said. "Senator Mitchell came in like the cavalry, and gave me $100,000, which enabled me to go right on TV in the Washington suburbs, where I was not well known, and had been Michael Barnes's primary base."

Mikulski easily defeated Chavez, and became the first Democratic woman elected to the Senate. Before long, she had plenty of company. But for her, the most memorable moment came during a fund-raiser Mitchell attended, where she convinced him to dance with her. "Senator Mitchell is a man of many talents, and he's swift on his feet, but one would not think of him as dancing with the stars," she said. When she held out her hand, he said, "Like in everything else you lead and I'll follow," which broke up the crowd. "He was there for his members," she said. "He campaigned for us, he believed in us, and he was really a good sport."

The coup for Mitchell's efforts, though, was the candidacy of Kent Conrad in North Dakota. Conrad would seem to have had no chance. He held the elected position of state tax commissioner, but was going up against a seemingly impregnable Republican incumbent in Mark Andrews, who'd also served eighteen years in the House, and was seeking a second Senate term.

Conrad had met Mitchell during the 1972 Muskie campaign, and told himself then, "This is a highly competent person." When they got together to consider the 1986 race, Conrad found, "You're dealing with someone who is very calm and analytical. He's always thought through not only the next move but the move after that, and the move after that, and so I went over with him my campaign plan and strategy."

Conrad was thirty points behind, and said, "I had no money, my opponent had a million dollars in the bank, and had gotten over 70 percent in the last election." After hearing his pitch, Mitchell "instantly recognized there was a possibility." The same day, Mitchell pledged to raise the maximum amount the DSCC could spend. "It really formed the foundation of my campaign," Conrad said, "and gave me credibility beyond the borders of North Dakota, and played a major role in my being able to squeak out . . . the greatest political upset in the history of my state." Then, and later, Conrad admired Mitchell's "ability to see beyond the conventional, inside-the-Beltway thinking."

On the Republican side, Alan Simpson of Wyoming, majority whip and a noted wit, saw the Conrad–Andrews race as the keystone to the Democrats' Senate victory. "It was the ultimate triumph within the triumph," he said, "that you have screwed thine enemy and won seats so that all of you could get back in the majority and chair committees and have budgets and power and fame again, instead of sitting in the back row and sucking canal water."

Conrad wouldn't have won without DSCC support, but sometimes senators managed to win without the party's help. One was Dennis DeConcini, elected from Arizona in 1976 at a time when the state was already solidly Republican and Bennett Johnston was DSCC chair. "They didn't give me hardly any money because they didn't think I had a chance," DeConcini said. "But when I came here, nobody could have been nicer than Bennett Johnson, and he apologized, kiddingly. He said, 'God, I didn't think you were going to win, or I would have dumped some money in there.'"

The sheer unexpectedness of the victory in November enhanced Mitchell's reputation among his peers, which had already been strengthened by his comeback win in 1982. Bob Dole had hoped to hold the majority, perhaps with the help of Vice President George Bush as the deciding vote, but instead was on the short end of a 55–45 split as Democrats gained eight seats. Dole assumed the minority leader role, where he remained throughout his later partnership with Mitchell.

Sometimes, parties win back a majority through open seats, and Democrats did pick up two, in Maryland and in Nevada, where Harry Reid won a seat previously held by Republican Paul Laxalt. But the 1986 victory was mostly achieved the hard way, by defeating incumbents, seven in all. In addition to Conrad and Daschle in the Dakotas, and Bob Graham in Florida, Democrats beat incumbents in Washington, Alabama, Georgia, and North Carolina. They held open seats in Colorado, where Tim Wirth succeeded Gary Hart, and in Louisiana, where John Breaux followed Russell Long. The only open seat Democrats lost was in Missouri, where Kit Bond defeated Harriet Woods to succeed Tom Eagleton. The Senate success also contrasted with House races, where the partisan division was almost unchanged; Democrats gained just two seats.

DeConcini had no doubt who was responsible, saying of Mitchell, "Everybody gave him credit for it. . . . When we won, everybody said George Mitchell was the guy, and nobody disputed that, not even Bob Byrd." Chuck Robb, who was elected to the Senate in 1988 after serving as Virginia governor, didn't like to go to fund-raisers because, he said, "I couldn't wax enthusiastic for someone I didn't believe in." He was happier when Mitchell was there. "I would talk a little bit, and introduce George, and George was the principal draw. I love introducing him because he was the real thing." Beyond fund-raising, Robb saw Mitchell growing as a leader. "He has all of the tactical skills, but he doesn't throw them in your face. That's the difference between leadership and simply being in charge."

12

THE SENATOR
AND THE COLONEL

The Iran-Contra scandal began quietly, much like Watergate, with a news
story about a plane being shot down on October 5, 1986, in Nicaragua.
The pilot, Eugene Hasenfus, was captured by Sandinista soldiers, part of the
army led by Nicaragua's ruler, Daniel Ortega. Ortega, a dabbler in Marxist
ideology and ally of Fidel Castro, was seen as a threat by the Reagan administration, which was supporting—some say organizing—the Contra rebels fighting
the Sandinista regime. It turned out that Hasenfus was running supplies to the
Contras, and the former US marine was being paid with American money—an
apparent violation of the Boland Amendment that Congress had enacted in
1984.

In a speech given at Boston University Law School in 1989, George Mitchell explained what happened next. "Three years ago this month, an airplane
piloted by Eugene Hasenfus was shot down over Central America. With that
incident, the Iran-Contra scandal began to unravel. Questions about Hasenfus
and his ties to our government were followed by a published account in a Mid-
eastern newspaper of American officials visiting the Ayatollah Khomeini of Iran,
carrying a cake in the shape of a key and a Bible. Most Americans found those
accounts literally unbelievable." But they turned out to be true. "In the following weeks, we learned that our government had sought to secretly sell weapons
to Iran in exchange for our hostages while calling publicly for international
refusal to bargain for hostages. We learned that the money from those weapons
went into a Swiss bank account controlled by Americans, one a staff member of
the National Security Council in the White House, the other a retired military
officer." Though he didn't name him here, Mitchell included Oliver North

in this description, the key figure in subsequent congressional investigations. Mitchell concludes, "We learned that some of the money was given to the Contra forces fighting the Nicaraguan government, although Congress had refused to finance those forces."

That the whole Iran-Contra affair was so seemingly unbelievable, ironically, hampered Congress's ability to enact reforms aimed at preventing its repetition. It was all too credible to most Americans that Richard Nixon maintained an "enemies list" and sought to discredit opposition politicians such as Ed Muskie. By contrast, Ronald Reagan's 1980 election victory over Jimmy Carter was achieved in large part because of Carter's perceived ineptitude concerning the American Embassy hostages, and Reagan's vow never to negotiate with Tehran. Its secret reversal seemed out of character. The tangled skein of testimony to a joint Senate-House investigation added to the sense that Iran-Contra was a perplexing, confusing mess. Yet the high drama of another confrontation between a president and Congress through televised hearings did capture the nation's attention, and Maine figures again played a large part in the proceedings.

The Tower Commission convened by President Reagan and chaired by Senator John Tower, with Ed Muskie also serving, was the first to report. It found that, indeed, the administration had sent arms to the Ayatollah in response to Reagan's heartfelt concern over several high-profile Americans, including a CIA station chief and an administrator at the American University in Beirut, who had been taken captive by shadowy terrorist groups. The commission also found that profits from the arms transactions—the Iranians were charged far more than the weapons were worth—were diverted to covert aid benefiting the Contras.

The Senate Intelligence Committee was also briefed on Iran-Contra, but the testimony was classified, and their report limited. Senator Bill Bradley, who served on the intelligence panel, later said there was "very clear evidence of Reagan's involvement," and that the subsequent investigating committee hearings "were an anticlimax, because in some ways the committee refused, or did not take as aggressive action as it could have." Patrick Griffin, from the majority leader staff, said, "They could have taken Reagan down and I believe they chose not to."

Those decisions could be traced, in part, to the Senate chair of the select committee, Daniel Inouye of Hawaii, a World War II hero who became Byrd's choice, even though he initially considered naming George Mitchell. Most of *Men of Zeal*, the account of the hearings Mitchell co-wrote with Bill Cohen, is presented jointly, but in a section in Mitchell's voice, he wrote that Byrd "was concerned that appointing me as chairman might appear partisan," because Mitchell had just served as DSCC chair. "While I would have liked to be chairman, I recognized it made sense to appoint Inouye," he said, citing Inouye's service on the Watergate investigation, and "a reputation for fairness and a lack of partisanship." Mitchell then added, loyally, "He went on to justify Byrd's decision by doing a very good job in a difficult situation." Byrd then made Mitchell the second-ranking Democrat. "As I drove to the Capitol," Mitchell said, "I thought that this appointment would change my life, for better or worse." Then he added, cryptically, "It did."

Naming the select panel did not come without controversy. Byrd and Bob Dole both decided Congress needed to investigate, but not all Republicans agreed. David Durenberger of Minnesota, a moderate who often worked with Democrats, served on the Intelligence Committee with Bradley, and tried to talk Dole out of it. "Byrd conned Dole into this whole Iran-Contra committee," he said. "The important thing is that Reagan learned a lesson, that future presidents learn a lesson. . . . You can't do this in public, it isn't going to work."

Reagan addressed the nation in November, and, after the Tower Commission reported, spoke again on March 4, 1987. "A few months ago I told the American people I did not trade arms for hostages," Reagan said. "My heart and my best intentions still tell me that's true, but the facts and the evidence tell me it is not."

The arms deal itself was an apparent violation of the Arms Export Control Act of 1976, which prohibits arms sales to nations designated as sponsors of terrorist acts; the Reagan administration had designated Iran under the act in 1984. Byrd chose Mitchell to give the Democratic response to Reagan's speech. Mitchell said it was not an auspicious debut. "A dispute broke out among some of the technical staff people about whether I should rely exclusively on the teleprompter or whether I should have a written text in front of me. Apparently the teleprompter had malfunctioned." Out of what Mitchell termed "an excess of caution," he was given the text, but later was told "people could hear the papers shuffling. It wasn't too effective." Mitchell also hadn't seen the president's speech beforehand, so his remarks were speculative rather than responsive.

The Senate voted in January 1987 to form a select committee, and the House followed suit. The two committees were later merged, which provided awkward moments; the procedure hasn't been repeated since. The first order of business was to name and staff the two committees. Improbably, both Maine senators were picked. Byrd, though naming Inouye chair, insisted Mitchell serve. Bill Cohen was asked because Byrd had already named David Boren, chairman of the Intelligence Committee, and Dole believed Cohen, as vice chair, should be there as Boren's counterpart. The partnership between the two Maine senators led not only to *Men of Zeal*—the best contemporary account of the Iran-Contra hearings—but to a deepening relationship that endured beyond their Senate years.

After the chairman, the most important selection was vice chair. The deal Byrd and Dole worked out included this important role for the top Republican. Dole chose Warren Rudman of New Hampshire. Mitchell already knew him well. Rudman had been state attorney general before being elected to the Senate, and was a skilled prosecutor and interrogator. He was irreverent about party loyalties, and retired after serving two terms, in 1992. Rudman counted as a major achievement that he helped convince George H. W. Bush to name a New Hampshire protégé, David Souter, as his first nominee to the Supreme Court.

Rudman had a reputation for calling things as he saw them. When he joined a former Mitchell staffer on a flight following the Supreme Court's 2000 decision in *Bush v. Gore*, ensuring Bush would become president, he said, "Your guy got screwed." Rudman said he didn't seek the Iran-Contra assignment. "I got a call from Bob Dole, who said, 'You're going to be the top Republican on the committee. I'm jumping you over a lot of other people because you've got great experience.'" Rudman said he and Mitchell worked together. "We discussed witnesses' testimony or staff virtually on a daily basis," he said.

On the House side, Lee Hamilton, an Indiana Democrat, chaired the select committee, while Dick Cheney of Wyoming, formerly Gerald Ford's White House chief of staff, was the ranking Republican.

RICH ARENBERG HEADED MITCHELL'S STAFF TEAM. In appreciation of Mitchell's work at the DSCC, Robert Byrd named him to a largely ceremonial post that, nonetheless, put Mitchell in the ranks of Senate leadership. The Senate's president pro tempore is the only member, other than the vice president, named in the Constitution, and is third in line to the presidency, after the vice president and House speaker. By tradition, the post is held by the senior member of the majority party. When Hubert Humphrey returned to the Senate after serving as vice president, Mike Mansfield created the post of deputy president pro tem. Byrd revived it for Mitchell. Arenberg then decided to staff the Mitchell leadership office. He was replaced in the Senate office by Martha Pope, who had started on the EPW Committee, and was serving as Mitchell's legislative director.

The Iran-Contra hearings were exactly the kind of challenge Arenberg was hoping to find. When Attorney General Ed Meese made the first report on what soon became "Iran-Contra," Arenberg saw the possibilities. He told Mitchell, "There are probably six or seven Senate committees that have jurisdiction here . . . and I have the feeling this is going to wind up being the perfect situation for a select committee." Because of Mitchell's service as a federal judge, Arenberg thought he'd be "perfect" as chair. Did Mitchell want him to approach Byrd's staff? It was characteristic of Mitchell, Arenberg said, that while he grasped the logic, "He wasn't willing to be . . . as presumptuous as I was willing to be in approaching the leader." What Mitchell did tell Byrd was that, if there was a committee, he wanted to be on it.

For those who later doubted the need, after the Tower Commission and the Senate Intelligence Committee inquiries, and the subsequent independent counsel investigation, Arenberg emphasizes that, while Reagan recovered his standing with the public before leaving office, that wasn't clear then. "It's easy to forget how hamstrung the Reagan administration was at the time, with the scandal exploding all around them. . . . It was very important for the Congress to get the facts out and find out exactly what had happened."

Each senator on the committee also picked an attorney to be part of the general staff. Mitchell chose Jamie Kaplan, partner in a Washington law firm, whom he'd known since he was US Attorney. Kaplan worked closely with Tim Woodcock, Cohen's choice, who later became mayor of Bangor; Kaplan and Woodcock are still friends today.

Kaplan had never been to Maine before becoming a law clerk for Judge Gignoux. He met Mitchell at the Portland courthouse, "and George was kind enough to take me under his wing," even helping him get a cable TV hookup. Kaplan became a Mitchell tennis partner, and they continued to play together in Washington. He enjoyed working with the lawyers appointed by all the senators, both Democrats and Republicans, though "George received priority treatment."

Soon after his appointment, Kaplan noticed things had changed from the days when he and Mitchell had an easy, bantering relationship. He got a late-night call at home from Mitchell, who said, "Jamie, this is the Senator." When Kaplan replied "Which senator?" Mitchell became "a little flustered and, frankly, ticked off." At the Capitol, "He'd talk to me, looking straight forward, and I'd say something like, 'George, I'm over here.' It wasn't like we could walk through the halls of the Senate as equals. That was how members dealt with staff, and I had become staff."

In initial negotiations, Mitchell said some Republicans wanted the hearings to last only two weeks—clearly impossible, given the scope of the inquiry—but even the three months of approved hearings provided constraints. The preliminaries took longer than expected, and when the hearings opened on May 5, there had already been maneuvering behind the scenes. One critical call was Inouye's decision to provide immunity to both Lieutenant Colonel Oliver North, the former marine at the heart of the investigation, and Admiral John Poindexter, the National Security Advisor.

Kaplan wasn't privy to those talks, but got the distinct impression Mitchell did not agree. Mitchell later observed that North was eager to tell his story, and that immunity, or the lack of it, wouldn't likely have altered his testimony. The numerous grants of immunity complicated the task of Lawrence Walsh, the special prosecutor who later brought criminal charges, because he had to show that evidence did not derive from the congressional testimony. Even in cases where he did win convictions, several were reversed on appeal. It was the beginning of what, at least to some Senate Democrats observing the proceedings, was an unimpressive performance from Inouye.

The hearings started slowly. Investigators wanted to build a record of what had happened, and concentrated first on the Contra connection because witnesses were more available, even though the arms-for-hostages sales were the focus of public concern, and foreign policy significance. Reagan officials were still negotiating terms, and the committee's time was fast disappearing. In *Men of Zeal*, Cohen and Mitchell detail why the Contra connection was a sideshow, and a confusing one. While the administration presented the Sandinistas as a mortal threat, this was hard to take seriously, given the size and poverty of Nicaragua. And Congress had hardly been consistent on military aid. After several iterations of the Boland Amendment, at the time of the hearings, Congress had approved arms sales. This gave administration supporters like Dick Cheney room to criticize Congress.

One aspect of the Contra testimony that greatly concerned Cohen and Mitchell was "the Enterprise," a free-floating, open-ended, covert-action operation that North and others were running from the White House basement. The profits from arms sales, repeated in other venues, would finance new ventures the president would know little about, and which would be secret even from the NSA and CIA. Because their cover was blown when the cargo plane went down, the conspirators never expanded their operations, but these secret, unaccountable covert activities were what Mitchell later argued was the central danger. Jamie Kaplan called the Enterprise "a remarkable delegation of authority to people who had no relationship or accountability to the US government running around with missiles and other weaponry."

There was also an "epidemic of amnesia" Kaplan observed from early witnesses, which he said "was as prevalent as any Ebola outbreak you could imagine." The committee heard, over and over, "I don't think, I'm not sure, I don't recall." Even those who'd chatted freely with reporters somehow found it difficult to remember things under oath. Unlike Watergate, where stonewalling was largely confined to keeping congressional committees from seeing documents and hearing tapes, the Iran-Contra witnesses kept the select committee at a distance from the facts.

Mitchell kept focusing on the real and harmful effects of the secret initiatives that he believed had not only undermined American credibility, but also thwarted US policy. In an op-ed published during the hearings, Mitchell pointed to something that was often missed: The illegal arms sales to Iran had a material effect on the outcome of the Iran-Iraq war that had been raging for nearly a decade. It included an almost unimaginable loss of life.

In the early years, Iraq had advanced into Iran's territory, but, armed with bartered American weapons, Iran was turning the tide. Mitchell wrote that, "In December [1986], Iran launched the first of a series of mass attacks in the vital sector at the head of the [Persian] Gulf. These attacks have brought its forces within shooting range of Kuwait, which harbors petroleum reserves larger than either Iran or Iraq." He said the arms-for-hostages deals had given Iran 2,008 TOW missiles, which he describes as "an extremely efficient and portable anti-tank weapon." Made by Raytheon, and still available today, TOW stands for "tube-launched, optically tracked, wireless-guided." The TOWs allowed Iran's "human wave" attacks to succeed after previously being thwarted by Iraqi tanks.

The new parts for Iran's Hawk missiles were perhaps even more damaging and, Mitchell said, "enabled Iran to reactivate . . . missiles the U.S. had supplied to the previous regime but which had deteriorated with age and poor maintenance." Such clarity was hard to maintain in hearings that featured a largely uncooperative cast of characters much larger than Watergate.

IT WAS THE APPEARANCE OF OLIVER NORTH, however, that threatened to turn a frustrating inquiry into a full-fledged disaster. In his first days of testimony, North had his questioners on the defensive, and established the aura of a military hero before Congress in a way not seen since Douglas MacArthur gave a riveting speech after being dismissed as Korean War commander by Harry Truman. *Men of Zeal* details the reasons nearly everything went wrong.

First was the selection of the chief Senate counsel, Arthur Liman, as recommended by Mitchell and Alabama Democrat Howell Heflin. The *Washington Post* called him "perhaps the top trial lawyer in New York, and one of the best securities and white-collar crime lawyers in the country." Liman had a distinguished legal pedigree, experience as both prosecutor and defense attorney, and "his penetrating intelligence was apparent after just a few minutes of discussion," Cohen and Mitchell said. But "No one ever paused to consider how Liman might project on television or how the American public might react to an aggressive New York lawyer."

The setting also worked in North's favor once he began ignoring questions and speaking repeatedly about his commitment to his country. Trying to accommodate twenty-six members of the House and Senate, and their staffs, in the

Russell Office Building's caucus room wasn't easy. The architect of the Capitol came up with a two-tiered seating arrangement that enabled the committee to be close to the witnesses, but also, on television screens, loom over them. *Men of Zeal* reports, "We had transformed the hearing room into a mini-coliseum, and we appeared as the equivalent of Roman potentates, turning thumbs up or thumbs down on the stoic Christians."

North would have made an impression in any setting, however. Cohen said recently that he had no inkling of what to expect, based on the committee's private sessions with North and his attorney, Brendan Sullivan. "He was soft-spoken, he was polite. He didn't make any unreasonable demands," Cohen said. That all changed, though, just before North was to appear in public. Sullivan presented a long list of demands. North would testify for no more than three days. He'd turn over documents only for a limited period. He could not be re-called. If the demands weren't met, Sullivan said, North would refuse to testify.

Mitchell, with two other Democratic senators, Howell Heflin and Paul Sarbanes, wanted to call North's bluff. In *Men of Zeal*, Mitchell writes, "I believed that Sullivan was bluffing and that he very much wanted North to testify publicly as long as he had immunity. It seemed to me that North's best hope of avoiding criminal conviction was to testify and then to get the criminal charges dismissed on the grounds that the prosecution . . . had been compromised."

Mitchell said later that he wonders what might have happened had he pushed the matter to a vote, but he didn't. Some members without Mitchell's courtroom experience were ready to meet all the demands, and Inouye and Rudman negotiated an agreement that met most of them. Cohen and Mitchell observed, "The committee's letter was a fig leaf to cover the embarrassment of what had happened. . . . Oliver North and the committee had gone eyeball to eyeball, and the committee had blinked."

When North appeared, Mitchell was impressed. "The first thing I noticed was the uniform. Then the medals: a chest full of them. His handshake was tight, even hard, as though he was trying to make a point. His eyes were clear, his gaze was firm, his smile quick. Before he said a word, I knew Oliver North would be a very tough witness." Cohen said, "The uniform means a lot," and decided questioning North might be difficult. "It was dangerous. We all sensed it." Yet under military protocol, North, who had resigned from the Marine Corps, shouldn't have been wearing the uniform at all.

Chief House counsel John Nields was the first to question North, and, Kaplan said, "He was a very nice guy and a very, very good lawyer, and he thought he was going to kill Oliver North." Nields, however, "didn't antici-pate the extent of the difference in the forum. This was not a deposition or a cross-examination of witnesses, but a legal proceeding without any procedural constraints." Nields also provoked a hostile reaction from viewers when, impatient at North's evasiveness, he said, "You put some value, don't you, on the truth?"

It went downhill from there. Some Republicans lobbed softball questions that invited North to talk about himself and why he had done what he did, and there was no effective rebuttal, under the ground rules Sullivan demanded. Mitchell said of North, in his memoir, "He not only admitted that he lied; he boasted about it. He had to lie, he said, to save lives. But that too was a lie." This wasn't evident to most television viewers, however, whose numbers during North's testimony were far greater than those who'd watched Watergate unfold. There were some critical questions for North, but he evaded or ignored them. Those who tried to point out the inconsistencies in North's accounts got the same treatment as those who invited North to expound on his patriotism. Even evidence about the free installation of a private security system at North's home allowed him to indignantly attack those who questioned the need for it.

By then it was Friday afternoon, and George Mitchell was the next questioner. He'd prepared for the occasion, but now realized his prosecutorial brief might be equally ineffective. The misty-eyed North had captivated the viewing audience, and no one could break his rhythm. It was late, and Inouye and Hamilton recessed the hearing. Mitchell had the weekend to figure out what to do.

Mitchell and Kaplan talked briefly before Mitchell returned to Maine. Kaplan said, "I didn't know what he was going to do—it was one of the few times I wasn't sure how he was going to handle something." Kaplan figured Mitchell would be working long hours, but didn't expect he would need much from him. "You're a senator, I'm not," he remembers saying. "I have some thoughts, but I don't have this kind of experience." Still, he was surprised when he didn't hear anything. One call Mitchell did make was to Harold Pachios, which didn't surprise Kaplan. He said Pachios "was much more familiar with the political arena. He's very close to George and has wonderful judgment."

The conversation between the two wasn't recorded, but both have a strong sense of what was said. Mitchell said Pachios "made some very commonsense and helpful suggestions, guiding me in the direction of what I should take in my questioning." What they agreed on was that trying to get North to stop making speeches and answer specific questions wouldn't work. Mitchell would have to make a speech of his own. Pachios is still amazed Mitchell credited him with the idea, repeated it in *Men of Zeal*, and still refers to it in speeches. "I've never known that to happen," Pachios said. "In all my years following politics, participating in it, I have never known of an elected politician who was praised for doing something, and gave any credit, even one percent, to anybody else. It's unique, in my experience."

Mitchell canceled events on Saturday, but kept an appointment, with Cohen, to attend the launch of a guided-missile cruiser at Bath Iron Works. He figured he'd complete a first draft by Saturday night, then polish it on the flight back to Washington. North had been testifying for four days, and Sullivan no longer objected to extending his testimony. Mitchell decided he needed to take on North's contention that the American people "ought not to believe, as a consequence of these hearings, that this government cannot or should not conduct covert operations." Mitchell knew that no one had suggested banning covert activities, so he wanted to dramatize the point that it was not secret missions themselves that were the problem, but how they had escaped the government's control. As he listened to Pachios, though, he realized he had to be simpler and more direct. He recalls Pachios saying, "North said that you guys should vote aid for the Contras for love of God and country. That's outrageous. It's insulting. You can take that and turn it around."

THERE WAS A HEAT WAVE OUTSIDE THAT JULY Monday morning. In the caucus room, Mitchell faced the cameras and said he had a statement. He departed from his prepared text in several places, skipping, for instance, the account of his own background he'd used so effectively many times before. He turned to North, and began:

> You have talked here, often eloquently, about the need for a democratic outcome in Nicaragua. There's no disagreement on that. There is disagreement over how best to achieve that objective. Many agree with the President's policy; many do not. Many patriotic Americans, strongly anti-communist, believe there's a better way to contain the Sandinistas, and to bring about a democratic outcome to Nicaragua and to bring peace to Central America.
>
> Many patriotic Americans are concerned that in the pursuit of democracy we not compromise it in any way here at home. You and others have urged consistency in our policies; you have said repeatedly that if we are not consistent, our allies and other nations will question our reliability. That is a real concern. But if it's bad to change policies, it's worse to have two different policies at the same time—one public policy, and an opposite policy in private. It's difficult to conceive of a greater inconsistency than that. It's hard to imagine anything that would give our allies more cause to consider us unreliable than that we say one thing in public and secretly do the opposite. And that's exactly what was done when arms were sold to Iran and arms were swapped for hostages.

Now, you have talked a lot about patriotism and the love of our country. Most nations derive from a single tribe, a single race; they practice a single religion. Common racial, ethnic, and religious heritages are the glue of nationhood for many. The United States is different: We have all races, all religions; we have a limited common heritage. The glue of nationhood for us is the American ideal of individual liberty and equal justice. The rule of law is critical in our society. It's the great equalizer, because in America everybody is equal before the law. We must never allow the end to justify the means where the law is concerned. However important and noble an objective—and surely democracy abroad is important and is noble—it cannot be achieved at the expense of the rule of law of our country.

Now, you have addressed several pleas to this committee, very eloquently. None more eloquent than last Friday, when in response to a question by Representative Cheney, you asked that Congress not cut off aid to the Contras for the love of God and for the love of country.

Mitchell looked North in the eye, and said,

Now I address a plea to you: Of all the qualities which the American people find compelling about you, none is more impressive than your obvious deep devotion to this country. Please remember that others share this devotion and recognize that it is possible for an American to disagree with you on aid to the Contras and still love God and still love this country just as much as you do. Although He's regularly asked to do so, God does not take sides in American politics. And in America, disagreement with the policies of the government is not evidence of lack of patriotism. I want to repeat that: In America, disagreement with the policies of the government is not evidence of lack of patriotism. Indeed, it is the very fact that Americans can criticize their government openly and without fear of reprisal that is the essence of our freedom, and that will keep us free.

I have one final plea. Debate this issue forcefully and vigorously as you have and as you surely will, but, please, do it in a way that respects the patriotism and the motives of those who disagree with you, as you would have them respect yours.

Jamie Kaplan was sitting behind Mitchell, looking directly at North, and was struck by what he was seeing, as well as hearing. "He basically keeps North in his seat, and George becomes the focus of the hearings for the first time. I'm watching this, and I'm thinking, this is a truly brilliant tactic—and I don't use the term *brilliant* with any regularity. Listening to it, it's both spellbinding, and, at its base, emotionally charged and touching." He also saw North and

Sullivan had no idea how to respond. "To give his mantra after that," Kaplan said, "would have seemed trite." The chairman called a recess.

Kaplan then had an embarrassing moment. He was so moved that when he and Mitchell stood up, he went to shake his hand. Mitchell looked at the proffered hand and said, "No, that will look contrived." Kaplan quickly realized he was right. "I was his guy. For me to shake his hand *would* look contrived. I was just overcome, like everybody else. He'd created this moment, and he wanted it to be right."

The reaction to Mitchell's statement was swift. Lauren Higgins, whose Senate office was across the hall from the front desk, helped served as a backup when the receptionists' lines were busy. "For days, the phones were just constantly lit up, as one line went down it would come back up, and we were constantly answering the phone out back," she said. "It was just overwhelming to hear all these people calling from all over the country, not just from Maine, and what that statement meant to them and how proud they were." Back in Portland, Jeff Porter experienced the same thing. "We got deluged with calls," he said. "He went from being a senator who wasn't too well known around the country to being at the top of everybody's list very, very quickly."

Mitchell says in his memoir, "The response was immediate and overwhelming. Before I finished speaking, every line in every one of my offices was busy. By the thousands they came in, first the telephone calls, then the telegrams, then the letters. Most were favorable. The unfavorable, although few in number, were intense in their hostility." His own assessment was, "I don't think I dented Ollie North's image one bit. I'm sure the supportive comments to him far outnumbered those I received. But at least I got across a different point of view."

WHEN MITCHELL WAS PREPARING TO CONFRONT NORTH, he may have remembered Ed Muskie's Election Eve address of 1970. He was deeply involved in Muskie's reelection campaign, and assisted in the speech preparation, as Muskie turned Richard Goodwin's text into his own. He may also have been influenced, less directly, by Margaret Chase Smith's "Declaration of Conscience," which she delivered on the floor of the Senate on June 1, 1950. Mitchell and Smith became friends during his Senate years, and at the time Mitchell entered politics, Smith's oration was the most famous political speech ever made in his home state. Coming near the beginning of what came to be known as McCarthyism, Smith's address made her a national figure.

The three speeches have a common theme: the need for principled patriotism in a nation that derives its strength not from common origins in race, religion, or ethnicity, but in its respect for the rule of law, a belief in individual liberty, and a tolerance for dissenting opinions. Whether by accident or design, these three Maine senators became leading exponents, at intervals nearly a generation apart, for the American political creed and the principles underlying it.

The speeches are also strikingly different, written for varied occasions and circumstances, employing words and rhetorical structures in sometimes idiosyncratic ways, and reaching different conclusions about what the nation should do in response to threats to its traditions. The first two were frankly political appeals. When Ed Muskie paused and said to viewers, "That is a lie. And the American people know it is a lie," everyone knew who he was talking about. He was contesting the charge, leveled in dozens of campaign appearances by Richard Nixon's vice president, Spiro Agnew, and then by the president himself, that Democratic liberals in Congress, Muskie included, were unpatriotic, even disloyal, and—at least on that occasion—Muskie's point of view prevailed with the voters.

Smith's statement also had a political context. She was speaking not across the partisan aisle, but to senators from her own Republican Party—chiefly Senator Joe McCarthy, whom she didn't name, but also others, including her own colleague from Maine, Owen Brewster, whose defeat for reelection she helped to bring about. Where Muskie had employed a measured, reassuring tone, Smith's "Declaration" was far more strident, even alarmist. Her speech is remembered not for its contemporary impact—it produced no response similar to the statements by Muskie and Mitchell—but as, in retrospect, the first direct criticism of McCarthyism on the Senate floor.

She began by saying, "I would like to speak briefly and simply about a serious national condition. It is a national feeling of fear and frustration that could result in national suicide and the end of everything that Americans hold dear." The reference to "national suicide" is startling, but at the time struck many as apt, given the alarms about the rise of Communism in China and Southeast Asia, the atomic bomb test by the Soviet Union, and the criminal conviction of State Department adviser Alger Hiss, whom she names. Smith repeats several times that the Senate had been "debased to the level of a forum of hate and character assassination sheltered by the shield of congressional immunity." Smith found it galling that McCarthy could level whatever charges he liked without any consequences. She was saying that McCarthy was a coward—a charge especially effective coming from the sole woman senator.

The appeal of Smith's words is more complicated than either Muskie's or Mitchell's because, while making it clear McCarthyism was her main target, she also said the Truman administration bore responsibility for the "feeling of fear and frustration." Truman's upset victory in 1948 had angered Republicans, who'd endured four consecutive victories by Franklin Roosevelt. Smith shared these sentiments. "Today we have a Democratic administration which has developed a mania for loose spending and loose programs," she said, then added, "America is rapidly losing its position as leader of the world simply because the Democratic administration has pitifully failed to provide effective leadership." Republicans could win a fair electoral fight, Smith said. There was no need for "the Four Horsemen of Calumny—Fear, Ignorance, Bigotry, and Smear."

If Smith's language is heated, she also included an appeal to what she calls "the basic principles of Americanism," hewing closely to the Muskie and Mitchell themes: "The right to criticize. The right to hold unpopular beliefs. The right to protest. The right of independent thought." These statements remain in collective memory, while her partisanship has faded.

Smith and Muskie were delivering conventional political addresses, honed and edited. Smith had considered her "Declaration" for some time, and six fellow Republicans, including Vermont's George Aiken and Oregon's Wayne Morse, formally joined her remarks. Muskie had a script and an assignment. Their speeches are lengthy, and sometimes digress.

Mitchell's "God does not take sides in American politics," by contrast, was written on deadline, and is tightly constructed and finely tuned to its purpose. As delivered, its six hundred words do not match the brevity or eloquence of the Gettysburg Address, but they still make a powerful impression. Even what he left out is telling. Mitchell had written about his experience as a federal judge in welcoming new citizens, including the fresh detail that "to this moment, it was the most exciting thing I have ever done in my life." The story would have been effective, but Mitchell realized, while speaking, that it would have diverted him from his intense focus on Oliver North.

Mitchell was addressing a former marine lieutenant colonel across the hearing room, but he was also making a statement about his own place in politics, one that Democrats have often failed to do when in opposition or under duress. In the context of Iran-Contra—with a persistent effort by Republicans, led by Dick Cheney, to discredit the proceedings—Mitchell was also playing a partisan role. But he did so with an appeal to reason, precisely describing and analyzing what had happened, and without any overt political appeal. It was a mark of his leadership style that can be said to have begun with this speech.

THE IRAN-CONTRA AFFAIR ENDED, FOR MANY, INCONCLUSIVELY. On one central question—what President Reagan knew—it was especially difficult to judge. Reagan was present at meetings where arms-for-hostages trading was discussed, and approved the original trade, for five hundred TOW missiles, which was supposed to result in the release of all seven hostages, though only one was freed. He also participated in discussion of subsequent trades that were no more successful, and moved forward over the objections of Secretary of State George Shultz and Defense Secretary Caspar Weinberger.

It's less clear whether Reagan knew about, or understood, the diversion of profits to the Contras. Jamie Kaplan says that Reagan had seen a memo from CIA Director William Casey laying out much of the plans during the 1985–1986 period, when North was most active. "But quite honestly, we thought there was a possibility that he'd never read it," he said. The select committee was granted access to Reagan's diary, which wasn't much help. "While he noted matters of importance," Kaplan said, "there's no reflection in the diary that he knew about the diversion, or that he'd signed off on it." One lesson, Kaplan said, is the futility of using extra-governmental channels to accomplish foreign policy aims. In the end, few hostages were returned, more were taken, the Contras never threatened the Nicaraguan government, and the disarray of American foreign policy prevented any serious efforts in the Middle East to build on Jimmy Carter's success in convincing Israel and Egypt to sign a peace treaty.

The committee report's executive summary includes a detailed account of what took place during Iran-Contra and what went wrong. It found Watergate-like episodes. Private fund-raising for the Contras that Congress had permitted resulted in a disinformation campaign, with $1 million spent to defeat congressional critics. One of the most prominent, Representative Michael Barnes, lost his Senate primary in 1986 to Barbara Mikulski. There were astonishing mishaps, such as the $10 million donation to the Contras from the Sultan of Brunei that was lost because it was deposited to the wrong Swiss bank account.

In light of what happened later, one report of North and Richard Secord's negotiations with Iran stands out. North "told the Iranians that the President agreed with their position that Iraq's President, Saddam Hussein, had to be removed, and further agreed that the United States would defend Iran against Soviet aggression. They did not clear this with the President, and their representations were flatly contrary to US policy." While Reagan may not have known about all the covert operations, the report found that he had made numerous false statements. It said evidence that could have determined his knowledge had been shredded by North and Fawn Hall when Attorney General Ed Meese's internal investigation failed to secure North's office. Finally, the report largely exonerated Vice President Bush from any direct role.

The majority report was signed by all Democrats and three Republican senators, including Cohen and Rudman. The minority report, signed by all six House Republicans and two Republican senators, was largely the work of Representative Dick Cheney. Rudman was terse in his assessment, calling the minority report "a piece of trash."

Lawrence Walsh prosecuted many of the key Iran-Contra figures, including Oliver North and John Poindexter. He brought criminal charges against fourteen defendants, and eleven were convicted. One case was dismissed after the government failed to turn over key documents. Two defendants were still awaiting trial when President George H. W. Bush pardoned them, and four others, on December 24, 1992, as he was leaving office. This didn't ignite public outrage as the Ford pardon of Nixon had, but Walsh said it "undermined the principle that no man is above the law," and that "The Iran-Contra cover-up, which has continued for more than six years, has now been completed."

Mitchell focused on the preemptive pardon for Defense Secretary Caspar Weinberger. While noting the irony that Weinberger "was one of the few persons in the Reagan administration who vigorously opposed the arms for hostages swap," Mitchell said short-circuiting the process was a mistake. He concluded, "What began in the 1980s as contempt for democratic processes and the rule of law by one president ends in the 1990s with contempt for democratic process and the rule of law by another president. Although the American people learned something from the Iran-Contra tragedy, it appears, sadly, that no president did."

Mitchell also drew a larger lesson. In an article for the *Kentucky Review*, "The Constitution and the Liberal Arts," he wrote, "Admiral John Poindexter and Colonel Oliver North expressed the view that in the dangerous world in which we live the president must have unrestricted authority to conduct covert operations. Their faith in this president would invest the presidency itself with unlimited power to commit American resources, personnel, and policy to secret actions in foreign lands. But such a process in my view is fundamentally inconsistent with democracy. The essence of self-government is information. If Americans cannot know what their government is doing, they cannot assent to it if they agree, and they cannot try to change it if they disagree. Despite the authority and trust that all presidents have, the American people demand to know what their Chief Executive is doing."

Jamie Kaplan had a more visceral response to contentions that any errors committed during Iran-Contra were minor and forgivable. Not long after concluding his committee assignment, he gave a talk at a high school in Kennett Square, Pennsylvania, as a favor to a relative, a Republican, who was appalled by what the hearings revealed. Afterward, a teacher stood up and said, "Everything you're saying seems OK, but what you're ignoring is that Oliver North is an American hero." Kaplan thought for a moment, then said, "If you consider your American heroes people who lie outright to the Congress, abuse executive authority without a thought, who operate enterprises using US-manufactured armaments, and trade in a manner antithetical to the stated foreign policy, who work with people outside the government in a totally unaccountable manner, and who potentially profit personally from some of those activities—if you consider people who act like that an American hero, then yes, Oliver North is an American hero."

North entered politics. In 1994, after Virginia Democrat Charles Robb was weakened by personal scandals, North joined the Senate race and won the Republican nomination, though John Warner, Robb's Republican Senate colleague, was so outraged by North's candidacy he helped convince an independent to enter the race. After an initially lackluster campaign, Robb narrowly won reelection. North later became a television host for the Fox Network.

The hearings cemented the friendship of George Mitchell and Bill Cohen. Mitchell's new chief of staff, Martha Pope, said that during the hearings the two felt so comfortable together, they "slipped out" to watch a basketball game on television; Cohen had been a basketball standout at Bangor High School. The Iran-Contra assignment served as a cover story, and "when the press found out . . . all hell broke loose with the phones," even though they were just watching the game. Pope noticed that "the relationship improved after that, and Mitchell kind of laid down the law to his staff—that he wanted things to improve. We got our marching orders."

Tom Daffron, Cohen's chief of staff, saw the two as complementary. "George has a lot of administrative skills and he's a manager. . . . That's not Bill's shtick. He's sort of an evangelist; he likes to go out and make a speech, get on the floor, get in committee, ask a lot of tough questions." He also noticed a fundamental compatibility. "Mitchell's and Cohen's voting records are a lot closer than you might think, particularly when so much of the stuff impinged on Maine. . . . You'd see them over on the floor, talking to each other all the time." Bob Tyrer, Daffron's successor, said the two staffs still competed for recognition and headlines, "but there was a mutual respect between Cohen and Mitchell, so that always stopped at the water's edge."

Tom Bertocci, who served in Mitchell's Belfast office, often saw the two together when they returned to Maine. Cohen was much more informal with staff: "It was always Bill this, Bill that, and lots of palling around," he said. Mitchell was more remote. "The Senator always treated me generously and thoughtfully . . . but he did maintain a clear distance."

Reflecting on the bipartisanship that then seemed to be thriving, Barbara Mikulski said, "Look how Bill Cohen and George Mitchell worked together. It's the stuff of legend. And now it's the stuff of almost ancient history, regrettably, but those two really worked together."

IT WAS COHEN'S IDEA TO WRITE *Men of Zeal*. Mitchell had written dozens of legal briefs and hundreds of speeches, but he hadn't considered such a venture before. Cohen was already a prolific author, with two books of poetry, two Washington books, including a journal of his first year in the Senate, and a spy thriller he co-wrote with Gary Hart. He also had an agent who'd sounded out a publisher, Viking Penguin. Mitchell had proved adept at writing his Iran-Contra speech on deadline, and the same would be true for the book outline that became *Men of Zeal*. They had just over three months to assemble and refine their accounts of the just-concluded hearings. "I had no idea how the business end of it worked," Mitchell said. Cohen told him, "It was unusual that Maine had two senators on the committee, and it might make a good book, and he added "I owe Bill a debt of gratitude for getting me involved."

They divided up the chapters roughly in half. Each chapter focuses on a single witness, and is narrated mostly in the first person plural, though where each played a distinctive role—such as the Oliver North response—they speak in their own voices. Cohen's suggestions went first to Rich Arenberg, who'd agreed to help coordinate the project. "The book ultimately had to read as if it had one author, and yet their initial writing styles were so diametrically opposed," Arenberg said. "George Mitchell was a federal judge, [and] there's a lot of his persona that reflects that . . . short, declarative sentences, very concrete, solid, very clear. People would always tell me they'd go read his floor speeches to see the clearest exposition of an issue . . . he'd work at it and polish it. Bill Cohen, on the other hand, had a clear writing style but very florid. He's a novelist, he's a poet, and he loves to elaborate."

Cohen suggested chapter titles, sometimes delivered in a phone call at two a.m., Arenberg said. "As far as George Mitchell's concerned, the chapters ought to be titled chapter one, chapter two, chapter three, chapter four." Some of Cohen's titles were perfect: "Top Gun," for the Oliver North chapter, or "Beauty and the Beasts," for Fawn Hall, North's secretary. One suggestion that didn't make the cut was "Three Blind Meese."

The authors leave little doubt about their views, but *Men of Zeal* is more discursive than didactic. They do frame the issue squarely through their choice of a quotation from Justice Louis Brandeis that produced the book title: "The greatest dangers to liberty lurk in insidious encroachment by men of zeal, well-meaning, but without understanding." The book sold well, and effectively launched Mitchell's career as an author. Since then, he has written four more books.

While the two haven't collaborated as authors since then, they continue to produce fruitful suggestions. In a 2009 interview, Cohen, speculating on how Mitchell might be remembered, said, "If you had to make the movie, or a book, it would be called 'The Negotiator'; that would be George." Five years later, Mitchell used it as the title of his memoirs.

During the Iran-Contra hearings, Cohen had plenty of opportunity to observe Mitchell, and said of the speech to North, "That was the moment, with all the pressure and the tension and the fact that Ollie North was such a captivating figure, and we were the bad guys. . . . How George handled the issue was a moment when his colleagues saw him in a light that said, 'This is going to be our next leader.'"

THE YEAR OF
TWO ELECTIONS

G eorge Mitchell had to wait eight years after his loss in the 1974 governor's race for a chance to test himself before Maine voters again. And it was just eight years after his arrival in the US Senate that he had the opportunity to perform on a much larger stage. At the start of 1988, he was in the unusual position of conducting two political races in the same year, one familiar and relatively safe, the other, a leap into the political unknown.

Mitchell had been preparing to seek reelection, if his comment to David Johnson is taken at face value, since shortly after his 1982 election to a six-year term. He began concerted fund-raising in 1987, not long after he wound up his duties with the DSCC, and he made it sound as if he were starting from behind. The first meeting of his finance committee, again chaired by Scott Hutchinson, was on January 24, and Mitchell wrote to the committee that "in order to concentrate my efforts, I refrained from raising money for my own reelection campaign. Therefore, I must begin immediately to raise the money necessary to win." In a more general fund-raising appeal, he wrote that the DSCC assignment "left me no time to raise money for my own reelection campaign. And it has made me the number one target in 1988 for the Republican Senatorial Campaign Committee. They will pull out all the stops to regain control of the Senate in 1988. That means millions of dollars of funding for my opponent." His staff and supporters, however, were confident, especially after the Iran-Contra hearings, that Mitchell would be reelected, and as 1988 began, no one had yet stepped forward to run against him.

The other race was for Senate majority leader. Despite the Democrats' return to the majority with the 1986 election sweep, Robert Byrd was hearing grumbling about his performance as leader, as he resumed the majority leader post he'd last held in 1980. Bennett Johnson of Louisiana had let it be known he might mount a challenge, but drew little support and announced for Byrd, who was chosen again. When television came to the Senate in 1986, it opened up a window on floor performances by both Byrd and Bob Dole, and although Dole wasn't a natural, Byrd's style seemed from another era. With House Speaker Tip O'Neill effectively neutralized by Ronald Reagan's mastery of the airwaves, Democrats were beginning to look for something different from Byrd's courtly bows to tradition. Byrd was preparing his Senate history for publication, and, in 1988, as he assessed his chances of beating back a more serious challenge— Johnston and Daniel Inouye had already announced—he considered another opportunity. John Stennis, one of the last of the Southern lions, had become Appropriations Committee chair in 1987, but he was eighty-six, and ailing, and decided not to seek another term. Byrd then vacated the leadership post to claim Appropriations, a position he held, when Democrats were in the majority, until he died in 2010.

While Mitchell didn't openly challenge Byrd, when the leader made his decision in April, he was ready. Since the Iran-Contra hearings, colleagues had expected him to run, and with Reagan term-limited, it seemed possible Democrats could control the House, Senate, and presidency for the first time since Jimmy Carter's single term. Johnston and Inouye had far more seniority and credentials, but Mitchell had assets, too. First, though, he would have to secure another term from the voters back home.

REPUBLICANS NEEDED TO FIND A CANDIDATE. Olympia Snowe, who passed on the 1982 race, displayed no interest in taking on Mitchell this time, either. The other Republican congressman elected in 1982, John McKernan, had run successfully for governor in 1986, and switched seats with Joe Brennan in the First District.

In October 1987, Sarah Sewall, Mitchell's foreign policy aide, returned a call from a reporter at the *Kennebec Journal* in Augusta. Diane Dewhirst, the press secretary, had already left for the day, and since the reporter asked for Sewall by name, she assumed it involved foreign affairs. When she called back, however, the reporter raised an entirely different subject. Sewall wrote down the conversation:

Reporter: The Republican Party is trying to get your father to run against Senator Mitchell. How do you feel about that?

Sewall: I have no comment.

Reporter: Then this is news to you?

Sewall: Could you hold a minute? [pause] Sorry, where were we?

Reporter: I was asking if you knew about the requests for your father to run against Senator Mitchell.

Sewall: No, I didn't.

Reporter: I just thought it was intriguing that both your parents—your father and your stepmother—are both active Republicans, and that you're working for a Democrat.

Sewall: That's correct.

There were more questions about what Sewall did, her title, and her age—twenty-six—and then this closing exchange:

Reporter: And what would you do if your father ran; would you still work for Mitchell?

Sewall: I just began working for the Senator; I have a commitment to him. I have nothing more to say. Thank you for calling.

January, the traditional time for announcements, came and went, and it wasn't until March that a Republican finally stepped forward. He was Jasper Wyman, known as Jack, part of a family whose frozen blueberry business was, and still is, the largest in the United States. An ordained minister, Wyman was executive director of the Maine Christian Civic League, an organization of evangelical Protestant churches largely from the "Bible belt" of rural, inland towns. The league had begun as a temperance organization, and began to grow again during the 1970s, becoming the linchpin of the anti-abortion movement. By the 1980s it had begun to organize against proposed anti-discrimination legislation to protect gays and lesbians. Wyman was not exactly what one might have expected, though. He was uncomfortable with the anti-gay focus, and eventually left the organization, and Maine, to work in prison ministries. His only previous political experience was two terms in the Maine House, from 1976–1980—as a Democrat. He switched parties, and, eight years later, was the only Republican interested in taking on Mitchell.

Wyman wrote a fund-raising letter dated March 16, 1988, addressed to "Dear Christian Friend." It began, "After a great deal of prayer and careful deliberation, I have decided to be a candidate for the United States Senate this year. I have never been more needful of your prayers and support. You should know that I have sincerely sought God's will in this important matter. I have concluded that this is in keeping with God's purpose for my life, and it is an undertaking that God would have me assume."

He said, as Christian Civic League director, "I have not been afraid to step out and lead the fight for morality and justice in our society. . . . Our nation desperately needs strong moral guidance and leaders with integrity and commitment to our traditional life and family values. My campaign will present the deeply contrasting philosophies of Senator George Mitchell and myself." He also noted that "my opponent has already raised $1.5 million," and said, "I pray that you send me a substantial campaign donation." He concluded, "I did not seek this service, yet it has beckoned me, and I will not turn my back on the obligations and opportunities that it represents. I am, first and foremost, committed in my heart and mind to honoring my God and the Lord Jesus Christ in all that I do."

Wyman's explicit appeal to Christianity was part of the "evangelical right" that coalesced after the *Roe v. Wade* decision and became a major factor in Reagan's campaigns and subsequent Republican politics. Wyman rarely returned to the religious themes of the fund-raising letter, and instead focused squarely on traditional political issues, many with scant appeal to faith-based voters.

Chris Potholm, a Bowdoin College professor and political adviser to Bill Cohen, told Wyman that the race was "a chance to redo your image." Potholm reasoned that Wyman "had been the Christian Civic League, he'd been against the gays, he'd been a champion of anti-abortion, he had a two-to-one negative ratio." While Wyman couldn't expect to win, Potholm told him, he could be a credible candidate with Cohen's support. Potholm gave Wyman a lengthy briefing, with the current Republican slant on issues like nuclear missiles that were Cohen's specialty on Armed Services. "Jasper was extremely pleased with this approach," Potholm said, "so he went around taking the very high road. . . . I don't know if his base even voted, but he had the best time, and he was just smiling."

Cohen himself, however, managed to get into trouble with the Maine Republican Party. *Men of Zeal* had just been published, and Cohen and Mitchell made several appearances in Maine on their book tour. Unlike 1982, when Cohen sent his top aides to assist Dave Emery, during the 1988 campaign he was making common cause with Mitchell on Iran-Contra. He told Maine Republicans, who "were really unhappy with me," that, "We had this experience, this is a nonpolitical book." He acknowledged that, 'Yes, I'm with George Mitchell and, yes, I'm the co-chair of Jasper Wyman's election bid.'" It didn't satisfy party officials. The book tour spanned September and October, and the GOP chairman suggested Cohen should leave the party. A state committee motion to expel him, however, was defeated.

Mitchell waited for Wyman to enter, then made his own announcement on April 5. He emphasized ties to Maine: "For eight years, I've attended diligently to my duties in Washington and also returned home to Maine regularly, on weekends, during Senate recesses, to meet and talk with Maine people from every walk of life, in every part of the state. I've listened to their opinions, I've heard their concerns, I've been heartened by their hopes."

Mitchell again cited Joshua Chamberlain, the Civil War hero, and later, everyone's favorite Republican governor, to contest the Reagan view of government as a problem, with the passage he'd first employed in the state government section of Ken Curtis's 1966 Maine Action Plan. The Chamberlain quotation concludes that government "should combine the insight and foresight of the best minds of the state for all the high ends for which society is established and to which man aspires. That gives us much to do."

More than a century later, Mitchell sought to bring Chamberlain's words up-to-date. "Americans are engaged in a continuing debate over the proper role of government. Some hold that government is an evil force, alien to the people, suppressing freedom, draining society of its energy and enterprise. Surely there are governments in the world—past and present—that fit that description," he said. This was not Chamberlain's, or Mitchell's, view. "There are others who believe that, properly directed and restrained, government can be a force for good, that it can through collective action meet the needs of people that cannot otherwise be met. That outcome requires energy, effort, generosity, optimism, and idealism. And those qualities are what Americans have in abundance." Mitchell's statement would serve for both races he ran that year.

His campaign brochure repeated his 1982 themes, with the slogan, "An Effective and Responsible Leader for Maine and the Nation." It focused on his work as chairman of the Environmental Protection subcommittee, and on Social Security, now buttressed by health care, and his success in removing Maine from the Department of Energy's unavailing search for a second high-level nuclear-waste site. Mitchell said, "Nothing is more important than protecting Maine jobs and creating new jobs for Maine people"—something every candidate says, but he had specifics, citing work for Bath Iron Works and the Portsmouth Naval Shipyard. Mitchell also mentioned his efforts "to protect the fishing, potato, and shoe industries from unfair imports," and other projects of benefit to Maine—a breakwater at Eastport, initial funding for the Brunswick-Topsham bypass, and creating a formal boundary for Acadia National Park. Mitchell said, "Budget deficits are the most pressing economic problem confronting our nation." This was to become his central concern. There was no mention of Iran-Contra.

After long years in Ed Muskie's shadow, it must have been gratifying for Mitchell to read a Muskie fund-raising letter on his behalf. Muskie did feature Iran-Contra prominently, after paraphrasing theologian Reinhold Niebuhr: "There is just enough bad in human beings to make democracy necessary, and there is just enough good to make it possible." The passage on Iran-Contra focused on Muskie's own participation, however. "As I said in the press conference following our submission of the Tower Commission report to President Reagan, the policies which fueled this affair were wrong policies, and they were the president's policies. An over-obsession with secrecy apparently compelled abandonment of vital checks and balances and caused a major operation to slip into the hands of Lieutenant Colonel North and those he assembled to pursue it. These events have taught a painful lesson in history."

While Mitchell rarely referred to his larger ambition during the Maine campaign, it did come up in fund-raising. He wrote to supporters that he sought "to build upon our success in 1986 and strengthen the Democratic majority in the Senate. And that will be especially important if I am elected majority leader." Another sign his national prospects affected his approach to issues came on campaign finance disclosure. Post-Watergate, Mitchell had been a radical, in the 1974 campaign releasing his income and net worth, and challenging other candidates to do the same. Answering a questionnaire from the Portland newspapers in 1988, he supported only the minimal disclosure requirements for Congress, and referred to a joint response from the Maine delegation. The question was whether "candidates for national office should disclose their net worth and other information from their tax return." They responded: "We feel that the level of information you request not only goes beyond the requirements of US law, but also goes beyond the bounds of privacy that all American citizens—including elected officials—are accorded."

While Mitchell's 1988 victory seems foreordained, he expected a frontal attack from Republicans about abortion and other "social issues" that often favored the GOP at the time. The Republican Senatorial Campaign Committee's donation to Wyman was just $32,000, though. Mitchell realized his opponent had other disadvantages. In a recent interview, he recalled that he'd campaigned for Wyman in his legislative races, and said, "I knew Jack very well, and I did think highly of him. But when he changed parties, he had the worst of both worlds. Republicans didn't really trust him, and Democrats were angry at him for switching parties." It also didn't help Wyman that his last major appearance before Maine voters, in 1986, featured him spearheading the Christian Civic League's anti-pornography referendum. After leading early, it was roundly defeated after opponents attacked the referendum as censorship, and produced a television ad featuring an image of burning books.

Bob Squier, a nationally known consultant, did Mitchell's polling and advertising for the 1988 race, and initial surveys showed striking differences from 1982. Squier-Eskew Communications found Mitchell had a 76 percent favorable rating among Republicans, and commented, "For some senators, 76 percent within their own party is a worthwhile goal." And while Wyman was initially known to 52 percent of voters, most regarded him unfavorably.

Left behind by the switch was Lee Bobker of Vision Associates, who had hoped to work for Mitchell again. After being given the news by Larry Benoit, Bobker wrote to Mitchell on January 14, 1988, and referred to his "emotional devastation." Mitchell responded with an unusually personal note, which began, "I've come to regard you as a good and valued friend," adding, "My decision was not based in any way on dissatisfaction with you or your work product. To the contrary, I believe that your work is of the very highest quality. I have said often, and repeat now, that the television ads you made for me in 1982 were among the best I've ever seen, and were a principal factor in my winning that election. This year we anticipate a highly negative campaign featuring so-called social issues. To help us counter that, we wanted someone with experience in such campaigns. . . . That is why we chose Bob Squier's organization."

Mitchell attached a postscript saying he'd gone back to the 1982 scripts, including one from a Portland senior center. "I saw, talked, and played cribbage with many of the same people. It brought back a flood of memories and made the writing of this letter all the more difficult."

THE ISSUES OF THE MITCHELL–WYMAN CAMPAIGN were those that dominated politics in the 1980s—taxes, defense, and patriotism. Wyman had, like most Republicans, including that year's presidential nominee, taken a pledge against raising taxes. Mitchell responded on May 13. "Yesterday my opponent pledged that if elected he would not vote to raise taxes. I have been asked if I will make a similar pledge. I will not." Mitchell pointed out that senators serve for six years. "To make such a categorical statement now, about what one will or won't do for the next six years, without regard for circumstances or the national interest, is not a responsible approach."

Then, Mitchell subtly turned the tables: "What if there is a war? In virtually every war in American history, taxes have been raised to defend the nation's security. If my opponent says he wouldn't vote to raise taxes in the event of war, then he is willing to risk our nation's future for short-term political gain. If, on the other hand, he acknowledges that he will vote to raise taxes in the event of a war, then his pledge is meaningless."

On domestic issues, Wyman supported eliminating funding for Amtrak, the passenger train agency, and for Conrail, the reorganized freight carrier—even though the government had already sold its Conrail interests. Mitchell was cultivating support for restoring passenger train service to Maine, which bore fruit the following year.

On defense, Wyman criticized Mitchell for not supporting Reagan's proposal for a new intercontinental ballistic missile system called the MX, and the "Star Wars" missile defense system. Mitchell responded by referring to Congressional Budget Office estimates that the two systems, with the full "Astrodome" missile defense, would cost $1 trillion. Mitchell said he instead favored the "Midgetman" single warhead missile that would circulate on railcars to avoid detection by Soviet satellites.

Wyman also tried to capitalize on an exchange Mitchell had on *This Week with David Brinkley* in September over a recent Supreme Court decision that upheld a Jehovah's Witness claim against being forced to recite the Pledge of Allegiance. It paralleled a later decision to allow flag-burning as a form of protest. Mitchell's adversary, Representative Lynn Martin, an Illinois Republican, interrupted Mitchell after he said, "The issue is freedom of speech" by interjecting "Oh, that's bosh."

Mitchell then compared forced recitals of the Pledge to loyalty oaths. He said, "There are places where loyalty oaths can be forced—Nazi Germany was one, Soviet Russia was another—but in the United States, we don't force people to make loyalty oaths . . . and that's why the Pledge means something here." It wasn't Mitchell's most articulate response, and Martin pounced on the Nazi analogy, as did Wyman. Mitchell issued a clarifying statement, saying, "The real issue has been obscured by those who seek to use the Pledge of Allegiance for political gain by impugning the patriotism of their opponents. . . . I favor the Pledge of Allegiance and recite it often. But I do so voluntarily, as a free person whose heart and mind tell me that we are fortunate to be Americans." It was reminiscent of the Iran-Contra hearings.

There were lighthearted moments, too. Mitchell, a classical music fan, must have enjoyed a "Mozart for Mitchell" fund-raiser at Ellsworth City Hall, featuring two string quintets. It was preceded by dinner at the Hilltop Restaurant, where Mitchell had first met Paula Silsby years earlier.

His Washington staff saw the 1988 campaign almost as a triumphal march. Anita Jensen said, "It seemed like there was almost nothing he could do wrong. . . . It was just amazing." Jeff Porter, who accompanied him frequently, was struck by Mitchell's persistence in attending every public event his staff could find. Mitchell and Wyman, he said, were "very respectful. Whatever the exchanges in print or on the airwaves, they'd always go out of their way to shake each other's hand, so it never got nasty or personal."

In September, Wyman told a reporter he had "almost insurmountable disadvantages," adding, "Senator Mitchell had raised $1.5 million before I was even asked to run. We'd be within five points of George Mitchell if we had as much money as he has. We could even do it with half of what he's got." By then, in addition to the $32,000 from the RSCC, Wyman had raised only $99,000. One poll showed Wyman with only 10 percent, to an astonishing 80 percent for Mitchell. Wyman told the reporter, "I'm certainly not going to tell you we're in any danger of closing in on him."

Mitchell had raised all the money he needed, just over $2 million, and shut down fund-raising in April. The national contacts he had made through the DSCC paid off, and Mitchell would never again have difficulty raising money, in or out of government. Barbara Keefe, who served as campaign treasurer in both the 1982 and 1988 campaigns, said the contrast was striking: "Fund-raising was a lot easier. I mean, they couldn't write checks fast enough."

Mitchell began returning contributions, and wrote to donors, "The support I have received has been overwhelming, far exceeding my expectation. I have already raised enough money to adequately fund my campaign. Accordingly, I am returning your contribution." Not everyone was pleased. The response from some contributors, Mitchell said, was "What—my money isn't good enough for you?" On August 1, Larry Benoit told Mitchell there was still $1.3 million available. About 70 percent would go to ads. The campaign asked supporters still interested in helping to hand out bumper stickers, signs, and brochures.

Wyman proposed debates on July 21, and Mitchell accepted five days later. The debates were unlikely to enhance his chances, but he never thought of turning down the challenge; he saw it as his responsibility to engage publicly with his opponent. There were four televised debates, the last one ten days before the election. They reprised earlier exchanges on defense and budget issues, and Chris Potholm thought Wyman scored a palpable hit when campaign funding came up.

"Mitchell was the king of PAC men," Potholm said. "He set the indoor record for PAC contributions against Jasper Wyman." Mitchell had acknowledged that PACs were getting out of hand, and that public financing was a better option. During the debate, Wyman said, "I've got this wonderful idea, Senator Mitchell," as Potholm recalls. "The best way you can strike fear into the heart of these PACs is to give me your PAC money." Mitchell, according to Potholm, was momentarily speechless. After the last debate, Wyman was walking beside a reporter on the way out, who asked him to assess his chances. "I'm going to lose," he said. "I don't see any other possible outcome." It may have been the first such pre-election admission in Maine political history.

On Election Day, Mitchell made a historic sweep. His winning percentage, 81 percent, is still a record for any statewide race. He received 452,590 votes to Wyman's 104,758. Mitchell carried Cumberland County by five to one, and it must have been satisfying that in Lewiston, where Jim Longley had beaten him decisively in 1974, he rolled up a margin of seven to one. After carrying only four counties in 1974, and all but one county in 1982, Mitchell not only won every county by wide margins, but he also took all but one of Maine's 493 incorporated cities, towns, and plantations. The lone holdout was the Washington County hamlet of Talmadge.

Mitchell's extraordinary vote did not extend to the Democratic presidential candidate. Vice President George H. W. Bush won 56 percent over Massachusetts governor Michael Dukakis—the last time to date that a Republican nominee carried Maine. Wyman congratulated Mitchell, predicting he would "serve with honor and integrity." Of himself, he said, "I have no regrets about the campaign I have waged against virtually insurmountable odds."

A few days after the election, reporters noticed the curious result in Talmadge, where voters had favored Wyman, 18-12. Then, as now, Talmadge had just over sixty residents. Other Washington County towns and cities favored Mitchell by big margins. Mitchell devotes a short chapter to Talmadge in his memoir, more space than he uses to cover the rest of the 1988 Maine campaign. Given his new visibility in Washington, when he returned to Maine and made Talmadge his first stop, he had a contingent of national reporters following him. The Talmadge visit had almost been scrubbed earlier because of the opposite problem. He had asked Mary McAleney, his new personal office chief of staff, who'd grown up in the area, to look into a possible meeting, and, she said, "He was nervous that nobody was going to show up." The staff called each registered voter and invited them. McAleney said, "It turned out that the person who was the town clerk was someone whose family I had grown up with." When she checked back, the clerk said, "We're all excited because we've never had a senator come here before. . . . We understand that he likes chocolate, so we're baking some food for him to take with him, because we know he works so hard, he doesn't have time to eat lunch." When Mitchell inquired again, McAleney assured him he'd get a friendly reception. "That crowd doesn't feed people they don't like."

He first met a class of third graders at the Princeton airport whose teacher had won a national environmental award—the kind of invitation Mitchell found impossible to resist. In Talmadge, though, Mitchell found himself confronting a heckler, a retired military enlisted man who, after the meeting, told Mitchell he had "always wanted to get an officer," but also said, "You've got a lot of guts to come here." For the rest of the crowd, much larger than the thirty who'd voted, the man's admission he was from New York City was more than enough explanation. And Mitchell did get an answer to why Talmadge favored Wyman: The pastor of the Baptist Church where the meeting was held said, "Abortion was the issue here."

MITCHELL HAD WAITED, UNLIKE DANIEL INOUYE and Bennett Johnston, for Byrd to announce his departure as majority leader before starting his own campaign. Some of Mitchell's staff believed Byrd hoped Mitchell would succeed him. A larger group thought Byrd, leaving Senate leadership after eighteen years, was indifferent to who might follow.

Patrick Leahy of Vermont, who later chaired the Judiciary Committee, was an early Mitchell supporter, and says he was the first to publicly announce support. Leahy thought Byrd had worn out his welcome with the caucus, saying, "With the exception of Mike Mansfield, leaders don't last that long." Leahy figured Byrd just found the Appropriations Committee "far more appealing." Dale Bumpers of Arkansas was a rare breed, a Southern senator with progressive instincts. He believes Byrd "sensed a growing antagonism toward his leadership style, and thought he might be a loser if he hung around much longer." Johnston inclines more toward Leahy's view, saying that, while he'd chaired the Energy and Water subcommittee on Appropriations, even twelve years after his now eventual retirement, he wouldn't have enough seniority to become Appropriations chair. "That's a prize of great worth," he said. Rich Arenberg, on Mitchell's staff, said Byrd was also attracted by the idea that, with Stennis's retirement, he would also become president pro tem and remain in leadership.

Patrick Griffin, who had left Byrd's staff to partner with David Johnson and headed Inouye's PAC, said he "was helping Senator Inouye become the heir apparent to Byrd." Inouye was the initial front-runner, but "the whole thing turned upside down on Iran-Contra." Together with his DSCC performance, the hearings turned Mitchell into a formidable candidate. Griffin said of Mitchell, "He showed real leadership there, in contrast to Inouye, who was trying to exercise a different kind of leadership. It was when they really believed in bipartisanship, and not to take a president down simply because they could." While Inouye announced well before Mitchell, Griffin said he wasn't aggressively pursuing votes. He could see the momentum shifting, and told Inouye, "These guys are fading on you." When Inouye responded, "They gave me their word," Griffin said, "I think you'd better check on their word."

Bill Bradley had been among the first to suggest Mitchell enter the race. He and two Democrats Mitchell was close to, Paul Sarbanes and Jim Sasser, met with Mitchell "to try to facilitate George's elevation to leader." Bradley said, "If you're going to be a Senate leader, what you need above all else is patience and a strategic sense, and George had both of those." Bradley thinks Inouye "waited a little too long" to intensify his campaign. Mitchell said Max Baucus was the first to approach him. Baucus, from Montana, served on the EPW Committee with Mitchell and later succeeded him as subcommittee chairman. Baucus told him a lot of other senators were thinking along the same lines. It was two days later, Mitchell said, that Bradley approached him "and bluntly urged me to run."

Ted Kennedy was probably in Mitchell's camp, but as a senator whose seniority rivaled Byrd's, he was keeping his own counsel. Kennedy and Mitchell had the kind of friendly but intense rivalry of two senators who excelled in their chosen fields. After losing to Byrd in the 1970 whip election, Kennedy had risen to committee chair, heading the Health, Education, and Labor Committee and producing a virtual blizzard of progressive legislation. A 1984 handwritten note from Kennedy to Mitchell after their joint appearances in Lewiston and Biddeford on behalf of the Mondale-Ferraro ticket suggests the tone of their relationship. After thanking Mitchell, Kennedy says, "Through my travels across the country into twenty-one states, I have never heard a longer warm-up speech." Apparently, Mitchell didn't always observe the lesson he'd learned from Muskie.

The eleven Democratic freshmen who came in on the 1986 wave may have been Mitchell's biggest asset. Tom Daschle, who became a protégé, said Mitchell "became immensely popular with the class of 1986, in part because of his accessibility and the amount of help he offered" as DSCC chair. He said Mitchell was "as instrumental as anybody in Congress in persuading me" to leave his House seat and run for the Senate. Of the eleven freshmen, all ended up backing Mitchell except for Harry Reid of Nevada, who was close to Johnston, and John Breaux, who, as the other senator from Louisiana, could hardly be expected to back anyone else.

While Byrd remained neutral, there are indications that Mitchell was getting favorable treatment from Senate staff. Martha Pope said Joe Stewart, Senate secretary, "had a horse in the race and it was Mitchell. He had worked a very long time for Byrd, and had been involved in a lot of leader races, and he was giving the impression of being evenhanded with Inouye and Johnson, but he was helping Mitchell with the members, in terms of their interest in committees and assignments."

When Baucus, and then Bradley, urged him to run, Mitchell made up his mind quickly. He had come a long way since being the senator with an asterisk. "After I was elected in 1982, and by such a convincing margin, I think it's fair to say that attitudes toward me changed," Mitchell observed. "I acquired perhaps a little more legitimacy in the eyes of other senators." He also thinks becoming deputy president pro tempore contributed to the changed views. He developed an affectionate relationship with John Stennis, the president pro tem. When, after Stennis's retirement in 1988, a building was being named for him at Mississippi State University, he invited Mitchell to speak. "I loved him, really," Mitchell said. "We didn't agree, obviously, on every issue, but he was a very kindly, courtly gentleman and he took a special interest in me."

Mitchell maintained good relations with many Southern senators, including Howell Heflin of Alabama, with whom he'd served on the Iran-Contra committee. The class of 1986 had a sizable number of Southerners—Richard Shelby of Alabama, Wyche Fowler of Georgia, Terry Sanford of North Carolina, John Breaux of Louisiana, Bob Graham of Florida, and, from a border state, Barbara Mikulski of Maryland.

Mitchell's own view of his role had changed, which he often illustrated by telling a story attributed to Harry Truman. When Truman entered the Senate, he was awed by the institution and its members, and wrote to his wife the first day, saying, "I'm sitting here in the Senate and I look around at these other senators and I wonder, what am I doing here?" Several years later, he wrote another letter, and this time he said, "I'm sitting in the Senate looking around at these other senators and I wonder what are *they* doing here?" Mitchell knew both of his opponents well, and played tennis often with Johnston. One advantage he had was that, with the long track records of Inouye and Johnston, he knew immediately why a senator might favor one of his opponents, allowing him to sharpen his own presentation.

The courting of senators in leadership races is among the best-kept secrets in Washington, in that what happens behind the scenes is rarely leaked to the press. Much of the campaigning is public, or appears to be, but because it's by secret ballot, there's no way to be sure how someone will vote, and, unlike votes on legislation, consequences are hard to enforce. Inouye seems to have believed he had enough votes to be selected over Johnston, but the situation changed rapidly after Mitchell entered. Mitchell not only met with each Democrat personally, except for Inouye and Johnston, but also made many follow-up visits.

Rich Arenberg provides a glimpse of Mitchell's method. "He counted votes in a very careful, factual way, and paid attention to what they said. He didn't count a vote unless it was pretty explicit. I have the impression that if they said, 'I'll vote for you, George,' he'd say, 'On the first ballot?' He was always very conservative about what the head count was, and I believe he knew from day one to when those votes were actually cast exactly how many votes he had, and in the end he was exactly right."

Public support like that from Patrick Leahy was helpful, but those votes counted the same as those who were keeping quiet. Mitchell knew John Breaux would support Johnston, but still pressed him for a commitment on a second ballot. Breaux saw why Mitchell might be gaining an edge. "Bennett had sort of had his chance before against Byrd, and that didn't go very well," Breaux said. "And I think maybe some people thought this house was too parochial and wanted someone from the Northeast who was more of a traditional, more liberal Democrat."

Mitchell knew Dale Bumpers would also be voting for Johnston. "That was just a calculated political vote," Bumpers said, "because if Bennett was elected leader, I'd become chairman of the energy [sub]committee. That's the way things work around here." Mitchell continued to pursue Bumpers. When he called him in Boston to ask for support if there was a second ballot, Bumpers said yes.

Jeff Bingaman of New Mexico was a senator with no obvious allegiance, but he gravitated toward Mitchell. "It seemed as though George was the early front-runner," he said. "Much of what we deal with here involves thin slicing of legal issues . . . and nobody is better equipped to do that and to succeed in that environment than George. He had a very keen legal mind." Bingaman also thought Mitchell saw further ahead than most. "He was not just making the trains run on time; he knew what was in each train."

The Democratic class of 1988 was much smaller than 1986, and Chuck Robb found himself courted repeatedly. He was, ideologically, more aligned with Johnston, but thought Johnston was taking him for granted. "He just thought I ought to be with him," Robb said. Inouye, on the other hand, made him a promise. "If I'm elected," Inouye told him, "I'll give you the desk LBJ had in the Senate"—an attractive offer, since Robb was Johnson's son-in-law. "I had a high regard for both men," he said, but he wasn't interested in a quid pro quo—"that's why I'm not a good horse trader." He remembered the Iran-Contra hearings, and saw leadership qualities in Mitchell. "He has a calm, reasonable delivery and never appears to lose control. He can deliver a very pointed message without looking like he's bleeding from the eyeballs or doing something that would cause people to think he was not rational. He could eviscerate an opponent in an oral argument without the opponent ever realizing he'd just removed his heart and lungs." Yet Mitchell, Robb said, didn't alienate opponents. Some leaders, "If they know they've got the votes, will absolutely shut you out rather than worry about the next time." Robb said Mitchell "was just one of those who could bring people together."

As senators firmed up their commitments after the November election, there was unanimity that the new leader should offer a break from the past, as represented by Byrd. Patrick Griffin provided this assessment of his former boss: "He had an incredible mind, incredible discipline, but his social skills were quite limited. He could speak to an audience, but he had a hard time developing any intimacy. There were serious questions about his ability to trust."

Jim Sasser thought Mitchell won votes by "the manner in which he ran his campaign, and his judicious and fair-minded personality. Everyone thought that if George Mitchell were majority leader, everyone would get a fair shake, and he wouldn't play favorites . . . and this put everybody's mind at ease."

With such a small electorate—fifty-five Democratic senators—comparisons were important. By this measure, Mitchell also stood out. He had outperformed Johnston in the job the two had in common, DSCC chairman. And on the Iran-Contra committee, he had risen in the public's estimation while Inouye had declined.

With the November 29 vote approaching, Mitchell knew he had a substantial lead. He was hopeful of a first ballot victory, which would require twenty-eight votes, and almost sure he'd prevail in a second ballot. There was one more obstacle, however. A few days earlier, Byrd had asked to meet with him. In his memoir, Mitchell writes, "I sensed what was coming and steeled myself as I entered his large and impressive Appropriations Committee office in the Capitol building. He seated me in a soft cushioned chair and pulled up a small wooden chair on which he sat directly in front of and looking down at me, our knees almost touching. . . . Although I had guessed right about what he would say, it still hit me hard when I heard it."

Before Byrd announced in April that he was withdrawing from the majority leader race Inouye and Johnston had already entered, Mitchell had promised to vote for Byrd, and Byrd now asked him "to honor that commitment by withdrawing from the race." Byrd said Mitchell lacked experience and seniority, and that if he withdrew and threw his support to him, Byrd could still win. Mitchell pointed out that the earlier pledge no longer applied, and declined to withdraw, and records this reaction: "He was a great man, strong and proud, and he was reluctant to cede power. In a perverse way I admired him more than ever." It seems unlikely Byrd expected Mitchell to step down. It may just have been a final test. Byrd, however, told Mitchell he wouldn't vote for him.

As the fifty-five Democrats assembled in the Old Senate Chamber, Mitchell believed he had twenty-eight votes, just enough to win outright. He thought Inouye would get fourteen votes and Johnston thirteen. Press coverage of the race favored Johnston, with many interpreting Johnston's comments as predicting he would win. Later, Johnston said, "I don't think I ever put it quite that strongly. I think I said that with the commitments and the leaners, I thought I could win." The prior weekend's coverage might have led one to think otherwise. Rich Arenberg, who knew the count, wasn't swayed, but he did wonder. "I learned a rule of thumb I've always followed since then, that what's really going on in a leadership race is inversely proportional to the amount of smoke and fury you see on the outside, because there's no reason to play that outside game if you're winning the inside game." Mitchell himself made few predictions. A rare exception was when, in late October, he told a Portland reporter, "I believe I'm going to win."

Mitchell admits he was nervous. "I'd read all the stories about 'senators don't keep their word,' and 'you can't be too sure.' I really didn't believe that and I still don't. I thought that people who committed to me were committed." John Glenn agreed to make Mitchell's nominating speech. Byrd presided from the rostrum while the three candidates were seated together. The paper ballots each contained a single, handwritten name when they went into the ballot box. Byrd announced the results: "Mitchell, twenty-seven, Inouye fourteen, Johnston, fourteen." Mitchell was one vote short. "One senator had not kept his commitment to me," he wrote in his memoir. "Instantly the face and name of that senator came to my mind. I don't know how or why I knew who it was, but I did know, with absolute certainty."

Before anyone else spoke, Johnston rose and moved that Mitchell be elected majority leader by acclamation. He said later, "I knew where every vote was, and it seemed to me not a winnable race for either one of us," and told Inouye what he was going to do. Inouye then seconded the motion. Mitchell recalls that "instantly the other senators stood, applauding and shouting their consent." Martha Pope, however, got the impression Inouye wasn't happy about Johnston's motion. Of the former front-runner, she said, "He wanted it to go to a second round, and he got boxed in." Johnston, she said, knew one of the two of them would be eliminated before the second round—though since they were tied, it wasn't immediately clear who that would be. Johnston, she said, "didn't want to be dropped, because he'd blown so much smoke downtown about how he was ahead," she said.

While pleased with the outcome, Mitchell was still disturbed about the missing twenty-eighth vote. After "a blur of press conferences, congratulatory calls, meetings and more meetings," he didn't get home until eleven p.m., and was asleep when, sometime after midnight, the phone rang, and he answered. After he recognized the voice, he said, "I know why you're calling." There was a long pause. Mitchell explained that he didn't know how he knew, but he did. After hearing the senator explain why he went back on his word and voted for Johnston, Mitchell said, "I accept your apology. You've shown a lot of guts in calling me. You had no way of knowing that I knew. As far as I'm concerned it's over. It's behind us. . . . Let's concentrate on the future." In an earlier interview, he added that the senator "went on and had a very successful career in the Senate and I went on and became majority leader, and I helped him quite a bit in some matters later." The two "remain good friends to this day," Mitchell said.

The missing vote is an experience Mitchell hasn't entirely left behind. It's unclear whether anyone other than the two of them knows the senator's identity. No staff members admit to knowing, and those asked say they wouldn't disclose the name even if they did. On that point, Mitchell is emphatic. "I assured him that I would never disclose his name to anyone," he wrote. "I never have. His name will go with me to my grave."

So far as can be determined, there were no hard feelings or repercussions from the leadership race. Mitchell had started out feeling that "I'm not in the same league as these guys," and afterward said, "I really did like both men and regarded them as friends." Johnston said, "It was always friendly between me and Mitchell. George said he would appoint me to the Intelligence Committee, which he did. It was not a problem in the caucus." Johnston was also impressed with Mitchell's subsequent performance, saying, "He just drove the Republicans crazy, because he didn't give them anything they could put their hands on. He was so articulate and would make the Democratic position out to be so logical and appealing that it was hard to be against him."

Alan Simpson, the Republican whip, said of his caucus, "They were all a little surprised that Mitchell beat Bennett Johnston. Bennett was an old pro, Louisiana politics, anything goes." Inouye, he said, might have been seen as too old, and "he didn't like some of the harsh combat that goes with leadership. George didn't mind that at all, and neither did Bennett. You have to have a little of the go-for-the-jugular in you to be leader."

How surprising is it that Mitchell was elected majority leader? Seniority alone is usually not the deciding factor. Lyndon Johnson was elected leader during his first Senate term, though he had served in the House for many years before succeeding in his second try for the Senate in 1948. There were special circumstances, though. Johnson was the protégé of Richard Russell of Georgia, as he had been of Speaker Sam Rayburn in the House. Russell probably could have been leader, but as an avowed segregationist, he didn't want to serve under Harry Truman, who'd just integrated the armed forces. Johnson's two predecessors as Democratic leader, Scott Lucas and Ernest McFarland, had lost their seats in reelection bids in 1950 and 1952. Johnson advanced first to whip, then to leader after the 1952 election, and became majority leader in 1954 when the Democrats won a slim majority. Like Mitchell, the "master of the Senate" also served just six years as majority leader before accepting John Kennedy's offer of the vice presidency.

Tom Daschle became Democratic leader, following Mitchell's retirement, after also serving eight years, following his switch from House to Senate in 1986. Daschle won by just one vote over Chris Dodd of Connecticut, a Senate veteran. Dodd, however, was a last-minute replacement for Jim Sasser, who unexpectedly lost his seat to Republican Bill Frist.

In neither case were there the same obstacles that faced Mitchell. He ran against two better-known, much respected, and senior figures, and won by a surprisingly large margin. In that respect, if no other, this 1988 election victory resembles the one Mitchell won in 1982.

As MITCHELL PREPARED TO TAKE UP HIS NEW DUTIES, he was single again, something he never sought and had long hoped to avoid. He and Sally were divorced in March 1987, and he remained unmarried until near the end of his Senate tenure.

Najeeb Lotfey, Mitchell's accountant, remembers him calling the office and saying, "I have something terrible to tell you—the most terrible thing in my life is happening." Mitchell said the divorce was amicable, and that he wanted Lotfey to continuing assisting Sally with her finances—as he later did with their daughter, Andrea, as well—and that Mitchell would pay whatever was needed. Lotfey sometimes visited Sally at the Channel Road house in South Portland where she continued to live until her death, "and I could tell that it was an amicable separation," he said.

Larry Benoit heard that after the divorce, Republicans were polling to see what effect it might have on the 1988 Senate race. "Because it was coming through as a press question, I had to go in and tell him," Diane Dewhirst said. "And that was hard. It was hard to do, and hard to watch him. . . . It was painful to tell him, and he looked pained."

Janet Mitchell said the family continued to include Sally in various events, and she believes George and Sally "remained very good friends." But she added, "It was a very difficult life for her." Sally had briefly tried living in Washington, and even went with Mitchell on one of his early "CODELs"—for congressional delegation—on a trip to the Soviet Union. Yet she never got used to politics, in Maine or Washington, and when it became clear he would run again for the Senate the following year, they decided to part. Mary McAleney knew her well. "I was always fond of her," she said. "She was just a private person, a very private person."

Like several others close to Mitchell, she contracted cancer. Sally Heath Mitchell died at home, at the age of sixty-nine, on October 26, 2003.

14

TAKING IT
TO THE TOP

The post George Mitchell assumed when the Senate reconvened in January 1989 had been substantially enlarged by two of his predecessors, Lyndon Johnson and Mike Mansfield. Senate Democrats created the position of party leader in 1920; Republicans followed suit in 1925. Before that, the Senate had been run by the party conferences, a collection of senior members, and business proceeded, by later standards, at a snail's pace. The US Senate once operated more like the House of Lords than the House of Representatives, which initiated and crafted most important legislation, with the Senate primarily deliberating on its merits. That began changing with the ambitious domestic agenda put forward by President Woodrow Wilson and the direct election of senators in 1914. The early leaders' tasks were primarily to manage the floor, assisted by the whips, positions created a few years earlier.

The majority and minority leaders weren't even necessarily the heads of their caucuses. When Senator Robert Taft rose to prominence among Republicans during World War II, he preferred to exercise power as conference chairman. The Republican leader was a figurehead who did Taft's bidding. Today, Wallace White's name is unfamiliar to most Americans, and even those from his native state, yet White is the only Mainer besides George Mitchell to have been majority leader. The genial White was so oppressed by Taft's demands that he repeatedly tried to resign, but Taft thwarted him. White had to leave the Senate to step down, which he did in 1948, with Margaret Chase Smith succeeding him.

Lyndon Johnson was the protégé of Richard Russell, but began exercising substantial power in his own right, in part because Dwight Eisenhower saw the job of president as managerial, with a modest legislative agenda. Under

Johnson, the Senate was far more likely to take the lead on major bills, a process accelerated by the 1958 class of liberals. This role was consolidated by Mike Mansfield, who enjoyed by far the longest stint, from 1961 to 1977, and managed to move legislation without Johnson's arm-twisting, enlisting cooperation from Republican leaders Everett Dirksen and Hugh Scott. To the extent Mitchell had a model, it was Mansfield.

After reaching the helm, one of Mitchell's first calls was to Bob Dole. When they met, Mitchell said, "The first thing I did was congratulate him, and he congratulated me." He then told Dole, "I haven't been here very long. . . . I've observed how difficult these jobs are in the best of circumstances." Like his staff, Dole was surprised by Mitchell's victory over Johnston and Inouye, and was curious about what Mitchell would say. It was, "I'll never surprise you. I'll always give you fair notice of what I plan to do so you can respond." Dole readily agreed.

The "surprises" Byrd had sprung on Dole contributed to tension between the two. Dole said recently, "The leader can't be on the floor all the time. I could have always sneaked some amendment through, and he could have done the same, but we agreed early on to notify each other." Mitchell then made a second pledge: "I'll never embarrass you." Because of the complexity of Senate procedures, "nobody gets 100 percent of their way," he said. "Since we have to come back to work together every day, no matter who's won or lost the previous day, it's a lot less difficult if we haven't embarrassed each other." Somewhat to his surprise, Dole found, "We never had a cross word in all that time. We carried the Democratic or Republican flag on the floor, and sometimes it gets a little hectic, but we both kept our word."

After that first meeting, Mitchell honored a Dole request Byrd had neglected. As Mitchell delicately put it, "There had been some disagreement over office space. And the majority leader controls the space on the Senate side of the Capitol, so I told him he could have whatever office space he wanted. I wanted to accommodate him to make certain he didn't feel in any sense disadvantaged." And Dole recalls, "We used to meet in his office or my office, every day. It really didn't make any difference which one. We got along famously."

Back in Maine, Tony Buxton thought there were deeper reasons for the extensive cooperation between majority and minority leaders. "Dole was impressed by Mitchell's level of analytical skill," he said. They had served on the Finance Committee when Dole chaired it, from 1980 to 1984, yet their relations there were formal and constrained. Though he usually concealed it, and disliked people talking about it, Dole effectively lost the use of his right arm after being wounded in World War II, and couldn't even use it to shake hands.

Buxton said, "Bob Dole began his life by giving his life to his country. Mitchell understood that, and tapped into it." Dole was a decade older and had more seniority, and Mitchell was deferential without being obsequious. Informed recently about Mitchell's age, Dole quipped, "Ah, a mere youngster."

One of Mitchell's staff members was involved in a poignant incident with Dole. Deb Cotter, daughter of Colby College president William Cotter, had been hired as a receptionist and had been promoted to legislative assistant when she suffered a massive stroke, the result of a congenital birth defect, that paralyzed her left side. After many months of rehabilitation, she was able to return to work. She met Dole on a ceremonial occasion, and, knowing about his disability, offered him her left hand as they posed for a photo. "It's my weak hand, so I couldn't let go of him and we got tangled up," she said. "It was pretty embarrassing, but at least I know how he feels sometimes . . . when people tried to shake his right hand."

Jim Sasser, who chaired the Budget Committee and was close to Mitchell, offered a more partisan appraisal of the Mitchell-Dole relationship, but concedes that "there was no going back on a commitment. Once they'd made a commitment, they stuck with it. And they got along reasonably well. Senator Dole is not so difficult to get along with until he starts losing, and when he's backed into a corner he can be pretty waspish and angry. But all in all, considering the tough issues that came through the Senate . . . they did about as good a job as could be done in trying to hold the place together and represent their own side of the aisle."

Diane Dewhirst, who moved to the majority office as communications director, said the relationship thrived in part because of their sense of humor, with Dole more mordant and Mitchell gentler. "They laughed a lot, they worked very hard, they were honest with each other," she said. "Their staffs worked together all the time." Dewhirst added that they would provide a heads-up about fractious members of their own caucuses, warning about Howard Metzenbaum, "who's going to blow this whole thing up," or, on the Republican side, John McCain, "who's coming in to get us again on catastrophic health care." They installed a hotline. "It wasn't used hourly, but it was used a lot," she said. "When it would ring, Mitchell would pick it up." Later leaders abandoned the hotline. Dewhirst said that on Election Night in 1994, after Democrats had lost their majority, she remembers Mitchell saying, "I should congratulate Dole." After she called to arrange it, however, Dole's office called back, saying, "He doesn't want him to have to walk through all this. Senator Dole's going to come down to see him."

One reason the offices coordinated smoothly was Dole's choice as chief of staff, Sheila Burke, a self-described "McGovern Democrat" from California. Dole had hired her for her health care expertise when he chaired Finance, and decided she should head his majority office staff after Howard Baker retired in 1984. When the news of Burke's hiring broke, there was a swift and furious reaction from other Republicans. Dole said it blew over quickly. "She had the skills, she was an expert on health care, and she was able to get things done with people on both sides of the aisle. I didn't delve into her politics. There were a few that grumbled, but when they got to know Sheila that all stopped."

Burke said she benefited from a close relationship with her counterpart, Martha Pope, who had moved to the majority office. Burke thought the Finance Committee connection was important, too, because there were "remarkable people" serving on it, including John Chafee, John Heinz, and John Danforth among Republicans, and Democrats Abe Ribicoff and Daniel Moynihan. "Early in the Reagan administration there were a lot of pitched battles, and Finance was in the middle of those, whether it was TEFRA or DEFRA, or OBRA or COBRA, we had a whole series of them," Burke said. On the committee, she observed Mitchell having "extraordinary insight, a strong sense of his sur- roundings. He was very patient, but very focused." Dole, she said, never let disagreements get out of hand. He would say about another senator, "He is not my enemy, he is my opponent; he is someone with whom I disagree." Burke thought this came from Dole's wartime experience. "He's *seen* the enemy, and he knows what they look like."

John Breaux contrasted the Senate later with what Dole and Mitchell were able to accomplish for six years. "The atmosphere today is that my team has to win, and your team has to lose, and they can never meet in the middle where both sides could win." Mitchell and Dole in effect said, "We've got to make government work," and, Breaux said, "Dole was flexible with Mitchell. They were from entirely different backgrounds, but they were good friends, and that helped make the Senate a better place."

Some Maine friends noticed an immediate difference when Mitchell became leader. Severin Beliveau, a "superlobbyist" at the State House, also special- ized in getting access for Washington clients. When he asked Mitchell why a particular bill wasn't brought to the floor, he was told, "Because I don't want to do it." When Beliveau shot back, "Who the hell are you to make that deci- sion?," Mitchell responded, "I'm the majority leader. I'm in charge." Beliveau persisted, saying the decision was unfair, and was told, "I decide what's fair and unfair." Beliveau observed, "It was a polite exchange, but he knew his territory, and he protected and defended it."

As MAJORITY LEADER, MITCHELL HAD a staff of fifty, and the first months were a rapid but disciplined round of hiring, with decisions about who would serve where, and how best to adjust his committee assignments to reflect his new responsibilities. Mitchell never considered giving up either Finance or EPW, and remained on Veterans' Affairs. He did yield his environmental subcommittee chairmanship to Max Baucus, a reliable ally, and, on Finance, the health care subcommittee chair to Jay Rockefeller.

Martha Pope was the obvious choice as chief of staff. Unlike David Johnson, who left for the private sector, and Rich Arenberg, who preferred policy—he had moved to the Intelligence Committee staff—Pope seemed to have no ambitions beyond serving Mitchell in whatever capacity he required. Amid spacious new quarters, Pope decided not to have an office at all. She occupied a small desk in the reception area outside Mitchell's office, allowing them to be in constant communication. But Mitchell was equally choosy about his personal office. He planned to appoint Gayle Cory as Senate postmaster, and filled the void with a staff member who combined several of Cory's and Pope's qualities—complete loyalty and an intimate knowledge of Maine.

Mary McAleney had worked on Maine campaigns before joining Mitchell's in 1982—for Muskie in 1976, and Phil Merrill in 1978. She made a quick transition to scheduling and moved up after Cory left for the post office and Pope for the majority office. At the time, the Senate was nearly all-male, and even in Senate offices it was unusual to have a high-ranking female staffer, let alone three. Some were skeptical of McAleney's credentials, and she could see their point. "When he asked me to take over the chief of staff work, he could have chosen among hundreds of people," she said. But "he wanted someone who would take care of Maine, and did understand about the ways and workings of Washington, and understood the staff." McAleney said when she went to work for Mitchell, "He was a junior senator from the minority party, from a small state," yet "the wonderful thing was that as he grew, his staff grew. He was always . . . wanting to make sure that people from within were promoted."

McAleney was conscious of the dual role she'd now have to fill, encompassing some of Cory's tasks as well as Pope's. The move of Cory to the post office, suggested by Pope, was precipitated by the illness of Cory's husband, Don, who'd had surgery and faced a long recovery. "We worked all sorts of hours," Anita Jensen said, "and Gayle knew she couldn't work those hours." Estelle Lavoie said Cory's value to Mitchell came through their long relationship, because they were contemporaries, but mostly through her presence. "She had such a warm personality that everybody liked her, and people from all over the state would come to Washington and stop by to see Gayle," Lavoie said. "There was just a constant parade of people." Jensen added, "Everybody in Maine knew her, so she was like a walking advertisement for Mitchell."

McAleney couldn't entirely replace Cory, but she provided similar help to younger staff. Ann Tartre, daughter of a Biddeford insurance agent, was hired by McAleney at age twenty-two, and said McAleney made the transition easier: "She really made it feel like a place that was safe and still connected to Maine." When John Hilley took over for Pope in the majority office in 1991, when she became Senate sergeant at arms, he relied on McAleney implicitly, saying, "Since I know nothing about Maine, I was fortunate that this wonderful, smart, dedicated, knows-everything-about-Maine person was there. . . . I would have been totally incompetent to try to interject myself into that." McAleney said she learned from Cory's persistence. "She taught you to live by your wits. She tracked down Leon Billings once on the Airline, on Route 9, by calling the county sheriff." When McAleney found someone in Lewiston unreachable at five a.m., she said, "I called the Lewiston cops and asked them to go over and tell her to put her phone back on the hook."

Not a conventional chief of staff, McAleney shared her boss's aversion to hierarchy. The Senate had new personnel policies, and "Donna [Beck] and I had to go to these godawful, painful sessions, and one of the things they wanted us to do was draw an organizational chart," McAleney said. "I ended up drawing a chart that looked like a wagon wheel." When she showed the chart to John Hilley, "We all started laughing." Keeping track of hours wasn't her style. "We had no leave policy. There were people who had serious medical issues, but we never kept track of anyone's hours, or vacation time." It was assumed everyone would work the necessary hours, and lots of them.

Over time, she noticed changes in Mitchell's relationship to office staff. Since he was only rarely in the Russell Building, most contact was by phone or by visits to the Capitol. "He depended on longtime staff more and more," McAleney said. "He'd say, 'I can't keep this up, I don't have time.' He was depending on people like Anita more and more." Jensen found it unnerving that Mitchell would call staff directly, rather than through a receptionist. "He scared the living hell out of half that staff because he would buzz through to your telephone. Ed Muskie never did that," she said.

Pat Sarcone was Mitchell's new scheduler and personal assistant, after Cory's departure. She grew up in Iowa, worked for Senator Harold Hughes, then joined John Culver's staff, where she met Martha Pope. Pope helped her find work, first at the Democratic Policy Committee, then in the majority office. Without Cory's familiarity, she often wondered, "When do you interrupt him, when do you go to the floor to pull him off, because you always have calls from the president, members of Congress, Cabinet members, and he's in the middle of a floor debate." She said, "By the time we finished the first year or so, I pretty much knew when to interrupt and when not." She remembers Mitchell at work in the 1990 budget negotiations and on the Clean Air Act, "which we negotiated in our back room," she said. "Senator Mitchell's dogged determination to get a resolution of a bill was amazing to some people. It would be three o'clock in the morning, and he'd still be going strong, and people would say, 'Is he still going?'"

MITCHELL'S ABILITY WITH THE NEWS MEDIA was part of the rationale for electing him majority leader, and he cultivated a cool, though not detached, style. Mark Shields, who interviewed him many times, found Mitchell "a very effective advocate. He was reasonable and spoke in a non-polemical way. You never saw a personal attack from George Mitchell." Nor did Mitchell appear to speak off the cuff. "It was like he was presenting a brief," Shields said. "It was always well-organized and well-crafted. I always assumed a lot of preparation had gone into it." Congressional leaders, Shields said, "are usually skilled at the inside game, but only a few can also play the outside game"—and puts Mitchell in that category.

Diane Dewhirst said Mitchell was especially effective with "bigfoot" reporters—such as E. J. Dionne of the *Washington Post*, and Walter Pincus, an Intelligence specialist—who wrote interpretive and agenda-setting coverage, and influenced their peers. "Word had spread that this guy was on the up-and-up, and he was really smart," she said. Reporters could find it frustrating that "Mitchell never gave a lot to the press, he never gave them everything they wanted, and he never dished on anybody," she said. "But he helped them understand. And while he never gave them any scoops, I would like to think that he educated them and also prevented them from making mistakes." During Mitchell's first four years as majority leader, he played the Washington role—along with House Speaker Tom Foley and Majority Leader Dick Gephardt—of leading Democrat.

Television network reporters were insistent on access, and Dewhirst, along with Pope and Hilley, urged Mitchell to do background briefings with exclusive information. He always said, though, "I'm not going to do that. I'll explain, but I'm not going to dump on my colleagues." If they persisted, he'd say, "I'll do that when you tell me I don't have to ask them for another vote." At one point, five reporters—Cokie Roberts, Bob Schieffer, Brit Hume, Andrea Mitchell, and Candy Crowley—were invited in so Mitchell could hear their complaints. Dewhirst remembers thinking Mitchell would cover by blaming her. "I thought, 'Oh man, he's going to cut my legs out.'" But Mitchell "said the exact same thing to them that he said to me."

The Maine press got an unusual amount of attention, in Dewhirst's eyes, even from the majority office. "He would always return phone calls, always spend time with them when he was up there, even when he had to travel to do fund-raising for the DSCC. He was always connected home." She wondered about Mitchell's policy never to criticize colleagues, even off the record. "I still felt that he could have been a little more forthcoming, to show a little leg at times. . . . But he, for the most part, got pretty darn good press, largely of his own doing."

From the Republican side, Bob Packwood thought Mitchell was a good spokesman for his party, though he noted, "He's not a William Jennings Bryan orator; that is not his forte." Packwood added, "On television, the media would call him 'cool.' It's that logic. But on *Meet the Press*, I'm not sure if George were the guest that the audience would necessarily stay glued to the television set."

ON THE WHOLE, MITCHELL BENEFITED FROM the contrast with Robert Byrd as leader. Sheila Burke, Dole's chief of staff, characterized Byrd as "a very formal, disciplined man who had a very strong point of view about the leadership and about the Senate." While Dole learned to get along with him, Burke said Byrd "was quirky. He would go into his office and close the door and play his violin, or his fiddle, for hours." Dole, she said, "has the patience of Job, and could ride through that, but it wasn't the normal kind of discourse where you can just pick up the phone." By contrast, with Mitchell, "it was a much more predictable, much freer relationship . . . and it was not unusual for them to wander down the hall to one another." The two developed a level of trust that occasionally unsettled their own members. "We literally would have conversations that our caucuses would never want to occur," she said, where the two of them were "unbelievably frank," often when "some member was just out of control."

Dole recalls Byrd telling him, "Let's try to get along even though you're too partisan." Dole said he wasn't close to Byrd, but "I used to ask his advice because he knew the rules, and he'd tell me, even though it wasn't in his interest." He resists any suggestion he and Byrd clashed often, and said, "It was a good relationship, but it wasn't a real friendship." Mitchell is in a different category; Dole calls him "my good friend."

Dennis DeConcini saw Dole and Byrd as similar in that "they wanted to be sure that everything was going to go the way they had planned," contrasting them with Mitchell and Howard Baker, who "were the most outstanding leaders because they were willing to take some risks." With Byrd, "If you crossed him, you could pay a price." The tension between Byrd and Dole produced the filibusters and all-night sessions depicted in Mitchell's "cot story" with John Warner. When he returned as majority leader in 1987, DeConcini said, "Byrd thought nothing of keeping us here three days, and hauling in the cots. It was always a threat for anybody who was going to filibuster."

Bob Packwood was not a fan of Byrd. He viewed Byrd as an "accidental leader" after Mansfield's retirement, saying, "You can get advanced to a position that's beyond your leadership capabilities." The late-night sessions were grueling, and Packwood said of Byrd, "He had no sense of balance." But he viewed Mitchell as "a natural leader," who "understood that ninety-nine other senators had an additional life. Bob Byrd never understood that."

Mitchell was always respectful of Byrd, but liked to tell a story that displayed their differences. Queen Elizabeth made a state visit, with Mitchell attending the state dinner as leader. He introduced Byrd, who was hard of hearing, and mentioned that "Senator Byrd can recite from memory the name and the date of rule of every one of your predecessors." Byrd then "took that to be an invitation to recite these names," Mitchell said. "It was just amazing. After a couple of minutes, he'd covered fifty or one hundred years, and the queen said, 'Well, Senator Byrd, those were all before my time.'"

MITCHELL STAKED A CLAIM FOR HIS POLICY OBJECTIVES, as well as for his leadership of the caucus and the Senate. In a statement to the Democratic Leadership Council on March 11, 1989, he addressed the centrist organization with a nod to history—noting that the first Congress set up the federal judicial system, wrote the Bill of Rights, and is often called "the most productive session in history." He then observed, "We are in a new era. The New Deal and the Reagan reaction to it are over. We face new circumstances." His priorities included responding to Mikhail Gorbachev's leadership of the Soviet Union, safeguarding the environment, and "reawakening the spirit of citizenship." He said, "President Bush has repeatedly stated his desire to work in a close, bipartisan spirit to forge American policy," and added, "Congress does not want to and should not try to micromanage either diplomacy or arms procurement. But Congress will insist on the full exercise of its powers." He was specific, saying the War Powers Act, passed over Richard Nixon's veto in 1973, needed reworking.

On domestic policy, he vowed to focus on "What must government provide each American, and what will each American do for his country?" He said, "One answer has been that government owes its citizens nothing but defense against external threats, and citizens owe government nothing but the payments of taxes," Mitchell said. "At the other extreme, the answer has been that government must protect its citizens against every contingency, and the citizen's only duty is to make clear his changing needs." Mitchell, as John Kennedy had, emphasized the mutual obligations of citizens and their government and, in the spirit of New Deal experimentation, said, "To advance those general beliefs through specific actions is a challenge renewed for every Congress and every Administration. It does not require or prohibit any particular idea." To a considerable degree, this speech summed up the course of his leadership over the next six years. Ten days later, he added a codicil, reiterating that the federal budget deficit was the biggest challenge Congress faced. "It is difficult on a scale that goes beyond the simple politics of President Bush saying 'read my lips' on taxes, and the Congress saying there are needs out in the country that we have to meet."

WHEN HE FIRST TOOK TO THE FLOOR OF THE SENATE as majority leader, Mitchell knew how tightly Senate rules and traditions constrained action. Knowing this, and trying to make the body function, were two different things, however. Later on, Mitchell could sound philosophical. "The Senate is in microcosm the ultimate in the belief that we've got to divide power, and the most effective way to prevent bad things from happening is to prevent anything from happening," he said. Unlimited debate—which doesn't exist in the House—makes life complicated for both majority and minority leaders, who spend much of their time negotiating agreements needed to open debate. Any bill can be amended, at any time. "Most people are shocked to learn that amendments are frequently offered when a senator sits at his desk and writes something down on a piece of paper, walks up, and hands it to the clerk," Mitchell said. "That's an amendment, and there's no limit to it." As a result, "You spend sixteen hours a day negotiating."

Characteristically, Mitchell uses an anecdote to illustrate. After one laborious negotiation with Dole, debate was about to open when a young staffer burst in and announced a senator was, despite the agreement, objecting. When Mitchell asked that the senator come to the floor, he was told he was home in bed. The aide said, "He's watching this on TV." Mitchell then told the aide he was creating a new rule—"A person who is lying down in his bed at home cannot express an objection." The following day, the angry Democrat confronted Mitchell, who stood his ground. "If you've really got an objection, you've got to stay here and sweat it out like the rest of us."

After he left the Senate, Mitchell was working with British prime minister John Major toward a peace accord in Northern Ireland, and recalls Major complaining about a rogue member of his party holding up an important vote. Major told Mitchell "it was unfair and an abuse of the process," and asked what he thought. Mitchell said, "When I was Senate majority leader I had that happen fifteen times a day, every day." Holds on presidential nominations were particularly notorious. "You've got to go and wrangle with every guy that's got an issue," Mitchell said. "You end up in hundreds and hundreds of side issues—in reality, non-issues—trying to keep the wheels turning and the process moving forward."

Despite the numerous obstacles, Mitchell was well regarded by many colleagues for his skill in removing them. Fritz Hollings, a conservative Democrat from South Carolina, said simply, "He was the best." During thirty-eight years in the Senate, Hollings said, "I don't know of a better senator, in that he was just highly intelligent, he did his homework, he listened, and he knew how to get things done—which is exactly our trouble in Washington today. They don't have any idea of getting anything done." Chuck Robb saw Senate life as "controlled chaos," and said, "George's ability to control chaos, and to enjoy controlling chaos . . . was one of his gifts." Jay Rockefeller emphasized Mitchell's sterner side. "He'd make jokes, but the Mitchell smile, it comes and goes quickly, it doesn't tarry," Rockefeller said. "Maybe he could have allowed more flowers to bloom, in that there was a sort of grimness in his leadership."

Majority leaders, and their parties, can benefit from the "outside game," but their core responsibilities lie within the Senate—on the floor and in the caucus. Since caucus meetings are private, there are no records, but there's no doubt a leader always has to be in control. Mitchell had a lighter hand than Johnson or Byrd, but he had his ways of bringing Democrats around. Bob Kerrey of Nebraska said, "If you can't manage the caucus, you're not going to be majority leader for very long. The second most important thing is being able to lead the floor debate . . . and third, but less important, is the way you present yourself to the nation."

Charles Kinney said Mitchell decentralized leadership after Byrd. "When Senator Byrd was leader, he was in charge of it all—chairman of the Democratic Policy Committee, chairman of the Conference, and Democratic leader." Mitchell appointed Tom Daschle, from the 1986 class, as co-chair of the Policy Committee, and gave him substantial responsibilities. "It was a dispersal of some authority," Kinney said. "But nobody had any second thoughts about Senator Mitchell being in charge. He didn't need the titles."

John Hilley said Mitchell built strong relationships with the key committee chairs and gave them room. "He made a point of being very close to the people he needed to be close to, such as Lloyd Bentsen on Finance," Hilley said. On the Armed Services Committee, "Sam Nunn, who, on a political spectrum and the nature of their states, they had their differences, but there was always a sense of respect, admiration, and friendship." Joe Biden on Judiciary, and Ted Kennedy on Health, Education, and Labor, were in the same category, Hilley said.

Mitchell's circle of friends among Senate Democrats included Paul Sarbanes, Jim Sasser, and Don Riegle. Hilley said Sarbanes would often visit Mitchell after sessions. "Sarbanes liked to come in at nine p.m. and talk. He's in his own right probably one of the smartest senators who's ever served," he said, but also "much harder to get to know, and befriend. Sarbanes was someone he could have a quiet time with, eating his cucumber sandwich for dinner." Those outside Mitchell's inner circle didn't feel excluded. Dale Bumpers said, "I didn't hesitate to approach George if he didn't approach me about a burning issue. George came to me on occasion and asked what I thought," but Bumpers didn't expect constant attention.

Dennis DeConcini noticed Mitchell, in looking for votes, developed an alternative to the strong-arming associated with Johnson or Byrd. He often saw Mitchell in the private Senate dining room. "He'd come to lunch and ask your opinion," DeConcini said, "and then when you got up, he said, 'Dennis, can you come around later in the week? I'll call you.'" When the appointment was kept, "He would have the key senators on the issue he wanted to talk to you about, Kennedy and Biden, or Stennis and Nunn, and that's how he worked. And it was very persuasive. It was peer pressure, but not in a way that you felt offended, or that if you didn't do this, you're going to be punished." Though Byrd named DeConcini to the Appropriations Committee and Steering Committee, he also "paid a price" when he opposed Byrd. "Mitchell never expressed that," DeConcini said. "If you voted against Mitchell, at least with me, he just accepted it. . . . If you wanted to offer an amendment and he was on the floor, he didn't say, 'I'm sorry, you didn't help me last week,' he said, 'Sure, get in line.'"

Charles Kinney said Mitchell chose different settings for persuasion. "If there were distinct differences between two or more members of the conference, they were not addressed in the large room setting," Kinney said. "He didn't waste his time with that. He would have private meetings with senators in his back office. They would get the issue thrashed through. . . . When he stood as chairman of the conference, he was in charge. There was not a lot of nitpicking or griping."

When Mitchell became leader, some of the Senate's old Democratic lions returned to prominence. Teddy Kennedy was one whose committee work was rejuvenated, even though a Republican still occupied the White House. In a 1989 year-end memo to Mitchell and Daschle, his cover letter provided the tone. "As we discussed, National Service legislation and the Family Planning reauthorization are ready for floor action upon our return in January, and legislation to provide Health Care for All Americans, my top priority for next year, should be ready for floor consideration shortly after the Pepper Commission reports on March 1." The memo also outlined bills such as the Excellence in Teaching Act, Family and Medical Leave Act, Civil Rights Act, and Food Safety Amendments, as well as initiatives to regulate tobacco, help cities with AIDS funding, prevent homelessness, and limit age discrimination.

Mitchell chaired the conference, shared leadership of the Policy Committee with Daschle, and kept a close eye on the Steering Committee. These behind-the-scenes groups could have a significant effect on legislation. Lauren Higgins, who worked in Mitchell's Senate office before departing for law school, returned to work on the Policy Committee staff. Byrd treated the staff as his own, but Mitchell "created a committee that served as a resource for other Democratic senators," she said. "It was a way to help Democratic staff and senators prepare for legislation and big debates on the Senate floor." On the other hand, Dennis DeConcini said the Steering Committee had sometimes strayed from the leader's direction, so Mitchell more closely controlled nominations. Mitchell had been a committee member himself, and DeConcini said he "figured it out right away; he said, 'DeConcini and Sasser, some of the young guys are rolling the chairman.'" DeConcini decided, "This guy's really smart. And Byrd's smart too, but I don't think he had this figured out."

MITCHELL'S LEADERSHIP STYLE FIGURES PROMINENTLY in most descriptions of his tenure, and while there are similar themes, people saw different aspects. There's widespread agreement about what Mitchell refers to as his "patience muscle," and the ability not to lose control despite numerous provocations. Tim Agnew, head of the Finance Authority of Maine, who often had business in Washington, says Mitchell "just has a manner about him that calms people down and makes people try to figure out solutions rather than figure out ways to keep fighting." When Harold Pachios watched Mitchell at work, he decided that his friend was someone who could "suffer fools gladly." No matter how casual the acquaintance, Mitchell was attentive. "All it took was someone saying, 'I want to talk to you.' Here's the Senate majority leader, listening intently, paying close attention, and according that person enormous respect. I don't know another human being who can do that . . . he never tunes out anyone."

Patrick Leahy saw Mitchell's technique most often in the caucus room, where "he would call on different people, make sure that people got heard, but then would use that same negotiating ability, and say, 'Well, now here's the situation we have,' and 'Don't you think we should do . . .'" Leahy said, "He'd tell them the conclusion, and usually we'd have agreement." Mitchell did enjoy recesses, however, according to Leahy. "He'd say, 'This is a really good job if you're all gone and I don't have to be taking care of all your needs.' I think it was said only half in jest."

Carl Levin used a baseball analogy to compare Mitchell to Byrd. "Mitchell played a game of hardball, but it seemed like softball. Byrd played a game of hardball that seemed like hardball." Mitchell, Levin said, was able to get his way without seeming aggressive. "He has a demeanor and a bearing that was, and is, extremely pleasing and nonthreatening. As tough as he is, it's a velvet glove there on the outside." Bob Kerrey was struck by "an unusual combination of gentleness, very considerate, very respectful," but on the floor, "He's quite determined, knows what he wants and has got a pretty good idea of what he needs to do in order to get there."

Bob Graham said Mitchell used his analytical abilities well. "He had an uncommon ability to articulate his position in ways that drew people to his side." Graham said that at the time, "I would suggest that a third of the senators were basically centrist, and I would put George in that category." Mitchell did, however, "have a reputation for being stubborn, and some people thought he was a little inflexible," he said.

Ed King, a Texan who worked for Byrd and then carried out various foreign policy assignments for Mitchell, got to watch him often on the floor, and detected a more Machiavellian side. He recalls maneuvering with the Bush administration over Central America that produced a tactical advantage for Democrats, and said, "Mitchell had them right where he wanted. He was one of the most underrated partisans I've ever seen, because this guy goes for the jugular, but he does it with a smile, and he does it so nicely and smoothly that nobody knows it." King said Mitchell's message to the Policy Committee staff, on a rare visit, was simple: "You do the policy, I do the politics." He relied on staff to draft floor statements, but added his own angle, King said. "Mitchell was the best weaver and dodger I have ever seen in politics." Foreign policy debates were the most theatrical. When Mitchell and Dole appeared together on the floor in these situations, King knew what to expect. "They'd go at it," he said. "Dole would come out first with a ripper, and Mitchell would come winging and dinging him right back. Press gallery's writing it up. We already knew what the vote would be, because they'd agreed ahead of time . . . so that was the game."

Barbara Mikulski became an unabashed admirer, and had her own analogy about Mitchell's floor leadership. "He was like Clark Kent sometimes, with his horn-rimmed glass and his very quiet manner. People say, 'Well, he's just a quiet leader,' but then he emerges as a superhero and begins to move this legislation. He led by example. People had so much respect for him. They wanted to cooperate with him."

Charles Kinney often compared Mitchell, implicitly or explicitly, with Byrd, his former boss. While Mitchell didn't have the same seniority, he learned quickly, Kinney said. "The Senate rules are more intricate than most anything you can imagine, and the leader has to understand them. Senator Mitchell did understand the rules . . . and he knew the questions to ask the parliamentarian to get the result he was seeking. . . . It's sort of like a maze, and if you don't pick the right avenue you'll hit a brick wall."

Kent Conrad remembers votes where he felt he had to disregard Mitchell's pleas, such as on the "carbon tax" in the 1993 Clinton budget he believed would hurt North Dakota, a major oil and gas producer. "He never raised his voice with me," Conrad said. "He would get a glint in his eye and I knew he was upset, and he would push me, push me as hard as he could to get me to relent, but when it became evident I could not and would not, he moved on." Another time, Conrad said, "He was pretty vexed with me, but he didn't show it much, he didn't show much anger, but I could tell, watching those jaw muscles tighten, that he was not at all happy with me."

Patrick Leahy had a lawyer's appreciation for Mitchell's technique. "He could figure out the position he wanted to take, and then convince you that it was yours. . . . As a trial lawyer, we always try to do that. We know the conclusion we want the jury to reach and have to convince them it's their idea. And George would do that all the time." Diane Dewhirst agreed. "One of his talents was that he would listen, so you never, ever had a circumstance where he was asking a question that had just been answered. . . . He would listen to what the question was, pull something from what somebody else said, and then take it in the direction he wanted to go."

Estelle Lavoie once answered a reporter's question about whether Mitchell was an effective leader by saying it was no longer possible to operate like Lyndon Johnson, "who used to browbeat people and threaten to take away their committee assignments. . . . You can't operate that way, you can only achieve your goals by the use of reason and persuasion." Mitchell, Lavoie said, "was the antithesis of Newt Gingrich, who operated by name-calling, by trying to annihilate the opposition."

MITCHELL HONED HIS DEBATING SKILLS BEFORE ascending the rostrum, and deployed them to considerable effect. Harry Reid, who became whip in 1995 and then leader after Daschle's defeat for reelection in 2004, and who lacked the gift himself, said, "George Mitchell was a terrific extemporaneous speaker, and now having had his job, I understand how the asset he had was so important, because we're always asked on a minute's notice to start saying something. He was very good, the best I've seen here."

When Mitchell was leading debate, even his own caucus had to stay on their toes. Bob Kerrey admired the daily interchanges between Mitchell and Dole, who he said "could hit the ball pretty far himself when it comes to a debate," but saw Mitchell as on another level. "You had to be very, very prepared when you were debating with Senator Mitchell," Kerrey said. "He would listen closely to what you were saying, leaning in, and it wasn't like you felt like you were going to become his prey in a physical way, but intellectually, he certainly could. He'd say, 'Now, yesterday you said something entirely different, Senator Kerrey.' I mean, could I explain? And you'd think, 'The line has been set and the hook is sunk.' You could learn a lot listening to Senator Mitchell."

Asked if Republicans tried to undermine Mitchell, Warren Rudman said they did. "That's normal, but we weren't very successful at it. He was always one step ahead of everyone. George had this amazing ability to see around corners. It's like a good chess player. George was always thinking three moves ahead, and that is a skill that's rare among legislative leaders. Those who have that ability are the great leaders."

Mitchell rarely lost his cool, but it did happen. Lula Johnson, from the floor staff, remembers one particular incident: "It was late one evening when he was getting into a shouting match [with] a Republican member. It was looking pretty bad, because we have a press gallery, and that's what they want to hear." It went on, and then Johnson said, "I think it was Martha Pope who convinced Senator Mitchell that he needed to take it off the floor into his office . . . and they came back, they were smiling and patting each other on the back."

WAS MITCHELL A LIBERAL? IT DEPENDS on who you ask. Most Republicans saw him that way, but many Democrats would have agreed with Bob Graham's assessment of him as a centrist. Aside from budget issues, his voting record is remarkably similar to Bill Cohen's. In their day, both Cohen and Mitchell were in the middle of their respective parties' spectrum of opinion, but difficult to pigeonhole. As leader, Mitchell had to represent the caucus, so his own views were sometimes suppressed, though more often he moved the collective view in his direction.

He was certainly a different kind of liberal from Ed Muskie, who came to prominence when public spending was viewed quite differently. Barbara Trafton, who co-chaired Mitchell's 1982 campaign, remembers a conversation with Muskie where she said, "I'm so tired of everyone always saying the Democrats are the party of big spenders." Muskie "sort of looked at me with his little wry grin, and said, 'Barbara, both parties are big spenders. What it is, is what they spend on, it's the priorities. So don't be embarrassed that your party spends money. . . . Be proud of what they spend it on." Mitchell, by contrast, was always careful about voting for spending or tax increases, and his focus on reducing the federal deficit was intense.

Chuck Robb, on the conservative end among Democrats, said of Mitchell, "He's not easy to put in a box. I suspect he's really more liberal than he's viewed, because he approached the job in a less antagonistic way. . . . He was probably a fairly conventional, as opposed to hard left, liberal in most things. But he didn't wear his ideology on his sleeve in a way that made you either be enthralled by him, or out to do him in." Robb tried to recruit members for the fledgling Democratic Leadership Council, and Arkansas governor Bill Clinton was initially a tough assignment. Mitchell spoke on several occasions to the DLC, even though, Robb said, "George probably was under some pressure not to have much to do with us, but I don't remember him ever saying anything that led me to believe he was not supportive."

Bob Packwood entered the Senate from Oregon in the Republican Party's liberal wing, though he skillfully represented the Reagan administration during the tax reform debate of 1986. He and Mitchell served for years together on Finance, and he described Mitchell as "liberal, no question about it." But Packwood added, "He's not going to be swept off his feet by fads. . . . He understands where you've got to compromise your liberality to get half of what you want, and then two to four years later you work on the other half; that part he understands. Others don't understand that."

Mitchell was so wary of being typecast that when the Supreme Court handed down its June 1989 ruling that flag-burning was a protected form of speech, he immediately recognized it could reopen the patriotism wars. The decision, wildly unpopular in early polls, was by 5–4 vote, but not the typical liberal-conservative split. Justice John Paul Stevens wrote the principal dissent, arguing that flag-burning was a form of conduct, not a means of expression—a position Mitchell seconded.

Mitchell criticized the decision, but the House quickly did more. Before a month had passed, House Speaker Tom Foley cleared a floor vote on a constitutional amendment to ban flag-burning. The ball was suddenly in Mitchell's court. Since Iran-Contra, Mitchell had witnessed the implosion of Michael Dukakis's 1988 presidential campaign under sustained attack by the Bush forces. Dukakis enjoyed a sizable lead following the summer conventions, but by fall he had fallen behind and carried only nine states. One of the attacks created by Lee Atwater featured Dukakis's statement that he was "a card-carrying member of the ACLU." Dukakis had barely responded. Mitchell wasn't about to make the same mistake.

A week later, he took his case to the American Legion Convention in Bangor, an annual stop. Rather than his usual report from Veterans' Affairs, he devoted his speech to flag-burning, which had already elicited a petition for a constitutional amendment from the group. "I know that many of you disagree with me on this issue," he began. "Perhaps most of you do. Especially for that reason,

I believe you are entitled to hear, and question, and of course disagree with my views. That is what democracy is about." Mitchell reviewed the decision, and said the five judges in the majority "were wrong," but added, "Under our system, once the Supreme Court has ruled, that ruling is the law of the land."

He then reviewed the case for an amendment. "I oppose and condemn the burning of the flag. I find it offensive and obnoxious. I'm proud to be an American. But I do not support changing the Constitution." Mitchell then spoke of the adoption of the Bill of Rights, and the text of the First Amendment guaranteeing freedom of speech. "Never in two hundred years has that amendment been changed or amended. Never in two hundred years has Congress been able to make a law abridging the freedom of speech." He said, "Some of those pushing this proposal want to make it appear that the question is not that contained in the words of the amendment, but rather: Are you for or against the American flag?" The amendment the House was considering, Mitchell said, was so broadly worded that it could curtail not only speech, but also the right to trial by jury in flag cases. "You fought for the flag," Mitchell told the veterans. "You also fought for the freedom protected by the Bill of Rights and represented by the flag." News accounts say the speech's reception was quiet and respectful.

Mitchell made a floor speech using similar themes and, for the only time as majority leader, distributed it with a personally signed note to every senator. Bob Packwood described what happened next. "The House passes a constitutional amendment, but we're just up against the August recess, and we didn't do anything. We went home for the month and discovered that the public wasn't all that upset, and by the time we got back after Labor Day, the issue was gone. We then passed a statute which everyone knew was clearly unconstitutional, but that satisfies the zealots, and it's the Supreme Court that has struck it down again. That's an ultimate in long-term strategy." Packwood said it fulfilled the role the Founders had designed for the Senate.

MITCHELL'S PARTISAN ROLE HAS OCCASIONED much debate, in large part because "partisanship" is often an all-purpose tool to deplore whatever might be wrong with Congress. Alan Simpson, as the Republican whip opposite Mitchell's deputy—first Alan Cranston and, after 1990, Wendell Ford of Kentucky—was well positioned to observe. Even when he was playing a partisan role, Mitchell didn't alter his usual demeanor, Simpson said. "We'd be sitting in the cloakroom, watching floor debate. The sound would be down. And I'd look at George, speaking very calmly, and I couldn't hear his voice, of course, and I'd say to Dole, 'I wonder what he's doing now, what's he talking about?' Dole said, 'I don't know; it's something bland and insignificant.' Well, I turned the sound on, and he was ripping George Bush to shreds, without a bit of facial expression. And he had that way of doing that, a most amazing propensity."

Simpson admired Mitchell's decisiveness. "He was persistent. When he had the bit in his mouth, as we say in the West, he could ride hard, and he could push hard. He'd say, 'I'm tired of this diddling around, and we're going to call a cloture vote and you guys are going to pay.' And whenever he made a threat, he carried it out, instead of this gumless mumbling where you say if the Republicans do this again, we're going to be up all night for three nights in a row, and then nothing would happen. But if George got up and made that kind of statement, we knew he wasn't joshing—he was going to pull the trigger."

After Mitchell kept the Clean Air Act on the floor for twenty-five days in 1990, Simpson liked to kid him, saying, "George, you should have a whip here, some kind of instrument to give us a flog." Mitchell's reply, he said, was, "No, I don't need that, I just expect you to do your work." Simpson said, "We'd laugh about that," but added, "All he expected was that you do your work, and you do it for the country, not for your party. And yet he was a partisan guy. George Mitchell was an awesome partisan, but the partisanship ended if it was country-first time."

Steve Symms, an Idaho Republican who served with Mitchell on EPW, saw partisanship as healthy, within limits. "Ronald Reagan was a partisan, and of all the presidents I worked with, he was probably the best at getting what he wanted from the Democrats." He recalls Mitchell lambasting Republicans, "really giving them heck on the floor." Afterward, Mitchell came over and said, "Steve, I wasn't talking about you. I just want you to know that. . . . These other two guys, they're way too partisan." In 1986, Mitchell had been in Idaho for the DSCC backing a popular former governor, John Evans, who Democrats hoped could oust Symms. "George was trying to engineer a campaign to beat me," Symms said, but "he respected other people even though they might not agree with him. There was no personal animosity. . . . I was glad to have him as majority leader. I'd rather have had a Republican, but of the Democrats, he was fine with me."

Dole said partisan differences can't always be bridged. "There are some issues that are highly partisan, you can't come to agreement, so you debate," he said. "George and I always had a vote, though. Harry Reid, he just stacked up the bills, with no vote. The Senate ought to act, whether we like it or not. If you're a leader—and we don't elect nonpartisan leaders—you stand up for the party and its principles. We both tried to do that, even though we were close friends. The Republicans would blame me for giving in to Mitchell, and the Democrats blamed Mitchell—blamed him for doing the right thing."

Years later, Rich Arenberg, serving on Carl Levin's staff, assessed Mitchell's Senate years. "He'll certainly be remembered as one of the most effective Senate leaders, somebody who was a voice of reason, who was very effective in the partisan wars but, at the same time, understood the value of reaching across the aisle and getting things done. That's something I've thought a lot about since, as the Senate has become more and more polarized. . . . Mitchell, given a choice between solving a problem and having an effective wedge issue, he would almost always choose trying to get the solution. . . . As time has gone on, we see both caucuses in the Senate choose the issue over the solution."

THESE WERE THE EARLY YEARS OF THE PARTISAN WARS that began in the House, and climaxed with Newt Gingrich's insurgency and the Republican takeover of both House and Senate in 1994—the first time in forty years Republicans were fully in charge. Mitchell never served opposite House Speaker Jim Wright because Wright was Gingrich's first, and largest, target. Wright was found culpable of manipulating a book deal to pad his income, and resigned. His majority whip, Tony Coelho, left rather than face investigation of his fund-raising techniques. The skirmishes within Congress expanded, too, with such episodes as the House Bank scandal. While Gingrich, as minority whip, was focused on House ethics, Mitchell soon was dealing with charges that five senators—the "Keating Five"— had improperly intervened with regulators on behalf of Charles Keating, eccentric head of a large savings and loan. Keating became the face of the S&L crisis, the largest banking collapse since the Great Depression wiped out most banks.

Keating looked the part. He left behind a bizarre, ten-page defense with the Senate Ethics Committee which did little to alleviate suspicion, and much to confirm he was indeed responsible for defrauding depositors, and the government that guaranteed deposits. The Keating Five scandal came uncomfortably close to Mitchell. One of those accused was Alan Cranston, the majority whip. There were three other Democrats—Dennis DeConcini, Don Riegle, and John Glenn—and one Republican, John McCain. After a lengthy inquiry, the Senate Ethics Committee found Cranston had violated Senate rules, but the others were only reprimanded, prompting widespread criticism, as well as demands for reform. Mitchell renewed his call for public financing of congressional elections, but it would be nearly a decade before a much more modest measure, the McCain-Feingold Act, became law. Cranston, who had prostate cancer, decided not to continue in leadership, and retired in 1992 at age seventy-eight.

Dennis DeConcini also retired, in 1994, though he believes he could have defeated John Kyl, the Republican who took his seat, and had also taken donations from Keating. DeConcini said it was sometimes hard to distinguish routine fund-raising, with its overlapping and multiple connections, from what happened with Keating. His fund-raiser told him that he'd need at least $4 million for the 1994 race, and the September before, he told himself, "I don't want to do this." DeConcini had heard that Dole was intervening with the Ethics Committee on McCain's behalf, and decided to see Mitchell. "When I asked him to intervene for me, he said no, he couldn't do it. He said 'Dennis, I don't think you're going to get hurt by this, and I know you didn't do anything wrong,' but he wouldn't intervene, which was probably the correct ethical thing to do."

Feeling ran high throughout the winter of 1990–1991. In a private letter about the Keating Five case, a moderate Democratic senator from North Carolina and former governor, Terry Sanford, wrote to Archibald Cox, the former Watergate prosecutor fired by Nixon, and now head of Common Cause. "It is sad and I am ashamed of you," Sanford wrote. "Common Cause has obviously not studied the evidence, obviously is not concerned with justice, not with the common cause, but rather with its own selfish cause. . . . We were unwilling to join the lynch mob you have so assiduously organized."

Cox replied that, "Having long admired your public service, I read with great sadness the statement of the Senate Ethics Committee . . . and now your own sorry letter. . . . The strong editorial condemnation of the inaction of the Senate Ethics Committee in newspapers throughout the country suggests that what you hear is not a lynch mob but the sober voice of the American people."

The ethics wars extended elsewhere. David Durenberger, a moderate Republican from Minnesota, often worked with Mitchell, and was ensnared in a controversy over his real estate dealings, claiming expenses for his own condominium that led to him being "denounced" and fined by the Senate in 1990, and also led to federal criminal charges in 1993 that were dismissed. He also decided to retire in 1994. Durenberger believes his own party was responsible. "I knew it was more of a Republican effort to get rid of Republicans, certain kinds of Republicans, and it wasn't by accident that people like me . . . were not getting the kind of support they needed from their party." He was satisfied by the treatment he received from the Ethics Committee, and from Mitchell.

Much of the most damaging information about the Keating Five was leaked by sources at the Ethics Committee, something that concerned and frustrated Mitchell, but he could do little in the absence of agreement with Republicans. That turned around quickly later in 1991, however, once the nomination of Clarence Thomas to the Supreme Court became a pitched, and largely partisan, battle.

The selection of Thomas gave credence to Mitchell's theory that the Bush administration's attitude toward Congress had changed from warily cooperative to downright hostile after the 1990 midterm elections. Bush's first high court selection, David Souter, was a moderate, and his sponsor was Warren Rudman. The Thomas nomination came after Thurgood Marshall resigned on June 27, 1991, citing failing health. Marshall was considered the court's most liberal member, and his replacement by Thomas, from the far right, is what shifted the balance decisively toward the conservative bloc that has controlled many important decisions ever since. It was not ideology, though, that created the firestorm over the Thomas nomination, but leaks from the Judiciary Committee. Anita Hill's testimony was initially heard behind closed doors, and her explosive allegations of sexual harassment against Thomas might never have been heard publicly without the leaks.

Republicans were outraged, and demanded an investigation. Mitchell reminded them that they seemed not to care about leaks when those under scrutiny were Democrats, as with four of the Keating Five. Mitchell took to the floor to lay out his case. "There is no credible argument against the simple fact that leaks will occur so long as a staff member anywhere in this body believes his or her senator will condone a particular leak. A double standard for leaks—tacit approval of those that serve our interests, condemnation for those that don't . . . is precisely what keeps leaks going," he said. "Despite the uniformity of verbal outrage about the Thomas leaks, when it comes to actually doing anything realistic to stem leaks, the double standard prevails again." Mitchell said that all leaks should be condemned equally, and mentioned not only the Keating Five, but also President Bush's nomination of Timothy Ryan as director of the Resolution Trust Corporation, the agency created to manage the S&L bailout. Though Republicans sought a special prosecutor for the Thomas leaks, they wouldn't agree to include the Ryan and Keating investigations. A smaller-scale probe was launched, which, as a former prosecutor, Mitchell thought was unlikely to produce any substantive results, and it didn't.

MITCHELL SERVED WITH TWO PRESIDENTS, George Bush and Bill Clinton, and was an active participant in the 1992 campaign that ousted Bush and brought Clinton to the White House. He sees the Bush administration divided in half: During the first two years, both sides worked productively together to pass a wide range of ambitious, even monumental, legislation, including the last bipartisan budget plan, the Clean Air Act, and the Americans with Disabilities Act. The second half, Mitchell said, followed Bush Chief of Staff John Sununu's announcement to congressional leaders shortly after the midterm election, "You can go home as far as we're concerned. We don't need anything more from you."

There were irritants on both sides. Before the Thomas nomination, there was the Tower nomination—Bush's pick of John Tower for Defense secretary, a conservative Senate Republican from Texas—with a different ending. Tower was the only one of Bush's Cabinet picks to face significant opposition, but it started early, and grew. Bush no doubt thought that, like Jimmy Carter's nomination of Ed Muskie as secretary of state, Tower's status as a senator would produce a favorable reaction. He reckoned, however, without Sam Nunn, chairman of the Armed Services Committee, where Tower had been ranking Republican. Nunn was aware of allegations that Tower was an alcoholic—a condition that had ended the Senate career of Thomas Dodd, and shortened others. Tower was also accused of mistreating female staff, an issue that ultimately forced Bob Packwood to resign, in 1995. The Senate's old boy network was fraying.

Because of the awesome responsibilities involved, Nunn felt Tower was unfit to serve. Mitchell agreed. Carl Levin said, "Mitchell was helpful in gaining the support to defeat that nomination." Democrats had enough votes to deny confirmation, but Mitchell was wary of making the issue partisan. In the end, he could convince only one Republican—Nancy Kassebaum of Kansas—to vote against Tower; three Democrats ended up voting to approve the nomination, which was defeated, 53 to 47—the first time a new president's Cabinet nomination had been rejected. Bill Cohen voted for Tower, then was put on reporters' short lists as his replacement.

Coming early in the administration, the Tower nomination could have derailed cooperation between Mitchell and Bush, but did not. Bush was restrained, though he did say Tower had been subjected to "groundless rumor." Mitchell said the Senate was not trying to weaken the president: "From the bottom of my heart, this is not the case." Mitchell said he believed the fight would do "no permanent, long-lasting damage" to relations within the Senate. Some Republicans disagreed. Bob Dole said "we should hang our heads." He had earlier proposed allowing Tower to serve six months to see if he could abstain from alcohol. Steve Symms said, "It was mostly Sam Nunn's doing," but agreed that Mitchell played a role. "That was the low point of my time in the Senate, because he was by far the most capable defense guy."

The Senate quickly confirmed Bush's next choice for Defense, Dick Cheney, who gave up his congressional seat. During the Persian Gulf War of 1991, Mitchell attended a briefing at the White House where Cheney delivered the administration's plan to expel Saddam Hussein's forces from Kuwait. "He had the facts and the issues well-organized and -presented," Mitchell said. He wrote a note and passed it to Bush, and said, "You don't have to answer this, but you should thank us for turning down John Tower and letting you get this guy." Bush didn't respond.

By the time of Clarence Thomas's nomination, John Sununu, in Mitchell's mind, had already declared war, and Bush's choice was clearly predicated on having a black justice replace the first black justice—even though his views, on civil rights and many other issues, were diametrically opposed to Marshall's. Bush was daring Democrats to vote against a candidate of color. Until Anita Hill's allegations became public, few were willing to contemplate doing so. Democrats now had fifty-seven seats, and Thomas was confirmed, 52 to 48— the closest tally in a century for a successful high court nominee. The vote did not fall entirely along party lines. Eleven Democrats supported Thomas, most of them Southerners who were intensely worried about Republican challengers. One of them, Richard Shelby of Alabama, became a Republican after the 1994 election. Three Democrats who initially supported Thomas, including Harry Reid, voted against him. Two Republicans opposed the nomination, Jim Jeffords and Bob Packwood. Bill Cohen supported Thomas.

From the floor, a somber Mitchell spoke of "this terrible episode." In a speech to Planned Parenthood two days after the vote, Mitchell said, "Recently, while in Maine, a woman came up to me and said, with great emotion, 'Please vote against Judge Thomas, because if he's confirmed, the right of choice will be lost.' I told her that the right of choice was lost when George Bush was elected president. Judge Thomas has been confirmed and will soon be sitting on the Supreme Court. There he will vote to restrict the right of choice by women."

Working with Bill Clinton as president was a challenge of a different order. Mitchell said later that he enjoyed working with Bush. "When President Bush first entered office, in his inaugural address he offered a hand of friendship, physically and orally, to us. . . . We accepted and we wanted to work together, and we had a number of notable successes of cooperation." Still, he said, "It was much easier with President Clinton." That was not a universal view.

The Democrats did try to do things differently. The beginning of the Carter administration had been a moment of extreme Democratic disunity. Bennett Johnston had been Jimmy Carter's state campaign chairman, but was "very disappointed" by Carter's frosty relationship with congressional leaders. "After he was defeated" in 1980, Johnston said, "he didn't come back to Washington for over a year, and when he did have some kind of dinner, not one member of Congress was invited. A lot of us were very hurt."

By contrast, Mitchell organized a congressional unity event at the Waldorf in New York immediately after Clinton's election, even though a second Southern Democratic president faced skepticism within the party. Mitchell ensured that all the senators who'd sought the nomination against Clinton were there.

Dick Gephardt, the House majority leader who worked effectively with Mitchell on budget issues, said there were inherent tensions with the new president—not least because few Democrats, including Mitchell, had ever served under a Democratic president. Gephardt was stunned when Clinton finally produced a health care bill late in 1993, and expected Congress to pass it intact. "This was a case where the White House kind of wrote a bill and handed it to the leaders in Congress and said, 'This is what we want.'"

John Hilley disliked the stimulus bill Clinton expected Mitchell to push through the Senate. Clinton had campaigned on the issue, arguing effectively that Bush had ignored the lingering recession, but he'd also presented a budget that called for significant budget cuts and tax increases. Hilley said Republicans contended that Clinton wanted to drive up the federal deficit before cutting it. "It was a horribly ill-conceived bill to start with, of which we'd not had sufficient input," Hilley said. "They hadn't devised their own program, so they threw it to the Appropriations Committee"—chaired by Byrd—"which did what appropriators do, which is ladle it out to their various interests. When we got to the floor, we got slaughtered."

Patrick Griffin, who'd left his partnership with David Johnson and was working at the White House, was appalled by the level of disorganization under Clinton's first chief of staff, Mack McLarty. After McLarty's replacement by Leon Panetta, he said, "It became much more rational, but it was still a pretty dysfunctional place."

A key moment with Clinton came, according to Jay Rockefeller, when the president showed up, unannounced, at a Senate Democratic caucus. "Mitchell, very nicely but very firmly, said, You are the executive branch, we are the legislative branch; we are now meeting to discuss policies," Rockefeller said. "This is our time, and I would ask you please not to be here." After a tense moment, Rockefeller said, "The president and the Secret Service and all just left. And it was a magnificent moment . . . because it shows the strength of the Senate, and the power of a firm leader."

THOUGH HE WAS NOW SINGLE, MITCHELL'S personal life during his six years as majority leader was limited, mostly by his twelve- to fourteen-hour workdays. He dated several women, one of them named in the Washington press—Janet Mullins Grissom, Bob Packwood's former chief of staff, who was then legislative affairs director for the State Department.

Classical music was a consolation. Mitchell said he has had no musical training, but likes to have the radio on, tuned to a classical station, whenever he's at home. "I don't really know much about music," he said. "I'm a listener, not a student." He remembers that one night, tired after arriving home at eleven p.m. from the Senate, he put on a recording of Rachmaninoff's *Symphony No. 2* and noticed a haunting melody. "I must have played that record every night for the next two weeks," he said.

He had less time for personal reading. It was the first time since his apprenticeship with Elvira Whitten all those years ago, Mitchell said, that he was no longer able to keep a book going from his nightstand.

Some things didn't change, however. Despite being scheduled to the hilt, and dependent on others for food and transportation, Mitchell still occasionally got behind the wheel even as majority leader. Kelly Currie was a young intern who later became one of Mitchell's most trusted aides, on a par with Martha Pope, and he often was the chauffeur in Washington. Currie immediately noticed Mitchell's encyclopedic knowledge of Washington streets, dating from his days as an insurance claims adjuster. "He always had great advice, and there were actually times when he wanted to drive. He was just like, 'Move over, I'm driving.' He likes to drive fast, too. . . . He knew DC really, really well, so I learned DC really well, partly because he knew it so well."

George Mitchell's class photo from Waterville High School, late 1940s.

A family photo of Mitchell's parents, Mary and George Sr., with the house at 49 Front Street where he grew up.

Frank Coffin swears in George Mitchell as a US District Court judge in 1979; Mitchell served only six months on the bench.

Surrounded by his family, George Mitchell shakes hands with Ed Muskie after being sworn in as his successor in 1980. Sally Mitchell is at left; daughter Andrea is to the right.

In an expansive moment, George Mitchell rallies supporters during the 1982 Senate race, accompanied by Ed Muskie.

George Mitchell served with Bill Cohen (right), seen here in 1980, during his entire fifteen-year US Senate career.

George Mitchell meets with President Bill Clinton in the Oval Office in 1994.

Barack Obama's first official appointment in 2009 was his selection of George Mitchell as Middle East Special Envoy. They are joined by Mitchell's second wife, Heather, and Secretary of State Hillary Clinton (far right).

15

THE BEDROCK
OF GOVERNMENT

Presidents are supposed to bring their agendas before the people, but that's not expected of majority leaders. With their managerial roles paramount, and given the Senate's uniquely fractious nature, most Senate leaders have little time or energy to devote to thinking about the course of the nation. George Mitchell did so, however, and set himself the unenviable but essential task of putting federal finances back in order after a decade where they had veered alarmingly out of control. The Reagan tax cuts and defense buildup created an annual deficit in peacetime the likes of which had never been seen before—and most of Washington, including the next president, appeared uninterested in doing anything about it. Over the next six years, Mitchell led efforts under two different presidents to restore the federal budget and the national economy to balance. And he succeeded.

Mitchell believed, above all, in fiscal prudence. He was not drawn to tax cuts or tax increases, and was skeptical of both. He had strong views about what constituted a fair system of taxation, but he also saw taxation not as an isolated issue, as Ronald Reagan had, but as the necessary support for the national government's programs and commitments. In a floor speech, he quoted George Washington, at the end of his presidency in 1796, who said, "Toward the payment of debts there must be revenue; that to have revenue there must be taxes; that no taxes can be devised which are not more or less inconvenient and unpleasant."

Fiscal responsibility was not only good policy, but good politics, he believed. In a speech to the AFL-CIO on February 20, 1989, Mitchell said, "We continue to lose presidential elections while winning congressional and gubernatorial elections. And I believe that one of the reasons for that inconsistency is that state and congressional Democrats have continued to identify with the economic aspirations of average Americans, while presidential Democrats have not," and added, "The presidential Democratic Party has come to be seen as the party that does not put economic growth high on its priority list."

Mitchell had also said, "The New Deal and the Reagan reaction to it are over." He may have been premature about the latter assertion, but continued to draw inspiration from the New Deal, even though he frankly described the tangible achievements of Franklin Roosevelt as less lasting than many believed. In a speech the previous summer at the University of Maine at Machias, before a performance of *Sunrise at Campobello*, set at Roosevelt's summer home off the Maine coast, he dwelled on FDR's "defeats." These included his unsuccessful bid for the US Senate from New York in 1914, and his presence on the 1920 Democratic ticket as vice president, with its landslide loss to Warren Harding and Calvin Coolidge—and being struck by polio. "Before he was forty years old, he had been defeated both statewide and nationwide, and was permanently crippled. How easy it would have been to give up, to accept what fate then appeared to dictate: the life of a comfortable invalid."

Mitchell made no reference to his own political career, which had similar reverses. He said of Roosevelt, "But of course he didn't give up. Tonight's play tells part of his story. It is one of courage and resolve in the face of adversity." Mitchell, like Roosevelt, labored long and hard over the words he used in public. "He knew," Mitchell said, "as one biographer put it, 'that those words would constitute the bulk of the estate that he would leave to posterity.'" That judgment, Mitchell said, was correct. "Except for the one great public policy monument that today remains intact, the Social Security system, most of Roosevelt's programs and policies are no more." Agencies famous in their day—the Civilian Conservation Corps, the Works Progress Administration— disappeared with World War II. "Roosevelt's true legacy—the only thing above all others that he gave our nation—was the idea that in a democracy where the people are sovereign, the government must do more than simply observe its citizens' economic, political, and civil liberties. Roosevelt's legacy was to empower Americans to act through their government for their own common good." To renew that legacy, Mitchell believed, the nation's fiscal house must first be put back in order.

Mitchell had sought appointment to the Finance Committee to bolster his political fortunes. Once there, he worked diligently to master the terrain. The Finance Committee is one of the Senate's oldest and most powerful committees, with an expansive jurisdiction encompassing not only the federal financial system, but also such key jurisdictions as Social Security and health care, issues which engaged Mitchell perhaps as much as any other. He needed an experienced hand for his committee staff, and chose Tom Gallagher, a South Dakota native who, like many of his generation, found Washington a magnet for his career ambitions.

Gallagher graduated from the Kennedy School at Harvard—"Washington's a kind of Emerald City if you have a master's in public policy," he said—and went to work for the Congressional Research Service. He moved to the Senate Budget Committee to work for Ed Muskie, where he told himself, "This is a really safe job because, unlike working for an individual senator where your job insecurity comes every six years, I'm working for the majority party, and Democrats are never going to lose their majority." Then came the election of 1980, "and a lot of Democratic staff were out looking for jobs." Gallagher, after Mitchell succeeded Muskie, was able to move to Finance.

Gallagher had the benefit of an unusually flattering reference from John McEvoy, one of Muskie's former chiefs of staff who became staff director for the Budget Committee. McEvoy called Jim Case, in Mitchell's office, and told him Gallagher would be perfect—that he'd worked for the Budget Committee for four or five years, and had a PhD in economics. Gallagher witnessed the call, then said, "I haven't worked for you for four or five years, it's one year, and I don't have a PhD." McEvoy's reply was, "No charge." By the time Gallagher was hired, David Johnson had come aboard, but he apparently agreed with McEvoy's assessment.

One thing that immediately impressed Gallagher about Mitchell was his presence on the floor. For most senators, a constant task for the staff was to clean up remarks for the *Congressional Record*, official publication for floor proceedings. "Every few years somebody like *Reader's Digest* would expose the scandal that the *Congressional Record* isn't really the verbatim record of what was said on the Senate floor," Gallagher said. He recalls another staffer saying, "OK, here's the start of the sentence on page forty-seven; I think he ended it here on page fifty-three, if we just kind of move these together and block this out." It was, he added, "horrible work." But not for Mitchell. "I just stopped doing this for Senator Mitchell, because I never had to make any changes. Not only did he speak in complete sentences, but he spoke in well-ordered paragraphs."

Gallagher said Mitchell didn't have a natural bent for Finance Committee work. "Economics wasn't really his strong suit, so I probably had more freedom to roam. Obviously, being the lawyer and judge that he was, he was more drawn to those kinds of issues and foreign policy, and less drawn to the core economic issues." It was during the debates over the Reagan tax cuts that Mitchell first took notice of the Social Security cuts the president had also proposed, "and that became a big issue for Senator Mitchell, and most Democrats, in the run-up to the 1982 midterm election."

WHILE STILL A BUDGET COMMITTEE MEMBER, Mitchell had given a 1980 floor speech in favor of a $22 billion tax cut—$39 billion annually—that would be dwarfed by the package Ronald Reagan rolled out after his election. While Mitchell had strong doubts about the size and distribution of the Reagan plan, he voted for it after it had been scaled back from three annual 10-percent across-the-board rate reductions to an initial cut of 5 percent, and 25 percent overall, along with a top rate reduction.

"I felt that reducing the top rate from 70 percent, where it had been, to a lower figure made sense," he said. The new top rate was 50 percent. Initial budget projections once the tax cut took effect were so alarming that Bob Dole, the Finance Committee chair, introduced a tax bill the following year. The Tax Equity Act of 1982 was the first of several revenue increases Dole authored. He didn't see it as a "tax increase," merely a "loophole closing," a distinction that has since faded. Mitchell thought the bill's increases far from equitable, and voted against it.

Aside from tax bills, Mitchell's first years on Finance were relatively uneventful. He wasn't a major player in the Social Security rescue plan, the 1983 package that made major changes both in benefits and taxes. The early retirement penalty was increased, and full retirement age delayed, while the payroll tax went from 5.1 percent for both employers and employees to 6.2 percent. That was primarily the work of Dole and, on the Democratic side, Daniel Moynihan.

The tax climate changed sharply in 1984, as Reagan sought reelection with the "Morning in America" campaign, and Walter Mondale challenged him about mushrooming deficits. Mitchell got a new Finance staffer as well. Gallagher moved to the International Trade Commission, and was replaced by Bob Rozen, looking to relocate after five years with Senator Wendell Ford of Kentucky, the state where Rozen had grown up. He said of Ford, who became Mitchell's second majority whip in 1990, "Senator Ford was a very good Democrat and could be counted on to vote with the party, but the state is rather conservative, and I thought my political views were more in line with Senator Mitchell's." Rozen had earlier interviewed with Lloyd Bentsen, the ranking Democrat, but didn't get the job.

Rozen found Mitchell different, both personally and politically. "When I worked for Wendell Ford, every day he would come back by your desk, he would walk through the office," he said. "Quite often he'd answer your phone if it was ringing, just to be funny to whoever was calling." Mitchell never would have done things like that, Rozen said. "He was very nice, he was reserved, kind of the Yankee reserve." Like Gallagher, Rozen was impressed by Mitchell's demeanor on the floor. "There were times when I would write a floor speech or a statement for the committee, and I wouldn't be convinced of what the arguments were, but when I heard it given I would be convinced," Rozen said. "He had a voice that had a lot of gravitas in it." As a questioner, Mitchell "was a real gentleman," he said. "If he had a person from the executive branch who was testifying, he would have us call and tell them what the questions would be so they wouldn't be caught off guard. . . . As a staffer, I always tried to do that, but he'd want to warn them."

Mitchell often challenged his staff. "Regardless of the issue, when you told him what he should do, he invariably disagreed and argued with you," Rozen said. "He was always complaining, 'No, I can't do that,' or . . . 'No, I don't agree,' but he would quite often do it." Rozen found this "amusing," and Mitchell's Socratic technique had less of an edge than it did with Muskie. Rozen said, "You respect people more who challenge you, who don't just cave in when you disagree, so I think part of that was just his personality, wanting to challenge and draw you out and make you justify your advice."

After Reagan's reelection, Rozen documented the existing and future consequences of the administration's economic policies, marked by significant domestic spending cuts but much larger defense increases, and, of course, mammoth tax cuts, truly "the largest in history." For fiscal 1982, the deficit was $45 billion, $17 billion higher than Carter's blueprint. The following year, the deficit doubled to $92 billion. The third Reagan budget doubled the deficit again, to $189 billion. The Congressional Budget Office projected $200 billion deficits "as far as the eye can see," and some second-term deficits were even larger.

In a memo to Mitchell, Rozen wrote, "It's no mystery why President Reagan has yet to propose a balanced budget. Most observers agree that any real solution to the deficit problem will require revenue increases and a slowdown in the Reagan military buildup, as well as continued restraint on domestic spending. If revenues are not increased and military spending growth is not slowed, balancing the budget will require virtually dismantling most of civilian government." Rozen then commented on Reagan's latest proposal—a balanced budget amendment to the Constitution. "Having no constructive plan to offer, President Reagan and his Republican allies have instead opted for a political ploy—their current media campaign for a balanced budget amendment." He concludes, "Despite all the Republican rhetoric and fancy television advertisements, the basic fact remains that solving the deficit problem does not require amending the Constitution. The way to solve the problem is to formulate a plan for balancing the budget and then to implement that plan. So far, President Reagan has refused to take the first step." The balanced budget amendment remained part of Republican campaigns for years, and was a key element in Newt Gingrich's 1994 "Contract with America."

The Reagan deficits were truly unprecedented for peacetime. The last surplus was in Lyndon Johnson's final budget. From 1970, when the deficit was $2.8 billion, it increased sharply by 1975 to $53.2 billion under Richard Nixon. Nixon's deficits were $70 billion over five years; amid "stagflation," Gerald Ford ran deficits of $180 billion for three years. Reagan's eight years produced $1.4 trillion in deficits.

The leading exposé about the Reagan budgets was William Greider's lengthy insider account in *The Atlantic* about his college classmate David Stockman, head of the Office of Management and Budget, or OMB. It's best known for Stockman's assertion that, contrary to the public emphasis on tax cuts for everyone, the Kemp-Roth bill, with its across-the-board cuts, "was always a Trojan horse to bring down the top rate." The other memorable passage concerned the bidding, joined by House Democrats, over which party could provide the biggest corporate tax breaks. "The hogs were really feeding," Stockman said. "The greed level, the level of opportunism, just got out of control." The central problem, however, Greider presented almost as an aside: Wall Street banker Henry Kaufman's assessment that "cutting taxes and pumping up the defense budget would produce not balanced budgets but inflationary deficits."

The immediate challenge of reining in deficits fell to Bob Dole as Finance chair, and he produced almost annual bills to stem red ink. Mitchell generally opposed them because Dole's changes were regressive. Mitchell took his lead not from Dole, but from the former Democratic chairman, Russell Long, who retired in 1986. Despite his concerns, Mitchell never introduced legislation that would have rolled back the Reagan reductions and, while Reagan was in office, they doubtless wouldn't have gotten very far. Mitchell observed, "Reagan was a brilliant guy politically, and one of the reasons is, he had very clear views on things, and had a capacity to disregard facts inconsistent with his views. He always said he'd never raised taxes, but he signed this bill in 1982, which at the time was the biggest tax increase in history. But it didn't have a personal income tax increase. In President Reagan's mind . . . the words 'taxes' and 'personal income taxes' were interchangeable."

While Dole's efforts didn't earn Mitchell's vote, they did win Tom Gallagher's respect. "Starting in 1982, Senator Dole took it upon himself to address the deficit," said Gallagher. "He was determined to try to close the budget gap, to play the role of the fiscally responsible moderate Republican, much to the chagrin of die-hard Reagan supporters." Internal Republican conflicts over taxes were growing. Gallagher said, "I remember where some conservatives came in, saying, 'Yeah, we're going to shoot all the liberals, starting with Bob Dole.'"

THE FINANCE COMMITTEE EFFORT THAT did engage Mitchell was tax reform, which came to the fore in 1986. During the 1970s and '80s, tax shelters for investors grew by leaps and bounds, and expansion of businesses preferences in the 1981 Kemp-Roth bill had, ironically, dramatized the tax code's failure to efficiently raise revenue. Mitchell introduced his own tax reform bill in 1982, and said, "After a year and a half on the Finance Committee, it is clear to me that what we need is not just a more fair tax system, but a tax system that does not invite contempt and does not encourage cheating. Our current tax laws are so riddled with special treatments, exclusions, and preferences that the average person can no longer understand what the tax laws mean. By simplifying the tax code and modifying or eliminating these special tax breaks, tax rates could be lowered substantially without sacrificing total revenues. The result would be that higher-income persons currently paying lower amounts of taxes would pay more, and the majority of taxpayers would end up paying less."

Republican members had other ideas. Some said a flat tax, uniformly applied, would take care of tax shelters. But Mitchell said there was no need to scuttle progressive rates. "Some of the flat tax rate schemes could easily end up overtaxing those at the lower end of the scale, and produce a minimal tax burden on persons with high income," he said on the floor. "Our tax code has always taken into account the ability to pay. We should not sacrifice that well-tested principle." Mitchell was assigned to open and close the Democratic response to Reagan's State of the Union address on February 4, 1986. He said, "On the budget, we must finally make real choices. We can no longer rely on rhetoric which refuses to face the real world—which pretends we can have un-limited military spending, and unrestrained tax breaks, and a balanced budget, all at the same time. It hasn't happened. It won't happen. It can't happen." In an echo of Ed Muskie's Election Eve speech, Mitchell concluded, "And when he says it again, as he often has, the President is wrong. And the American people know he's wrong."

Tax reform might improve at least one part of that equation. Bob Packwood had succeeded Dole as committee chair when Dole became majority leader, and led the first round of discussions. The resulting bill, in Bob Rozen's estimation, fell far short. "The bill Chairman Packwood put together was a disaster. He basically took care of his constituencies and didn't move the ball toward reform. That process failed."

Packwood admitted as much, and started over. Instead of inviting lobbyists to explain why their preferences were essential, he reduced preferences to zero and asked why they should be restored. Rozen said Bill Bradley took the lead among Democrats, and Mitchell joined him in advocating broad-ranging reform. Packwood named a six-member working group from the twenty-member committee to assist him. Daniel Moynihan joined Bradley and Mitchell for the Democrats; John Chafee, John Danforth, and Malcolm Wallop were the Republicans. "There were things we were adopting that George didn't necessarily agree with," Packwood said, "but he understood that the bill was a good bill, and he would sort of reserve his rights and say, 'At some point I may try to remove this, but let's go ahead.'" While some deductions remained relatively unscathed, such as for mortgage interest and charitable donations, the Finance Committee scrapped a host of exclusions, and eliminated the most egregious tax shelters. This produced a dramatic reduction in rates without sacrificing revenue, as Mitchell had long advocated.

Mitchell liked the overall approach, but had doubts. The primary one is that he believed the new top personal income tax rate of 28 percent, initially 27 percent, was too low. Just five years earlier, the top rate had gone from 70 percent to 50 percent. Now it was scheduled to sink to a level not seen since before the Great Depression, when federal spending was a tiny fraction of subsequent levels. To get there, Republicans proposed raising the capital gains rate, on "unearned income," from 20 percent to the same 28 percent level. Mitchell was suspicious. It was an article of Republican faith that the capital gains rate needed to be lower than "ordinary income" in order to provide investment incentives. He noted that Reagan had proposed a 35 percent top rate. Mitchell recalls telling the working group, "I'll vote to get it out on the floor, but . . . I'm going to offer an amendment to put the rates back where they were." The idea, Mitchell said, "was to retain the differential not by lowering the rate, but by keeping the maximum rate at 35 percent." Packwood let Mitchell offer his floor amendment, but Bradley disagreed. He thought amending the bill would doom it, and he and Mitchell had a lively debate in the Democratic Caucus.

Later, Mitchell asked John Chafee, his Republican counterpart and friend on Finance, as well as EPW, "How could all these Republicans vote to eliminate the capital gains differential?" Chafee's response was, "They want the lower rate more than anything," and added, "And as soon as it's the law, they'll come back on capital gains"—another Trojan horse.

The Mitchell Amendment was one of the major floor debates on tax reform, and took place on June 18, 1986. It occupies thirty pages in the *Congressional Record* and lasted five hours. Mitchell said his primary objective was to provide greater tax relief for the middle class by reducing the lowest rate from 15 percent to 14 percent, keeping the 27 percent rate, and adding a 35 percent rate for income above $68,000. The amendment was complex, but the effect was easily understood. The Republicans would get their preferential treatment for capital gains, but higher-income taxpayers would shoulder more of the load.

After four hours of debate, Majority Leader Dole asked about a dinner break, but advocates such as Pat Leahy and Frank Lautenberg of New Jersey pressed on. Mitchell had a show of his own. The Senate had recently approved televising sessions on C-SPAN, and Rozen prepared charts and illustrations, with the help of one of Mitchell's young staffers, to illustrate the amendment for viewers. "Now they've got a big production center that churns them out, but . . . we were the first ones to do charts," Rozen said. "We showed how the rich were going to pay more, and it was all going to go to the middle class, and it was a very compelling argument." Rozen wanted to be available to Mitchell, and "I didn't want to be the person to turn the charts . . . so my able assistant, Grace Reef, was the chart-turner. The *New York Times* did a story about the use of charts, and featured Grace, because she was the chart-turner for George Mitchell."

Reef remembers the occasion. It was her first time on the Senate floor, and the charts weren't cooperating. "There I was, with a roll of electrical tape, trying to get them to behave," she said. She remembers Rozen telling her, "This is the foundation for becoming a legislative assistant."

Bill Bradley regretted opposing the Mitchell Amendment; he'd made similar proposals. "I could almost give his speech because I gave that speech thirty times in 1981," Bradley said. He'd recommended the tax reform approach to Walter Mondale. "Since Reagan was the great tax-cutter, Democrats were going to get tarred for a tax increase," Bradley said, "so why doesn't he advocate lower rates and fewer loopholes?" Mondale wasn't interested.

Finally, Packwood called for a vote, and the Mitchell Amendment was defeated, 71–29. Every Republican opposed it, and while Mitchell did win a majority of Democrats—which he said was surprising, given Bradley's prominence on tax reform—many leading Democrats, including Hubert Humphrey, Lloyd Bentsen, Chris Dodd, Daniel Moynihan, and Ted Kennedy, opposed him. When the Senate-House conference report came back, Mitchell voted for it, but said, "I believe it is fundamentally flawed in one major respect. I am deeply disappointed that this legislation abandons our historic commitment to a progressive system of federal income taxation. The essentially flat rate structure of this bill . . . is inconsistent with basic American concepts of fairness."

Rozen said Republicans anticipated big political gains from tax reform. "Republicans felt it would be a landmark bill, something they could boast about for some time, and the American people would embrace because tax rates were reduced," he said. "And it really didn't work out that way." One reason, he decided, was that a seemingly minor change altered the employer withholding rates by which most Americans pay taxes. The old rates resulted in over-withholding, meaning people got big refund checks because too much was being taken out. The results were counterintuitive. "They got smaller refund checks back, and that kind of soured them on this tax reform," Rozen said. "Even though . . . their taxes were cut, to them the most visible thing was the refund, and it was smaller."

MITCHELL HAD LOST ONE ROUND IN A BATTLE he knew would continue, but he had a signal victory on another front. Cuts to domestic programs had not been across the board, but were concentrated in agencies such as the Department of Housing and Urban Development, whose staff was cut by 30 percent, and its oversight capabilities decimated. The resulting scandals that surrounded HUD Secretary Samuel Pierce didn't unfold until later, but reduced federal support was creating, in Mitchell's view, an affordable housing shortage amid the 1980s real estate boom. With less direct federal spending, housing subsidies were increasingly created through tax shelters. While the shelters were inefficient and largely ineffective in producing housing, their virtual elimination through tax reform could have turned a shortage into a crisis.

Bob Rozen said reviving the old shelters wasn't viable. "They were poorly designed for the purpose of creating affordable housing. They weren't specifically targeted to reducing rents." So, with Mitchell's permission, Rozen designed an alternative as part of the tax reform bill. "This was something I cared about, and he cared about, and he pretty much gave me free rein because he trusted me," Rozen said. "We just totally reworked the program, creating a credit-based system rather than a deduction-based system. We made a lot of changes in the committee, further changes on the floor, further changes in conference, and Mitchell had a major floor amendment. Ted Kennedy was a big supporter, and we worked it out with Chairman Packwood." Mitchell headed a task force with Republican John Danforth that improved the program in 1989, and it was made permanent in 1993. "It's a real legacy program, and it's become the primary means of building affordable housing. And Mitchell was the first member of Congress to get behind it and move it," Rozen said.

Mitchell, in his memoir, called the Low Income Housing Credit a "minor bill that had a major impact," but it wasn't clear that it would pass muster; the whole idea of tax reform was to do away with preferences, not create new ones. "There are some areas of our economy where there is no market in which profit-seeking enterprises can operate successfully," he wrote. "One such market is in the provision of housing for families with very low income." The reason the tax credit works better than deductions to taxpayer-investors is that, by targeting credits to developers, it swaps debt for equity. Because developers know precisely how much they'll gain from including low-income units in a larger development, they can use the credits with banks to help finance the whole project. Because of Rozen's efforts, and his clear explanation of how the tax credit would work, Mitchell gained nineteen co-sponsors for his amendment, including five Republicans.

Joe Wishcamper, a Portland developer and Mitchell supporter, was one of many developers who'd used HUD's Section 8 subsidies to rehab buildings and build new ones. But "like every other program that private industry gets hold of, there were a lot of abuses, and people were basically ginning up losses that shouldn't have existed to be able to raise more money, and the government eventually decided it needed to crack down," Wishcamper said.

While it still exists, the Section 8 program is much smaller, and to make the numbers work, it needs to be combined with tax credits, he said. Wishcamper was among the first developers nationally to understand and use the program, building nearly ten thousand units in thirteen states. Wishcamper wasn't surprised that Mitchell won over skeptical senators; he'd dealt with him earlier as an attorney on real estate deals. "His intelligence wasn't overbearing," Wishcamper said of Mitchell. "I could sit down with him and talk about an issue. He was probably honing the skills he eventually was so successful with, which was to be more intelligent than anybody else in the room, but not having anyone else resent it."

When Mitchell attended housing events, "He did something extraordinary," Rozen said. "The low-income housing community really appreciated all he did, and they would invite him to come to groundbreakings and speak. And whenever he did . . . he would always call me out and say, 'It was really Bobby that did it.' But it wasn't me, because no matter how much work I did, he was the one willing to put his name on it."

MITCHELL'S FRIENDSHIP WITH JIM SASSER ALSO brought him the aide who became his last Majority Office chief of staff. John Hilley was the Budget Committee's staff director, where Sasser had succeeded Lawton Chiles as ranking

Democrat, then chairman. "That's why I got to know George Mitchell, because throughout the 1980s and early '90s, budget matters were at the fore," Hilley said. After talking with Martha Pope, who was leaving for the Senate staff in 1991, Hilley thought he'd move to the Democratic Policy Committee, but instead was told the chief of staff job was his, "which I was very, very happy to take." His first sustained exposure to Mitchell had come the previous year, when he was Sasser's staff representative at the Andrews Air Force Base "summit," called to negotiate a budget agreement with the Bush administration. "I think the reason he wanted me to be chief of staff is because he understood that the budget's never-ending," Hilley said. "And this was the age of trying to fill the deficit hole, and it was the primary focus of domestic policy from 1981, when the budget was first blown open, to 1997, when we were finally able to balance the budget again."

By this time, Mitchell's skills on economic issues had advanced to the point where Hilley called them "unbelievable. . . . He had a clear analytic mind and a very reasoned way of approaching everything, but he was also incredibly numerate, so that quantitative issues were easy for him. So there was never this issue of 'I don't understand,' or 'Do that again.' He was very easy to deal with. . . . I was very fortunate to have a boss who was smarter than I am."

When George Bush presented his first budget in January 1989, Mitchell was unimpressed. A new president usually introduces his most important programs there, but there was little in the Bush budget that differed from the Reagan blueprint. The new president had said in his inaugural address that the nation had "more will than wallet," but there was no plan to combat a rising deficit. What Bush did have was a plan to cut the capital gains tax; John Chafee's prediction had been borne out.

Mitchell believed this was no time to be cutting taxes. He had built his case steadily over previous sessions, and offered a concise overview in 1988 remarks to the National Economic Commission, one of many groups charged with finding some solution, any solution, to the deficit—as long as it wasn't too painful. "The federal government today collects roughly the same amount of revenue, as a percentage of GNP, as it did during the 1970s," Mitchell told the commission. "However, to raise that revenue, the government now relies to a far greater extent on regressive taxes than it did a decade ago. The correspondingly smaller role of the progressive income tax means that the highest-income families in America have benefited from substantial tax reduction in recent years, while all other income groups bear heavier or constant burdens. In effect, the federal government has replaced billions of dollars in tax revenue from the wealthy with billions of dollars of borrowing to finance the deficit."

Mitchell pointed out that, compared to 1977, the lowest tenth of Americans, by income, were paying 20 percent more in tax, while the highest tenth were paying 20 percent less. He addressed the frequent claim that the wealthy were paying more taxes; this was, he said, because they had a greater share of national income. "According to the CBO, the share of income claimed by the top 1 percent increased by 46 percent, while their share of taxes increased only 23 percent." By contrast, "the lower half of taxpayers saw their income share fall 9 percent, but paid only 6 percent less in taxes." In a 1987 floor statement, he said, "What has happened in this country in the last seven years is that we have pursued a two-track policy on taxes. We have reduced the income tax, which is based on ability to pay, and we have increased every other federal tax, all of which are unrelated to ability to pay."

The Bush administration thought it had a good counterargument and, at the beginning of the capital gains debate, it also appeared to have the votes. A substantial number of Democrats were on record, or leaning toward, capital gains cuts, and Bush could expect support from virtually every Senate Republican. Joe Lieberman, a freshman Democrat from Connecticut, told the *Washington Times* that he supported the plan because of indirect benefits. Workers would "get a job if they have none, or a better job if they are employed," he said. Bob Rozen commented, in a memo to Mitchell, "This is a case of a new senator, unfamiliar with economic debate in Washington since 1981, who is a sucker for the arguments about the great things that will occur if the rich don't have to pay taxes."

In a letter to Mitchell on January 31, Bush asked for prompt consideration. "The subject of capital gains has, in the past, led to partisan conflict," he wrote. "In some cases, it has engendered demagogic argument and counterargument. I'm sure none of us would wish to see a repeat performance." In the letter, Bush suggested that Mitchell defer to the favorable judgment of Alan Greenspan, who'd taken over as Federal Reserve chairman from Paul Volcker in 1987, and was to serve until 2006.

Bush's trump card involved studies showing that cutting the capital gains tax increases revenue. That idea had been thoroughly discredited concerning taxes on ordinary income, with the Reagan deficits one result. But the immediate effect for capital gains seemed positive. Mitchell said that was because, unlike ordinary income, where the tax is paid when income is earned, investors can choose when to sell stocks or bonds, in effect timing their taxes. In a recent interview, he said he wasn't opposed to lower capital gains rates per se.

"Properly structured and targeted toward small businesses—particularly start-ups—a capital gains differential can make a difference, but not in the manner proposed by President Bush, which increased the deficit by reducing revenues," he said. "Now, they always argue that when you create the differential, there's an increase in revenues. That's a one-time deal, a short-term deal, because a lot of transactions then occur. But the inevitable result, after that initial bump, is that revenues go down." He added, "I never doubt the sincerity of those who believe that cutting taxes raises revenue, but I think they're wrong. The evidence is overwhelming. . . . The history of the last twenty years pretty clearly supports that view." But Mitchell knew this was a technical argument, and hard to explain. He needed something better to head off the Bush plan.

Mitchell's strategy used the Congressional Budget Office's estimates of who would benefit. After the Reagan tax bill made across-the-board cuts, dramatically reducing progressivity, Democrats instructed the CBO to do a distributional analysis of each tax bill. What it showed for a straight capital gains cut was devastating: Fully 60 percent of the benefits would go to those earning more than $200,000, while just 8 percent would go to those earning less than $50,000, further reducing progressivity. But that still wasn't enough. Few voters paid much heed, although by now reporters were paying attention. The vote count remained discouraging. Bob Rozen calculated that eleven of the fifty-five Democrats, led by Bob Graham and Richard Bryan of Nevada, already supported Bush's plan. John Hilley said, "Capital gains cuts are very popular among senators, not only the business elements, but the timber, mining, and other interests, so it cuts a lot of ways."

From his Budget Committee experience, Hilley knew that if the capital gains plan remained in the budget bill, there was no way Mitchell could stop it, since the "budget reconciliation" vote takes only a simple majority. Lloyd Bentsen, who'd succeeded Packwood when the Democrats regained the majority, had already prepared an intricate revenue plan for the budget. The only way capital gains could be removed, under Senate rules, was if all "extraneous" provisions were scuttled. "I'll never forget the meeting we had with Lloyd Bentsen, who as a powerful chairman had put all sorts of wonderful provisions in," Hilley said. He recalls Mitchell saying, "Lloyd, the only way we're going to beat this is to strip the reconciliation bill of all the provisions, and I know you have more to lose than anybody." Bentsen, who Hilley said "didn't bat an eye," replied, "If that's what you want, Mr. Leader, that's what we'll do."

Even with capital gains out of the budget, the odds were still daunting. Rozen said some Democrats were so incensed at Mitchell's stance they threatened to vote against a debt ceiling increase. "There was a lot of high drama," he said, "because if you didn't raise the debt limit, things shut down." Ultimately, Rozen said, "The key to it was that there was the media attention to the unfairness of it, and secondly, he went toe-to-toe with these Democrats in his caucus, and urged them—and it was a matter of personal intervention—'Do this for me, you don't need this, it doesn't make sense, it goes against what we did a few years ago.' And they decided, based upon the force of his personality and argument, to back down."

There had been plenty of capital gains debates, and Rozen was able to supply an entertaining stock of quotes from senators who, three years earlier, had insisted it was just fine to have capital gains taxed at the same rate as ordinary income. Packwood asked and answered his own question on June 9, 1986, opening the tax reform debate by saying, "So, can we do without a capital gains tax [rate] in this country? I think we can if the rates are kept low enough." Nine days later, Packwood was among many senators to oppose the Mitchell Amendment, which would have set the top rate at 35 percent and kept capital gains at 27 percent. Packwood said the differential would revive the tax shelter game: "We will be lucky if some of them pay anything, because we will have given them the tax dodges to escape paying taxes again." Bush's new plan, with the top rate now 28 percent, would reduce capital gains back to 20 percent.

John Chafee said that "by restoring the differential between capital gains and ordinary income, the Senator from Maine is leading us into that old quagmire from which we are trying to extricate ourselves." And Phil Gramm of Texas, Democrat turned Republican, said, "I am sure the Senator from Maine is very sincere, but the Mitchell Amendment is the same old siren song: Let us take something away from one group and give it to another group."

Pressure on Mitchell increased when the House passed the capital gains cut in September, with one-quarter of the Democrats joining a united Republican caucus. Packwood, now ranking Republican on Finance, didn't appreciate Mitchell's strategy. Packwood claimed the CBO was "estimating a $17 billion revenue loss over five years," while the administration projected a gain. The difference, he said, was "infinitesimal" in terms of "trillions of dollars in transactions." Still, "George was able to take that and say, 'Are you for the rich or are you not for the rich?' . . . He was able to portray that battle as elite and rich vs. the common man." Steve Symms remembers Dick Darman, Bush's budget director, visiting the Republican Caucus, and urging them to stay in session over Thanksgiving and Christmas, if necessary, to push through the capital gains cut.

Mitchell needed forty-one votes to maintain a filibuster, and though some Democrats defected, proponents never got close to sixty votes. Although Mitchell was still speaking against the capital gains cut the following February, by November it was essentially over. The *Wall Street Journal* was impressed. A front-page story was headlined, "Mitchell Defeats Capital Gains Cut Almost by Himself," and began, "Senate Majority Leader George Mitchell lay down on the tracks in front of the capital gains freight train, and he has walked away with a smile. Until recently, the low-key lawmaker was criticized for being too accommodating to President Bush. Not anymore. Through a combination of cajolery and commitment bordering on obsession, the Maine Democrat fought the White House's proposed cut in capital gains taxes and won." It also reported that, while Bush vowed to keep fighting, "White House aides privately acknowledged that Senator Mitchell derailed the capital gains juggernaut."

THERE WAS NO RELIEF FROM BUDGET PRESSURES as 1990 began. Mitchell had found Bush's 1989 budget proposal unsatisfactory, and the new one no better. The deficit problem that had been ignored the previous year ended up taking most of 1990 to resolve. Not everyone thought the deficit would be a high priority. *Congressional Quarterly* had summed up conventional wisdom by saying "The last thing anyone expects George Bush to do as president is balance the federal budget. Chances are he won't try."

A year later, things had changed. Congress now agreed, though with dismay, that the savings and loan crisis could only be resolved by a bailout. The agreement, which Mitchell shepherded through a reluctant Senate roiled by the Keating Five scandal, called for $50 billion in the next budget, declining in subsequent years. The administration wanted the S&L funding "off budget," meaning it wouldn't count against the deficit—as opposed to the Social Security surplus, which it did count. Democrats said S&L funding was a regular budget item. A compromise put $20 billion on budget, and the rest off. Mitchell's performance won him plaudits from Treasury Secretary Nicholas Brady, who said, "Your efforts were instrumental in ensuring that the legislation was kept on track with its essential reforms intact." Brady added a handwritten note, saying "You are a leader. This note comes with thanks for your intensity and understanding," and was signed "Nick."

Another factor prompting deficit reduction was that the Gramm-Rudman budget act was beginning to bite. The law, also co-sponsored by Democrat Fritz Hollings, who got left off the shorthand version, set a series of deficit targets. While no one knew whether Congress could actually meet them, disregarding them could be politically perilous. The next target was $100 billion. While OMB projected a deficit of $116 billion, a manageable number, the CBO estimated $141 billion, which was not—and in Congress, the CBO numbers were what counted. In the end, the deficit was higher than either estimate. The resulting "sequestration" would have cut deeply into both domestic and defense spending.

Within the Bush administration, there were three who dealt directly with Mitchell on the budget: Dick Darman, budget director; John Sununu, chief of staff; and Brady. The big issue for Mitchell was Bush's "Read My Lips" pledge, made repeatedly during the 1988 campaign, that he would never sign a tax increase. While initially a tactic to win over reluctant Republicans in the primary, where Bush faced Bob Dole and Jack Kemp, among others, it was considered sacrosanct by Sununu, a former New Hampshire governor, where taking "the pledge" against a sales or income tax had become part of the state's political DNA. Darman and Brady were more agnostic about tax increases, without which Mitchell had decided there could be no deal. Darman was the stronger personality, but Brady was close to the president. The dynamics among the three would be critical as the debate continued, from mid-May through late October

The first step, since the White House sent conflicting signals, was a meeting with key congressional leaders, including, from the Senate, Jim Sasser as Budget Committee chair and Wyche Fowler from Appropriations. The meetings got nowhere, for a familiar reason summed up by Sununu. He said of congressional leaders, "If they want to come to the table and say they put tax increases there, it is their prerogative to put them on the table, and it's our prerogative to say no. And I emphasize the 'no.'"

Darman came to see Mitchell to explain a possible agreement. The two got along well. Mitchell said of Darman, "He was highly intelligent, articulate, with a wry sense of humor and an occasionally sharp tongue." He told Mitchell that when the leadership group assembled, "Out of this discussion, a tax increase will emerge." When Mitchell asked him to explain, Darman "fluttered his hand, in a rising fashion," and said "Well, it'll just emerge." Mitchell "fluttered back," and said, "I don't think this is good enough. We want to know what does the president propose, because we're concerned that you guys are trying to play a political trick on us."

And so it went. On June 20, Darman announced "a new proposal," but, said Mitchell, "the only thing new in it was the insertion of the word 'new' in the description." It was a discouraging time. Bob Rozen's handwritten notes from a "leadership summit" recorded that, "President doesn't want to do anything. Complete failure of presidential leadership. Won't go to people or propose a plan. Doesn't want to be involved in process." Rozen also believed the White House thought Democrats' insistence on tax increases paired with spending cuts would crack over time, but it didn't. Mitchell made sure of it.

Finally, Mitchell got a call at six a.m. one morning from Sununu, who asked him to come to breakfast at the White House. Mitchell soon found out that Tom Foley, House speaker, and Dick Gephardt, majority leader, were also attending.

Mitchell was hosting a lunch at the Capitol before Nelson Mandela's address to a joint session of Congress, but he accepted Sununu's invitation without hesitation. At 7:30, they had breakfast with Bush, Darman, Brady, and Sununu. Mitchell suggested Foley and Gephardt ride with him, and by the time they got to the White House they had a strategy.

Foley, who some suspected was the weak link, presented the congressional position. The two sides exchanged briefs, which Mitchell said was "very cordial and civil." Then the president said to Darman and Sununu, "Why don't you go into the next room and draft up a statement?" They were gone only briefly, so Mitchell figured the statement had been prepared earlier. It included the phrase "tax revenue increases." When it was presented, and "before anybody said anything," Mitchell said, "Mr. President, this is very positive, but I would like a few minutes." He, Foley, and Gephardt caucused. Mitchell thought, "They're trying to get away with finessing it." And he told Foley and Gephardt, "They think they can explain it away." They agreed on a counteroffer.

When they returned, Mitchell told Bush that "this is not a 'Statement by the President,'" despite the headline saying that, and he eliminated references to "we" to make it clear Bush was speaking. The crucial sentence in the original read, "It is clear that both the size of the deficit problem and the need for a package that can be enacted require all of the following: entitlement and mandatory program reform; tax revenue increases, growth incentives; discretionary spending reductions; orderly reductions in defense expenditures; and budget process reform." Though the sentence included "tax revenue increases," Mitchell added a caret to the first part and inserted "to me," so it now read "It is clear to me." After another change, altering the statement that budget negotiations "should reconvene" to "will resume," all parties endorsed the wording, though the statement remained unsigned.

Mitchell asked if he could keep the paper, and Bush agreed. The congressional leaders quickly returned to the Capitol, with Mitchell calling his aides to arrange a press conference. He suspected what would happen when Sununu called Newt Gingrich, House minority whip, but already in effective control of the caucus, as longtime Republican Leader Bob Michel's influence waned. Sununu attended a House Republican caucus, and Republicans called their own press conference, insisting that the "Read My Lips" pledge still applied, and whatever the president said wouldn't bind House Republicans. It was an act of rebellion Bob Dole never would have countenanced. But Mitchell and the House Democrats got there first. And Mitchell had the piece of paper, stating clearly that Bush had broken his pledge. Jim Sasser said Mitchell called him during the return trip, "and he was exuberant. And I was exuberant, too, when he told me what had occurred. And I was particularly exuberant that he had it in writing."

Bush addressed the nation and Mitchell followed him, saying the Democratic leaders supported the president. Later, Mitchell decided he'd erred by not trying to tease out what "tax revenue increases" actually meant. "The problem was that while he'd agreed to tax increases, we weren't specific, and so we had another four months of terrible, rancorous debate over what increases, and by how much."

Mitchell was proud of that moment, reproducing the statement in his memoir, and it became almost legendary to his staff. Bob Rozen was blunter than Mitchell about how precarious the Democratic front had been. "Early on, the House wanted to fold on this, and Mitchell and Sasser were adamant—they were not going to do this until the president eats his words, basically." While agreeing that the statement "seriously eroded" Bush's position with Republicans, Rozen said, "It had to be done, and it really was done only because Mitchell and Sasser were relentless." Gephardt agreed, saying, "George Mitchell, of the three of us, was the toughest and strongest and most steadfast in really facing the president down to get him to do what he knew he had to do."

While it seemed like a breakthrough, the "Statement by the President" didn't galvanize the budget talks, which dragged on. Thinking a setting away from the Capitol might help, congressional leaders agreed to a "budget summit" at Andrews Air Force Base after Labor Day—but most of the parties, and all of the disputes, came along with them. Mitchell pressed ahead, but there were distractions. Saddam Hussein's forces invaded Kuwait on August 2, shoring up Bush's popularity, which had been in decline since the capital gains defeat, backing down on taxes, and a perception the administration was adrift.

Bill Frenzel of Minnesota was ranking Republican on the House Budget Committee, then serving the last of ten terms, when he encountered Mitchell at the Andrews summit, and found him "a strong, if not dominant figure," saying, "I was rather surprised at his technical competence. He knew a great deal about the budget." Frenzel said the Andrews talks, while not the end, were helpful. "One of the problems was that we had literally dozens of supposed negotiators, but many of them were just part of the Greek chorus sitting in the background. People would come and go, telephones would ring. Thank God we didn't have cell phones then. . . . We didn't complete work, but we cleared a lot of brush down there."

The Andrews episode had its comical aspects. Jim Sasser recalls that some Republicans didn't bother even to feign interest. "Newt Gingrich didn't participate at all, just sat there and read a newspaper while the rest of us were around the big table trying to work out a budget," Sasser said. Sununu "put his feet up on a table, and I remember Senator Byrd lecturing him that that was improper conduct."

On October 2, negotiators announced an agreement. Dick Gephardt said, "Mitchell was critical in helping keep the Senate folks in line. He had some pretty strong characters to deal with, like Senator Byrd and others, who really didn't want to do any of this. But George . . . kept everybody moving in the right direction, and after a lot of fits and starts we finally got something together."

Meanwhile, Republicans were anxious about the approaching congressional elections, and Bush had come to realize he needed a deal before a likely invasion of Kuwait; he was soon dispatching 200,000 troops, followed by 200,000 more. But Rozen said Democrats were dismayed Bush continued to rule out an income tax increase, while renewing his push for a capital gains cut. This produced some of the $500 million package's odder elements, such as the excise tax on luxury goods, including yachts, expensive cars, and high-priced jewelry. But it was a deal, and the CBO said it met budget targets.

Gingrich wasn't quitting, though. The theory behind the agreement was that it was bipartisan, with unpleasant elements for both sides. Even without an income tax increase, Gingrich saw the increased revenues as a betrayal, and began organizing against the bill. Despite the support of Michel, Foley, and Gephardt, the budget deal was defeated on October 5, 254–179. At that point, House Democrats decided to use their majority to pass a bill more to their liking, while hoping Mitchell could convince Bush, and Senate Republicans, not to block it. The House adopted a new top income tax rate of 33 percent, with a surtax for incomes above $1 million, for an effective top rate of 36.3 percent. Mitchell pushed the Andrews deal through the Senate to convene a House-Senate conference. The conference sped through the spending cuts, and settled on a top rate of 31 percent, plus increases in alcohol, tobacco, and gasoline taxes. The White House signed off. The House approved the agreement 228–200, and the Senate, 54–45. Bush signed it into law on November 5.

Newt Gingrich's first major political gambit backfired. Bill Frenzel said, "The Republicans cut their own throats." He was impressed there was any deal at all, and it was the last time the two parties worked cooperatively on a deficit-reduction package, a quintessentially painful proceeding. "The country and the Congress prospered as a result of that act," Frenzel said. "The people who did the heavy negotiating did a splendid job. It was great for the country, and I keep praying for another one of those agreements."

Bob Kerrey thought that, despite appearances, Bush and Mitchell had a "special relationship" during this period. "President Bush got a lot of criticism for supporting a tax increase, but deserved a tremendous amount of praise, actually, bringing Democrats more towards the center, in some cases center-right, with Paygo and other procedures you'd normally think of as coming from conservative Republicans." Bill Bradley, who was up for reelection, had seen a backlash in New Jersey after Governor Jim Florio, a Democrat, had raised taxes after his election in 1989, and was grateful Mitchell gave him a pass on voting for the deal. Bradley told him "a vote for it was death in New Jersey." After Bradley's narrow win, Mitchell called to say, "You were right. If you'd voted for it you would have lost." Bradley said that while Mitchell was disappointed in his vote, "He was always realistic. . . . If you couldn't be with him and told him, he'd understand, and he'd always have three or four votes that he held back."

In his memoir, Mitchell contrasted the 1990 budget agreement with what came later. "When measured against the needs of the country it was a modest result," he wrote. "When measured against the difficulty of adopting anything that inflicts sacrifice on any segment of society, it was a significant accomplishment. I hoped that from the pain and bitterness of our experience we all had learned valuable lessons that we could apply to better effect in the future. But obviously that didn't happen."

THERE IS A MYTHOLOGY OF WHAT HAPPENED between Bush and Mitchell. No less an ally of Mitchell than Harold Pachios insists that his friend "tricked" the president into signing a tax increase, "and we've had nothing but trouble from the Republicans about taxes ever since." Clearly, Bush had underestimated the difficulty the budget agreement would create for him among Republicans. He had an assertive primary challenger, Patrick Buchanan, two years later, whose entire strategy seemed to be reminding voters about the broken pledge.

Alan Simpson, the Senate Republican whip, dismisses the idea Mitchell ever employed trickery. "I've always said if you have integrity nothing else matters, and if you don't have integrity nothing else matters," Simpson said. "And that's George; he had that. There wouldn't be anybody who would at the end say 'George Mitchell tricked me,' or 'He ran a fast one on me.' And I can tell you, I know people like that." Bill Cohen said the budget agreement's tax increase "still resonates with Republicans. They saw it as a breach of faith," adding, "Bush did the right thing, but paid for it."

In a 2014 interview some twenty years later, Mitchell said, "There was no trickery. If you go back and check the record, which I've done, the Republicans were deeply split internally." Democratic senators such as Sasser, Sarbanes,

Riegle, and Fowler were effective in the floor debates, Mitchell said, in pointing out how regressive the tax package the Republicans had insisted on really was. "You get a distribution that shows a huge tax cut for those at the very top, and increases for everyone else. And as these distribution tables were coming up, the Republicans in Congress were panicking because of the midterm elections. That was the factor that drove things."

John Breaux said Mitchell's abilities often confounded the opposition, and did so here. "He was always strongly assertive, and he was also very smart. I wouldn't say how much smarter he was than the president, but there was no question that he knew the subject, and could argue the merits on just about anything with clarity. And it was more than just political posturing or repeating what somebody else had told him. . . . Knowledge is a very powerful weapon in this city, and George had it."

THERE WAS AN IMPORTANT FOOTNOTE to the 1990 budget debate, one so consequential it may ultimately dwarf that agreement in significance. The 1983 Social Security package raised the basic contribution rate by 20 percent, with the aim of generating surpluses over the next forty years in anticipation of the retirement of American's largest generation—the baby boomers. But the law hadn't specified how the federal government should account for the surpluses. The law's authors had decided to postpone any Social Security and Medicare tax increases until near the end of the Reagan administration, safely beyond their next reelection campaign. By 1990, though, surpluses began appearing, and the Bush OMB decided they should appear "on budget," that is, included in the calculation of the current deficit, and made available for current spending. Many lawmakers, and not only Democrats, were outraged. How could the ambitious reform law achieve its goals if the surpluses intended for the baby boomers' retirement were instead diverted to current spending?

Daniel Patrick Moynihan decided he had a way to dramatize and, possibly, turn back the Bush plan. Rather than creating a "lock box" for Social Security, as Democrats later proposed, over and over, Moynihan decided to take a page from the administration's contribution to the budget negotiations. Called "pay as you go," or Paygo, the idea was that if any lawmaker wanted to increase spending, he or she would have to find a revenue source to match. The rule, though sometimes waived or disregarded, is still part of federal budget procedures.

Moynihan proposed a Paygo in reverse for Social Security taxes. Rather than accumulating surpluses immediately, Moynihan proposed reducing the tax rate back to 5.1 percent from 6.2 percent, and only beginning to increase it in 2011. There would be no surplus to fight over, and no one would be tempted to spend it elsewhere. What followed was a pitched, but largely inside-the-Beltway battle. It turned out the public wasn't much concerned over which rate was used—perhaps another case of payroll withholding muting concerns over taxes.

Moynihan was a noted orator and respected thinker, and he made his case well. On December 29, 1989, he introduced his plan, saying, "I make this proposal because it has now become clear that the administration intends to use the Social Security payroll tax as an ongoing, permanent source of revenue for the general purposes of government. There is a word for this—the word is 'thievery.'"

Moynihan had been pushing Mitchell on the issue. The previous January, he'd written to the new majority leader about keeping the Social Security surplus "off budget." He said, "It will be painful to balance the budget. But the reward will be vastly different from the satisfaction that is said to come from performance of duty. The reward will be the transformation of the American economy." When the debate over the surplus was reaching its peak, in July 1990, Moynihan wrote Mitchell, "I see that you and I vote together more often than any other two senators. Which may give you cause for alarm, but is reassuring to me." *Congressional Quarterly* calculated that Moynihan and Mitchell voted together 95 percent of the time, although Mitchell also matched Ted Kennedy 94.7 percent. Moynihan didn't give up. In October, he pronounced, "We are embezzling the pension funds of working men and women."

After holding his fire, Moynihan finally acted, attempting to attach his Paygo amendment to another debt ceiling bill. He had won Mitchell to his side, who urged the caucus to back the amendment. Unfortunately for Moynihan, the one Democrat who outranked him on the Finance Committee, Chairman Lloyd Bentsen, decided to oppose him, splitting the caucus. With Republicans following Bush's lead, the Moynihan amendment was defeated. Lobbying had produced equally mixed results. The AFL-CIO firmly backed Moynihan, but AARP, with its millions of members, decided not to support the proposal "at this time."

Budget Committee Chairman Jim Sasser pondered the difficulties of protecting Social Security while ensuring that taxes were allocated to their intended purpose, and employed a form of gallows humor: "We are reduced to deciding whether the trust fund's surplus is safer being misused, as it is today, or is it safer just reducing it so it cannot be misused."

Estelle Lavoie, who had worked on Social Security earlier for Mitchell, was disappointed. "The surplus over the years wasn't put into a bank account. It was spent by Congress annually to lower the deficit," she said. "So what the Treasury Department did was write bonds, or the equivalent of a promissory note, to the Social Security Trust Fund, saying, 'OK, we took $50 billion from your trust fund and we'll give it back someday.' So there's a five-drawer file cabinet at the Social Security Administration in Parkersburg, West Virginia, that is full of these bonds."

It's true that neither the United States nor any foreign nation has ever accumulated a savings account the size of what the Social Security Trust Fund would be today, had not the government essentially spent it. It could have been used, however, as an investment tool, as some have urged the government to do with annual revenues, and could have stemmed increases in the national debt driven by interest payments. Politicians still refer to the Social Security surplus, but the issue has long since faded. Yet in a very real sense, there is no reserve for the baby boomers' retirement wave.

A LITTLE MORE THAN TWO YEARS LATER, Mitchell was struggling to get agreement on Bill Clinton's first budget. The recession of 1990–1991 had hit the Northeast particularly hard, and when Clinton took office, the idea of another deficit-reduction package was even less appealing than the first one had been. Yet Mitchell believed it was necessary, and so did the president's economic advisers. The recession had deepened the short-term deficit, so reductions expected from the 1990 agreement weren't achieved.

Mitchell had thought from the beginning that the scale of the agreement possible under Bush wouldn't solve the deficit problem, and he was an important voice as the Clinton team decided what to do. As soon as the president proposed tax increases in January, Bob Dole told Clinton he could expect no Republican votes. He'd observed what the tax increases Bush agreed to had done to party unity, and with the Democrats in control of House, Senate, and the presidency, he saw no reason for Republicans to help. Democrats had increased their Senate seats to fifty-seven, and their House majority was healthy. With greater party discipline, House passage seemed secure—although in fact it was a lengthy struggle—but the Senate was a question mark. Southern Democratic senators were averse to any tax increases, and Clinton was proposing a lot of them.

Mitchell wrote to Clinton on February 12, saying the plan relied too much on tax increases. He said, "This may doom enactment of the economic program while giving the Republicans political advantage." He recommended a top income tax rate of no more than 36 percent. He also had suggestions about the energy or "BTU" tax that, in the final version, was simply a 4.3 cent gasoline tax increase. Mitchell opposed eliminating highway "demonstration projects," such as the new Portland–South Portland bridge for which he had secured funding.

Jim Sasser recalls how close Clinton came to backing a reduction in Social Security cost-of-living increases, which Republicans proposed, and to which Tom Foley had agreed. Sasser said Mitchell came back from one leadership session and said, "I'm the only one who's not agreeing." Sasser said, "It was unfair to do that, because, number one, the Social Security Fund was generating enormous surpluses, and secondly, this was going to hurt the older people who were neediest of all. We also thought it was going to be a political disaster, because we saw what had happened to the Republicans in 1985," when they voted for a similar reduction. Sasser believed the 1985 vote played a part in Democrats retaking the Senate the following year. He angered Clinton by writing an op-ed for the *Washington Post* about preserving COLAs—cost of living adjustments—but still thinks it was a wise move when Mitchell prevailed.

Then there was the stimulus bill, the first Clinton economic proposal to go to the floor. Like John Hilley, Bob Kerrey took a dim view. "It was $50 billion, and it looked like it was going to stimulate a few interest groups," he said. "And the economy was recovering. I didn't think we needed a stimulus. . . . What I thought was necessary was to balance the budget."

In a March 24 floor statement, Mitchell offered a sustained defense of the Clinton budget. "The budget resolution we're debating is evidence of the enormous and welcome change in the nation's debate over spending, national priorities, and national needs," he said. "The national debate has become serious, after years of budgetary flimflam. The budget the president proposes contains real, achievable, and sustainable spending cuts—not unspecified spending cuts in some indefinite future, but specific spending cuts that will come to pass. We're taking seriously our responsibility to future generations to put our fiscal house in order." He condemned the Republican alternative, which capped domestic, but not defense, programs. "If the simple act of imposing a 'cap' on anything through the budget process had the effect of cutting the deficit, we wouldn't have a deficit. This amendment is tantamount to wishing the deficit away."

Hilley did vote counts, and Mitchell decided that at best, he could get fifty votes for the budget, which, like its predecessor, was designed to reduce the deficit by $500 million over five years. It divided evenly between spending cuts and tax increases; the Bush agreement relied more on cuts. Mitchell got the budget through the Senate, but the House-Senate conference added revenues and subtracted cuts, and some senators were balking. "If you wanted a bucket of cold water on you about the joys of doing the heavy lifting for a new administration, which was taking a constructive but politically perilous path, that was it," said Hilley. "That was very, very difficult, and the truth is, President Clinton came in with a bunch of neophytes. These guys were showing up at my office and saying, 'Now, tell us about this federal budget. How does this work?'" Hilley respected George Stephanopoulos, the communications director, "but he wasn't a legislative guy."

Six Democrats were still undecided, and Bob Kerrey was one of them. "I thought that additional spending cuts were warranted, so I'd basically, in my own language, put myself in a position where I'd have to vote no," he said. He was watching C-SPAN when a Democratic press conference began, and he saw Dick Bryan, Sam Nunn, Bennett Johnston, David Boren, and Frank Lautenberg say they were voting no—five of the six. Kerrey said, "I don't know why I wasn't invited to that press conference. If I had, there would have been six of us saying 'We're going to vote no.'" He then went to see Bob Dole, to find out what would happen if the budget failed. "I just wasn't confident it would get any better, so I voted yes. I made my decision, wrote a speech, and went and saw a movie." The movie-going was to avoid the press, camped outside his office. "It's an object lesson," Kerrey said. "I never again was the last person to make up their mind about a controversial issue."

Kent Conrad was among those senators who wavered before voting yes, and credited Mitchell with "an extraordinary effort" to keep the caucus together. In a 2009 interview, he said, "That package made a profound difference for this country, because it put us on a path not only to balance, but to actual surpluses, and even, for a period, of not raiding the Social Security Trust Fund. It was a remarkable accomplishment, and if those gains hadn't been squandered by the succeeding administration, this country would have avoided this extremely serious downturn that we're now confronting. And George Mitchell really led that effort."

The *New York Times* devoted an editorial to Mitchell's role, headlining it, "The Quiet Man Who Got the Budget Through."

> Mr. Mitchell, the majority leader, irritated other Democrats in Congress, especially Rep. Dan Rostenkowski of Illinois, as he kept pushing for ways to tinker with the bill. He would bring along one senator by proposing an increase in something, while keeping another in the fold by urging that a cut be made.
>
> It was exhausting. It got none of the attention received by [Bob] Kerrey or by other lawmakers whose votes made news. Mr. Mitchell was not even much noticed when he closed the final debate, alternately attacking Republican arguments as "false" and patriotically defending the bill as essential to Mr. Clinton and the nation.

The very characteristics that deny Mr. Mitchell attention—the control of his temper, the willingness to yield center stage, and the sometimes tedious command and explication of detail—were essential to success.

He insisted he had applied just two standards in his maneuverings: whether a change would "help us pass the bill" and whether it was "good public policy." But in the process he had to cajole and plead and, above all, exercise what he told the House Speaker, Thomas S. Foley of Washington, was "the best developed patience muscle in Washington."

Bill Clinton's thoughts are not on record, but Mitchell heard from Roger Altman, the deputy Treasury secretary, who wrote, "This is just a note to say how much I admired your handling of the reconciliation bill. It was really masterful. Were the lead in anyone else's hands, it wouldn't have passed."

16

ENVIRONMENT IN THE BALANCE

Unlike George Mitchell's achievements on the Finance Committee, where he built from scratch, there was a dominating presence behind his work on Environment and Public Works, starting with the name. Ed Muskie was the first chairman of the Senate Budget Committee, but his efforts in building the old Public Works Committee into what was, at the time, the most legislatively fertile committee in Congress, was his most remarkable achievement. Though Muskie never chaired EPW, his subcommittee produced most of the important environmental legislation of the 1970s—laws that have stood the test of time. When Mitchell inherited Muskie's seat, and later his subcommittee chairmanship, he was joined not only by Muskie's staff, but also by expectations, both in Maine and nationally, that were difficult to meet.

Muskie often said he went to Washington because of his frustration over trying to clean up rivers in Maine. Air pollution in the 1950s was considered "a Los Angeles problem," not a national concern. Water pollution "was very visible, but we weren't able to do very much with it," Muskie said in a 1991 interview. He did convince the Legislature to enact a scheme of water quality standards, but the system "did nothing about improving it if it was below what people regarded as acceptable standards." When, in his second term as governor, he attempted "to use those standards to try to upgrade the quality of important waterways," he said, "That got absolutely nowhere." A 1971 Muskie biography reported that Maine, already concerned about an aging population because of out-migration, was so desperate for industrial jobs that, "If environmental pollution is the price that must be paid for gaining industry, Maine has been all too willing to pay it." Yet things were changing. The Clean Air Act of

1970, and the Clean Water Act of 1972, became the foundation of efforts that culminated in George Mitchell's full-scale rewriting of environmental law fifteen years later.

By the late 1980s, the atmosphere around environmental legislation had changed markedly. Charlene Sturbitts, the environmental aide who transitioned from Muskie to Mitchell, said, "Where Senator Mitchell came in . . . the Clean Air Act was extraordinarily complex compared to what the Clean Air Act had been when Muskie started. . . . He had a lot of catching up to do." Earlier, there was a real demand for national legislation, as Don Nicoll, Muskie's chief of staff, pointed out. "The nature of the problem was that you see, taste, and feel the effects of pollution. It was hard to argue credibly that nothing should be done."

Another factor was that, initially, "Industries were not very effective in countering the arguments for a cleanup." Demand for change was so strong that the 1970 Clean Air Act included requirements for technology that didn't yet exist—and the inability of the automobile industry to produce that technology prompted the 1977 rewrite. Nicoll said that on EPW, "There were a number of Republicans for whom conservatism and conservation went hand in hand." As another biographer put it, after Muskie began traveling the country for field hearings, he "became a pollution evangelist, speaking almost exclusively about pollution problems." Two short films EPW commissioned, *Troubled Waters* and *Ill Winds*, were in high demand on college campuses and in high school classrooms.

Political rivalry also pushed environmental legislation forward. One newspaper columnist decided President Nixon's "elevated rhetoric" about the need to protect the environment "clearly means he expects Muskie to be his 1972 rival." Nixon's surprise creation of the Environmental Protection Agency in 1970, which has since become a powerful regulator on a par with the Food and Drug Administration and the Securities and Exchange Commission, was prompted in part by his concerns that Congress was moving ahead without him. The duel continued after Nixon proposed a Clean Water Act but balked at the price tag of $24 billion. Congress overrode his veto, leading Nixon to refuse to spend the money—a tactic that became known as impoundment. Congress passed a law prohibiting the practice, and the Supreme Court, in a rare intervention involving executive and legislative branches, ruled that the president had no authority to withhold Clean Water money appropriated by Congress.

Muskie however, wasn't just riding a wave of popular enthusiasm, Sturbitts said. She noticed "how dedicated he was to doing the right thing in a legislative context, not ever taking the easy way out, even if it was less controversial or would take less time. . . . I just marvel at this incredible skill at being able to think strategically about how to get to an end point and bring people with him. And that included knowing when to compromise, so you didn't end up with nothing." By Mitchell's time, the political tide had headed in the opposite direction and President Reagan was so confident of the appeal of his anti-environmental stance that he sought repeal of both Clean Air and Clean Water acts.

The environmental subcommittee, whose membership remained largely unchanged, was important to Mitchell's development as a legislator. Muskie had taken senators of diverse viewpoints and backgrounds—some had close ties to coal mining—and allowed them "an opportunity to participate regardless of their point of view, and have full expression of their perspectives," Don Nicoll said. "The doors were never closed, not to members of the committee, or to the outside. And this proved quite an experience. . . . It was a combination of his style of encouraging debate and rigorous intellectual honesty and pushing members and staff to be clear about what they were doing and why."

Howard Baker, future Republican majority leader, joined the subcommittee in 1967, and admits that debates with Muskie were often lively. "I also had a temper at times," Baker said. "The wags around the Senate staff said we would regularly get into shouting matches, which is an exaggeration, but we sometimes did. I'd look around and the staff would be cowering, wondering how they were going to repair the rift, but there was no rift. Muskie and I took care of that. When it came to business, we were almost always together," Baker said—and he provided strong support for the Clean Air and Clean Water Acts. Baker may have gotten on the EPW Committee to look after the Tennessee Valley Authority, the New Deal–era public power agency, but he gradually became a committed environmentalist. After Mitchell joined, Baker rounded up support for Mitchell's first acid rain legislation, which provided stature for him in his 1982 race against David Emery.

CLEAN WATER LEGISLATION, HOWEVER, was where Mitchell made headway first, not only in getting bills out of committee but onto the floor. Muskie's experience was instructive. He had proposed a clean water bill in 1968 that would have enacted tough standards on offshore oil drilling, then becoming widespread. The petroleum interests had enough influence with the House to produce a much weaker bill, which they pushed through to conference just as Muskie was campaigning with Hubert Humphrey. Muskie refused to budge, and the bill died, but the following January offshore wells blew out in the Santa Barbara channel near California's prized beaches, and the reaction led to the more comprehensive bill enacted in 1972. Mitchell was aware that environmental disasters can result in swift congressional action—but only if legislation is ready to go. The

1972 Clean Water Act also set an important precedent for cleaning up industrial and municipal sewage discharges. Earlier laws depended on establishing a causal link between discharges and water quality; the new one set standards for each industrial plant, including provisions for "best available" technology. Funding was $14 billion over four years, with the federal government bearing 75 percent of the cost for municipal treatment plants.

Overall, the 1972 legislation worked well. Rivers around the country, and particularly in the Northeast, were visibly cleaner, and fish and wildlife were beginning to return. The rivers' ability to cleanse themselves exceeded expectations, and though sediments often contained toxic materials, the water itself showed dramatic improvement. Although the original funding was running out, there was still plenty to do, and the Reagan administration was almost implacably opposed to new domestic spending. Mitchell and the environmental subcommittee faced a tall order in securing any reauthorization, much less a bill that would address "non-point" source pollution from agriculture. Their efforts seemed about to bear fruit in 1986, but the conference negotiations dragged on, and because the bill gained final passage just before Congress adjourned, Reagan was able to pocket-veto it.

Mitchell started over in the new Congress, this time backed by a Democratic majority that made him subcommittee chair, facing a president in his last two years. Charlene Sturbitts had decided to move on. She was replaced by several specialists, in line with Mitchell's increasing committee responsibilities.

For water issues, he chose Jeff Peterson, initially on loan from the Environmental Protection Agency to Mitchell's personal office. Peterson had been a McGovern delegate in 1972, something that earned ribbing from other staff. "I took some serious shots over that, and I was educated as to my obvious failings at a young age, and that I should have had the insight to recognize that Senator Muskie was the way to go," he said. "And I'm mostly convinced they were right." Peterson had a family connection to Maine, and had noticed the new senator working his way up. He wanted to work on policy, not just implementation, and his offer to relocate to Mitchell's office was accepted. Peterson's boss at EPA, Jack Ravan, had been AA for Strom Thurmond, and believed that "federal agencies often didn't really have a clue what was going on" in Congress. He encouraged the move.

Mitchell's predecessor as subcommittee chairman was John Chafee, and Peterson noticed their affinity. "There was always a very strong and warm personal relationship between Mitchell and Chafee," he said. "Chafee was really a wonderful person, as well as a wonderful politician, and a great environmentalist." In his first year, Peterson handled the Clean Water bill while Sturbitts worked on Superfund reauthorization. He found both the committee staff and Mitchell's office congenial. "We worked very comfortably together with the Chafee staff," Peterson said. "It helped that they both had strong environmental interests, were from two small states, and their constituencies had a lot in common." On Mitchell's staff, "People liked working together. It wasn't like we were lone wolves competing for ten minutes of face time with the senator." Together, Chafee and Mitchell ushered in a brief but potent period of bipartisanship that lasted until the 1990 election.

Peterson communicated with Mitchell primarily by memo, which suited them both. "I liked being able to use a memo to force myself to be concise, but also to look over the big picture and become more confident of what I was saying," he said. It helped "that the senator actually read the memos. If I thought they were going in without being read and understood, that would be different." It worked "when he was not distracted by a million other things," as sometimes happened after Mitchell became majority leader. Peterson credits Mitchell with "a higher tolerance for the written word than most other senators," and he developed a system, based on a tip from Martha Pope, to complete the circle. On memos suggesting action, he put three boxes, marked "yes," "no," and "discuss," and Mitchell almost always responded. "Usually I got a yes, occasionally a no, and almost never got 'discuss,'" Peterson said. When Mitchell used memos in committee or on the floor, "I was amazed that he would deliver the material very effectively, almost verbatim. Other times he would ad lib and improve it dramatically. . . . He treated a lot of the memos as he would have briefs, with a lawyer's outlook."

Peterson eventually joined the committee staff, and the Clean Water Act remained his focus. It was clear that changes would be needed to attract Republican support. "President Reagan was very interested in getting the federal government out of the sewage treatment business, and saw it as a program that could be ramped down," Peterson said. It was Chafee who first suggested substituting a revolving loan program for the grants David Stockman and OMB put on the chopping block. "Senator Chafee felt like that was a key idea that could bring the president along," he said.

Mitchell was skeptical. He wasn't sure a loan fund would provide sufficient financing for states like Maine, which had many small treatment plants that needed upgrades. As ranking member, Peterson said, "He could have killed the idea outright." Yet Mitchell, "to his credit, was willing to listen to how an idea would work, and after the public hearing, decided it could." The loan program became a template for the Safe Drinking Water Act as well, but the program never worked exactly as the subcommittee envisioned. The federal budget still provides annual appropriations, because loan funding hasn't met demand, which increased markedly when EPA began regulating "combined sewer overflows," storm-water runoff that once bypassed treatment plants. Yet the reauthorization—the last to date—won bipartisan favor and ensured the law's future.

Mitchell created new programs within the bill, such as regulation of toxic contamination and a new National Estuaries Program. The latter, Peterson said, was ingenious. Rather than having the federal government acquire land directly, the bill left it up to each governor to decide about participation. The EPA provided grant funding for planning and technical assistance, and states nominated estuaries. Because coastal ecosystems had more development pressure than freshwater wetlands, the voluntary aspect proved appealing. Casco Bay near Portland became one of the first protected estuaries, and the program was also popular in Chafee's Rhode Island. To date, twenty-eight estuaries have been protected nationally, and "the states worked with the Sierra Club and Audubon as very constructive partners," Peterson said.

One of the thorniest issues involved toxic chemicals released in industrial processes. The initial Clean Water Act focused mostly on organic substances that can be removed in conventional sewage-treatment plants. Many toxins remained despite treatment. The provisions Mitchell backed, and often wrote, took the approach not of regulating each specific chemical—a herculean task—but authorizing states to apply standards through discharge permits now required for each industrial plant. The EPA was required to update guidelines for toxic chemicals every three years, and devise a plan every two years to tighten standards for those dangerous to health. The provisions called for joint enforcement by the states and federal government. Mitchell referred to it as "a second-generation program to achieve greater control over toxic water pollutants." The record also includes numerous testimonials. Chafee said working with Mitchell "has not only been an intellectual pleasure but a great personal pleasure. He is a man who knows the Act." Lloyd Bentsen praised Mitchell's "incredible hours in very productive work."

Unlike other environmental bills, the House passed similar Clean Water protections before the bill went to conference. This still took nearly four months, in part because of complex state funding formulas. Provisions for $18 billion over five years to capitalize the revolving loan fund became contentious. "We had countless long, convoluted meetings with EPA," Peterson said. "How do you judge fairly, how do you come up with a good number that is the true need . . . and is that also a politically acceptable solution?"

One protracted dispute pitted Lloyd Bentsen against Daniel Moynihan over appropriate shares for Texas and New York. "They were major figures in the

Senate, and neither one wanted any perception that somehow they'd been gotten the better of," Peterson said. "And everything had been worked out . . . but we were still hung up" over the New York and Texas shares. "Finally, Senator Moynihan turned to him and said 'What'll it take to make this deal?' And Moynihan just scraped off the top of his allocation what he thought he needed to get Senator Bentsen to agree. . . . That was not something staff could have ever done; it was a personal gesture on Moynihan's part."

As subcommittee chair, John Chafee claimed principal credit for the Senate bill, but Mitchell and he had worked so closely together that, at times, it was difficult to determine which provisions had been suggested by each senator. The conference agreement from 1986 had been a solid one, and Reagan's pocket veto seemed unlikely to hold.

The White House may have thought a new Congress would be less insistent about Clean Water, but if so, it was mistaken. House and Senate leaders agreed the bill should have priority, and it became H.1 in the House and S.1 in the Senate. The House moved swiftly to pass the Water Quality Act of 1987, and the Senate followed suit. Reagan vetoed, denouncing it as "loaded with waste and larded with pork." While insisting "cleanup of our nation's rivers, lakes, and estuaries is, and has been for the past fifteen years, a national priority of the highest order," he said any new federal funding would be inappropriate. "This is a matter that historically and properly was the responsibility of state and local government," he said, though states had never done much to respond to polluted waterways. Reagan also claimed the new non-point source program would become "the ultimate whip hand for federal regulators," placing intolerable burdens on family farms.

Congress wasn't impressed. "I believe President Reagan has listened to the wrong advice," said Representative Arlan Stangeland, a Mississippi Republican. "This body needs to send a strong message to the president and the American people that this Congress won't tolerate delays in cleaning up American waters." The House overrode the veto 401–26 on February 3. In the Senate, Mitchell, now subcommittee chair and the bill's floor manager, addressed Reagan's principal complaint, saying the bill wasn't a "budget buster," and complied with the 1981 budget caps. The Senate override was 86–14. It was a harbinger, as Reagan was increasingly unable to make his vetoes stick.

Jeff Peterson, when asked about Reagan's seemingly quixotic veto, said, "Republican presidents always veto clean water bills." The record shows that not only Nixon and Reagan, but also Dwight Eisenhower vetoed Clean Water bills. The modest 1960 measure Eisenhower vetoed was then enacted under John Kennedy.

Peterson said Mitchell deserves the acclaim he received for his work as majority leader in pushing through a new Clean Air Act. "That's probably fair in the bigger picture, although a lot of the stuff he did on water is probably not as well understood or recognized as it should be," he said. Peterson was also struck by Mitchell's detailed attention to Maine. Mitchell "wanted to get it right, for Maine and also the country." Peterson had worked for Mitchell for more than eight years when Republicans took a majority in 1994. He could have continued on the subcommittee staff, but decided to return to EPA, where he now serves as Water Program director. He looks back on the Mitchell years as the peak of his career, and said it was "an exceptional experience. . . . The challenge of the work put it right up there for anyone interested in public policy."

WHEN MITCHELL BECAME MAJORITY LEADER, he made it clear he intended to vigorously pursue a new Clean Air Act, which had last been reauthorized in 1977. His efforts in the previous session had come to naught, and he saw 1989 as his best opportunity. His authority as leader was still largely untested. The ability to move important legislation through Congress might seem the leader's key role, but some of his predecessors, and successors, didn't have the knack. On March 24, an incident in Alaska gave him an unexpected opportunity.

Previous oil tanker disasters had provided warnings, unheeded, that a grounding could produce an environmental catastrophe. In 1976, the *Argo Merchant* ran aground off Nantucket and Cape Cod, but the 8.5 million gallon spill drifted away from shore. In 1978, the *Amoco Cadiz* spilled its entire cargo, 67 million gallons, off France. When the *Exxon Valdez* hit a reef in Alaska's Prince William Sound, the legislative response was dramatically different. Mitchell had introduced oil spill prevention legislation three times before, beginning shortly after he had entered the Senate. It was based on Maine's 1969 statute enacted after a much smaller spill in Casco Bay; Portland is one of the largest oil-shipping terminals on the East Coast.

But even some advocates of greater national protection decided congressional action required preempting existing state laws. As Mitchell explains in his memoir, "I feared that the industry would persuade friendly members of Congress to support a weak national law that would eviscerate stronger state laws like Maine's." That danger seemed greater in the House, which had important friends of the industry. "The debate over this issue was contentious, even acrimonious at times," Mitchell said. "The chairman of the committee wouldn't even permit a hearing to be held," he once told a reporter. "Not only could I not get to first base—I couldn't [even] get out of the batter's box."

After the *Exxon Valdez* ran aground, with a third mate at the helm and a disabled radar system, Mitchell was ready. The spill, which continued for days, leaked eleven million gallons of the fifty-five-million-gallon cargo, decimating one of the world's most fertile fishing grounds. Mitchell reintroduced his legislation and gave a floor speech. The results were immediate. "It was a banner headline across the nation," said communications director Diane Dewhirst, "and you're like, of course, he's the Senate majority leader. . . . The megaphone, and the timing of when to do things, makes all the difference in the world." Of Mitchell, she said, "If he were here, and candid, I think he would say, 'Whoa, I get it now.'"

Mitchell deflects credit, as he often did. "It had nothing to do with me or my ability to persuade others, because I tried for nine years and I couldn't persuade anybody," he said. "This was a dramatic change that occurred because of an external event, unplanned and unexpected, that simply changed the way people thought." In his memoir, he said it was "politically impossible" to oppose the legislation, but that understates his role. Plenty of environmental disasters have occurred without prompting any significant congressional response. The *Exxon Valdez* spill legislation was comprehensive. It recognized state laws, as Mitchell insisted, and required tankers to be constructed with double hulls—a step the industry insisted was unnecessary.

Since 1989, there have been no comparable tanker accidents. Major oil spills have involved pipelines and drilling rigs, including BP's Deepwater Horizon blowout in 2010. The Gulf of Mexico was one region where Mitchell was unable to secure "strict liability" that would have mandated compensation for all damages. BP ultimately settled for $18.7 billion after five years. The *Exxon Valdez* case took far longer. A jury assessed a $5 billion punitive damage award against Exxon. It was reduced to $2.5 billion by an appeals court. It wasn't until 2008 that the US Supreme Court decided punitive damages couldn't exceed actual compensation, reducing the required payment to $500 million. The eighteen years of litigation would have been unnecessary had a spill law already been in place.

When Mitchell announced agreement on the bill August 3, he said, "I am pleased that the Senate is taking action on this important legislation. Congress is often criticized for being slow and indifferent, but I note that the US Senate is passing oil spill legislation just four months after the tragedy in Alaska. To move legislation of this complexity took the dedication and concern of many members"—and, on his script, he penciled in the names of Max Baucus, John Chafee, Fritz Hollings, Ted Stevens, and John Breaux. It was not, as he has called it, a "minor bill," but a signal legislative achievement just seven months into his tenure as majority leader. It also suggested avenues for pursuing a new Clean Air Act.

Initially, Mitchell's efforts on Clean Air closely resembled his experience with oil spill protection. Charlene Sturbitts had also had to look for a job in 1980, and found the transition to Mitchell's staff a bit bumpy. "The activity level in a personal office is always frenetic. The activity on a committee is more measured," she said. "The hours are a lot more irregular in a personal office. You're there whenever the Senate is in session because you're advising your senator on legislation, so you really need to be there. In the time I worked for Senator Mitchell there were a lot of long nights, probably many more late nights than early nights, but that was part of the excitement, really being part of the legislative process." She guided Mitchell through the debate on coal-burning power plants a week after he became a senator, and acid rain became part of the Mitchell portfolio. "We put together the very first acid rain bill in late 1981, and that was the beginning of what became the provision that was enacted in 1990," she said.

Even earlier, Mitchell was given a small platform after Senator Gaylord Nelson of Wisconsin invited him to co-chair a subcommittee hearing on acid rain on September 23, 1980; Nelson, who had served three terms, was another Democrat who lost his seat that November. In his remarks, Mitchell said the Senate had just approved a "massive coal conversion program" to displace imported oil, and he'd been unable to convince the Senate to include environmental standards. He said, "Acid rain has only recently attracted the attention of scientists and policymakers in this country," but pointed to findings that it had already killed all fish life in 170 lakes and ponds in New York state, and caused an "eightfold increase in the acidity of Maine lakes from 1937–1974." In Sweden, scientists were finding sharply reduced rates of forest growth. "Despite these alarming initial indications that acid rain may be a potential environmental disaster, we are embarking on an energy program based in large part on coal," he said. Even then, he was calling attention to the "real economic losses" for natural resources the data implied.

After the Democrats' loss that November, "there wasn't as much interest . . . in who was going to be the ranking member" of the subcommittee, Sturbitts said. She had a talk with the committee staff director, John Yago, who was skeptical that Mitchell should be selected, saying, "He's so junior"—in fact, he had the least seniority of any committee senator. Her argument was the same as Mitchell's when he joined the Finance Committee: "We really need this, he needs to be elected, and this is going to be an important part of it." He got the job.

By April 1981, Mitchell was conducting his own hearings on acid rain, including one in Augusta. He invited Ron Irwin, a Canadian member of Parliament who chaired its acid rain subcommittee. Canada was much more united about acid rain, perhaps because it was far more receiver than contributor due to prevailing winds. Mitchell took note, saying, "Acid rain generated in the United States and exported to Canada is severely straining US-Canadian relations. We are neighbors and friends, and we want to maintain good relations with Canada. But unless the United States reduces its largest contributions to Canadian acid rain levels, the historic relationship of Maine and the Canadian provinces may be sorely tested"—and, he added, "by a problem for which the people of Maine are not responsible." The threat to Maine, he said, was unmistakable. At the time, forest products industries represented "43 percent of the value of all products produced in Maine." As with Muskie's argument that water pollution was a national problem, Mitchell said, "No matter how stringently our local industries control their pollution, acid rain levels in Maine will increase unless emissions are controlled at the source"—primarily heavy industry and power plants of the Midwest.

Mitchell continued to speak out for the next nine years, and the Canada card proved useful. Sturbitts said reducing acid rain pollution was Mitchell's distinctive contribution to the 1990 legislation. "It was the first new regulatory program in Clean Air since the act had been written. People talked to me about Mitchell being the guru of acid rain." Ann Tartre, a younger staffer, remembers the later hearings that led to action, with the same emphasis on tangible results. "Hearing him say, over and over, 'It's going to cost us a lot more to do nothing than it will to implement these changes,'" provided "a very strong argument."

Mitchell knew that while Ronald Reagan was president, progress wouldn't be easy. In answering questions for a Maine Democratic straw poll in October 1983, he was unstinting in his criticism. "Until Ronald Reagan became president, protection of our environment was not a partisan issue. Republicans and Democrats worked together for over a decade to enact and enforce national laws to protect the very basis of a healthy life: clean air, pure water, and unpoisoned land. This was not the result of a passing fad or partisan fancy. Environmental laws respond directly to pollution that causes injury, sickness, and death. They are our commitment to leave our children the heritage of a clean land. . . . What has Ronald Reagan done? The American people braced themselves for a presidency of a man who, as a candidate, said that trees cause pollution. But his actions have been worse than our lowest expectations. Ronald Reagan has shattered the bipartisan consensus for a healthy environment."

Earlier that year, while accepting an award from the Natural Resources Council of Maine, Mitchell broadened the focus. "Seventeen days after its inauguration, this administration reinstated federal permission to export hazardous products without the informed consent of the recipient country," he said. "Eighteen months later, the U.S. cast the lone negative vote of 147 nations against an initiative to prohibit such hazardous exports. In the fall of 1982, the U.S. again cast the lone negative vote against a proposed UN World Charter for Nature."

Eventually, Reagan eased his stance. After the head of the Superfund toxic waste cleanup program, Rita Lavelle, was convicted of lying to Congress, and served six months in jail, and his initial EPA administrator, Anne Gorsuch Burford, was forced to resign, Reagan turned to the first EPA administrator, William Ruckelshaus, appointed by Richard Nixon in 1970. Mitchell said Ruckelshaus's confirmation was "the first step toward restoring EPA's badly damaged credibility and effectiveness." But he didn't relent. In a 1988 speech at College of the Atlantic in Bar Harbor, Mitchell said, "This decade has seen the highest average temperatures ever recorded—in a century of rising temperatures." And he recalled the response of the Reagan administration to the scientific finding that CFCs—chlorofluorocarbons—used in refrigerants and aerosols were depleting the atmospheric ozone layer that protects the Earth against ultraviolet radiation. Mitchell quoted Ernest Baynard, assistant secretary of energy, who'd just been confirmed, saying there was no reason to act because it "would be folly to come up with a solution to the problem before we know what the problem is." His boss, Energy Secretary Donald Hodel, suggested sunglasses and sunscreen might be adequate.

By the mid-1980s, Charlene Sturbitts was ready to move on. "I began to see a change, which I think persists today, which is that I don't see senators getting as immersed in issues," she said. "I don't see the legislative process being played out as it was in the 1970s, with real markups, where people debate issues and listen to their colleagues. . . . And on the Senate floor as well, there used to be real debates. Occasionally there still are, but beginning with the 1980 election where so many new senators were elected, and they defeated really seasoned senators, they came in and were part of the Reagan Revolution, and they weren't necessarily interested in legislating. I just saw that evolve into more of the norm." Sturbitts went to law school, practiced law, and later returned to government in the Department of Energy.

Her air quality portfolio went to Kate Kimball. A young lawyer, Kimball had worked on a project for the EPW Committee after the Three Mile Island accident in 1979, joined the staff of Representative Alan Mollohan as legislative director, then returned to EPW in 1984 to work on nuclear issues. When Mitchell expanded his staff, she became his EPW designee. As with Jeff Peterson, Kimball and Sturbitts overlapped a year. The Mitchell environmental staff was beginning to diversify and, Kimball said, aides were becoming specialists, including Peterson for Clean Water, and Kimball's future husband, Bob Davidson, for wildlife conservation and wetlands—what Sturbitts called the "bugs and bunnies" issues.

From the beginning, Kimball had no doubt she wanted to work for Congress. "Bobby Kennedy had been my senator for a while when I was young, and that convinced me Washington was where all exciting and good things happened," she said. It turned out that 1986 "was a big year for the environment." Not only was the Superfund hazardous waste cleanup finally reauthorized, but the Safe Drinking Water Act was passed, and Mitchell was making headway on acid rain. At the EPA, William Ruckelshaus turned the job over to a career EPA staffer, Lee Thomas, and Kimball got the feeling Thomas "really wanted to do something positive." Investigations of suspected toxic waste contamination had produced new finds, so many that she said, "There wasn't a state, and not many congressional districts, that didn't have a Superfund site." The program lapsed during an eight-month House-Senate conference, but its eventual return brought environmental legislation back into public view.

Mitchell "encouraged you to do your best work," Kimball said. "He was smart, he would notice nuances in memos, and was a close and retentive reader. If I was sloppy he would notice it. He was very logical. Any time you have a very observant audience, it makes you want to do better. He made me do my best work because he had standards, and he would take even the worst work I produced and end up being eloquent. And if I gave him quality work, he would make it even better. He was as good as you can get for that job."

Mitchell began to realize that presenting clean air just as an environmental issue might not be enough to create momentum. As Kimball put it, "Opposition was centered in the petroleum and chemical industries, and in the auto industry, but it touched every major industry, in almost every state." By this time, "Elected officials were generally neutral or hostile. Only a small group wanted it to happen." Mitchell began to hold hearings on, and gave speeches about, the health effects of dirty air. Diane Dewhirst noticed the shift during a 1987 hearing which featured pediatricians, the American Lung Association, and experts on asthma. "He was taking the clean air issue and turning it into a health care issue," she said. "I give Senator Mitchell, Kate Kimball, and Martha Pope a lot of credit for devising that, and approaching clean air not just as a tree-hugger issue but as a health issue."

Mitchell's second book, *World on Fire*, published in 1991, focuses on the environment, and one chapter summarizes testimony from that hearing, which took place on February 3, 1987. The title is "Unsafe for Human Health." In his testimony, Mitchell quoted Lee Thomas's article in the *EPA Journal* saying, about the greenhouse effect and ozone depletion, "If we wait until health and environmental impacts are manifest, it might be too late to take adequate steps to address these problems. We must realize that there will always be scientific uncertainty associated with these complex problems. We will have to be prepared to act despite these uncertainties." Mitchell drove home the point. "I would argue in the present circumstances, the EPA cannot afford to wait . . . for more precise research data on the adverse effects of acid air pollution on the lungs," he said. "Considerations of cost and benefit pale, I think, when they are applied to the health of children. Any parent who sat by the bedside of a child with asthma would hardly consider cost-benefit issues."

Though the Democrats had the majority by 1987, Mitchell's effort to advance the Clean Air Act that year got nowhere. Ronald Reagan was still president, and it was hard to conceive of him signing any environmental bill Mitchell would consider worth passing. Mitchell had devoted his Democratic National Convention speech in 1984 to a critique of Reagan's environmental record. He lampooned Reagan reelection commercials, which showed him as a "friend and protector of the environment," with backdrops from Chesapeake Bay and "a cave in Kentucky," contrasting them with "this president's disastrous environmental record."

He also had a tricky obstacle in Majority Leader Robert Byrd, who wasn't opposed to a Clean Air Act, but was opposed to anything that steepened the decline of West Virginia mining jobs. This was a big problem. West Virginia, and other eastern mining states, produced anthracite coal that was high in sulfur—a key chemical constituent of acid rain. Softer bituminous coal from Western strip mines has far less sulfur—it's now the primary fuel for coal-fired plants—and Western senators objected to the pro-Eastern bias of the draft Mitchell presented. Kate Kimball remembers those meetings, and not with pleasure. "He gave so much to Byrd that we weren't getting the reductions we needed. It's not like Byrd was wrong. Coal employment was plummeting, and entire communities were disappearing, but that doesn't mean it's OK to pollute," she said.

Negotiations with Alan Simpson of Wyoming, minority whip, were equally frustrating. It was a rare moment when Kimball disagreed on tactics. "Senator

Mitchell would offer something. There were objections, and then another, new set of objections to the new offer," she said, and remembers thinking, "He's playing you, and I don't like it." Finally, the deal fell apart. Of the committee, she said, "They all hated it. I could see how much they hated it." Mitchell decided by 1988 to shelve the bill. As 1989 began, two things had changed that improved prospects for Clean Air. Robert Byrd was no longer majority leader, and Ronald Reagan was no longer president.

In his memoir, Mitchell praises George Bush's "courageous decision" to break with the environmental policies of the Reagan administration. "Suddenly, dramatically, the question shifted from 'Will there be a clean air bill?' to 'What will be in the clean air bill?'" he wrote. But it wasn't that simple. In other contexts, Mitchell was much less flattering about Bush's role. In *World on Fire*—written when the Clean Air Act had made it through the Senate in May 1990, but when success was still far from assured—he painted quite a different picture. He wrote, "Mr. Bush had proclaimed himself the Environmental President; his speeches were filled with the rhetoric of the green movement. But when it came to real action, to specific legislation, the Bush administration's deeds did not match the president's words. In my office, as we hammered out the clean air bill—word by word, line by line—there was no environmental rhetoric from the president's men. Their concern was the cost to industry—the auto industry, the oil industry, steel, chemical, coal, utilities. We can't do this; it will cost too much. We can't do that; industry can't afford it. Over and over they urged less control, stressed cost, argued for delay. I sometimes wondered if they had read the Environmental President's speeches!"

Mitchell was usually careful to praise Bush, however. In a letter to John Sununu on July 27, 1989, Mitchell called attention to his public statements, and in answer to a reporter's question, said, "Let me emphasize . . . the mere fact that [Bush] has not continued the policies of the Reagan Administration of blanket opposition to clean air legislation is of enormous significance, for which the President deserves great credit."

The first step, as always, was to shape the bill in committee, starting with Mitchell's environmental subcommittee. Though he had passed the chairmanship to Max Baucus, Mitchell remained intensely involved. Alan Simpson had already gotten a dose of Mitchell's interrogations. "We were on Environment and Public Works together, but he just as well could have been on Judiciary because of the questions he asked," Simpson said. After a series of probing inquiries, he said, "Senator Mitchell, I'm very pleased that I never had to practice before you in your court." Mitchell replied, "You should be very pleased. You'd never have made it." Simpson decided Mitchell was joking, and added,

"He has a great sense of humor . . . and an extraordinary way of taking a complex issue and putting it in understandable terms with patience—God, the patience; I would have lost my mind on half that stuff."

Mitchell gathered the principals and said, "What do you have to have in this bill?" Simpson reminded Mitchell about the 1987 bill: "If you put that requirement that every bit of coal has to reduce 15 percent of its carbon, regardless [of whether] it's low-sulfur coal, that one's a fake." Mitchell assured him the 15 percent requirement was out.

John Breaux was impressed with Mitchell's ability to go one-on-one with Boyden Gray, Bush White House counsel, initially the administration's chief negotiator. Mitchell, he said, "was a strong pusher to keep that thing going. I remember many, many meetings . . . when we were regulating sulfur dioxide emissions, and Boyden Gray was calling for less and less regulation. And George was very strong in helping to keep that deal together. Had it not been for him, it would have fallen apart."

The committee bill, reported out in November, was even stronger than Mitchell had hoped, and by design. In his memoir he said, "We all knew that the Senate committee bill would be the high-water mark . . . and that we would have to compromise it down with the White House." The strategy made sense, though there was a big gap between the administration's estimate—that its proposal would cost $20 billion a year—against $40 billion for the committee bill. After all, with Howard Baker's help, the subcommittee reported out an acid rain bill in 1982, though it quickly died. Now that Mitchell was majority leader, expectations were much higher, and the committee bill wound up encouraging unrealistic ideas of what could be accomplished.

Mitchell had created impetus through his emphasis on health, and it helped persuade his key partners on the committee—Baucus, as chairman, and Republicans John Chafee and David Durenberger, who he said were "both moderate Republicans, both very strong for protection of the environment and both extremely significant participants in the Clean Air revisions." The link with health, he said, was nearly indisputable. "We live in an age of incredible scientific discovery, and it's become increasingly obvious that health and the environment are inextricably and deeply interrelated. I don't see how any reasonable person can dispute the premise," he said. "History is pretty clear that some of the most dramatic and devastating of ancient plagues and epidemics were the direct consequence of poor sanitation, particularly the absence of clean water. And the same is true of clean air."

Baucus wrote after the vote, "Many thanks for your assistance in passing clean air legislation out of committee. In fact, were it not for you, we'd still be thrashing about in the weeds." A few weeks earlier, Baucus had written, "You more than any other senator are responsible for the passage of Clean Air. I helped. You are the prime mover." Bob Graham of Florida wrote, "Your long-term dedication to strengthening the Clean Air Act is an inspiration. . . . I have been around politics for twenty-four years, and have never seen a display of greater patience and persuasion over such an extended period of time." John Kerry sent a note saying, "I am prepared to help you with the Clean Air bill in (almost) any way you want." When it passed the Senate, Kerry sent champagne, and Mitchell replied, "I appreciated the champagne, which I've shared with my staff."

There were some disappointments in the committee bill, particularly concerning "mobile sources"—cars and trucks. The key House players included Henry Waxman of California, the environmentalists' champion and chairman of the health and environment subcommittee, responsible for developing the clean air bill; and John Dingell of Michigan, committee chair of Energy and Commerce, whose district was the locus of US automobile manufacturing. The two sparred for years, with Dingell adroitly defending the industry, aided by his labor allies, who saw threats to union jobs. Dingell entered the House in 1955; Waxman, in 1975. Their rivalry continued unabated until Waxman ousted Dingell as committee chair in 2009. They both retired from Congress in 2014.

Mitchell's problem with vehicle emissions was that he had no hope of moving the House further than Waxman was able to push Dingell. After preliminary talks Waxman was able to gain somewhat tighter standards on new cars than the 1977 backtracking Ed Muskie oversaw, but they were widely considered disappointing. Asked what prevented tougher standards, Kate Kimball has a short answer: "John Dingell."

By 1990, large urban areas were in "non-attainment," the Clean Air Act's term for failure to provide breathable air. "People are not having to wear masks now, which is where we were headed," Kimball said. Ground-level ozone, a lung irritant, is strongly associated with vehicle exhaust, and was increasing. Air quality alerts were issued regularly not only in California, but along most of the East Coast, including Maine. "One of the problems with regulation is that no one knows exactly how much it's going to cost," Kimball said. "They were able to use that uncertainty effectively."

The circumstances of Dingell's chairmanship were, in her view, unique. "The auto industry employs so many people in Michigan, or did then, that employment was highly concentrated, but not the interests on the other side." Though it was an advance over 1977, the 1990 law "had a much weaker standard than we would have liked." While the Obama administration has used the

Clean Air Act more vigorously than the Clinton administration, and, especially, the second Bush administration, regulatory changes for cars and trucks have come in mileage standards, not emissions controls. Better mileage is not a good environmental substitute, Kimball said. "You can build cars with good mileage that are very dirty." Electric cars—"zero-emission vehicles"—now gaining in popularity could have been pushed forward two decades earlier.

Drafting the Clean Air Act was arduous, Kimball said. "It was a group thing. After a while, it was hard to say where the language had come from." She was thirty-four at the time, and had never before assumed such responsibility. "I was thrown into a big role in a hurry, and I was so nervous about it." She credits Martha Pope and Diane Dewhirst for supporting her through marathon sessions, "and all my little meltdowns." The back-and-forth between subcommittee and committee, House and Senate, and the administration, could be dizzying. "It was all a team effort, but the teams kept changing."

Kimball noticed that Mitchell took a different approach from staff in decisions about what provisions made it, and which were scuttled. The staff's perspective was, "We need to get the air clean enough," and they bristled at amendments that reduced that possibility. Mitchell had a different standard, she said: "Is it better than current law?" If it was, he was generally willing to make concessions and move on to the next issue.

THE BILL EPW SENT TO THE FLOOR WAS STRONGEST on reductions from power plants, and less effective on vehicle emissions. It would have been an enormous advance on existing law, but Mitchell soon found himself under attack from an unexpected source: the environmental groups that had applauded his work since he came to the Senate. He might have anticipated the criticism. Muskie had been lambasted by Maine environmental groups for making concessions, to the point where some threatened a primary challenge against him over his alleged perfidy. When Muskie compromised a point in the unsuccessful 1976 negotiations, he earned a press release from Barbara Alexander, representing the Maine League of Women Voters, that began: "For the senator known as 'Mr. Clean' in the nation, Senator Muskie has performed miserably." It went on for two pages, single-spaced, and was featured prominently in Portland and Bangor newspapers. It produced, a reporter said, a "beet red reaction" from Leon Billings, Muskie's top aide.

Mitchell was taken aback by the intensity of the outrage. "Something had happened which I had not anticipated," he wrote in *World on Fire*. "The committee bill had become the minimum acceptable bill to most of the national environmental organizations and much of the press." When the Senate agreed on a framework proposal on March 2, 1990, the *New York Times* called it a "dilution," and made a point-by-point comparison of the "stronger" committee version and the "weaker" compromise. "That perception made more difficult the task of getting the compromise bill passed by the Senate," he wrote.

As majority leader, Mitchell was used to having his every move subjected to scrutiny and criticism. But this hurt. The most prolific attacks came from the Sierra Club and the Natural Resources Defense Council (NRDC), but he was not exempted by groups in Maine. "I think the only time in my life I ever got a full headline across the top of the *Portland Press Herald* front page," he said, was when a group of state environmental commissioners—including Maine's Dean Marriott—held a press conference to attack Mitchell. When the bill ultimately passed, in some ways stronger than the one the Senate first considered, things turned around. "The real irony is the next year, after we got the bill done, they all appointed me 'Man of the Year,'" he said. "They gave me trophies and plaques and I'd go and speak to their groups so they could tell me how grateful they were—the same groups that [just] the year before had vilified me."

Alan Simpson, often far to the right of Mitchell, and somewhat to the right on clean air, sympathized. "I came out of a negotiating session at two o'clock in the morning, and this group was there, the real greenies, and there were also some real rape-and-ruin guys there, too, but this was a circle of greenies, and they were saying, 'We're going to make them pay.'" When Simpson asked who they meant, they said, "We're going to defeat Mitchell and Chafee." Simpson shot back, "You must be the dumbest bastards in the whole village. George Mitchell and John Chafee do more for the environment on each side of the aisle than any of you jerks, with your 100 percent purity." He said, "That earned me some great fame with that group."

If the environmentalists' criticism stung, it was their challenge to his political judgment that bothered Mitchell more. They'd gotten the idea the committee version was so popular in the Senate it could easily withstand a filibuster. "Not only could we not get the sixty votes necessary to end a filibuster, we couldn't even get a simple majority," he wrote. "In their view the only remaining obstacle to a glorious victory was my unwillingness to bring the bill to the floor for a vote. Although no one directly called me a coward, that was the implication." Mitchell knew that if he pushed for a vote, and it failed, the bill was dead. The environmental groups refused to believe him. Mitchell remembers them saying, "We've canvassed them, and if you just bring it up and force it, they'll vote for it." Finally, he asked for the sixty names, and was immediately struck by some of them. The ever-changing negotiating group was meeting in Mitchell's large conference room, and he went to speak with John Heinz, a moderate Republican from Pennsylvania—a major coal state. Mitchell said, "I appreciate your support," causing Heinz to sit bolt upright and ask, "What are you talking about?" Mitchell said, "I've just been informed that you've committed to vote for cloture." Heinz, Mitchell said, "practically shouted," saying, "Are you crazy? I can't do that." The groups still weren't persuaded.

The environmental groups apparently didn't know how to count votes in the Senate, taking favorable comments from a senator, or staff, as a solid commitment. And there was another consideration, as Kate Kimball saw it. "These national groups—the NRDC, the Sierra Club—gave Mitchell grief on everything." And, she said, "Do you really want to have the environmental groups think it's a good bill? It would be the kiss of death to be that environmentally friendly . . . it's not like the ranks were swelling with people who wanted to do the environmental thing." At times, she was irritated as much as Mitchell. "They were completely unrealistic. We were holding on by a spider's thread, and they were so convinced of their own political skills and strategy that anybody who didn't buy in was making a huge mistake. They were so sure they were right."

In the end, Mitchell's course wasn't altered by the criticism. He had many other things to worry about. Seemingly endless negotiations continued in the majority office, at his insistence, so he could keep a close eye. Initially, Mitchell and a few senators faced Bush officials, testing the parameters of the "environmental president." The talks grew, with more and more senators and staff, and two rows of chairs flanking the conference table. "Soon they were packed in, many of them standing, from early morning until late at night," Mitchell wrote. "More participants meant more discussion, more debate, more controversy. The issues were many, and technical. Few of the participants had a perfect understanding." He credited Kate Kimball with having "mastered every detail of every aspect of the issue."

One of the most controversial proposals was the administration's plan for a "cap and trade" system to allow expanding industries to, as their critics saw it, buy a "license to pollute" from companies below agreed-upon emissions caps. The administration saw it as an efficient way to lower pollution levels, instead of "command and control" regulation. Using market forces was a novel strategy, and Mitchell, at first, was skeptical it could actually work, and not just lead to more delays in improving air quality. He eventually came around, and helped push negotiations toward tighter standards. "The administration was less concerned because we were using a form of the allowance system they had proposed, which made them happier," Kimball said. "Senators were of course terribly concerned about exactly . . . who the winners and losers would be."

With talks dragging, Mitchell entered the room, "and told us we had forty-five minutes to work it out. I'm sure I gave him a look of, 'Are you out of your mind?'" After another staffer said it was impossible, Kimball said, "I told him he'd have to tell Senator Mitchell the bad news to his face because I wasn't going to do it for him." The deal was reached. "That's an example where Mitchell's careful use of his authority made the difference," she said. "That was the only time I recall him telling us that the clock's ticking, you have to finish."

In *Washington at Work*, Richard E. Cohen's blow-by-blow account of the 1990 Clean Air Act, Mitchell's insistence on keeping negotiations where he could monitor them, he writes, "challenged the bill's opponents to an endurance test. During the seemingly endless meetings the air quality in Mitchell's office ironically would become so poor that the site was known as the 'locker room.'" It was in the same "environmentally sanitized" conference room after enactment that Mitchell told reporters about his "patience muscle," which he said "has been remarkably strengthened in the past two years." But for weeks, "the talks continued into the night, and the pizza delivery man arrived with stacks of boxes," while lobbyists waited outside "to get a few valuable morsels of information. And pizza boxes piled up outside the normally majestic Room S-224." Though seemingly chaotic, the process was more orderly than on the House side, where Cohen quoted one participant saying, "There were so many deals on the table that it was hard to keep track of details, even by members who were sponsoring them. It was like a bazaar."

WHEN THE BILL REACHED THE SENATE FLOOR, "There were literally hundreds of amendments," Kimball said. Most were easily brushed aside—the conference-room deals held—but not all. The biggest threat came from the senator Mitchell had just succeeded—Robert Byrd. In 1988, Byrd had been offered a favorable deal, but by 1990 the bill looked very different. Western coal was already cheaper, and its price advantage would grow if utilities had to install expensive "scrubber" systems to remove sulfur from Eastern coal. Byrd realized that, with the Bush administration's support, he had little prospect of winning on emissions levels, and pursued a different tack—federal compensation for miners displaced by the new law. The Byrd Amendment provided a stern test of Mitchell's leadership and, unlike the budget talks, he was largely on his own.

In his memoir, Mitchell is diplomatic. "On the coal miners, we had struggled for years to find the right balance, without success. Byrd had participated in a few of the negotiating sessions but, unsatisfied by what was on offer, withdrew to enlist the support of other senators and to draft his own legislation. It provided for substantial benefits to coal miners who lost their jobs." The benefits were substantial indeed, and their $500 million annual cost drew an immediate veto threat from Bush. Mitchell sensed the amendment was a deal-breaker. With plenty of other industries adversely affected, the Byrd Amendment could fuel endless demands.

Mitchell had his Finance aide, Bob Rozen, do an analysis, and the results were startling. Byrd had asked for three years of benefits, starting at 70 percent of total compensation; Mitchell had counteroffered at six months, and suggested that, rather than just coal miners, benefits go to all states with unemployment 115 percent of the national average, and to industries losing more than 15 percent of their workforce. Under Byrd's amendment, coal miners would do much better than laid-off steelworkers. Another key difference was how many miners would qualify. Byrd specified a "direct" connection with job losses. Mitchell wanted "direct and primary." Rozen calculated that Byrd's plan would provide miners with compensation of $41,240 for jobs that paid only $36,660.

Byrd had long been skeptical about the Clean Air Act, though careful not to make his concerns public. According to Charles Kinney, his aide, he repelled efforts by Henry Waxman to engage in talks. "The House kept trying to send it over, and Senator Byrd got to the point where we, the floor staff, were admonished very sternly to read every word that came from the House to make sure Clean Air wasn't in it, any facet of it."

Mitchell had already turned back several well-intentioned efforts to improve the Clean Air Act he knew would sink it. At a March 8 press conference, many erstwhile Democratic allies, including John Kerry, Brock Adams, Joe Lieberman, Timothy Wirth, and Alan Cranston, advocated much tighter mobile source controls. Frank Lautenberg of New Jersey led off, saying, "Motor vehicles emit 56 percent of all the air toxics." Improved public health surely required more, they argued. It pained Mitchell to reject their amendments. He said, "I was placed in the extremely awkward position of having to oppose strengthening amendments by Democratic senators that I personally felt should be in the bill. But I knew the president would veto it if we did. . . . Senator [Al] Gore offered a strengthening amendment, and I had to oppose that. John Kerry offered one. Tom Harkin offered one. All good friends of mine, all offering what I thought were sensible measures that I wished we could have put in."

Floor debate on the Byrd Amendment was scheduled for March 29, and Mitchell said in his memoir, "I woke up with a throbbing headache, a sore throat, and a very runny nose. On any other day I would have stayed in bed." Instead, he convened the Senate in discouraging circumstances. Byrd had made twenty-five "house calls" to senators, reminding them that, as Appropriations chairman, he could decide the fate of any project they wanted. "He's everywhere. I've never seen the likes of it," the *Washington Post* quoted one senator as saying. Mitchell rose to open debate and saw "the gallery was full, the chamber was packed." He knew already that a majority of Democrats would be voting with Byrd. They each came to his office to deliver the news. "It felt like a rapid series of hammer blows, each hurting more than the one before," he said. Most said they couldn't risk crossing Byrd.

Mitchell knew the vote would be close. He had Bob Dole's support, and Republicans brought along by loyalty to Bush, but he needed every vote. As the secretary called the roll, it was too close to call. Mitchell knew who was still uncommitted, and realized it would come down to Joe Biden, who favored the bill, but wavered over Byrd. Biden left the chamber to take a call from John Sununu at the White House. Unlike on the budget, Sununu was a Clean Air ally. A trained engineer and former governor of a state burdened by acid rain, he rallied the troops. When Biden asked "point blank," as he then told the Senate, whether Bush would veto the bill with the Byrd Amendment attached, Sununu "guaranteed" him the president would. Biden voted no, and the amendment failed, 50–49. Only fifteen Democrats joined Mitchell.

Martha Pope witnessed Byrd's long memory. When, during a heated exchange months later, Biden "was trying to claim credit for something," she said, Byrd pointed at him and said, "You forsook me." Pope said Byrd mounted a copy of the roll call on his office wall behind his desk "so people could see it as they came in to ask for money for their projects, and it was kind of hard to go to the 'lick log,' as he referred to himself, when you knew you had voted against him, so you had to spend many a day trying to get yourself back into his good graces."

Mitchell, and, to some extent, Byrd, moved on. Four years later, Byrd wrote Mitchell a note, in his inimitable style, after the Senate turned back another attempt to pass a balanced budget amendment. It reads, "I express my commendation as well as my thanks for what I know was a tough but courageous vote. . . . Make no mistake: It was a vote to save the Constitution, and we can sleep well in the knowledge that we have handed to our children and grandchildren a Constitution as whole and intact as we received from our forefathers. Lord Nelson's dying words were, 'Thank God I have done my duty.' I thank God that you did yours."

There was only one amendment Mitchell couldn't head off, and it was significant. Tom Daschle organized his Midwestern colleagues behind "oxygenated" additives to gasoline. Methanol, from natural gas, and ethanol, from corn, were leading candidates, and Daschle found strong support across the political spectrum, even though the committee bill didn't address fuel content. Richard Cohen, reporting from the floor, could see that Mitchell's demeanor was different. His "opposition to the Daschle amendment was accompanied by a symbolic wink to senators who cared about where he stood. The signal was that its passage would not threaten the broader deal. He remained off the floor until the end of the vote and made no effort . . . to keep wavering senators on his side. The fact that Daschle was a close political ally of Mitchell . . . may have been another vital factor in the outcome. And Mitchell perhaps determined that since the amendment likely would pass no matter what he did, he should avoid a precedent that might encourage the approval of other, more harmful amendments." It was approved, 69–30. Later, ethanol, amounting to 10 percent of gasoline, was criticized by environmentalists as inefficient and wasteful, involving a federally subsidized crop. Its inclusion in the Senate bill made certain it would remain.

Along with the acid rain provisions and mobile source reductions, the Clean Air Act set the nation on course to eliminate CFCs, then drastically depleting the protective atmospheric ozone layer. It also buttressed the EPA in regulating air toxics, and substantially increased enforcement in "non-attainment" areas that included most major cities. It was a longer and more complicated law than its 1970 or 1977 predecessors. Kate Kimball said, "Industry always takes the position of 'Quit telling us what to do. Set goals and we'll take care of it.'" But Congress found, "If you say, clean up your air, and you give them all the freedom in the world, nothing happens." The result is that "Legislation gets more and more detailed, more prescriptive." The Reagan years, she said, "brought a sea change where people felt they could push back." At one time, Japanese car manufacturers seemed unconcerned about congressional mandates, but by 1990 "they had joined the Big Three. . . . There were no longer any outliers."

Even after Senate and House passage, there were still twists and turns. Perhaps the most consequential involved a major miscalculation by the White House. Mitchell, while fending off some of the "hundreds" of amendments, had offered a deal. He had committed to a "no changes" policy through Senate consideration, and now—anxious to keep Bush on board—offered the same deal the rest of the way. The White House turned him down. After the Senate approved the bill on April 3—it had been on the floor since March 5—Mitchell was dismayed when "the White House undertook a major effort to further weaken the bill in the House." Though the agreement had expired, "I felt it was inconsistent with the spirit of our negotiation. I had already spilled a lot of political blood to get the agreement . . . speaking and voting against my friends and their amendments. It was too late for me to abandon the course I had chosen. We had the agreement and I had to honor it, which I did. But I didn't feel right about the way it ended."

He wondered, though, if the White House knew what it was doing. While Mitchell had allowed the administration into his inner sanctum, a highly unusual tactic, the House leadership excluded the White House. Roger Porter, handling the final steps for the administration, apparently thought he could get John Dingell to eliminate provisions the White House found problematic. But Dingell had no real concerns other than sections that affected the automobile industry. Some House provisions ended up being tougher than the Senate version. Mitchell felt vindicated. The alleged "dilution" of the committee bill to keep debate going resulted in a bill stronger than the administration wanted, and better than Mitchell had expected after the bruising battle over the Byrd Amendment.

His colleagues recognized that Mitchell had done something extraordinary. Republicans were among the most appreciative. Dave Durenberger saw how often Alan Simpson conducted shuttle diplomacy between the committee and Dole's office, and how closely minority and majority leaders worked together. "George would never take anything to the floor until we knew we had the majority," he said. "We knew what amendments were likely to come up, we knew how we were going to deal with them, and that was all because he did this shuttling back and forth between his conference room, the Dole group, and the floor."

Another Republican, John Warner, said Mitchell's small group meetings were effective. "He was masterful at persuasion, in a way you left thinking you could take a measure of credit for passage of the bill. In his office, he quietly rewrote basically a new bill, while the Senate was out there arguing over the committee bill." At the House-Senate conference, Warner saw Mitchell's "ingenuity in attaining a greater number of new policy decisions," while the House negotiators "seemed tempted to trade and give ground to the Senate on policy if they could get their projects." But Steve Symms, though he served on EPW and admired Mitchell, was dead set against the bill. "I thought what we needed to do . . . was to encourage people to get more money so they could buy new cars," he said. "I had a lot of fun on the floor, raising a ruckus."

When it was over, Mitchell called Kate Kimball to the floor for a bow, "which is something he is not prone to do," she said. "I appreciated that very much." The final negotiations had been a forty-eight-hour marathon in which neither she nor Mitchell had slept, and she called her turn on the floor "a very strange experience. Senators were gracious to me and thanked me, even when I had been a little cranky to them and their staffs. It was a wonderful moment. . . . I'm grateful both that I could be there, and that I didn't have to keep doing it."

The signing of the bill was delayed until after the November midterm election. Congress had completed work on October 27, ten days before the election, but Bush didn't hold the ceremony until November 15, nineteen days after passage. It was, Richard Cohen wrote, awkward. Though everyone was invited, and Mitchell and Dole attended, Bush surrounded himself solely with members of his administration. Two of them, Vice President Dan Quayle and First Lady Barbara Bush, Cohen said, "had virtually nothing to do with the bill." In his remarks, Bush "barely acknowledged the countless hours consumed by the coterie of members of Congress or the battles they had endured in drafting the several-inch stack of legislation before him." It was only after the presidential photo op that Bush, "in an unplanned and awkward move," invited House and Senate leaders forward, with Mitchell among those shaking his hand. "Perhaps still smarting from the wounds of the earlier budget battle, Bush did not even stage the ritual of handing pens to the chief legislators responsible for the new law."

Observers at the time didn't seem to take in the full significance of what had been accomplished. Cohen, who chronicled the process over two years, was tepid. After asking rhetorically, "Will the new law help to clean the nation's dirty and toxic air?," he said, "Probably, yes." Some principals also offered equivocal opinions. Yet a quarter-century later, the law's scope has become monumental. It was the last reauthorization of the statute Ed Muskie wrote in 1970, despite many new attempts, most recently in 2009. The Clean Air Act has become the nation's bulwark against global warming; no other equally effective national or international agreements have yet been devised. Much of the reach of legislation like the Clean Air Act can be discerned only long afterward. It was not until 2014 that a United Nations study first reported that the atmospheric ozone layer was showing signs of recovery, though previous studies had found that the problem wasn't getting worse. The ozone layer is expected to recover to its 1980 levels only in 2050. And it was in 2013 that two scientific studies showed red spruce in New England—the "canary in the coal mine" for acid rain—was now growing vigorously. One researcher said, "They're growing better than they ever have in recorded history."

Kate Kimball said that in drafting the act, Mitchell recognized the problems he'd identified wouldn't be quickly solved, so it was important to ensure that future regulators had sufficient scope for changing circumstances. The Bush administration enforced the law with some vigor, but the Clinton administration pushed forward more slowly—and progress stopped altogether during the second Bush administration, where, as in the Reagan administration, former industry lobbyists occupied top environmental posts. The act has achieved a second life under the Obama administration, which has moved decisively on many fronts. Laws, Kimball said, "are really only words on a piece of paper until they're implemented. This law has a lot in it that can still be used by administrations that take a greater interest in it. It has enough strength that it could do a lot more good, still. It was designed with that in mind."

THE CLEAN AIR ACT WAS THE MAJOR environmental accomplishment of Mitchell's tenure as majority leader, but there were many other bills of significance. One of Kimball's favorites was the Federal Facility Compliance Act, introduced in 1990 and enacted two years later. Federal agencies, most prominently the Defense Department, sought exemptions from the hazardous waste regulations that had begun with the Resource Conservation and Recovery Act of 1976, and were expanded in the Superfund program. As a candidate, Mitchell noted, President Bush had said, "some of the worst offenders are our own federal facilities. As president, I will insist that, in the future, federal agencies meet or exceed environmental standards: The government should live within the laws it imposes on others."

As president, however, Bush took no action, so Mitchell exhorted Congress, saying, "This is a fundamental question of public health protection and equity." He rejected the idea that federal agencies should comply "only with those environmental requirements that are convenient and inexpensive." Mitchell said the proposed law would "clarify" requirements, even though Maine Federal District Court Judge Gene Carter had already ruled that "Any intelligent person reading the statute would think the message plain: Federal facilities will be treated the same as private institutions so far as enforcement of . . . hazardous waste laws are concerned." Kimball said that, to a degree, there's been better compliance since. At least when the military has closed bases and turned them over to states and the private sector, hazardous waste cleanup has been included.

The North American Wetlands Conservation Act, written and steered to enactment by Mitchell in 1989 with little controversy, has since distributed more than $1 billion to preserve coastal and freshwater wetlands. It enjoyed strong support from sporting and conservation groups, required relatively little funding, and has benefited from $3 billion in matching funds.

There were failures, too. When alarming levels of radon gas began seeping into homes in Pennsylvania from groundwater, Mitchell thought Congress should act. Jeff Peterson said, "It was a good example of Mitchell being willing to look at a complicated issue that wasn't the popular issue of the day in the environmental community. . . . It was clear that as big a threat as it was, it was really just part of other issues related to indoor air pollutants." Mitchell introduced bills in three different sessions. None was enacted, though news coverage "raised the visibility of the issue a lot," Peterson said. Kimball said when she inquired whether indoor air pollution should be considered during Clean Air Act discussions, "The answer was no." Peterson also held meetings and prepared drafts to reauthorize the Clean Water Act in the early 1990s, but none advanced beyond committee, and the 1987 law remains the last word.

Mitchell saw losses, as well as wins, as part of his job. It was most important to him, Kimball said, that issues were raised, explored, and debated, whether or not Congress ultimately acted. She once told him a floor amendment he wanted advice on that called for a study was "a bad idea," and simply a delaying tactic. Mitchell's response was, "Why are you afraid of more information? If you're right on the policy, more information is not something you should be worried about." She observed, "That's the kind of adult tone he had as subcommittee chairman. It's also been advice I've heeded since then."

Mitchell was equally effective on Finance and EPW, his major committees, but he seems to have had greater warmth for his environmental colleagues. After the chairman, Democrat Quentin Burdick of North Dakota, who rarely created a fuss, and Republican Steve Symms, who often did, left the committee, he paid affectionate tribute to both. Burdick had died on September 8, 1992, and Mitchell spoke at his funeral. "Quentin Burdick was tireless and devoted to duty," he said. "He never saw that duty as a burden. Rather, he saw it as the privilege it is, the privilege of serving others. . . . Quentin wasn't much given to long speeches. That alone distinguished him from the rest of us in the Senate." Burdick had been on the committee when Mitchell joined it in 1980 and, Mitchell said, "To the very end, even as his body began to fail, his mind remained clear. . . . His sense of humor got us through some tense times. I know I speak for every member of that committee—they're here today—when I say: We loved Quentin Burdick." He recalled the many cribbage games he'd played with Burdick, which seemed a natural common interest, "since the winters in North Dakota are like those in Maine. I thought I was pretty good, but I wasn't as good as Quent. He loved to beat me, and he usually did."

Mitchell spoke at Symms's retirement dinner a week later. Mitchell said, "It came as no surprise when I read that the first farmers in Idaho were New England Yankees," and devoted most of the tribute to their common interest in transportation. Symms had a passion for passenger trains, helped Mitchell to move the 1991 intermodal transportation bill, and voted to override President Reagan's transportation bill veto in 1987. Mitchell gave him credit for including national recreational trail provisions. Yet he couldn't resist a little needling.

After saying Symms "has always and consistently been the man with the funniest quips," he added, "Steve's ability to bring a touch of lightness and humor to serious committee business has often contributed to a positive outcome—even when it's not necessarily the outcome he might have preferred."

As he negotiated the Clean Air Act, Mitchell was speaking out in a larger context. In an address to the American Society of International Law on March 29, 1990, he said, "Climate change will affect the life of every human being. Some nations have recognized that action cannot wait." He'd been aware of the issue for some time. One bargaining chip on Clean Air with President Bush—an effective one—involved Bush's close relationship with Canadian prime minister Brian Mulroney, the Conservative Party leader. Mitchell said, "More than a decade ago, Canada established the Canadian Climate Program to identify the sensitivity of agriculture, fisheries, forests, and other sectors to climate change." He said the *Climate Change Digest* published there was "beginning the process of public education."

Mitchell wrote *World on Fire*, his first solo performance as an author, in large part because of his concern about climate change, and whether governments would act effectively to combat it. He likened the atmospheric environmental issues to the Four Horsemen of the Apocalypse—global warming, ozone depletion, destruction of tropical rain forests, and acid rain—and in later chapters added global population growth. The "distress signals" evident in 1990 carried "ominous messages. They tell us that the world is about to grow warmer, warmer than any time in recorded history, and that the warmth will bring catastrophe."

As on other issues, he was disappointed with President Bush's actions. He pointed to a meeting of the Intergovernmental Panel on Climate Change. The president's speech "had been highly anticipated" in asserting American leadership, Mitchell wrote. "Instead, after much-publicized infighting within his administration over the tone and content of the speech, the president delivered a flat, narrow address which left his listeners unimpressed and his nation uninspired." Bush called for more study; Mitchell quoted a World Meteorological Organization official saying, "The global warming to which we are already committed is irreversible. . . . By the time we detect it, it will be too late." Mitchell acknowledged that the United States was contributing a disproportionate amount of greenhouse gases, was "one of the planet's biggest energy wasters," but said it should act, and not just from obligation. "We must lead because we can lead. . . . No other nation has shown a stronger commitment—in money and in know-how—to cleaning up its own environment."

Mitchell published *World on Fire* in 1991, but it achieved little notice. The book came out the same week Allied forces invaded Kuwait to expel Iraqi occupiers. "I had scheduled a promotional tour, but the whole tour was canceled," he said recently. "Sales were low, and the book didn't get a lot of attention. And about eight months later, Al Gore published his book [*Earth in the Balance*]. Mitchell said, "It was a better book, and it deserved to do better."

Some Mitchell staffers disagree. *World on Fire* and *Earth in the Balance* cover the same territory, from startling changes in coastlines to the plight of nations like Bangladesh, whose very existence is threatened by rising sea levels. For Kimball, *World on Fire* "was a fine book; it was right about so many things." She points out that Mitchell held the initial congressional hearing on climate change, featuring NASA scientist James Hansen, the first federal researcher to speak out. Kimball said that on climate change Mitchell "was willing to stake his political reputation on it. He just didn't have the single-minded focus that Gore did."

The EPW committee changed drastically after Mitchell retired. A panel once dominated by New Englanders of both parties used to working together acquired a Western, and much more conservative, tilt. Kimball said the current Republican chair of the committee, James Inhofe of Oklahoma, is "a climate change denier," and has written a book about it called *The Greatest Hoax.*

Mitchell has called climate change "one of the great human challenges of our times, and this century. The failure to address it in the wake of the overwhelming evidence is alarming." He adds, "There has been some progress, but far from what's needed to be commensurate with the problem."

WORLD VIEW

Before he became majority leader, George Mitchell had scant opportunities for involvement in foreign policy. He didn't serve on the Foreign Relations Committee, and he came from a small state far from the centers of power, which didn't encourage his interest. Mitchell's first major speech in the Senate, however, was on nuclear arms control. Even before the nuclear freeze movement gathered momentum in 1982, he was concerned about the consequences of the massive arms buildup the Reagan administration was seeking, and which Congress largely approved.

After his speech, Mitchell noticed that nothing appeared in the newspaper, even though Maine had a Washington reporter. "I asked him why," Mitchell said, "and he said, 'Nobody in Maine cares about that stuff.'" Mitchell's reply was, "I hope they do, because it's important," but called it "a good lesson" in what reporters deemed newsworthy. And, while he'd always been interested in foreign affairs, "I hardly ever went on a foreign trip before I became majority leader."

Mitchell was doubtless aware that senators who got too involved in foreign affairs often paid a price. In the years just before and after he joined the Senate in 1980, three chairmen of the Foreign Relations Committee lost reelection bids—J. William Fulbright of Arkansas, Frank Church of Idaho, and Charles Percy of Illinois. Fulbright lost in a 1974 Democratic primary to Dale Bumpers, while Church fell less than 1 percent short against Republican Steve Symms in 1980. Percy, a Republican, lost to Democrat Paul Simon in 1984. Fulbright's and Percy's defeats were widely attributed to their less-than-unstinting support for Israel.

Mitchell did speak out in opposition to Ronald Reagan's nuclear arms buildup and his defense policies in general—a sometimes tricky line, given that

Maine manufacturing jobs were ever more concentrated at Bath Iron Works and the Portsmouth Naval Shipyard. Mitchell had been elected in 1982 despite the president's personal popularity, and he doubtless believed most Mainers shared his views about nuclear confrontation with the Soviet Union.

After Reagan's State of the Union address in January 1984, Mitchell spoke on the Senate floor, noting that when Reagan delivered the line, "Nuclear war cannot be won, and must never be fought," he received "the most spontaneous, longest, and loudest applause of the evening." Mitchell said, "The United States and the Soviet Union are engaged in an unrestrained nuclear arms race," and detailed how Reagan's applause line differed so dramatically from his previous statements and positions. He said Reagan opposed the Nuclear Test Ban Treaty negotiated by President Kennedy in 1963, the Nuclear Non-Proliferation Treaty signed by President Johnson, as well as the SALT I and SALT II treaties concluded by Presidents Nixon and Ford. Although as a candidate in 1980, Reagan had promised an "immediate" resumption of talks, he instead waited seventeen months, and then suspended them again.

Mitchell chronicled Defense officials' "provocative or inaccurate comments" about nuclear war. "They included talk of 'prevailing' in a nuclear war, firing a weapon for 'demonstrative' purposes, and tolerating a 'limited exchange' of tactical nuclear weapons." And while these statements were often "clarified" later, Mitchell said they had an "electric effect on the listening public, especially in Europe," arguing that "the Soviets moved quickly to magnify and exploit it." Mitchell said Reagan had driven a wedge between the United States and its European allies, who were still committed to detente, and noted that when the UN General Assembly voted 111–1, with 35 abstentions, to ban all nuclear testing, the United States was the only "no" vote. Reagan's record on arms control, he said, "is perfectly consistent—and consistently wrong."

At a Jefferson–Jackson Day dinner on October 18, 1986, just before the Democrats retook the Senate, he provided a different perspective following Reagan's initial failure to reach agreement with Soviet leader Mikhail Gorbachev at the Reykjavik summit. Mitchell said, "President Reagan's strong political position has given him the opportunity to take an important step toward world peace. If our history is any guide, the prospects are good that he will take that step. In the American experience, it is often the presidents who make the most dramatic reversals who have the greatest successes. President Roosevelt was called a traitor to his class when he fought the entrenched economic interests. President Nixon reversed two decades of Red China–baiting when he recognized that nation. . . . That opportunity still exists for Ronald Reagan." Despite being "the only American president to have publicly opposed every major nuclear arms control agreement," Reagan did change course.

IT WAS NOT UNTIL 1983, AS HE SETTLED into a six-year term, that he began looking for an aide to handle foreign policy issues. Until then, he had relied on Mike Hastings, and others, on defense issues, mostly involving Maine shipyards and military bases. Sarah Sewall had a family connection to Bath, where her father Loyall Sewall's family home eventually became part of the Maine Maritime Museum. The connection included Gayle Cory and her brother, Buzz Fitzgerald. After studying at Groton, and while a junior at Harvard, Sewall received an internship at the Institute for Policy Studies, where she was assigned to do research studying parallels between the movement to abolish slavery in the nineteenth century and the campaign to abolish nuclear weapons in the twentieth century.

"That was a wonderful assignment that completely flummoxed me," Sewall said. "I would go to the Library of Congress, sit in the beautiful dome, studying what on earth I should read to try to answer this question." But Sewall was now "hooked on Washington and politics and this nexus of political activities and normative questions about international stuff." She also went to Oxford as a Rhodes Scholar, where she traveled to the Soviet Union and as far as Burma, and interned for Representative Olympia Snowe before landing at the Center for Defense Information. The think tank was run by a left-leaning former admiral, Gene LaRocque, who was so impressed by her use of the word "adumbrate" that he mentioned it whenever they met. She'd been studying satellites and space-based weaponry, and decided that "this notion that the U.S. and then the Soviet Union would knock out each other's eyes and ears that were so important for strategic stability was really insane." She was working on the technical details, budget impact, and secrecy concerns when Ronald Reagan "gave his Star Wars speech on March 23, 1983, and it became a big issue."

Sewall did some soul-searching, at the suggestion of a friend, who asked her, "What are the things you believe in? What are the kinds of things you want to do? Who are the people who believe those things?" She said, "Through that discussion in a very structured way that I would have been incapable of doing on my own . . . the answer was George Mitchell." She called Cory, who told her Mitchell didn't have any openings. But she kept calling, and one day Cory called back to say, "He's going to hire a foreign affairs LA [legislative assistant]; you should come in and interview." She did, Cory vouched for her, and, despite the "awkwardness" of her father's Republican Party service, Sewall was hired. She was twenty-two. "I ended up getting this job that was exactly what I wanted to do. I just felt like the luckiest person on the planet . . . and the learning curve in this job is just exponential—it's better than school," Sewall said. "I don't imagine I will ever have a job that is more fun and more rewarding."

Staffing a very junior senator from the minority party who served on no relevant committees left Sewall with an apprenticeship writing memos and advising Mitchell on floor votes. But she soon developed more substantive efforts, one involving the Nuclear Non-Proliferation Treaty designed to prevent the spread of nuclear weapons, but long neglected. Mitchell, she said, "had a very progressive view on arms control issues generally." She became friendly with staff from Mark Hatfield's office, a liberal Republican, and James Exon, a conservative Democrat, and they developed a proposal to cut off funding for nuclear tests that later won Senate approval. "Between Hatfield and Exon and Mitchell, we built a coalition," she said.

After Mikhail Gorbachev halted nuclear testing in 1991, George Bush suspended tests the following year, and they've never resumed, despite suggestions the United States might need tests to ensure its nuclear arsenal's viability. "I remember when Senator Mitchell gave his speech about what it meant and why it was important, just having that extraordinary thrill . . . that strong analytic and empirical work, and savvy politics, could make a difference, and I was just joyous," Sewall said. Looking back more recently, she said, "Everyone said it couldn't be done," because, "nonproliferation had been so weakened by bellicose Reagan policies that it nearly expired. The U.S. nearly violated the treaties we had signed." Bush had also opposed the moratorium, but the Senate twice enacted it. Sewall said "the one-year moratorium gave space for broader agreement" after Gorbachev reciprocated. It's "an important legacy," she said, "not of partisanship stopping at the water's edge, but finding common cause across the aisle."

Mitchell also took on a much knottier problem in the War Powers Act, the resolution Congress passed, over Richard Nixon's veto, in 1973. It attempted to reassert the constitutional war-making power by requiring notification by the president when committing US forces abroad. The act has never worked smoothly, and some presidents, including Reagan, ignored it. Mitchell had doubts about its constitutionality, and, as with nonproliferation, tried to build a coalition. Sewall said the War Powers Act was "far from ideal legislation," because it "skirted the fundamental question of who's responsible" for overseas deployment. While these circumstances might, to some degree, be inevitable because of the Constitution's provisions that the president is commander in chief, while only Congress can declare war, the specific timetables in the law are now "painstakingly quaint," Sewall said. Further, she believes the law provided "perverse incentives" for both Congress and the president in diffusing responsibility. Still, she "literally didn't know what he was going to do," and wrote briefs on both sides.

Whatever his doubts about the War Powers Act, Mitchell believed he was bound to follow it without a court ruling or congressional changes. "We agreed the law was problematic, it was really a dysfunctional law, but that the situation triggered the law," Sewall said. Mitchell has already seen the consequences when a president deployed troops abroad solely on his own authority. When 241 American service personnel, including 220 marines, were killed in a terrorist attack in Beirut, Reagan hadn't even notified Congress of the deployment. After an Iraqi jet attacked the USS *Stark* in 1987, during the Iran-Iraq War, killing 37 Americans, Reagan again did not consult Congress.

Mitchell introduced reform legislation in 1987. He enlisted important supporters, Majority Leader Robert Byrd and Armed Services Committee Chairman Sam Nunn, whom Sewall characterized as "not his normal political bedfellows." It would have removed the timetable requiring withdrawal of forces within sixty days without congressional approval, and instead put the onus on Congress to specifically require withdrawal of forces, or end funding—as it did in Vietnam, and official support for the Contras. The existing law required troops to be withdrawn unless Congress approved a deployment quickly. It seemed unlikely Congress would fulfill that responsibility. The major addition would have been a "Permanent Consultative Body," including members of the House and Senate, that would meet regularly, and not just when a deployment was contemplated. Included were legislative leaders and Foreign Affairs, Armed Services, and Intelligence committee members. Rather than relying on the appropriations process, "funds would automatically be cut off if Congress voted to withdraw troops," according to the bill summary.

After the *Stark* attack occurred on May 17, 1987, Reagan ordered military action without involving Congress. Mitchell prepared a response to a Reagan radio address on October 10, then decided not to deliver it. In the prepared text he said, "I share some of [the] concerns" of those who believed the War Powers Act exceeded congressional authority, yet he said the law was "binding until the courts determine otherwise." The president, he said, "must either openly challenge the constitutionality of the law, or he must obey it."

By April 1988, Reagan had authorized more aggressive action in the Persian Gulf, directed not at Iraq, but at Iranian ships and oil platforms. In a May 19 statement, Mitchell said, "The Administration did not appear even to understand the law with which it claimed to be 'conforming' but not complying." While many in Congress supported military action, debate over the War Powers

Act's provisions continued. "In a few weeks' time the Senate may again consider a resolution pursuant to the law that the President will not obey," Mitchell said. Despite Democratic majorities, Congress didn't send Reagan any legislation to reform the law. Mitchell made another effort after becoming majority leader, designating new legislation as S.2, but with no result. The stalemate continued, as it does today, with the law still in effect in its original form, and the underlying conflicts unresolved.

While domestic matters consumed most of Congress's time and attention, it can fairly be said that Mitchell became majority leader at a momentous time in international affairs. In his first year as leader, the Berlin Wall fell and the former Soviet "satellite" nations asserted their independence, while China cracked down on demonstrators in Tiananmen Square. In his third year, the Soviet Union collapsed.

He started, as he always had, by reaching out. His aide at the Democratic Policy Committee (DPC), Ed King, said that on one of his first days as majority leader, Mitchell said, "Where's Pell's office?" Claiborne Pell, a former Foreign Service officer who spoke four languages, had been elected a Democratic senator from Rhode Island in 1960. While best known for the federal college grants that bear his name, his longtime ambition was to chair the Senate Foreign Relations Committee, which he achieved after the 1986 election. Pell was known as an eccentric for wearing old suits, driving used cars, and dabbling in the paranormal—but voters didn't care. His third reelection victory, in 1978, was over John Chafee, and he served six terms. Mitchell showed deference to a senior senator, and the unannounced visit to his office delighted Pell. King said Mitchell told Pell, "Anything you need to have done, you tell Ed to do it," and "If you have anything you want to talk to me about, any time of the day, you just call me." Though Pell wasn't a forceful chairman, Mitchell kept in close touch; King attended Foreign Relations staff meetings regularly.

Sarah Sewall also moved to the DPC, and while her duties expanded considerably, she wasn't happy about the move. She was surrounded by an all-male staff, considerably older, put in place by Byrd, and decided she worked harder than any of them while being paid less—not the first time that issue came up. She also missed the frequent contact with Mitchell, now reporting to a boss whose attention was inevitably more divided. The Mitchell staff, she said, was "a close-knit group of people who cared about each other." At the DPC, "I was young, and confronting an older white male staff doing their work in a very different way. I was representing a new boss, but I wasn't given authority. It wasn't an easy transition."

Sewall wrote a memo on December 13, 1988, making recommendations about Mitchell's new majority leader duties. "You will have many visits from foreign heads of state, many of whom you may want to receive," she wrote. "You will be deluged with requests from foreign and defense ministers, only some of which you may want to see. Ambassadors will be constantly knocking, and you should probably be selective about whom you receive." She also noted, "Sometimes State will ask that you see an official; the degree of coordination and cooperation here will depend on your relationship with Secretary [James] Baker." In a section where she recommended staff screening and memos identifying possible problems, he wrote in the margin, "I agree." He did not always take her advice. As majority leader, Mitchell was in constant demand as a co-sponsor. On April 7, 1989, she recommended Mitchell sign or co-sponsor only one of four requests, but he approved all four.

Another task was dealing effectively with Senate opposition, and Mitchell was challenged early and often by Jesse Helms of North Carolina, ranking Foreign Relations member, and a stronger personality than Pell. Ed King, five years older than Mitchell, loved a good battle, and was impressed by Mitchell's handling of Helms, who was often vociferous, put holds on nominations, and was known, alluding to the James Bond character, as "Senator No." On the floor, King said, Helms "would put up what we called 'the ton'; he'd come up with a hundred amendments, because he's going to grind us down." Mitchell assigned the staff to prepare a rebuttal to every amendment, and distribute the answers to other Democrats. "We'd take them to the floor and we'd vote them, and we'd be there all day, half the night, if that's what it took," King said. Mitchell's persistence paid off. "The rest of the Republicans weren't with Helms, and they started disappearing and his votes started disappearing, and pretty soon he'd begin to drop those amendments."

Though Mitchell hoped to cooperate with the Bush administration on foreign policy, he was sometimes disabused. A crisis in Panama had been brewing for more than a year. On February 26, 1988, President Eric Delvalle attempted to dismiss Manuel Noriega as head of the armed forces but, instead, the National Assembly voted to remove the president. Noriega remained de facto leader and, on March 15, survived a coup attempt. After Mitchell told the Lewiston *Sun* "the U.S. supported Noriega because he helped the Contras and is anti-communist," Sewall wrote a March 29 memo gently correcting her boss about Noriega's "anti-communism," pointing out that he and Panama's former military leader, General Omar Torrijos, provided support for the FSLN, the Sandinistas, during the Nicaraguan revolution in 1978.

After Torrijos's death in 1981, "which Noriega may have engineered," Sewall wrote, Noriega "squelched the transition to civilian rule" Torrijos had planned. He later provided aid to the Contras, while maintaining friendly relations with Nicaragua's government, and Cuba. She called Noriega "a consummate Machiavellian, who until now successfully played all sides against each other." The reason Noriega retained US support was that, as early as 1966, he cooperated with the CIA. "He has assisted the U.S. in several important drug busts, thereby keeping the U.S. away from his personal massive involvement in illegal drug activity," Sewall said.

When George Bush took office, he decided Noriega had outlived his usefulness. Bush steadily increased the pressure, backing more coup attempts and attempting to sway an election in May. He authorized "Operation Just Cause" on December 20, 1989, sending 28,000 troops and 300 aircraft to the small nation to oust Noriega. Ed King said Mitchell was blindsided. King was accompanying Mitchell on an official trip to Mexico City, along with Jim Sasser, when Diane Dewhirst called him at eleven p.m. and said, "Have things broken loose in Mexico City?" The Panama invasion had begun, she said, and the CIA had informed Mitchell's staff "there's going to be riots in Mexico City," and Mitchell needed to leave.

King said the administration knew all along about the Mexico trip, yet provided no warning. "They hung him out there," King said, "and he was furious, which he should have been. It was just terrible." Mitchell and Sasser went to the US ambassador's residence, then "we got the cars and raced out to the military airfield, moved the plane over and loaded up, and came back to Washington," he said. In King's experience, Mitchell was never visibly angry, "but you knew . . . he and Sasser were sitting there with long faces, and they were sleepy, and they were not happy campers."

By that time, Mitchell and Bush had clashed about several international incidents—the most serious, China's crackdown on pro-democracy demonstrators in Tiananmen Square and elsewhere, starting in the spring of 1989. As democracy protesters began making headway in the Soviet bloc, Chinese students tested the regime's tolerance for dissent. But while Mikhail Gorbachev wanted to bring both economic and political reform to the Soviet Union, it was soon clear that China's Communist Party would tolerate only economic change. At first the protesters were marking the death of Hu Yaobang, a reformist general secretary from 1980–1987 who was purged for not cracking down on previous protests. After his state funeral in April, students began gathering in Tiananmen Square, Beijing's historic public gathering place, and soon camped there. On June 3, the party leadership, badly split, ordered troops into the square.

When Mitchell heard the news at about two a.m., he called Diane Dewhirst to say he wanted to make a floor statement that morning. Ed King said Mitchell was outraged, saying, "They're murderers." He focused on what lay within Congress's responsibility—previous moves to grant Most Favored Nation (MFN) trading privileges that were making the United States China's biggest export market. And so began a long struggle with the administration about China policy.

When it became clear the crackdown wasn't going to change the administration's attitude, Mitchell began building his case. One useful document was a State Department report he frequently cited. It began, "The human rights climate in China deteriorated dramatically in 1989. On March 5–7, People's Armed Police used indiscriminate and excessive force in suppressing demonstrations in Lhasa, Tibet, killing scores of persons. These killings and other serious rights abuses, however, were dwarfed when the leadership ordered the People's Liberation Army and other security forces to suppress forcefully a peaceful, student-led movement seeking greater freedom for China's people. At least several hundred, and possibly thousands, of people were killed in Beijing on June 3–4. The Beijing massacres were followed by a drastic, country-wide crackdown on participants, supporters and sympathizers."

Later that year, Mitchell was visited by a Bates College professor, Yang Ye, and Mitchell quoted him in a floor speech, contesting the idea that democracy was an alien concept in China. Yang Ye said, "The fundamental concepts of democracy and freedom are not incongruous with the Confucian values of benevolence, humaneness, and individual dignity. What is alien to Chinese civilization, in my opinion, is the Marxist-Leninist theory of class struggle and violence, a theory that is preoccupied with differences and based on hatred." Mitchell added, "I am moved by his words."

When Mitchell prepared his trade bills, which proposed limitations on China's MFN status, he was careful to spotlight existing trade disputes. He worked with Nancy Pelosi in the House, already rising in leadership, in whose San Francisco district human rights was the foremost concern. When, in May 1990, Bush announced he would renew MFN status without conditions, Mitchell made a measured but forceful statement. "I very much regret his decision," Mitchell said. "It is inconsistent with American values, it is contrary to American interests, and it is profoundly wrong." Bush had sent a high-level delegation to China just a month after Tiananmen, and his national security advisor had toasted the regime in December. The president said "a signal would be forthcoming" that China was improving its human rights record. Mitchell said, "President Bush's own State Department reported a few months ago on increased repression inside China. Defecting Chinese officials and escaped student leaders have added damning details." He concluded, "The President's repeated concessions for the Chinese government have been met with intransigence. The answer is not more concessions."

A few weeks later, China ignored the first anniversary of Tiananmen, and so did Bush. Mitchell quoted Bush as a presidential candidate in 1980 criticizing Jimmy Carter for establishing formal relations with China. "China, whose primary interest lies in a strong, steadfast American presence in the world, has now seen just how easily we can be pushed around," Bush said. "The Chinese realize that we have given all and gained nothing." Mitchell said, "It is doubly tragic for Americans that the silence of the Chinese regime is echoed in our own country, by our own President." He concluded, "All tyrants hope to rewrite history and wipe from memory the atrocities they commit. All democratic people know that it is the force of memory which keeps alive the force of freedom in the world."

Mitchell didn't give up. When on May 16, 1991, Bush again renewed MFN status, Mitchell introduced legislation to condition renewal "on reciprocal action by the Chinese government to end its violation of international standards of human rights, its unfair trade practices, and to cooperate with the world community in restricting the proliferation of chemical, biological, and nuclear weapons technologies." None of the bills made it to the president's desk, however.

When Bill Clinton took office, Mitchell had hopes he might condition trade on human rights improvements, and at first, seemed to be making progress. But Treasury Secretary Robert Rubin ultimately convinced Clinton that the United States would pay too large an economic price if trade were curtailed, and Clinton announced that there would be separate tracks for economic and political issues—essentially, a continuation of Bush's policies. Anita Jensen, his speechwriter, said Mitchell's many speeches "really got under the White House's skin. They hated that; it drove them nuts." But Jensen disliked writing them, and believed Mitchell was indulging a quixotic crusade. She was relieved when Clinton became president, and the criticism stopped.

Sarah Sewall didn't cover China issues, but also didn't share her boss's passion. She said recently that she used American policy in China as a case study in a course she taught at Harvard's Kennedy School. "Ultimately, every presidential candidate takes a human rights perspective on China, and finds himself adopting a different policy in office," she said. "China's enormous economic power suggests that no administration could have made a significant difference." That, she said, "is one of the benefits of being in Congress. You can take a position different than you would in the Executive Branch."

Mitchell, however, believed that forceful, earlier action by President Bush could have made a difference, but executive authority proved superior to any legislative strategy he could muster.

IF CHINA PROVED A DEAD END IN PROMOTING human rights, there were better prospects in the Soviet bloc, and many hopes were soon realized. Mitchell's first major foreign trip as a senator came in 1985, shortly after Mikhail Gorbachev took power, when he was included on a CODEL—congressional delegation— trip to Moscow, his first meeting with the last Soviet premier. "I went as a junior member of a delegation to Soviet satellite countries, to Hungary and then on to Moscow," Mitchell told an interviewer. The delegation met with Reagan before departing. "A bipartisan group of us had a very long meeting with Gorbachev, just after he took office," Mitchell said. They must have seen something in each other; Mitchell was soon convinced that Gorbachev had made a decisive break with the past, and that his reformist instincts were genuine—something George Bush was still questioning when he took office.

Dennis DeConcini went, and remembers an example of Mitchell's prankish- ness. "He took a picture of me sleeping on the plane and handed it to me on the floor, and said, 'If I don't get your vote, I'm going to turn this over to the *Arizona Republic*.' I was snoring, just a terrible picture." Diane Dewhirst, who was along for several, said the trips could by no stretch of the imagination be called junkets, more ceremony than substance. "Mitchell didn't partake of any of that," she said. "They were heavily scheduled, absolutely brutal."

Not everyone was as impressed by Gorbachev. Bill Bradley, who joined Mitchell on a later CODEL to Moscow in 1990, remembers their meeting as "his usual Gorbachev-in-power performance, as opposed to Gorbachev now, who actually talks. Then, you'd have a meeting and he'd speak fifty minutes and give you ten minutes." But for Mitchell, the relationship continued even after Gorbachev fell from power in 1991.

When he became majority leader, Mitchell identified relations with the Soviet Union as a crucial international issue. He delivered a lengthy statement on January 13, 1989, just before the presidential inauguration, fixing responsi- bility for conflict clearly on the other side. "Following World War II, hostility and competition between the United States and the Soviet Union cast a dark shadow across the globe," he said. "The Cold War was born of broken prom- ises at Yalta, the Soviet denial of Eastern Europe's right to determine its own future. The Soviets set their sights on further territorial and political expansion, according to the Marxist doctrine of international class struggle." Yet, he said, relations with the Soviet Union were "in a process of transformation," which he welcomed. Mitchell said the rise of other powers, and the "stunning examples of emergent power in Germany and Japan" were also transformative, and "we need not see this realignment of power as threatening," because it could lead to "a more balanced and cooperative approach to global problems, including the search for peace."

He praised Gorbachev's "extraordinary leadership," and said, "Gorbachev's greatest strength is his ability to admit the truth: Communism is a failure as a system of economic organization. That is the central economic lesson of the twentieth century." He took note of Gorbachev's moves toward democracy, but said, "The reforms are unlikely to affect the Communist Party's grip on political power," and noted "the inherent gap between the rhetoric and reality of perestroika." It was an optimistic speech, and Mitchell wanted to see how far the boundaries could be pushed.

Mitchell didn't believe Bush shared this optimism. Though the Tiananmen Square protests were crushed in June, peaceful uprisings were gathering force across Eastern Europe. By September, Poland was moving toward significant reforms, and on September 18, Mitchell said Bush's "reaction to this stunning opportunity has been inadequate and uninspired," adding, "There appears to be a basic ambivalence within the Bush administration about the dramatic transformation now under way." Mitchell said this was "difficult to understand," given that US policy had always been "to promote greater autonomy and freedom. Instead of encouragement and engagement, the administration has adopted an almost passive stance," he said. And then, in a phrase that stung, Mitchell said, "The Bush administration seems almost nostalgic about the Cold War." How a more forceful response might have affected events is difficult to say, but Mitchell was resolved to exercise congressional prerogatives.

Sarah Sewall was in her element as an analyst of the dynamic between majority leader and president. She said recently, "There's a huge difference between being in Congress and critiquing foreign policy, and having to carry it out." She said Mitchell's main point was that "We needed to think creatively and question the assumptions of the last forty years," while Bush "wanted to put policy back in the box." Mitchell was able "to take satisfaction in being able to question old assumptions and open the way for a broader conversation." And while Bush "didn't want to seek counsel," she believes Bush understood that Mitchell supported his underlying policy, "but used pressure and prodding." While she thinks Bush knew what had to be done, "Mitchell had a greater ability to communicate and was much more effective than the administration team," she said. Mitchell was "filling a vacuum."

Earlier in the year, Mitchell had struck up a relationship with Yevgeny Primakov, a "moderate reformer," according to Sewall, who was close to Gorbachev, served in several roles, and was now chairing the Supreme Soviet, which Gorbachev hoped would assist in decentralizing power. Primakov had visited the United States earlier, but his appearance before the Senate on October 27, 1989, at the invitation of Mitchell and Dole, marked the first time he'd led a delegation. In a memo previewing the visit, Sewall called him "an interesting character, an academic turned political leader, an establishment figure in a moderate reformer role, a foreign policy expert now focused on domestic political workings." She said he supported "greater independence for Poland and Hungary, and he may be a key person trying to help chart a new Soviet relationship with Eastern Europe."

After the visit, the Americans and Soviets issued a "Joint Communique of the Delegation of the Supreme Soviet of the USSR and the US Senate." The document referred to the "parliamentarians of each country," making the point that both now had elected leaders, even though the Supreme Soviet was hardly democratic. The communique didn't gloss over remaining issues, and the Americans "raised a broad range of human rights issues, including freedom of emigration and religion." Unlike China, the Soviet regime was listening. Primakov's visit also served as a political road show. He made stops in California, Pennsylvania, and New York, visited Kansas with Dole, and came to Maine with Mitchell, who introduced him to his family in Waterville—an itinerary hard to imagine just a few years earlier.

Events were moving more swiftly than anyone anticipated. The ferment in Poland and Hungary arrived in East Germany, once the locus of Soviet control; on November 9, the border between East and West was no longer patrolled, and Berliners began dismantling the Wall. On November 19, Mitchell, noting the impending "Malta Summit," where Bush and Gorbachev would mark the end of the Cold War, spoke briefly. "In Eastern Europe we have witnessed monumental changes that many never believed could occur," he said. "Solidarity, only recently banned, now leads Poland. . . . Hungary is preparing for free multiparty elections. . . . Even Bulgaria is led by a reformer who has pledged to turn Bulgaria into a modern democratic and law-governed state. If there were doubts about the enormity of the transformation under way . . . they most surely have been erased by the figurative, and now literal, destruction of the Berlin Wall."

If the Cold War had ended, the fate of the Soviet Union was still in question. Gorbachev's strategy of devolving power had led to the "loss" of the Eastern European states of Hungary, Poland, and Czechoslovakia, and East and West Germany were discussing reunification. But there was a distinction in Gorbachev's mind: Those countries had never been incorporated into the Soviet Union. The Kremlin maintained the fiction that they were willing participants in the Warsaw Pact alliance.

It was at this moment, in the spring of 1990, that Mitchell and Dole undertook a more ambitious visit to the Soviet Union. After a preliminary meeting with Soviet Ambassador Yuri Dubinin on April 5, the CODEL visited West Berlin and East Germany, and had three days of intensive meetings with Soviet Foreign Minister Eduard Shevardnadze, Primakov, Presidential Council member Aleksandr Yakovlev, Supreme Soviet Chairman Anatoliy Lukyanov—and spent two hours with Gorbachev. They also met with leaders of Lithuania, which had declared independence.

At one point, the trip was nearly canceled. Sarah Sewall wrote a memo to Mitchell on April 2, beginning, "If you have any doubts about the advisability of traveling to Moscow, you may want to speak to Baker about it. Since it will be very difficult logistically to arrange for alternative travel plans, time is of the essence." The administration, and Secretary of State Baker, had been giving mixed signals about congressional trips, as politicians, intrigued by democratic change, flocked to the spectacle of a great Cold War power being transformed; Ted Kennedy planned a nearly simultaneous visit. The Mitchell-Dole team and the administration came to an agreement. Baker traveled to the same destinations a month later, and the Senate leadership and State Department teams were mostly in harmony.

Sewall provided an overview on April 4 of what Mitchell was likely to find. She said, "Gorbachev's position as head of state has become more significant than his leadership of the Communist Party, and he appears prepared to embark upon new, more radical economic reforms." The first popularly elected body, the Congress of People's Deputies, with duties loosely defined, would choose the Supreme Soviet, from which Gorbachev had stepped down. Gorbachev appointed himself to the most powerful position, president, but pledged after a five-year term to hold multiparty elections. The Communist Party, which the populace blamed for the nation's problems, was in trouble. "This restructuring leaves the Communist Party adrift, but the ship itself is sinking," Sewall wrote. "Polls reveal that no one believes that the Communists can effectively lead the country." After seventy years where all power flowed from the Party, this was radical reform indeed.

Sewall had a prescient observation about Gorbachev. "Judged solely by the difficulty his opponents would have in removing him, Gorbachev is in his strongest position to date. But his popularity continues to decline. . . . Glasnost and democratization, while appreciated, do not satisfy people's immediate concerns. In fact, they exacerbate the underlying tensions by providing freedom for popular protest . . . and allowing demands for secession or greater autonomy from Moscow."

Mitchell was encouraged that, for the first time, the Soviet people were talking openly about the nation's problems. He told Dubinin he was struck by a comment that "self-flagellation is our national sport," and that he'd found "a tremendous spirit of openness." In transcripts of the meetings, there's a glimpse that this moment was the best chance for the Soviet Union to make an effective transition to democracy. The session with Yakovlev, a prominent reformist, was telling. Yakovlev said Gorbachev's recent internal reforms were significant. "What is happening here is that we have proclaimed the construction of a law-based state. This is not easy. There are many obstacles: lack of legal practice, the political culture, and in many cases, lack of a common culture. We have no historical democratic experience."

Yakovlev was pressed by Jim Sasser about possible aggressive moves by Moscow toward Lithuania. Unlike the Eastern Bloc, the Baltic States had been annexed to the Soviet Union after World War I, although the West had never recognized this action. Sasser told him that "any untoward action will strengthen the right wing in the United States, just as Lithuanian actions may be strengthening the right wing in the Soviet Union." When they discussed the failing economy, Yakovlev was willing only to endorse a "regulated market economy" for fear of creating chaos.

The Gorbachev transcript shows a leader in deep trouble who doesn't realize it yet. Gorbachev ruminated on the difficulties of democracy in a nation with no experience of it. "It can be said we have the same Congress as you do, perhaps more complex," he said. "For that reason, I don't think it will be easy to propose or enact laws." He spoke of "radical reform" of the economy, but was vague about concrete steps. He called Lithuania "a stupid situation," and blamed leaders there for pushing ahead with independence after the Soviets had promised negotiations. At the end, Mitchell asked how Gorbachev was "holding up under all the pressure." The response: He was "holding his own."

When Mitchell arrived home, he had a brief moment of public diplomacy. He was greeted at the airport by reporters clamoring for comment on Soviet moves toward Lithuania. Moscow had declared a partial economic embargo; there were rumors troops would be sent. Mitchell said, as he had in the private meeting, that military action would be unwise. In the end, Gorbachev let the Baltic States go, solidifying his democratic credentials but further undermining his support at home.

There was another round of visits in 1991 as the Soviet Union entered its last days and Boris Yeltsin emerged as the first popularly elected president of

Russia in June. Yeltsin had initially supported Gorbachev while mayor of Moscow, but was purged after complaining about the slow pace of reform. He made a spectacular comeback, and was clearly the people's choice, with Gorbachev consigned to limbo. An August coup by Communist hard-liners failed, and enhanced Yeltsin's standing while ending Gorbachev's authority. Just after the June election, Yeltsin was invited by Mitchell and Dole to address Congress, but Mitchell didn't see in him the leadership qualities he'd glimpsed in Gorbachev. Sewall provided the flavor in saying, "The greatest benefit presented by Yeltsin's visit to the U.S. is the opportunity to support his goals rather than his personality," although she conceded, "This trip could free him from the drunken bumbler image created during his last visit."

The failure of democratic reform within the Soviet Union was dramatized by a meeting Mitchell had with Gavril Popov, mayor of Moscow, on October 18. Popov told him that, after the August coup attempt, there were three paths. "First, we had a chance to re-create a democratic government for the whole country to move toward reform," which "unfortunately did not happen." The second option was for Yeltsin's Russian government to lead the whole country, and "since the government of Russia is mostly democratic we hoped it would take over and solve the problems." The new republics, however, feared Russian dominance. "So this was opposed by both democrats, who feared re-creating an empire, and the Communists, who were afraid of democracy spreading." The new republics would give up nuclear weapons, but democracy wasn't their guiding principle.

In 1992, Mitchell invited Gorbachev, now a private citizen, back for another congressional appearance. On May 14, Mitchell paid him a handsome tribute. "You prompted a profound yet peaceful transformation of your nation and those around you. Your action began a process that has helped redefine international politics. By helping to end what you have called 'the vicious circle' of the Cold War, you have made it possible for the international community to redirect its energies and resources toward the many pressing and common problems we on this planet face. Rarely can it be said of an individual that he has fundamentally changed the course of history. There is no doubt that you have done so."

In his toast to Gorbachev the same day, Mitchell recalled the Soviet leader's December 1988 speech to the UN General Assembly, and depicted Gorbachev as a global statesman: "He called for revitalization of the United Nations and democratization of the global dialogue. He stressed the importance of international law. He cited the need for international cooperation on issues as diverse as equitable economic development, protecting the environment, and eliminating hunger." If, as Mitchell pointed out, Yeltsin was the first Soviet leader to be purged and then revive his political career, then Gorbachev was the first Communist

Party head to make a graceful exit. Yet, as it would have been impolite to point out, Gorbachev couldn't finish the peaceful revolution he'd begun.

AFTER MITCHELL LEFT THE SENATE, HE BEGAN WORK on this third book, *Not for America Alone*, published in 1997. He hired two researchers to help with this unusual work of nonfiction, which includes a brief account of growing up in Waterville, his debts to his parents, and reflections on the momentous events he had witnessed, and participated in, as majority leader. It features a short history of the twentieth century conflict between East and West, and provides a glimpse of what Mitchell might have produced had he followed his youthful ambition to become a history professor.

Not for America Alone is an argument for internationalism, and its thesis is that the American system of government is a gift to mankind—not, perhaps, always in its execution, but in the universalist ideas it has embodied for more than two centuries. In a speech from this period, Mitchell said, "The U.S., not Japan or Germany, was the model for change in Czechoslovakia, Poland, and Russia. Havel, Walesa, Yeltsin looked to America. We symbolize and stand for fundamental freedoms, universal human rights, and the dignity of working men and women."

In the book, he recalls once again the citizenship ceremonies in his federal courtroom, and writes, "We Americans are the most fortunate people ever to have lived." Unlike some on the left, Mitchell never imagined that Marxism, theoretically or in practice, offered a desirable alternative. He provides a short, sharply etched portrait of Karl Marx—whom he calls "the angry modern Moses bearing the tablets of the new law"—that leaves no doubt. Yet he understands Marxism's appeal, and includes as a chapter title, "The Dazzling Bolshevik Sun." Mitchell depicts America during the Great Depression, when he was born, making the case for reform rather than revolution, even amid what he calls "a long nightmare of joblessness." He stresses that, like most major upheavals, it was completely unexpected. "The American people were as absolutely unprepared for the Great Depression as if it had been a volcanic eruption in Kansas or Nebraska."

The reformer was Franklin Roosevelt, whom he calls "the only confident man in America." Mitchell surveys the results of the New Deal in 1933, with passage of bank regulation, TVA, Civilian Conservation Corps, and regulation of the agriculture and industrial sectors—and, even more important, the Second New Deal of 1935, when overwhelming Democratic majorities in Congress enacted Roosevelt's plan for Social Security, the National Labor Relations Act, and the other underpinnings of contemporary public life. He concludes, "Within weeks after Roosevelt took office, the country seemed a new place. Hope was reborn."

Yet Mitchell is also frank about Roosevelt's boldness. "In effect, there was a sort of constitutional dictatorship in operation, such as one might see in a country on a war footing." Observers as intelligent as Edmund Wilson and Walter Lippmann expected Roosevelt to assume dictatorial powers, but Roosevelt himself said, "I have no inclination to be a dictator. I have none of the qualifications that would make me a successful dictator." Europe, Mitchell points out, was much less fortunate. "That Hitler and Stalin should have lived and held power at the same time was perhaps the greatest single misfortune to befall the twentieth century."

Mitchell brings the story up to contemporary times, and reflects on Mikhail Gorbachev as a world leader. While he supported Gorbachev's reforms, sometimes enthusiastically, Mitchell says he never believed they would work the way Gorbachev intended. Roosevelt, he said, "preserved and strengthened democratic capitalism and in the process doomed communism." The weaknesses of the Soviet state were internal and structural, and its economy "simply never worked right. It had never met its people's needs," Mitchell wrote. What's important about Gorbachev "is neither his many strengths nor his inevitable weaknesses. Rather, it is that at a crucial time in history, he helped free his country from an evil, totalitarian system and set it on a path to a better, democratic future. In so doing, he induced the final collapse of communism as an effective ideology." Communism, he wrote, "was founded on a big lie and nourished on many small lies."

THE END OF THE COLD WAR AND THE FALL of the Soviet Union had unexpected consequences, few more dramatic than Saddam Hussein's invasion of Kuwait on August 2, 1990. At first, President Bush seemed not to know what to do. His ambassador to Iraq, April Glaspie, had notoriously failed to issue a warning when meeting with Saddam eight days earlier. Democrats in Congress, including Mitchell, believed the Reagan-Bush "tilt to Iraq" during the seemingly endless Iran-Iraq War had emboldened Saddam to enlarge his domain without fearing the consequences. After the urging of Republicans at home and leaders such as Britain's Margaret Thatcher, Bush decided the New World Order he envisioned required the occupation be rolled back.

Bush focused first on the UN Security Council, building support for an Allied effort to evict Saddam's army. He won a series of resolutions escalating pressure on Iraq, culminating in Resolution 678, approved November 29, which authorized the use of force, unless Iraq complied with previous resolutions by January 15, 1991. Bush had already dispatched 200,000 troops to the Persian Gulf, then sent 200,000 more. It wasn't clear Congress would even be involved, inevitable though its vote might seem in retrospect. Mitchell and Speaker Tom Foley talked about a possible recall of Congress in October, but Bush made no request. Everyone was in uncharted territory. During the Cold War, a military operation of this size was unlikely, but with the Soviet implosion, and its leader advocating sharp reductions in nuclear and conventional forces, the United States had no military rivals. Americans had fought on behalf of allies in Korea and Vietnam, but it hadn't launched an invasion on this scale since D-Day.

While ambivalent about the need for congressional involvement, the president actively courted support, and Mitchell was among the leaders who traveled to Saudi Arabia, which had fatefully agreed to host US operations. Bush sent a handwritten letter to Mitchell from Camp David on November 24. It reads, "Just a quick note to thank you for coming all the way to Saudi Arabia. I am convinced the trip sent good signals to our troops. You leaders being a key part of it was, in my view, important. Thanks for breaking away from a Maine Thanksgiving to lift the morale of some great kids."

There was no thought, as in 2002, of pushing up a vote authorizing force to before the midterm elections, which resulted in Republican gains before the invasion of Iraq in 2003. No one expected the easy victory that ensued in Kuwait, and initial estimates from the Pentagon were grim. Sarah Sewall said, "The intelligence was very dire about the prospective costs and casualties." The war began with air strikes on January 16, and she remembers the day before, visiting Arlington National Cemetery with a friend, "sobered by what we thought would be the costs on an invasion." It was clear, "in retrospect, that DoD overestimated Iraqi capabilities," but no one said so at the time.

Mitchell advocated sanctions, and there was a tight regimen specified in the UN resolutions. He was backed by several military experts. Admiral William Crowe and General David Jones, former chairmen of the Joint Chiefs of Staff, said sanctions could work against Saddam. Crowe testified, "I personally believe they will bring him to his knees. If in fact the sanctions will work in twelve to eighteen months instead of six months, the trade-off would, in my view, be more than worth it." In retrospect, Sewall said, "The arguments about sanctions were inconclusive. As we say now, it was not a slam-dunk that they would be effective." Yet Bush had already "created a fait accompli through the troop buildups," she said. "The march to war affronted congressional sensibilities."

Mitchell finally got Bush to agree that Congress should vote, and the Senate prepared two resolutions—one conforming to the UN mandate, the other outlining stepped-up sanctions but not authorizing invasion. Bush formally requested the resolution on January 8. In a letter to Mitchell and other congressional leaders, he called for votes in the House and Senate to "adopt a resolution stating that Congress supports the use of all necessary means to implement UN Security Council Resolution 678." He said, "Such action would send the clearest possible message to Saddam Hussein that he must withdraw without condition or delay from Kuwait." Just a week before the planned invasion, the statement might seem pro forma, but Congress prepared for debate with the utmost seriousness.

Mitchell's position on the resolution was unknown, even to his staff. He "kept his cards very close to the vest. It wasn't clear what his personal opinion was. I could have seen him going either way," Sewall said. What was important to Mitchell, she said, was that the Democratic Caucus work through the issues and come to consensus. "He had a president who clearly was going to war, and he had a rank-and-file membership that was confused and uncomfortable." In the meantime, she drafted the sanctions resolution Mitchell could offer on the floor. "There was a wide variety of opinions in the caucus, and many, many meetings on how to proceed," she said. "There were pivotal moments with individual senators." She saw "the brilliant way he listened to inchoate comments and read between the lines, between argument and emotion, or argument and politics, and watching him process everything." Mitchell coordinated closely with Dole before the vote, knowing "the mechanics of the Senate require cooperation." In the end, she said, "The Senate worked in a wonderfully efficient way."

Ed King agreed that the staff process faithfully reflected Mitchell's methods. King said, "He wanted you to show him where you thought things were, and then he would decide where he wanted to be. And it wasn't important whether you agreed or not, because you were a staffer. He was going to go where he wanted to go, but you were to provide him with the wherewithal to get there."

Democrats decided to vote against Bush's resolution, though there were "defectors," Sewall said, "who fared better for having defected," including Al Gore, planning a run for president. It wasn't an easy decision, and Mitchell, once the caucus had voted, used his persuasive powers to convince others to go along. Chuck Robb, a former marine serving his first term, had been promoted to leadership as chair of the DSCC. He had concluded that "General Schwarzkopf and his team had done the things necessary to carry out the plan," and he planned to vote yes. But Mitchell "and my normal allies, particularly on defense matters, Sam Nunn, Lloyd Bentsen, John Glenn, Howell Heflin, and several others had all sort of been preempted." Nunn, in fact, "was even asked by George to lead what would be the opposition to the president's initiative." But because Robb had already spoken out, Mitchell said, "He's been very up front, he's out in front on this, I'm not going to ask him." Robb said, "It was a very wise, conscientious move on his part not to attempt to get me to do something, as a matter of conscience, I couldn't do."

Dale Bumpers was persuaded to vote no, though he later called it "a wrong vote." He said Mitchell "demonstrated his best qualities when we were debating." And, when he was asked to defend Bill Clinton during the Senate impeachment trial in 1999, the first person he called for advice was Mitchell. Carl Levin ended up with the same conclusion as Bumpers, after voting no. He said of Mitchell, "We were both wrong, but he was persuasive." Levin said he was also influenced by Joint Chiefs Chairman Colin Powell arguing privately against the invasion. Jay Rockefeller said Mitchell was "the only majority leader in the twenty-five years I've been here who ever called me at home and asked me to vote a certain way." He was planning to vote no, and, when Mitchell called, "I was shaving and had to put the phone right in the middle of my shaving cream, so I wasn't happy." Bob Kerrey, characteristically, would have preferred another option. "I was very uncomfortable that we appeared to be fighting a war just to drive Iraq out of Kuwait. It wasn't about freedom; it felt more about oil." Kerrey said he thought Mitchell should have supported the Republicans if they'd agree to amend the resolution.

Among Republicans, Alan Simpson thought Gore vexed Mitchell, which he said was confirmed when Gore sought him out, along with Dole, to ask, about the debate, "How many minutes will you give me tomorrow if I support the president?" Dole asked how many minutes the Democrats had offered, which was seven, and Dole offered him fifteen of his own twenty minutes, while Simpson chipped in five, "so you'll have twenty minutes." When Gore replied, "I'll think about this carefully," and left, Dole told Simpson, "Put him down on our side, we've got him." John Warner said Mitchell "spoke against the timing, very eloquently and very fairly." But to Warner, the "rampant death, destruction, and challenges to sovereignty in full view every day" in Kuwait necessitated his vote for the resolution.

In his floor speech, Mitchell emphasized constitutional questions. He said that, as commander in chief, Bush was within his responsibilities to deploy troops. "But if he now decides to use those forces in what would plainly be war, he is legally obligated to seek the prior approval of Congress." And, he said, "The grave decision for war is being made prematurely." The vote on January 12, after two days of debate, was close—fifty-two in favor and forty-seven opposed. Ten Democrats, mostly Southern, voted for the resolution, while two Republicans opposed it. Sarah Sewall said she still doesn't know whether

Mitchell's vote against the resolution represented his own opinion, or that of the caucus.

After the vote, Mitchell got a note from Paul Wellstone, the Minnesota senator who had been elected just two years earlier. He said, "I am profoundly sad about where we are heading in the Gulf. Rushing to war is a terrible mistake. But getting to know you has given me a lot of hope about public service. I have tremendous respect for your ability and integrity. . . . Every time, even when you don't agree with me, you have been fair, kind, and supportive. You make it easier for me to vote my conscience and for that, I thank you. You are a great majority leader."

Once the war began, Mitchell was steadfast in support of the president's policy. He chose that year to make the Democratic response to the State of the Union address, and on January 31 provided a full menu of policy alternatives for the home front, as well as taking note of a recession beginning to take a toll on jobs. Mitchell still had a few points to make about Kuwait. "Before the war began, we debated openly, as democracy demands," he said. "We agreed that Iraq's aggression was brutal and illegal, and that Iraq must leave Kuwait, by force if necessary. The difference was not in the goals, but in the means: whether force should be used immediately, or only as a last resort if other means failed. No one will ever know if another course would have worked. Now that war has begun, we must be unified in purpose, and we hope and pray that it will be swift and decisive, with the least possible loss of life."

He offered a reminder about consequences from previous policies. "When the war's over, there's one lesson we must never forget: The dictator we help today may turn his weapons on us tomorrow. We can't repeat that mistake. Out of the tragedy of war, we seek a world in which the force of law is more powerful than the force of arms. We seek a world in which justice and human rights are respected everywhere. Students massacred in China, priests murdered in Central America, demonstrators gunned down in Lithuania—these acts of violence are as unacceptable as Iraqi soldiers killing civilians. We cannot oppose repression in one place and condone it in another."

UPHEAVAL IN THE COMMUNIST STATES and the Gulf War were the largest international events during Mitchell's six years at the helm, but there were others where he played a significant role. One where he struggled to find his footing was the emergence of Nelson Mandela as South Africa's leader-in-waiting once the white minority government released him after twenty-five years in prison. Mitchell received sharply conflicting advice from his staff. The question was how Mitchell should present Mandela to the Senate when he spoke. Anita Jensen was sharply skeptical, and prepared a "lukewarm rather than enthusiastic" draft. "It's not clear to me from media accounts whether the man remains a committed democrat or what distance he intends to place between himself and the more radical fringe of the ANC," she wrote in a June 22, 1990, memo. "His wife, who is with him on this tour, is generally accused of having her bodyguards kill a young black South African and has been criticized by other black leaders. The intra-black fighting in the nation is as bloody as the black-white conflict. It's not clear to me that democracy as we understand it is Mandela's goal, or the goal of any potential leader down there."

Sarah Sewall, writing the same day after seeing Jensen's memo, dissented. She rebutted each point, and wrote, "To impugn Mandela for the behavior of his wife while he was imprisoned is unfair." She also said, "Mandela's commitment to democracy is unmistakable given that he wants one man, one vote democracy. It is [F. W.] De Klerk who does not want democracy as we know it; he envisions 'group rights' that will provide special protection to whites." She conceded that Mandela's "view of liberation" included violence "when peaceful means were not an option for blacks in South Africa," and said she was "disturbed" by the ANC's refusal to formally abandon armed struggle, "although it does not visibly continue," and saw this as a negotiating strategy, with violence to be renounced later—a theme that ran throughout Mitchell's later involvement in Northern Ireland.

Mitchell ended up splitting the difference. He used an "inoffensive" quotation Jensen had chosen where Mandela committed himself, while entering prison, to achieving "a democratic and free society" after fighting against both "white domination" and "black domination." But Mitchell rewrote the rest, emphasizing Mandela's "lack of bitterness toward those who unjustly imprisoned him for more than a third of his life." He connected Mandela to the democrats of Eastern Europe, Lech Walesa and Vaclav Havel, and to Martin Luther King's "I Have a Dream" speech. He concluded, "Even as we do what we can to help your people achieve freedom in their land, your presence inspires us to rededicate ourselves to that great task in our own land."

THE CHAOS THAT FOLLOWED THE END OF US military involvement in Vietnam continued to spread years later. Not long after the collapse of the Khmer Rouge regime in Cambodia, following one of the largest genocides of the twentieth century, a united Vietnam, under Communist control, invaded and occupied Cambodia. The Reagan and Bush administrations provided covert military aid to non-communist opposition groups, but Mitchell was concerned they were ignoring the reality that the Khmer Rouge was dominating the resistance. He resolved to quietly convince the Senate to use funding to get the administration's attention. Mitchell's concerns prompted several letters from the White House, including one from Secretary of State James Baker on July 18, 1990, and another from NSC Advisor Brent Scowcroft, assuring him a "restructured" aid program was working. But he wasn't satisfied.

Sewall was in Mitchell's office at eleven p.m. one evening when Baker called. Mitchell had prepared with his committee chairs an amendment cutting off aid to the Cambodian opposition, and Baker had gotten wind of it. Sewall figured Baker would call, and had briefed Mitchell. As the secretary of state protested, Sewall said, "I remember the smile on Senator Mitchell's face. It was just like the Cheshire cat, because he knew he had him." She later described Mitchell as "uncharacteristically gleeful." Because he knew he had the votes, "There was nothing the administration could do. Covert assistance was discontinued, and that was a critical factor in establishing a UN-led peace process," she said. Mitchell believed, she said, "This wasn't a way to halt violence, and it provided indirect support for genocide." Successful peace talks "then opened the way for a very different foreign policy chapter, a better place than if we'd continued to fuel a war." Sewall called it "an extremely satisfying moment. . . . I was proud to work for Mitchell, and that Congress was actually exercising its oversight role."

A COUNTRY UNIMPORTANT IN THE SCALES of superpower rivalry, but close to Mitchell's heart, was Lebanon. The homeland of his mother's ancestors had also been that rarest of things—a democracy in the Middle East, the one thing it had in common with its powerful neighbor, Israel. By the 1970s, however, Lebanon had come undone. The unique power-sharing arrangement in which the president was a Maronite Christian, the speaker of Parliament a Shia Muslim, and the prime minister a Sunni Muslim, came under strain with the rise of religious-based militias among Christians, Muslims, and Druze, then collapsed into civil war in 1975. Syrian troops arrived in 1976, occupying much of the country until 2005. The Palestinian Liberation Organization had moved into a vacuum in southern Lebanon, prompting an Israeli invasion and occupation in 1982 that lasted until 2000.

Mitchell believed the cosmopolitan, tolerant culture of Lebanon, and its free-market economy, provided a model for a war-torn region, and did what he could. As one of few senators with ties to Lebanon, he was in strong demand as a speaker. In October 1980, shortly after joining the Senate, he addressed the Second World Maronite Congress in New York, and stressed Lebanon's link to his country, and his family. "We Maronites are no strangers to injustice, to war, and to disunity," he said. "For over fifteen hundred years, Lebanon, like America throughout its history, has been a haven for the oppressed, where people of all faiths have lived in free and secure community. A free Lebanon is of great value to itself, to the region, and to the whole world." He said, "Being here tonight with you, my fellow Maronites, I cannot fail to mention my mother, the source of my Lebanese heritage, and to me, the living embodiment of the Lebanese Maronite character." Not for the first time, he paid tribute to her. "She taught us the simple principles by which she lived: faith in our Lord and our Church; love of our family; devotion to our country. There may be more sophisticated principles in which one can believe, but there are none more meaningful or lasting. My debt to my mother cannot be calculated, let alone repaid. Whatever I am, whatever I do, I owe to her." In another venue, Mitchell summed up Lebanon's contemporary plight as "a tragedy of location" caught between more powerful, warring neighboring states.

Mitchell, at the end of the Gulf War, joined with Bob Dole in writing to President Bush on March 1, 1991, saying "The end of the war will not end the problems and challenges of the Middle East," and urging "serious attention to the nation of Lebanon." Sanctions levied on Iraq had also "severely disrupted" Lebanon's economy, already "devastated by fifteen years of war." Mitchell and Dole said they were "especially troubled that the expansion of Syrian authority" in Lebanon "occurred following Syria's decision to join the international coalition against Iraq and Secretary Baker's meeting with Syrian President Assad." It would be a "terrible tragedy" if Syria saw its cooperation as permission "for broader aggression in Lebanon," and they urged Bush to make Lebanon "a central concern of American policy in the postwar period. We cannot achieve a 'new regional order' in the Middle East if we exclude Lebanon."

Lebanon's traditions of tolerance also made it a terrorist target. The American University of Beirut paid a particularly heavy price. Its president, Malcolm Kerr, was assassinated outside his office in 1984. Thomas Sutherland, dean of agriculture, was kidnapped by Islamic Jihad, a pro-Iranian group, in 1985, and not released until 1991. Joseph Cicippio was held from 1986 to 1991. Alan Steen, a journalism professor, was captive from 1987 to 1991, after being kidnapped along with a computer science professor, Jesse Turner. All were American citizens, and some were among the hostages futilely bargained over during Iran-Contra. Their release followed the Taif Agreement, which, while not ending Syria's occupation, helped normalize Lebanese affairs.

Mitchell spoke at the 125th anniversary of the American University on November 8, 1991, shortly after Turner's release, and anticipating the others. "The taking of hostages is a particular tragedy because it is an affront to the very ideals upon which the university was founded," he said. The university, he said, "has become a symbol of Lebanon itself: diverse, dedicated, full of talent, energy, and intelligence." Mitchell, while suggesting the Taif Agreement was a thaw, not a solution, looked forward to a day when foreign troops would finally be gone. "Lebanon was once a land of industry and tolerance," he said. "This is the true spirit of the Lebanese people. This is the spirit that will save the nation."

One tangible achievement, though not brought to fruition until after he left the Senate, was convincing the State Department to lift a ban on travel by Americans. Lebanon was included on the State Department's terrorist watch list. Brett O'Brien, hired in 1989 to work at the Democratic Policy Committee, encouraged his counterparts at State to ease the ban, but got nowhere. Mitchell said they should see Warren Christopher, who had just taken office as secretary of state for Bill Clinton. O'Brien said they had an attentive audience, as Mitchell explained "his own heritage, his family's history in Lebanon, the opportunity that he had in coming to the United States . . . and his desire, along with that of many Lebanese-Americans, to give back to Lebanon." O'Brien said, "It really was that first meeting, where he had a chance to talk with Secretary Christopher in a very personal way," that made the difference. Christopher agreed to undertake a review, and the travel ban was lifted in 1995.

Often, there was little Mitchell could do to change events. But Sarah Sewall observed the features that later led to his prominent roles in the Middle East. "What was important was his unique position as someone who had credibility as an Arab-American, but wasn't Muslim," she said. Mitchell also maintained good relations with the Jewish community in Maine, and with AIPAC, the American Israel Public Affairs Committee, the principal pro-Israel lobby. Mitchell, she said, brought a "balanced approach" among the "oddly unstable coalition of Druze/Maronite/Muslim." If not unique, Mitchell was unusual. "Very few people possessed those qualities," she said. Bob Dole, by contrast, was often "perceived as anti-Israeli," and there were similar issues with James Baker. "Mitchell could be assertive without losing that balance and sense of perspective," Sewall said. "The importance was less what he was able to do than that he forged and reforged himself as a diplomatic force."

SARAH SEWALL WORKED FOR MITCHELL FROM 1983 to 1993, and later served in the Defense Department under Bill Clinton, and the State Department under Barack Obama. She felt both the closeness that some longtime staff members experienced, and also the boundaries he maintained. "The interesting thing about Senator Mitchell was how warm his public persona was, but in many ways how cool his private interactions with his staff were," she said. "Not that he didn't have warmth—but he clearly perceived his role as a senator as requiring a degree of distance." Even with colleagues, she said, "there were degrees of that. So his buddies from Maine, his longtime whatever they were—chess or checkers or card-playing buddies—are in a different category from his close Senate colleagues, different category from his Democratic colleagues, different category from the Republicans he really didn't like." In her experience, "You feel very close to the person that you represent, particularly if you do the kind of writing that I did for him, because it's your job to be in their head and to understand how they think."

Sewall came to see Mitchell almost as a surrogate father; Loyall Sewall had died at age sixty from the effects of alcoholism. "Senator Mitchell was sort of the closest thing I had in my life to filling that slot, so I think that's for me why the distance was always a little bit hard, because you'd see him treat other staff very familiarly, and you always wonder, 'If I didn't work for him, would he treat me like that?'" Still, she said, "The formality did have an edge of discipline to it that I think was helpful . . . in listening to him talk about Muskie, I would hear the reasons why he adopted the persona he did as senator, because I suspect they lie in his relationship with Muskie."

Other staffers had moments where boundaries suddenly appeared. Bob Carolla, who worked on defense and Maine issues, had arrived when Mitchell's office was relatively small, and noticed a generational shift as many younger people, in their early twenties, were hired after Mitchell became majority leader. Carolla discovered half a dozen were living in the same house in Arlington. Mitchell almost had to create distance, he realized. On the night Carolla's son was born, "I got a phone call at home, and it was the senator calling to congratulate me," he said. "I was sort of wired and I started to recount what it had all been like. And the senator had a real reserve with the staff, especially if it had anything to do with medical or health issues, or anything people would think of as private or personal, it was almost like a squeamishness. Over the phone I could just sort of sense his tone, backing off, and so I quickly thanked him" and hung up.

After Clinton was elected, Sewall left the DPC, and was nominated and confirmed for the new post of deputy assistant secretary for peacekeeping at Defense. She never got to work for the boss who selected her, though—Morton Halperin, a Defense reformer, like Clinton's first Defense secretary, Les Aspin. Jesse Helms took a dislike to Halperin, and blocked his confirmation for more than a year until he withdrew. Sewall left the administration after she delivered triplets in 1996. After stints of teaching and think-tank work, she served on the Obama transition team and, then, when the triplets went to college, joined the administration in 2014 as Undersecretary of State for Civilian Security, Democracy and Human Rights, managing a staff of two thousand.

Her new boss, John Kerry, has a different style than Mitchell. "Kerry had been a driving force in foreign policy his whole Senate career," she said, and his work at State is "very much a matter of what his personal relationships were like, a form of personal diplomacy." Mitchell, she said, didn't focus primarily on relationships, "but was more like a student mastering the material. By virtue of his role as a legislator, he was not an actor, but focused on the broader picture and arguments."

Looking back, "What I miss about working for him is that it was a time that sustained hope in our political system," she said. Though their subsequent contacts have been infrequent, "You always hope he's going to say, 'I have this great new project, I'm going to bring democracy to Burma, come do it with me.' But it hasn't happened yet."

18

WHAT AILS
THE PATIENT

George Mitchell's legislative record from the other subcommittee he chaired, Health Care on Finance, is less well known than his environmental work, but it ended up playing a large part in his Senate leadership, and resulted in several important successes, as well as his biggest disappointment. The Finance Committee was even less generous with minority staff than Environment and Public Works—only the chairmen chose staff—and Estelle Lavoie handled all of his Finance issues for his first three years on the committee. It wasn't until 1984, when he was moving up the Health Care subcommittee ladder, that he hired a legislative aide for committee work, Christine Williams, whose focus soon narrowed to health care as Mitchell became more legislatively active.

Williams grew up in Massachusetts and became a social studies and political science teacher in her home state of New Hampshire, and in South Dakota and Brunswick, Maine. After working on Ted Kennedy's presidential bid in 1980 as a volunteer, she decided to go to Washington to see what she could find. "Unfortunately, it was 1981, and Ronald Reagan had just been elected, so it was not a good time to be a Democrat coming to Washington looking for a job, because there were a lot of people out of work," she said. Mitchell was still an appointed senator, but in February 1982 Williams was hired to run the mailroom, "which was not a great job, but it was a foot in the door, and after six months of looking I was happy just to have a job," she said.

As some of the old Muskie hands, including Lavoie, departed, Williams moved up. Mitchell became ranking subcommittee member in 1985—serving opposite John Chafee again, as he had on EPW—then chairman in 1987. Mitchell worked on several ambitious bills that year, but the staff shortage was daunting. Williams says it was fortunate a Robert Wood Johnson fellow joined the staff, Greg Paulson, a mid-career geriatrician, who understood the clinical background and played a key role in drafting a nursing home reform bill.

When Mitchell left the Senate in 1994, Williams was stunned, and remembers a conversation about job-hunting with Diane Dewhirst, where Dewhirst said, "You'll never have another job like this again," and deciding, "She was right." Yet there were occasional stormy moments. Williams had been arranging witnesses for a subcommittee hearing, and knew Mitchell had a strict rule that twelve witnesses was the maximum. Another staffer kept pushing for another witness, and finally she gave in. When Mitchell saw the list, she started to explain that her colleague had insisted, but Mitchell said, "He doesn't know, but you do." She said, "He was really kind of upset." She later visited him in his office to request that, should he feel the need to reprimand, "It would be better if you and I had the conversation in private." Mitchell "just nodded," but she heard from others, "Wow, the senator is being really nice to us today," and knew he'd acknowledged her point.

Other times, she expected a reaction but didn't get one—as when she provided faulty information about an abortion vote, which was "really serious." She never had any difficulty with his level of understanding, however. Her background as a teacher sometimes caused her to over-explain, as when she said, "And Senator, another way to understand this is," he interrupted to say, "Chris, I got it the first time." She said, "He quickly became very knowledgeable and well-versed in many of the intricacies of health care," even though, when he started, he often said, "I'm not an expert."

Mitchell suggested there might be reasons why he learned quickly. After assuming the subcommittee chairmanship, he spoke to the American Society of Anesthesiologists on May 4, 1987. The speech included an elaborate presentation on escalating costs of physician services under Medicare Part B, rising at an annual rate of 18 percent. He then made this statement: "While it is true that I do not have a medical degree or a background in health policy, I do approach health issues from a very important perspective. I am a hypochondriac. I like to think I'm a *recovering* hypochondriac, but a hypochondriac nevertheless. And so, my job is perfect for me—I get to be around physicians, learn about new diseases, and talk about health issues on a daily basis."

The nursing home bill was the first major health care legislation Mitchell guided to passage, and it reflected his concern that neither financing nor oversight of nursing homes was handled effectively by states or the federal government. Greg Paulson drafted the bill in 1986 while Williams handled the political aspects. It was based on recommendations from the Institute for Healthcare

Improvement, which contended that since the federal government was the principal funder of nursing homes, there ought to be basic standards for care. It wasn't ripe for passage in 1986 and, in 1987, Democrats decided to include the Federal Nursing Home Reform Act in budget reconciliation, which made it more difficult to filibuster, and probably impossible for President Reagan to veto.

The legislation has been described as "the first major revision of the federal standards for nursing home care since the 1965 creation of both Medicare and Medicaid," and remains in effect. "It really is a landmark piece of legislation in improving the quality of care in the nation's nursing homes," Williams said. She also remembers the late-night Senate-House conference sessions. "Mitchell and Chafee were negotiating opposite Henry Waxman and Pete Stark," Williams said, "both from the left coast." The congressmen were suspicious of the bipartisan legislation Mitchell had prepared. While Waxman was gentlemanly, if steely, Stark, who chaired the Ways and Means health subcommittee, was known, as one source put it, for his "ornery disposition and record of bizarre insults." At two a.m. on the final night of bargaining, the two Senate negotiators adjourned to a back room. It was so small only the two senators had chairs, "and the rest of us sat on the floor," Williams said. Finally, Chafee said, "I guess we'll have to go along with them on this," to which Mitchell replied, "Yes, but let's make them wait awhile."

Because the bill passed as part of the budget, Mitchell didn't get the recognition he might have otherwise, but it was certainly noted by his peers, the industry, and consumer groups. Williams, who worked in health care for the rest of her career, said, "Of course, as soon as you pass federal regulations, people are looking for ways to get around them." Assisted living facilities, the courts have found, are not covered, and have multiplied around the country. "There's been a tremendous shift from nursing homes to assisted living," Williams said. "There's no real federal regulation, and state regulation varies enormously." Those taking care of elderly parents often ask her, "Why don't we get more help? Why doesn't the government do something?"

Despite having taught in Brunswick a few years, Williams knew few people in Maine, but was impressed by the quality of industry leadership, including the Maine Long Term Care Association. "It's usually the case that Maine is ahead of the curve," she said. "When we did nursing home reform, Maine had already met the standards. But across the country, many, many states had not met them." The commitment was put to the test when, amid a major state budget shortfall following the 1990–1991 recession, Maine governor John McKernan sought a federal Medicaid waiver that would have limited nursing home eligibility to those with monthly incomes of less than $423, down from $1,302. At the time, only two thousand of Maine's ten thousand nursing home residents paid privately. Williams's note on the memo says, "This waiver request is a very bad idea," and the Legislature rejected it.

Williams counts long-term care as one of the major unsolved problems of American health care. Mitchell was involved, for instance, in a proposed pilot program that would have allowed federal employees nearing retirement age to switch their government-paid term life insurance for long-term care insurance, but the numbers didn't work. Williams said the United States is far from the only nation with inadequate coverage, and financing a universal system faces daunting obstacles. But Mitchell did achieve one breakthrough on Medicaid funding. Under the initial rules, when a spouse got funding for nursing home care, the remaining partner—usually female—was often left destitute. The Spousal Impoverishment Act Congress adopted allows states to recover expenses from estates only after both partners have died. It also reserves a portion of pensions from requirements couples "spend down" their savings before qualifying for Medicaid.

The bill started with a visit to Mitchell's Augusta office, where Mary McAleney was then located. A representative from legal services for the elderly came in to talk, accompanied by an elderly woman. "As most women had done, she had stayed home and run the house and brought the kids up. He was the one that had the pension," McAleney said. "When he went into the nursing home, the fees for the nursing home took all of his pension before Medicaid kicked in." She called Williams to say, "This is horrible." Williams already knew about a House bill addressing the issue, and promised she'd take it up with Mitchell. "Because somebody from Maine had brought that to him he had a face on that," McAleney said. "He worked hard on the bill. And when my dad went into the nursing home, my mother was able to live" on her own, she said.

When the time came to move the bill from Finance to the floor, Mitchell considered who could benefit the most from managing it. Like all health care legislation, both Finance and Health, Education, and Labor have jurisdiction, and Barbara Mikulski, serving her first year, had responsibility for HEL. "It was his right in many ways to take it to the floor," Mikulski said, but Mitchell told her, "This is your first bill, and you've told me what it meant to you because of your father, why don't you . . . take the lead?" She said, "He helped me shepherd that amendment through, he always had my back. . . . It was Mikulski-Mitchell, but it really could have been Mitchell-Mikulski." The legislation, she said, made a major difference. "AARP has told me we've kept at least a million people out of poverty."

Williams sometimes was willing to push Mitchell harder than other staff. Her year as a VISTA volunteer at the Rosebud Reservation in South Dakota left her with a vivid impression of tribes caught between two worlds, and when representatives of the Micmac tribe in far northern Maine came to visit, she listened carefully. The Micmac live on both sides of the Maine–New Brunswick border, and had little standing with either national government. Without federal recognition, they could share in none of the benefits available to the Penobscot and Passamaquoddy tribes from the 1980 land claims settlement. Mitchell wasn't enthusiastic. "I don't want to get into that," he told Williams. "We did this in 1980; it was very contentious. I don't want to reopen that." She persisted, saying, "These people are really, really poor." On why they hadn't participated earlier, she said, "They didn't even know this was going on."

Eventually, Mitchell allowed her to pursue the project, and, several years later, the Micmac were federally recognized. Williams well remembers the day the tribe came to Washington to thank Mitchell. He was by then majority leader, and "We sat in his office, and I didn't even sit at the table, because he was still sort of irritated with me. I had sort of dragged him into this." Several of the Micmac began crying, and she remembers them saying, "We never thought we'd see this day, you don't know how much this means to us." When he responded, Mitchell said, "Well, you've got a big champion in my office," which she said meant to her, "You did the right thing." She called it "very New England," and said, "He never effusively praised people, but you knew. I mean, I felt not only vindicated, but that he appreciated it in spite of everything."

ONCE THE CLEAN AIR ACT WAS COMPLETED in 1990, Mitchell felt he could turn his attention to another pressing national issue. In 1991, building on his experience with nursing home reform and long-term care, he introduced his first national health care reform bill. Support for a unified system, which always polls well before details are included, was building once again. Neil Rolde, a former Democratic legislator, took on the task of opposing Bill Cohen's second reelection bid in 1990. Rolde staked his campaign on a national health care plan, and did surprisingly well, winning 43 percent, a much better showing than most little-known candidates against Senate incumbents.

The following year saw the political tsunami of Harris Wofford's stunning upset of Dick Thornburg in the Pennsylvania special Senate election to succeed John Heinz, who had died in a plane crash. In Washington, the Pepper Commission, led by longtime Florida representative Claude Pepper, issued a comprehensive report about American health care. It found costs were rising at two to three times the rate of inflation and, despite Medicare and Medicaid, care was uncoordinated, the medical profession was overspecialized, there were enormous inefficiencies, and governors were lobbying hard over rising state costs. Ted Kennedy had filed reform bills for two decades, but now had plenty of company, including Mitchell.

The moment seemed ripe for change. After the November 5, 1991 special election, *BusinessWeek* proclaimed on its cover, "Roar of Discontent," and quoted Burton Yale Pines of the Heritage Foundation, saying, "The blessing of the Pennsylvania election is that it came one year before President Bush has to face voters. He'd be resoundingly rejected if the election were held today." It also reported, "Medical costs have risen faster than the rate of inflation for fourteen of the past fifteen years, and now account for 12 percent of GNP." And it quoted Democratic strategist Celinda Lake saying, "Health care could well be the Social Security of the '90s—an issue that defines a political party to an entire generation." In one of Chris Williams's strategy memos, she wrote, "State governments cannot sustain current spending trends. States now spend 17 percent of their revenues on health care costs. Ten years from now it will be 27 percent." Countering Republican contentions that any national system would lead to rationing, she said, "Health care is rationed in America today. It is rationed by price."

The Mitchell bill, HealthAmerica, S. 1227, was introduced in June 1991 and covered 347 pages. When he presented it, Mitchell said it would preserve the existing public-private system, but add a requirement that employers cover their employees, the so-called "employer mandate." He said, "This program will replace the existing Medicaid program for all services except long-term care. All persons who are not eligible for employer-based health insurance will be eligible to receive health benefits through Americare. Americare is a dramatically new public program. Federal standards will be set for eligibility, benefits, and reimbursement."

One reason Mitchell proposed replacing the federal-state Medicaid program was that governors and legislatures were cutting coverage. A 1988 memo from a Robert Wood Johnson fellow said, "Medicaid currently covers just over 40 percent of the poor people in this country, down 20 percent in the past decade." On expanding coverage, it said, "As poor people have little ability to pay even a token amount for health coverage, it appears, and most agree, that Medicaid is the most appropriate mechanism."

Mitchell said his plan would include tax credits for small businesses and reform of the small group insurance market, with private insurance limited to 15 percent overhead on premiums, down from 25 percent; the Affordable Care Act standard is 20 percent. He also said, "Federal and state governments must share the burden in reforming the health care system." He said Congress was setting itself a large task. "Reforming the health care system will be difficult. While most of us believe there is a serious problem, few can agree on a solution. A perfect solution does not exist. Some argue that the United States should adopt a Canadian model of national health insurance. Others argue that tax incentives to businesses with no requirement to provide coverage is the answer." He concluded, "The legislation we are introducing today represents a compromise between those two views, keeping in mind our own traditions and values as Americans."

Williams had a brief moment of panic just before the bill was introduced. She had been up late the previous night to make final changes before it went to the Congressional Printing Office. She was stunned to find the next morning that it was printed only on one side of each page, rather than the usual book-like format. An already-long bill would look longer—an inevitable criticism whenever major legislation is presented. And that was the first point Republicans made. Mitchell asked about the curious printing oversight, and Williams said it was her mistake. "I was delirious from having not slept for several days," she said. Mitchell quickly thought of a solution. "Let's get a scale out here and let's weigh our bill, and let's weigh the Republicans' bill." He then said, "What do you know? The Republicans don't have a bill, their bill weighs zero, because they're not prepared to address this issue." Williams appreciated the theater, calling it a brilliant improvisation, but added, "That was the least of our problems in getting this bill passed."

Mitchell didn't expect to get any Republican co-sponsors, and the principal Democrats on the bill were Ted Kennedy, Don Riegle, and Jay Rockefeller—all Northern liberals; when Mitchell became majority leader, Rockefeller succeeded him as health care subcommittee chairman. Mitchell wanted to attract David Pryor of Arkansas, whose health care aide, Chris Jennings, worked frequently with Williams. Pryor "loaned" Jennings to the Clinton health care effort in 1993. But Jennings looked at the Mitchell bill, and said, "The small business lobby will never accept this," referring to the employer mandate.

Behind the scenes, there were already obstacles. On February 27, Williams reported, "The Finance Committee staff believes that this proposal must have significant cost-containment provisions. This has been a major contention with Kennedy's staff. We had a problem with David Nexon of Kennedy's staff on Friday. Apparently, David called a number of major health care provider groups . . . and told them that Senator Rockefeller was pressuring you to accept a single-payer model. By the time this misinformation got to the Maine Hospital Association, it was reported you were advocating a single-payer model." Williams said she had "taken care of the problem," but added, "It points out how strongly Kennedy's staff (and maybe Kennedy himself) feel about not having any controversial cost-containment piece."

Eventually, the Republicans did come up with a statement of principles. It included opposition to regulations, mandates, and additional payroll taxes, but it did embrace universal coverage, saying, "We believe the following three goals are fundamental: Quality of care must be maintained. Every citizen must be covered. The growth of health care costs must be restrained." Among the twenty-four signers were Bob Dole, Dave Durenberger, and Bill Cohen.

The System, the most exhaustively detailed account of the Clinton health-care plan, by *Washington Post* journalists Haynes Johnson and David Broder, covers this period, and claims Mitchell was angling to get a "big bill" before George Bush so he would veto it and hand the Democrats a 1992 campaign issue. This seems unlikely. Mitchell was, first and foremost, trying to achieve consensus among Democrats, and his failure to attract Pryor was a sign Southern Democrats weren't going to come aboard.

Without such a consensus, Mitchell traveled. He held field hearings in Tampa, Atlanta, Cleveland, Detroit, and Denver in December. He reported on the trip in a floor speech January 22, 1992. "As we begin the second session of the 102nd Congress," he said, "I want to express, in the strongest terms possible, my intention to move forward in reforming the nation's health care system. . . . Last December, I traveled to five cities across the country in an effort to learn more about the problems with the nation's health care system, and to seek viable solutions for reform. The eloquent, often tragic testimony from ordinary citizens who have been failed by the system has reinforced my determination to enact meaningful health care reform legislation as soon as possible. This is a matter of urgency—it cannot wait for the turn of the century, or even the next election. . . . Our current health care system is failing millions of American families—resulting in bankruptcy for many, worsening of illness for others, and death for some who might have been saved with appropriate treatment."

Mitchell also took to the op-ed pages, and critiqued Bush's response. He said, "I do not welcome criticism from those who have no alternative proposal to put forth. Unfortunately, to date the Bush administration has only had time to attack this plan. I am pleased that the president will finally become involved in the health care debate." In the *Christian Science Monitor*, he said Bush "conceded the central point of health care reform—that it is a right for all Americans, not a privilege for the well-heeled or safely employed." Mitchell added, "Time passed him by. . . . The debate about health care is no longer about 'socialized medicine' versus the illusion of a perfect free-market system. The debate today is how well a plan meets a pressing national need." By declining to regulate the insurance market, Mitchell said, "The president's plan is woefully inadequate. It is not a serious effort." Limiting malpractice claims and promoting managed care, its principal elements, was far from enough, he said.

Bill Cohen, testifying on the Mitchell bill, was more supportive of insurance reform. "Ironically, the very people who need care most are the ones who cannot get insurance and are therefore excluded from the system," Cohen said. "Insurance companies must stop competing with each other about whom to exclude and start concentrating on how to make affordable policies available for all Americans."

A for-profit hospital lobbyist gave a telling depiction of the industry's response in a memo to Williams. He said, "Here are the confidential specs: 'Praise Mitchell, Criticize Mitchell bill.'" The memo said the public response would be, "We are deeply concerned about Senator Mitchell's proposals to place government at the center of so many important spending decisions. . . . A health care system in which government, either directly or indirectly, controls prices and sets budgets will lead, inevitably, to serious shortfalls in quality and access." The private message was this: "The entire response is now being drafted, but of course no final decision has been made on the substance of that response. In fact, no final decision will ever be made in order that we may remain open-minded and objective."

Mitchell's bill was also attacked from the left. Sidney Wolfe, who had been crusading for years, appeared on a radio interview with Mitchell and Chafee on June 23, 1991, and said, "What Canada did twenty years ago essentially eliminated the health insurance industry . . . they save an enormous amount of money, enough to pay for the system." He said of Mitchell's bill, "It's an old out-of-date kind of idea, and though it might pass, it can't work." Later, he renewed the attack, sounding like the national environmental groups about clean air. "We don't like it at all," Wolfe said, "and the idea that the standard for legislation should be can it pass . . . is ridiculous. Before too long, four or five years, we're going to have a Canadian kind of system, a single-payer system."

Mitchell never introduced or supported a bill using the Canadian model. Williams said, "He wasn't opposed to the concept. Ted Kennedy was the leading proponent of a single-payer system, but Mitchell believed it was just not going to happen." In a June 22, 1992 speech to the National Council of Senior Citizens, however, he followed discussion of his bill's features with this comment: "It would move toward a single-payer system—the only way to ensure a national health care budget that the nation's people can afford."

Before the Mitchell plan of 1991 and the Clinton plan of 1993, there had been, for reformers, a disturbing incident involving previous Medicare legislation—the Catastrophic Health Care law. In 1987, Secretary of Health and

Human Services Otis Bowen, a former Republican governor of Indiana and a physician, convinced Ronald Reagan the Medicare system fell short in covering seniors for expensive procedures. There was bipartisan support in both houses of Congress, with Appropriations Chair Dan Rostenkowski, Waxman, and Stark taking the lead in the House, while Dole and Mitchell rounded up Senate votes. There was a broad recognition that lower-income seniors could be bankrupted, and funding was provided through the first income-based Medicare premium, with wealthier seniors paying more. Up to that time, there had been a flat rate.

Before the law took effect in 1989, Rostenkowski was confronted by a group of fifty angry seniors after an event in his Chicago district, who insisted that "middle class" seniors would be charged exorbitant rates. Rostenkowski tried to jog away instead of answering, saying, "These people don't understand what the government is trying to do for them." Within days, anti-reform groups were amplifying the charges, and Rostenkowski introduced legislation to repeal the law. Mitchell and the Senate reluctantly went along, and except for a few provisions—such as the Mikulski-Mitchell spousal impoverishment amendment—catastrophic coverage was gone. "It was the first time we ever tried to get an income-related premium," Williams said, which Mitchell believed was fair, "because lower-income seniors were paying a much larger share of their income."

MITCHELL, ALONG WITH TOM FOLEY AND Dick Gephardt, was invited to Little Rock to talk about legislative issues a month after Bill Clinton's election in November 1992. "The issues were pretty clear to everyone," Mitchell said. "Health care was among many." One of the first questions was how health care legislation would be presented. Mitchell's own experience, failing to gain consensus among Democrats, made him wary. The 1992 election barely altered the partisan balance; Senate Democrats gained one seat, and now held fifty-seven, though three newcomers were women—Dianne Feinstein, Barbara Boxer, and Carol Moseley Braun.

Mitchell also recalled that the Nursing Home Reform Act was folded into the budget resolution so only a simple majority was needed. Mitchell thought he could get fifty votes for health care reform, but he was dubious about sixty. He recommended Clinton consider adopting health care reform as part of his budget, and the administration considered but dropped the idea. There was no bill ready to go, unfortunately, and doing something of this complexity through budget reconciliation would have been difficult. "I recognize that the Senate process enables delay and obstruction much more than it permits swift action and movement toward the passage of legislation," Mitchell said, discussing adoption of the Affordable Care Act in 2010. "The more complex the legislation, the more those principles apply. It would be hard to be more comprehensive and complicated than health care, which of course represents a very substantial portion of our national economy, and which affects every single American. It's unavoidable that as an American, from the moment of birth to the moment of death, you have some contact with the health care system."

Even though Mitchell was concerned from the beginning that the Senate might not have the votes, he doesn't fault Clinton's decision to do the budget first. "That was a big part of the discussion" in Little Rock, he said. "What's the order we do these things? . . . I think his decision to complete his economic program before he went to health care was the right one, viewed in retrospect, but there were other views. Senator Moynihan wanted to do welfare reform after the economic plan, and push health care even further back."

When Mitchell presented his annual budget address on January 21, 1993, he included a lengthy passage on health care, and what lay ahead. "The single most difficult, controversial, and potentially divisive issue this Congress will face is health care reform. Reform is essential, because we have a system that delivers less care for a higher price than any other in the world. Reform demands change in the behavior of health professionals, insurers, and patients. Change is often difficult. It is often resisted for that reason. But without serious, substantial change in our system, we cannot come to grips with the economic health of the country, because health care costs are what is driving the deficit today. If we want to reduce the deficit, we have to restrain health costs. If we don't reduce health costs, all the calls for restraint and reductions in the rest of the federal budget will produce no more deficit reduction in the future than they have produced in the last dozen years."

While the budget address suggested the economy and health care were intimately connected, Mitchell later provided a different perspective. "The economic program was so important, it did so much good, that I think the judgment of history will be that Clinton did the right thing doing that first," he said. "But it made it more difficult to do health care, because the economic program passed without a single Republican vote."

Chris Jennings had worked several years for David Pryor before being detailed to the White House effort, and remembers Pryor had been "immediately impressed with Mitchell." Though he was a Southern moderate more naturally inclined toward Bennett Johnston for majority leader, Pryor, "without hesitation, embraced Mitchell," Jennings said. "He just saw in him a capability and potential that he thought needed to be cultivated, and he wanted to hook himself to the train." Pryor was usually cautious about commitments, but not here. "He was one of the members who spoke in favor of Mitchell to become the majority leader when it wasn't clear he was going to be."

Jennings himself was struck that Mitchell "felt this was a time when health reform could happen. It was an issue he felt very deeply about. He thought there was a very good chance to get something done, and he wanted to be around to do it." Mitchell's reading, he said, "was very encouraging to someone who followed the game pretty closely." Jennings also said he thought Clinton agreed with Mitchell about proceeding with reform through the budget. "He felt health care had to be part of the budget . . . for obvious reasons related to long-term solvency, and fiscal issues."

Moynihan was opposed to giving health care priority; he now chaired Finance because Lloyd Bentsen had accepted Clinton's offer to become Treasury secretary—what Clinton later called his biggest Cabinet mistake, because of Moynihan's intransigence. The budget reconciliation effort finally ran aground on the rock of Robert Byrd's opposition. As Appropriations chair, Byrd helped call the shots, and was adamantly opposed to inserting a huge new bill into the budget. He was repeatedly asked to relent, but refused.

According to *The System*, Mitchell was dubious about a non-reconciliation health care bill from the beginning, and believed "The odds for passage would have been zero had it not been for the intense public efforts of the President and the First Lady." The authors quoted him as saying, "No president in my time here has taken on an issue of such significance. The presidents I've served under are Carter, Reagan, Bush, and Clinton. Certainly none of them has gotten so deeply involved in this issue personally, acquired the knowledge, and pursued it with such doggedness."

A staff summary of Democratic senators' views on health care in May 1993 showed them all over the map. A few were uninvolved, but most had strong, and conflicting, views. David Boren was concerned about small business and tax increases, and favored a "market-oriented approach." Byrd was listed as someone who "needs education." Kent Conrad emphasized cost controls. Christopher Dodd was worried about insurance companies in his home state of Connecticut. John Glenn believed that "doctors are unfairly characterized as the villains." Russ Feingold, just elected, thought a long-term care benefit was a necessity, and favored a single-payer system.

WITH THE POSSIBILITY OF AN EARLY BILL FADING, Clinton announced formation of the White House Task Force on Health Care Policy, co-chaired by an aide, Ira Magaziner, and Hillary Clinton. The president made a fateful move, with consequences he—as someone new to Washington—may not have fully understood.

By delegating strategy and even drafting to a separate task force, he not only cut out congressional committees, but even his own chiefs at Health and Human Services and Treasury. The task force process, which took six months, was both too rushed, in the sense of major decisions made on tight deadlines, and too lengthy, in that Congress was already headed toward summer recess by the time it reported.

Senators were impressed by Hillary Clinton's knowledge and demeanor. Mitchell co-hosted a health care forum in Orono, and saw how assured she had become on the subject, even though she had no previous background in health care. She wowed other congressional leaders during a five-day blitz immediately following the task force announcement. Jay Rockefeller thought the First Lady was almost over-prepared. "I remember watching her in front of the Senate Finance Committee, and she was way too good, she knew too much. It was embarrassing to the members, because most of them didn't know as much as she did . . . but they prided themselves on caring about health care."

Ira Magaziner was a policy expert, an academic, who'd never worked in politics. Bill Clinton chose him because he believed Magaziner was the most articulate advocate he'd found, but in Washington, clashes began immediately. Chris Williams had spent many hours with aides for the three senators who co-sponsored Mitchell's 1991 bill. Things got so intense, she recalled, that a Rockefeller aide rejoiced that she could go on maternity leave and attend no more meetings.

The Clinton task force was like nothing Williams had ever seen before. It started with five hundred members, and grew from there. There were twenty committees, and staffing all those meetings was daunting. "It was almost impossible to stay on top of all this stuff when there were so many different groups," she said. After a while, "It was like being locked in a room with no way out." Williams believes the "underlying concepts were good," but the bill "quickly became too complex; it got overloaded with detail." Some task force members tried to work out every policy detail, and Magaziner created "tollgates" for final reports. She said, "Ira didn't know much about the ways of Washington. . . . These committees met day and night, probably twelve hours a day. . . . It was a really bad process, and it's one of the things we told the Obama folks, 'You don't want to repeat this.'"

The task force bill weighed in at well over a thousand pages, and Mitchell and Williams worked, she said, "to slim it down," but it was a still a vast, complicated draft when introduced. Some concepts, such as the regional health care alliances setting budgets and organizing providers, weren't fleshed out, and were dropped. The effort faced repeated delays even after the budget was approved in

June. There were many distractions for the White House, including the failure of two female nominees for attorney general over "nanny tax" issues, the "gays in the military" standoff with Sam Nunn, an abortive mission to Haiti, and the "Black Hawk down" fiasco in Somalia. Few were related to health care, but all took a toll on moving legislation forward. Clinton quieted the doubters with a masterful address to Congress in September, but it was another two months before the task force bill was ready.

Mitchell spoke at this juncture to a New England Summit on Health Care Reform, with Ted Kennedy, on December 7, and outlined his own ideas. "A viable solution must meet several principles," he said. "First, any reform plan must provide all Americans with access to affordable health care. Second, any viable reform plan must control health care costs. . . . Third, states must have the flexibility to design a system that will meet their own needs. Fourth, meaningful reform must place an emphasis on primary and preventive care. We now spend too much money making people well after they've become sick. . . . Finally, a viable reform plan must retain consumer choice." Mitchell said, "As we proceed, we must remember what President Clinton said when he presented the Health Security Act to Congress. He said that he is willing to compromise, but that he will not sign a bill that does not assure health care coverage for every American. It is my belief that we will not send him such a bill."

Evidence continued to mount about problems needing solutions. Maine lobstermen once had an association health insurance plan purchased by almost all of its 1,200 members; by 1992, only 300 did, because the family policy increased from $180 a month to $510 a month between 1985 and 1992. The US Chamber of Commerce found its members had seen premiums double in six years, and said the organization "supports the need for universal coverage, and recognizes that it can only become a reality and be paid for through the shared responsibility of employers, employees, and government." It said, "It appears that the president's plan incorporates these principles." There were discordant notes, however. The Heritage Foundation dismissed the Clinton plan, saying, "Rather than competition, or even managed competition, the plan is Canadian-style rationing encumbered with vast insurance cartels."

The most heartening development for Mitchell was when Bob Dole appointed John Chafee as the lead Republican on the "Bipartisan" or "Mainstream" health care caucus. Not long after the Clinton plan finally appeared, Chafee introduced his own legislation, with twenty-two Republican sponsors, including Dole. Mitchell said, "It was a pretty good bill. It didn't have what I would have preferred, and it was not as far-reaching as the administration's bill.

. . . But I talked with him immediately thereafter, and we saw the possibility, the prospect of being able to do something on health care."

Mitchell said Chafee's plan "wasn't too far off" from what became the Affordable Care Act, sixteen years later. "The biggest difference was that we had the employer mandate, so they went to the Heritage Foundation and came up with something called the individual mandate," he said. It was their personal relationship, as much as Chafee's bill, that gave Mitchell hope. They had success with the Clean Water Act and Clean Air Act, and though the obstacles to health care legislation were larger, it wasn't implausible they could be overcome. "I think I was probably more optimistic than he was, but we talked regularly, and I really thought we could put this thing together," Mitchell said. "In retrospect, I was overly optimistic, and sort of trying to convince myself, maybe. But there was clearly a bargain to be made. If we would give up on the employer mandate and accept the individual mandate, they might accept some other stuff that we had to have."

Chris Williams was happy she'd be working with Chafee's staff. "He was one of the best senators I'd ever seen, a wonderful man. He was one of those old-time Rockefeller Republicans," she said. "Nobody did more to expand Medicaid than John Chafee. He was a gem."

Dave Durenberger was another Republican active in the bipartisan group. Though he didn't see the employer vs. individual mandate as crucial, he could see it divided the Finance Committee. After the Pepper Commission, "We were pretty much in agreement on most items, but the employer mandate, the pay-or-play, that came out of that divided Republicans and Democrats," he said. "It also was the beginning of a partisan divide in the Finance Committee, where universal coverage was more important to Democrats than payment reform. To us, payment reform was more important."

But the bipartisan group soon encountered the same problems Mitchell had among Democrats. "The big problem for us was that we had been at this for all our lives in the Senate, and regardless of who the president was, we wanted to get something done," Durenberger said. "And the Clintons just weren't cooperating, and on our side the guys that had come over from the House, the Gingrich gang, were committed to Bill Clinton getting nothing done, including health care."

John Breaux, closer to the Clintons than most senators, tried to undertake shuttle diplomacy for the bipartisan group. He said problems started with the task force. "Months and months passed before we ever got their proposal, and Moynihan was particularly agitated," he said. "He didn't want to trash the new president—and Mitchell [didn't either]—but I think there was a lot of feeling that this was not a good approach; it cut out the Congress." Breaux said Republicans were more likely to vote for health reform in 1994 than later, "because of Dole's and Mitchell's relationship," he said. "I think had they been involved from the beginning, it would have been easier . . . than it would have been today. Because there's a lot of Republicans now . . . who don't want to get anything done."

Mitchell, according to *The System*, carried around a three-by-five index card containing a line from the Republican bill he read aloud frequently. It was "Subtitle F, Section 1501. Universal Coverage Requirement." The provision read, "Effective January 1, 2005, each individual who is a citizen or a lawful permanent resident of the United States shall be covered under a qualified health plan or an equivalent health plan." Mitchell then said, "There it is. A Republican bill which provides for universal coverage and a mandate to achieve it." Under the rules as Mitchell understood them, this meant Republicans were committed to the goal, and would supply the votes whenever Democratic votes alone couldn't surmount a legislative obstacle. And he said, of senators elected in 1986, "We never had a partisan disagreement" on the Finance health care subcommittee. He recognized bipartisanship was in short supply in the House, and said, "If you take a group of people who begin a process with the goal of getting the job done, you can figure out how to get the job done. If you begin a process where people have the goal of preventing something from happening, they can think of ninety-three reasons why it can't be done." He insisted, "There are still plenty of Republicans in the Senate who genuinely want to get something done."

The Senate Finance and Health, Education, and Labor committees went to work. While Ted Kennedy, chairing HEL, was strongly committed to a single-payer system, he was cooperative with the Clintons, as he'd been with the 1991 Mitchell bill. David Nexon, his health care aide, worked with Kennedy from 1983 to 2005, and probably knew the subject better than any congressional staffer. He started in Washington at OMB, and helped with the administrative merger of the Medicare and Medicaid programs. Nexon had learned to roll with the punches. When Ronald Reagan was elected, he continued at OMB. "As a career civil servant, I did enjoy working with [David] Stockman, even though I disagreed with [many] of his views. He was a very bright, engaging kind of a guy." But when it appeared Reagan would be around for a second term, Nexon moved to Kennedy's committee staff, then known as Labor and Human Resources. Kennedy had been an advocate even longer, which Nexon said began with a visit from labor leader Walter Reuther in 1970, when Kennedy was choosing between chairing the health or education subcommittees: "Reuther convinced him that universal health care was the next big issue." Nexon said working with Kennedy was "inspirational without ever being overt," because "there was just this expectation that you were there to make people's lives better. He was working harder than anybody else you could imagine, so you were inspired to work just as hard as you could." The basic attitude was "an entrepreneurial approach—let's find the problem, let's figure out a solution to it, let's get it enacted."

Kennedy dealt with being called the Senate's "leading liberal," Nexon said, through hard work and charm. "On a personal level, he had good relations with almost every member of the Senate. I wouldn't say one hundred members liked him, but it was pretty close. Just about everyone who knew him personally liked him, no matter how antagonistic they were to many of his views." Nexon said Kennedy was initially concerned about Bill Clinton, because of the criticism the Democratic Leadership Council, which Clinton chaired, meted out to "what Kennedy thought was the nature of liberalism." But the two worked well together, and Kennedy was "thrilled" after Clinton's September speech.

After Clinton pledged universal coverage, Nexon heard Kennedy say, "I've been waiting twenty years to hear a president say that." He wasn't deterred by the task force process, even though Nexon also remembers meetings lasting "till two in the morning, night after night after night." When the Clintons said any member of Congress could join, "Kennedy took them up on it." The meetings often left Nexon shaking his head, though. At one, "There was a lively fight over whether we should ration care, which was absolutely ridiculous politically, but Ira [Magaziner] brought in all these academics who didn't have a clue. . . . We spent hours on that thing."

Mitchell struck Nexon as "an absolutely brilliant man." Since he wasn't on the HEL committee, Mitchell played no direct part in the two-week health reform markup, but it went as well as could be expected, given Republican concerns. Nexon said, "We were stumbling out at the end with a brief moment of elation when we voted the bill out of committee with [Jim] Jeffords's support, in addition to the Democrats."

Nexon had a different interpretation than Mitchell of Dole's appointment of Chafee to the bipartisan caucus. "Dole was very smart to appoint Chafee . . . because that made it very difficult for Chafee to move early to work with Clinton and Kennedy. . . . He had a very good staff, and they managed things very shrewdly, but the problem was, the shrewd management ended up in keeping something from happening, instead of producing a bill." Nexon believed "Chafee was sincere, but most of the guys who signed on were not." While Kennedy usually got along with Bob Kerrey, Kerrey gave what Nexon called "a sanctimonious speech" over his involvement with the bipartisan group that sent Kennedy over the edge. His boss "pounded on the table," and said, "You're the one who's hanging us up. . . . I want you to sign. Are you with us?"

There were no similar strains in the Kennedy–Mitchell relationship, Nexon said, and he sensed Kennedy occasionally changed Mitchell's mind about strategy. "Kennedy would drop by after hours, off the floor, have a little chat with Mitchell, and Mitchell would come out with a different view." As opposed to Kennedy, who could be effusive, Nexon found Mitchell "a very internal, inner-directed guy," and said, "It's interesting that a guy with that personality became leader, because the leader's got to keep the caucus together. Mitchell did it to a significant degree by force of intellect; he listened to people, and then he'd figure out how to thread the needle." Nexon said that Kennedy "had tremendous respect for Mitchell," and became adept at reading his moods. After seeing Mitchell, he might say, "Well, I didn't talk to him. I could tell George was just as tight as a drum. . . . It wasn't the right time." Nexon said Mitchell deferred to the president, though he did cut some independent deals, such as a tentative agreement to win AARP's support with prescription drug coverage.

When Kennedy died in 2009, after voting in committee for the Affordable Care Act, Nexon realized he was "except for my family, probably the most important person in my life. . . . And while I knew he had incurable cancer, there was some emotional level at which I didn't think he was going to die. He always seemed so indestructible." It was during the events around Arlington Cemetery and the memorial services, with crowds lining the street, that he felt the "recognition of him as a human being and as a public servant that . . . was cathartic and helped deal with the loss."

THERE ARE NUMEROUS ACCOUNTS OF WHEN health care reform began to unravel, and they differ not only in details but in who was responsible. There's little doubt, though, that when the bill that Kennedy's committee had crafted went to Finance, it encountered a stone wall in Daniel Patrick Moynihan. He was a curious creature in the Senate—an intellectual and academic who claimed he wasn't really a legislator, but who had outsized ambitions about crafting federal policy. When he wrote his famous report about the plight of the black family in America, he was working for Joseph Califano, secretary of Housing, Education, and Welfare for Lyndon Johnson. Despite the outrage it created among liberals, and black political leaders, Moynihan intended it as a sympathetic depiction of the enduring ravages of slavery and racism. His basic solution—a guaranteed annual income, something far out of the mainstream—found an unlikely advocate, for a time, in Richard Nixon.

Moynihan came to the Senate in 1978, just two years before Mitchell, but he gained committee seniority rapidly because several incumbents lost in 1980. Bill Clinton's regrets about appointing Lloyd Bentsen followed an acrimonious personal split between Moynihan and both Clintons, but also differences on policy. Moynihan championed welfare reform, which he envisioned far differently than the bills Clinton ultimately signed under a Republican Congress. Health care wasn't a major interest; some committee staff believed he was ill-informed, and he disliked the responsibility of overseeing a major health care bill. Bentsen was more conservative than Moynihan on health care, but Bentsen could make a deal. It was by no means clear Moynihan would.

Harris Wofford, who was serving his last year—he lost narrowly to Republican Rick Santorum in 1994—was close to Moynihan's wife, Liz, and said Moynihan was offended by the Clintons' approach. "This plan is too over-reaching, and nobody consulted me or listened to my advice," is what Wofford remembers Moynihan saying. "The way it came up, it's dead on arrival." At one point, Wofford's wife, Clare, and Liz Moynihan put together a dinner that included Moynihan and Bob Kerrey in an attempt to map out a new strategy. At the dinner, Moynihan told Wofford, "You've got to realize that the first Clinton term is going to be a catastrophe, and nothing can save it or this health care plan, but there's a chance that we can teach him to govern, and his second term will be satisfactory."

The System quotes an unnamed "leading Senate Democrat" saying Moynihan had "a very, very poor relationship with the majority leader," but that seems a canard. The evidence suggests Moynihan was impressed by Mitchell's intelligence, respected his judgment—but wasn't going to be deterred by any leader, in that respect closely resembling Robert Byrd. Moynihan wrote Mitchell erudite but chatty letters and, when Mitchell left the Senate and was rumored to be the next baseball commissioner, invited him to the Moynihan family estate, near Cooperstown, New York.

One note, ominously, is devoted to the theory of a Princeton economist, William Baumol, from the 1960s, arguing that a lack of productivity in the service sector inexorably increases costs—and applying the theory to health care. Charlene Sturbitts, who'd observed Moynihan frequently, said, "He had big thoughts and he liked to express them, and it was always interesting, [but] it didn't necessarily advance the legislative ball." David Nexon, Kennedy's aide, blamed Moynihan chief of staff Larry O'Donnell for some of the conflict. In meetings with Kennedy, he said, Moynihan would be "all sweetness and light," saying, 'There's enough here for you and me, Ted, we'll work together.'" But when Nexon met with O'Donnell, "He was just like the Prince of Darkness. His goal in life seemed to be to elevate Moynihan at the expense of everybody else, including the ability to pass a decent bill."

Harold Ickes joined the administration in January 1994 as one of two deputy chiefs of staff, primarily, in his words, to do "damage control" on health care. He quickly took stock of the Senate, and realized he could count on Kennedy— "an absolute stalwart"—and Mitchell, whom he'd met during the 1972 Muskie campaign, but not Moynihan. The damage there was on view over the Memorial Day weekend when Tim Russert, who'd worked for Moynihan, interviewed him on a Sunday talk show. "It was on that program that Moynihan basically declared health care dead," Ickes said. "I don't think he used the word, but anyone with any sophistication quickly came to understand that health care was not going through the Senate Finance Committee, or at least health care as drafted."

The size of the rift was visible almost as soon as the committee began its closed markup session, where deals are traditionally made. Chris Williams was stunned by the treatment she got from Moynihan, who banned her. Mitchell told her Moynihan insisted she was "impeding the process." In reality, little markup was going on. When Moynihan had the committee quickly vote out the bill, it had glaring flaws. If it was going to be saved, Mitchell was going to have to do emergency surgery on the floor, on a bill even more complex than the Clean Air Act.

A wild card throughout the debate was the "Harry and Louise" political ad campaign produced by the insurance industry. The ads started quietly and built from there, becoming what Mitchell said was, at the time, the most expensive issues campaign ever directed at Congress. The industry turned against the Clinton plan as soon as it learned the alliances would set global budgets, but the assault was indirect—raising questions about whether Americans could keep their doctors, without claiming directly that the Clinton plan would interfere. Mitchell said polls showed the commercials had only a slight effect on public opinion, but a much greater impact on House and Senate. "A couple of actors pretending to be husband and wife talked about the bill in a negative way, and it caught on," Mitchell said. "It was a very effective advertising technique . . . and the Republicans began to coalesce against it."

Harold Ickes said the campaign "played an absolutely critical role" in undermining support. The message, he said, was "This is big government; it's going to take away your doctor, and you're not going to have any choice left." And the campaign "beat that drum day in and day out with just absolute singular focus." Republicans, he said, "are very good at that. We Democrats think that if we've said something once, it's enough, and we then go on to say something else. The Republicans understand that focus, focus, focus, repetition, repetition,

repetition." The campaign, he said, "fit their philosophical bent as well as their political bent." David Nexon said Harry and Louise ramped up just as the bill's momentum was dissipating. "People have argued about the impact, but I think it had a pretty profound one," he said.

After the Memorial Day recess, Mitchell decided to try to salvage something. The Clinton plan was clearly not viable, but no one else had produced anything to replace its universal coverage. He had had it with Moynihan, telling Kennedy, in Nexon's words, "I want you to do it, Ted; I can't work with the other guy." There were still a few encouraging signs. As late as September 1, the National Governors Association addressed congressional leaders, saying, "We are writing to you once again to reaffirm the commitment of the nation's governors to bipartisan health care reform legislation this year." But Mitchell also heard from James Exon, the Nebraska Democrat who had earlier warned that "time, politics, pressure, and confusion have engulfed this critical issue." On July 14, he wrote, "If you ask me to jump off a cliff with you on this, I'm not saying no now, but I'm not reaching for your hand, either."

It was during Mitchell's attempts to move the Clinton-Mitchell bill that overt conflict with the White House began. The new version, unveiled in August, applied the employer mandate only after five years, in any state covering less than 95 percent of its population—a "hard trigger." The Medicaid program would be expanded to 200 percent of the federal poverty level, and there would be subsidies if employers increased insurance coverage. It wasn't clear whether this would produce universal coverage, but Mitchell knew it was the maximum he could hope to achieve. Mitchell did sell the idea to the Clintons, and warned everyone their only available target was Republican moderates. He could already see that those organizing against the Clinton plan could easily overwhelm the "town hall" events the Clintons planned to revive interest. *The System* reports him saying that supportive congressmen "may have a town hall meeting, but the town hall meetings are all going to be packed by the insurance industry and the NFIB. . . . You won't be able to turn the public debate in the way you hope unless we engage the moderates." Ira Magaziner, now in a supporting role, said about Mitchell's analysis, "The truth is persuasive, as it always is."

There were probably too many headwinds even before Mitchell put the bill on the floor in August. Harold Ickes said Hillary Clinton took a long time to accept that the original bill wouldn't fly and, before the Memorial Day recess, made "an impassioned plea to the legislative leaders that this had to be done, the people wanted it, America needed it." And while he said "There was no question that she was right on all those scores," he doubted her contention that "When members go back home on recess and they hear from constituents, they will come back and this health care bill will be passed." Ickes said Mitchell was more persuasive when he responded, "Hillary's missing the mark on how much public pressure is going to be brought to bear on us as we go back to our states," adding, "I think it needs to be reworked." Chris Jennings said Bill Clinton had taken too many political hits. "All these things over time tended to undermine the president's popularity. . . . It's almost palpable in Washington about what he can pursue in terms of [an] agenda." Patrick Griffin, Byrd's former aide, was critical of Mitchell for bringing the bill to the floor, saying, "It just protracted the debate and kept us looking terrible, longer, up until the election."

Mitchell tried to negotiate with moderate Republicans, but this wasn't like any negotiation he'd ever seen. One of the first signs came during the Finance Committee markup. Mitchell said to Chafee, as they entered the committee room, that he would introduce Chafee's own bill as an amendment, to force the Republicans to vote on it. "Don't do that," Chafee said. "You'll embarrass me and you won't gain anything." Mitchell didn't really intend to use the amendment, but said it showed "how far things had drifted from where they were at the start." Every attempt Mitchell made to trade concessions for commitments failed. "The Democrats kept moving toward the center, while the Republicans kept moving to the right, so that we were chasing after them . . . and they were moving away from us faster than we were able to move toward them." Chris Williams began to realize there was another problem: "It turned out that a lot of people's second choice was to do nothing."

There was little to fall back on. Opponents of reform were united, while supporters were scattering. Mitchell said recently, "Most supporters of the bill were interest groups interested only in their portion of the bill. You couldn't get them to moderate their demands for the greater good. They wanted 100 percent of their issue as the price for supporting the bill, and you couldn't give sixteen different groups 100 percent." He realized, too late, that "There never was the kind of broad-based, overarching demand for health care. There were a lot of different individual demands. And gradually, it drifted against us."

Many senators, including Bob Dole, were unhappy Mitchell kept the Senate in session into August, and tempers were running short. Mitchell had just addressed the Tuesday caucus lunch when two Democrats came up to him, an encounter "I remember just as if it were yesterday. One of them said to me, in a low voice but with a lot of anger, 'Are you trying to defeat me? You keep this goddamned bill on the floor another week, you'll beat me in November. . . . You've got to get this bill off the floor.'" The other senator then approached and said, "You've got to keep this thing going. It's the right thing to do. We need it, and we're winning politically." For Mitchell, "It just symbolized the way the issue was tearing our caucus apart."

Soon, Mitchell knew it was over. The final day of Senate debate featured Moynihan and Rockefeller arguing over subsidies for physician training. Rockefeller said rural areas needed more physicians; Moynihan insisted that New York's inner-city hospitals needed every dollar. Williams said Mitchell listened to the debate, then said, "I cannot have two Democrats, the chair of the Finance Committee and the chair of the health subcommittee, at each other's throats arguing over our bill. That's it, that's the end."

Mitchell had already announced in March he was leaving the Senate. In April, he publicly turned down Clinton's offer to appoint him to the Supreme Court—his second such refusal, since Clinton had also inquired about the first high court vacancy the previous year. Mitchell said he wanted to stay on to enact health care, but by summer's end, it all seemed like a mirage.

IN THE AFTERMATH, MITCHELL SAID LITTLE, but did offer remarks to the Blue Cross and Blue Shield Association on October 5. He did not mince words. "This year, it was possible to frighten Americans by suggesting that all government standards and regulations would only result in less health care. In future, as employees face higher costs and diminished choices, it won't be government they'll be scared of. It will be their own insurance company." Mitchell said he wanted to preserve the best features of the existing system. "I tried to do that with a bill which would have taken millions of Americans out of government-paid Medicaid and put them into the private health insurance system. My plan was attacked as a 'government' plan. Of course it wasn't. I predict that when Congress considers the negative effects . . . from halfway reforms, it will be driven back to the obvious answer—that the only reform possible is one that seeks to provide for universal health care coverage, however defined." He said, "I hope that despite the disappointments of this year, all parties have learned enough from the process and about the issues that when Congress next faces the reality of the rising federal health care budget, constructive reform will be achieved."

One puzzlement was the role of Bob Dole. At the start, though he told Clinton and Mitchell there'd be no Republican votes for the budget, he never said that about health care, and Democrats assumed Republicans would be open to some version of reform. Dave Durenberger was among those who believed Dole's intention to run for president in 1996 was significant. His likely opponents were running to his right, and, Durenberger said, "You can't be president without being a party's nominee, and you can't be the nominee if Phil Gramm and a whole bunch of these other guys are saying, 'No health care, no Clinton health care.'"

Dole recently responded to an observation by Mitchell that, during the final negotiations, "The Republicans kept moving the goalposts." Dole agreed, and said, "It's fair to say that we not only moved the goalposts, we took down the goalposts." By that time, "There was no way I could get Republicans on board. The conservatives thought I was playing games with George, but what they were really afraid of was that I was going to get something passed." In the end, Dole decided it was enough that he had appointed Chafee to the bipartisan group, and that if there was something that would have worked, Chafee would have found it. Dole said, "I remember telling them that, if they could sell the bill to Sheila"—referring to Sheila Burke, his chief of staff—"I'll vote for it." But that never happened.

Mitchell rarely spoke of it at the time, but there was another difficulty often ignored in accounts of the demise of health care reform—the role of the House of Representatives. Ordinarily, the House is better at passing legislation quickly than the Senate. There is no filibuster rule; a majority is a majority. The Rules Committee sets strict limits on floor amendments. Party discipline is stronger. Yet under Speaker Tom Foley, the House rarely delivered on major legislation. While during the spring, Dick Gephardt sounded optimistic about a compromise, no House health care bill even made it out of committee.

Pressed at the time on the disparity, Mitchell told an interviewer, "We not only have to pass the bill in the Senate, but then we have to go over to the House and pass it there, too." There was more than one weak link. And though most of the dismay among Democrats focused on Moynihan's role, there was no doubt Republicans tried to jam the legislative machinery. David Nexon recalls ranking Republican Bob Packwood's comment to an interviewer that, "We've killed health reform, now we've got to make sure our fingerprints aren't on it." Packwood later conceded, "The strategy was there to kill this bill."

Bob Rozen did the financial analyses for the almost innumerable versions of health care Mitchell presented. Now a senior accountant with Ernst & Young in Washington, he isn't given to overtly dramatic responses. When asked about the failure of health care reform, though, he paralleled Jeff Peterson's comments about Republican presidents' vetoes of Clean Water bills. Rozen said, "Republicans never vote for health care reform bills proposed by Democratic presidents." That, too, is consistent with the facts. When Barack Obama proposed health care reform in 2009, and Congress wrote and enacted it, it received not a single Republican vote—not even from Senator Olympia Snowe, who voted for the Affordable Care Act in committee but opposed it on the floor.

Chris Williams thinks this was by design in 2009, but may not have been foreordained in 1993. "There was a big shift in the Republicans on the Finance Committee," she said. Originally, Chafee, Packwood, Durenberger, and Heinz had been available votes. "They understood health care, and the need, and they were sympathetic to the individual mandate," she said. By Obama's administration, "It was strictly political opposition. All the moderates had left the Senate."

The passage of the Affordable Care Act—through budget reconciliation in 2010, after the Democrats lost Ted Kennedy's seat in a special election—prompted bittersweet reflections among Clinton-era veterans. Jay Rockefeller, still a senator, described the Affordable Care Act process as "messy," to the point where voters lost interest and ended up with "the worst possible interpretation" of what was happening. He was appalled by Democrat Ben Nelson of Nebraska, who held out for special treatment for his state, though the Nelson amendment was swept away when the House version was ultimately used for Senate reconciliation. "My own view is that over time, people will see it for what it is," Rockefeller said, "and that it's an enormous improvement. . . . There's just a wealth of things." Obamacare became a reality, unlike Clinton's plan. Mitchell said the Affordable Care Act is "a tremendous accomplishment" for Obama and Congress.

Chris Williams stayed to the end of Mitchell's Senate tenure, and remained in health care. She'd been impressed by work in Maine that measured outcomes and practice variations, sponsored by the Maine Medical Association. In 1989, Congress enacted Mitchell's Medical Outcomes Research Act, creating the Agency for Health Care Research and Quality. The idea was to examine why physicians prescribe and handle patients so differently, and how to improve performance. Williams went to work for the agency, finishing out her career. "A lot more attention is being paid to this now," she said, "but we still haven't solved the problem."

Williams worked for Mitchell for nearly thirteen years, and said "Obama reminds me a lot of George Mitchell. . . . Mitchell's not quite as photogenic and charismatic, but he's very inspiring, he's sincere, he's the child of immigrants himself. I just loved working for him, and I loved working for the people of Maine."

19

SENATOR FROM MAINE

O f all his state's senators, George Mitchell may have the most intimate relationship with Maine and its people. He was not only junior senator for
nearly fifteen years, he was—in the Lincolnian sense—of Maine, by Maine, and
for Maine. It began with his upbringing in Waterville, and the devotion of his
parents to their adopted state and country, but has continued, uninterrupted,
ever since. It's one of his few regrets, for instance, that he never served in state
government. When he remarried in 1994, his new wife Heather lived in New
York City, while Mitchell was anxious, after leaving the Senate, to return to
Maine. "So we compromised, and decided to live in New York." Yet he never
gave up the idea of living in Maine, and after years of summer visits, built a
house on Mount Desert Island, where his family spends part of each year.

Jeff Porter, who eventually ran the Lewiston office and was often involved
when Mitchell was in Maine, was surprised that "even as majority leader, he
was still home three weekends out of four." Porter said Mitchell "really loves the
state," and that "he needed the time with his family where he could just totally
be himself. . . . It kept him grounded. Here he is, Senate majority leader, and
he's clicking on all cylinders, and people are telling him how great he is. But
you come back to Maine and you're doing a town meeting, you have somebody
calling you every name in the book, and you have to be sharp all the time. I think
he loved it. . . . He got strength from it." Porter never found that Mitchell "hid
behind staff." He scheduled meetings with almost any Mainer who requested
one, and "never went 'Washington.'"

In the Senate, Mitchell's commitment to Maine became evident in whom he
hired. "I was lucky that Senator Muskie had assembled a first-rate staff that I

inherited and gradually built on," he said. While he hired Mainers in the early years, it wasn't until he became majority leader that he "suddenly found I had authority over much larger activities. . . . The budget then was $100 million a year, and there were thousands of employees. I wanted to be able to give as many youngsters from Maine as possible the chance, provided they were qualified and capable and interested in working. I knew there was a good work ethic in Maine." The employment effort bore fruit. "For quite a while, if you got on an elevator, or took a tour of the Capitol . . . chances were pretty good it would be a young man or woman from Augusta or Presque Isle or Rumford who would be showing you around," he said. And many worked their way up. Chris Williams started in the mailroom. Kelly Currie, whom Mitchell chose for his staff in Northern Ireland, began "moving boxes around" as an intern, and is now a defense attorney in New York City. Gary Myrick, who started out of college, is now Harry Reid's chief of staff. Mitchell said, "I don't go to the Senate much anymore, but I run into people who say, 'You remember, you hired me?'" Mitchell confessed, "I don't remember everyone, actually. There's just so many of them, and it's quite a while ago."

Jim Case, his first chief of staff, noticed Mitchell's willingness to promote from within. "He was very loyal to people, very loyal to his staff, as he should be; they were loyal to him, too," Case said. "The number of Maine people he placed in different situations in Washington during his tenure was amazing." Mary McAleney said the standard practice was to hire students right out of college and provide a ninety-day paid internship. "There wasn't one of them that got off the bus or the boat or the train or out of their car that didn't have the opportunity for a job, whether it was parking cars, working in the copy room, the mailroom, working on the door in the Senate, running the elevators, you name it," she said. "In that ninety days, they'd have money, they'd have a job, and if they hustled, they would figure out how to get a permanent job."

It often worked. "You wouldn't think the elevator would lead to much, but if a kid was smart and learned to recognize every senator, and learned to watch and listen for the train, to make sure these poor guys wouldn't have the elevator shut in their face—I know two or three who got hired by other senators because of that," McAleney said. The Mainers were so reliable that the deputy sergeant at arms, Bob Bean, was surprised when one showed up late. "Are you sure you're really from Maine?" he asked, and told McAleney, "I've never met anybody from Maine who didn't show up to work on time." Rich Arenberg, another chief of staff who worked for senators from much larger states, saw how Mitchell could spot good candidates. "In a six-year term, Senator Mitchell would probably shake hands with almost everybody in Maine as he traveled around the state," he said.

"At times, he even managed to pull branches of the family tree out of people's backgrounds that they weren't all that sure about and they'd say, 'That's right, he was my aunt's father's brother-in-law.' . . . He knew all those connections."

The same held true for departures. Kelly Horwitz, the inadvertent cherry blossom princess who started in the mailroom, admits she was angry when Mitchell decided to leave the Senate, saying, "He pulled the rug out from under us and walked away and decided to have his own life." She stayed on the floor staff when Tom Daschle succeeded Mitchell, but decided to apply to law school. She enlisted Anita Jensen's help, but Mitchell told her to write her own letter of recommendation—"one of the hardest things you can be asked to do," she said—and he then offered to lend her money for school, as he'd done for other staffers, and she accepted. When Horwitz graduated, she was hired by Warren Christopher and chosen for a task force vetting vice presidential candidates in 2000—a group she realized might include Mitchell. She said, "This was not too long after the whole Monica Lewinsky scandal, and relationships between older politicians and younger women may not be viewed in the best light." When she next spoke to Mitchell, she promised to repay the loan, with interest, and said, "I'm concerned about what people would say about you." Mitchell, she said, "got this look on his face like it was the first time it had occurred to him. . . . I think his motives were so pure that it never crossed his mind that other people could twist them into something he never intended."

Mitchell provided help to any of his now-numerous staff who were job-hunting. In 1994 Brett O'Brien, who'd worked on defense issues, heard that Dick Gephardt was looking for a defense specialist for the House majority office. "I had a couple of initial interviews, and . . . it was looking like a real opportunity," he said, and asked if Mitchell would call Gephardt before the final interview. Mitchell said, "No, I'm going to call him before your interview and after the interview, and let's see what we can do to make this happen." O'Brien got the job.

Mitchell's policy on visitors was unusual, an example of a strategy adopted for a short-term reason that also served for the long run. "For most of my Senate career I came to Maine every weekend," he said. "I made a public promise that I would have a private meeting with any citizen of Maine. . . . That wasn't so hard to do when I made the promise, because I was way down in the polls and . . . not many people cared about talking to me." In later years, "the list got very long. But I kept the promise. I used to sit in my office in Portland or in Bangor or in Presque Isle on weekends and meet people one at a time for as long as anybody wanted to meet with me."

The reason why so few legislators or congressmen have such a policy was plain. "I found that many people came in who disagreed with me," Mitchell said. "That's the reason they came. . . . But for the most part, if I had a rational basis for my decision, if I could explain it in a way that was reasonable, even if people didn't agree. . . . They would say, 'Well, OK, I don't agree with you, but I understand the reason.'" And, Mitchell said, "I think that's true whether you're dealing with constituents, with corporate leaders, with presidents, or with anybody else."

The welcome mat affected organization of the Senate offices. Lee Lockwood—who grew up in Texas, graduated from Duke, and worked for Muskie—was hired to handle correspondence when Mitchell became majority leader, and said the Mitchell office was more relaxed and informal than Muskie's. But she also discovered that Mitchell's policy of answering "all mail, not just mail from Maine," had made her job larger than she'd expected. "It went from however many letters a week to five times that much. We had, depending on the issue, five thousand letters a week. And I'm glad it was before e-mail. I don't know what they do now, I cannot imagine." The physical bulk alone was impressive. "It came in by the bagful. . . . You're dealing with enormous piles of paper all the time." Although many were form letters, and got a similar response, there were many personal messages, too. "I felt at the end of it . . . I had probably written to most everybody in the state of Maine, or at least seen a letter from them," Lockwood said. She decided to leave after the Clinton inauguration. "I would bring mail home and spread it out on the floor, five hundred letters . . . and I don't know how I did it all. I was just really tired and didn't want to do it anymore."

Bill Hiss, a Bates College admissions director who later worked with Mitchell setting up a statewide college scholarship program that became the Mitchell Institute, first saw him at a town hall meeting at the Auburn police station. "The room was pretty crowded, there were probably thirty or forty people, and the senator stayed there for two hours, simply answering people's questions and allowing them to speak," he said. "I'll never forget that afternoon," Hiss said. "The senator's seat was absolutely bombproof. The people of Maine would have voted Senator Mitchell back in office until they took him out feet-first. And yet he felt an obligation to . . . take on all comers, and answer all questions, listen to people's sometimes grumpy opinions. . . . And he did it with decency, courtesy, and sympathy." It was, Hiss said, "an example of American democracy working as it should."

Not every delegation member took this approach. Bob Tyrer, Bill Cohen's chief of staff, said Cohen "never had any enthusiasm nor the ability to show any false excitement about partisan politics or campaigning, or fund-raising . . . so if someone was going to call the Republican chairman in Franklin County and yuk it up with them and see how their uncle's knee operation went, that was more likely to be me." Tyrer had studied Margaret Chase Smith's loss to Bill Hathaway, though, and knew things were different in Maine: "If you skipped the potato blossom festival or the chicken-throwing contest too many times, it became less and less OK to say, 'Hey, remember, I'm really busy writing laws.'" When Mitchell was appointed—"a slightly accidental senator," as Tyrer put it—and the two began doing joint appearances with school groups, he noticed Mitchell's diligence. "Senator Mitchell would come over afterward, and say, 'Now, I got the name of that guy, third in the back row, who said his parents were from Rockland, but do you have the names of the other three kids? Because I want to send them a note.'" Tyrer said, "It became, over time, a kind of gallows humor, because you could not be ill in Maine, you could not be dead in Maine, without Senator Mitchell being the first one to call. . . . It used to drive us crazy." When Cohen would call, the response often was, "Oh yes, I was just talking to Senator Mitchell." Tyrer said, "You could never get the drop on him . . . and it was him, it wasn't staff-driven."

Steve Hart, who'd worked on other Maine campaigns in 1982 before joining Mitchell's staff, saw how Mitchell, as majority leader, "tried as hard as he could to make sure the people of Maine didn't think he'd left them behind." Hart said Mitchell dealt with the volume of requests by becoming still more efficient. "He was amazing to get his picture taken with these constituents. He would be in front of the fireplace and they would come in and get their pictures. . . . If you put together ten of those pictures, and they'd take them in two minutes, he didn't even change his posture."

David Johnson recalled that, when he and Mitchell were working late, Mitchell got rare moments of pleasure by calling Maine letter writers and surprising them. What Johnson doesn't say, as Mitchell relates in his memoir, is that the letter writers almost always had something critical to say, perhaps accounting for their surprise. On other occasions, Mitchell wasn't the only one taking the brunt. He held field hearings in Maine not just on his own legislation, but any federal issue affecting the state. Some were on subjects that would cause most politicians to flee, such as the Department of Energy's short-lived search for a second high-level nuclear waste repository along with one already selected in Nevada. Another was a US Forest Service proposal to designate as wilderness a section of the White Mountain National Forest that lies in Maine. Steve Hart staffed Mitchell on EPW, and remembers them both.

"We went into one high school auditorium and the entire room was full of people holding 'no' signs," he said. "Very ugly, very angry, difficult issues." That hearing, he said, was "awful," and the one on the Caribou-Speckled Mountain Wilderness, eventually established, was "very unpleasant." When

Cohen and Mitchell jointly sponsored a Northern Forest study, there was another "awful" hearing in Bangor's city council chambers. Hart said, "It was so small half the people who were accusing him and Cohen of being Communist couldn't get in the room, and we went back and had a second one in the Bangor Auditorium." He recalls Mitchell "was very gracious through the whole thing, and bore up well to the criticism, a lot of it very unfair, vitriolic, almost nutty." Back to Washington, Mitchell told him the nuclear dump site search should end—"Let's deauthorize it because we don't need it," which Hart hadn't thought of, and Congress approved.

Mitchell, as all senators do, helped constituents having difficulties with the federal bureaucracy, but often went further than staff expected. Bob Carolla had been dealing with the case of a young sailor the US Navy had charged with desertion, who was being held in Louisiana where his family couldn't visit. Clyde MacDonald told Carolla, "Everyone in town says this is a really good young man . . . he was away from home, and he was overwhelmed." Gayle Cory agreed the case was worthy, but Carolla was told by the navy, "There's absolutely no way. This kid's going to be court-martialed." Mitchell called the secretary of the navy and, as Carolla put it, "used up a silver bullet, and you don't have many." After the sailor was transferred to Newport, Rhode Island, at Mitchell's request, the navy decided it wouldn't fly the witnesses there, and he was given an ordinary, rather than dishonorable, discharge.

Kelly Horwitz handled the case of an elderly Russian immigrant to Maine "who was getting all this press" because she wanted to become an American citizen before she died. There was a private bill on her behalf, which Cohen supported, but, Horwitz said, it was "a somewhat dicey proposition" because private bills could be precedent-setting. It was 1993, and Mitchell planned to run for reelection. She said, "You don't want to be portrayed as this mean man who let this woman die without becoming a citizen." Mitchell didn't push the bill, the woman died, and Horwitz heard him say later, "I should have listened to Kelly."

SOMETIMES, MITCHELL'S LEGISLATIVE SUCCESSES LED to headaches back home. That was true for the Clean Air Act's new emissions standards, which the EPA began implementing in 1994. EPA decided to make Maine a test case for "enhanced" emissions testing, even though the state had never done any testing before—unlike many large urban areas, which were already regulated under previous rules. The tests, aimed at curbing ground-level ozone, would be conducted not only in Portland, but also along the coast, with its many rural counties. Regulators may have counted on Maine's "green" reputation and Mitchell's favorable standing, but Mainers had a lot of old clunkers, and their owners feared they wouldn't pass. CarTest, a private company, set up the inspection stations, and the tests became an instant public relations disaster. There was an uproar at the Legislature, and lawmakers who'd voted to implement the tests, including some Republicans, came under heavy fire, and several lost their seats. Finally, EPA announced in October that it would suspend the tests to allow state officials to consider alternatives.

Mitchell, the law's principal author, walked a fine line. In public statements, letters, and op-eds, he defended the law. He said air pollution took a heavy toll, "as much as $50 billion each year in lost work days and extra health care costs." He took issue with opponents' contentions that Maine's ozone pollution came from other states. "That claim cannot be substantiated by existing evidence," he said, adding that Maine, depending on weather patterns, was also sending air pollution to its neighbors. "We will either agree to control and reduce pollution and take the necessary steps . . . or we will continue to suffer from air pollution. Those are the choices available." Opting out of a regional solution would be a mistake, he said. "If Maine is not a member of the Ozone Transport Region, it will lose all leverage over the pollution-control efforts in states to our south, which contribute much of our excess pollution." Maine was then experiencing more than a dozen "ozone alert" days each summer. Mitchell acknowledged the car testing program could be revised. "It is the states, including Maine, which make the decisions about how to reach those goals. The specific actions each state or region takes will be decided at the state level, the best place." Ultimately, Maine devised a new plan relying on reformulated gasoline, and restricted emissions testing to Cumberland and York counties.

Mitchell spoke out on behalf of his old friend Joe Brennan, making his fifth and final run for governor, having narrowly lost to John McKernan in 1990. Mitchell said Brennan, who'd voted for the law in Congress, "demonstrated his leadership when he stood by a law which is aimed at protecting the health of all the people of Maine. . . . Joe Brennan understands that clean air means a strong economy, and that a job means nothing to those who can't go outside or go to work because of health problems associated with polluted air."

Brennan was in a tight four-way race with Angus King, an independent, who'd worked for Bill Hathaway but left the Democratic Party after going into business; Republican Susan Collins, in her first statewide race; and Green candidate Jonathan Carter. Collins's candidacy never took off, and the stretch run was between King and Brennan. King suggested in a September debate that Maine had a disadvantage by being placed in the Ozone Transport Zone, where new pollution sources had to be offset, unlike others states. Responding to a question from an attorney representing corporate interests, King said, "The real question is that the Clean Air Act amendments of 1990 are a no-growth law imposed on Maine and not imposed on seventeen or twenty other states. Minnesota, Arkansas, South Carolina, South Dakota do not have that offset requirement." He called emissions testing "kind of the tip of the iceberg. I think it's the wrong policy at the wrong place at the wrong time." King received 35.4 percent of the vote, beating Brennan by 8,000 votes, less than 2 percent.

Starting with his 1982 campaign, Mitchell steered a different course than Muskie in dealing with the press. While Muskie sometimes shunned reporters, Mitchell reached out to them. Yet he had his battles. Clyde MacDonald was more than happy to go toe-to-toe with the *Bangor Daily News* and its editorial editor, Paul Reynolds. "Even in its worst days," MacDonald said, the paper "always had a policy of allowing critics to respond." He said, "I used to joke that in the first two or three years I worked for Senator Mitchell, I spent as much time in the *Bangor News* office as I did in my own office. We were always negotiating how to correct this or that." To one suggested correction, Reynolds said, "We can't use that. It makes me look like a fool." MacDonald said, "I just looked at him, and said, 'Well?'" MacDonald got along better with later editors. About one, he reported to Mitchell, "This guy was hired as a hatchet man, but he doesn't have the stomach for it, and I think we can work with him." MacDonald said Mitchell's regular visits to newspapers, including weeklies, created good relationships and, unlike battles with Paul Reynolds, "I never chastised them or gave them a hard time if they didn't print something they should have . . . because I realized they were under the gun."

Mitchell did sometimes respond, at length, to editorials he felt distorted or misconstrued his position. In a seven-page response, he took issue in May 1991 with an editorial in the *Kennebec Journal*, headlined, "Mitchell Unmoved on Brady Bill." He said it "misrepresents my position and mistakes the issues involved." As majority leader, Mitchell was in a ticklish position on gun issues. Many Democratic senators represented urban states that had enacted background checks and other restrictions. Maine, by contrast, was a largely rural state with low crime rates and high levels of gun ownership. He said, "The Brady bill would require those twenty-six states, including Maine, which have not voluntarily done this, to establish a seven-day waiting period," but "would not require any background checks to be made." This meant, he said, "nothing is likely to happen under the Brady bill" without a national computerized registry. Mitchell also referred to the NRA's alternative of an "instant check" system, and suggested the two approaches be combined, which "should create the minimum inconvenience necessary for persons without prior criminal records." Mitchell evinced some frustration, saying, "Your editorial doesn't even mention these proposals of mine, even though I have repeated them publicly many times. That omission creates a highly misleading perception of my position." It wasn't until November 30, 1993, that a new version of the Brady bill became law.

Sometimes, even his own party took issue with his stances as majority leader. In 1990, a crime bill included several new death penalty provisions; adding them became a bidding war between the two parties. Mitchell voted to strike the provisions, but only twenty Democrats and five Republicans favored his amendment. Those supporting death penalty additions included senators normally among Mitchell's closest allies—Bill Bradley, Christopher Dodd, John Kerry, Paul Sarbanes, and Jim Sasser. The Maine Democratic State Committee proposed to vote on a resolution that began, "The MDSC is deeply disappointed that Senator Mitchell has abandoned our long-standing position against capital punishment by votes in favor of the recent crime bill." Maine had abolished capital punishment in 1876.

In response, Mitchell asked committee members to discuss the situation with him, and said, "The resolution is inaccurate. I oppose capital punishment." In a deleted section was this statement: "I am surprised that, less than three months before an important general election, the State Committee is devoting its time to debating a resolution critical of a Democratic senator. May I suggest that you consider devoting the committee's time to helping Democrats win." An earlier draft included the sentence, "I suggest that, at least between now and the election in November, you consider resolutions relating to the Republican members of Congress." As usual, Mitchell was prolific in endorsements of Democratic candidates for the Legislature and Congress, often with personal messages; since becoming majority leader, requests had risen markedly. The proposed resolution was dropped.

Mitchell rarely turned anyone down. His friend Harold Pachios said, "George Mitchell is different than any other politician I've ever known. I have not asked him for many favors, but I've always known that anything he could do to help me or my family, he would do. He'd never say no." Even in later years, Pachios said, "He's a busy guy . . . but anyone who's an acquaintance, trying to make a connection or have him put in a good word, he's found a way to do something positive. That's always amazed me. . . . He's never sought to insulate himself from people, even from people he doesn't know well. And if he can't do it, he'll tell them." Pachios said, though he'd met many "brilliant and disciplined people," that "when it comes to making connections with other human beings, he's the best."

Patrick Leahy, first elected to the Senate in 1974, and still serving, saw Mitchell as "a New England Democrat, basic values, FDR, sensitivity to the people who really needed government help." Leahy thought it started early. "He'd seen, in the mills in Maine, the needs of people, parents, immigrants. This was the America of great dreams, and I think he wanted to make sure that we were doing things to keep that dream open for anybody, no matter where they came from, or what background they came from, and not just for a select few."

ANYONE ELECTED TO THE CONGRESSIONAL DELEGATION becomes aware that defense issues are Maine's bread and butter. When Mitchell served, Loring Air Force Base in Limestone, Brunswick Naval Air Station, and Portsmouth Naval Shipyard in Kittery were all major sources of well-paid government jobs. The Pratt & Whitney aircraft engine plant in North Berwick and Saco Defense were important private defense contractors. But by far the biggest destination for federal defense dollars was Bath Iron Works, at times Maine's largest private employer, and a magnet for skilled tradespeople. Maine has almost always had a congressman on the House Armed Services Committee, and usually in the Senate, too. When Mitchell arrived, that senator was Bill Cohen, who later added Intelligence, and it was at BIW their rivalry was keenest.

Mitchell devotes a chapter in his memoir to "My Friend Bill Cohen," and describes his attempts to achieve parity with the shipbuilders' unions, among the strongest locals in the country, and an anomaly in Maine. It was a rare election morning the gates weren't crowded with hand-shaking politicians, Republicans along with Democrats. The biggest events at BIW were ship launchings, which, before a land-level dry dock was built, were visually spectacular, as ships slid down the ways before thousands of cheering spectators. Cohen had every advantage over the new junior senator, and Mitchell found it frustrating. Mitchell was used to Cohen speaking first at joint appearances, and said, "He always finished by saying he had to go to an important meeting; then he would hand me the microphone and leave. Since he had talked so long the audience was invariably smaller and exhausted by the time I started speaking." The navy cruiser and destroyer launches at BIW— there were many amid the Reagan defense buildup—were particularly difficult.

One day, he decided to ask Bath Iron Works president Bill Haggett, visiting Mitchell's office, why he only invited Cohen to speak at launches. Haggett "looked at me as though I was crazy, paused, then replied, 'Well, I like you, but you're the junior senator, not very well known, with no clout. He's the senior senator, a member of the Armed Services Committee, and the chairman of the seapower subcommittee. . . . Who would you invite?'" Mitchell acknowledged the point, but said Haggett, after "a long and embarrassing silence," seemed to feel sorry, and said the yard would have a small launch in February, when the cold would keep away the crowds, and Mitchell might be invited. "I don't think Bill will mind too much," Haggett said.

Mitchell prepared "a short, but I hoped an effective speech," and bundled up. Just before the launch at 1:15 p.m., sitting next to Haggett, Mitchell noticed "to my astonishment, there seated at the other end of the front row, was Senator Cohen." When Mitchell asked Haggett why Cohen was there, he made a palms-up gesture and said, "What could I do? He just showed up." Mitchell said he ruefully admired Cohen's speech. "Without notes, speaking confidently and with obvious knowledge and authority, his presentation was perfect, right down to the timing. Just seconds before the deadline, he thanked the crowd and basked in their applause." Then came the crack of the champagne bottle and the band playing. "My name had not been mentioned," Mitchell wrote. "I hadn't said a word." Mitchell says, apparently not entirely in jest, that the incident motivated him to run for majority leader. "I would outrank Bill Cohen! I would be introduced first, speak first, and then leave just as he was being introduced."

Mitchell did become intimately involved in BIW affairs, and his six years as majority leader were a tumultuous period. The Reagan buildup crested and receded, and by 1990 there were more layoffs than hirings; unions were restive, and had even gone on strike. In 1991, during a conference at BIW, a navy employee inadvertently left behind bid documents from a competing yard. Haggett first had them photocopied, then realized his transgression, reported it to the navy, and resigned, abruptly ending twenty-eight years at BIW; two vice presidents also resigned. His successor was Buzz Fitzgerald, Gayle Cory's brother and Mitchell's friend. The senator and new BIW president realized a crisis was at hand, and BIW's very survival could be at stake.

Along with the sudden change of leadership and navy downsizing, BIW was still burdened by debt from a leveraged buyout dating from its unsuccessful ownership by Congoleum, the flooring company that became a "conglomerate," a short-lived business fad for acquiring unrelated companies. "The competitive pressures were relentless," said staffer Bob Carolla. "The navy was taking a new path, and it wasn't clear how big a role BIW would play." The first battle concerned which shipyards the navy would select for bids. For destroyer- and cruiser-class ships, it had relied on three—BIW, Ingalls in Mississippi, and Avondale in Louisiana. The navy decided it would include only two shipyards for its DDG-51 destroyer class, its major procurement focus by the mid-1980s. Avondale became the odd yard out, but Bennett Johnston didn't give up, and, according to Carolla, the shipbuilding dispute got tangled up in the 1988 majority leader race. Johnston tried to force through an amendment to return work to Avondale, and Mitchell reacted as angrily as Carolla had ever seen. "This isn't about a fair-play amendment, this is a sore loser amendment," he said on the floor. Carolla thought, "I can't believe he said that," then realized, "That's actually what it was; he really got to the heart of it."

With Ingalls and BIW competing head-to-head, the navy said both yards would be guaranteed work, but depending on price and performance, one might get an extra ship. Given their size, approaching $1 billion per ship, that was a big bonus. The two-yard arrangement has continued, though the navy usually provides equal work to each yard. Navy planning sometimes ran afoul of congressional appropriations, though. Brett O'Brien recalled a crisis during the Democratic National Convention in 1992. The Senate had authorized one more destroyer than the House, and the conferees were about to meet. O'Brien heard that Senate negotiators planned to accept the House's lower number, and told Mitchell to find Ted Kennedy, who'd taken over from Cohen as seapower subcommittee chairman. Mitchell made his pitch, which was successful. "I was trying to deal with this at a level that couldn't get any further," O'Brien said, "and he was willing to take time out of what must have been a million responsibilities . . . to make this work."

Steve Hart said "earmarks" exploded after 1994, "when the Republicans came in . . . and made earmarks a mechanism for consolidating political power," with Newt Gingrich's majority leader, Tom DeLay, leading the effort. "When I was there, it was what people were expected to do to represent their state." He said, "Mitchell asked for one of the destroyers, he didn't ask for all of them," adding, "He's not like Byrd, asking that you move entire agencies to West Virginia." Bob Carolla said there was tension between Mitchell's responsibilities. "There's no clear dividing line between when a Maine issue ends and a national one begins," he said.

THE END OF THE COLD WAR, added to deficit-reduction budgets, put a serious crimp in defense spending. The Pentagon tried to cut back weapons programs, but Congress resisted, and also refused to close bases. Congressional leaders authorized a series of base-closing commissions to, in essence, do what Congress was unwilling to do through the budget. Key votes on the first commission occurred in 1988, before Mitchell was majority leader. He immediately recognized the commission could threaten Maine bases, given the state's small size and lack of clout, particularly with a two-member House delegation. Sarah Sewall wrote a May 9 memo on the defense authorization bill, with the commission included. "The provision is sound policy," she wrote. "Despite the existence of obviously obsolete or redundant bases, not one has been closed since more stringent closing regulations were imposed in 1977, and three new ones have opened. In the third consecutive year of declining real defense expenditures, it is time to do away with unnecessary infrastructure." Nonetheless, she said, "It would be perceived as contrary to Maine's interests to support the provision."

The biggest concern was Loring, with its aging B-52 bomber fleet providing first-strike capability against the Soviet Union, which was now disarming. The US Air Force proposed closing Loring earlier, but Muskie and Cohen beat back the effort. Speculation was intense that Loring would be on the first list. Sewall recommended Mitchell oppose the commission, and he did. In a floor speech October 12, he said, "Congress, with its constitutional mandate to provide for the common defense, has a responsibility to consider each base opening. It similarly has a responsibility to consider each base closing. This measure would, in large part, deprive Congress of this right and duty." The commission was approved, however. There were five rounds of closings, in 1988, 1991, 1993, 1995, and 2005, and 350 installations have been closed. Loring wasn't on the first list, but Pease Air Force Base in New Hampshire was—the first base to shut down, in 1991. The commission faced resistance from the navy, and former Senator Thomas Eagleton singled them out for "stonewalling." Another round was scheduled for 1991.

Another likely target was the Portsmouth Naval Shipyard, as the navy pared down from eleven shipyards to the four that remain today. Mitchell and Cohen recognized the closure possibility and, with Mitchell now majority leader, the delegation was better positioned to play defense. Portsmouth had built no new submarines since the 1960s, but it had a steady business overhauling Los Angeles–class subs. Mitchell learned that, while the yard was productive overall, its efficiency plunged sharply in winter—a disadvantage against the other overhaul yard on the East Coast, at Charleston, South Carolina. He attempted, along with Cohen, to convince the navy it should build a dry dock next to the subs berthed along the piers. The navy wasn't receptive. It had no similar facilities, and hadn't planned major new investments in an overhaul yard. Mitchell persisted.

Bob Carolla inherited the project from Mike Hastings and, in 1985, said the dry dock "was a concept, not even a model, to cover one of the berths, literally put a super dome over it." Workers then had to exit the main building, bundle up, and carry their tools into the submarine, often overheated. Admiral Bruce DeMars was submarine fleet commander, and in early 1989 Mitchell and Cohen met with him and Navy Secretary William Ball. It did not go well. Debate on John Tower's nomination as Defense secretary was going on in the Senate chamber, casting a pall over the proceedings; Ball had served on Tower's Senate staff. Carolla remembers DeMars, who "had a very imperious manner about him, and an engineer's mind," kept saying "There's no way we're going to build this." Cohen became incensed, and even Mitchell was exasperated.

Carolla tried to understand DeMars's position, and finally realized he thought the "super dome" would prevent movement of the big cranes that transferred heavy components. Carolla sought another meeting with DeMars, which was also testy, but the admiral talked about smaller modules that might overcome his objection. Working with the yard commander and with the union chiefs, they developed a revised plan that, DeMars admitted, could work. He told Carolla, "I continue to question whether this is needed," but signed the authorization. As majority leader, Mitchell focused on funding, while Cohen moved the project ahead in committee. The dry dock was approved and built, just in time. Carolla estimates efficiency improved 20 to 30 percent, enough to put Portsmouth ahead of Charleston during the 1993 round, when it was clear one would be axed.

The preliminaries began in 1992, and Brett O'Brien accompanied Mitchell on a tour to show the commissioners Portsmouth's improvement. There were several senators along, and it was planned that each would address an aspect of the yard's performance. After discussion, they decided Mitchell would give the whole presentation; O'Brien prepared the draft. "On the bus ride, he took the speech, reworked parts, really brought together what I had done in a much more dynamic arrangement, and he told me to go seat to seat, and consult with every other member." O'Brien said, "That was a significant moment of keeping the team together at probably the most critical and perilous moment . . . he really made a very compelling argument." Portsmouth was spared, and Charleston was closed. Carolla said the experience showed "how much decisions made in one year could have major consequences much farther down the road."

In 1994, the Clinton administration, still seeking a peace dividend, requested another closing round—the last, except for a small list in 2005 that included the Brunswick Naval Air Station. Mitchell was taking no chances, seeing how close Portsmouth had come to extinction, taking six thousand jobs with it. Deputy Navy Secretary Richard Danzig headed the 1995 commission, and when he visited, Danzig intended it as a courtesy call. Instead, O'Brien said, "Senator Mitchell bombarded him with charts and graphs and studies." Danzig, he said, was "taken aback, but very impressed that a year and a half ahead," Mitchell announced his retirement, though he had "focused on this and reaching out to him . . . to defend the base." Although the commission added Portsmouth to the 1995 list, it then voted against closure, and the yard remained open.

Things did not go as well with Loring. Since it had escaped the first round and Pease was closed, there was some optimism it might survive. But it was targeted in 1991, and, despite attempts to convince the commission to close Plattsburgh, New York, instead, it remained on the list. Plattsburgh was closed in 1993, as were nearly all the old Strategic Air Command bases. Mitchell had convinced the air force to modernize the base earlier. Alan Dixon, a Democrat on the Armed Services Committee, wrote Mitchell on May 8, 1987, informing him that Loring would receive $4.3 million in building improvements, plus a $13.1 million refueling project. The air force had just built new dormitories when the closing was ordered.

It was a difficult moment for Mitchell. Congressional rules specified the list must be voted up or down in its entirety. After the commission vote, there was little to do, and Mitchell never considered forcing rejection. "The loss of Loring was traumatic," Brett O'Brien said, "and folks in Aroostook County weren't sure what the future would hold." Limestone had barely existed as a town when the air force built Loring after World War II, and many thought it would become a ghost town. With the corresponding decline in potato farming, the future for Aroostook looked bleak.

Mitchell worked to contain the damage. One possibility arose from another defense consolidation, centralizing the Pentagon's finance and accounting operations. Kelly Horwitz, who worked with another young aide, Sandy Brown, remembers frantic hours as they finished the application and delivered it across the Potomac in Crystal City. "The thing about Crystal City is that everything is named Crystal—Crystal Drive, Crystal Lane—and here we were, right down to the wire, driving around this government wasteland of buildings. . . . It was like something out of a comedy movie . . . trying to figure out where to drop this application." They made it, and a Defense Finance and Accounting Center was built at Loring. And, even though there was a Job Corps center in Bangor, Mitchell convinced the Department of Labor to open another in Limestone. Employment has never approached Loring's personnel, but Limestone survived, and the former base has become a small manufacturing hub.

Even minor effects from base realignment drew Mitchell's attention. The navy stopped using a pipeline from Harpswell to the Brunswick Naval Air Station, and closed the oceanfront property that off-loaded tankers. Gordon Weil, who much earlier served on Joe Brennan's staff, was a Harpswell selectman, and his wife, Roberta, advocated turning over the old fuel depot to the town. By that time, the federal government was supposed to be compensated, but Mitchell inserted a provision in the defense appropriations bill to transfer it at no cost. "He was majority leader, and that was the kind of thing that majority leaders could make happen," Weil said. The navy cleaned up hazardous waste, and the town took ownership, though not without some grumbling. "I put on the warrant that we should name it after Mitchell, and explained why—that we wouldn't have had it without him," Weil said. "One of my selectman friends didn't like the idea of creating a park, so we called it a field." Mitchell spoke at the dedication of the George J. Mitchell Field. Weil said, "I thought there should be more things in this state named in honor of his efforts, but I guess that will come in time, but at least in Harpswell, we did something for him, and he did something for us."

MITCHELL DIDN'T SHY AWAY FROM TRADITIONAL Maine interests, fisheries and farming, though the work was less eventful, and often involved navigating the federal bureaucracy's intricacies and the overlapping jurisdictions of congressional committees. One example was a fish inspection bill, an idea Mitchell got after reading about disease outbreaks from contaminated seafood, and hearing from Maine fishermen. This almost unregulated industry was becoming more prominent in American diets, and because much fishing took place far offshore, beyond state jurisdiction, Mitchell thought there should be a federal role. Bob Carolla was among the staffers who spent many hours on the bill. The Maine sardine council was among the backers. "In theory, the Food and Drug Administration was supposed to be monitoring, with the National Marine Fisheries Service [NMFS], but they weren't doing much of anything," Carolla said. "This came after a couple of summers in which medical waste was washing up on beaches."

There was a conflict over jurisdiction between the Department of Agriculture, which oversaw aquaculture, and NMFS, with a smaller budget, and located in the Department of Commerce. There were also concerns from consumer groups that a relatively modest seafood inspection bill might weaken meat and poultry inspections at Agriculture. While the USDA "loved the idea" of taking on fish inspection, Carolla said, many others did not. Mitchell included the legislation in the 1989 farm bill, but committee issues dogged it, and it was removed and introduced separately. The proposal gained the animus of Ted Stevens of Alaska, notoriously irascible, who, Carolla said, thought Alaska had the only marine fishery of significance, and couldn't imagine why anyone would inspect seafood. Stevens vowed to filibuster the farm bill, not realizing the inspection provisions had been removed. Mitchell had to instruct Stevens there was already unanimous consent on the farm bill, but he could contest the inspection bill. When Stevens did, "We beat him pretty handily," Carolla said. Heading back to the majority office, he noticed that Mitchell was uncharacteristically gleeful. "He did a little bit of a jump, almost like a jig—it's very vivid to me, and definitely like a little hop."

The triumph was momentary. The appropriations bill got bogged down in conference and Congress adjourned. "In the next Congress nobody wanted to touch the issue again," Carolla said. "Of all the issues I handled, that's probably where I felt most ambivalent." The debate did lead to "heightened concern about how seafood was being handled, and elevated it on the public agenda," he said.

Maine's agricultural interests were the primary reason Mitchell initially opposed NAFTA, the North American Free Trade Agreement, the pact Bill Clinton pursued through "fast track" authority, though, as majority leader, Mitchell shepherded it to passage with mostly Republican votes. "One of the first things you discover when you do agricultural policy in Congress is how parochial it is," said Steve Hart. "Mitchell's involvements in agricultural issues were just like most senators'. . . . We spent a lot of time dealing with potatoes." One successful effort was blueberry research, which helped solidify Maine as nearly the sole US producer of frozen wild blueberries. At times, Mitchell got involved with maple syrup and dairy products—though, to the relief of longtime staff, cow jokes did not reappear. Some staff members would freelance, Hart said. "Clyde MacDonald was an enthusiastic supporter of growing cranberries, and he actually pulled us in," though to no great result.

The jousting over agriculture could lead to unusual deals. The Food and Drug Administration was setting maple syrup standards, and Vermont and Maine already had a rule that no water could be added. The FDA rule would preempt the state standards, so Vermont, the largest producer, needed help to contest it. Vermont's Jim Jeffords was a much-sought-after vote on the Clinton health care plan, and to help persuade him, Mitchell worked on syrup standards. "I remember meeting with the FDA, and they just were not going to budge," Hart said. "So we had to do something legislative. We ended up putting this exemption for maple syrup standards in the Nurses Training Act."

No item was too small for Mitchell's attention. Mary McAleney said that after Mitchell became majority leader, she was attending a caucus lunch when Mitchell motioned her over. "The senators are in this horseshoe and they all have their little sandwiches and their chips and their sodas," she said. Mitchell told her, "This water's not from Maine. There's no water here from Maine." He proposed a solution: "Call up every bottling company in the state and figure out how many of them want to send bottled water down here, and we'll buy it." A small company responded, and water started arriving, an incident that still amuses McAleney. "He was thinking about Maine, thinking about bottled water from Maine."

AS MEASURED BY DOLLARS, THE BIGGEST IMPACT on his home state from Mitchell's Senate tenure was transportation funding. He brought millions of dollars in discretionary spending for highways and bridges, and was the father of the Downeaster, securing grants and equipment to restore passenger train service to Maine after an absence of forty years. In addition to becoming majority leader, he continued to serve on EPW, where the public works side came to the fore as Congress considered a major multiyear reauthorization.

The biggest prize for Mitchell in the 1987 reauthorization had been securing $24 million for the Topsham-Brunswick bypass, the Coastal Connector, which cleared a bottleneck in downtown Brunswick that produced the "thirty-minute mile" on Maine Street—the time it took to navigate that stretch each rush hour. The four-year reauthorization was much larger than previous bills, financed by a five-cent increase in federal fuel taxes—the last such increase enacted for transportation. The increase prompted Reagan's veto, overridden 67–33, exactly the number needed, as thirteen Republicans deserted the president, though not Bill Cohen. Mitchell commented, "We repeatedly told the president not to pick fights on issues that don't warrant them." Cam Niven, publisher of the Brunswick *Times Record*, wrote, saying "Congratulations on a remarkable achievement."

The 1991 reauthorization was an even larger undertaking. An aide who worked on the bill, Grace Reef, said it "rewrote all the highway laws"—only a slight exaggeration. The Intermodal Surface Transportation Efficiency Act, or ISTEA, set transportation policy on a new course that reflected Mitchell's interest in the environment, as well as roads, bridges, and trains. The legislation included requirements for air-quality improvements, and emphasized federal support for "intermodal" connections, particularly rail lines that could connect to ports, airports, and freight hubs, while, Reef said, "providing more flexibility for states to set regional priorities." It gave higher standing to multiple-use projects. Pedestrian and bike trails were funded on a small, but permanent, basis.

Reef, who worked with Sandy Brown, is an example of how Mitchell developed talent by providing significant responsibilities early on. Both Reef and Brown started working for Mitchell in their early twenties. Reef ended up with a variety of issues, including the child care tax credit, a rare federal support for working parents. This represented another elaborate collaboration between Finance and Health, Education, and Labor, and reflected competing aims of senators as diverse as Chris Dodd, Lloyd Bentsen, and Orrin Hatch. It also presented a familiar problem. "There are many views brought to the table when you bring twenty different children's groups together, including some who, if it wasn't 110 percent their way, then it was the losing way," Reef said. Mitchell mediated many disputes. A final obstacle concerned a church–state issue: whether parents who sent their children to church programs would qualify—at the time, Reef said, 30 percent of the total. Because the credit was claimed by the parents, rather than a payment to institutions, the bill passed muster. "Senator Mitchell is the kind of person who could let people rant and rave and just get it all out, and at the end of it they're somehow appreciative of him, but it was kind of a crazy time," she said.

Transportation funding seemed more straightforward, but Reef was quickly disabused of this notion. "The only thing more political than the dicey emotional arrangement . . . of the child care issue was highways," she said. Reef had begun in 1987, but the 1991 version involved a lot more staff work. Maine had a particular problem with federal highway funding because the original formula for interstate highways gave it a minimum allotment, similar to New Hampshire and Vermont. But Maine had more than twice the interstate mileage as either northern New England neighbor, a perpetual disadvantage, and has never attracted enough support to change the formula. Instead, Mitchell worked within the discretionary provisions and obtained funding to finish the Topsham-Brunswick bypass and build three major new bridges—a replacement for the Million Dollar Bridge between Portland and South Portland, the Casco Bay Bridge; a new bridge alongside the Carlton Bridge across the Kennebec between Bath and Woolwich, the Sagadahoc Bridge; and a second bridge between Waterville and Winslow, named for Don Carter, a Waterville legislator.

The highway package alone totaled $186 million, and provided nearly ten thousand construction jobs. Much of it was from the "disproportionate share" account, reflecting the difficulty each state had in raising matching funds. Mitchell campaign architect Larry Benoit, monitoring things from Maine, said, "They did very well with that." He noted that a Florida newspaper rated the effectiveness of congressional members' ability to get legislation passed, and its significance. Mitchell not only made the "All Star team," but was rated the top slugger, Benoit said.

Reef, then twenty-five, made an error during debate over the distribution formula, which, notwithstanding its other provisions, requires each state to get back at least 85 percent of the money it sends to Washington. Reef checked with the EPW committee counsel, rather than the Budget Committee. He assured her everything was okay, but it wasn't. Robert Byrd, who she said "knows more about money than anyone else on Earth," noticed the discrepancy, and proposed an amendment. "We ended up with a formula fight for three weeks on the Senate floor," she said. The hardest part was telling Mitchell. His response was, "You asked *who*?" She said, "I remember the way he looked at me, and I just felt like I really disappointed him. . . . It was like your dad is disappointed in you, and it was a huge fiasco." With John Hilley's help, she tried different formula variations until one finally received fifty-one votes. Lloyd Bentsen decided Texas was getting shortchanged, and screamed at Reef. "They really shouldn't do that, but they can have any kind of behavior they want," she said.

There were many other aspects of the transportation bill, and some pitched battles. Steve Symms, despite his conservative leanings, liked transportation funding. "That's one thing George and I always agreed on," he said. "You show me a place that doesn't have a good road, and I'll show you a business that's going broke. . . . This country's got a huge infrastructure problem because we've underfunded highways." Symms joined forces with Mitchell on an amendment to build a high-speed rail line in Texas—something Bentsen opposed because he thought it would hurt then-fledgling Southwest Airlines—but the House refused the provision in conference. Another Republican, John Warner, was impressed by how EPW united around new concepts. "The beautiful bike path along the Potomac River from DC to George Washington's home in Mount Vernon, was expanded in ISTEA," he said. "The committee [members] were all supporters of the environment and America's great outdoors."

While Mitchell was happy to help Maine in any way he could, the part of ISTEA that meant the most to him was passenger rail. It harked back to his days in Waterville when freight trains ran past his bedroom window, and his father's keen interest in trains. The last passenger train left Portland's Union Station in 1960, and the following year the station was demolished to make room for a strip mall—a loss that energized Maine's historic preservation movement. Mitchell was determined to bring back passenger service, but he wanted to do it right. Ad hoc ventures, such as a train that briefly ran from Manchester, New Hampshire, to Boston in the late 1970s, vanished without a trace. A campaign promise from Jimmy Carter to Governor Hugh Gallen, it failed in part because the only departure was at five a.m. Amtrak had fought for its life throughout the 1980s, as David Stockman used it as a litmus test for congressional will in cutting domestic spending. But Mitchell was convinced it could work, and ISTEA presented the opportunity.

"I have no idea why my father was fascinated with railroads," Mitchell said. "He could tell you the history of every railroad, every mile of track in South Dakota, and this place and that place. He devoured railroad magazines." Mitchell didn't share the obsession, but he did think of his father when he joined EPW and realized, "Maine was one of only two states in the country that did not have passenger rail service." He decided to get to know Graham Claytor, head of Amtrak, and the two hit it off. Mitchell told him, "I know you support rail, you run the doggone thing, and I'm shocked to find out that my state is one of two that doesn't have passenger rail service. You should at least study the possibility of bringing it back."

Wayne Davis, a Portland bank executive, disliked flying and took his business trips by train. He was appalled by the dismal service, which worsened as Congress squeezed funding to Amtrak. Davis formed a group of rail aficionados, calling it TrainRiders/Northeast. He began writing the congressional delegation about improving service. At the time, the most common reaction to the train campaign was, "Why would you want to do that?" Ending passenger rail service was planned in conjunction with building interstate highways and expansion of air travel. Except for freight, railroads, most planners believed, were obsolete.

Davis said recently he had no idea whether anyone was reading his frequent letters, but Sandy Brown was putting them in front of Mitchell. Mitchell invited Davis to meet for lunch in Portland, and Davis found him attentive. Mitchell thought the biggest obstacle was the perception that the public had no interest. "We concluded that if anything was going to change with passenger rail, it would be born from the street level, not the state capital," Davis said. "It had to start with the people." So TrainRiders undertook the arduous task of collecting enough signatures to get a measure on the 1990 ballot. "We had no guidebook on how to do this," he said. The traditional means for those who don't hire signature-gatherers is to set up tables at polling places. But 1989 was an off-year election, and the group gathered only 40,000 of the 53,000 that would be needed. It was then the middle of winter, with few places people gather in numbers. They decided to try the Maine Mall. "Today, we wouldn't be able to do it, but back then, they said yes," Davis said. After watching volunteers drag tables and chairs through the snow, the mall owners—"who liked the idea of a train"—provided furniture. They submitted 60,000 signatures, but petitions continued to pour in. "We had a stack higher than I was. In the end, we had more than 90,000," Davis said. The effort removed any idea Mainers were indifferent to trains. Transportation Commissioner Dana Connors then convinced the Legislature that nothing in the petition required new state spending, so, lawmakers approved the initiated question without sending it to referendum, a rare occurrence.

Mitchell had the evidence he needed. During his dealings with him, Davis was amazed the majority leader always seemed to have time for him. "If I came up to him at the end of a meeting, he'd say, 'Walk with me.'" On one occasion,

Davis accompanied Mitchell to his room at the Holiday Inn, talked while he packed, and concluded the conversation in the elevator before Mitchell disappeared into a waiting car. "He always had suggestions, and they were good ones," Davis said.

Grace Reef was among several staffers looking for a way to fund the service, which would originate in Boston's North Station and run on MBTA tracks to Haverhill. Beyond that were rickety rails good enough for low-speed freight, but inadequate for passenger service. The initial run would reach Portland, with up to half a dozen stops. Reef was making rounds during late-night committee sessions when she found an Appropriations subcommittee marking up the transportation bill. The talk was about discretionary projects, and Reef said Mitchell had a rail project "ready to go." She was then asked, "How much do you need?" When she said $30 million, they penciled it in. Reef still isn't sure if this was appropriate. Mary McAleney said, "The rail service was always in the plan, and if it didn't work this way, we would have found another." The hasty insertion did cause some difficulty; funding was directed to an agency that didn't ordinarily handle interstate trains, but corrective legislation smoothed the way.

Mitchell had secured a pledge from Graham Claytor that Amtrak would provide top-flight equipment—not new trains, but the next best thing. Amtrak was introducing new Acela cars for service from New York to Washington, and Metroliner equipment was retired, and reconditioned for the Downeaster as the Capstone line. Davis believes up-to-date equipment played a major part in the train's immediate success, exceeding ridership projections in its first year. "I still get calls from my friends in New York State, who tell me, 'You have all the good ones. Why can't we get some?'" Because Claytor had pledged that the $20 million in equipment would be provided "at no cost to the state of Maine," the state pays only a modest ticket subsidy. "Every president of Amtrak, and their accountants, has tried to figure out how that happened," Davis said. "They still want Maine to pay." Because of difficulties in negotiating agreements with the track owners—Guilford, since renamed Pan Am—it wasn't until 2001 that the first trains pulled into Portland. Service was extended to Brunswick in 2011.

Wayne Davis saw the Downeaster as just the beginning. Mitchell appointed him to the National Commission on Intermodal Transportation that ISTEA authorized. He traveled around the country for hearings and briefings. He was the only citizen among a sea of transportation officials and lobbyists. He was told, "I was the only one without an ax to grind. They couldn't threaten my funding because I didn't have any." The commission recommended high-speed rail service along California's Alameda corridor that was eventually built. It also recommended a train tunnel be constructed between South Station and North

Station in Boston as part of the "Big Dig"—the completion of Interstate 93, with the Central Artery moved underground, and a tunnel built to Logan Airport.

Mitchell obtained funding for "slurry walls" to frame the "Big Dig" tunnel space for eventual rail construction, which would have allowed direct service from East Coast points to Maine and beyond. The train tunnel wasn't built, though proponents still push for it. Davis said, "If we'd done it, we'd already have direct service to New Brunswick and the Maritimes. The Canadians wanted it, and wanted to invest in it." In a 1992 speech to TrainRiders/Northeast, Mitchell called the connection between North and South stations "an important element of making the Portland-to-Boston link an integral part of the Northeast rail corridor." He provided his own vision of the transportation future, which, he said, went far beyond the renaming of the "highway" bill as "surface transportation." He said, "Thirty years ago, transportation planners regarded passenger rail service as a relic of the nineteenth century, unable to compete either in capital costs or operating efficiencies in a modern, highway- and airway-dominated world. But like so many visions which seem simple and easy, this one turned out to be wrong." He said airliners "have given us speed unknown to earlier generations," but "at the price of distant airports, wasted travel time, and high prices." Mitchell said, "Passenger rail today is a sensible alternative and complement in many parts of the county. It's an idea whose time has come, and gone, and now come back again."

THE AIR TRAFFIC CONTROLLERS STRIKE THAT Ronald Reagan broke in 1981 by firing the controllers echoed in labor-management relations in Maine. Reagan's aggressive response stunned the Professional Air Traffic Controllers Organization (PATCO) union members, Bob Carolla said, who had supported Reagan over Carter in 1980. "Reagan sent the message that if you go on strike, you're going to be replaced. Unions were starting to take the hits that they've continued to take since then."

The consolidation of New England rail lines as Guilford Transportation under the ownership of Timothy Mellon, heir to the Andrew Mellon fortune, seemed initially promising, but soon turned sour as relentless cost-cutting led to several strikes by the mid-1980s. Mitchell worked behind the scenes, trying to keep the parties at the bargaining table, but Guilford's lawyers pursued other avenues. They decided to lease the Maine and other New England lines to Springfield Terminal, a subsidiary, and apply lower short-line pay rates from the Delaware & Hudson, another system Guilford absorbed. A strike by Maine Central employees soon spread to other lines, and courts upheld secondary picketing. Mitchell and Cohen wanted the president to declare a cooling-off period, and, after the senators kept "baying at the door of the White House," as Carolla put it, Reagan did. But negotiations went nowhere, walkouts continued, and, in 1988, a federal arbitrator ruled in the unions' favor. Guilford responded by taking the Delaware & Hudson into bankruptcy, shedding union contracts, and reducing its New England workforce from 2,000 to 1,200. Carolla remembers other railroad executives would check in during the long conflict, often to say, "We're not like Guilford." Guilford proved a frequent obstacle to restoring and then improving Downeaster service on its tracks. It resisted higher speed limits necessary to run passenger service, even after required track improvements were made at federal expense, and refused to talk with Amtrak officials. The federal DOT's Surface Transportation Board ordered Guilford to honor its Amtrak contracts, and Downeaster service finally began on December 14, 2001.

Mitchell had even less success during the bitter International Paper strike at the Androscoggin Mill in Jay, which began in June 1987 and lasted more than a year. IP was one of the companies emboldened by the PATCO fallout, and warned that if unions didn't accept pay cuts and other concessions and went on strike, they would be replaced. The company quickly did just that, and hundreds of non-union workers, many from Southern states—"scabs," according to the strikers—drove through the mill gate past angry picketers.

Two months later, Mitchell gave a speech to the Maine AFL-CIO. "I've been deeply moved by the plight of those on strike," he said. "The Jay workers face a double tragedy—the financial and emotional drain of the strike, and the long-term threat to the community they live in. Jay has been a community, but the bitterness of a strike like this—bitterness caused by real pain and suffering—cannot be erased as though it never happened, even if the strike were resolved tomorrow. . . . It bothers me to see people and a community in Maine torn apart like this." Mitchell made it clear he supported the workers. "Working men and women must have the right to organize, the right to bargain collectively, the right to have management give them a fair hearing and a fair answer, the right to withhold their labor. I strongly support those fundamental rights." But he also said "the principle of nonintervention is the only right one" under the law. "Those who think my intervention in the strike would somehow end it are mistaken," he said. "It would not cause the company to change its position. It would only cause the company to get other elected officials to take its side."

At the end of the strike, the company imposed its terms, unions were decertified, and there have been no paper mill strikes in Maine since. The multinational companies that owned the large Maine mills—IP, S. D. Warren, Champion, Boise Cascade—made few investments and sold their Maine holdings within the decade. Employment at the Jay mill dropped from 1,400 to 865 over two decades, then to 565 after layoffs in 2015.

ONE OF MITCHELL'S MOST TIME-CONSUMING ENDEAVORS—establishing a permanent boundary for Acadia National Park on Mount Desert Island—also provided unanticipated benefits. Estelle Lavoie had worked on the issue for Muskie before Mitchell inherited it. "I ended up spending six years [on it], which I didn't anticipate when I accepted the assignment," Mitchell said. "I later joked that this was the best training I ever had for my experience in Northern Ireland and the Middle East." While Lavoie left Mitchell's office in 1984 to attend law school, Mitchell remained enmeshed in the details.

"Acadia was the only national park created entirely on land that was donated to the government," Mitchell said. First protected as Lafayette National Monument in 1916 by order of President Woodrow Wilson, it became a national park by an act of Congress in 1929. Donations, encouraged by the Rockefeller family and other wealthy summer residents, didn't cease when the park was created, and boundaries were left undefined. "The land was spread out over ten towns [and villages], and officials became upset because it became quite common for wealthy individuals to donate their homes and estates to the park," Mitchell said. "The towns would lose the property off the tax rolls, and it wasn't very usable as a park to have twenty acres and a house somewhere miles away from . . . the national park."

The debate among the towns, the National Park Service, and the National Parks Conservation Association became heated. After meeting with all sides, Mitchell saw possibilities for negotiation. "The town of Bar Harbor owned some land that was now smack in the middle of Acadia National Park, and some parts of Bar Harbor, places where there had been large estates, were owned by the park," he said. He worked to arrange land swaps, "so they could get these properties back on the tax rolls, and the park would come close to establishing a contiguous landmass." There were many parcels, and because Mitchell often met with each owner, years went by. Finally, in 1986, Mitchell proposed and Congress enacted a permanent boundary, with the legislation also requiring a master plan and procedures for future acquisitions—authority the park had lacked. "It was met with widespread but not unanimous approval," he said. "Some people didn't like it. I got some flak. It's impossible to satisfy everyone."

Mitchell made his first trips to Mount Desert Island in January and February, "and it was really cold and difficult." He returned in more benign seasons, and the place began to grow on him. When he moved to the Portland area, his family had summered on Drake's Island in Wells. Now, he started renting cottages on the southern end of MDI, and did so for nearly two decades. Once he left the Senate and remarried, he began thinking about more permanent arrangements, and bought a hilltop site near the village of Seal Cove in 2000, where a single-story, shingle-style house now hugs the ridgeline.

When Mitchell heard the Coast Guard was decommissioning lighthouses along the East Coast, replacing them with automated beacons, and planning to sell them, he sponsored the Bicentennial Lighthouse Fund to encourage their transfer to nonprofits and individuals who would protect and restore them. An appropriation for the Portland Head Light, now owned and operated by the town of Cape Elizabeth, was a model. Though broader legislation wasn't enacted until after he left the Senate, nearly all historic lighthouses in Maine have been preserved.

On May 10, 1989, a flash fire caused by construction leveled one of the mouse facilities at the Jackson Laboratories in Bar Harbor. The mice, used for genetic testing, represented some of the world's most important genetics stocks, a role that has only grown with the explosion of molecular biological research. Ken Paigen, the lab's director, announced plans for rebuilding, but the fire severely disrupted research, and the nonprofit didn't have the resources for a lengthy fund-raising campaign. Mitchell asked what he could do to help. Chris Williams was assigned, and Mitchell told her, "They say they need $20 million to rebuild. See if you can get it for them." The largest customer for the Jackson Lab mice was the National Institutes of Health, and Williams saw that Mitchell wanted to be sure rebuilding was a national priority, not just for Maine's benefit. The lab received a $19.5 million loan, and, in Williams's estimation, Mitchell and his staff "did 95 percent of the work," even though the entire delegation signed on. When the new buildings were dedicated, there was some consternation that only Mitchell's name was on the plaque. It was later reworked to read, "through the leadership of George Mitchell and the support of the Maine Delegation." Paigen wrote on September 27, 1994, to thank Mitchell for a parting gift—waiver of the $500,000 loan interest, which Paigen called "essential to our future success." Since the fire, the lab had added 160 jobs.

Mitchell likes to tell a story about another rebuilding that took place a few years earlier, when the Jordan Pond House burned down in an off-season fire. Its splendid view toward "the Bubbles," twin pink granite peaks at the far end of the pond, is one of the most famous scenes in Acadia. Finding that, through regular appropriations, it would take five years to fund a replacement, Mitchell sponsored a bill that allowed construction to start the following spring. Not long after the restaurant reopened, Mitchell was meeting friends there, and one hadn't appeared. He went to find a pay phone—he reminds audiences that "we didn't have cell phones in those days"—and spotted one in the lobby. In his various tellings, Mitchell points up the contrasts between Maine and Massachusetts, a long-running source of friendly rivalry and ribbing with Ted Kennedy and others. The District of Maine was originally attached to Massachusetts. Maine, a magnet for settlers by the turn of the nineteenth century, got consent to separate only in 1820, when the Jefferson Democratic-Republican Party, growing rapidly in Maine, threatened to outnumber ruling Federalists, the party of Washington, Adams, and Hamilton, whose last stronghold was in Boston. In speeches, Mitchell likes to remind listeners that "Massachusetts was once part of Maine."

There are different versions of the Jordan Pond story, depending on the audience, and Mitchell includes a short rendition in his memoir. The scenario positions Mitchell, after finding the pay phone, next in line behind an increasingly irate tourist, who's from Massachusetts, and is plugging quarters into the phone and swearing about the inability of Mainers to keep even a pay phone in operation. The man keeps inserting quarters, and swearing, and Mitchell sees that a line is forming behind him. His immediate neighbor notices him and says, "Aren't you the new US senator from Maine?" Mitchell acknowledges this, and the two chat. After a while, Mitchell asks, "And what do you do for a living?" The man leans forward and confides, "I'm a telephone repairman. And as soon as that guy from Massachusetts uses up all his quarters, I'm going to fix that phone." At least in Maine, the story always gets a laugh.

AS A FORMER POLITICIAN IN HIS NATIVE STATE, Mitchell stands out as unusually devoted to the party that created him. His nephew, Jim Mitchell, who ran as a Democrat for Congress in 1994, said "he was always very concerned with the strength of the party; some of that was because of his own history." When Jim Mitchell did fund-raisers with his uncle in Washington, "We raised more money than the party had raised in a decade." He noted Mitchell's service as party chairman, and said, "He had a real interest in seeing the organization strengthened as a critical part of how to advance the cause of the Democratic Party."

Even when a candidate wasn't winning acclaim, Mitchell didn't hesitate. Following his narrow victory in 1994, Angus King had become so popular as governor he was expected to be reelected by acclamation in 1998. No prominent Democrat volunteered to run. The nomination went to Tom Connolly, a little-known Portland lawyer. Tony Buxton's law school was giving Mitchell an honorary degree, and Buxton, Mitchell's long-ago campaign manager, was marching alongside when Mitchell said, "I'm going to endorse Tom Connolly tomorrow." When Buxton said, "That's great," Mitchell added, "Some people have told me not to do it, because he's not a serious candidate in their mind. But he's the Democratic nominee, and I'm a Democrat." Buxton was impressed because "He didn't have to do it. . . . There were a lot of Democrats who endorsed Angus King because they thought it was to their personal advantage. George saw it differently."

In 2008, Tom Allen gave up the First District congressional seat he'd held for twelve years to run, unsuccessfully, against Senator Susan Collins. Allen said Mitchell did everything he was asked. "He was fabulous. He came to an event in New York, he raised money for me from friends, he spoke for me, and for several days near the end of the campaign, he was in Maine promoting my campaign . . . and it meant a lot. I just think he felt I was the best candidate, and he was going to do everything he could to help me, despite a schedule which, when he left the Senate, didn't slow down very much."

Eliot Cutler had returned to Maine after years spent working abroad and was preparing to run for governor in 2010 when he came to see Mitchell, whom he'd worked for during the 1972 Muskie campaign. "You're a lifelong Democrat," Mitchell told him. "If you run as a Democrat, I'll support you." But Cutler rejected the advice, ran as an independent, and Mitchell endorsed the Democratic nominee, Libby Mitchell; the two are not related.

When there wasn't an election on, Mitchell was more than happy to reach across the aisle. Not long after he was elected in 1982, he invited Margaret Chase Smith back to the Capitol for her birthday; it had been ten years since her departure from the Senate, and she hadn't returned. "At the time," his aide Mike Hastings said, "the legislative branch only had two limousines, and Senator Mitchell arranged for one to carry me out to Silver Spring, to Margaret Chase Smith's house, to pick her up and bring her back to the Capitol." Hastings had never been in a car with a phone, and, five minutes before arrival, he alerted Gayle Cory, who had Mitchell standing on the steps. Smith "took him by the arm, and he led her into the building, and he took her to the members' dining room and they sat down and began lunch." Mitchell had written personally to each senator, "and serially they came into the dining room to wish her a happy birthday, and some of them brought a rose. So she ended up by the end of the meal with this bouquet of roses, and she was just beaming."

Hastings reflected on a campus appearance at Colby that Smith had made in May 1970, just after the Nixon administration's invasion of Cambodia ignited student protests. During an antiwar rally at Colby College involving two thousand students from around Maine, Smith insisted the United States didn't have any troops in neighboring Laos, to which a demonstrator, a former Marine lieutenant, responded, "If we don't have troops in Laos, why was I shot there?" Smith turned to an aide, but could not produce an answer. Talking with her on the way home, Hastings said, "The lady in the back of that car was the sharpest person alive; I mean, she was on the top of her game when George Mitchell invited her to the Senate. Her memory was great. She was up-to-date on world affairs, and I never could really reconcile the image that came out of that 1970 demonstration and the impression I got in the backseat of that limousine." After the lunch, Mitchell escorted Smith to the Senate gallery, then went back to the floor, where, Hastings said, "for the next hour, senators gave speeches about her career, and it was just a wonderful thing."

20

TWILIGHT

George Mitchell entered his last year in the Senate sensing he would not be running for reelection that November. He said later he made the decision over the Christmas holidays—the time he had long reserved for pondering his future—but he didn't announce it publicly until March 4, unusually late in the election cycle. In another account, he said he came to the realization that he would not run again while listening to Bill Clinton deliver his second State of the Union address, on January 25, 1994.

Most of his staff had no idea what he was thinking until he called them together in the Mansfield Room at the Capitol that March day, although his inner circle realized he was indeed pondering retirement. It seems likely Mitchell came to the decision in stages, that he had never seen another six-year term as certain, and that the decision was affected by external as well as internal events. When he did make the announcement, he offered the hope that, with political considerations put aside, he could be more effective in pushing the president's health care legislation through to passage. Whatever its genesis, the decision became part of a web of political events and unanticipated consequences that not only brought to a close a five-year period of extraordinary bipartisan legislative accomplishment, but also marked the effective end of the dominant Democratic majorities in Congress that had lasted for the better part of four decades. In the two decades since, Democrats have controlled the White House and Congress simultaneously for just two years.

In his memoir, Mitchell leads up to his decision to step down by recalling a moment when he "exaggerated to make a point" by constructing a monthly Senate calendar marked with the remaining time slots if all the requests to avoid votes were granted. "As you can see," he said, "they cover only two to six o'clock in the morning, Tuesday through Thursday. So if I accede to all your requests, the Senate can only vote in the middle of the night in the middle of the week!" When one senator, a "good friend," came up afterward and said, "You've got a tough job, but nobody forced you to run for majority leader," Mitchell had to agree—but it's also clear that, the more diligent he was in running the Senate, the more consuming the job became. Nonetheless, his retirement announcement stunned most of his staff, surprised his constituents, and led to later second-guessing about the course he had taken—though Mitchell himself seems to have had few second thoughts.

One thread that led to his departure began with a seemingly casual meeting at the US Open tennis tournament in Queens, New York, the previous summer. Mitchell had untangled a typical snag in the Senate over a routine measure, to grant Most Favored Nation trading status to Romania, which been liberated from dictator Nicolae Ceausescu's rule. There was no objection; the Foreign Relations staff simply hadn't finished the paperwork. The bill was enacted, and Mitchell was touched by profuse thanks from the Romanian delegation, led by tennis star Ion Tiriac. Mitchell got to play in a doubles match with Ilie Nastase, another Romanian star, who had won seven Grand Slam titles in the 1970s. Tiriac also offered tickets to the US Open, which Mitchell declined; he was already attending his first Open with a group of friends, including his brother, Paul. But Tiriac left a phone number in case he changed his mind. After a semifinal match, one of the friends inquired about getting tickets to the finals, and Mitchell called the number. Thirty minutes later, tickets were delivered to his hotel room with a business card from Heather MacLachlan.

At a pre-match reception the next day held by Nastase, Mitchell said he "encountered a tall, very attractive woman with long black hair." Nastase introduced her as Heather MacLachlan, Mitchell thanked her "for the speed and efficiency with which she'd arranged delivery" of the tickets, and his group watched Pete Sampras win the final match. Mitchell checked up on her, finding that she was a Canadian whose ancestors made their way from Scotland to Montreal; Ion Tiriac was a former boyfriend. She was thirty-five; Mitchell was sixty. He discovered that she was "highly regarded" as a tennis promoter, "having been the first woman to represent a male professional player, and she directed several tournaments in Europe." He notes, "The next day I sent her a thank-you note."

Unless Mitchell was being unusually reticent, it wasn't love at first sight. The September 14 note reads, "Thank you for your kindness and assistance during this past weekend. I had a wonderful visit to New York, and I appreciate your help in making my stay so enjoyable. Thanks again, Heather, for your help and hospitality," and signed "With best wishes." A handwritten addition is, "Thanks for the last minute help!" Yet within a week they had dinner, and "within a month we were seeing each other regularly," he wrote. Mitchell even permits himself a rare philosophical reflection. "Life is both a mystery and a surprise. So much that we do, or don't do, is the result of chance, the fickle dictator who rules and roils our lives."

MacLachlan attributes her success in tennis to being able to speak French. "I was sort of a temporary replacement for the assistant to the executive director of the ATP, the Association of Tennis Professionals, and just a lucky break that I think probably wouldn't happen today," she said. "So I was in the right place at the right time basically. It was a very small business. I was fortunate to start when it was making the transition from sport to really big business," in 1979. She was then traveling forty-five weeks a year on tour, with successive home offices in Paris, London, Monaco, and then New York. She said of Mitchell, after she sent the tickets, "ever the gentleman" had told her, 'I'd like to reciprocate the hospitality. If ever you're in DC, I'd like to give you a tour of the Senate." She was traveling there the next week. "We agreed to meet for lunch, and then we met for dinner, and it was after really one dinner I thought, 'Wow, this man's very special.'"

She does not share Mitchell's low opinion of his athletic skills. "I certainly wasn't around those early years when he was playing basketball with his brothers, so I can't pass judgment on those years. But he's a very, very good, unassuming tennis player," she said. "He didn't pick up a racket until he was forty, so his form is perhaps not the best, but he has an incredible focus, and he's smart, and those are things you really need in tennis. You have to strategize and you have to never look back, never worry about the point you missed, and try and keep your cool and to just persevere, one point at a time. And so as a result, he's an incredible tennis player."

It was a long-distance courtship, with MacLachlan continuing to tour and Mitchell leading the Senate. Yet the relationship became serious quickly. "As a matter of fact, we were a little apprehensive to make an announcement, because it was so quick," she said. "We met in September, and it would have been the following spring that we made the announcement, although we'd made the decision together much, much earlier, and we were married the following December."

Politics wasn't a big part of the relationship. "I don't see him as George Mitchell the politician," she said. "He became my husband quite quickly, and his ego is pretty much in check. . . . What makes him so special is that there's a sincerity and a moderation and a sense of humbleness that you don't find in many people anywhere, especially those in positions of power. . . . What struck me immediately that is quite unusual, that he is very consistent. The man you see is the man you get. There's really nothing very hidden about him."

After he made his spring announcements, Mitchell said his impending engagement did not affect his retirement decision, and that MacLachlan had urged him to run for reelection if he wanted to. Behind the scenes, it was more complicated. "When we decided to get married, he was not sure what he wanted to do, whether he wanted to stay, whether he wanted to run for reelection," she said. "I think that obviously had a little bit to do with me. I think he recognized that married life is a strain when you are a public official, and . . . it had affected his first marriage. And he was very committed to this marriage." She also ended up turning down a job prospect, as commissioner of the women's tennis tour, left the business and, after her children entered school, became a literary agent.

Mitchell later admitted personal considerations were a factor in his leaving the Senate. When he turned down a job offer to become president of Disney Entertainment, even before he left the Senate, he said, "I told them that I was really honored and flattered, as I was, but I had made a decision about retiring in part because I was going to get married . . . and my wife-to-be had lived in New York for some time, and she wanted to live there."

Charlene Sturbitts thought personal aspects were paramount. "It was a terrible loss for the Senate, just an immeasurable loss," she said. "But I thought it was terrific that he was going to have more of a personal life, and that's what it appeared was the motivation for him leaving."

Barbara Mikulski remembers the relationship bloomed about the time rumors about Mitchell becoming baseball commissioner were at their peak. She could tell her male Senate colleagues were envious. "The men never said this around me, but they were overheard in the locker room—this spectacular woman, and a little bit younger, and then being baseball commissioner. They thought it was going to be a dream," she said. "Actually, what turned out to be the dream was Heather, and it's just wonderful to see them together and their devotion to each other. . . . I saw this relationship grow, and this wonderful smart, savvy gal, who first of all understands the life that George lives," including service in Northern Ireland and the Middle East. "It was pretty good," Mikulski said. "I thought it was pretty wonderful, actually."

Bob Kerrey retired for similar reasons in 2000, and said he was also affected by Jim Exon's decision to retire four years earlier. "I was about to get married, and the woman I was intending to marry wanted to have a baby," Kerrey said. "And I'd raised two kids in politics, or participated in raising two kids in politics, and I didn't want to do it again."

Bill Cohen also left the Senate, two years after Mitchell, and also was married again the same year, to Janice Langhart, a television journalist, with whom he wrote a book, *Love in Black and White.* Bob Tyrer, his chief of staff, said he was surprised when Mitchell departed, but said, although Cohen was nearly a decade younger, "They were at an age where there's still much to contribute, but if you keep staying for six years at a crack, then the number of sixty-two-year-olds people hire is smaller than the number of fifty-six-year-olds people hire. So I came to have more sympathy for his view that there were other things to do in life." A few months later Cohen was Bill Clinton's secretary of Defense.

A MONTH AFTER MITCHELL ANNOUNCED HIS RETIREMENT, Harry Blackmun decided to leave the Supreme Court at the end of its term. When Byron White retired the previous year, Mitchell had also been sounded out for the appointment, which went to Ruth Bader Ginsburg, but it was just two months into the new administration, and both Clinton and Mitchell recognized it would be an awkward time to replace the Senate leader. This time, Clinton was more determined. He clearly wanted Mitchell on the court.

In his memoir, Mitchell writes, "Early the next week President Clinton called and told me he had decided to nominate me to succeed Blackmun. I thanked him and told him that I was honored and flattered. As a lawyer and a former federal judge, I regarded membership on the Supreme Court as the pinnacle of professional accomplishment." Mitchell said he thought confirmation would be assured, but he raised health care, as he had a month earlier, as a reason not to accept. "For a few days there was speculation in the press about a scheme in which I could be nominated and confirmed, but then delay my departure from the Senate until health care was completed," which, Mitchell said, "I regarded as nonsense."

After a few days considering the offer, Mitchell turned it down. "I told the president that because I thought there was a reasonable chance we could pass a good bill in the Senate, I would stay to finish the fight for health care reform," and said, "While heartened by my assessment of the chances for reform, he was disappointed by my decision." Of his own qualifications, Mitchell said, "While I believed I could do a good job on the court, I knew that there were many others who could serve as well if not better; among them was Stephen Breyer, the man ultimately chosen."

Not many people have turned down a Supreme Court seat; the reaction was swift. Ed King, Mitchell's foreign policy aide, had a typical response when he said, "I was really amazed that he didn't take it," because "all he had to do was say he wanted it." But opinion was divided, even within Mitchell's family.

His brother Robbie thought the Supreme Court was exactly the right way for Mitchell to complete his public service. Robbie's widow, Janet, said he believed Mitchell would be "a ground-breaking jurist" and a rare "man of the people" on the high court. Janet herself wasn't so sure. "I don't think he would have been happy there," she said. "It would be too quiet, too isolated, and not involved with enough different people. He had unique things to offer to the world, and I think he wanted to explore that." Berl Bernhard, his co-manager of the 1972 Muskie campaign and future law partner, said, "The Supreme Court, that damn thing. If George could have been chief justice he might have accepted it, but I don't think he would have otherwise."

Tony Buxton doesn't think Mitchell would have accepted appointment under any circumstances, and sees a parallel between his decision to leave the Senate and not to accept the Supreme Court offer. "He made a decision that he was going to be married, and that was more important," Buxton said. "The wonderful irony of George Mitchell's life, is that here's this person blessed with such an analytical mind that it was almost his entire person for the early part of his political career, and then what bloomed in him, because of defeat, was a great emotional capacity, to the point where he treasured love over fame."

On March 12, David Souter, whose Supreme Court nomination Mitchell steered through the Senate in 1990—despite opposition from the National Organization for Women, he was confirmed 90-9—responded to Mitchell's retirement a week earlier with a handwritten note. He thought Mitchell might have a judicial appointment in his future—in contrast to his friend Tom Rath, another former New Hampshire attorney general and Republican kingmaker, who had helped quell Republican doubts about Souter. "Tom Rath and I agree that the Senate is about to take too heavy a hit. We part company on what should happen after that. I hope you'll move over to this side of First Street. Tom hopes you'll become baseball commissioner so he can be your deputy (i.e., can muscle you out and succeed you in the job). Whatever you do, I hope you'll have the joy and satisfaction I wish for you. Grateful as I am for your service to us all."

WHEN THE STAFF ENTERED THE MANSFIELD ROOM, a grand, ornate, high-ceilinged chamber on the Senate side of the Capitol, few of them knew exactly why they were there, though there was a sense of foreboding. Chris Williams said the meeting was called hastily; although the only staff members who'd been given the news were Martha Pope, John Hilley, Mary McAleney, Larry Benoit, and Diane Dewhirst, Benoit realized someone was spreading the word in Maine, and it would be only hours before reporters started calling. Williams, who was to be married in three weeks, said, "As soon as I entered the room I knew something was up." She huddled with Steve Hart and "a handful of us who had been with him for ten years," and when she heard him say, "I'm not going to run again," she said, "I was in complete and total shock. It was as though a bomb had gone off." As the news began to register, she said, "I remember thinking, 'This is what death is like.' And I say that because it's like you know someday you're going to die, but you don't really believe it, you're in denial. You have to be in denial, or you wouldn't go on." She had thought, in a general way, that "Someday I wouldn't be working for Mitchell anymore. I'm sure there'll be a day when I'll get another job, or he'd leave the Senate. But when that day came, it was like, 'This is it; it's over.' I just sobbed, I sort of get choked up even thinking about it now."

Jeff Peterson had a cooler reaction. He remembers the "funny chairs" in the Mansfield Room, "they were kind of gilded, and sort of lined up." He said, "And we just filed in and we were all sitting, waiting, and then Senator Mitchell came out and gave a nice talk, explained he was retiring. We were all pretty stunned. . . . Here he was, in a very important, powerful position in the Senate, and really, to all appearances, absolutely on top of his game. . . . And it never occurred to me that he wouldn't be there for a long time." Peterson was in the last row, and, he said, "Maybe we all still had kind of stunned expressions on our faces when he finished and he was getting ready to leave." Peterson decided it was one of those rare occasions where Mitchell had miscalculated his effect on an audience. "For whatever reason, he was walking by, or he stopped to answer a question, and he put his arm on my shoulder. That was not something he would usually do, or ever, and I think it was a little gesture of conciliation. He knew he'd delivered hard news, because we all understood this was changing everything . . . but he was trying to offer some kind of statement about how important the collective group of us [was] to him. It certainly made me feel better about the whole idea."

Grace Reef's reaction was more like Chris Williams's. "I hadn't been thinking at all about what I would do next. I was totally shocked," she said. "It was like someone had died." Anita Jensen, who was sitting nearby and saw her crying, told her to brace up. Some of the staff began to leave during the remainder of the year, but Reef said she "stayed to the end. I didn't want to leave. I didn't want to move on."

Mitchell wasn't as calm as he looked. In his book, *Making Peace*, he said that when he was taping the announcement to be broadcast back in Maine, he uncharacteristically had to do three takes. "I found, to my surprise, that it was hard to say the words now, when it really counted, as opposed to when I had been just thinking about it."

His Senate colleagues had varied reactions. Jim Sasser, who was close to him, saw the price Mitchell paid because of the way he chose to do his job. "The majority leader really has no rewards to give or punishment to mete out, to bring people along . . . on votes that are politically risky; it's a difficult process," he said. "If you get elected, that bolsters the ego, and of course a lot of the folks who get there had a pretty substantial ego in the first place. . . . George was very patient. He'd listen to them, sort of like a psychiatrist giving them oral therapy sometimes; he'd listen and slowly bring them along. Some were more difficult than others. Some almost drove him to distraction. The truth is, you could see George aging as majority leader. It really took a toll on him."

Bob Kerrey felt the loss immediately. "I was somewhere between surprised and very disappointed," he said. "When you've got a leader and the leader walks off the field, that was a difficult moment for us." Barbara Mikulski's response was more like that of Mitchell's staff. "I couldn't believe it," she said. "He was a very good leader, and we were more than satisfied with his leadership." Harris Wofford, among those senators defeated for reelection that November, summed up his reaction as "sorrow," but said, "He retired with dignity."

Southern caucus members emphasized a sense of personal, rather than political, loss. John Breaux was among those encouraged to run as Mitchell's successor, but decided he was too conservative. The retirement "was very unusual for a majority leader who had the support of the caucus. No one was ever going to run against him. . . . Maybe he just felt there were other ways to provide public service." Bob Graham said Mitchell "should be remembered as one of the great Senate majority leaders. And had he decided to continue, chances are that he would be the majority leader today. I was never quite clear as to why George retired as early as he did." Howell Heflin spoke about Mitchell near the end of the session, on October 7, saying, "Although he has only been majority leader since 1989, he has in those short five years become synonymous with the body like few others have, and we have come to take him for granted in many ways. When most people use the term 'partisan,' they do so in the pejorative sense. They use it to imply blind allegiance to a political party or cause, without regard to right and wrong, or what is in the best interest of the country as a whole. Senator George John Mitchell, however, is a partisan in the very best sense of the term—in the sense that was meant before it became distorted by the politics of obstruction and destruction."

Republicans also saw him through the lens of their own experience. Warren Rudman, who worked with Mitchell on the Iran-Contra committee and again after their Senate years, served only two terms himself, retiring in 1992. "I remember George was shocked when I announced I wasn't running," Rudman said. He wasn't surprised by Mitchell's decision, and said, "You're trying to run a place that's run, so-called, by the inmates, and that's hard to do." Rudman said, "I think what I did had some influence on him." Alan Simpson did register surprise, but said, "When I got to '96 and wanted to retire myself, I wasn't surprised at all, because it's like wearing away a rock, and with George, I'm sure it was the same way."

Ted Stevens, who despite their occasional clashes had a soft spot for Mitchell, wrote a note on March 7. "You have made the right decision, but I'll miss you next year," he wrote. "In 1984, when I was sixty, I told Howard Baker I would retire that year. He talked to me for two hours about why I needed to stay. Obviously, I stayed and he didn't! Since I have a few years more on my life than you do, my advice to you is to find a wife. None of my business, but as I look back at my life, I was rudderless after Ann was killed in an airplane crash. My grandmother used to tell me that women are hard to live with, but it's harder to live without them." Stevens served until 2009, completing forty years in the Senate, and was himself killed in an airplane crash in 2010.

Tom Daschle, who succeeded Mitchell as leader, was more surprised than anyone. "It just shocked me, because I was sure he was going to run, it was just assumed, and he was a relatively young man at the time," he said. After serving ten years as leader, Daschle found, "It's one of the toughest political jobs in Washington. You don't have nearly the support that a president does, but you have many of the same roles." He now sees Mitchell might have "felt somewhat relieved to turn over all of this to somebody else, but there's always a bit of reluctance, a sense of disappointment that you're leaving."

Mitchell has rarely discussed his decision to step down. He has said he might have sought one more term if he didn't continue as leader. Like Robert Byrd, he might have considered an important committee chairmanship had one been available, but none was. One of his few regrets was the impact on Maine. In an interview with Jim Brunelle in the *Portland Press Herald* published December 1, he said, "Because of my position, I've been able to be very helpful to Maine. I thought that if I leave, nobody is going to be in precisely that same position. But then I decided that if I succumbed to that logic, I could never leave." Others have not been shy, though, about speculating.

Working with Bill Clinton couldn't have been easy, not only because Clinton's lack of experience in Washington led to difficulties in the crucial first months, but because Clinton did not often show the discipline to proceed, step by step, through the difficulties of the legislative maze. Mitchell had made his own decisions for four years; now, he had to defer to a much younger president who reached the White House more through charm and magnetism than steady political achievement. Yet no one has detected a hint of disloyalty from Mitchell toward Clinton; their relations have remained cordial, and it seems unlikely the relationship played any significant part in Mitchell's retirement.

Mitchell's brother John was characteristically blunt when he recently assessed the reasons. "He did want to make more money," he said, and Mitchell had expressed concern about providing for his new family. In a note to his brother at the time, John sounded plaintive, writing a postscript, "I hate giving up being an important guy in DC. The legend of Swisher will fade away!!"

Gary Myrick, the young aide who sometimes drove Mitchell home when sessions ran late, remembers one night, when "neither of us [was] especially chatty, especially at midnight or whenever it was." Myrick asked him if he was having any fun, and Mitchell said, "No, it's really not that much fun." Myrick thought of that conversation on March 4. "Being senator could be a great job. I'm not sure about being majority leader," he said. "It's a very, very, very lonely job, where you have all the responsibility and none of the tools to actually get the job done except for sheer will and hard work. And after a time, it will drag you down." Tom Allen, who was elected to Congress in 1996, but saw Mitchell in Washington before that, called it "a killing job." He once asked Mitchell how he was doing. The reply was, "I'm just trying to figure out how to keep doing this job." Allen said, "You could see the pressure, the weariness almost at times, that comes from doing a job that requires that much intensity, emotion, concentration over such a long period of time."

Scott Hutchinson, who'd worked on all of Mitchell's campaigns, had a different perspective. Hutchinson thought Mitchell changed, "and became a different person in terms of his wishes or desires, thought process and his commitment," he said. "After he got to be the Senate majority leader, after the bloom wore off the rose, he didn't care about it anymore." Anita Jensen said Mitchell told her, when he retired, that "the thing he hated most about being majority leader was that the guys, meaning the senators, would bring their personal problems to him, and he really hated being Dear Abby." Larry Benoit said he had the same impression. "It was a job that had become all-consuming, and it wasn't sustainable," he said. "That's what happens to really talented people—they just get more and more work piled on them. I know his colleagues called upon him for lots of advice that had nothing to do with legislative issues, personal stuff. He'd tell me he'd leave the Senate at ten o'clock at night, and at eleven his phone was ringing at home. So it was a grind."

DURING HIS LAST TWO YEARS IN OFFICE, Mitchell worked persistently on legislation he hoped might be a legacy, an issue that had concerned him since he was first elected—campaign finance reform. The high-water mark for reform came right after the Watergate scandal in the form of the Federal Election Campaign Act of 1974, which established voluntary public financing for presidential elections that, for a time, took most of the private money out of top-of-the-ticket races. Had it been in place two years earlier, it would have immeasurably helped Ed Muskie's cash-strapped campaign, and it played a significant part in elevating Jimmy Carter in the Democratic field of 1976. At least through the 1984 election, the system worked smoothly for presidential races, with major party nominees, and most primary candidates, accepting federal funding and the attached spending limits. But the Supreme Court, through its curious 1976 decision in *Buckley v. Valeo*, which left in place contribution limits while striking down spending limits, created unintended consequences in another portion of the 1974 law, one that created political action committees. PACs, for post-Watergate reformers, were a means of creating greater accountability through required disclosure of campaign contributions. They were included in response to the virtual shakedowns of corporate donors by the Nixon White House that led to felony convictions for a number of business owners. By eliminating spending limits, *Buckley v. Valeo* invited "bundling" of contributions to create rapidly growing pots of campaign cash.

By the mid-1980s, Democrats were moving to rein in PAC spending and tighten contribution limits. The early leader was Senator David Boren, a conservative from Oklahoma who won the support of Majority Leader Robert Byrd, who in turn tried to force action in the 1987 session, but failed to overcome a filibuster despite eight attempts. At the most heated point, Byrd ordered marshals to carry Bob Packwood to the floor, after the ranking Finance Republican refused to appear for a vote. Mitchell inherited the legislation from Byrd and was, if anything, even more committed to reform, though he didn't employ Byrd's tactics.

Fred Wertheimer was president of Common Cause, and de facto leader of a large coalition supporting campaign finance reform. He regarded Mitchell as his most steadfast and unstinting ally. Wertheimer recalled how close Congress had come to creating a public financing system for its own elections; in 1974, the amendment passed the Senate but fell short in the House. Fifteen years later, Common Cause was still battling just to get back to that point. The organization was founded by John Gardner in 1970 as a "citizens' lobby," after Gardner decided, "Everyone's organized but the people." Its first major goal was ending the American role in Vietnam. "As I have pointed out," Wertheimer said, "I stopped working on the Vietnam War in 1975, and unfortunately I've never got to stop on campaign finance reform. John Gardner used to say reform is not for the short-winded, but he never told me it was thirty-seven years and counting."

Wertheimer had high hopes for Mitchell's effort. "He had a very straight-forward style of communicating, soft-spoken in many ways, and was extremely tough-minded, both in terms of his view about public policy and his leadership capacity with the Democratic Conference. He had a real combination of leader-ship skills, and a patience to build what you had to build to get to the end of the game." Wertheimer observed, "His opponents, particularly Republican opponents, always thought of him as a very tough partisan, but that was not the way he came across publicly. The tough partisan aspects came into play when-ever he was involved in fights with them, because he was very strong and very strategic, and very effective, in my view."

It took several tries, but by 1991 reform legislation had come into focus. There were three key elements: The first was a prototype for public financing of congressional races—a modest start creating a precedent to build on. Sec-ond came tougher disclosure requirements and contribution limits for PACs. The third was a ban on "soft money," another financing innovation intended to get around contribution limits. "Soft money" involved PAC and individual contributions routed through state party organizations, then redeployed back into congressional races. The courts upheld the end run, and, absent further action from Congress, the loophole was growing rapidly. While by today's standards, the amounts raised in the 1980s seem quaintly small, there was rising public concern, and demands for action, which Mitchell intended to harness. The main vehicle in the 1991–1992 Congress was the Boren-Mitchell bill, and Common Cause and the reform lobby got all of the major presidential primary candidates to endorse it; along with deficit reduction, campaign reform was also Ross Perot's signature issue. Late in 1992, enough Republicans came on board to enact the bill, though they knew it faced a likely veto from President Bush, which he supplied.

Along with two others bills Bush vetoed—the Family and Medical Leave Act, and the "motor voter" registration bill to enlist state motor vehicle agencies in signing up new voters—campaign finance reform was supposed to be atop the congressional agenda for 1993; Clinton pledged to sign all three. But while the first two were swiftly enacted, campaign reform languished. The problem was not with the bill, nor the schedule, but with House Speaker Tom Foley. Wertheimer said, "Foley, who one would not describe as an assertive speaker on most occasions, basically said to the president, 'Don't tell us when to deal with the issue, we'll decide when to deal with it. You've got the budget to deal with, you've got health care, this is about us.'" Foley kept the bill in committee until December 1993, even after Clinton finally introduced his health care plan. Wertheimer was frustrated that Clinton, after submitting a strong bill in April and urging Congress to act, "disappeared on the issue for the rest of the session. He basically didn't lift a finger to help get this done. If he had, I think we would have gotten it done." Mitchell moved the Senate bill to the floor in June, but that created another dilemma.

There was a split between House and Senate Democrats on reform. House members liked the idea of public financing, which would come with free or low-cost television time; fund-raising occupied an inordinate portion of their two-year terms, and most House incumbents didn't have access to big donors, who were focused on Senate races. House members were more dependent on PAC contributions, and resisted any new limits. Senators, by contrast, were suspicious of public financing, because even small-state senators had national appeal, and incumbents had huge financial advantages. PAC limits concerned them less, because expanding their donor base was relatively easy.

Mitchell took vote counts, assessed the possibilities, and called in Wertheimer. Republicans were already filibustering, and, Mitchell told him, "We can't break this filibuster. We either have to drop public financing or we're going to have to pull this bill." Wertheimer asked for time to get more Republicans to support ending the filibuster, with the bill put on hold. But Mitchell said, "We can't do that. If we pull the bill, it's not coming back in this Congress." Wertheimer still wasn't convinced, and said, "We have a Democratic Congress, and a Democratic president. Everyone's on record saying they want to do this, and we have to keep fighting." Mitchell disagreed. He suggested passing the bill in the Senate, sending it to the House to see if it could add public financing, then going to conference and getting Senate negotiators to accept limited public financing. Mitchell said, "I'm not making this decision. This is your decision, and I need the answer tomorrow."

Wertheimer said, "I'd never run into something like this before. We had a very large coalition . . . and I had to make a decision." If he called a meeting, he knew it would quickly turn to quarreling, but if he didn't consult his partners, "They would be furious." Finally, after consulting Boren and a few key allies, Wertheimer agreed to the Senate version without public financing, igniting the reaction among reformers he'd foreseen. Foley still refused to schedule a vote for another five months. Wertheimer saw Majority Leader Dick Gephardt as more likely to stand up to dissident Democrats pressuring Foley. He knew Gephardt supported public financing, and made his case. "You guys are crazy," he told Gephardt. "The institution needs this system, and everyone's going to do OK. Democrats always think the Republicans will kill them under any system, and

Republicans always think that any limits on money are going to kill them, and everyone gets it wrong. . . . The real issue with public financing is it provides substantial resources to run against incumbents, and it's an incumbency issue, not a party issue." He realized, listening to Gephardt, that this was exactly the point: "Underlying all of this was the notion that the Democrats had been in power for forty years, and things were just fine, and why should we rock the boat?" After the Republican landslide in 1994, he saw Gephardt again, who told him, "Well, I guess we made a mistake." Later, Wertheimer said, Gephardt provided crucial support in enacting the soft-money ban contained in the McCain-Feingold Act as of 2002, but in 1994, "They just sat there, and wouldn't enter into a deal."

Mitchell wasn't giving up, despite the long delays, but new obstacles were emerging. State party chairs, taking in the implications of the soft-money ban, were organizing against reform. Labor unions were incensed about PAC limits. In the early years, unions were reasonably successful in competing against corporate PACs, and in some key races felt their PAC money had made the difference. Mitchell assigned Bob Rozen to run the numbers on various versions of the bill, and, though Rozen had no previous experience in the area, he learned quickly. Rozen said Mitchell opposed the use of soft money as DSCC chair, and felt even more strongly about it as leader. "What motivated Mitchell was he thought it was very bad for the system, very bad for Congress, and for presidential candidates to be taking this kind of money," Rozen said. "He also felt that fundamentally, long term, there's always a lot more rich people, and corporations, who support Republicans, and we're never going to be able to win that game."

Rozen attended many stormy meetings. "Mitchell came under a huge amount of pressure from labor, and from Democratic officials, national party, and state parties, they just thought we were idiots, they thought we didn't know what we were doing," he said. Rozen contrasted this experience with his day job, on Finance, where "Everyone tells you how great you are, how smart you are, they kiss up to you, but on campaign finance issues all I had was people telling me I was an idiot. . . . I was destroying the party, I was destroying labor, I was destroying Emily's List—at the time, a new PAC supporting liberal women. When McCain-Feingold finally passed, Rozen said, "It democratized the system . . . and the gratifying thing was, the Democratic Party did better than ever. The Internet was developed and it was easier to raise money from average people, but I also think people are more inclined to give if they think their giving makes a difference. And if they see wealthy people and corporations giving money, enormous sums of money, their attitude is, they don't need my money because they've got this big money."

At the peak of lobbying by Democratic constituencies, Mitchell got a letter from forty-eight state Democratic Party chairs protesting the soft-money ban. The only states not signing were Maine and Utah; Wertheimer said the Utah chair had been a Common Cause board member. Rozen recalls two meetings in particular. The first, involving labor, began with Mitchell and Martha Pope joining him, "and they were just irate, and they were not shy about it, they were quite vociferous." After ten minutes, Mitchell was called to the floor, Pope went with him, and Rozen was left as the sole target.

The second meeting, with state party chairs, was preceded by a session with Sam Gejdenson, a House Democrat from Connecticut who passionately opposed reform. "Gejdenson couldn't stop talking," Rozen said, "and Mitchell was trying to read a briefing to prepare for the meeting and Sam Gejdenson just wouldn't shut up, and finally I asked Mitchell if he wanted me to tell Sam to shut up. . . . Finally he shut up, Mitchell read it, we went in, and the state parties yelled at us as well." Mitchell, Rozen said, "showed a lot of bravery on this. He did the right thing. It was something he really believed in, and he struggled to bring everybody else along, particularly Gephardt and some key members of his caucus."

The House finally passed a relatively weak bill in October 1994, and pushed for a conference, which Mitchell knew was futile because Republicans would filibuster the conference report. Nonetheless, he did what he was asked. "He was a great leader on this," Wertheimer said. "He managed the conference on this, and he managed it well." When the bill returned, Republicans killed it. Sam Gejdenson was one Democrat who survived that November, winning reelection by four votes among 186,000 cast.

Wertheimer said the McCain-Feingold bill that passed eight years later was essentially the same, minus public financing, as the Boren-Mitchell bill that failed in 1994. By then, he said, PAC spending had tripled. "We could have established the principle of congressional public financing, at a minimum in the House, we could have established free TV time, and ended the soft-money system eight years earlier," he said. In 2010, the Supreme Court swept away the contribution limits of McCain-Feingold and almost all other limitations on individual spending in its *Citizens United v. Federal Election Commission* decision, overturning dozens of state statutes in the process.

In March, Mitchell had little idea what the coming year might bring, and it's unlikely it was at the forefront of his concerns. Political service, and retirement from political service, represents an intensely personal decision rarely influenced by questions of "what if." But if Mitchell failed to make such calculations in the spring, by fall he was well aware what was happening. He has rarely commented on politics, as such, since leaving the Senate, though he does use his historian's eye when asked to. A rare glimpse is provided in his 1997 book, *Not for America Alone*, which he began planning just after the 1994 elections. He focused not on the politics surrounding Newt Gingrich's takeover of the House Republican leadership, which was well under way during the last Congress in which Mitchell served, but on the campaign document that represented his program, the Contract with America.

Mitchell writes, "Many Republicans have claimed that in November 1994, American voters repudiated the New Deal and all it stands for—particularly the role that government plays in American society. The Republicans' "Contract with America"—which called for deregulation of an overly regulated economy, downsizing government, "devolutionizing" duties to states and cities and away from the federal government, privatizing tasks the government now does, term limits, a balanced budget amendment to the Constitution, and reducing Medicare spending, even as more Americans become eligible—was effectively marketed as something the American people wanted enacted into law."

Commentary on the Contract that fall emphasized that it was "poll-tested," and only elements that got 60 percent from voter surveys were included. Mitchell debunks that claim. "Wholly apart from the wisdom of legislating by public opinion poll, the assertions of support for the Contract were untrue," Mitchell said—crediting "an enterprising reporter named Frank Greve" from Knight-Ridder for asking follow-up questions, and getting the pollster, Frank Luntz, to admit he'd done the survey "for himself," and who said the polling materials were "private information." The Republican National Committee switched tracks and claimed there was no polling, that "We did what we did because it was good policy, not because it was popular," said RNC communications chief Chuck Greener.

Greve's story appeared a year after the election, and, Mitchell notes, wasn't followed up by the Associated Press, *New York Times*, or *Washington Post*. Nor did the account change the existing story line. When Haynes Johnson and David Broder published *The System* in 1996, they presented the health care battle as an epic contest of Americans' vision of the future as enunciated by Gingrich and Clinton, with the outcome still in doubt. Gingrich, however, resigned his speakership and seat in Congress in 1998, shortly after the political gains he promised Republicans if they impeached Clinton failed to materialize.

Mitchell didn't doubt the outcome of this contest over the future of government. "We should not confuse novelty with change," he said. In his book, he mounted another defense of New Deal values. "Roosevelt brought about true change when he provided a degree of stability to the lives of ordinary citizens. Instead of destitution after job loss, Americans could count on unemployment insurance to help tide them over. Instead of an old age of indigence and loss of self-respect, Americans could build on the base that Social Security assured them." In contrast, "Nothing in the Contract carried similar assurances. Nothing in the Contract altered the relationship of today's working families with the economy, with their workplaces, with their status in our society. And to the degree that some elements of the Contract threatened to reduce the scope of the social safety net, it represented a threat to families' economic security. By targeting laws and regulations that protect our health and safety, the Contract revealed its desire to reestablish conditions that earlier generations repudiated. But in the end, it was the Contract itself that was repudiated." Only one item in the Contract—a pledge that the federal government abide by the laws it applies to private entities—was ever enacted. Mitchell concludes, "We are passing through a period when, for political purposes, enemies must be created in the absence of real ones. A decade ago it was Soviet power. Today it's government itself."

But in the moment, Mitchell had ceded his own power. Chris Williams reports that Mitchell, after a negotiating session involving Gingrich on health care in 1994, "came back really shaken," and told her, "The Republicans just want to kill whatever the Democrats propose." Charlene Sturbitts had deplored declining interest in legislation among senators much earlier. "Staff take their lead from their member, and a member who wants to legislate has to have a staff to actually accomplish that," she said. "And if your senator is more into sound bites than legislating, then you're not going to learn how to do it."

Carl Levin sounded a warning a week before the 1994 election. In a floor statement, the Michigan Democrat said, "The recent Gingrich-style GOP— Gridlock-Only Party—is on a collision course with traditions of compromise and conciliation. The victims of this collision won't just be members of Congress; they'd be all of us. If our government can't work for the common good, then all Americans suffer and the United States is weakened."

Though Bob Dole remained Republican Senate leader, and perhaps owed his majority to Gingrich's campaign, Alan Simpson was deemed not conservative enough to remain whip, and lost the position he'd held for eight years to Trent Lott in a 27–26 caucus vote; Lott became leader when Dole resigned in 1996 to pursue his presidential bid. Simpson was typically droll in his assessment: "We all knew that Newtie Gingrich could throw firebombs from the top of the castle steps and the parapet, with a catapult." Nor was Dole impressed by the new

House speaker's abilities. At an early meeting, Gingrich complained that people seemed to take an instant dislike to him, almost as soon as they met him. "Why do they do that?" he asked Dole. The reply was, "It saves time."

The Contract with America was one cause of the Democrats' 1994 electoral debacle. Another was their own disarray. But Mitchell thinks one factor that came into play had nothing to do with Gingrich—the Senate's filibuster rule. "When you're an individual senator and a filibuster occurs, you just go do other things usually, unless you're involved in the issue," he said. "But when you're majority leader, you've got to deal with the problem. It's an enormous issue." Mitchell researched the subject. "In the one hundred years between 1800 and 1900, there were about sixteen filibusters in the Senate," he said. "In the last two years of my tenure as Senate majority leader, 1993 and 1994, I filed motions to invoke cloture . . . more than seventy times." Mitchell was amazed at the lengths to which Republicans would go to tie up business. One military nominee "was going to be elevated from two-star general to three-star general, and those have to go through the Senate, and usually they're done in a routine manner," he said, but a late filibuster blocked the promotion. "The Republicans had a very clear strategy," Mitchell said, "and that was to prevent anything from happening in the Senate and then claim Democrats couldn't get anything done. It sounds cynical, and I guess it is. Although both sides have done it at various times, the most difficult part to accept is that it clearly worked." In his view, this episode started the filibuster wars that raged in subsequent sessions, and continued afterward. "What really changed is attitude," Mitchell said. "The Senate has always had its rules and its procedural mechanisms, which if exploited to the hilt, could be used for delay and obstruction. But there was a sense of institutional loyalty, of comity, of accommodation, in which senators refrained from using every mechanism for obstruction . . . and that gradually eroded." At the end of the 1994 session, Republicans were threatening to filibuster even naming members for conferences with the House.

Tom Daschle, who defeated Chris Dodd by one vote to become Mitchell's successor, thought there was another overlooked factor—the House Bank scandal. While the House institution, which the Senate has never adopted, didn't resemble a bank in any real sense, revelations about casual practices that allowed members to overdraw their accounts proved damaging. "It was mostly Democrats, and so it was viewed as a Democratic scandal, and that also was catalytic in bringing about a change in mood," Daschle said.

The failure to enact health care was the most visible shortfall as the election came on, but there were plenty of other possibilities, particularly the Clinton budget that had raised the income tax and gasoline tax. The omnibus crime bill had dozens of new penalties and longer sentences, but all the controversy was about the "assault weapons" ban Dianne Feinstein insisted be included. Harris Wofford was convinced it was responsible for his defeat in Pennsylvania. "We wanted her to bring it up after the election," he said. "I am a great friend of Dianne's, and people pleaded with her . . . but she passionately believed in it. I had no choice but to vote for the ban," he said. "But that turned it into a real gun owners' crusade against me."

In Maine, Mitchell had also unintentionally handicapped his potential successors among Democrats, in part by the late retirement announcement. First District Congressman Tom Andrews, an avowed liberal in his second term, quickly jumped in, but he had a fatal flaw. To demonstrate his commitment to reducing defense spending, Andrews, alone among the delegation, voted in favor of the 1991 base-closing commission list that included Loring Air Force Base. While not likely to hurt him in his own district, it made him hugely unpopular among voters in the Second District, where the base had just closed. Olympia Snowe, who had waited for this opportunity for twelve years, and had served sixteen years in the House, was the easy winner. By giving up his seat, Andrews opened the way for Jim Longley Jr., son of the former governor, a Republican, who pulled off an upset in the First District, though he lost the seat two years later to Tom Allen, more moderate than Andrews.

The lone success in Congress for Maine Democrats that November was in the Second District, where Mitchell's nephew, Jim, faced state senator John Baldacci, his cousin, in the primary. Baldacci won the primary, enlisted Mitchell's help, and was elected in November, serving eight years in Congress and two terms as governor. Larry Benoit, who'd left Maine to serve just over a year as Senate sergeant at arms, stayed in Washington and became Baldacci's chief of staff. "We pulled in a lot of Mitchell people," Baldacci said. "I was very lucky to be able to have that as an advantage." He was one of just two Democratic freshmen to win a previously Republican seat that year.

As MITCHELL PREPARED TO LEAVE OFFICE, the tributes began. Bob Carolla was among the few called to the Mansfield Room who'd figured out what Mitchell was going to do. "The announcement was one of the times when I felt proudest of him," he said. "He showed a strength of following his own star in ways that were unpredictable. Who leaves at the top of their game? Well, sometimes that's the best time to leave." Carolla himself later moved to the National Alliance on Mental Illness as communications director. He remembers Martha Pope, shortly after Mitchell's announcement and the annual salary review, saying, "Congratulations. The good news is that you've gotten a raise in pay. The bad news is, you don't have a job." Carolla still thinks Mitchell made the right decision. "Some of the senators who are still there, who are or have been in positions of power, are in their seventies or even eighties. And I think the place does something to you. I'm just proud of Mitchell that he didn't buy into that."

The *Maine Sunday Telegram* published a special section that included responses from national leaders. Bob Dole said, "When future historians write about the office of majority leader, I think they will conclude that one of the most effective senators to serve in that office was my friend, George Mitchell." Dick Gephardt said Mitchell "is a man who gives politics a good name." Bill Cohen observed, "The fact that he can put up with ninety-nine inseparable egos . . . marks him as one of the truly extraordinary human beings on the planet." George H. W. Bush offered a conventional tribute, though he did say, "under that friendly veneer, there was steadfast partisan opposition." Bill Clinton was expansive. "He has this almost magical blend of ability and discipline, of pragmatism and principle, of flexibility and fight. His powers of concentration and persuasion are legend. He really does bring a sense of balance to every debate. No matter how strongly I feel something, if he thinks I'm wrong I'm afraid to talk to him, because I think there's a 90 percent chance he will convince me I had it wrong all along." Clinton connected Mitchell to his roots. "You can't be an immigrant's child in this country and become majority leader of the Senate . . . without knowing your primary obligation is not to solve every problem that's before us, but to leave this country well-enough off that the American dream is still alive for everyone that comes after us. I have known very few Americans that remotely embody the quality of this country in the purest sense as well as George Mitchell."

There were private tributes, too. Birch Bayh, the senator from Indiana who served three terms and was defeated for reelection the year Mitchell joined the Senate, wrote on April 4: "I must confess that I have mixed feelings on hearing the news. Part of me thinks from the public perspective, the Senate will not be the same without your strong and perceptive leadership. You have provided a persuasive voice for all of the big issues of importance to our country. In this time, particularly, you convey trust and believability." Bayh also said, "The other part of my mind thinks like a friend and as a private person who has some small idea of the kind of burden you have been carrying. . . . There comes a time when it's right and human to say 'enough.' You made the decision voluntarily; the people of Indiana made it for me. However, as I look back to those days, as much as I wanted to win . . . the people made the choice that was best for me personally. Of course, I miss seeing you and the 'troops' regularly. When a Clarence Thomas comes along, I wish . . . ! But you can bet I don't miss fund-raising and those backbreaking schedules."

Nancy Chandler, who had known the Mitchells since Waterville days, also penned a letter, on March 20: "Bruce and I were so happy for you when we learned about your decision to hang up the Senate career. It is tough to walk away from a seat of such political power, and all of those wonderfully bright people on your staff. It takes strength, and we applaud you! You have given much to Maine and our country. You have brought public respect to your office and work—a challenge for any politico these days!" And she went back to the beginning. "Your announcement caused me to reflect on a conversation I had with Prin and Swisher some thirty-two years ago. We were living upstairs at 14 West Street, and they were so excited you were coming back to Maine to pursue a political career. I can remember John saying, 'George will be governor of this state someday,' and how surprised we were, never having met you. I thought to myself, he'll have to get by Bruce Chandler first! It wasn't many years later we were talking about your becoming president someday. A guy from Arkansas intervened. There are lots of twists on the road, and we never know what the next bend will bring." It was still before Mitchell's engagement announcement, and she said, "For you, I wish a life of fulfillment and joy and hope as you enter the last quarter you can take it a little easier, and perhaps have time for a partner to enjoy it with you. It is one of life's supreme joys."

Mitchell became more reflective once he again had time to himself. He often recalled his friendship with Marshall Stern, the lawyer from Bangor who Mitchell said "had a very great and generous heart. He was forever contributing to good causes, and trying to get me involved." Mitchell also knew Stern's father, Ed, one of Muskie's most devoted supporters. Mitchell loved to tell a story about Ed Stern, who routinely allowed Democrats to put his name on ballots for the Legislature, never suspecting that anything would come of it. But in 1964, with the Johnson landslide, he was elected and quipped, "I demand a recount!"

Mitchell had delivered the eulogy at Ed Stern's funeral and, six months after Mitchell left the Senate, Marshall Stern was killed in what Mitchell called "a horrific automobile accident" that also severely injured his son, Jason. The crash had occurred after Jason, a budding photographer, had returned to Maine from Israel, and they were delivering legal papers to meet a deadline. On their way home to Bangor, their car was demolished by a pickup truck that veered into their lane. Mitchell gave the eulogy at Marshall's funeral. Jason Stern went back to law school, but things weren't right. "For a variety of reasons which I don't really know or fully understand," Mitchell said, Jason took his own life. In his memoir, Mitchell suggests the young man suffered from survivor's guilt. The two occupants of the other vehicle were also killed; he was the only one who lived. "It was impossible to adequately describe the sadness and sense of loss that enveloped Jason's funeral as I delivered yet another eulogy," he wrote. Remembering his friend Marshall Stern, Mitchell said, "There's hardly a day goes by that I don't think of him, particularly when I'm on Mount Desert Island in the summer, because Marshall had a home there, and he introduced me [to the island]."

Mary McAleney didn't entirely like the talk about retirement because, she said, she didn't believe Mitchell ever saw himself leaving public life. "It wasn't his intention to retire, it was to do other things with his life," she said. "He saw that in six years, there would be other doors that would be closed. I always expected him to look for something new to do, something more to learn, to tackle yet another unsolved challenge." Don Nicoll saw Mitchell's decision as one that distinguished him from Muskie who, Nicoll said, "never had a career plan." Nicoll said, "A key to understanding George, in addition to his intellectual capacity and his affability and his desire to be liked, which were driving forces for him, was his enjoyment of being in the world of the power brokers, and a drive to succeed financially as well as professionally. You can just see that throughout his career."

Mitchell's peers evaluated him as a leader differently than outsiders. Bob Kerrey said, "The changes in the law that he brought to bear were significant in and of themselves, so he's got a significant legacy of accomplishment." Kerrey's next observation concerned education. "George prided himself on giving commencement addresses, and my guess is there are young people who were in those audiences who had their lives changed by his words and presence and deeds." Finally, Kerrey said he and others asked themselves, "I wonder if George Mitchell would do it this way?" He added, "'You're behaving like George Mitchell' is a compliment, a high compliment."

Republicans also observed him closely. Alan Simpson thought Mitchell was tougher than Howard Baker, saying, "Baker was just one of the most popular leaders of all time, a very wonderful guy with patience, great patience, like George, but without the sometimes hardness that George would come to where he said, 'This has to be done.'" For Bob Tyrer, Mitchell's leadership harked back to Lyndon Johnson. "Mitchell became leader during the last period of time where the job was as significant as it once was under Senator Johnson. . . . I think he caught the last tail of what has now become a truly hellish and thankless job that you can tell, with all due respect, does not tend to be held by hugely distinguished individuals." Steve Symms, who knew Baker, Byrd, Dole, and Mitchell during a relatively brief Senate career, saw Byrd and Dole as alike in their intense focus on the Senate as a life unto itself. Baker, he said, "respected the fact that people had lives and people wanted to get home for the weekend," a trait Mitchell shared. "With George, it was nice to be in the Senate when you had a leader who actually realized some people had other things in their life they wanted to do."

A FINAL QUESTION ABOUT MITCHELL'S SENATE YEARS is why he never ran for president. Many on his staff, and around the chamber, expected him to do so. Bob Carolla remembers Larry Benoit saying, when the majority leader race was developing, "If he doesn't get elected majority leader, then we should just go ahead and start running for '92." Tony Buxton saw Mitchell exercising national leadership when John Sununu, after the 1990 election, told Democrats, "The country's doing fine, we're not going to do legislation, you guys might as well go home." Buxton said, "That created a political vacuum, and George filled it. He didn't seek it, but the country needed to have some things done, and he stepped up."

Mitchell did consider running for president, once, for the 1992 campaign. "I had, by then, served two years," he said recently. "There had been some tough times, but it had generally gone pretty well. I had a broad base of support among Democratic senators, several of whom—I don't want to exaggerate the number, but maybe as many as a dozen—had come to me and said, 'You know, you really ought to think about running for president.'" Mitchell believed he had a substantial group of potential donors, some of whom urged him to run. "So I did think seriously about it," he said. "I ultimately decided against it, for several reasons. I had been majority leader for only two years, and I was already aware—keenly aware—that the burdens of that job were huge, and totally consuming. And I couldn't figure out how I could run for president and serve as Senate majority leader. In fact, four years later, Bob Dole tried to do that, and he couldn't." After seeing what it took, "literally seven days a week, twelve hours a day, deluged with requests and demands," he decided, "How can I possibly run for president and do this job?" His assessment was, "I didn't think that the odds were so good on my being elected president that it would be worth giving up being Senate majority leader." He had also gauged the political outlook. "The second factor was, about the time I was considering it, Bush was at the absolute peak of his popularity. It didn't look like anything remotely resembling a sure win. It looked like a very tough fight to defeat him. There was a big primary field, and a couple of my Senate colleagues did run. They were not among the group urging me to run." Mitchell had meetings with his top staff to discuss running, "and then I concluded that I simply couldn't reconcile the demands of being majority leader with a campaign for president. And I decided not to do it."

Harold Pachios admits to some disappointment Mitchell never ran for president, but understands the reasons, including what happened during his first marriage. "He was not that ambitious for the presidency that he would spend two years doing only that," he said. "There was already an accumulation of things that you saw when he left the Senate." Once he remarried and had children again, Pachios thought there was no chance Mitchell would be tempted. "He wasn't going to put them through that."

Gordon Weil often heard Mainers talking about a Mitchell candidacy. "You've heard lots of people say he should have been president. . . . There's no question, as I look at the people who were available to run, that in every respect he was more qualified." Weil looked back to Muskie in 1972 and said, "Muskie's problem was that, while he probably would have been a good president, he was a terrible candidate. He thought he should be given the presidency." Weil believes Mitchell wouldn't have made that mistake. "Mitchell understood you had to run for it, that nobody owed you that." And in 1992, Weil said Mitchell would have won. "His style as conciliator, negotiator could sell to people that they ought to support the Democratic ticket," he said. "I think he would have been a splendid president, because he knew how Congress worked . . . knew the full range of issues. He should have been president."

Berl Bernhard, who knew both intimately, also thought Mitchell would have been a better candidate than Muskie. "He was always productive," Bernhard said of Mitchell. "George has hidden somewhere, in his soul and his physical makeup, staggering amounts of energy, which he does not show all the time. Ed, by contrast, would be the no-energy personality; he was exhausted all the time." Bernhard said Mitchell "had a good grasp of the English language, and a real capability of relating complex issues to the needs of a good civil society."

Bill Clinton ran for reelection in 1996, and, unlike Ted Kennedy, Mitchell would never have considered challenging an incumbent Democratic president. As 2000 approached, there were still those hoping for a Mitchell candidacy. Dick Gephardt, who'd run in 1988 and would run again in 2004, thought that Mitchell would be a good successor to Clinton, and he urged Mitchell to run. "He was the best leader I saw in my time up there," Gephardt said. "George Mitchell was tough when he needed to be, and he was willing to lead and take a stand and fight for it. He would have had a great set of skills to lead the nation."

Even as late as 2004, when Mitchell was seventy, there were those thinking of him in a national race. One was Angus King, who'd completed two terms as governor in 2002. "I remember being at this meeting in Augusta, the one where he gave this analysis of Iraq, and I raised my hand and said, 'Senator, would you please run for president?' And he would have been elected in 2004, if he had run; he would have gotten the nomination against John Kerry, and he would have beaten George Bush." King said in a 2009 interview, "George Mitchell is one of the two or three most able public officials of his generation. He should have been president. And I can't think of anybody else I would say that about." King said Mitchell's "synthesis of high intelligence—and when I say that, I mean off-the-scale high intelligence—and adherence to principle is an almost unique phenomenon." He said, "If things had been slightly different in timing, he would have been president, and would have been a great president." Eighteen years after Mitchell left the Senate, in 2012, King was elected to his seat.

21

A PEACE THAT PASSES
UNDERSTANDING

For a decade before George Mitchell went to Northern Ireland on an economic mission in 1995, the governments of the United Kingdom and the Republic of Ireland had been making progress toward normalizing relations, which had remained somewhere between chilly and frozen since the 1921 partition of the rural, Catholic, agricultural South and the urban, Protestant, manufacturing North. Partition, which reduced the original nine counties of Ulster to six—creating a more dominant Protestant majority in the new state of Northern Ireland—had, from Britain's perspective, solved one problem but created another. Relations between minority Catholics in the North and the dominant Protestants worsened over time, and the 1968 street protests that led to "the Troubles" became the first armed conflict in the British Isles since the end of the brief but savage Irish civil war in 1923, with pro-treaty and anti-treaty forces battling for ten months. The intensified fighting that succeeded "Bloody Sunday" in Londonderry in 1972, after British troops killed thirteen unarmed Catholics, had been briefly lifted by the Sunningdale Agreement the following year. It brought about a power-sharing government in the North, including both Catholics and Protestants. Yet the government was short-lived, falling the next year after the revolt of many of the same politicians, including, on the Protestant side, Ian Paisley and David Trimble, with whom Mitchell later negotiated for more than two years. Since 1974, Northern Ireland had been ruled directly from London, with Stormont Castle, seat of government in Belfast, standing empty.

The first evidence of a thaw came through the Anglo-Irish Agreement of 1985, signed by British prime minister Margaret Thatcher and Irish taoiseach

Garret FitzGerald, who committed their governments to finding a peaceful solution to the northern conflict, which had settled into rounds of terrorism and
bombing, both in the north of Ireland and London, carried out by a revived
Irish Republican Army and Protestant paramilitaries. But subsequent British-
led negotiations produced little, with each round ending in recriminations
and walkouts. The new prime ministers, John Bruton for Ireland, and John
Major for the British, who had succeeded Thatcher when she was ousted by
her own Conservative Party, were ready for a new approach. They consulted
US president Bill Clinton about the possibilities. Clinton was sympathetic. He
had just lost his congressional majorities in the 1994 election and, under such
circumstances, presidents often look for opportunities abroad. He'd already
asked Mitchell, when he turned down the Supreme Court appointment, if he
would be open to other opportunities, and Mitchell said he would be. Yet it
was an intricate and convoluted process by which Mitchell went from leading
a trade delegation in 1995 to assuming his role as independent chairman of the
Northern Ireland peace talks the following year.

Mitchell was already familiar with some of the players and diplomacy between
the British and Irish governments. In 1988, Sarah Sewall wrote a memo for
Mitchell as background for an Irish newspaper interview. It recapped declining
public confidence in the Royal Ulster Constabulary, the all-Protestant force that
policed Northern Ireland. The RUC's record included targeted killings, cover-
ups, and thwarted investigations, along with the shooting by British officers of
three IRA men in Gibraltar. On the other hand, the United States had agreed in
1986 to eliminate from the US-British extradition treaty the "political exception"
protecting IRA fugitives, legislation Mitchell voted for, in recognition of progress
represented by the 1985 Anglo-Irish Agreement. The United States also provided $120 million in economic aid to Northern Ireland over three years, though
the support had lapsed. The "MacBride Principles," calling for religious nondiscrimination by companies doing business in Northern Ireland, were getting
increased attention, particularly after the "Sullivan Principles" brought about a
successful economic boycott of South Africa's white minority government. In
Maine, the Legislature had voted to divest the state's investments in companies
not adhering to the MacBride Principles by 1992, but Governor John McKernan
vetoed the bill. Still, the nondiscrimination movement suggested an avenue for
Mitchell when the possibility of new peace talks emerged.

Mitchell had several meetings with Dick Spring, the Irish foreign minister
who served from 1993 to 1997 and was influential in portions of the peace
talks. Spring, a former rugby star, got on well with Mitchell. The two had met
in November 1993 and again on September 29, 1994, and admired each other's

diplomatic skills. In a memo prepared for Mitchell, Ed King wrote that Spring "has been a staunch advocate for negotiating an agreement based on equity for the concerns of both sides. It is his expressed view that unionism and nationalism can and should coexist peacefully in an ultimately unified Ireland. He thinks the key to this is for both sides to agree to respect the political rights and traditions of the other." In more practical terms, the IRA had announced a lengthy cease-fire, and, for the moment, it was holding.

For a new mission involving the former Senate majority leader, Clinton's assignment for Mitchell seemed puzzlingly minor. Mitchell was just supposed to organize a trade conference, bringing together business owners from both sides of the political and religious chasm in Belfast. It focused on a problem Mitchell had already observed—that conflicts are often begun and continued by young men who have no place in school or in the workforce, and no prospects. Some suspected the limits on Mitchell's charge reflected the State Department's traditional pro-British bias, and the so-called "special relationship" among intelligence agencies.

Patrick Griffin, David Johnson's former business partner now with the Clinton administration, got a call from Mitchell as he was leaving the Senate, asking about the prospects for working on Ireland issues. When Griffin said he could check, he remembers Mitchell saying, "This is what I want. Go fly it, test it." After discussing it with Clinton, the president referred Griffin to Tony Lake, the National Security Advisor, and a career Foreign Service officer. Griffin said Lake vetoed any notion of giving Mitchell broad responsibility. "Tony was a real Anglophile," Griffin said. Lake was concerned that a high-level appointment would be "tipping our hand," perceived as putting pressure on the British government. Griffin said, "Tony and I were sending cards, rewriting the sentences of what Senator Mitchell was going to do on his starting venture, and it was really dumbed way down. I think Mitchell was disappointed."

David Pozorski, a Foreign Service officer who worked for Richard Holbrooke in Germany before being designated for Mitchell's staff in Northern Ireland, agrees with Griffin's assessment. "The State Department historically was reluctant, always supported the United Kingdom in Northern Ireland matters," he said. "So the State Department was the place to be, but the president set the policy." Though Pozorski originally was supposed to be Mitchell's "minder" for the State Department, Clinton approved reducing its influence, and "the State Department played a minor role," Pozorski said.

Lee Umphrey got the call to do advance work for the economic conference in Northern Ireland that Clinton had approved. Umphrey staffed Senator Claiborne Pell on the Foreign Relations Committee staff until 1989, then moved to

Maine to work for the US Department of Labor at Job Corps centers in Bangor and Limestone—the latter the one Mitchell was influential in securing after the Loring closing. It took longer than expected to get the conference organized, and by the time it occurred Mitchell was already involved in preliminaries for the international peace talks that began in June 1996. The conference brought together business owners from the predominantly Catholic West Belfast area and the Protestant East Belfast district—about two hundred in all. Umphrey soon realized that "these are people who have never talked to each other, and many of them hate each other." Yet during the conference, some of the grievances the business and economic development officials expressed created tentative bonds. "They realized that there really were inequities in the way services were provided," he said. And they were interested in the idea of the United States providing export markets, something they hadn't considered before.

Mitchell, already busy with the peace talks, opened the conference and spoke for ten minutes at the Stormont Hotel, Umphrey said. "He set the tone, and it seemed to help people focus on why they were there." He had brief instructions, and was told, "Make sure everyone feels comfortable with each other." The "fear of a blowup" was on the organizers' minds, but it unfolded smoothly. It was an opportune moment to talk about business opportunities. "Shipbuilding was dying," Umphrey said. The "peace walls" that separated Catholic from Protestant neighborhoods were still growing higher and longer, but the conference got people thinking differently, he said. "The question became, 'How do we identify the skills we need, and translate that into finding jobs for the young people.'"

As Umphrey watched Mitchell talking to participants, he saw the abilities that allowed Mitchell to keep peace talks going among the seventeen political parties then active in Northern Ireland, ten of which participated in the peace talks. "The situations were constantly changing, but his demeanor, action, and ability to connect with people did not," Umphrey said. "He could be energizing without necessarily being warm. I never heard anyone say, 'He didn't listen.'" Another trait Umphrey observed was that Mitchell "constantly focused on the outcome. He'd say, 'Why don't we do this?' or 'Why don't we try this?'" Mitchell "had the ability to be directive without people knowing it. It was not leading the witness, but clarifying people's thinking." Umphrey said Mitchell knew that doing this takes a lot of time, and occurs gradually. He could be equally directive with staff. "If you're doing something, he can give you a look that just tells you. You can see that he thinks it should have been done differently."

By the time David Pozorski arrived, Mitchell had already taken two trips to Northern Ireland, and a third not long after the economic conference, which

Pozorski said "turned out to be quite a success, sort of a big-tent event." During these discussions, he said, Mitchell "met representatives of all the political parties, in addition to the government leaders in the UK and Ireland."

Mitchell's own impressions are recorded in his book, *Making Peace*, published in 1999. "I gained a sense of the importance attached to American involvement in Northern Ireland," he wrote. "Although my role was minor, there was extensive media coverage of every meeting; my discussions with the community groups were carried live on the radio. I met for the first time many of the men I would come to know well in the coming years. . . . I was impressed by their involvement in economic issues, by their candor, and by the extent of their mistrust of the 'other side.' I didn't know at the time how mild these comments were in comparison to what I would hear later."

Mitchell said of the North, "Its people are productive, literate, articulate. But for all its modernity and literacy, Northern Ireland has been divided, by a deep and ancient hatred, into two hostile communities, their enmity burnished by centuries of conflict." As usual, Mitchell delved into the historical background. "The events of recent years can be understood only in the context of the long history of British domination of Ireland. In the early seventeenth century, about the time the British began the colonization of North America, they undertook the settlement of Ireland; it was called 'the plantation.' The policy encouraged settlers from England and Scotland to go to Ireland, the lure being grants of land. As in North America, the settlers landed on the east coast and gradually advanced westward, pushing the native inhabitants ahead of them."

The seeds of partition were sown early. Within the North, Belfast became the Protestant capital, while Londonderry was dominated by Catholics. When Northern Ireland became a separate state in 1921, Mitchell notes, in the words of a unionist leader, the goal was "a Protestant Parliament for a Protestant people." Even in Londonderry, where Catholics were a majority, Protestants retained control through gerrymandering.

AT THE TIME THE NEW TALKS BEGAN, conservatives were in charge of both Ireland and Britain, though in Ireland's case the distinctions were hard for outsiders to understand. Fine Gael, led by Garret FitzGerald, was descended from Michael Collins's pro-treaty forces, which had accepted partition. The Anglo-Irish Agreement was concluded after FitzGerald launched the New Ireland Forum in 1984 to discuss new ways to consider the island's ongoing conflicts. Fianna Fail, the "liberals," led by Eamon de Valera, were anti-treaty and fought and lost the civil war, but dominated the fledgling Irish government. Fianna Fail, as the more "nationalist" party, committed to reunification by any means necessary, was distrusted more by the British than Fine Gael, though in practice neither of the main Irish parties had accomplished much toward stemming conflict in the North.

Margaret Thatcher, while rejecting any change in political status, was more comfortable dealing with FitzGerald, who served from 1982 to 1987. Within the North, among the Protestants, the major split was between "unionists," with parties led by David Trimble and Ian Paisley, who emphasized the union with Britain, and "loyalists," more working-class and populist, who wanted Protestant dominance, but had no warm regard for the British. Protestant paramilitaries were more "loyalist" than "unionist." Among Catholics, the split was between parties committed to nonviolent reunification, with the largest bloc led by John Hume's Social Democratic and Labour Party, contrasted with the IRA and its political wing, Sinn Fein, increasingly under the dominance of the charismatic Gerry Adams. Adams attempted, then and later, to ignore the divide between Sinn Fein's political aims and the IRA's bombings and targeted assassinations, which prompted loyalist retaliation.

Mitchell noticed other points about the task ahead. One was the importance Catholics placed on self-government. While the Protestants, particularly the unionists, sometimes seemed indifferent to a Northern Ireland parliament, that was not true for Catholics. "For them, it was critical to achieving an agreement," Mitchell said. "It was central." Northern Ireland was a small place—just 5,500 square miles compared to Maine's 35,000 square miles, and densely populated, 1.7 million at the time, compared with Maine's 1.2 million. Among Protestants, Mitchell knew he'd have his hands full with Paisley, who refused to meet with him. Bill Clinton visited the British Isles in 1995. Mitchell wrote, "The president and Hillary Rodham Clinton were warmly received in London, cheered in Belfast, and embraced in Dublin. Huge crowds greeted them with a rousing enthusiasm." Paisley did meet with Clinton, and Mitchell attended. It was the end of a very long day, and Paisley lectured the president for half an hour on the unionist cause, barely allowing Clinton a word. It was, as Mitchell would discover, a typical performance.

During Mitchell's three visits, British officials acquired confidence in him, and proposed, with the agreement of the Irish government, to appoint him independent chairman of what was initially the "decommissioning" report—the first time they'd delegated key negotiations to an outsider. The British believed the key to peace talks was getting the two sides to disarm, and that an international group could convince Sinn Fein and the loyalists to get their followers to stand down. In pursuit of that objective, the British added retiring Canadian Defense Forces chief John de Chastelain to the three-member panel. The Irish picked Harri Holkeri, former prime minister of Finland. The three met for the first time in December 1995, following presentation of the decommissioning report. Mitchell commented, "We never had a serious disagreement, substantive or personal. My two colleagues and their staffs were a pleasure to work with: fair, open-minded, willing to work hard." And, he added, "De Chastelain and Holkeri deserve a lot more credit than they have received."

Mitchell chose Martha Pope as his chief of staff, following her service in his Senate office, the majority office, and as Senate secretary. David Pozorski represented the State Department, but functioned independently. The third member of the team was Kelly Currie. He was officially the press secretary, but, like Pope, played several roles, included consultation with the British and Irish governments. He had been introduced to the Mitchell family at Swisher's summer basketball camp, something John liked to recall. Currie became an instructor, and John said that, like his brother, "I never hired anybody unless they knew their stuff." Currie had left the Senate office in 1990 to go to law school, and went to work for a New York firm in 1994. When the decommissioning panel was arranged, Mitchell asked if Currie could take leave. Mitchell said, "The governments are telling me it's going to be six months," and Currie's law firm agreed it was a good opportunity. "Of course, it ended up being a lot longer than six months," he said. Currie arrived in June 1996.

The Mitchell team settled into a routine, mingling with the de Chastelain and Holkeri staff during off-hours. They stayed at the Europa Hotel, which had a reputation as the "most bombed hotel" in Europe, although during the talks it was surprisingly quiet, with only one bomb scare. Martha Pope called it "a fairly miserable existence," not because of the hotel, but because she was living out of a single room. "We had a driver and a car, and we were all jammed in" for the daily ride to Stormont. "Mitchell would ride up in front with the driver, and the three of us would be in the back. . . . Finally they found a bed-and-breakfast Kelly and David and I could move into," allowing them to cook and share meals with the Finns.

The talks had been delayed by the IRA's spectacular bombing of Canary Wharf in the Docklands section of London in January 1996, ending a seventeen-month self-imposed cease-fire. The half-ton bomb killed a night watchman and caused $100 million in damage. Prime Minister John Major, who'd welcomed the prospect of talks, called it "a dark shadow of doubt," though British intelligence officials decided Gerry Adams hadn't known of the plan, carried out by a splinter group calling itself the "Real IRA."

Sinn Fein was barred from the opening of the talks, which were attended by both Paisley and Trimble. A one-time Paisley protégé, Trimble headed a rival and larger unionist party, the Ulster Unionist Party, or UUP, while Paisley led the Democratic Unionist Party, or DUP. The British push for prior surrender of arms had fallen flat. Sinn Fein, along with Protestant paramilitaries, refused any advance handover, and the talks began by focusing on political matters. Mitchell credited Major with allowing the talks over objections by his security agencies and some Cabinet members, especially after the disarmament bid failed. "He started the process, and that was probably the most difficult part," Mitchell said.

Mitchell began with individual and group meetings with various political parties; general sessions were formal and brief, and rarely polite. The first meeting with Paisley and Trimble went especially badly. David Pozorski recalls, "At that meeting they both told Senator Mitchell to pack his bags and go home, this wasn't going to work, he was pro-Irish. And Senator Mitchell, as always, stoic, and at the end of the day both the Irish and the British government, which is the government with influence over the DUP and UUP, said, 'Senator Mitchell stays.'"

Mitchell acknowledged the situation was delicate. Seven of the ten parties supported his selection as chairman, and, he said, "Paisley led the opposition." Trimble's deputy leader, John Taylor, was "negative," and Taylor told reporters Mitchell's appointment "was the equivalent of appointing an American Serb to preside over talks on the future of Croatia." Yet Trimble said nothing, which Mitchell saw as significant. "Trimble could have made it impossible for me to assume the chair by joining them in outright disapproval. But he didn't." Trimble later explained that, with seven of ten parties supporting the appointment, he didn't want unionists held responsible for ending the talks before they began. He intended to use his leverage to deny Mitchell discretion and authority, insisting the parties themselves would define his role—a process that took many months. Paisley and other dissident unionist leaders walked out—not the last time this traditional tactic would be employed. But the talks began.

The early months featured sessions that were more recitals of grievances than attempts at finding common ground. One reporter quoted Mitchell as saying he'd sat through a seven-hour speech, which he said wasn't true, "But we did have many long speeches of a couple of hours or more," he said. "I was criticized for letting people talk for so long, but I decided it was part of my job to keep the process going. If the talks ended at that point, it was clear they would not resume."

Nonetheless, even Mitchell's legendary patience was sorely tested over the next two years. "Day after day, I was listening to essentially the same speeches, over and over again. Letting everyone have their say meant hundreds and hundreds of hours." He had also decided setting "rules of relevance" was pointless, because digressions often provided the only scraps of new material. Gradually, slowly, "They began to feel more comfortable with the process, and with me," he said. "Allowing the length helped me in the end. When I found trust growing tangibly, I was able to move to become a mediator, not just a presider."

Mitchell also provided humor, though sparingly. One quip that went down well was his comparison of his role to Rodolfo in Verdi's opera, *La Bohème*. He said, "I know Rodolfo's going to sing the same words every time, and it gets me prepared to come back to Belfast, because the one thing I know is that I'm going to have to sit here and listen to you guys saying the same thing over and over again, every time."

There were aspects Mitchell found even more difficult than leading the Senate. Though the formal negotiations were limited to ten political parties, "not once did we have them all in the same room at the same time." Mitchell also found it sobering that among the negotiators were men who had undoubtedly committed criminal acts, several who'd served time, and some who may have committed murder.

Mitchell knew he had to create some structure for the talks to get anywhere. He divided the detailed negotiations into three "strands," representing different aspects of a potential agreement, covering political, economic, and governance issues. One strand was devoted to agreements between the Irish and British governments. Even when one strand seemed hopelessly bogged down, there was usually some progress elsewhere, thus avoiding a sense of utter gridlock. Even more important was a code of conduct Mitchell wrote that became known as the "Mitchell Principles," adopted as the standard for parties to participate. Mitchell knew that all sides respected the written and spoken word, and the MacBride Principles had been one of the few initiatives that had promised tangible gains for the Catholics as they contested Protestant domination. The principles were contained in the decommissioning report and, in an artful way, kept that debate alive while recognizing there would be no prior disarmament.

There were six Mitchell Principles in all. The parties committed themselves:

- to democratic and exclusively peaceful means of resolving political issues;
- to the total disarmament of all paramilitary organizations;
- to agree that such disarmament must be verifiable to the satisfaction of an independent commission;
- to renounce for themselves, and to oppose efforts by others, to use force, or threaten to use force, to influence the course of all-party negotiations;
- to agree to abide by the terms of any agreement reached in all-party negotiations and to resort to democratic and exclusively peaceful methods in trying to alter any aspect of that outcome with which they may disagree; and,

- to urge that "punishment killings" and beatings stop, and to take effective steps to prevent such actions.

Mitchell felt the principles met the unionist objections to Sinn Fein participation and, when Adams and his chief lieutenant, Martin McGuinness, accepted them, it led to resignations by other top party officials. After the Paisley walkout, Mitchell announced, and the parties agreed, that the principles would be mandatory—a decision that initially barred Sinn Fein, but worked eventually in favor of those who wanted an agreement. Mitchell thought Paisley and Adams were indeed "polar opposites" in many ways, but had some things in common, including "an unerring instinct for the TV sound bite," which, he realized, "was becoming an important part of political leadership" in British-Irish as well as American politics. The talks survived, and Mitchell began getting good reviews. John Alderdice, leader of the small Alliance Party, a rare nonsectarian participant, said, "George is so good and so universally praised that we may be expecting too much of him. It's a messianic role he has now."

THE FIRST YEAR OF TALKS WAS THE MOST DISCOURAGING for Mitchell. "I never felt it was hopeless," he said, and, in a statement he's since repeated many times, he added, "There is no conflict that is insoluble. Conflict is created by human beings, and can be ended by human beings." It was the personal crises of the year that proved most daunting. Earlier in 1996, he had endured the deaths of Ed Muskie, his political mentor, and Gayle Cory, one of his closest aides. Her daughter, Carole, recalls that Cory's death occurred just a month after Muskie's; Gayle had been too ill to attend that service or that of a favorite uncle. In his eulogy, Carole said, "George talked about how upsetting it was, speaking at one service after another, but that my mom's passing was the most upsetting for him."

In July, Mitchell was told that his brother, Robbie, diagnosed with bone marrow cancer four years earlier, was failing. Agreement on an agenda and a framework for negotiations was nearing success, and Mitchell felt he couldn't leave. He'd seen Robbie earlier that summer, and they talked by phone frequently until Robbie couldn't manage it. Robbie's wife, Janet, said of him, "They tried a lot of things, and he loved his doctors. He used to drive from Waterville to Boston every three weeks for transfusions and treatments." Robbie even managed to get to Red Sox games. "He was very valiant," Janet said. "He lived his life to the last."

Mitchell was torn. He consulted Robbie's doctor, who told him it was likely he still had more than a week to live, by which time the agenda would be settled. Robbie died just a few days later. "Heather and I spent the longest and saddest weekend of our life together, in a hotel room in London," Mitchell said.

"There I second-guessed myself and replayed in my mind my life with Robbie. I flew back to Belfast on Sunday evening, once again filled with doubts about being in Northern Ireland." He vacationed on Mount Desert Island in August, and returned to Belfast after Labor Day in a more hopeful mood. But not long after, Heather, who was pregnant, called him during the night to say she was ill. He flew back to New York, but Heather lost the baby. A few days later, during a walk across the city, the contrast between the beauty of a September day and their own mood oppressed him. "We had never felt worse, as we walked, slowly, silently, sadly." Yet when she spoke, she told him, "You've got to go back. It's the right thing to do."

Heather Mitchell said she worried about her husband's safety more than her own. She met with a State Department representative who had evaluated security, "and he came to report to me, trying to reassure me, but in fact he horrified me more than anything." What he told her was, "The chances of him being the victim of an act of violence are greater on the streets of Washington or New York City," which she said "did not reassure me at all." Her husband told her, "I'm not a target. There is violence, there's plenty of it, but it would serve neither side to come after me." But she thought he said it "just to appease me." Her own evaluation was, "The risk was there, and he could have easily been the victim of an act of violence, intentional or random." She visited later, while pregnant with their son, Andrew, during "marching season," the Protestant ritual celebrating British military victories over the Irish, which frequently led to street violence. "I was requested by the British and Irish governments to leave," she said. "They felt more comfortable having the pregnant wife out of Belfast." The talks were held in a drab office building at Stormont, not the empty castle next door, in deference to Catholic sensibilities. Martha Pope said there was virtually no security. "We were never under any threat," she said. "The Republicans, Sinn Fein, had no interest in harming us in any way."

Later, perhaps in compensation, Heather found Mitchell an unusually attentive father. For a father-son event called "Doughnut Day" at Andrew's preschool, Mitchell worried about missing it because of a meeting at the White House involving Gerry Adams. She told him not to worry. "It doesn't matter. He's four years old; he's not going to remember. There's going to be plenty of Doughnut Days." But Mitchell was insistent. "I told him I'd be there for Doughnut Day, and I'm not going to miss it."

TOWARD THE END OF 1996, THE POSSIBILITY of another presidential appointment came up. Mitchell was widely rumored as a candidate to succeed Warren Christopher as secretary of state; Christopher, like Defense Secretary William Perry, told Clinton he wouldn't be staying for a second term. Mitchell supporters sometimes sound certain Clinton planned to make the secretary of state offer in December, but was deterred by Hillary Clinton's preference for a woman. Lee Umphrey remained in touch with Pope and Currie, and said Mitchell's office was anticipating a call from the White House. When the call came, it was from Vice President Gore, who told Mitchell he wasn't being selected. The new secretary was Madeleine Albright, who'd worked for Mitchell, and got her start in politics, during the 1972 Muskie campaign.

In a 1998 interview, Mitchell said he did have a long meeting with Bill Clinton to discuss Cabinet possibilities—including Bill Cohen for Defense—but, as with the rumored 1994 baseball commissioner post, Mitchell said of State, "the position was never offered, so I don't know what he might have been thinking." He added, "There's no benefit to looking back and agonizing about what might have been, and I'm pleased with the way things turned out."

The evidence suggests it's unlikely Clinton would have tapped Mitchell. It would have almost certainly meant him resigning as chairman of the peace talks, which he'd spent more than a year organizing and getting under way. Clinton also strongly believed an agreement was possible, and it's doubtful anyone could have taken over for Mitchell successfully. Second, it seems clear Clinton focused early on Cohen, and it would have been extraordinarily unlikely that any president would choose two former Maine senators for his Cabinet. After Clinton's stinging midterm losses in 1994, he recovered to win reelection, and employed a version of Dick Morris's "triangulation" strategy to run between Republicans and Democrats. Adding a prominent Republican to his Cabinet was integral to the strategy, and Cohen, among the most qualified possibilities, fit perfectly.

FOR KELLY CURRIE, THE WINTER OF 1996–1997 was the low point of his time in Northern Ireland. "It was difficult because there was a lot of violence on the ground still," he said. "Belfast is pretty far north, and so in the winter the days are short, it starts getting dark early. . . . Folks burn peat in some of their houses, like in little woodstove kind of things, so there's this smell of burning peat, not unpleasant, just distinctive. So I can recall just a long, rainy, cold fall and winter, the smell of peat burning as you're walking around Belfast."

Martha Pope mapped logistics for the innumerable meetings involving a constantly shifting cast of characters. "For months, years, we would have a topic and we would all sit in a room and we'd go around the table with the different parties," she said, "very deliberately placed and arranged so the wrong people wouldn't have to sit next to each other. People would give their views, and sometimes it was dignified and sometimes it was a harangue, and it felt as though no progress was being made. But I do remember reminding some of the parties that progress *was* being made, just the fact that everybody was at the table, and that these issues were being aired." Toward the end, she decided the talks needed to finish quickly, "because there wasn't anything new to say." She said it was Mitchell who ultimately made the difference. "One of Senator Mitchell's greatest contributions . . . was that he held the talks together for two years in the face of what everybody thought was failure. People thought we weren't making progress, and yet he had the stature, and the patience, and the gravitas, to keep those talks together until the circumstances were correct on the ground for an agreement to be reached."

Currie saw Mitchell's political experience as crucial to navigating among a large and diverse group of elected officials, saying, "I think he could relate to all of them because they're all people who are in public life and had to go face the voters. [He had an] intuitive understanding of what those people needed as part of a deal to satisfy their constituents."

A crisis in the talks that jolted Mitchell and his team was the astonishing revelation in the Sunday papers of December 1 that Martha Pope was having an affair with Gerry Kelly, a prominent Sinn Fein member. It was astonishing because it was completely untrue. Pope had never met Kelly, did not know who he was, and rarely had a free evening for anything beyond the negotiations. The story featured most prominently in the tabloids—the *Mail on Sunday* in London, and the *Sunday World* in Dublin. The stories had plenty of individual shots of Kelly and Pope but, of course, none of them together. It seemed inexplicable, but Mitchell pieced together a plausible scenario. From other press reports, it was clear John Major was urging the IRA to declare a comprehensive cease-fire that would allow Sinn Fein to join the talks, and that unionists—Ian Paisley in particular—would do whatever they could to prevent that from happening. Paisley seemed unusually well-informed about the alleged Kelly-Pope liaison.

Mitchell, after consulting Pope, denounced the stories as false—but when British security services commented, they referred to Mitchell's denial rather than refuting the story themselves. The hoax may have been launched by a poorly lit British surveillance photo of Kelly with a woman an intelligence officer decided was Martha Pope. That too was a problem, because participants were supposed to be immune from spying by either side. Pope, at the center of an international media maelstrom, was unflappable. Recently, she said it was the intelligence services that "ended up discrediting themselves because they tried to discredit me." She took the allegation seriously, "because I had been head of US Senate security, and I had a career to protect." The scheme quickly unraveled. Pope hired a lawyer and filed a libel suit and, in one of the fastest settlements in British legal history, won compensation of what she confirmed was "six figures." The papers printed retractions in Sunday editions a week later, on December 8.

Mitchell was still perplexed, because it made no sense to him that British intelligence services would undermine their own government. He does allow, in *Making Peace*, that "Another widely discussed conjecture held that there were those within the British security service who were opposed to the entire peace process and especially to American involvement; in effect they refused to accept their own government's policy and were working to sabotage it. . . . When the prime minister rejected their assessment that Martha was involved, they leaked the documents." Mitchell said, "I had no way of assessing this theory. I don't know whether any document existed, or whether Paisley had any role." He denounced what had been done to his top aide: "In all my years in politics, I have never been involved in anything so despicable. A woman who devoted her life to public service had her career threatened by a totally false report that was given worldwide coverage. Only her courage and determination—and the truth—had saved her." Pope's judgments are lower-key. She said the attempted smear "didn't have any effect whatsoever, and I felt strengthened in my determination that the talks must continue."

THOUGH THE TALKS DID CONTINUE, by the summer of 1997 everyone, including Mitchell, could see they were flagging. They needed new energy, and got it through elections in both Britain and Ireland. John Major, who Mitchell consistently credited with the idea and design for the peace talks, was in a precarious political position. When Margaret Thatcher was deposed in 1990, Major had been her choice as successor, but hardly anyone thought he could win an election. When he did, in 1992, it was a stunning upset over Labour Leader Neil Kinnock, whose once-promising career ended. By 1997, Major trailed in the polls, and Labour's new rising star, Tony Blair, ran a "New Labor" campaign that paralleled Clinton's "New Democrat" mantra. An admiring Mitchell called Blair's campaign "masterful."

He also summed up the tangle of Irish politics that spring. John Bruton had led a coalition government since December 1994, and had brought in Mitchell's old acquaintance, Dick Spring, as foreign minister and deputy leader; Mitchell said Spring "proved himself to be an effective advocate and a skillful negotiator." The Irish economy was doing well, and Bruton decided to seek a majority during the break called for the British election. The Irish government said earlier the talks wouldn't be recessed to accommodate their election, which Mitchell said "was another example of the importance the country's parties attached to peace in Northern Ireland."

Bruton's gamble failed. Fianna Fail formed the government with a smaller party on the left, and Bertie Ahern was named taoiseach—and became the longest-serving Irish leader since Eamon de Valera. Mitchell said Blair and Ahern were in tune from the beginning, saying they "quickly developed a warm personal relationship and an ease and candor in working together that would prove to be essential to the agreement reached on Good Friday." David Pozorski could sense the change in mood. "We had new leaders in both the UK and Ireland, both of whom were even more committed to the progress and eventual success of the talks than their predecessors," he said. Ahern and Blair, he said, "both put their personal prestige on the line." In straight political terms, Blair's position was stronger than Major's. He had such a commanding majority that the Northern Ireland unionists couldn't have threatened his government—an assurance Major never enjoyed.

With new leaders in office, Sinn Fein was finally prepared to join the talks. It was here that Ian Paisley made a critical miscalculation. Blair visited Belfast shortly after the election, and his speech there on May 16 earned an excellent review from Mitchell. "It was his first trip outside of London since becoming prime minister, an important gesture that was not lost on the people of Northern Ireland. There, in a balanced and well-crafted speech, he reached out to both unionists and nationalists." Blair challenged Sinn Fein, saying, "The settlement train is leaving. I want you on the train. But it is leaving anyway, and I will not allow it to wait for you. You cannot hold the process to ransom any longer. So, end the violence now." Coming from another leader, this might not have had the desired effect, but Mitchell could see it put Sinn Fein on the spot and forced it to decide.

Blair made another critical decision, naming Marjorie "Mo" Mowlam as secretary for Northern Ireland—often a graveyard for British political careers. Mowlam had all of Blair's energy and a trait he didn't possess: fearlessness. She roiled political parties around the British Isles, but gained immense popularity among voters. As Mitchell described Mowlam, "She has a decidedly nonpolitical approach—she is blunt and outspoken, and she swears a lot. She is also intelligent, decisive, daring, and unpretentious. The combination is irresistible. The people love her, though many politicians in Northern Ireland do not."

In a startling move, Mowlam decided to visit loyalist "political prisoners," in the Maze prison, which held hardened combatants from both sides. The loyalist paramilitaries were shunned by the prominent unionist parties, and Paisley was outraged, claiming it gave credibility to terrorists. But the visit increased rather than decreased Mowlam's standing. With Sinn Fein's announced intention to comply with the Mitchell Principles and enter the talks, Paisley led a walkout, assuming this would end them. Mitchell said, "The decision by Paisley and [Bob] McCartney"—Paisley's deputy—"to quit the talks was predictable. . . . Yet if their objective was, as they repeatedly insisted, to end this process, then their walkout was a fateful error."

Paisley believed David Trimble, despite presiding over the largest Protestant party, would quickly follow. As Mitchell wrote, "from June 1996, when the talks began, until July 1997, when they left for good, Paisley, McCartney, and their colleagues made life miserable for Trimble and the UUP." They'd repeatedly thwarted Trimble's strategy, especially over decommissioning, where they took a hard and inflexible line. The talks resumed on September 9 with unionists absent, but Trimble signaled he wanted to return. An IRA spokesman tried to imply that the Mitchell Principles would be binding on Sinn Fein but not the IRA military wing, and Trimble came back on September 23 to contest Sinn Fein's participation. He then accepted the three commissioners' ruling that the IRA statement was not conclusive, and stayed in the room from then on. Paisley had maneuvered himself out of his decades-old stranglehold over peace talks.

Martha Pope saw age-old fault lines shifting. "Much of the animosity with the talks was not republican vs. loyalist, even though they could have, as in the past, been engaged in attacking one another. It was between loyalists and unionists that animosity was the highest, and between unionists and the British government." She credited two loyalists, David Ervine and Gusty Spence, with playing a constructive role. Earlier, Ervine "was caught with a bomb in a car, and they tied a rope around his waist . . . and made him defuse the bomb before they hauled him off to prison." But like many others, he'd decided to trade political violence for participation in the talks. "David and Gusty learned to think for themselves," she said, "and when Sinn Fein walked back into the talks, the unionists Paisley and Trimble walked out. But Trimble eventually returned and he was between the two loyalists when he did that. The fact that the loyalists didn't walk out was huge."

When Sinn Fein did come back, she was impressed with both Gerry Adams and his principal deputy, Martin McGuinness. McGuinness was reported to have been the IRA's chief of operations, one of the "hard men," as they were known, but he joined Sinn Fein and rose in the ranks. Pope said the two "were very intelligent, sophisticated negotiators, and they had been at it longer than the loyalists, and there was a sense of self-assurance there that the loyalists did not initially have." Pozorski agreed about Ervine. "He was, at least for my tastes, certainly one of the most sensible, practical, rational participants," he said.

Mitchell had time to observe Gerry Adams, and found that his political style, so different than most of the key negotiators, repaid study. Mitchell said Adams had first been arrested in his early twenties. The British adopted internment—preventive detention—in response to the first outbreaks of violence in the late 1960s, and began locking up suspected IRA leaders; while imprisoned, Adams was allowed to participate in secret talks with the British government, which failed. After being released in 1977, he was rearrested the next year and held for seven months on suspicion of being an IRA member, but charges were later dropped. Mitchell observed: "As has happened so often in so many societies, his imprisonment deepened his commitment to the cause for which he was incarcerated." His supporters compared Adams with Nelson Mandela, emerging from long confinement to ascend the world stage. After joining the IRA's political wing, Mitchell wrote, "He then began the long, slow process of transforming Sinn Fein from a political pariah to a mainstream party. Wounded once in an assassination attempt, he had lived much of his adult life on the run. Yet he has survived, and flourished, in the face of setbacks that would have defeated most men." Bill Clinton had materially assisted Adams's rise, both at home and abroad, when, over the State Department's vehement objections— Adams was on its terrorist watch list—he granted Adams a visa in 1994, a move Mitchell supported. Adams took part in meetings with Congress, and at the White House.

The forgotten man in most accounts of the Good Friday Agreement—though he shared the Nobel Peace Prize with Trimble—was John Hume, leader of the largest Catholic Party, the Social Democratic and Labour Party, or SDLP. Mitchell said, "It was not surprising that the Catholic civil rights movement found its voice in Londonderry . . . in the person of John Hume. Young, articulate, a natural leader, he grew up resenting the injustices he felt were being suffered by Catholics. But he could not support the response of those nationalists who supported the use of force to expel the British from Northern Ireland. He advocated peaceful protest. He didn't want to throw the unionists out; he wanted to live with them— as equals." During the talks Hume was not a problem. Amid clashes of towering egos and vividly expressed grievances, he rarely raised his voice, yet Hume was essential to the result, which would have been impossible without his support, and his deft maneuvers between Sinn Fein and the loyalists.

Sinn Fein was suspended once more, a month, for violating the Mitchell Principles, but with Paisley out and Trimble back in, the lineup for the final negotiations was set. This didn't mean, however, there was a clear path to agreement. At times, even Mitchell became so frustrated by the participants' ability to find fractures and differences in even innocuous phrases, like a dog worrying a bone, that he nearly despaired. When the final negotiations began in October 1997, Adams and Trimble, and their deputies, still weren't talking with each other, "but only through me," Mitchell said.

He completed the final ground rules a few days before Andrew MacLachlan Mitchell was born on October 16, Mitchell's second child and first son. "Late in the middle of one night I sat watching Andrew sleeping," he wrote. "I began to imagine what his life would be like, lived, as it would be, almost entirely in the twenty-first century. I then started to think about how different his life would be had he been born a citizen of Northern Ireland." In a story Mitchell has told many times since, he wondered how many babies had been born there the same day as Andrew. He called his staff and, due to meticulous record-keeping, soon got the answer: sixty-one children. As in his confrontation with Oliver North, Mitchell was able to personify what this meant—what so many people had argued about, fought and died for, for so many years—in a compelling way. "Why should people have to live like that?" he wrote. "This conflict was made and sustained by men and women. It could be ended by men and women. And I knew those men and women. They were there, in Stormont. . . . For the sake of those sixty-one children, and thousands of others like them, we had to succeed. All of the doubts about my role in Northern Ireland vanished. No matter what, I would see it through, all the way to an agreement. . . . I felt an overpowering urge to touch my sleeping son. I picked him up and held him close for a long time. He couldn't hear me, but I told him that for him and his sixty-one friends in Northern Ireland, I was somehow going to get this job done, and when I did I would refer to it as Andrew's Peace."

Mitchell set a deadline for the end of the talks—Good Friday, a date of great significance to both Protestants and Catholics—which fell on April 10, 1998. He acted after one of the worst days in the long wrangling he'd listened to for more than two years. "Much has been said and written about my patience. I do have a lot of it, but I felt that I had just about used it up," he said. "Rarely in my life have I felt as frustrated and angry as I did on that day." The arguments he was hearing sounded just like those he'd heard at the start. He cut through them with his first and only demand of the talks—that they conclude by April 10, or be disbanded.

It was a gamble, though not as much of a gamble as it might have appeared. Mitchell employed a similar tactic during a crucial moment of the Clean Air Act negotiations in 1990, and recognized that a deadline would concentrate discussion in a way seemingly impossible otherwise. The authorization the Irish and

British governments had provided expired in May. While it might be possible to extend the date, that wasn't something Mitchell considered. In a 1998 interview, he said, "There was a greater sense of hope and optimism in the couple of weeks before I proposed the deadline," but "There had been a surge of violence since Christmas, and I knew the talks would probably not survive another major incident."

The talks proceeded along different channels. Tony Blair and Bertie Ahern announced their own, supposedly unalterable agreement on British-Irish issues a few days before the deadline, only to have Mitchell help revise it when the unionists wouldn't accept. For the nationalists, the prospect of shared self-government kept Hume on board. The realization the British would no longer provide unconditional backing prompted Trimble to stay. Bill Clinton stayed up all night during the final session. Mitchell, according to Pope, didn't sleep for two days prior to April 10. But on Good Friday, everyone signed.

When it was clear on the last night that the agreement would hold, Mitchell recorded his response in an unusually personal way. He discovered, after two years in the drab Stormont building, that there was a shower next to the office Tony Blair used during his visits. At five a.m., Mitchell retreated there. "It looked as though everyone in the building had used it that night. The floor was covered with water. A pile of used towels was stacked along one wall. The mirror was completely fogged by steam. There was no dry place to put my clothes when I took them off. But none of that mattered." He said, "As I stood under the showerhead, letting the hot water roll over me, I had one thought: We're going to do it! We're going to do it! . . . My eyes misted over, and my tears mingled with the water running down my face."

John Hume, meanwhile, was sitting quietly in the conference room and, Kelly Currie said, "His eyes teared up and he really couldn't talk any more and he said, 'Thirty years.' There was a man who really spent his life working toward this goal."

MITCHELL SOMETIMES RECALLED THE TALKS' EARLY DAYS when, after being only briefly a stranger, older women would stop to talk with him on the streets of Belfast. "They almost always offered words of gratitude and encouragement," he wrote. "Thank you, Senator." "God bless you." "We appreciate what you're doing." But the sentiments were followed by what Mitchell called "the fear." "You're wasting your time. We've been killing each other for centuries and we're doomed to go on killing each other forever." For once, the conventional wisdom, if that's what it was, was wrong. The Good Friday Agreement ushered in a lasting peace. After the final ceremony, Kelly Currie was walking out of the hotel as two elderly women walked in. "They called out to Senator Mitchell, 'Senator, senator,' and wanted to come over and shake hands," he said. "They said 'Thank you, for our kids and our grandkids.' . . . I had no idea whether they were nationalists or unionists, but they were just happy about the future."

Martha Pope thought there were at least three reasons why the talks succeeded despite so many predictions of failure. "Circumstances on the ground were so bad that both sides—both sides—wanted it to stop," she said. She said the initiative launched by Clinton, and carried out by Mitchell, was fundamentally different than what previous British governments had done. They'd wanted to keep "the troubles" in-house, committed, as they were, to the idea Northern Ireland was an integral part of the United Kingdom, even though the British public was tired of the effort and expense involved. Allowing the United States to lead through a former Senate leader was also a gamble, though a successful one. Mitchell, she said, "had the gravitas and the intelligence to keep the talks going longer than anyone thought possible. He gave the talks legitimacy" that previous rounds had lacked. Finally, Tony Blair's firm line with the unionists was a turning point, she said. While his initial speech was headlined by the demand Sinn Fein join the talks, he also told unionists they wouldn't be rewarded for bad behavior. Pope, like Mary McAleney earlier, was mildly surprised when Mitchell chose her over others with weightier qualifications. "I'd never done foreign policy before," she said, and when Mitchell asked her, she said she'd have to think about it. In Belfast, though, she found, "It really was much the same as working in the Senate. The same clash of personalities, the same need to know who to trust, and who not to trust."

Mitchell's staff liked to joke that the Good Friday Agreement was "Sunningdale for slow learners," and in fact the 1998 solution did resemble its 1973 predecessor in outline. But there is a vast difference between a peace on paper—which many have long been able to map for Israelis and Palestinians, and for Greeks and Turks on Cyprus—and a lasting accord all sides agree to and are willing to defend. That was emphatically not the case with Sunningdale, but it was true on Good Friday in Belfast.

Four months after the agreement was signed, a powerful bomb went off in the marketplace of the quiet town of Omagh, in County Tyrone, on August 15, killing twenty-nine people and injuring hundreds. It wasn't until 2015 that a suspect was charged. It was the biggest test of the Good Friday Agreement, which had been ratified in May by voters in both the Republic of Ireland and Northern Ireland. The peace held. There were no retaliatory bombings. Both sides seemed to recognize that the choice was between peace, or continuing violence.

The next test came in 1999, when Northern Ireland began forming its first government in a generation. Talks didn't go well, and reached an impasse. Both governments appealed to Mitchell to return, and he did. The sticking point was that the IRA, once again, refused to commit to disarming, which the agreement said must be done, though without setting a timetable. Once again David Trimble faced the most pressure, and decided to go ahead anyway. On November 28, his UUP ended a boycott that had delayed naming a twelve-member Cabinet, which would include two members from Sinn Fein. The *Washington Post* reported, "Today's vote was testament to the negotiating prowess of George Mitchell, the tireless problem-solver who brokered the Good Friday deal in 1998 and then watched in dismay as the agreement turned to eighteen months of angry stalemate." The new understanding was that the government would be formed and the IRA would begin disarming "soon." That turned out not to be until October 2001, when Adams, realizing terrorism had acquired a new and ominous dimension after September 11, convinced his party it was time to move on.

Mitchell told the *New York Times* he returned reluctantly. "It was a very difficult thing for me," he said. "But my wife was the one who said, 'You'll never forgive yourself if you don't do it.' Of course she was right." This time, it took only three months, rather than three years. Martin McGuinness, who had become Sinn Fein's chief negotiator, said that for the first time, the talks were "cordial." A negotiator from John Hume's SDLP said "trust crept in." Mitchell disagreed. "Trust is an overstatement," he told the *Times.* "But at least they stopped insulting each other, and that's what enabled us to reach agreement."

The fortunes of those who signed the agreement took varying arcs. David Trimble, after steering his party through the first years of self-government, feuded with Paisley's DUP, and lost his seat in Parliament in 2005. Gerry Adams's stock continued to rise, and Sinn Fein surpassed the SDLP as the largest Catholic party. Paisley vowed in 1999 he would never stay in the same room as Martin McGuinness, and campaigned against the agreement even while joining the Northern Ireland government. Some supporters faulted Paisley for not picking an Education minister in the first Cabinet, when a lottery-style process was used. That portfolio went to McGuinness, who was credited with improving schools long riven by sectarianism. In 2007, many were astounded when Paisley took his seat as the government's leader while McGuinness became deputy leader.

Mitchell was appointed chancellor of Queens University in Belfast, a largely honorary but prestigious post he held for ten years, until required to step down to become President Obama's Middle East envoy. He thoroughly enjoyed the role, he said, because he got to give lots of speeches to attentive undergraduates. In a recent television documentary, he acknowledged that, while peace has come to Northern Ireland, the communities remain deeply divided. The "peace walls" erected all over Belfast remain in place, though in recent years there have been experimental "openings." Mitchell said that peace and reconciliation, while often paired, are really two different things—and reconciliation often takes much longer. In a 2014 op-ed, novelist Colum McCann wrote, "Forging a continuing peace process means understanding that there are always going to be several viable truths. The peacemaker—as Senator George J. Mitchell, who negotiated the peace, learned in 1998—must show the tenacity of a fanatic." McCann said, "It is, of course, naive to expect total reconciliation. Some grievances are so deep that the people who suffered them will never be satisfied. But the point is not satisfaction—the point is that the present is superior to the past, and it has to be cultivated as such."

Since 1999, Mitchell hasn't been recalled as a negotiator in Northern Ireland. The experience stayed with him, though. He'd been moved by the testimony of one of the survivors of the Omagh bombing, Claire Gallagher, just fifteen, who was blinded by the blast but refused to hate her attackers, becoming a witness for peace. One affecting moment in the television documentary is a scene where Mitchell and Gallagher sit together. She clutches his hands and seems, even as he prepares to leave, reluctant to let go. When he and Heather became parents of a daughter three years after Andrew was born, they named her Claire, in honor of Claire Gallagher. At the end of *Making Peace*, Mitchell envisions himself sitting in Stormont Castle at an assembly of the Northern Ireland Parliament with Andrew—a scene included in the documentary. He wrote, "There will be no talk of war, for the war will have long been over. There will be no talk of peace, for peace will by then be taken for granted. On that day, the day on which peace is taken for granted in Northern Ireland, I will be fulfilled."

22

THE UNENDING CONFLICT

In his early Senate career, George Mitchell wasn't much involved in foreign affairs, or in the Middle East, though his support for democracy in Lebanon began almost as soon as he took his seat. He did take a stand, though, as a supporter of Israel. A speech in April 1982 to the Israel Bond Dinner in Chicago featured strong and, for Mitchell, almost strident criticism of the United Nations General Assembly for its "attack on the meaning of the words with which we communicate."

After its founding in 1964, the Palestine Liberation Organization and its leader, Yasser Arafat, suffered a number of crushing defeats in the late 1960s and '70s. After the Six-Day War in 1967, Israel occupied the West Bank and Gaza, where most Palestinians lived. The PLO's expulsion from Jordan after the failed "Black September" coup attempt in 1970 against King Hussein left it without a territorial base. Its murder of eleven Israeli athletes at the 1972 Olympic Games in, of all places, Munich, stirred worldwide revulsion. And it had become a pariah with Egypt, the most powerful Arab state bordering Israel.

The one place the PLO made headway was with the "Third World" or "non-aligned" nations at the UN, which adopted one anti-Israel resolution after another. Mitchell was incensed by what he saw as the hypocrisy of nations such as "the Soviet Union, Cuba, Uganda, Vietnam, Iran, Nicaragua, and Poland," declaring that Israel was not a "peace-loving nation," and hence, ineligible for membership. Nor did he hesitate to label the action anti-Semitic. "The purpose of this resolution was not merely to provide another forum to attack Israel; it also called for an international boycott," he said. "The goal is to isolate Israel as thoroughly in the community of nations as Hitler isolated the German Jews within his Third Reich."

Mitchell, along with fifty-four co-sponsors, had proposed, and the Senate unanimously adopted, a resolution that "any action to expel Israel from the UN General Assembly will be met with US withdrawal from the General Assembly, and US funds as well." He added, "Ironically, our State Department would have preferred a less resounding expression of congressional opinion." Mitchell continued in this vein, in a style one rarely observes in other speeches: "If the demagogues of the Third World want to exercise their rhetoric at the expense of democratic nations such as Israel, they should be on notice that the United States, the world's leading democracy, will not sit idly by."

Eight years later, the stridency was gone, but the position on Israel was essentially the same. The majority leader spoke to AIPAC, the American Israel Public Affairs Committee, on June 11, 1990, and said, "This afternoon I joined several other senators in introducing a resolution in the Senate calling upon President Bush to suspend the dialogue with the PLO until that organization condemns the recent terrorist attack on Israel and expels Abu Abbas from its Executive Committee." Abu Abbas, the *nom de guerre* of Mohammed Abbas, had led the 1985 hijacking of the *Achille Lauro* and the murder of Leon Klinghoffer, and five years later his Palestine Liberation Front had attempted an assault on Israeli beaches. Mitchell noted the "high hopes" that attended the PLO's 1988 declaration accepting Israel's right to exist and to renounce terrorism. Mitchell's summary was succinct: "The attempted attack on Israeli civilians violates the PLO's pledge to renounce terrorism. The PLO's attempt to term the attack a military operation is unacceptable. As one participant in the attack admitted, 'The aim of the operation was to murder civilians.' That's terrorism. There is no way around the term."

Mitchell wasn't reflexively pro-Israel. In 1988, he declined to sign a letter, initiated by Dennis DeConcini, Charles Grassley, Patrick Leahy, and Alphonse D'Amato, urging that Arafat be denied a visa to speak to the UN and the National Press Club until the PLO formally recognized Israel. Other co-signers included Daniel Moynihan, John Kerry, Al Gore, Jim Sasser, and Warren Rudman. Mitchell refused a second appeal, "a full court press," wrote Sarah Sewall, who said the letter was irresponsible, though adding, "the issue is symbolic for the Jewish community, and may be publicized." Sewall also outlined concerns that resulted from the new tone set by the George H. W. Bush administration and Secretary of State James Baker, who had earlier been Reagan's Treasury secretary. She analyzed AIPAC's concerns about a recent Baker speech, and said, "The speech, which stressed the importance of the US-Israeli relationship and was wholly supportive of the Israeli election proposal, lacked the rhetoric to which the Jewish community has become accustomed to under Reagan. . . . For many Jews, even appearing to equate Israel and the Palestinians is tantamount to abandoning Israel." Still, neither Mitchell nor Dole was willing to endorse AIPAC's letter to Bush.

Mitchell won the trust of key Israeli leaders during his years as majority leader. One important issue was the resettlement of Soviet Jews after Mikhail Gorbachev allowed their wholesale emigration. In 1992, Israeli ambassador Zalman Shoval sent a formal note to Mitchell thanking him for steering a $10 billion loan guarantee for new housing through the Senate, then added a hand-written message. "I appreciated that you always found the time to listen—and the will to help."

MITCHELL'S FIRST MISSION TO THE MIDDLE EAST came long after his departure from the Senate, when Bill Clinton asked him to chair an international commission that became known as the Sharm el-Sheikh Fact-Finding Committee. Following the Gulf War of 1991 and the containment of Iraq, both Israel and the PLO looked more favorably upon negotiations and, through a backchannel not connected to either government, began direct, secret negotiations in Oslo that led in 1993 to an accord that prescribed a limited "land for peace" exchange between Palestinians and Israelis. The agreement ratified the PLO's renunciation of terrorism and created the Palestinian National Authority, or PA, with governance over small portions of the West Bank and Gaza. But the interim agreements suffered several reverses by the late 1990s, including the assassination of Israeli prime minister Yitzhak Rabin in 1995, and by 1998 Clinton began to take a more direct role in encouraging talks. Prime Minister Ehud Barak, elected in 1999, urged Clinton to seek a final settlement, and marathon sessions took place at Camp David in July 2000, involving the president, Barak, and Arafat—modeled on the talks convened by Jimmy Carter that led to a peace treaty between Egypt and Israel in 1979. The talks failed, however, and Clinton looked for some means to maintain the momentum he felt had been created into a new administration, which would take office six months later.

The Israelis were deeply suspicious of UN sponsorship, so international oversight was delegated to the European Union. Mitchell, the commission's chairman, was joined on the five-member panel by former senator Warren Rudman; Turkish president Suleyman Demirel; Norwegian foreign minister Thorbjørn Jagland; and Javier Solana, the EU's foreign and security policy chief. The commission was created at the end of the Middle East Peace Summit at Sharm el-Sheikh in Egypt on October 7, 2000. The appointments were announced on

November 7, and the commission began work a few weeks later, submitting its report to President George W. Bush on April 30, 2001. It was an intensive five months of work.

The impetus for the commission was the outbreak of the Second Intifada, a violent resistance movement among Palestinians they said was touched off by Israeli opposition leader Ariel Sharon's visit to the Temple Mount in Jerusalem, the holy site seen as sacred by Jews, Christians, and Muslims. The official charge was to investigate the causes of the violence—which had brought the peace summit to an end—but from the beginning, Mitchell conceived a larger aim. Through rigorous investigation, reporting, and analysis, he hoped to lay the groundwork for a more successful American-led peace effort by the Bush administration, which would soon take office. In an interview a few months after the report was submitted, Mitchell said that he had discovered "a total lack of trust" among the two sides, and that the progress represented by Oslo had long since been frittered away. The compressed timeline meant that he had "only a couple of days to figure out precisely what needed to be done," and the crucial meetings took place at the Waldorf Astoria Hotel in New York City. Mitchell asked Kelly Currie, who had gone back to his New York law firm, to act as his personal aide. He was joined by Jim Pickup, an attorney from Mitchell's Washington law firm.

The commission staff was led initially by a State Department professional, Larry Pope, who'd been recommended to Mitchell by Madeleine Albright. Pope, not related to Mitchell aide Martha Pope, was a former ambassador to Chad and Kuwait who had also worked on counterterrorism in Iran and Iraq. He became a Middle East expert through thirty-one years in the Foreign Service. Pope was a Bowdoin graduate and had family ties to Maine, but his involvement in the Sharm el-Sheikh effort didn't go smoothly. His deputy was Fred Hof, who had military as well as State Department experience, where he was seen as a protégé of Richard Armitage, designated as deputy secretary of state by George W. Bush. Hof had been an army attaché in Beirut, and had served in the Defense Department's International Security Affairs office.

The final American staff member was Brendan Melley, a former army officer and intelligence consultant chosen by Warren Rudman, who'd met him through the Defense Foreign Intelligence Advisory Board that Rudman chaired at Clinton's request. Melley said the Palestinians and the Israelis were both acutely aware of commission members' backgrounds. "For Senator Mitchell, attention was paid to the fact of his Lebanese Christian ancestry," he said, and while "few knew it at the time, Senator Rudman's parents were Jewish." Clinton also thought the gesture of bipartisanship would be reassuring, and their close relationship from the Senate helped Mitchell and Rudman work harmoniously together. Rudman noted that he was the "only person ever named to chair the President's Foreign Intelligence Advisory Board by a president of the opposite party," a highly confidential role. "We had some major problems which I helped Clinton solve," he said, "which I can't talk about."

For Melley, the initial meeting at the Waldorf Astoria was disorienting. "I ended up in New York on the day after Thanksgiving," he said, "and completely impressionable, walking into a situation at the Waldorf, with the elegant rugs and long chandeliers, to an upstairs room. I have a room to check into, it's a complete whirlwind, there's State Department staff shuffling things around, I'm told, 'Oh, you're here with Senator Rudman, go sit here.' And then we're in a small conference room and I'm within two hours of arriving, getting the lay of the land, and there are representatives from the government of Israel, the Palestinian Authority, making their initial cases on the intifada and what they wanted the commission to do."

He hadn't met Mitchell before, but he had an uncle who was an education lobbyist in Washington who knew Mitchell well. The new chairman's reputation from the Senate, Melley said, was that "he was known to be partisan as needed, when he was up on the Hill, but more importantly he was known by his judgment and the way he considered issues." After seeing Mitchell that first day, Melley observed that "He has a quiet, commanding presence. Because of his intellect and the depth of his experience, when he talks to you, or when you're talking to him, he is one of those people who can convince you that he's nowhere else in the world but listening to you. And in a room full of people with different points of view, he was very ably going around the room and letting everybody have their say."

When they reconvened in Gaza, with a group of forty Palestinians, Melley said, "Each of them wanted a chance to speak, and he gave them each a chance. And, unlike the rest of us who had jet lag sneak up on us within twenty minutes, he was able to." Mitchell took charge immediately, Melley said. "He was recognized as chairman; he did not need to assert his authority, it was established." And when everyone had spoken, Melley noticed Mitchell was able "to summarize in a way that met his objectives, and the objective of what we were trying to do, but reflecting points from each of the participants. So he might be rejecting 75 percent of what you said, but he's referring to the 25 percent he's accepting, and thereby convincing you with eye contact that, OK, he's heard you."

Rudman found the pace difficult and sometimes exhausting. He had vivid memories of the commission's first trip to the region, including the Gaza meeting, and made it sound breathless. "It was hectic as hell. The thing I will never forget is being driven in SUVs from Tel Aviv down to Gaza, across the Gaza Strip, and then picked up by Palestinian PLO security, and then being driven to Yasser Arafat's home on the Mediterranean and sitting at a huge table with thirty or forty Palestinian leaders and interpreters, sitting next to George Mitchell for two and a half hours and carrying on a dialogue about where we thought this ought to go, and then having dinner with Arafat, and then intelligence came in from the Israelis—we had an Israeli guy with us—that there was an ambush up the way we came, waiting for us, so we went a different way to get back to Ben Gurion International Airport, got on the plane, and flew to Cairo. Oh, I remember that trip."

Mitchell knew he'd been handed a difficult task as soon as Clinton asked him to serve. Clinton told him both Barak and Arafat wanted him to be chairman, and Mitchell was pleased Rudman would join him. "He was a very close friend of mine," he said. "We were close before that, and we became even closer through that experience." The Sharm el-Sheikh summit had ended with a specific, though not exactly clear, charge, he said. "One of several things they agreed upon was to create a commission to look into what had happened and to report back to the leaders on what steps could be taken to accomplish those objectives—to end the violence, and get a resumption of negotiations. It was very sensitive, because they didn't want an inquiry which would attempt to assign blame. So the mandate, inherently, was to some degree contradictory, that we want you to find out what happened and report on it, but don't blame anyone . . . those were the constraints." The commission membership was announced on the day of the Bush-Gore presidential election, so who the commission would be reporting to was initially uncertain. Mitchell got a call from Bill Daley, later an Obama chief of staff, asking him to help the Gore team during the recount, but he had to decline.

Mitchell believed the commission threaded the needle in examining the causes of violence without taking sides, yet "We got some criticism later that we didn't more specifically assign blame," he said. "Most of the people who criticized hadn't read the mandate that we were given." Work on the ground was intense, but Mitchell was satisfied with the access given the commission. "We were very heavily protected," he said; at one point there were Israeli, Palestinian Authority, and EU teams guarding the commissioners and staff. Mitchell was ready to ask for more help. On another trip to Gaza, when he thought American security would be prudent, the embassy initially balked. Fred Hof reports that Mitchell said, "If you don't want to provide security, that's up to you. I'll go to the Norwegians or the EU, wherever I have to go." The embassy changed its mind. Mitchell said, "It was still hard to get around because it's not an easy place to travel in, but we were not prevented from going anywhere. We had full access," he said. That was eventually true, though not initially. Still, Mitchell couldn't fail to notice the disproportion in power and infrastructure on the two sides. The Israelis hosted their meetings in airy rooms with chandeliers and elegant furniture. Most meetings with Palestinian leaders took place in underground bunkers. The following year, the Israelis bulldozed part of Arafat's compound in Ramallah in retaliation for the continuing intifada.

Larry Pope, the first commission staff director, was direct about tensions behind the scenes. "From the beginning, the Israeli attitudes . . . and Palestinian attitudes were quite different. The Palestinians welcomed the committee, they wanted fact-finding done, they wanted an investigation," he said. "They took the position that the causes of the Palestinian intifada and the violence were entirely due to the Israeli occupation of their land, and in particular to the visit that Ariel Sharon . . . had made to the Temple Mount, the Haram esh-Sharif, a provocative visit in which he was accompanied by hundreds, if not thousands, of armed Israeli security personnel, which was designed to assert sovereignty." By contrast, "The Israeli position was, if we have to have this damn thing going on, it's fine, but we will put all of our trust in the new administration to ensure that our interests are protected. We're not entirely sure about this group of international statesmen. We think Senator Mitchell's probably all right, but we're going to make every effort to ensure that this rather peculiar international body is kept under control. And control was really the Israeli watchword."

The staff followed up on Mitchell's first visit, in which he was joined by Rudman and the EU's Javier Solana. They ranged widely, including, on the Palestinian side, visits to Bethlehem, Gaza, and Ramallah, where the PA was beginning to build a state-in-waiting, and had meetings with both Palestinian and Israeli human rights groups. "On the Israeli side, we ran into a brick wall," Pope said. "Although the Israelis had said all the right things to Senator Mitchell when he came out, about their willingness to cooperate . . . their effort was to control to the maximum extent possible, the operations of this group of people, loose cannons from their perspective." The Israelis had assigned a Defense Ministry official, Moshe Kochanovsky, to be the staff's "minder." There were several meetings, Pope said, "each more difficult than the last." Kochanovsky decided, Pope said, "that we should not interview anybody without Israelis present, so that if we were going to talk to Palestinians we would have to have an Israeli with us to ensure that whatever we heard was corrected by an Israeli." Pope called the demand "silly," and said he made it clear that, while an Israeli could be present, "we couldn't allow our operations to be hamstrung."

One thing Pope was insistent on, however, was that the staff be allowed to visit the Haram esh-Sharif, as Muslims called it, where they believed the Prophet Mohammed had ascended into heaven from the Dome of the Rock. The Temple Mount was within the same walled complex of holy sites, believed by Jews to be the site of the second Temple, destroyed by the Romans in AD 70. Access to the site, uneasily shared, was controlled by the Jordanian Ministry of Religious Affairs. "So very quietly, we contacted the Jordanians, and we said, we want to make a very private visit, no publicity whatsoever, to walk the ground up there where all of this started, and to see how it arose," Pope said. As he prepared to fly back to the United States to meet with Mitchell, Pope discovered that the Israelis knew about the proposed visit, "presumably by tapping telephones, which one assumes is normally done," he said. "They went through the roof." Pope even got a call from an Israeli television station hoping to cover the visit, "and the Israelis wanted to send armed personnel up there with us in order, again, to assert their sovereignty." When he briefed Mitchell at his Manhattan apartment, Pope said, Mitchell didn't object to the visit, and recalls him saying, "If you think you have to do that, fine."

The visit occurred while Pope was still in New York, and he called it "completely unexceptional." Brendan Melley was present. "It made perfect sense for us to go up there," he said. "We were pretty sure the Israeli government was not going to give us permission, but then we really didn't need permission," because the Jordanians controlled access for both sides. Melley called it, "a place of such importance to, and proximity within, for Jews, Christians, and Muslims. It's an amazingly powerful place." Rather than enter through the front door, as Sharon had, the staff came in the side, almost comically. "We were probably being watched; we looked like shoppers going through the old city of Jerusalem, and ended up, 'Oops, look, here's a door.'" They found a guard waiting, who said, "Come on in." Melley said, "We looked around the Temple Mount, it was still daylight, and it was a fascinating little fact-finding venture."

If the Israelis were annoyed before, they were now furious. They called in Pope and, in violation of protocol, left him cooling his heels for fifteen minutes. When he did see Foreign Ministry officials, they insisted he'd created a diplomatic incident. "We then had a talk with senior officials," he said, "and they yelled at me for a while and I yelled back at them." His opposite numbers "insisted on referring to me as former ambassador to Chad," and told him he "had done this terrible thing, compromised Israeli sovereignty over the Temple Mount." Pope knew he'd reached an impasse, called Mitchell, and offered to resign. "He tried to talk me out of it a little bit, but not too hard," Pope said. He suggested Fred Hof as his replacement and, after further discussion, Mitchell said, "All right, if you think you have to do that."

MILITARY SERVICE IS A COMMON TRAIT among most Israeli leaders since independence in 1948, and Fred Hof's army and Department of Defense background may have been reassuring, but whatever the reason, he didn't strike sparks as Pope had. The transition came just before the Bush administration took office. Hof said, "It's important to remember that the Israelis agreed to this fact-finding committee with a great deal of reluctance." Pope, he said, "was faced with . . . resistance from the Israelis, and some of it, for some reason, seemed to be personal. Eventually, he came to the conclusion, as a professional, that it would probably be better if he stepped aside."

Hof realized that because of his relationship with Richard Armitage he might also be more acceptable in drafting the report for the new administration. This was ironic, because Hof was a lifelong Democrat, and had joined Armitage as a business partner. Though Hof had never participated in politics, he said, "I remembering chuckling about it that my dad would be rolling in his grave if he thought I was being recruited to something on the basis of being a liaison to the Republican Party." The staff was based in Jerusalem. "We would be receiving statements from the parties, and other than that we would try to devise our own program of speaking to people and trying to get answers to the basic questions," Hof said. He now had less than four months. The Armitage connection did prove of value, he said. "We had a more formal link into the working level at the State Department."

The first task was to see if the Bush administration would accept the results of an investigative team Bill Clinton had appointed. Relations between the outgoing and incoming administrations weren't warm. Hof, through Armitage, was able to arrange an early meeting with the incoming secretary of state, Colin Powell. Powell, Ronald Reagan's national security adviser after the Iran-Contra debacle, had also served as chairman of the Joint Chiefs of Staff during the Gulf War of 1991 for the new president's father. He prevailed over Defense Secretary Dick Cheney's view that Saddam Hussein's retreating troops should be pursued into Iraq, and his appointment by George W. Bush was an implicit recognition of Powell's preference for diplomacy over immediate military force—though he was again pitted against Cheney, now vice president. Powell gave Mitchell a warm reception. Mitchell believed Bush should have the option of replacing him, and told Powell, "If you and the president would like, I will withdraw and permit you to appoint someone of your own choosing." He'd discussed this with his fellow commissioners, and said the group agreed it could be disbanded.

Powell, Mitchell said, was emphatic, saying, "We want you to stay. We want the commission to continue, and we want you personally to stay."

Mitchell then went to see Arafat, as well as Israel's new prime minister, Ariel Sharon. Sharon had benefited from a wave of support, at least among Israeli voters, after the Temple Mount visit and the violent response from Palestinians. He won the top post from Barak with 60 percent of the vote in the February 6 election. Because of the fractured nature of proportional representation in the Knesset, Sharon had to form a coalition with Labor to govern, and the new Foreign Affairs minister was Shimon Peres, who'd already served twice as Labor prime minister, and shared the 1994 Nobel Peace Prize with Yasser Arafat and Yitzhak Rabin for his part in the Oslo Accords. Peres's appointment was a boon to the commission.

In Mitchell's meeting with Sharon after the Bush endorsement, Mitchell told him, "If you want this to end, it will end. It cannot work if we don't have the full cooperation of both Israel and the Palestinian Authority." Sharon had, during the election campaign, called appointing the commission "a historic mistake," but in office, Mitchell said, he "didn't want the responsibility for this commission not proceeding. Neither did Arafat," though "They both had some reservations." Sharon's support was necessary, but it was Peres, according to Fred Hof, who cleared the way. Barak, facing reelection, had communicated suspicion and even hostility through his staff, but Peres supported the commission fully.

Hof still faced obstacles, however, with the Ministry of Defense. "I recall my first meeting with Israeli officials, when I was told, point-blank, they were concerned that one of our missions was to develop evidence of Israeli war crimes, evidence that would make it possible to indict Israeli soldiers and have them extradited for some sort of international trial," Hof said. When he asked defense officials, "Have you seen President Clinton's letters to Senator Mitchell, defining the mission?" he was told, "No, we haven't heard of such letters." Hof was able to tell them, "Here are copies, they're unclassified, there's nothing secret."

When American ambassador Martin Indyk went to see Sharon after the election, he got a more explicit answer than Mitchell. "I'm not really crazy about this committee, I don't like the idea of foreigners coming in and asking questions about the activities of the Israeli military," as Hof reported Sharon's words, who added, "Nevertheless, Israel is not a banana republic; my predecessor agreed, however reluctantly, and I intend to cooperate fully." Indyk told Hof, "I've just had the most extraordinary meeting with the prime minister–designate."

Hof, like Pope, never had a problem with the Palestinians. "Arafat had requested this committee in the first place; we received nothing but cooperation," he said. "Sometimes the cooperation was overwhelming. We could have spent all our time with Palestinian academics and government officials." But the change with the Israelis was dramatic. "All of a sudden, anything we asked for, anybody with whom we wished to speak, the answer was automatically, 'yes.'" With Peres's support, Sharon decided the "historic mistake" was acceptable, after all.

DRAFTING THE REPORT WAS A HIGH-PRESSURE OPERATION, and Mitchell, after directing the staff to do preliminary work, took charge. Hof hadn't seen this side of Mitchell, and he was impressed. The staff and commission returned to New York, and Hof thought the report was "95 percent finalized." But the remaining points were the hardest on which to get agreement. "The senator presided over that meeting, and what I remember specifically was Senator George Mitchell getting his way in every detail, big and small. It was quite a performance, the likes of which I have never, in my life, witnessed before or since."

Hof's account shows that Mitchell's working methods remained consistent from his Senate days. "He had a remarkable way of getting consensus, basically formed around the direction he wanted to go, using the words he wanted to use. He did it in an entirely gentlemanly and collegial manner. The closest he would ever come to laying down the law on a disputed point would be to say something to the effect of, 'Look, at the end of the day, this report belongs to all of us, but it's my name that's going to be on it, so this is really the way I would like to phrase this particular passage.' That's really the closest he ever came to a sort of 'Take it or leave it, we're going to do it my way' formulation." Hof said it was "remarkable seeing him in action, seeing how he could form a consensus around a half-dozen passages that the staff had been arguing about for the previous three weeks."

Brendan Melley, during occasionally chaotic staff conferences, decided he, as the fastest and most accurate typist, should take over preparing the draft, and this did reduce the chaos, he said. In the final conferences, he said, Norwegian Foreign Minister Thorbjørn Jagland was the toughest sell. Jagland "had a very dramatic flair when he objected to something," Melley said. "He was not always cal. . . . For him it was 'I must protest, I will go back,' and he would pound the table." Another Norwegian, who was "more collected and reasonable," nonetheless joined the protest. "We could see all the energy behind him, defying us and defying the Americans for putting in this language," he said. Mitchell was listening and, when the minister stopped, said, "Why don't we try this?" Melley said, "He pieced together a new sentence containing the parts of the other sentences, and in a creative way that kept our point in there . . . but avoiding the precise formulation the Norwegians were objecting to, and he did this while looking around the room. So this was from memory, he created a very long, multi-clause sentence—and we're all scribbling, writing it down—and there was a pause, and Foreign Minister Jagland said, 'Brilliant.' And that was the final point that needed to be resolved, and then there was full agreement on the report."

Melley reflected on what he'd just seen. "It was amazing to watch him. Somebody of lesser capacity might have written it down and sent us back" to work on it, "but this was in his head, he constructed this sentence based on those different ideas, and it met the objectives of everybody and everyone was happy."

The Sharm el-Sheikh report carried out the assigned mission but, with precise language, it makes many salient and telling observations about the conflict still unfolding. The major conclusions were unsurprising; it called on participants from the original summit, which included the major Arab states, "to recommit themselves to the Sharm el-Sheikh spirit and implement the decisions made there in 1999 and 2000." It proposed to end the violence by returning to existing agreements and have Israel and the PA "immediately resume security cooperation." Rebuilding confidence, it said, would require establishing "a meaningful 'cooling-off period,' and additional confidence-building measures." Israel should freeze all settlement activities in the disputed territories, it said, and the PA "should prevent gunmen from using Palestinian-populated areas to fire upon Israeli-populated areas." Israel should lift all border closures, pay the PA tax revenues due it, "and ensure that security forces and settlers refrain from the destruction of homes and roads, as well as trees and other agricultural property in Palestinian areas." It acknowledged that these tactics were motivated by Israel's security concerns, but said, "the economic effects will persist for years." And it endorsed joint vetting, by PA and Israeli security, of Palestinians working in Israel to ensure they were "free of connections to organizations and individuals engaged in terrorism."

The report documented curious behavior by former prime minister Ehud Barak. Sharon's intent for a show of force on the Temple Mount was well known, and, as defense minister, he was subordinate to Barak. The report shows that, despite appeals from both the United States and the PA, Barak refused to intervene. "Mr. Barak told us that he believed the visit was intended to be an internal political act directed against him by a political opponent, and he declined to prohibit it," the report said—even though the visit, and the violent reaction, probably cost Barak the election. In the first clashes, Israeli police fired hails of rubber bullets, killing four and injuring two hundred. The report also noted Israel's claim that the cause of the intifada was the breakdown of the Camp David negotiations in July, and what it called "the widespread appreciation in the international community of Palestinian responsibility for the impasse." The report commented, "In this view, Palestinian violence was planned by the PA leadership," and aimed, as the Israelis claimed, "at provoking and incurring Palestinian casualties as a means of regaining the diplomatic initiative."

Without assessing blame, the report made findings. One was that "We have no basis on which to conclude that there was a deliberate plan by the PA to initiate a campaign of violence at the first opportunity, or to conclude that there was a deliberate plan by Israel to respond with lethal force." About Sharon, it said the Temple Mount visit "did not cause the 'Al-Aqsa Intifada.' But it was poorly timed, and the provocative effects should have been foreseen; indeed, it was foreseen by those who urged that the visit be prohibited. More significant were the events that followed: the decision of the Israeli police on September 29 to use lethal means against the Palestinian demonstrators; and the subsequent failure . . . of either party to exercise restraint."

Concerning causes, the report focused on the Palestinian conviction that Oslo, and the Madrid Conference that preceded it, "heralded the prospect of a State, and guaranteed an end to the occupation and a resolution of outstanding matters within an agreed time frame. Palestinians are genuinely angry at the continued growth of settlements and at their daily experiences of humiliation and disruption as a result of Israel's presence in the Palestinian territories." When it turned to the Israeli perspective, the report said Israel acknowledged the settlements as "an outstanding issue," but said at Camp David and elsewhere Israel "offered to make significant concessions . . . in the context of an overall agreement."

A passage that bears Mitchell's imprint says, "For Israelis and Palestinians alike, the experience of the past several months has been intensely *personal*. Through relationships of kinship, friendship, religion, community, and profession, virtually everyone in both societies has a link to someone who has been killed or seriously injured in the recent violence. We were touched by their stories. During our last visit to the region, we met with the families of Palestinian and Israeli victims. These individual accounts of grief were heart-rending and indescribably sad. Israeli and Palestinian families used virtually the same words to describe their grief."

Most of the report, just thirty-two pages, not including supporting documents, contains detailed elaborations of the initial themes on ending violence, resuming security cooperation, and reviving direct negotiations. It particularly emphasizes the provocative effect of new Israeli settlements, and quotes Secretary of State James Baker, on May 22, 1991, saying, "Every time I have gone to Israel in connection with the peace process, on each of my four trips, I have been met with the announcement of new settlement activity. This does violate United States policy. It's the first thing that Arab governments, the first thing that the Palestinians in the territories—whose situation is really desperate—the first thing they raise when we talk to them. I don't think there is any bigger obstacle to peace."

Of the Palestinians, the report points out "disturbing ambiguities in the basic areas of responsibility and accountability. The lack of control exercised by the PA over its own security personnel and armed elements affiliated with the PA leadership is very troubling."

Mitchell believed the report did more than investigate events, make observations on the conduct of both sides, and delve into causes of the violence. Taken together, the detailed recommendations provided a path forward to ending violence and structuring new talks. Indeed, when the Bush administration, long afterward, unveiled its "Road Map" to a settlement, Mitchell staffers thought it replicated, almost word for word, major sections of the Sharm el-Sheikh report.

The report was presented to Colin Powell on April 30. He made it public on May 21 and strongly endorsed it, appointing the US ambassador to Jordan, William Burns, as his envoy to revive negotiations. Yet in the months that followed, the Bush administration made no visible effort to move things forward. Warren Rudman was disappointed in the response. "It's really a shame both sides of that dispute didn't really look at the report and say, 'This is the best we're going to get,' and do it, because it could have led to a far different situation than we're dealing with now." Asked if he saw any evidence of buy-in by the Bush administration, he said, "Not at all," though he added, "I can't say they didn't buy into it at all, but they had some problems, and they weren't tough enough, as far as I was concerned."

Mitchell was more neutral. "It was accepted by both sides, with some reservations, but no action was ever taken to implement it," he said. "Unfortunately, like so many other commissions or studies, it essentially went unfulfilled because there was no mechanism to implement the commission's recommendations." He added, "I believe there was resistance within the administration." Mitchell also spoke of what he'd learned "about the roots of the conflict, and to see firsthand the very high level of mistrust and hostility, hatred even, that exists between the two sides, and which makes resolution of the conflict very, very difficult." Larry Pope was blunt. "All of us were very well aware that this was a dicey business, to take what essentially was the policy of one administration and continue it on into the next," he said. "We all knew, Senator Mitchell better than any of us, that the Bush administration had a sort of hostility to the Arab-Israeli peacekeeping the Clinton administration had engaged in." Four months later, the attacks of September 11 were launched, and Middle East negotiations went to the back burner until the very end of the second Bush administration, in 2008.

Mitchell continued to speak out during the next year. In December, he said Arafat needed to do a better job combating terrorism in his ranks, yet also noted that the Israelis "have made a decision not to target Arafat. They have a military capacity to either kill or expel him because of the tremendous imbalance of military strength," he said in an interview. If Arafat were killed, he said, "the fear is that his successor would come out of Hamas or Islamic Jihad and be totally committed to the destruction of Israel and unresponsive to the US government."

As the years passed, Mitchell distanced himself from the Bush administration. In a 2006 speech at College of the Atlantic in Bar Harbor, he sharply criticized Bush, though without naming him, for his conduct of the "War on Terror." He said Bush's assertion he alone could decide what participants were "enemy combatants" lacked any legal foundation. "This is not based on any law," Mitchell said. "I am amazed any president would make such a claim, and I am more amazed that the American people have acquiesced with little or no protest." He said, "Ours was a great nation at birth. It is critical that we rebuild our historic relationships and our status in the world."

MITCHELL WAS SURPRISED WHEN HE RECEIVED a summons from Hillary Clinton, Barack Obama's designee for secretary of state, as 2009 began. In his memoir, he writes, "Shortly after the election in November, I'd had a brief telephone conversation with Joe Biden," who'd been Judiciary Committee chair when Mitchell was majority leader. "I congratulated him on his election as vice president, and we discussed my work in Northern Ireland and whether I might serve in the new administration. I said I would of course be happy to consider it. Two months had passed and I had forgotten about the conversation, but Hillary reminded me of it when we met." Heather Mitchell said, "George was very surprised to get a phone call . . . to go down to DC and have a discussion," but "I was not surprised . . . and I think it's one of those things, given his background and his experience, that he felt he had to try."

Mitchell had met Obama when he was still an Illinois state senator. On a fund-raising trip, a hostess told him, "This young man is very bright and is going places. I wouldn't be surprised if someday he got elected to the US Senate." When they met in the White House, Obama may have reminded him of his younger self; Mitchell was now seventy-five. "We talked for an hour, some of it trading stories about our service in the Senate," Mitchell said. "Although our meetings in Chicago had occurred several years earlier, he recalled them; he even remembered the jokes I had told. . . . When he asked if I would serve as his envoy to the Middle East, I told him that I would." It was Obama's first major appointment, becoming official two days after the inauguration.

It was no small thing for Mitchell to join the State Department, which has strict rules on divestment and disclosure. He had to resign from his law practice, where he was now chairman of the mega-firm DLA Piper, the largest in the world. He stepped down as chancellor of Queens University in Belfast, which was close to his heart. And he sold his small ownership stake in the Boston Red Sox. When Obama asked how long he would serve, he said two years.

Mitchell was as qualified a Middle East envoy as any diplomat assigned the task. He was an accredited peacemaker, after the agreement in Northern Ireland—a rare example of true power-sharing anywhere. His work at Sharm el-Sheikh impressed many Republicans as well as Democrats. And he was in tune with Obama's approach to the Middle East, and has consistently supported his policies, from the initial settlement freeze to the nuclear agreement with Iran. After the end of his service, he dismissed as groundless the contention that the Obama administration had endangered Israel's security. "One of the ironies of the criticism of the president is that the US-Israeli security relationship is the best it's ever been," he said in a 2012 interview. He said the administration "has provided extraordinary assistance, particularly in helping Israel to build and deploy an anti-missile system," the so-called Iron Dome.

Mitchell already knew many of those he would meet, but the top leadership on both sides was new. Yasser Arafat had died in 2004. Mahmoud Abbas succeeded him as PLO chairman, and was elected Palestinian president on January 15, 2005. The Palestinian leadership was already split, not between the PLO and earlier splinter groups, but between the Palestinian Authority and Hamas. In 2000, Ehud Barack unilaterally ended Israel's occupation of southern Lebanon, which had been launched in 1982 by Menachem Begin to counter PLO attacks from the area. In August 2005, Ariel Sharon withdrew Israeli forces from Gaza, dismantled settlements, and removed the settlers. The Bush administration pushed Israel to allow early legislative elections for the Palestinians, and in January 2006 Hamas scored a decisive victory, winning 74 of the 132 seats, while Fatah, Abbas's party, won only 45, though losing the popular vote by only 44–41 percent. While both the 2005 presidential and 2006 legislative election were judged free and fair by international observers, they then lapsed, as the rival parties settled into de facto power-sharing. In practice, Hamas has governed Gaza, after defeating PA forces there in 2007, while the PA and Fatah retain control of the West Bank. Hamas, unlike the PLO, hasn't renounced terrorism, or recognized Israel's existence. While Fatah is secular, Hamas has vowed to establish an Islamic State with Sunni principles.

Israeli prime minister Ehud Olmert of the moderate Kadima Party, was, like Ehud Barak eight years earlier, faced with early elections. He was already dogged by financial scandals that, in 2015, would lead to his conviction on bribery charges. Like Barak, he had pressed Palestinian leaders for a quick, comprehensive agreement at the end of an American administration, based on a map dividing territory between Israel and a Palestinian state. Though details were murky, Barak insisted, at Camp David in July 2000, that Arafat sign off on such a map, and Arafat's refusal ended the talks. In late 2008, Olmert presented Abbas with a map that, according to Israeli sources, included withdrawal from "93 percent" of the West Bank, but not including a "contiguous" state. Abbas turned down the offer, and in December new violence erupted in Gaza, bringing the talks to an end. Olmert then decided to step down as party leader in favor of Tzipi Livni, who had been closely involved in the talks with Abbas, and who led Kadima into the February 10, 2009, elections. The fighting in Gaza between Israel and Hamas ended only on January 18, two days before Obama took office. More than one thousand Palestinians were killed; thirteen Israelis died.

As with Camp David, there were retrospective assertions that Olmert and Abbas had been close to a deal, and that Obama had erred by instead seeking to restart the process. In his memoir, Mitchell singles out *Washington Post* columnist David Ignatius's October 16, 2011, assertion—after Mitchell's departure—that Olmert had offered "a miraculous package," and that "in one of President Obama's biggest mistakes, he decided to start negotiations over." Even aside from Olmert's imminent replacement by Benjamin Netanyahu, who rejected and denounced the Olmert offer, Mitchell said the assertions are unsupported. "If true, this would have been a serious mistake by the president. But it is not true; it is contradicted by the facts, most of them a matter of public record," he wrote. The failure in 2008 clearly influenced Abbas's approach to the new talks, through the two years they sporadically continued.

Those who knew Mitchell well offered strikingly different assessments of prospects at the start of his mission. Berl Bernhard, his law partner, was also involved in the Middle East through a nonprofit that raised money for West Bank housing projects. Bernhard said in February 2009, "It may be Mission Impossible. I made a bet with three Palestinians who were here yesterday, that George—should his system tolerate it—will resolve the Middle East dilemma within five years, or never. I took odds on it. I said, 'You don't know him the way I do; it'll happen.' Obviously, anything can change the scene, including more belligerency."

John Warner, Mitchell's Republican Senate colleague, who'd retired in 2008 after serving thirty years, said, "I was a little puzzled when he accepted this Middle East assignment, because it just seemed impossible. . . . But maybe, and I have to repeat, *maybe*, he sees some course to lessen tensions in the region that I don't." Harris Wofford, a Democrat, said, "I have a hope in the Middle East right now; the harsh logic of events is going to make it the time for Mitchell and Barack," and called Obama's Cairo speech in June 2009 "one of the most important things that's happened in foreign policy, in terms of America's role in the world." Wofford, who'd lived in a kibbutz in Israel with his wife in 1950, said, "I've been a lover of the pioneer state society they built before they had a state, but the tragic, vicious circle of the Palestinians and the Israelis is one of the greatest problems in the world."

Mitchell drew strength from his roots in Waterville's Lebanese community, which was so thoroughly acculturated into Maine that, when shopkeepers like Al Corey hung American flags outside their businesses, it didn't seem out of the ordinary. Colby professor Sandy Maisel saw Mitchell following a lecture just after the Israelis announced a major settlement expansion during Vice President Biden's visit, but Maisel found him "amazingly not discouraged."

Bob Dole, speculating about "why he gets these special assignments," joked that, "He's got an easier job trying to settle the Mideast crisis than he had working on health care." Fred Hof, from the Sharm el-Sheikh staff, said, at the beginning, "I understand the senator is reasonably confident he can make serious progress . . . but he's also aware that the complexity is daunting, and the past eight years have not simplified the task. On the contrary, it's become greatly more difficult." Hof said, "Eight years ago you at least had the semblance of two relatively coherent parties in terms of internal unity, and that's definitely a thing of the past."

In a Colby lecture on October 22, 2009, Mitchell recalled Northern Ireland and sketched out why he thought he could make headway. "For the first time in my adult lifetime, we have a president who placed this high on the agenda right at the beginning of his term, not at the end," he said, alluding to both Clinton and Bush. "That's a huge factor." He told the students about persistence. "If you take the position that you tried something that you believed in and it didn't work once, twice, or three times, that you're going to give up, you're going to find that you will go through life without solving a lot of problems that you could have solved," he said. In Belfast, "I was asked not dozens, but hundreds of times by reporters, 'Senator, you've failed. When are you going home?' Politicians held press conferences demanding I go home on a regular basis. I persevered because, although I was often discouraged, I always believed it could be done. . . . In Northern Ireland I had seven hundred days of failure and one day of success."

At Obama's announcement on January 28, the president said, "The charge that Senator Mitchell has is to engage vigorously and consistently in order for us to achieve genuine progress. And when I say progress, not just photo ops, but progress that is concrete." In an interview with an Arab television station, Obama said, "What I told him is start by listening, because all too often the United States starts by dictating." Mitchell did listen, spending the first months shuttling between Israeli and Arab capitals, talking to almost every head of state and many other officials as well. The Arab consensus was that talks couldn't start without a freeze on Israeli settlements. Mitchell then worked to achieve this, though he faced higher hurdles than previous negotiators. Prime Minister Netanyahu strongly resisted the idea, and Obama faced intense criticism in Congress, and not only from Republicans—even though George W. Bush had made the same proposal in his parting address as president.

Finally, Mitchell gained Israeli acceptance of a ten-month freeze, except in East Jerusalem, which Israel claimed to have annexed. But as Mitchell soon learned, he had an unpredictable negotiating partner in Mahmoud Abbas. At the very moment Mitchell was negotiating the freeze, Abbas told the *Washington Post*—"unhelpfully," is Mitchell's understated reaction—"that he hadn't been asked to participate, and that there was nothing for the Palestinians to do, that everything depended on the Israelis." When the ten-month moratorium was finally achieved, at a meeting in New York attended by Obama, Mitchell, and Abbas, the Palestinians' chief negotiator, Saeb Erekat, told Obama that the moratorium was "worse than useless" because it didn't include East Jerusalem, and allowed completion of units under construction.

What came next tried Mitchell's patience even more sorely. The moratorium began in November 2009, and, as he explains in his memoir, "By the spring of 2010," and since the beginning of the moratorium, "we had been unable to persuade the parties to resume direct negotiations, despite an intense effort. To try to establish some traction we suggested, and the parties agreed, that we conduct 'proximity talks' in which I would meet separately with each side." The "proximity' talks were notable for the complete contrast in styles, nearly as stark as the imbalance between the two sides' political and military power. Palestinians showered Mitchell with papers and charts, many similar or identical to documents presented during the 2008 Olmert-Abbas talks, which Mitchell had already read. The Israelis put virtually nothing on paper, insisting on oral exchanges only, and made numerous references to opposition to any talks by members of their governing coalition. "From the beginning to the end of my tenure, the Israelis took the public position that they wanted direct negotiations," Mitchell wrote. "Privately they insisted that those negotiations be entirely oral, with nothing in writing and no exchange of documents." The result was that "the proximity talks evolved into a one-sided affair in which the Palestinians provided me with detailed position papers . . . while the Israelis, up to and including the prime minister, said little and made clear their disdain for proximity talks. On one occasion, for nearly an hour, a midlevel Israeli official read aloud to me a document that his government had submitted in the previous round of negotiations . . . and which I already had." Mitchell realized the Israelis had a point. Despite abundant detail, the Palestinians were repeating what they'd already said in public, without any new offers. More than fifteen years after Oslo, it was difficult to see why Palestinians couldn't just sit down with Israelis and talk.

The moratorium clock was ticking, and it was in March 2010, during Biden's visit to Jerusalem, that Israel announced construction of 1,600 new housing units in East Jerusalem, despite promising Mitchell there would be "no surprises" during Biden's visit. The resulting furor did push Netanyahu to pursue diplomacy of his own, and Netanyahu met with Obama in July to try to convince him to push Abbas on direct talks. Mitchell's response to Netanyahu was guarded, though the prime minister's barely concealed hostility and contempt for Palestinian negotiators must have been trying. Aside from the settlement criticism—which Mitchell was careful to link to American policy dating back to Lyndon Johnson in 1967, just after the Six-Day War—he said nothing directly critical of Netanyahu or his Likud predecessor, Ariel Sharon, even concerning the 2005 Gaza withdrawal that produced the power vacuum filled by Hamas. The most Mitchell would allow is that the Gaza withdrawal, along with the Lebanon pullout before it, were "the right decisions for the Israeli leadership," but had "unfortunate consequences" in prompting new terrorist attacks.

According to Ed King, however, when Mitchell as Senate leader had his first meeting with Netanyahu—who'd served as Israel's ambassador in Washington and at the UN—Mitchell had a brief from Secretary of State Warren Christopher, who wanted him to push Netanyahu on settlements and closures of West Bank borders. King said of Mitchell, "He made every one of the [points], but he made them in a very gentle way. Netanyahu didn't give him one inch on any of those issues." After the meeting and Netanyahu's departure, King and Mitchell were gathering their papers when Mitchell, "who seldom said anything, he kept it to himself," turned to King and said, "Boy, he's a hard-ass, isn't he?"

Finally, the two principals agreed to four meetings, with Secretary of State Clinton joining Mitchell. The first, in Washington, was "largely ceremonial," Mitchell said. The next two were in Egypt, where Abbas attempted to pursue various issues, with Netanyahu resisting. He insisted they had to talk first about Israel's security concerns. At the fourth meeting, in Jerusalem, they did so, and Netanyahu made it clear what he had he mind. He'd been critical of Olmert's offer on many points, but focused on what he saw as a lack of security on the eastern West Bank border with Jordan—territory that once belonged to Jordan. At the meeting, Mitchell said, Netanyahu "read from a long typewritten statement, in which he declared that Israeli Defense Forces would have to be stationed within any Palestinian state, along its eastern border, 'for many decades.' He repeated the phrase several times, with increasing emphasis." Abbas immediately rejected the idea, though he said he'd consider a transition period for such security of "two to four years," later amended to "one to three years," Mitchell said. If Israel were to maintain control of the entire West Bank for decades, it would differ little from the current occupation.

In earlier meetings, the Palestinians attempted to hand documents to the Israelis, which they generally declined to accept. At the fourth meeting between Abbas and Netanyahu, Abbas heard the prime minister say, again, that no documents should be exchanged. This, Mitchell said, "obviously angered Abbas," who got out his briefcase, assembled a set of Palestinian position papers, and offered them to Netanyahu. "For a brief, silent moment, Netanyahu hesitated," Mitchell wrote. "Abbas, arm extended, looked directly at him, and their eyes locked; Secretary Clinton and I silently watched. Then Netanyahu reached out, took the documents, and laid them on the floor next to his chair." The meeting broke up; no more were scheduled. Mitchell said, "They all walked out the front door to their waiting cars. Thus ended the direct talks, the moratorium, and the document dispute. I never learned what happened to the documents on the floor."

Mitchell didn't resign as special envoy until April 5, but with the collapse of talks the previous fall, failure of efforts to revive them, or get Israel to renew the moratorium, the mission was effectively over. He said, "My two years were up, and as winter came to a close I decided to leave." He was asked to stay on for a short transitional period, and "On May 19, I returned to my family and to private life."

A year later, Mitchell was asked if he agreed with the apparent consensus that his mission had failed. He said he did. "The reality is that if you try to get a peace agreement, and you don't get one, then you failed to get an agreement." But then he added, "If that's the case, then ten presidents, nineteen secretaries of state, untold numbers of envoys and emissaries, and many Israeli prime ministers have all failed. Because we've been trying to get agreement since 1947, and there isn't any agreement yet." Israel signed a peace treaty with Egypt in 1979 after Jimmy Carter's Camp David talks, and another with Jordan in 1994, at Bill Clinton's urging, but has signed no similar agreement with the Palestinians.

While Mitchell paints a bleak picture of the Netanyahu-Abbas talks in his memoir, he's more positive about developments on the ground in the West Bank. He clearly admires former Palestinian prime minister Salam Fayyad, who served from 2007 to 2013, whom he credits with reducing corruption and creating detailed and durable arrangements for security cooperation with Israel. Mitchell said of Fayyad, "He set forth targets for the establishment of the institutions of government that would be ready to take over in the event an agreement was reached and they got a state." Mitchell noted that a 2011 World Bank report examined when the PA might be ready to establish a state, and its conclusion was, "They're ready now." Fred Hof believes the Palestinians, despite the rise of Hamas in Gaza, have made progress toward democracy. "With the Palestinian territories, there has been a tremendous development of NGOs dedicated to democratic governance," he said. "Palestinians, through all the travails over the past decades, have managed to maintain a decent educational system, and my sense is that if we can ever get to a stable, sustainable two-state solution, I think it is very probable, if not certain, that Palestine will be a functioning democracy."

Although Abbas's performance in the 2010 negotiations was frustrating, Mitchell credits him with one clear break from his predecessor. "While Arafat said he had renounced violence, there's no doubt he did not adhere to that fully," Mitchell said. Abbas, however, "has been clear and outspoken throughout his tenure in opposing violence, and stressing that the only way forward is through peaceful negotiation." For many Palestinians in the West Bank, at least, daily life is no longer viewed primarily through checkpoints and military control. Nonetheless, Mitchell doesn't believe time is on the side of those who still hope for agreement. "We grow older each day," he said. "We change each day—and that's true of countries as well as people." By not taking advantage of relatively peaceful intervals, the two sides, he believes, court disaster.

Though admitting that negotiations in recent decades have been largely fruitless, Mitchell finds alarming suggestions from American politicians that another war in the Middle East, especially with Iran, represents a rational policy goal. "There's a lot of reckless talk about war," he said in 2012. "We've just completed nearly a decade of war in Iraq and Afghanistan, and here you've got people in this country saying, 'Bomb Syria!' 'Bomb Iran!,' just like it's not a major thing. It's a *huge* thing to become involved in a war in this region."

In three different episodes of his life, Mitchell confronted "security walls" built to restrict the flow of people and goods—first in Berlin, where he was stationed as a young army officer, then in Belfast, where "peace walls" separate Catholic and Protestant neighborhoods, and finally in the West Bank, where Israel's continuing wall-building divides previously Palestinian areas from each other. He said, "I formed a belief that walls do provide temporary respites. That is, if the immediate objective is to separate, to reduce contact, to limit travel between the two, they do work for that purpose. But they don't contribute to the ultimate solution, because they don't address the root causes of the conflict itself." Israel, he said, is no exception. "There's no doubt that the wall erected by the Israelis to reduce access to Palestinians and other Arabs has worked in the short-term objective of reducing the number of suicide bombers . . . but it doesn't solve the ultimate problem. Indeed, the Israeli government that built the wall made clear it understood that it was a temporary measure." Since then, he said, the danger has shifted. "Israel's security is not so much threatened by suicide bombers as it is by rockets. The technology that is advancing in the use of rockets is a serious military threat to Israel's existence. . . . The wall will serve no useful purpose in preventing that."

Mitchell prefers to focus on the hopes of those he's met abroad. "Despite the many differences among peoples and among societies—color, race, religion, history, culture, how they live—there is a high degree of uniformity among the aspirations of people despite their differences," he said. "I've never been anywhere where people didn't think a very important part of their life is to get their children off to a good start. Parents want their children to be healthy and happy and get a good education, and to have a decent chance in life, better than what they've had. . . . Overall, people seem to want pretty much the same thing: a chance for personal dignity that comes with freedom and the right of self-determination, for opportunity, which doesn't exist for all the members of any society, including our own—although I think we come the closest to anybody in all of human history."

23

THE WORLD
OF PROFIT

When Ed Muskie left the Senate in 1980, he didn't have any specific plans. He doubtless hoped he'd be able to serve a full term as secretary of state, but even in May of that year it was far from certain Jimmy Carter would be reelected. Muskie joined a Washington law firm, but was resolute not to become a lobbyist among his old colleagues, as so many others have done. He once confided to a former staffer, however, that if he'd known how dull private practice would be, he'd never have left the Senate.

George Mitchell had no such concerns when he left office. Except for the dozen years he'd spent at Jensen Baird in Portland, he'd been in public service all his adult life, including stints in the army, with the Justice Department, on Muskie's staff, as US Attorney and federal judge, and finally, the Senate. Even during the Jensen Baird years, he was active politically, serving as state party chairman, Democratic National Committee member, managing Muskie's campaigns, and running for governor. As 1995 began, Mitchell was ready to try the private sector, and given his background, a law firm seemed the right fit. He had numerous offers, but decided to join Verner Liipfert in Washington, where his old political partner Berl Bernhard was long established, and now chairman of the firm. By then the firm's name had expanded to Verner, Liipfert, Bernhard, McPherson and Hand. Lloyd Hand was the former chief of protocol for the State Department, and the other partner, Harry McPherson, was former White House counsel for Lyndon Johnson and a longtime Mitchell friend. Mitchell says in his memoir, "It was one of the best decisions I ever made."

The firm was politically well connected, and Mitchell worked to broaden its appeal. When Bob Dole wound up his presidential run in 1996 and left politics,

Mitchell invited him to join. Dole said, "I had a lot of faith in Mitchell, and when he called he said, 'I've got to be out of town, but would you meet with Berl Bernhard and Harry McPherson and a couple of others?'" Dole signed on, but demurs when asked if he worked on any cases with Mitchell. "No, he was so far over my pay grade that I'd have sat back in awe," he said. "The guy is smart, but he doesn't toss it around, he doesn't rub it in." Only a few years later, Dole had to decide whether to stay on when Verner Liipfert pursued a merger with larger firms, and he ended up moving to Alston & Bird, where Tom Daschle joined him in 2005.

Dole saw this as returning Mitchell's favor. Mitchell "was a big factor" in convincing him to join Verner Liipfert, "just as I think I was a factor in getting Daschle into this firm," he said. Among the other political luminaries who joined Verner Liipfert were Lloyd Bentsen, former Texas governor Ann Richards, another Democrat, and former senator Dan Coates from Indiana, a Republican. Dole did think of staying on, but, he said, "It was a question of just getting too big. I remember the partner who came to see me to convince me to do it said, 'You'll be doing a lot of traveling, but you'll have a good time, we'll take care of you.' And that was enough for me, when I heard the word 'traveling,' because I'd had enough traveling for thirty years, fund-raisers and all that stuff." Mitchell, however, didn't have a similar reaction, and Dole's claim about not working on cases with him wasn't entirely true.

When Mitchell was mulling over leaving the Senate, he consulted Bernhard, who said, "I think he had made up his mind when we chatted. It was, 'Can you figure out a good reason why I shouldn't do this?'" From the beginning it was clear Mitchell wouldn't just take cases that came his way, Bernhard said. "We all agreed when he came here that he was a widely accepted and respected public official, high-level government leader, both national and international, and he would be . . . asked to, and would want to, give speeches where he could make some money, and we agreed that should happen. He also made it clear he wanted to go on some [corporate] boards, and we encouraged that. . . . There were expectations that were not predicated on his producing chargeable hours and big clients and so on, though as it turned out, he did do a lot of that."

When Dole joined, Bernhard was equally impressed. "We had this huge potential matter dealing with Lloyd's of London . . . and we had hoped to represent one of the very big players. And I remember talking with both Bob Dole and George about making a joint presentation to the client, which they did, and they were spectacular." Nor did Mitchell duck leadership roles. Bernhard had chaired the firm for twenty years, and wanted to step down. "He came in to tell me that was a wrong move to make, and I said, 'That's from your standpoint;

it's the right move from mine. But I'll tell you, George, you have responsibilities here, and I really think that you've got to take over as chair.'" There was "total silence," Bernhard said, "and then he got to the door, turned around, and said, 'I guess I'll have to do it, but I came in here to convince you to stay on.'" Bernhard didn't always persuade Mitchell, but when he did, that was it. "Once he takes on an assignment, it's a commitment," he said. "There is no one more determined, disciplined, and demanding."

After only two years, though, Mitchell pursued a second, part-time affiliation. Despite the "compromise" with Heather about staying in New York, he'd never quite given up his dream of living in Maine, and joining a Maine law firm at least allowed him to spend more time there. In March 1997, Preti Flaherty, home to many prominent Democratic lawyer-lobbyists, announced he was joining the firm as senior counsel, working out of the 443 Congress Street office in Portland. Harold Pachios, Tony Buxton, and Severin Beliveau were all partners, and all had chaired the Maine Democratic Party, while Pachios had run for Congress and Beliveau for governor. At the time, there were fifty-five attorneys. Mitchell didn't do any lobbying—aside from endorsing Democrats, he has stayed out of state politics almost entirely in his political retirement—but he did take cases suggested by other attorneys.

Tony Buxton hadn't worked regularly with Mitchell since the 1974 governor's race, and soon found that, whatever time Mitchell had in Maine—generally two days a month, plus phone consultations—he used fully. "He was by far the most easily accessible lawyer in our firm," Buxton said. "And when you called him up and said, 'I want your help on something,' he would, right then, say, 'OK, what do you want me to do?' . . . And you had to be ready for him, because when you put the phone down he would do it—as opposed to most lawyers, who will get to you in a month. He did not have a staff other than two assistants, he did not have an associate who was carrying his bags. . . . He just did things."

One case Buxton worked on with Mitchell involved the family of advice columnist Ann Landers, who had started a company called Millennium Vodka that marketed the Belvedere and Chopin brands, "and they were so successful that they acquired a competitor making the same thing . . . same bottles, same alcohol, and it was being done out of France and Poland." Legal issues arose from the intellectual property rights involved, and ultimately involved sixty-five countries, Buxton said. It was ideal for Mitchell, he said, "something involving international commerce, requiring people who can, by their presence in a room, be considered significant." The outcome benefited the client, with a French company ultimately acquiring Millennium. Buxton believes Mitchell found some of the cases as challenging as those he handled for Verner Liipfert, which at the time was comparably sized, with seventy attorneys.

Mitchell's Washington law firm got a lot bigger, however. It grew rapidly after he succeeded Bernhard as chairman, and had 234 attorneys and a large government affairs division, which now included former Republican House majority leader Dick Armey. But the September 11 attacks created a crisis. "We had a lot of clients in the transportation and international sectors," Bernhard said. "Business was down—way down." One possibility was to drastically downsize, but, with the agreement of the other partners, Bernhard and Mitchell went shopping for a possible partner. The receptions were not always warm, nor the prospects promising. After visiting one New York firm, Bernhard recalls Mitchell saying, when they got back to the lobby, "If this is what I've got to do to practice law, I'm not doing it."

In 2002, they found a match in the firm of Piper Rudnick, itself a product of a 1999 merger between Piper & Marbay in Baltimore and Rudnick & Wolfe in Chicago. A joining of equals, the Piper Rudnick deal was, at the time, the largest merger of law firms in US history. The legal profession had long been dominated by small family partnerships, and, even in large cities, firms with more than one hundred attorneys were rare. Retail advertising was discouraged by tradition, and by bar association rules. Piper Rudnick had done well, and was prepared to take on Verner Liipfert and its stable of highly visible former politicians. From the beginning, according to Harold Pachios, Mitchell was considered an asset. "He was part of the package they were interested in," Pachios said. "He was a perfect pickup for them. They got an attorney with an enormous amount of insight and knowledge, as well as a unique sense of business and entrepreneurship." Pachios said various high-profile Maine Democrats served in Washington and then joined law firms there, including Ed Muskie and Bill Hathaway, but Mitchell was "the only one who became a mega-lawyer." Speaking of the new firm, he said, "It didn't take them long to figure out what they had. George was a big producer of business."

Severin Beliveau also tracked Mitchell's ascent in the legal profession from his own position as one of Maine's most prominent lobbyists. "George saw an opportunity to make some money, and he fit right in with what became a huge international firm. He was wonderful with clients, he was superb at understanding the legal issues, and he could negotiate a deal." Of Mitchell's legal rivals, he said, "We all think we're big, but George was on a different level." Some skills from politics carried over, Beliveau said. "He's capable of understanding both sides of an issue, and he doesn't personalize it. He's not interested in putting opponents on the defensive or embarrassing them."

Piper Rudnick took another leap upward in size and scope two years later. Now with nearly 1,000 attorneys, it negotiated a deal to acquire the San Diego firm of Gray Cary, which had specialties in intellectual property and patent law. Gray Cary brought another 380 attorneys on board, but by the end of 2004 the new firm had become a three-way combination. The British law firm known as DLA, for the initials of its predecessor partners, was also on a growth campaign, and the American and British firms, each with more than 1,300 attorneys, combined on January 1, 2005, creating one of the world's largest firms with 2,700 attorneys. The official name was DLA Piper Rudnick Gray Cary, but it soon became known as DLA Piper, and grew to employ 4,200 attorneys in more than two dozen countries—the world's largest law firm. As the merger took shape, Mitchell was the consensus choice for DLA Piper's first chairman, a position he held until he became Middle East special envoy in 2009. Another result was that he and Heather continued to live in New York. As his responsibilities at Verner Liipfert increased, it made sense to relocate to Washington, she said. "We had bought a house, and our son had been accepted at school and we were really ready to move to DC, but then the merger happened, and they did have a very large presence here in New York, [so] we decided that we'd stay."

Even after formation of DLA Piper and, as the head of a law firm nearly a thousand times larger than the one in Portland where he'd long ago partnered with Mert Henry, some of Mitchell's old acquaintances saw little change in his demeanor, though conversations moved faster. Najeeb Lotfey, still his personal accountant, talked to him at locations throughout the world. "Whenever I need to talk to him, I don't hesitate to call, and whenever he needs to talk to me, he doesn't hesitate either," Lotfey said, but "more often than not I try him on a Saturday or a Sunday because during the week he's busy . . . or he's in faraway places. But he has called me from as far away as Egypt, as far away as Israel." Mitchell always called back, Lotfey said. "Of all the clients I have served over the years, he is probably the most responsive, as busy as he is. When I call, I hear from him within twenty-four hours, most often a lot sooner," though "We don't chitchat, we get right to the point."

While Mitchell's law firm showed rapid, even spectacular growth in employees and revenues, it wasn't all smooth going. For the new international firms, navigating dozens of different legal systems was a challenge. Another was keeping abreast of potential conflicts of interest, for which the possibilities multiplied as clients and attorneys crossed numerous boundaries. Mitchell was an old hand at this, but he wasn't immune to conflicts between the image and reputation he'd built over the years, and the companies he chose to represent.

Mitchell found himself in dilemmas created by his own success in the clearly distinct worlds of politics and law. His trials were perhaps most cogently summed up in a long profile in the *Boston Globe Magazine* on March 3, 2002, written by John Aloysius Farrell. It doesn't accuse Mitchell of wrongdoing, and deals with many aspects of his life and career, but its thrust is accurately summed up in the headline: "Integrity for Sale?" It was published just before Verner Liipfert merged with Piper Rudnick, and reflected Mitchell's work—when not in Northern Ireland or the Middle East—during his first six years with the firm. Mitchell had worked for some clients that raised eyebrows, including tobacco manufacturers and General Electric, which was resisting a cleanup of PCB discharges into the Hudson River. But the article began with a lesser-known case—that of chocolate manufacturers buying cocoa, their key ingredient, from the Ivory Coast—a country later shown to be using slave labor by children as young as nine. The US House had reacted by passing a labeling bill that would require manufacturers to certify, and state on packaging, that they weren't involved in "slave labor." The manufacturers decided these words would be confusing, if not disastrous, displayed on a product disproportionately consumed by children, and purchased by their parents. They went to work in the Senate, and hired Mitchell to represent them. The *Globe* profile concedes, "It's difficult to define just what Mitchell did in return for the fees that the venerable law and lobbyist firm he now chairs . . . received from the candy giants," but concludes that "access" to Congress is valuable only if it's discreet. It quotes a spokeswoman for the manufacturers saying, "We went to him, and he gave us advice. He certainly urged us to work with members of Congress, who were very concerned." In a settlement, the labeling requirement was dropped and the manufacturers given three years to ensure slave labor wasn't used in producing cocoa.

Mitchell's work for GE was brief, and not especially successful. The profile quotes his response: "I contacted EPA, I established a process for discussion and negotiation which unfortunately did not lead to an agreement, and then our representation ended." He added, "The purpose of the representation was to try and begin and complete a negotiation. I don't think there is anything wrong with that, and I absolutely don't subscribe to the view that I am doing bad things so that I can go do good things. I think both roles are perfectly defensible." Mitchell also commented on why a business might need such representation. "There are times when reasonable compromise is appropriate," he said. "There is a tendency on the part—and believe me, these are all friends of mine—of the environmental community to tar with a broad brush anybody who is willing to compromise anything." It wasn't until years later that GE began funding cleanups, and not until

2014 that GE settled a lawsuit filed by towns whose drinking water treatment plants had been compromised by PCB contamination.

It is the tobacco case, though, that caused the most difficulty with Mitchell's image, if not his reputation. In that sense, it was his Prestile Stream—roughly analogous to Muskie's embarrassment after he agreed to a nine-month downgrading of water quality on the Aroostook County river so a manufacturing plant could begin operating.

Berl Bernhard takes partial responsibility for Mitchell's involvement. After years of appearing impervious to lawsuits and political challenges, the tobacco industry was reeling from adverse court decisions and damaging revelations from former industry insiders that it knew about the multiple risks of cigarette smoking, but concealed them. In Bill Clinton's second term, there was strong pressure, from the president on down, for a deal that would, among other things, remove the industry's long-standing exemption from regulation by the Food and Drug Administration. The National Association of Attorneys General was a major player, and one of its principal consultants was Jim Tierney, a former Maine attorney general who, like Mitchell, won the Democratic nomination for governor—in 1986, over Severin Beliveau—but lost in November. Tierney was an association board member for many years, and still teaches state law subjects at Columbia Law School. Since a settlement was the goal, and Mitchell was an expert negotiator, Tierney urged Bernhard to convince Mitchell to allow the firm to represent the tobacco companies. Mitchell's degree of reluctance isn't known, but the contract was signed. Over two years, tobacco companies reportedly paid the firm $18 million.

Ultimately, congressional negotiations fell apart and the attorneys general reached a separate settlement that paid, over time, $246 billion into a fund that's supposed to provide perpetual revenue to each state. The money is intended to be used to combat smoking, and some states, including Maine, employ it that way, but the revenue is in fact unrestricted and is often treated like revenue sharing. There is still no FDA regulation of cigarettes.

In the profile, Mitchell explained his role: "We were approached and asked to participate in trying to reach a national settlement that would be beneficial to all concerned, that would, for example, bring tobacco companies under the regulation of the Food and Drug Administration, from which they were and still are exempt. They were willing to submit to that regulation. We were not involved in trying to defend past practices, trying to rationalize the industry. It was a very specific objective which we felt was in the public interest." That was all he was willing to say, and the writer observes, "Even when Mitchell was running for office or managing the Senate, he was a tough interview—giving little and parsing his words like a diamond cutter."

One of his partners, however, the old political hand, Harry McPherson, wasn't so reticent. In an interview with two journalists, one of whom had worked for him, and both acquaintances of forty years, he began in the same vein as Mitchell: "We agreed to do it because we thought it made a lot of sense in terms of the public interest." But McPherson then said, "Secondly, because it was very handsomely compensated work. I have a partner named Mitchell who is a guy who has the connection with the tobacco industry, and he then left it in my hands, to go off and try to keep the Irish from killing each other. So it is possible to be in a prosperous firm and not to lose all your values." Then he added, "I hope that's true, anyway."

Some neutral or sympathetic observers summed up Mitchell's problem in the profile. Larry Makinson, senior fellow of the Center for Responsive Politics in Washington, said, "If you really sit back and think how many surviving elder statesmen there are, it is a pretty short list, and George Mitchell is at or near the top. That can translate into cash. He had ultimate entree. Who in the world would not return George Mitchell's phone call? Who in the world would not deeply consider anything George Mitchell had to say? And the ability to open doors and have people listen to you is the highest-valued commodity in Washington." Makinson commented, "It is interesting: The loftier your reputation, the greater your value if you decide to become a lobbyist." Presidential historian Douglas Brinkley said of Mitchell, "He has no skeletons in the closet. He has never signed his name to something that demeaned his moral authority. The Mitchell name is like the Good Housekeeping seal."

Fred Wertheimer, who'd worked shoulder to shoulder with him on campaign finance reform just a few years earlier, provided thoughts that might have resonated with Mitchell. "The key to the wise man role is to do things in a way that can stand up publicly to the extraordinary reputation you have built," Wertheimer said. "Senator Mitchell has always been a careful person. He needs to be careful. I'm sure he knows that." Since the advent of DLA Piper, Mitchell hasn't represented any clients which might be compared to GE or the tobacco companies.

WHILE HIS LAW FIRMS BECAME MITCHELL'S MAJOR BUSINESS INVOLVEMENT, they were far from his only ones. Even before he left the Senate, Michael Eisner asked him to become president of Disney Entertainment. Mitchell declined, but did agree to join the board the following year—one of seven such corporate board appointments Mitchell accepted, spanning the next decade. Mitchell, after his early, embarrassing encounter with a former Muskie contributor during the 1982 Senate campaign, had won over the Hollywood crowd, some of whom became enthusiastic supporters and donors. Mitchell also joined the boards of FedEx, UnumProvident, and Xerox in 1995; Starwood Hotels in 1997; and Unilever and Staples in 1998. During the decade, his corporate board service amounted to a substantial annual income. Mitchell was impressed by several CEOs, and in his memoir singles out Fred Smith, who "invented the concept of express mail and created Federal Express," and Tom Stemberg, who "created and built Staples." In most cases, he served for six to eight years, though his involvement with Disney was the longest, more than ten years; he resigned on December 31, 2006. It was also the most consequential.

After announcing his Senate retirement in March 1994, Mitchell was feted in a variety of locales. An elaborate one came that summer, when he was invited to "a recognition and fund-raising event" at USC. "To my surprise, part of the program was produced by Disney Entertainment," he said. "It turned out that another member of the board [at USC] was also a board member of the Walt Disney Co., and several executives of the company were there, and I got to meet them." Frank Wells, Eisner's previous second-in-command, had been killed in a helicopter crash, and the board was looking for a quick and well-qualified replacement. Mitchell said no, explaining, "I had made a decision about retiring in part because I was going to be married." Their two choices of residence were New York and Maine, and California was a long way away. Mitchell later accepted Eisner's invitation to join the board, however, where he enjoyed the perks, "not the least of which is I got to take my kids to Disney World on several occasions, which they loved and I loved and my wife loved."

Eisner was the unchallenged leader of Disney, the man who had built it into an entertainment colossus far beyond the vision of its founder; he served as both CEO and board chairman. As Mitchell explains, "A number of American companies were, and many still are, run the same way. But there began to be some external criticism by corporate governance groups urging that the two positions be separated. . . . Some companies responded to that, some did not. Disney was one company that did respond." Mitchell, who'd been on the board for nearly eight years, was the board's choice in 2002 as presiding director—in theory, first among equals, but in practice he ran the board meetings. His final years on the board were eventful.

Eisner's decision to step down as chairman wasn't entirely the result of outside pressure. There was also internal dissension that soon came to a head. It had all begun cordially. The surprise entertainment at Mitchell's USC fete had been arranged by Stanley Gold, a Disney board member. Gold was the attorney for another board member—Roy Disney, Walt's nephew, who provided the family link to the company's storied past. Mitchell and Disney got on personally as well as professionally. "I had many warm discussions with Roy Disney . . . and his wife, Patty," he writes. "We shared an interest in and love for Ireland, where they owned a home and where I was then working most of the time."

Mitchell was also impressed by the company's performance during Eisner's twenty-one-year tenure. "In 1984, Eisner had become the chief executive of a company that was struggling artistically and financially," he said. "That year Disney had revenues of $1.45 billion and net income of $98 million. With energy, creativity, and a keen sense of the public's taste, Eisner led a sharp and successful expansion. By 1995, when I joined the board, revenues had risen to $12.15 billion and net income was $1.38 billion"—nearly equal to sales a decade earlier. Everything was going swimmingly. "New theme parks were opened and new attractions added at existing parks. The company entered the cruise ship business, as well as the live stage show business, creating long-running hits like *The Lion King* and *Beauty and the Beast*. The animated movie division churned out a series of hits, and the live-action movie business flourished. ABC television was acquired in 1996, and with it the spectacularly successful ESPN sports network."

Even the most successful companies have reverses, though, and Disney was no exception. In Mitchell's analysis, the contrast between Eisner's first and second decades, however understandable—high rates of growth are hard to sustain—began causing concern among board members. Growth in revenues, per decade, had dropped from 21 percent to 10 percent, and average net income growth had fallen faster, from 27.6 percent to 6 percent. And things were getting worse. "Disney's net income declined in five of the six years from 1998 to 2003," he said.

Disney and Gold worked closely together, and by the time Mitchell began serving as presiding director, things had soured between them and Eisner, and they soon emerged as the CEO's principal antagonists. The key blunder, in their view, was Disney's acquisition of Fox Family Worldwide, where the big asset was the Saturday-morning cartoon show, *Power Rangers*. At the time, most entertainment companies were starting or buying multiple new cable channels, for which—as the nation's habits shifted from broadcast to cable—there seemed unlimited demand. The timing was unfortunate. The sale, which involved $3 billion in cash and assuming $2.3 billion in debt, took place just before September 11, 2001, and the shocks that followed suggested Disney had overpaid. Disney and Gold became fierce critics of the acquisition. "I do not know whether that was the straw that broke the camel's back for Roy Disney and Stanley Gold, or whether there were other grievances more important to them," Mitchell wrote. "But they turned against Eisner, and Gold became increasingly critical of him, first in board meetings and then in public." Things got nasty. Mitchell observed that, beyond the theatrics, "What mattered was that the company wasn't doing well, and when a company doesn't do well, a natural reaction is to change its leadership."

Mitchell knew all the players well, and he respected Eisner's achievements. In a recent interview, Mitchell said, "Michael Eisner didn't found the Walt Disney Co., but for all intents and purposes he founded the modern Walt Disney Co., and was—is—still a truly remarkable and brilliant entrepreneur who took this small, foundering, and—I wasn't around at the time, but it's been described as a near-failing company—and transformed it into what is now one of the largest and most successful entertainment companies in the world. And he had strong support on the board while things were going well. But when a few stumbles occurred, and the returns weren't as good, not a large segment of the board—originally two members, Roy Disney and Stanley Gold—began an effort to oust Eisner." Mitchell's sense of fairness was offended by their focus on the Fox Family purchase. "There's no doubt in retrospect that the company did overpay, but what was of particular concern was that Stanley and Roy were huge proponents of the transaction when it was before the board. Stanley had strongly argued for going ahead with the deal. . . . I'd been in politics a long time, and I'd experienced that, but it made it very difficult." After Eisner stepped down as chairman and Mitchell stepped up to presiding director, he became a target, too. "It was very acrimonious," he said. "Those who opposed Eisner opposed me as well on the grounds that I was too close to him and I wasn't exercising enough independence."

At the end of 2003, Disney and Gold resigned and took their campaign public. "The campaign reached its peak of intensity on March 3, 2004, at the company's annual shareholders' meeting in Philadelphia," Mitchell writes in his memoir. "Over three thousand shareholders gathered in the grand hall at the Philadelphia Convention Center. Gold unleashed a stinging attack on Eisner and received applause for it. He also criticized me, but only briefly; I was just collateral damage." When the shareholders cast ballots, both Eisner and Mitchell were reelected, Mitchell with 76 percent and Eisner with just 57 percent. As Mitchell said, they were "both short of an overwhelming vote of confidence."

Just before the meeting, Eisner had asked Mitchell to assume full powers as board chairman, a much more demanding position. Mitchell said no, concerned it would look like they were panicking. After the meeting, the entire board renewed the offer. "I hesitated, torn between wanting to be of help to a company I had come to love and the concern that I was already too busy, and that this would be a long and painful effort not likely to end well." Mitchell met privately with Eisner, and said, "As is often the case with strong leaders, as the criticism mounted Eisner became more defensive and less willing to accept it." While Mitchell called the two former board members "excessively personal and unfair in their criticism," he also acknowledged, "their concerns were not unfounded." Mitchell decided to resign from other boards, from FedEx, Starwood, and Unilever, though he remained with Staples, to concentrate on the full-time job at Disney.

Fortunately for the board, and Mitchell, the company's performance improved, with revenues growing by 14 percent and net income by 83 percent in his first year as chairman. Eisner began to think of leaving, and by late 2004, with Mitchell acting as counselor, he planned his exit. Mitchell used his new powers to appoint himself chair of the selection committee. In the interview, he said, "Stanley and Roy were opposed to that as well. They brought a lawsuit alleging fraud in the process of selecting Bob Iger as Michael's replacement, which ultimately was withdrawn, and we were able to achieve unanimity of the board." He observed, "One of the problems on these large boards is that, very often, when you have a very strong CEO, members of the board will say things *to* him that are different from what they say *about* him when speaking with others. And so the CEO gets an inaccurate version of what his or her support actually is. I had to mediate that. I thought the world of Michael . . . and Bob has done a terrific job in succeeding him. You know, there's a time and place for everyone." Iger had been president and chief operating officer at Disney since 2000, and was Eisner's second-in-command.

The Disney–Gold dissension was an irresistible story. Mitchell received more press coverage for his Disney chairmanship than anything else he did between the Good Friday Agreement in 1998 and his report on performance-enhancing drugs for Major League Baseball in 2007. Understandably, reporters played up the conflict. A *Washington Post* story quoted the Disney–Gold statement saying that Mitchell's "selection as chairman is a terrible choice by this board. It is a grave disservice to their shareholders." The story also quoted Nell Minow, chairman of the Corporate Library shareholder activists group, saying, "Former government officials have generally not been good directors. But there have been notable exceptions. The jury is still out on Mitchell. If he pulls this one off, he'll go to the hall of fame." A *New York Times* story detailed the dissenters' contention that Mitchell couldn't be independent of Eisner, and said Mitchell "takes umbrage" at such talk. It also quoted Ted Kennedy saying, "He is a tough-minded person who has demonstrated he can deal not only with the sharp elbows of politicians, but can handle the elbows in the business world as well." And Eisner, recalling his initial offer to Mitchell in 1995, said, "I watched him in the Senate and I heard a speech he gave and I was blown away." The Maine stories were more flattering, and included Mitchell's self-assessments. About the shareholder vote, he said, "In any other endeavor in life, getting 76 percent favorable . . . would be very satisfying, but in this sense, I recognize that many stockholders are unsatisfied." He also said that while he admired Eisner, he was not a personal friend, and that he and Heather had dinner with Eisner and his wife only twice in ten years, contrasting his relationship with Fred Smith at Fed Ex, where the two shared tennis, socializing, and even a Thanksgiving dinner.

Mitchell's exit from Disney was announced on June 28, 2006, with an experienced corporate hand, John Pepper, former Procter & Gamble CEO, succeeding him. Things worked out well for almost all concerned. Mitchell returned to his law practice. Eisner started a new company, Tornante, which produces shows through a studio, Vuguru, that focuses on distribution through new media. And Disney regained steady growth and profitability. Pepper served until 2012, when Bob Iger became chairman and CEO.

In the New York area, Tuesday, September 11, 2001, dawned with a crystalline clarity to the atmosphere, and, as the sun rose, it became the kind of still, warm morning that, had it occurred later in the fall, would have been called Indian summer. George Mitchell was on his way to LaGuardia Airport, where he planned to catch a flight to Washington to give a speech. It was just four months after the Sharm el-Sheikh report had been made public, and there still seemed hope the Bush administration would use it to convene negotiations between Israelis and Palestinians. His speech, on Northern Ireland, would also address that possibility.

In a cab on the way to LaGuardia, there were confused reports of an attack on downtown New York. After he arrived, Mitchell heard an announcement that the airport was closing and everyone had to leave. No one seemed to know what was going on, but in the scramble Mitchell found a limo that he shared with a woman worried that her wedding would have to be canceled. On the way back to Manhattan, the passengers and driver listened intently to radio news reports. The limo crested the rise of the Triborough Bridge and Mitchell noticed, for the first time, that there was a clear view of lower Manhattan. Seconds later, the first tower of the World Trade Center collapsed. By the time they arrived at the Harlem River, the border between Manhattan and Queens and the Bronx, the bridge exit was closed. The driver headed north to see if any uptown bridges were open. None were. Manhattan was sealed off from the outside world. The driver said he was Palestinian, and didn't want to go farther, so Mitchell got out at 230th Street and began to walk. As he and hundreds of other pedestrians contemplated walking onto the bridge, one started, and the others followed. Mitchell spent the next five and a half hours making his way home to Broadway and 68th Street, via cab, on foot, and the C Line. Heather, Andrew, and Claire, an infant, were safe. He delivered the speech several weeks later, in a world changed by violence on an almost incomprehensible scale.

Mitchell had an inkling something like this could happen. His friend Warren Rudman had co-chaired, with Gary Hart, a National Security Commission that reported in February 2001 and gave what Mitchell termed "very explicit warnings" of terrorist attacks on an "unprecedented" scale. He'd been sobered by the level of hostility and hatred he'd witnessed during his fact-finding mission in the Middle East, and while what he saw that morning "still came as a shock," he said in an interview a few weeks later, it was clear to him that terrorist groups "had a lot of different efforts going on, on the theory that some will succeed, even though most will fail."

For a time, it seemed Mitchell would play another key role in investigating what happened on September 11 and in the months and years before in the Middle East, where many terrorist plots were conceived and carried out. Not long after the towers fell, calls began for a national commission to find out facts and causes, most loudly and persistently from congressional delegations in the New York and Washington areas. The Bush administration was preoccupied with launching the invasion of Afghanistan and then planning the invasion of Iraq, which it launched in January 2003, twelve years after George H. W. Bush ordered the invasion of Kuwait. Neither Senate Majority Leader Trent Lott nor House Speaker Dennis Hastert, both Republicans, pressed the issue, and it wasn't until late November 2002, fourteen months after the September 11 attacks, that commission members were named. Under ground rules agreed to by Congress, President Bush would name the chairman of the commission, and Senate Minority Leader Tom Daschle and House Minority Leader Dick Gephardt would jointly pick the vice chairman. There would be five Democratic and five Republicans choices for the ten-member commission. Bush announced his selection of Henry Kissinger as chair from the Roosevelt Room at the White House, while Daschle and Gephardt picked Mitchell as vice chair. Almost immediately, there was consternation and jockeying behind the scenes.

Bob Carolla, Mitchell's Senate aide, saw a parallel to the White House's resistance in an earlier investigation of a terrorist plot, the explosion of Pan Am Flight 103 over Lockerbie, Scotland, on December 21, 1988, which killed 259 people on board and 11 on the ground—an act now known to have been carried out by Libyan operatives. The airliner bomb plot occurred after George H. W. Bush was elected but before he took office, and he was reluctant to approve a congressional investigation. The impetus, Carolla said, came from the widow of a business executive lost on Flight 103, Victoria Cummock. "As often happens with bureaucracies, the White House and the FAA were stonewalling," he said. "None of the agencies wanted an investigation. The FAA didn't want to be accused of being responsible, the Department of Transportation didn't want to be held responsible, the FBI didn't want to divulge anything, same thing with the CIA." Some families managed to get meetings at the White House with Chief of Staff John Sununu, and even the president, but Carolla said the response was, "'We want to help and we're so sorry,' but nothing ever came of it." The families seemed to envision an Iran-Contra process, and "that wasn't going to be the level it would rise to," he said, but many felt Congress should do something.

"The person who broke through that stalemate was Vicki Cummock," he said. She had a family connection to Bob Dole, who met with her, and then recommended she see Mitchell. Carolla staffed the meeting, where Cummock said, "I really apologize for taking this much time. I know that a lot of people think we shouldn't be here in Washington." That brought Mitchell up short, and he said, "What do you mean? Who's saying that?" When she reported her discouraging reception at federal agencies and some congressional offices, he said, "It is your right in a democracy and under our Constitution to be here asking Congress and your government to do something." Carolla said, "It wasn't a lecture, but it was like a thirty- to sixty-second lesson in civics, and it was a very genuine one."

When Sununu heard that Dole and Mitchell would introduce legislation for an independent commission to investigate the crash of Flight 103, "All hell broke loose at the White House," Carolla said. An impasse was averted through agreement for a presidential executive order creating a commission, under terms acceptable to Senate leaders. The commission and its report became a model for the September 11 panel, according to Carolla.

The September 11 commission's chair and vice chair drew intense scrutiny. Some Democrats were outraged about Kissinger, who they believed played a questionable role as Richard Nixon's national security advisor and secretary of state—sometimes occupying both roles simultaneously. Vietnam, the "secret war" in Cambodia, and, particularly, the 1973 military coup in Chile that assassinated President Salvador Allende, they believed, compromised Kissinger. The *Guardian* said, "Several recent books and a documentary have questioned his honesty and integrity, and his appointment to chair the commission by President Bush was greeted with astonishment." Mitchell had no such baggage, but skeptics focused on his legal clients, which reportedly included foreign governments in the Middle East.

Discussions were private and haven't since been disclosed, but it appears Mitchell attempted to recuse himself selectively, but this didn't satisfy the critics. As envisioned, the commission work would be nearly full-time, though unpaid. On December 10, less than two weeks after his appointment, Mitchell resigned. In a letter he said, "Some have urged that I sever all ties to the law firm with which I am associated. Since I must work to support my family I cannot comply." He added, "I take this action reluctantly, as I wanted very much to be part of this important effort." Two days later, Kissinger, who had many more clients in the Middle East, also resigned. They were replaced, as chair, by Tom Kean, former governor of New Jersey, and, as vice chair, Representative Lee Hamilton, who'd been House chair of the Iran-Contra Committee.

MITCHELL HAD EARLIER SERVED IN A DIFFERENT role concerning September 11, one far less publicly visible, but which proved far more personally satisfying. The American Red Cross had launched a fund-raising effort called the Liberty Fund within days of September 11. The money poured in at a seemingly unbeliev-able rate. The response by Americans outraged by the attacks and eager to help victims and their families was overwhelming. At its peak, the fund took in tens of millions of dollars a day. A year later, $500 million had been distributed to fami-lies and another $125 million spent for cleanup costs, aid to disaster recovery workers, and administration. So much money was going to the Red Cross that other nonprofits worried their own donations would dry up, at least for a time.

The money was being donated, however, under what many believed were false pretenses. The Red Cross, under its strong-willed CEO, Dr. Bernadine Healy, decided that not all the money would go to September 11 families; some would be used for other projects she had long had in mind, though that wasn't made clear in the fund-raising appeals. What's not as well known is that the Red Cross—already struggling to respond to its greatest disaster on American soil—was also in orga-nizational chaos. The fund-raising controversy was just the tip of the iceberg. On December 27, 2001, Healy's replacement as interim board chair, Harold Decker, hired Mitchell as independent overseer of the Liberty Fund in an effort to restore the Red Cross's standing and credibility. He had much to do.

Healy had been hired in 1999, and there was soon tension between her and the board. If Mitchell was concerned about the size of corporate boards he served on, the Red Cross was even more unwieldy. There was a fifty-member board of governors, representing the fifty states, and it was slow to deal with a CEO increasingly resistant to board direction. Decker, a lawyer, public admin-istrator, and executive with Upjohn, the pharmaceutical company, for eighteen years, had been brought in by Healy in February 2001 to advise her on legal issues. He soon found bigger problems, however, and played a difficult role as liaison between board and CEO.

The Red Cross had earlier only with great difficulty navigated the crisis over AIDS-contaminated blood. After a federal investigation found serious problems, the Red Cross in 1993 signed a consent decree with the FDA to make improve-ments under court supervision. When Decker arrived, "It was an organization that was suffering a great deal of distress," he said. "There was a great deal of disorganization in the legal function." A previous general counsel had been summarily removed because of violations of the consent decree. "They just could not seem to get into compliance with FDA regulation," Decker said. "They had been regulated by the National Institutes of Health, and that was a much more relaxed relationship."

An even bigger issue, in Decker's mind, was Healy's ambitious plan for a makeover of the Red Cross from traditional functions, such as providing emergency blood supplies. Healy made large investments in a research institute and in developing a system to freeze blood and transport it long distances, rather than relying on local, fresh donations, as the Red Cross had always done. The frozen blood scheme, Decker was advised by experts at the Red Cross, was a distraction. "It's very impractical," he said, because freezing blood is prohibitively expensive. "The answer is to be able to line people up and tap into available sources from the human body. . . . No rational pharmaceutical or biologics company would attempt to freeze blood."

Healy had been director of the National Institutes for Health starting in 1991, where she began a women's health initiative, then became president of the American Heart Association in 1998. At the Red Cross, though, the organization experienced what Decker called "mission drift."

On September 9, a Sunday, Decker was in Memphis, Tennessee, meeting with representatives of Medtronic, and attempting to sell the money-losing research operation involving human bone and tissue. "The contracts that had been arranged for that particular business were very poorly done," he said, with "simply no way to get out of them." He flew back to Washington Monday night and was in his office Tuesday morning when his secretary called and said, "You should turn on your television. Apparently, a plane has hit the World Trade Center." He was just in time to see a plane striking the second tower. "Shortly thereafter we received reports that the Pentagon was hit, and then all hell broke loose, people running all over the area where our offices are," in downtown DC. Decker began to imagine what would come next. "We knew immediately we were going to be taxed greatly." At the ensuing staff meeting with Healy, blood supplies were a major topic. "Because it was following the Labor Day holiday, we were down to about a one- to two-day supply of blood, which is very low, dangerously low for the country," he said. The New York affiliate immediately began planning collection sites in Manhattan.

After a very late night, Decker returned to his office Wednesday morning and was confronted by a distraught Ramesh Thadani, head of biomedical services.

He'd been ordered by Healy to create a frozen blood reserve, which he and Decker knew was utterly impractical. Decker dreaded Healy's reaction. When he said, "Ramesh and I would like to talk to you about the frozen blood supply. . . . It was like somebody put air brakes on and she said, 'I won't yield on that subject.'" After he pointed out "we're two senior guys from the pharmaceutical industry, we just want to go through the positives and the negatives," she agreed to talk, but, "it was a pretty frosty reception." The meeting, Decker said, "deteriorated very quickly into a very acrimonious debate."

Healy also decided to go ahead with the Liberty Fund, officially the Liberty Disaster Relief Fund, without seeking board approval. The staff geared up for a massive campaign relying heavily on broadcast public service announcements. "Unfortunately, her fund-raising requests were not matched by her intended uses of the money," Decker said. "She went out with a very broad fund-raising request for families of victims and people immediately affected by the events of September 11. Later on, she announced she wanted to set aside part of the money for other purposes, which included the possibility . . . for what she called a strategic frozen blood reserve," and "a community outreach program designed to blunt ethnic intolerance." She also asked Decker to draft an after-the-fact resolution for the board to ratify her unilateral creation of the Liberty Fund. The board approved it, Decker said, "with a great deal of concern, and a great deal of apprehension."

Decker told Healy she was in trouble with the board. "They felt she was somewhat imperious, that she was single-minded, that she disregarded the authority of the board, that she was ruthless with employees." Decker said it "was a respectful talk, and she seemed to take the implied criticism quite well, but in the end it didn't seem to change her behavior." Decker was dismayed when he heard Healy attacking leaders of the Alexandria Chapter, which had led the response to the Pentagon disaster, which some criticized as slow. "She just blistered them in a public meeting out at the chapter headquarters," Decker said. The meeting of the board of governors on October 26 was surreal. "She resigned in a meeting that was broadcast live on television," he said. "She was making faces behind the chairman of the board as he was saying good-bye to her, and disavowing statements he was making by her actions behind his back on national television. It was really an ugly scene."

Sympathetic newspaper profiles at the time suggested Healy had tried to correct organizational deficiencies at the chapter level, albeit through heavy-handed methods. None of these accounts dealt with the blood freezing issue, the organization's troubled financial condition, or the decision to launch the Liberty Fund without board approval. Decker said, "Dr. Healy is a very strong-willed person. She's a very intelligent woman, and I guess the way I would say it is that it was like watching a Greek tragedy, where the protagonist has some marvelous gifts, but they also have some fundamental flaws. . . . Her flaw was that she failed to realize she had fifty bosses, and she was so strong-willed she was willing to take on many more challenges than I felt the organization was capable of accomplishing."

Decker became interim CEO. He told the board the Red Cross needed to abandon the subsidiary functions Healy had planned, and on November 10 presented a recovery plan that scuttled the frozen blood reserve. Decker knew the American Red Cross was a large operation—it had 36,000 employees and 1.2 million volunteers—and that it would be hard to turn it around quickly. He'd shut down the Liberty Fund—fund-raising would resume only months later—and organized a November 14 press conference that, he said, "went a long way toward releasing pressure." But Decker knew more was needed. Not only had public confidence been shaken, but internal disarray continued. He checked with the chief financial officer, and found there was a $400 million debt, $40 million in annual interest payments, and a margin of just 0.4 percent of revenue over expenses on blood operations, the mainstay of the Red Cross budget.

Decker consulted board chair David McLaughlin, and they decided to bring in someone from outside the organization. "We really needed somebody else to come in with a certain amount of credibility and gravitas with the American people who would not just provide eyewash for what we were doing, but someone who could provide substantive participation . . . for how we would deal with this massive amount of money we were the steward for, how we would distribute it, to whom, over what period of time, and for what purpose." This required someone "who had good analytical skills and an appropriate team," and "who was very articulate and speaks with clarity and force and imagination," Decker said. "And the person who came to mind pretty quickly was George Mitchell."

McLaughlin knew Berl Bernhard, and they arranged a meeting. Mitchell listened and "very quickly," Decker said, responded, "If I take this, I want agreement that part of my title will be 'independent'; no matter what else you put after it, I want it to be independent." They agreed on "independent public overseer." Jim Pickup, from Sharm el-Sheik, joined the staff team, along with Bernhard and a young Georgetown Law graduate, Jen Martin. Decker said the team "did a lot of the detail work that allowed Senator Mitchell to think . . . and to meet with people out in the field who were affected, and take their temperature and find out what we needed to do to satisfy their needs." Mitchell started at the end of 2001 and continued, often full-time, for nearly a year.

Decker continued damage control. He got a call from Eliot Spitzer, then New York state attorney general—no stranger to confrontation himself—who said,

"We've never met, but I've had a very confrontational relationship with your boss," and told Decker his office was trying to coordinate the many fund-raising appeals that had sprung up, and that Healy wouldn't cooperate. A subsequent agreement Decker brokered fell apart, but he told Spitzer, "Relax, things are changing." He said, "It helped when Mr. Spitzer knew that Senator Mitchell was going to be a part of the process."

Mitchell and his team helped with plans to reorganize the Red Cross's antiquated record-keeping—it still used paper copies to track blood donations—and cut back on extraneous spending. "The public assumed we were part of the federal government," Decker said, but federal contracts amounted to less than 3 percent of revenue. In his own account of the assignment, Mitchell glides over the organizational chaos, and doesn't mention Bernadine Healy—instead emphasizing the personal encounters with families and others whose lives had been uprooted. "One of the lessons," he said, "was the difficulty of applying the concept of fairness in a situation in which you had thousands of people, each of whom was in a unique circumstance, each of whom had some concept of fairness that applied to them but placed them at odds with others."

He details a meeting with a group of women, all of whose partners had perished. "It lasted for several hours," he said. "It was one of dozens and dozens of such meetings I had, trying to get a sufficient factual basis, an emotional understanding, and some conceptual rationale for how I would distribute these vast sums of money among these other people. Because I knew, the Red Cross had made clear, they would take my recommendation. Basically, I was going to decide where this money was going to go."

One woman, who had four children, said compensation should be based on the number of surviving children, "a very logical argument," Mitchell said. Another woman said, "I have two children, but one of them is retarded, and don't you think I and my child, now that my husband and their father is gone . . . need at least as much as someone who has four healthy children?" Another said her husband had been a waiter, and pointed out that the husband of the woman with four children had been a banker. "Don't you think that the amount of money or means we already have ought to be a factor?" It turned out that "of the twenty or so women in the room, no two of them were in identical circumstances. Each of them had a very powerful emotional case, and most of them were not only emotional but logical and persuasive." In his memoir, he says, "Each struggled with her grief, her needs, her embarrassment at talking about money with a man she had just met and a group of women she barely knew."

Mitchell reached tentative conclusions, and checked them with those who'd faced similar circumstances—such as the Oklahoma City federal building bombing in 1995. He doesn't reveal the formulas; the Red Cross had already said it would provide at least $30,000 to each family. He did announce four principles, however: "Meet the needs of those who suffered losses; honor the intent of the donors; provide assistance in a manner consistent with the mission and traditions of the Red Cross; ensure that all the money donated to the Liberty Fund would go to those who suffered loss on September 11."

The fund soon increased to $850 million, and for the nearly three thousand deaths in New York and Washington, each family received $109,000. Funding eventually exceeded $1 billion—perhaps an indication public confidence in the Red Cross had been restored. Mitchell said he learned a great deal through this experience. "Human beings are complicated, human lives are complicated, human societies are complicated, and it isn't always simple to decide what is the 'fair' way to do something. It takes a lot of time and effort, study and analysis of the problem, and most of all, hearing from those directly involved. They were the ones best in the position to know what to do, what not to do."

Decker said Mitchell made a memorable appearance at the Red Cross national convention in Phoenix. "His presence was very helpful," Decker said. "It had the effect of demonstrating to the employees and volunteers of the Red Cross that there was someone of prominence who was independently looking at what we were doing, keeping a scorecard, and putting his imprimatur on what we were doing . . . somebody who was part of the solution rather than part of the problem." Decker said Mitchell "is one of the most spontaneous and spontaneously intelligent people I have ever met. . . . He's someone who is able to apply a lot of imagination, and imagination is something you can't teach; you either have it or you don't, and he's got it. . . . People trusted him, because of the force of what he said, the clarity of his thinking, and how he had been proven right over time, over a long career as a legislator, as a judge, and as a negotiator. He's somebody who spoke with a great deal of moral force."

Mitchell's renewed full-time legal career has continued for more than two decades since his departure from politics. His choice of clients has gradually shifted from business representation, during his decade on corporate boards, to monitoring, overseeing, and mediating for nonprofit groups, athletic leagues, and other missions where he assumes the role of statesman more than attorney-at-law.

24

PASTIMES

George Mitchell's sister, Barbara, couldn't play baseball with her brothers growing up, but she could join them in their nightly sessions around the radio, listening to Boston Red Sox broadcasts. She said of George, "He always had a scoresheet and a pencil. He knew every player, and he remembered every game." Much later, on the campaign trail, Mitchell could silence a skeptic by asking a highly specific Red Sox question—a batting average or a pitching statistic—he knew would stump the challenger, but to which he, as a good attorney, knew the answer.

Even though Paul, like Swisher, was an excellent high school and college basketball player, also earning a scholarship to the University of Rhode Island, Paul's primary sport was baseball, and it was he who showed George the ropes. George was still in elementary school when Paul and John played high school baseball: John the shortstop, Paul in the outfield and the team's best hitter. George was more than six years younger than Paul, who got to play on the high school team when he was in the ninth grade. That required parental permission, because in Waterville, he was still in junior high. His father gave consent, but only on condition that Paul keep his grades up. And while George Sr. had virtually no apparent interest in his sons' basketball exploits, Paul said he did sometimes park his truck, part of his groundskeeping job at Colby College, outside the outfield fence, where he could keep track of the game.

If George was too young to play on the same team as his brothers, they could watch together, and his first opportunity came as a birthday present when George was in high school, with the Red Sox playing the Yankees at Fenway Park. As he relates in his memoir, "I was deeply impressed by the size and the beauty of the park. I had played in and watched a lot of local baseball games at which the attendance ranged from zero to a few dozen. To be among a crowd of 30,000 people watching a game was for me an unforgettable experience." The game went into extra innings, and in the top of the tenth, Joe DiMaggio, as big a star for the Yankees as Ted Williams was with the Red Sox, came up with the bases loaded. He struck a hard line drive to left field that went just foul over the "Green Monster," the thirty-seven-foot-high outfield wall. Two pitches later, "DiMaggio hit one harder and longer. There was no doubt this time as the ball sailed out of the park, high over the head of Joe's brother Dominic, the Red Sox center fielder." In the home half, Williams struck out to end the game, but Mitchell had seen the two best American League hitters in his first big league game.

As the older brother, Paul had memories of George at Fenway Park. One was George's picky eating. Before the game, he said, George spent so much time removing onions from a plate of spaghetti that they almost missed the start. They also stayed overnight at a downtown hotel, "an exciting first for me," Mitchell said, but there was only one bed. Paul slept in the middle, and in the morning complained that George had kept him up all night. "Not surprisingly, that was the last time Paul took me to a baseball game."

Mitchell's memories of baseball in his childhood are prefaced, as for other sports, with invidious comparisons to his own lack of ability. "I was not as good as my brothers in any sport," he said, and then, for emphasis, "I was so bad that not only was I not as good as my brothers, I wasn't as good as anybody else's brother. . . . With that came an inferiority complex, but the interest never waned." Mitchell said he liked all sports, but it isn't hard to infer that baseball was his favorite. "As kids we played all summer," he said. His baseball friend was Ronnie Stevens, and they chose Severns Field, on the old downtown Colby campus, for practice. Like countless boys before them, "Ronnie and I would go with a bat, three or four old balls, and he would bat and I would pitch three or four balls to him. He'd hit them, then he'd drop his bat, I'd drop my glove, we'd go out in the outfield, pick up the three or four balls, and then he would pitch and I would bat, just the two of us. We couldn't play a game, but we'd practice pitching and hitting and then throwing, and we spent many, many, many hours at that." They became "very good lifelong friends." As a fan, Mitchell could be equally focused. While serving as US Attorney, generally reluctant to take on any other commitments, even volunteer ones, he agreed on May 5, 1978, to serve an unexpired two-year term on the board of the Maine Sports Hall of Fame.

Mitchell was devoted to the Red Sox. Mike Aube, who served on the 1974 campaign staff, said, "His love for the Red Sox is just unbelievable." Aube witnessed one of those moments when Mitchell was having a hard time connecting to an audience, at Bowdoin College, and used his baseball knowledge to advantage. A student told him, "All you politicians are alike; all you want to do is talk. You have no connection to reality, what the pressures are, what are the things we really care about." Mitchell asked the student what he loved the most, and he said, "I love the Red Sox." Mitchell asked, "If I give you the starting lineup for the Red Sox and their batting averages, will you vote for me?" After the student agreed, Aube said, "George Mitchell went down the lineup, each player and what their batting average was." It was not, "'Oh, he's batting around .250,' but 'He's batting .263'; he knew them all, he had this great mind, as we all know, and the kid was blown away."

Chris Williams, who labored for many years with Mitchell on health care, found he rarely got off point. "Once in a while you might make chitchat about the Red Sox, but he wasn't a small talker," she said. Of the celebration on Election Night 1986, she said, "When we knew we had taken the Senate back, we had elected enough new Democrats, he stood up there on the podium and the first thing he said was, 'Well, this almost makes up for Bill Buckner,'" and the sixth game of the World Series a month earlier, when "Buckner let the ball roll through his legs and the Red Sox lost again."

Harold Friedman, husband of Mitchell's niece, Mary, remembers a Mitchell Institute event when "my brother and his wife from Detroit came out, and they met George, and my brother is a huge baseball fan, and he had one question for him, and that was 'What about the strike zone—isn't that really deteriorating in baseball?' . . . And there was George Mitchell . . . spending fifteen minutes talking to my brother about the strike zone . . . and [when] my brother walked away, he was on cloud nine."

Senators often found in baseball a common interest. Jay Rockefeller, asked whether there were baseball senators and football senators, said, "Everybody's a football senator for a while, but it's a much shorter season . . . and baseball is just built into the American psyche." The Red Sox were a good fallback with Mitchell. "You could approach him on a policy issue but just not human issues," Rockefeller said. "'Hey, how's it going, what's up?' That's not a George Mitchell conversation." Even though the Red Sox, despite "spending half my Harvard career at Fenway Park," Rockefeller said, "are my number-two team," it was a connection. "Baseball plays an important role, and particularly with a fellow like George Mitchell, who is not easily approachable."

Tom Yawkey, longtime owner of the Red Sox, died in 1976, and his widow, Jean Yawkey, continued the family tenure. After her death in 1992, the team was owned by the Yawkey Charitable Trust, and in 2001 trustees put the team up for sale. Various groups solicited Mitchell's support, and he joined one led by

Tom Werner, a television producer and later the team's chairman, and Maine ski area entrepreneur Les Otten. Mitchell also knew John Harrington, who'd functioned as team president during the trust's ownership, which also increased Mitchell's standing. The Werner-Otten group offered Mitchell a small ownership stake. The deal was clinched with the addition of John Henry, who'd bought the Florida Marlins in 1999 and sold them to pursue the Red Sox. In November 2001, the *Providence Journal* said Mitchell's involvement made his group the favorite, and Henry, who provided most of the cash, put them over the top, completing the purchase in February 2002. Another selling point was the group's pledge to expand seating and modernize Fenway Park on its existing footprint rather than build a new stadium elsewhere—a futile enterprise during the previous three decades.

Henry told fans after the purchase that his principal goal was to end the "Curse of the Bambino," an alleged hex put on the Red Sox after their owner sold his star pitcher, Babe Ruth, to the New York Yankees after the Sox won the 1918 World Series—their fifth title—to fund a Broadway musical. Ruth went on to hit 714 home runs, becoming baseball's greatest hitting star for the Yankees, who won twenty-six World Series from 1923 to 2000, while the Red Sox fell short year after year.

Mitchell was equally confident about ending the curse. At a campaign fundraising event in the summer of 2002, he told reporters, about his ownership stake, "It's very close between a neutron and what I own in the Red Sox," and said, following a sweep of the defending champion Arizona Diamondbacks at Fenway in June, "This is going to be the year." It wasn't, but fans didn't have to wait much longer. The Red Sox won the World Series in 2004, 2007, and 2013, and the curse is officially gone. When Mitchell was required to sell his Red Sox shares to join the State Department in 2009, he also had to step down as chairman of DLA Piper and chancellor of Queens University. Some who knew him best thought selling his Red Sox shares caused the most regret.

WHEN MITCHELL HAD LEFT THE SENATE IN 1994, there were far more reports of his becoming Major League Baseball commissioner than any other job. While all major US sports now use the commissioner model, baseball's position was uniquely powerful at its inception, when a sitting federal judge, Kenesaw Mountain Landis, was given nearly dictatorial powers by baseball owners in the wake of the "Black Sox" scandal in 1920, after several 1919 White Sox players conspired with gamblers to throw the World Series to the Cincinnati Reds. The commissioner's authority had declined markedly since Landis's death in 1944, however, and baseball had been riven by drug scandals and financial reverses since a federal arbitrator in 1975 created free agency for players in a sport that had no salary cap. Mitchell had gotten to know Bud Selig, former owner of the Milwaukee Brewers, and now acting commissioner, during his tenure as majority leader.

Selig had made himself synonymous with Milwaukee baseball. The Wisconsin city had landed the first franchise to move west following World War II, with the Boston Braves, who played second fiddle to the Red Sox, relocating there in 1953. The Braves already had several stars, including pitcher Warren Spahn and third baseman Eddie Matthews, and added their greatest player, Hank Aaron, in 1954. Aaron surpassed Ruth with 755 career home runs, but he did it with the Atlanta Braves, after the team left Milwaukee for the larger market of the Southeast, the first major league team below the Mason-Dixon Line. The Milwaukee Braves won the World Series in 1957, the National League pennant in 1958, and finished second three times in the pre–play-off era. Yet things soured between the city and team owners, attendance declined, and they decamped in 1966 after just thirteen years in the Midwest.

Selig, then just twenty-nine, headed the effort to return baseball to Milwaukee. He got exhibition games back into County Stadium, built for the Braves, and in 1968 convinced the Chicago White Sox to play ten regular-season games there. A 1969 Seattle expansion team, the Pilots, was in danger of folding, and Selig brought the team to Milwaukee in 1970 as the Brewers, where they've played ever since. Selig said, "The Milwaukee Brewers are here because I brought them here, and kept them here, and got a ballpark built"—Miller Field, which opened in 2001. Selig Drive connects the stadium to the interstate highway.

Yet if Selig was a youthful wonder as team owner, he was in a precarious position as acting commissioner. The owners in 1992 had fired Fay Vincent, deputy commissioner under the much-admired Bart Giamatti, the former president of Yale who died of a heart attack at age fifty-one in 1989. The owners had no plan beyond Vincent, and turned to Selig, one of their own, who stepped down from the Brewers to take the job. When owners repeatedly deadlocked over a successor, Selig remained acting commissioner for six years, getting the job permanently only in 1998, though his office remained in Milwaukee. Despite the shaky start, he served until 2015. Milwaukee was a "small market" club compared with teams from New York, Chicago, and Los Angeles that had far greater revenues, a disparity that continues to affect baseball's competitive balance, and later resulted in the first of Mitchell's baseball reports.

The year 1994 was a grim one. Labor relations with the players' union, never good since the advent of free agency, had worsened, and on August 11, the players went on strike and didn't return, canceling the World Series for the first time since John McGraw of the National League's New York Giants refused to play the American League champion Red Sox, in 1904.

Mitchell announced in March that he'd leave the Senate, and the baseball commissioner talk started soon afterward. Selig and Mitchell had met through a mutual acquaintance, and became friends. Selig is thought to have favored Mitchell as his successor, though it wasn't his call. Growing up, Selig's best friend was Herbert Kohl, the department-store magnate elected to the Senate in 1988; Kohl also bought the Milwaukee Bucks NBA franchise in 1985. Though Selig doesn't name him, it's likely Kohl was the mutual friend who introduced him to Mitchell. Asked about the commissioner's job, Mitchell uses the same formulation as for potentially becoming secretary of state—the job was never offered, so there was nothing to consider. Mitchell said that after the strike began in August, "The owners basically shelved any issue regarding a permanent commissioner until they were able to resolve the dispute with the players." That fits the facts; the strike dragged on until March 28, 1995, shortening the next season, and by that time the Northern Ireland prospect beckoned. Mitchell would seem to have been ideal for the situation, however. Like Giamatti, he was a lifelong fan, prominent and respected, and at the time had no ties to any team.

Mitchell said, "The discussions I had were general in nature. I did talk about it a little bit with Selig back in '94, but it never really progressed to the point that I got an offer. . . . Looking back, it's clear the owners wanted Selig." This seems unlikely. Baseball had never had a former owner as commissioner. The whole point of the job was to create an aura of independence from the owners who paid the commissioner's salary, and establish credibility with the players, fans, and public. While few of Landis's successors emulated his autocratic ways, Selig—with labor strife peaking—lacked cachet. There's evidence—as the press strongly suspected—that the 1994 commissioner talks with Mitchell were serious. Jeff Porter, who drove Mitchell frequently in Maine, said that during one trip, "He had a contract for the job that he was reading," but added, "If they really, really wanted him . . . he probably would have done it. But he wasn't going to lobby for the job the way other people did." Porter was undoubtedly not alone in wishing for that outcome. "That would be my ideal job. I'd love to be a staff member in the commissioner's office," he said.

Berl Bernhard, Mitchell's law partner, was also aware of behind-the-scenes movement, and said, "I had assumed, and George I think really hoped but didn't quite say it, that he would get the job instead of Bud Selig. And Selig had the inside move, because he theoretically owned a team, which he didn't really. I think George would have liked to have done that, I don't have any question about it." When George and Heather were married, Bernhard said, "I thought it was going to be all of Washington, but it turned out to be a typical George surprise. It was mostly his old friends from Maine. But one of the people sitting at my table was Bud Selig, and he was warm and pleasant with George, and I thought, what a bunch of BS. But then I realized it was a very smart move on George's part—that if there were a possibility that Selig for any reason couldn't or wouldn't take it, he would turn to George."

There's at least one more theory. The methods for selecting a baseball commissioner are opaque, but it's possible a single owner, or small group, could block a candidate they opposed. Sam Shapiro, former state treasurer, was close to Mitchell at the Maine Democratic Party. Shapiro said, "Everybody thought he was going to be commissioner of baseball. . . . And I happened to be flying back from the West Coast and sitting next to somebody who was a baseball umpire, out of Texas, and I said, 'Looks like our Senator Mitchell is going to be the next commissioner of baseball.' And he said, 'Well, he's not going to be.' And I said, 'Well, why do you say that?' He says, 'Well, I'm from Texas, and George Bush is not going to support him.'" Bush was managing partner of the Texas Rangers at the time, and the voting member. Shapiro said, "And George Bush the Second kept him from being the commissioner of baseball, because of what he felt George had done working for Clinton to defeat his father. I don't know whether George would have been better off or not, but I don't think so. I think George is better off, and certainly the world is better off."

IF MITCHELL WAS NOT TO BE SELIG'S SUCCESSOR, he did provide material assistance to his friend on several occasions. The first was an investigation into the economic and financial condition of baseball, which Selig commissioned in 1999. Since the strike, baseball had begun to recover, but its balance sheets were seriously askew. There were two problems: The first was that most teams were losing money. To the players this seemed impossible. Beginning in the 1980s, teams were sold to increasingly wealthy owners, prepared to spend whatever it took to win—and that meant acquiring high-priced veteran free agents. Even teams that could scarcely afford it were soon on spending sprees. Tickets soared in price, and fans often blamed "greedy" players, whose salaries were astronomical compared to those earned by Babe Ruth, Ted Williams, or Hank Aaron. If ticket prices were skyrocketing, they were still outpaced by the cost of player contracts, yet this was information the owners refused to share. There wasn't a single new collective bargaining agreement signed between 1975 and 2000 that didn't include a work stoppage. The 1994–1995 strike was just the most devastating.

The second problem was a lack of competitive balance. The "big market" teams had an inherent advantage because they had much greater broadcast revenues.

Unlike football, which shares all television revenue equally, and basketball, where shared national revenues are the most significant, baseball telecasts are mostly local events. It seemed almost impossible for cities like Pittsburgh, San Diego, Minnesota—or Milwaukee—to compete for division championships, let alone World Series titles.

As Mitchell explained it, "Selig called me and said there were serious economic problems with baseball. They feared . . . that the same teams were winning all the time and it was based on the high-revenue teams doing well, and the low-revenue teams were not. He was going to create a Blue Ribbon Commission to analyze and report and make recommendations." Mitchell wasn't formally designated the chairman, but functioned in that role. The other three members were prominent in their fields—Paul Volcker, former Federal Reserve Board chairman; Richard Levin, president of Yale University and a labor economist; and George Will, who frequently soliloquized about baseball in his *Washington Post* column and, Mitchell noted, "has written quite a few books about baseball, very knowledgeable, very interested in the subject."

The Commissioner's Blue Ribbon Panel on Baseball Economics issued in July 2000 a brief, substantive, and lucid report that set out the issues in unmistakable terms, and made clear recommendations that were adopted, in part, by the owners. The study period was 1995–1999, from just after the strike to the present. The report said revenues had doubled in just five years, from $1.39 billion in 1995 to $2.8 billion in 1999, but distribution was increasingly skewed and profits almost nonexistent. Local revenues were still dominant, growing from $1.2 billion to $2.2 billion, and revenue ranged from the soon-to-be-extinct Montreal Expos, $12 million, to the leviathan New York Yankees, $176 million. Overall payrolls had increased by 50 percent, but for the bottom half of teams, by less than 20 percent. The recommendations, it said, were intended to head off contraction—the possibility that some of baseball's thirty teams would be folded to preserve the rest. Debt levels were rising, from $604 million to $2.1 billion, and, it said, "Many clubs have reached dangerous levels of debt." There were already the equivalent of "fire sales" of financially distressed teams. In the previous five years, thirteen teams had changed hands, and in five instances the owners received less money than they'd paid for their teams. Only the Cleveland, Baltimore, Texas, and Cincinnati sellers made a significant profit. Current balance sheets were no better; only a handful of teams were profitable, and many were recording significant, unsustainable losses.

The conclusions were terse. "Large and growing revenue disparities exist and are causing problems of chronic competitive imbalance," it found. "These problems have become substantially worse during the five complete seasons since the strike-shortened season of 1994, and seem likely to remain severe un-less Major League Baseball (MLB) undertakes remedial actions proportional to the problem." It concluded that the "limited revenue sharing and payroll tax" approved in 1996 "produced neither the effect of moderating payroll dispari-ties, nor improved competitive balance. Some low-revenue clubs, believing the amount of their proceeds from revenue sharing insufficient to enable them to become competitive, used those proceeds to become modestly profitable." The financial turmoil, it found, was also having negative effects with fans. "In a majority of MLB markets, the cost to clubs of trying to be competitive is caus-ing escalation of ticket and concession prices, jeopardizing MLB's traditional position as the affordable family spectator sport."

With a membership that included two heavyweight economists, the report is dense with statistics, financial comparisons, and detailed analyses of quar-tiles, ratios, and thresholds, but it also includes salient observations that, when absorbed, must have seemed indisputable. "In 1999, one club's local revenues exceeded by $11 million the combined revenues of six other clubs," it reported. "From 1995–1999 every World Series winner was from payroll Quartile I, and no club outside Quartile I won even a single game in the series." More generally, "Sports leagues do not function as free markets. If they did, the clubs would be clustered in a few large markets. Rather, sports leagues are blends of coop-eration and competition—cooperation for the sake of producing satisfactory competitiveness." And, by that standard, there was far too little cooperation in baseball, as compared to other major sports.

To a large degree, that is still the case, but baseball made enough changes, in response to the commission's recommendations, for all thirty teams to survive, and for more of them to be competitive, although at least a third of the teams still have no realistic chance of winning a title. The commission recommended a 40 percent revenue-sharing level, and though revenue sharing increased somewhat, it falls far short of that level. The report found there are three com-petitive categories—"clubs that expect to perform well in the postseason; clubs that hope for an occasional 'dream season' to reach the postseason; and clubs that know going to spring training that they will not make the playoffs." That's still broadly true, but the report changed the game's structure and financial practices, though less visibly than the better-known report on performance-enhancing drugs that Mitchell completed, this time on his own, in 2007.

The most dramatic effect of the Blue Ribbon Commission was in the re-lationship of owners with the players. From hostility, rancor, and disbelief, bargaining sessions gradually shifted to wary, but respectful, negotiations. Players, and their agents, finally realized the owners hadn't been lying; despite increasing ticket prices by more than 100 percent over five years, most teams were still losing money. Since the report was issued, there hasn't been a single work stoppage in baseball, and each collective bargaining agreement has been completed on time.

Mitchell still sounds bemused about the earlier report's low profile. When the "steroids" report was distributed in 2007, "both Major League Baseball and ESPN put it up on their websites, and several million copies were downloaded," he said. That total exceeded the combined total of all downloads from Sharm el-Sheik and the Good Friday Agreement, he said. The total downloaded from the Blue Ribbon Commission report, he said, "was probably in the low hundreds." Between the dates the reports were issued, use of the Internet exploded, but even the greater number of users doesn't explain all the disparity.

By 2006, Bud Selig had an even bigger problem than baseball economics. The proliferation of performance-enhancing drugs was becoming impossible to ignore. The players' union had resisted attempts to create an effective drug-testing program, but the visual evidence was unmistakable. Barry Bonds, a slightly built Pittsburgh Pirates outfielder, an excellent fielder and contact hitter who'd averaged twenty home runs a year, developed into a power-hitting behemoth after signing a free-agent contract with the San Francisco Giants, averaging forty-four home runs for twelve years, with an upper body that looked freakishly overdeveloped. Bonds resembled Ted Williams as an almost incredibly adept hitter, and in having a relationship with reporters that ranged from surly to nonexistent. He hit five-hundred-foot home runs, often leaving the new Giants' stadium, and finished with 762. Fans also observed Roger Clemens—a former Red Sox pitcher, who, like Babe Ruth, joined the Yankees—demonstrating endurance into his late thirties not seen since the days of Walter Johnson and Cy Young. His twenty-win seasons and overpowering pitching continued beyond the age of forty as he helped the Yankees to more championships. Everyone knew this wasn't natural, but no one in baseball would account for it publicly.

Cracks in the facade had appeared, however. There were lawsuits and inquiries by prosecutors. A few players admitted steroid use, and several, now retired, talked about what they'd seen in locker rooms. Selig realized he had to act. He was often defensive, saying, "We had the toughest program in sports, but we were under some fire in Washington, I thought unfairly so, but that was irrelevant." Few outside the commissioner's office would have agreed baseball's drug testing in 2006 measured up to football, basketball, or the Olympics. Selig added, "I finally said to myself, with no support from any group, either my own office or any other, 'I need to bring in somebody from the outside to really examine the history of this thing. I mean, I have no secrets.' So I thought for a couple of weeks, who would it be? He had to be somebody, he or she, [a] statesman, [and] also have a great working knowledge of baseball." He also said, "It was the first time in American sports history that any sport had brought in an outsider in to examine the sport" —though that overlooked the first baseball commissioner, Kenesaw Mountain Landis, recruited as a judge to contain the Black Sox scandal. Selig said an outside investigation "was internally unpopular, was unpopular with the union," but, "My thought was that I was going to do it." When he considered candidates, "I had a bunch of wonderful names, but I kept coming back to George Mitchell."

There were two reasons to hesitate, Selig decided. "He did have a relationship with the Boston Red Sox." The second was, "He was a friend of mine." On the merits, though, Selig easily convinced himself. "He knew baseball; he was impeccable in terms of integrity, reputation. He was a great statesman, had been in Ireland . . . and I kept saying to myself, for the slight little negatives, this is a man to do it." In retrospect, he said, "It was the right decision. And today nobody quarrels with it. George Mitchell did a brilliant job; he was thorough, very smart, great relationship with a lot of the parties. The union refused to cooperate, but they could never really rip the senator, they just refused to cooperate." When it was over, Selig said, "My profound respect for him is even greater after that experience than it was before, and I didn't think that was possible."

Mitchell's connection to the Red Sox, and Selig, did prompt some criticism. A former federal prosecutor, John Dowd, who'd represented John McCain during the "Keating Five" Senate Ethics Committee investigation, took Mitchell to task for criticizing McCain, and then later having baseball interests while heading the drug investigation. After the report was issued, though, Dowd said he had no complaint about Mitchell's impartiality.

It started in March 2006. Mitchell was in Anaheim leading his last Disney shareholders' meeting, when, "Literally as I was walking out the door of my hotel room, the phone rang." He answered because he thought it might be about a meeting detail, but it was Selig. Mitchell said he couldn't talk long, but said, "I've never said no to whatever you've asked me, so I begin with an inclination to do this if you think it will be helpful." In his memoir, he says he added, "There's one thing I need to be clear at the outset. This won't be a committee, like the Blue Ribbon Commission; this will be just me. I'm your friend, but you understand that if I do this, I must have complete independence to follow the evidence wherever it leads and to report on what I find." Selig agreed almost immediately. They settled on a contract, and Mitchell brought in three DLA Piper attorneys; one of them, John Clarke, wrote much of the first draft.

Mitchell made no assumptions about cooperation, or the lack of it, but was thorough. He or members of his team conducted nearly two thousand interviews, and the commissioner's office, team personnel, law enforcement, and employees at testing labs were generally cooperative. Mitchell had no specific expectations about players, though he had served with the union's executive director, Don Fehr, in an earlier investigation concerning the 2002 Winter Olympics. "We had worked closely together," Mitchell writes of Fehr in his memoir. "I liked and respected him and got the impression that the feeling was mutual." But the experience was not repeated. "Our several discussions . . . were cordial but unproductive. He and the players were upset that Selig had not consulted with them about the investigation or my being chosen to head it. He insisted the Players Association had come a long way from its initial opposition to drug testing in any form, and he emphasized that the owners had not pushed hard for tougher testing. . . . He never declared that the Players Association would not cooperate in the investigation, but that's the way it turned out." Mitchell wasn't unsympathetic; expanded testing was approved in 2002, and his 2007 report said the new system caused some players using banned substances to switch from steroids to the then-undetectable human growth hormone to avoid failing tests. But the frequency of testing was still far below levels that might have exposed regular users, or restore public confidence.

Fehr may have believed Mitchell wouldn't name alleged individual violators without the union's cooperation, but if so, he was mistaken. The report names eighty-nine present or former players as likely users, and though it was a small proportion of those who'd played during that period, there were big names, and enough names to convince the public steroid use was both widespread and inadequately discouraged. Only one active player, Frank Thomas—who played for the White Sox and Toronto Blue Jays, and was later elected to the Hall of Fame—volunteered to speak with Mitchell during the eighteen-month investigation, in October 2007, just before the report was completed. Mitchell writes of Thomas, "There were no dramatic revelations; he conditioned his willingness to meet with me on the understanding that he would not identify other players. But he did express his views and he answered my questions. Although he would not name names, he was otherwise direct and forthright. He was clear in his belief that the use of performance-enhancing drugs in baseball was widespread and that it had an adverse effect on him and other players who did not use them. He was proud of his record and of the fact that he had compiled it the 'hard way.' To him it was a question of fairness. He didn't cheat, but he had to compete with players who did." Mitchell also spoke with one other active player,

Jason Giambi of the Yankees, who'd told a grand jury in May 2007 that he used steroids. Giambi appeared by agreement of the commissioner and the union.

Despite the players' noncooperation, Mitchell attempted to assess responsibility broadly. The report criticizes MLB's efforts to provide educational materials on drugs to players, as required by the 2002 collective bargaining agreement. It said, "Some criticized the perceived shallowness of the efforts, while others could not remember the programs at all, even though they were with the clubs when the programs were supposed to have been presented. Plainly, there is much room for improvement. In contrast, the issues of gambling, other threats to the integrity of the game, and players' safety receive prominent educational attention. Nearly everyone we interviewed could vividly recall an educational program addressing gambling." It also introduced the theme raised by Frank Thomas and taken up by other observers, and eventually more players, about the effects on others from those who cheated: "These players have been harmed by having to play against violators who gained an unfair advantage, and further harmed by having the legitimacy of their fairly earned accomplishments frequently questioned. The clean major league players deserve far better than they have had to endure."

A number of players, after reading the report, said they wished they had accepted Mitchell's invitation. Had more players come forward, the report could have been more comprehensive and, perhaps, better balanced. There was no doubting its effect, though. Evidence that so many players had cheated to boost their performance produced unprecedented interest, and revulsion against a perceived epidemic of performance-enhancing drugs. The union soon agreed to much more comprehensive and frequent testing, with stiffer penalties. Baseball then constructed the toughest anti-doping regimen in American sports, and has updated it since.

Mitchell said the public immediately focused on the named players, but that both sides took seriously recommendations for long-term improvements. More of them were implemented than had been the case with the Blue Ribbon Commission. The report also expanded its focus beyond "cheating" to document the harm steroids cause to those who use them regularly, including such adverse psychological effects as mania, depression, and increased suicide risk, "especially during withdrawal." While recognizing that steroids have therapeutic uses, it said doses players typically used "produce blood levels five to thirty times higher than any therapeutic use." Among other side effects were heart enlargement and heart attack risk. In a later interview, Mitchell pointed to "the alarming reality that hundreds of thousands of high-school-age Americans use steroids and human growth hormone and other such drugs. The best estimates range from 2 percent to 6 percent, but even the lowest numbers means several hundred thousand are doing this, with potentially devastating consequences."

In his memoir, Mitchell says players have become more vocal about performance-enhancing drugs, and quotes Mike Trout, a rising young star for the Los Angeles Angels, as saying, "I think you should be out of the game if you get caught. It takes away from the guys that are working hard every day and doing it all natural." The many legal proceedings and congressional investigations the report reflected and helped advance have produced few new facts or criminal trials, though Barry Bonds in 2011 was convicted of obstruction of justice, and acquitted of perjury, for statements he made to a congressional committee; the conviction was overturned on appeal in 2015. None of the suspected steroids users, including Bonds, Clemens, and Mark McGwire, have come close to election to the Hall of Fame, despite their stellar numbers.

Selig was grateful for Mitchell's work. "There's a huge change in the culture," he said. "We banned amphetamines, which we weren't even asked to do. There's no question people are now complaining that pitchers have taken over because they think the bans have worked so well, but that's OK, that's good." He said, "We had a cocaine problem in the '80s and they couldn't get a drug test improvement. We even had four players who went to jail, twenty-nine convicted, and they fought it. I know they were very unhappy about Senator Mitchell's report, but it turns out they couldn't be too unhappy. It was very factual, very well done."

There was intensive news coverage when the report was released on December 13. Frank Thomas told the *New York Times* he was surprised that five players who'd spoken out previously about steroids declined written invitations to meet with Mitchell. "It was weird," Thomas said. "The whole reason I did it was because I couldn't believe other guys weren't talking to him. I had nothing to hide." One of the five, Curt Schilling, who pitched the Red Sox to their first World Series title since 1918, said he "would have nothing to offer other than personal opinion and hypotheticals." Mitchell told the *Times* reporter that interviewing Thomas had been helpful. "I remember thinking, on the flight back to New York, I wished it were possible that others shared their views with me." Schilling, asked about the report, said, "I believe it, if that's what you're asking."

In a retrospective op-ed in 2014 for the *Washington Post*, Mitchell sketched what he thought were some lessons. "Some social problems persist despite laws to prevent them," he wrote. "Every society has laws against crime, but no one expects an end to crime; it's a continuing problem that must be aggressively deterred and punished. So it is with the use of performance-enhancing drugs in sports." He said attitudes have changed, and added, "I hope the tide is turning against it in all sports. . . . Learning that our childhood heroes are fallible is disillusioning. But we grow up and get over our disappointment, and we understand it as another example of life's complexity. Not every great human being is a great athlete. Not every great athlete is a great human being. Talent and morality may coexist, but they often do not."

ONE STRIKING ASPECT OF MITCHELL'S INVOLVEMENT with athletics is his competitiveness. His demeanor and methods sometimes misled people about this trait. Jamie Kaplan, his staff attorney for Iran-Contra, witnessed it often. When he was a law clerk, he and the federal court administrator drove to Mitchell's house in South Portland to deliver after-hours legal papers. "He had a basketball hoop in his driveway," Kaplan said. "We started playing 'horse.' So, George has his bathrobe on, it's Sunday morning, he might even have been wearing flip-flops. But he was not going to lose that game of horse. And we're all yukking it up, but George is not going to lose. . . . He always used to say, when it came to basketball, he never wanted to lose any game because he never won at basketball against Swisher. And he'd probably not admit that either, but he said, 'I take this stuff really seriously.'" Mitchell met the legendary coach of the Boston Celtics, Red Auerbach, when the two lived in Washington. They met through tennis. "Red was a tennis player, and a pretty good and cagey one," Mitchell said. "I'd been a Celtics fan for many years, of course; I knew all about him. We had several mutual friends." Mitchell recalled that the New England tournament–winning 1943–1944 basketball team from Waterville, which included his brothers John and Paul, also had a star named Ted Shiro. Later, Shiro had a tryout with the Celtics, and it was in sharing recollections about Shiro that Mitchell and Auerbach became friends, though Mitchell termed it "an acquaintanceship."

Auerbach was a notorious prickly character who wore his competitiveness on his sleeve, and Mitchell said, "As you'd expect, he was aggressive, argumentative—in a nice way!—and tricky on the tennis court, a lot of spin and misdirection and so forth." What Mitchell liked most about Auerbach was his storytelling. "He had a story about everything, and he'd lived through those great years with the Celtics and wasn't shy about talking about things," Mitchell said. "We'd sit there after playing tennis . . . and what you would normally think of as 'shooting the breeze,' but he was doing the shooting and I was doing the listening." Mitchell called it "one of the good fortunes of my life is to have known him," but, as an adult, basketball didn't engage his passions as baseball did. As a competitor, there was tennis.

His sister Barbara became Mitchell's doubles partner when they played against their older brothers. For the first time in athletic competition with them,

Mitchell was usually on the winning side. While Barbara probably enjoyed beating her brothers, too, she wasn't always satisfied with her partner. "Every ball was his," she said of George. "I was never able to get to anything that fell between us."

Harold Pachios joined Mitchell when he took up tennis in 1972, at age thirty-nine, though Mitchell became more serious after the 1974 governor's race, when he was reshaping his life and its direction. At the end of the 1972 Muskie campaign, Pachios said, "He took most of the summer off, and he and his wife rented a house down near Wells. . . . George had a pool table in the basement, and I'd go down there and we'd play pool, and there were some batting cages where you could practice, and we would go over there occasionally and hit. George was a pretty good hitter. Then we decided we'd take up golf"—Muskie's game—"and we played golf a few times that summer. George didn't like it very much, and he switched to tennis, and so I switched to tennis. . . . We started playing every Monday night, a group of us, there were eight, two courts, doubles. And I must say George got a lot better than I was. I always tried to figure that out, because we started exactly at the same time. It's because of his ability to concentrate and focus, and tennis really was a good game for George."

Other observers agree with Heather Mitchell that her husband's tennis form wasn't textbook, but that he was an effective shot-maker and strategist. The Portland tennis group varied over the years, and Mitchell became less active after he was appointed to the federal bench and worked in Bangor. Federal appeals court judge Kermit Lipez, then a young lawyer, was part of a foursome that often included Mitchell, Pachios, and Joe Angelone, the pizza shop owner. "We played doubles a lot, and that's probably how I spent most of the time with George in that period," Lipez said. "There was certainly an aspect of George's character that was revealed in his tennis game. First of all, George was too modest. . . . I know his brothers were great athletes, and he liked to portray himself as the non-athlete. . . . I suppose George was not quite as good as they were, but he clearly was a good athlete. He was very well coordinated, he was fast, but he was not schooled in the game of tennis, he was self-taught. So most of his shots were somewhat unorthodox, particularly his serve, which was not a thing of beauty. But his serve was deceptively effective, because it was precise . . . and it was always brilliantly strategic because it was always designed to expose the weakness in his opponent's game. And he was tenacious, he was like a human backboard, he'd always get his shots back. And he was highly competitive, not in an unpleasant way, but his determination to win was unmistakable." Lipez also contrasted tennis with Mitchell's performance during the 1974 governor's race. "There was a lot of good-natured kidding that would go back and forth, and this is the side of him that just never came out in that first campaign."

Jamie Kaplan played with Mitchell in Washington, and recalls a memorable match from before his Iran-Contra stint. He got a call at his law office from Gayle Cory, who said, "Can you leave work early? The senator is going over to Teddy Kennedy's house to play tennis." Kaplan and Mitchell were joined by Kennedy and Ron Brown, DNC chairman and later Commerce secretary for Bill Clinton. "Ted Kennedy was not a very good tennis player," Kaplan said. "But the great impression was that here's Teddy Kennedy in the privacy of his home, shouting on the court and having a kickback good time. George and I were the strongest tennis players on the court, and we're paired off against each other. But then afterwards we went into Kennedy's house and we're sitting around, having a beer, and I'm looking at all this memorabilia. . . . [I] felt almost like a kid in a candy shop." Kaplan said, "I always thought I was a better pure tennis player than George, but he was an absolute tiger as a competitor, and I'm sure he beat me more times than I beat him."

Mitchell had a variety of regular tennis partners in Washington, including William Webster, director of the FBI. John Breaux, senator from Louisiana, said that long after he and Mitchell left the Senate, they got together for a match in 2009, when Mitchell was seventy-six and Breaux was sixty-five. "He's still super-competitive," Breaux said. Of Breaux's Louisiana Senate partner, Bennett Johnston, Mitchell said in his memoir, "He was one of the best tennis players in the Senate, and I had shared the court with him many times."

Eliot Cutler had the future politician's critical appraisal of the present-day one. Cutler said of Mitchell, while noting "this was years ago," that "his tennis game was good, not great, but he's a good athlete . . . his court coverage was very good, and placement was good. Not a lot of power. But Jesus, he would contest every call. He could hit the ball five yards out of bounds and he'd claim it was in, he'd sort of start there. George is a terrific negotiator . . . he negotiates everything."

There were other criticisms of Mitchell's game. His sister-in-law, Janet, got to see him on her family's backyard court in Waterville built by his brother, Robbie, and said Mitchell's unorthodox serve often involved a foot fault as he stepped over the serving line, "but you could never convince him he was doing it." Tim O'Neil, president of Portland Glass, who played Mitchell often, said he was "very aggressive," and that "on his serve he's at least two steps into the court, because he's foot-faulting. If we could call foot-faults we'd probably all have won." O'Neil said Mitchell was so persistent in going after lobs most players would have given up on that he sometimes pulled a muscle. "I hated to have him as a partner in doubles and we lost, because he'd never say anything but you could feel the body language, and you knew damn well that when you screwed up it mattered." Nor did Mitchell go easy on female opponents. Marjorie Bride, who worked a year in Mitchell's Senate office, said of one match, "I remember getting trounced. I'm a pretty good tennis player, and he never let me up for air."

Mitchell's old friend, Shep Lee, the car dealer, said "George plays tennis the way he lives his life—honest, steady, no mistakes; he's a tough competitor." Walter Corey, a lawyer for Bernstein Shur in Portland who worked on Curtis and Mitchell campaigns, made a lengthy assessment. Corey said Mitchell wasn't a "ball hog" in doubles, "going after balls that weren't his," but he acknowledged the foot-faulting. "George would do it, not constantly . . . and when people would call him on that he would get sore and deny he had foot-faulted, but we never had the video running, and it was always a great opportunity to needle him and have some fun."

In later years, Mitchell could sound a nostalgic note. In a conversation with Lee and Pachios, he said that, in his new home at Seal Harbor, "I won my club championship this summer. Three times I've won the championship, two other times I've been in the finals. But the secret is to have a good partner, and I have a very good partner"—who was half Mitchell's age. He didn't forget his old friends. "It's always fun to play with Shep and with Harold, and we ended up with a group of friends, probably as many over the course of years as eight or ten people who played on a regular basis together. I miss that part of my life. It was wonderful."

MITCHELL'S BASEBALL REPORTS WERE HIS MOST visible sports assignments, but there were others. One he describes in his memoir was the scandal surrounding the selection of Utah's Salt Lake City as the site of the 2002 Winter Olympics. Mitchell had already agreed to chair the US Olympic Committee's ethics panel at the request of its chairman, Bill Hybl, when the scandal broke in 1998; it included allegations of bribery. Mitchell traces the roots to an earlier incident, when Toronto, believing it had made a "superior" presentation for the 1996 Summer Olympics, saw it go instead to Atlanta. Mitchell writes of the Canadians, "They concluded that they had been victims of a corrupt process in which the votes of IOC [International Olympic Committee] had effectively been bought. In polite but blunt language, the Canadians pried open the lid on a mess teeming with improper gifts, including cash payments, in exchange for votes. . . . The IOC peered into the mess, then replaced the lid and looked away. And what the Canadians feared soon came to pass."

For Salt Lake City, the memory of a failed bid by a neighboring state also fueled its pursuit. Denver bid successfully for the 1976 winter games, but rising costs required a public bond issue on the Colorado ballot in 1972, and voters rejected it. Salt Lake City was determined to succeed where Denver had failed. The city worked from 1989 to 1991 to secure the 1998 winter games. As Mitchell relates, "The city's Olympic Bid Committee made what its members felt was a persuasive effort and presentation. Included was the expenditure of over $250,000 on travel, hotel, entertainment, gifts, and payments of money to members of the IOC, their relatives, or friends. But when the IOC met . . . it chose Nagano, Japan. Stunned and disappointed, the Salt Lake City Bid Committee resolved to try again for the 2002 Winter Games."

The lines surrounding "gifts" were highly flexible, and, for Salt Lake City, trying again meant upping the ante. Mitchell describes this as "gift creep," and says, "They moved from goodwill gifts to strangers to payments specifically intended to get votes; from small, inexpensive items they graduated to lavish gifts, and ultimately to payments of substantial sums of money to individual IOC members." He comments, "The Salt Lake City Committee didn't invent the culture of corruption; they stepped into it and came to believe that in order to win, they had to match or exceed their competitors in the petty and grubby process of buying votes."

Bill Hybl may have had some inkling of this when he recruited Mitchell, and after the first allegations asked Mitchell to chair a separate commission to investigate. Mitchell had only two months to come up with a report, however. The tight deadline, he said, "precluded an exhaustive factual inquiry, which in any event would have been impossible because criminal investigations were under way in the United States, and most of the participants refused to talk." It may have reminded him of Iran-Contra. Nonetheless, Mitchell took the assignment, where he worked with Don Fehr of the baseball players' association; Ken Duberstein, former Reagan chief of staff; Roberta Cooper Ramo, former American Bar Association president; and Jeff Benz, a San Francisco attorney and champion figure skater. Mitchell said, "Although we did not identify the particulars of every improper transaction, we had more than enough information. . . . The Canadians had laid it out clearly eight years earlier."

The recommendations, made both to the USOC and the IOC, were intended to "eliminate the practices that contributed to the buying of votes," he said, and "to make fundamental structural changes to increase transparency and accountability to the public." The US Olympic Committee adopted all the recommendations. The IOC "made meaningful changes in its site-selection process, in some respects going further than our recommendations," but, on transparency, did little and, Mitchell said, "remains a relatively closed and tight-knit organization."

There remains substantial doubt whether the selection process is really "clean," though, to date, there have been no comparable scandals. In the federal criminal investigation, a federal judge threw out fifteen counts of fraud, conspiracy, and racketeering against Salt Lake organizers Tom Welch and Dave Johnson. Even so, the Salt Lake City case was frequently cited when US prosecutors indicted in May 2015 officials of the Fédération Internationale de Football Association (FIFA), the governing authority of soccer's World Cup, over site awards for future cups.

In 2012, the National Collegiate Athletic Association (NCAA), turned to Mitchell when a stunned nation confronted allegations that an assistant to one of the nation's most respected football coaches, Penn State's Joe Paterno, had sexually abused boys in locker rooms and at his home, under the guise of a program to help foster children. Jerry Sandusky was convicted on thirty-five of forty-eight criminal counts involving the abuse of ten boys over fifteen years, and imprisoned. Paterno resigned as coach and died, at age eighty-five, on January 22, 2012. Mitchell agreed to serve in one of his most sensitive roles yet, as monitor for the NCAA of Penn State's progress toward meeting an Athletics Integrity Agreement it signed in response to recommendations by former FBI director Louis Freeh, aimed at combating the "culture" in State College, Pennsylvania, investigators believed facilitated Sandusky's crimes. Mitchell was hired for five years, until 2017, but withdrew in February 2015 after submitting his tenth quarterly report to Penn State, the Big Ten Conference, and the NCAA. The report, which Mitchell said was positive, is not a public document. Mitchell cited personal reasons for withdrawing, and appointed Charles Scheeler, a DLA Piper attorney, as his replacement. After resigning as Middle East envoy, Mitchell had returned to the firm as chairman emeritus.

A FINAL EPISODE IN THE DEBATE OVER MITCHELL'S athletic career came in the form of "the Teddy," the Theodore Roosevelt Award, the NCAA's highest honor, which Mitchell received in 2010. Roosevelt's concerns over fairness and safety in college athletics led to creation of the NCAA in 1906. The "Teddy" is awarded annually; the first recipient, in 1967, was Dwight Eisenhower. Others honored include presidents Gerald Ford, George H. W. Bush, and Ronald Reagan; US senators John Glenn, Leverett Saltonstall, Bob Dole, and Bill Cohen; a Supreme Court justice, Byron White; and Cabinet members Bill Richardson and Madeleine Albright.

In his acceptance speech, delivered to the NCAA in Atlanta, Mitchell thanked both the organization and Bowdoin College, which he said "changed my life." He told about his selection by Governor Brennan as US senator, and provided the detail that Brennan called him at eleven p.m. and told Mitchell he needed an answer in one hour. He intended to announce the appointment at the State House the next day at noon. Mitchell said he consulted with his brothers, providing the familiar information that they "were great athletes" while he "wasn't as good as my brothers, wasn't as good as anyone's brother." He called his brother, John, who responded, "Look, everybody knows you're a born loser. You couldn't possibly win a statewide election. None of us can understand how you got to be a federal judge. We think you should stay where you are." Mitchell adds, "My other brothers said the same thing, in less polite language." That, Mitchell said, decided the issue. "I was so mad. I hung up the phone and called the governor. I said, 'Governor, I don't need until midnight. I have all the reassurance I need.'" In case his audience hadn't gotten the point, he said, "The only condition I imposed on the NCAA for accepting the award is that they make a video of it and send it to my brother, Johnny." He had noted that while Barbara was there, his brothers were not.

Mitchell's self-estimate is consistent with the award guidelines. While some of those receiving it, including Ford, White, Cohen, and Albright, were standouts, stardom isn't required. The NCAA says, "The 'Teddy' is presented annually to a distinguished citizen of national reputation. . . . The recipient must have graduated from an NCAA member institution and earned a varsity athletics award, or participated in competitive intercollegiate athletics."

The rivalry with Swisher continues to this day. When John stepped down as assistant basketball coach at Colby in 2011 after serving forty years, all but three with Dick Whittemore as head coach, he said of Whittemore, "I think we understood each other. I think he had respect for me and I had respect for him. He never listened to everything I said, and I didn't think he was right all the time, either." The same might be said of the Mitchell brothers. At the 2014 Mitchell Institute dinner in South Portland, in a ballroom filled with nearly a thousand supporters, George and Swisher continued to play their parts, with plentiful jokes by George about Swisher's hearing, or lack of it. The banter is still sharp, but also plainly affectionate, even loving.

In the end, it may come back to cribbage. On that field, the brothers competed evenly. Paul said of George, "He didn't win all the time, but he won a lot. You'd get caught up in it." Mary Mitchell Friedman, Robbie's daughter, remembers the games at the Front Street house of her grandparents, occasions where "we would spend just the most wonderful times with the cousins all running around outside and being adventurous, and the dining room table with the adults always filled with politics, as you can imagine, everybody shouting and yelling about their political passions." After Sunday dinner, when the dishes were cleared away, "there were these incredibly intense cribbage games between my dad and uncles. So they would play cribbage for hours, and they were all incredibly competitive because they were all fantastic athletes and came by their competitive natures naturally. And George, the youngest . . . got his vengeance at the cribbage table with all of them. It would always be very funny, because they would just erupt over a cribbage hand like it was scoring the winning touchdown."

25

LEGACY

Just six days after being sworn in to the Senate, George Mitchell delivered a commencement address at the University of Maine School of Law, on May 25, 1980, an engagement he no doubt made while he was still a federal judge. He introduced some themes that remained a feature of his remarks to graduates during his next fifteen years in office. "The only thing I remember about the commencement address at my graduation is that it was too long," he began. "I don't remember the speaker, or what was said. I expect that twenty years from today you will not remember today's speaker, or what he said. But I assure you of one thing: You will not remember that this address was too long. I have not been in the Senate long enough." In his own way, Mitchell was subtly separating himself from his predecessor, Ed Muskie, who Mitchell once cautiously told about his prolixity, and what Muskie then admitted was the charm of "the sound of your own voice." In a further bow to modesty, Mitchell said, "Although it is just a coincidence, I find it ironic that at this time I should be lecturing you. For, like you, I am about to embark on a new career. If it were possible to distill your collective wisdom and convey it to me, the result might be more profitable for both of us. But since that is not possible, you will have to listen for a few minutes."

Perhaps because of this disarming approach, and because word got around that Mitchell would speak briefly and to the point, he was soon in high demand as a graduation speaker. He spoke primarily in Maine, but occasionally elsewhere, and though it may not be possible to determine exactly how many graduation talks his political peers gave, it's unlikely any exceeded Mitchell's total. Over the course of his Senate career, he gave a commencement speech at each of the nearly 140 public high schools then existing in Maine, and usually made a follow-up visit as well. By 1983, he was revising and repointing his stump speech. Most follow the same pattern, unlike Mitchell's other speeches that were carefully tailored to a particular occasion, and likely for a simple reason: No one listening to a graduation speech by Mitchell was likely to hear another, so he worked primarily on polishing, with only a short passage devoted to the particular institution that invited him.

Mitchell's speechwriter Anita Jensen consulted the Congressional Research Service and came up with material Mitchell incorporated into his basic text. In a May 13, 1983, memo, she wrote, "The first report of a graduation ceremony took place at the University of Bologna in the mid-twelfth century. It took the form of a pageant and parade, but the report was made in a subsequent writing and does not expand on the basic fact." She said the first American commencement was at Harvard in 1642, and that CRS was still looking for a quote from it, which apparently was never found. Mitchell worked these nuggets into the address he gave at Colby College later that month, and began, "The graduation ceremony is an old and honorable tradition. The first known ceremony took place in the twelfth century at the University of Bologna in northern Italy. It is of course only coincidence that the city of Bologna also gave rise to the modern term 'baloney.'" The "baloney" joke may not have gone over; it's missing from subsequent versions. About Harvard, he said, "The first American commencement occurred in 1642 at Harvard. For those of you concerned about the length of this program, it may be comforting to know that at that first commencement, Harvard's nine graduates were subjected to three addresses, one in English, one in Greek, and one in Hebrew; the ceremony then closed with a lengthy discussion of philosophy, conducted in Latin. Let me reassure you by noting that I speak only English, and that the only thing I remember about the address at my graduation is that it was too long. With that memory in mind, I will today try to finish speaking before you finish listening." He managed to combine historical background with his pledge to be, above all, brief.

Mitchell took special care with his graduation speeches because he believed in the value of education above almost all else. His remark to the NCAA that Bowdoin College "changed my life" was not casual; it represented his considered conclusion about everything that had made him what he was. When he began speaking at smaller high schools in rural areas, one of the things he noticed was the small size of the college scholarship awards. In his memoir, he writes, "I recall vividly the two graduations that I attended on successive days. One was in a rural, poor area; there were twenty-one graduates. When the college scholarship awards were announced, they were for amounts ranging from $25 to $100. I was astonished. At best the recipient could buy a few books! At the other graduation, in a better-off suburb of Portland, several of the awards were in the thousands of dollars."

He was also struck by what he heard when he attended an "aspirations conference" at the University of Maine. Maine has an above-average rate of high school completion, but a much lower rate of college enrollment than other New England states. Part of this can be explained by the cost of a college education, but not all. Mitchell told an interviewer, "I listened to the other speakers, and I was not so much surprised as disappointed . . . that aspirations for Maine young people were not high, particularly those in the rural areas, those living in areas of high unemployment and low incomes."

Mitchell then said of his parents, "They placed a high value on education. Growing up, the life goal of many of the young men was mostly to get a job in the paper mill in Winslow. . . . It was a source of major employment in the Waterville-Winslow area and it paid well, in relative terms, and there was, at least at that time, the appearance of job security." After Kimberly-Clark acquired Scott Paper, it shut down the Winslow mill in 1997 to reduce tissue-paper capacity, the first major Maine paper mill to close, but far from the last. Mitchell said, "Higher education wasn't discussed very much at the time by myself or by many of those with whom I attended school or played with. . . . I was uncertain, insecure, lacking in direction, purpose, or self-esteem. I was sixteen years old when I graduated from high school. I saw the same emotions and reactions among several young people I met at the University of Maine conference, young Maine high school students talking about themselves and their futures in a way that, at least to some extent, reflected low aspirations."

He resolved to take the suggestion he'd also been offered at the conference—to speak widely and often to students about his own experience—"so they can see that someone from a background not much different from theirs was able to become a United States senator." When he decided to leave the Senate, his thoughts returned to that moment.

In 1992, Mitchell set a limit of $2 million for his expected 1994 reelection campaign. It was, he said, "a trivial amount by national standards," but then more than sufficient for Maine. When he decided not to run, he had to determine what to do with the money he'd raised. Under existing law, he could have simply kept it, but he never considered doing so. He was eager to earn his way in the private sector, and keeping money given for another purpose wasn't acceptable. He could have returned it all to contributors, but decided instead to provide a choice. They could get their money back, or allow him to use it for a college scholarship program Mitchell would set up to help students like those he'd met at the aspirations conference. About half the contributions were returned, and about $1 million remained. Bill Clinton agreed to headline a fund-raiser in Washington, which raised another $500,000. In his own remarks at the October 5 fund-raiser, Mitchell told the stories of the citizenship ceremony he'd presided over as a federal judge, and how Elvira Whitten, his high school English teacher, had given him books to read, and he said, "This is as important to me as anything I've done since I entered public service." In a handwritten addition to the text, he thanked David Johnson, his one-time chief of staff, for organizing the event.

Earlier, when he made the formal announcement of the scholarship fund on July 6, he said, "The scholarships will be granted on the basis of academic achievement, financial need, and community spirit and public service," which could have applied to most scholarship programs. But then he said, "Ability and a willingness to work hard aren't limited by geography or circumstance. They're found in small towns as well as large cities, in suburban communities and on islands. So I will provide that the scholarship assistance be distributed widely throughout the state: No high school will qualify for a second scholarship until each high school in Maine has received at least one scholarship." That feature was highly unusual.

The scholarship fund was initially entrusted to the Maine Community Foundation, which offers this service to many nonprofits, and it administered the fund from its inception in 1995 through 1998. Harold Pachios seemed to be an ideal choice to serve on the committee, but Pachios had a different idea about how scholarship money should be distributed. Pachios said he told Mitchell, "If you're going to raise all this money, make it like the Rhodes Scholarship of Maine. You pick ten kids, even five kids, every year, and they get full tuition for four years, and it becomes the most competitive scholarship in Maine, probably the most competitive scholarship given in any state. Five kids a year, full four-year scholarships, you're going to get the best, the very best."

The Rhodes Scholarships—named for Cecil Rhodes, a noted Victorian imperialist who was prime minister of the Cape Colony, later South Africa, and founder of Rhodesia—have been awarded since 1903 under terms of Rhodes's will. In 2015, there were thirty-two American Rhodes winners, and the program at Oxford University has helped launch the careers of many later prominent in government, including Bill Clinton; his classmate Tom Allen, congressman from Maine; and Sarah Sewall, Mitchell's foreign policy aide, and later, undersecretary of state. But Mitchell took a different path, and Pachios played only a background role in the Mitchell scholarship program.

Mitchell has often said, "After my family, it's the most important thing in my life"—and his family played a prominent role from the inception of the scholarship program. Barbara Atkins, his sister, led the effort, and she remembers that

Mitchell had a particular goal from the start. The first teacher who inspired him to love learning, Elvira Whitten, had died of cancer not long after he graduated, but Barbara said they were able to locate her daughter, who attended a scholarship event where Mitchell was able to thank her for what her mother had done. "It was a very emotional moment," she said.

Paul Mitchell also assisted, and said he took no convincing when it came to the value of public education. He pointed to the Educare Center in Waterville, a model preschool center providing comprehensive social services to the entire community, and funded initially by the Annie E. Casey Foundation, as an example of what can be done. The center was built on the same campus, and is connected to the George J. Mitchell School, Waterville's public elementary school. Paul was also among Governor John Baldacci's first nominations to the University of Maine System's board of trustees. Barbara earned her BA on the Orono campus, while Paul received a master's degree there. He said, "Colby, Bates, and Bowdoin do a magnificent job, but they don't have the facilities to handle the thousands of students that are going to require opportunities in college. . . . The University of Maine System is going to provide the education to the greatest number of young people for the future of this state."

Mitchell had given clear instructions about how he wanted the program to be structured, and called on a variety of people to help him carry it out. Mary McAleney, principal organizer of the high school graduation speaking effort, was involved, and remains a board member. "I have in his own handwriting changes in that program," she said, "to ensure that the impact would be greatest out in the rural areas of the state. One scholarship to a student in every high school was his dream. . . . And there were people who said, 'Well, that's unfair to Portland, where there's three hundred kids graduating,' but he said, 'That's the way I want it, because I want to do something for those kids.'"

Estelle Lavoie, who had worked for Mitchell and Muskie, was one of the first people Mitchell consulted about setting up the program, not long after his retirement announcement. "We came up with the parameters," she said, "that that money would be given to students going to a four-year college or university in Maine, and they would need to graduate from a Maine high school." He was also insistent that it benefit students who wouldn't normally be seen as scholarship candidates. She remembers him saying, "Estelle, there are always needy students," and she concluded, "He did not want it to be a program for elite students going to Ivy League schools. He wanted to try to lift people out of poverty, he wanted to help people on the merits. . . . If you want to better yourself, you should have the chance."

Mitchell also relied on Bill Hiss, admissions director at Bates College, whom he'd named to the federal Advisory Committee on Student Financial Assistance. Mitchell, as majority leader, made several appointments to the eleven-member group, and, when he was reviewing names, told this staff, "I'm going to put that fellow on from Bates. I don't remember his name, but Colleen Quint's husband." Quint had interned on the Mitchell's staff. Hiss served two terms on the commission, the second as a Republican appointee after Mitchell intervened on his behalf. "It was a very helpful and good committee," Hiss said. "It did the work which the Congress and the secretary [of Education] set it to do." The commission took the multiplicity of financial aid forms then existing, and dominated by the College Board, the SAT test-makers, who charged a fee; the forms were lengthy and complicated. The commission's proposal became FAFSA— the Free Application for Federal Student Aid—that's now the standard for college applications, after Congress accepted its recommendation. Hiss also helped preserve a little-known federal financial aid program called the Supplemental Educational Opportunity Grant (SEOG), which provides additional aid to low-income students beyond Pell Grants, when it was on the chopping block with the Republican-led Congress in 1995. He was able to show Mitchell's successor, Senator Olympia Snowe, that Maine students were heavily dependent on the program. Hiss said Snowe "sort of whistled through her teeth, and later got up on the floor of the Senate . . . and said 'Over my dead body are you going to get rid of the SEOG program.' And she was one of the pivotal swing votes, and the program has survived to this day."

Mitchell turned to Hiss for advice about his new venture. "The original concept was not the Mitchell Institute we know today; it was just a scholarship fund, and far simpler," Hiss said. Despite Mitchell's original intention of benefiting poor and rural students, this proved hard to accomplish in the early years. "If you look at the college destinations of the original program, when they were giving out twenty-five awards per year, and later on when the full Mitchell Institute was born, they were dramatically different," he said. "In the first years, because we were picking a very small number of students who basically were stars, the vast majority went to Bates, Bowdoin, and Colby. Later on, as the program became much bigger . . . by far the largest number of Mitchell Scholars is at the University of Maine."

Hiss also tried convincing Mitchell to alter his idea of requiring each public high school to be represented on the scholars list before any school could receive a second award. Hiss said, "Senator, this is the guy who's been running admissions offices for twenty years; let me offer you an alternate proposal." Hiss's idea was that the overall number of awards would remain the same, but wouldn't be as restricted by school. "Suppose there might be three just fabulous candidates at Bangor High School, and nobody too attractive at Mt. Blue, or pick any other school," he said. "And the senator very politely and very carefully listened to my thoughts, he thanked me for my opinions most graciously, and he sent me on my way. That wasn't what he wanted to do." And Hiss, too, has come around. "In retrospect, he was absolutely right," he said. "There are some high schools that are very small—Jackman or Katahdin. Vinalhaven High School might have only six or eight kids graduating. Is there one of those kids who needs the money, needs help, and has met the criteria? The answer is yes, absolutely yes." Yet the small number of scholarships and large number of high schools remained a dilemma for those making the awards.

One of them was Tim Agnew, CEO of the Finance Authority of Maine (FAME). Agnew had attended a Portland fund-raiser in October 1994, the counterpart of the event Bill Clinton headlined in Washington, and saw Mitchell's dedication in the gathering of five hundred people. "I saw the way he worked that room; he went around, and I don't think there was anybody he didn't know by first name, and I'd just met him a couple of times and didn't expect he would know who I was, but he knew exactly who I was. . . . It's a remarkable ability. I have a hard time remembering my kids' names at times."

After he joined the Mitchell Institute board, one of Agnew's favorite activities was spending three or four days each May reviewing the applications. "I like reading Washington County and some of the rural counties," he said, "because some of the stories are just remarkable in what some of these kids have overcome, with parents who died or have become incapacitated, who have no history of college, who have to work just to put food on the table, and yet have the determination to go on to higher education." By contrast, he said, "In Cumberland County, you tend to get a lot of kids like mine, who have all kinds of advantages, and it's just not as interesting reading."

THE FIRST AWARDS WERE FOR $2,500 AND WERE awarded to twenty-five students. The program made a modest splash in the press—nothing like it existed in Maine—but as Mitchell began making new connections in the private sector, he looked for ways to beef up its funding and broaden its mission. The breakthrough came when a private foundation, which was an anonymous donor, and remains so, offered a substantial challenge grant, contingent on matching fund-raising, that enabled creation of the Mitchell Institute in 1999. The greatly expanded scholarship program fulfilled Mitchell's original idea: to provide a graduate of each Maine public high school, now about 130, with a scholarship each year. An additional thirty nontraditional students, often adults going to college in their thirties and forties, are included annually. Students attending two-year programs, often at community colleges, are also now eligible.

The amounts of the scholarships have also increased substantially, to $8,000, distributed in equal installments over four years. In its first twenty years, the Mitchell Institute has distributed more than $12 million in scholarships; reflecting its recent growth, about half that amount has been provided over the last six years. Over time, the institute also developed a summer orientation program, summer internships, and an alumni support network. Additional support is also provided to scholars who've experienced life-changing events while they are in school. Perhaps the biggest change from the early years is that, starting in 1999, the institute hired a researcher to conduct studies on a variety of educational issues.

Barbara Keefe, who served as Mitchell's Senate campaign treasurer in 1982 and 1988, was a board member and a supporter of commissioning research, but found not everyone was. "Many of the people on the board felt that was unnecessary—that this was clearly going to be just a scholarship awarded to needy students who are academically successful in high school," she said. Mitchell supported the change in mission, though, and it was adopted. Another major impetus to research was a $10 million multiyear grant from the Gates Foundation, aimed at improving high school education. To Bill Hiss, the Gates grant meant the program had achieved critical mass. "The Mitchell Institute gradually has become a much more visible, respected, and potent player in public policy discussions, both on the state level and on the New England and national levels," he said.

Mitchell, however, "has always been cautious to make sure that the scholarship function stays at the core and the heart of the Mitchell Institute." The program has become so successful that it's attracted unexpected support, Hiss said. The Legislature funds an additional sixteen scholarships, one for each county, but in what Hiss said was "one of their more bizarre steps, they decreed that the money they gave would be allowed to have students go out of state," which Hiss said is most often "an Ivy League or a big research university."

The most notable research by the institute, among forty papers presented since 2000, was the "barriers" report from July 2007, written by research director Lisa Plimpton, which focuses on the transition from high school to college, and why Maine is so different from other New England states. Although 85 percent of high school students who entered the ninth grade in 2003 graduated four years later, only 50 percent enrolled in college that fall, far below other states; since then, the rate has increased to 53 percent. The lack of college attainment has been identified as one of the reasons why Maine's median income falls so far short of other New England states.

Mitchell himself often discusses this issue. "In terms of long-term unemploy-ment, an adult American who is out of work is more than three times as likely not to have a college degree. There are numerous studies that make clear that lifetime income is substantially higher for those who go on to higher education," he said, and the gap has increased. "We really need this in Maine, particularly in view of the sweeping information and technological change occurring through-out the world." The "barriers" report found that financial issues were promi-nent, as one might expect, but that issues in Maine's culture, and the many families where no one has attended college, are also important. Tim Agnew said, "In some areas of the state, there's a sense that the prior generation didn't need a higher education, and therefore this generation doesn't need it. There's a fear among parents that a higher education will only result in kids going away." Among the report's recommendations since adopted in Maine schools are dual attendance programs, where high school seniors take college courses, along with expanded career centers and advanced placement programs.

With the institute's expansion also came the need for staff, and Mitchell told Bill Hiss he'd like him to become the first executive director. Mitchell said Hiss turned him down because he liked his job at Bates, where he was now vice president for development. Mitchell said Hiss told him, "I have someone else I can recommend." It was his wife, Colleen Quint, now a lawyer specializing in education law. "So on Bill's recommendation and my own, we hired Colleen, who got it started, and it's developed tremendously," Mitchell said. Hiss admit-ted this caused some uncomfortable moments for him, since he'd served on the institute board from the beginning. "This is an obvious conflict of interest for me, to serve on the board while my wife is executive director," he told Mitchell, who he said replied, "Nothing doing. You're still the one who understands how to run a scholarship program, you have all kinds of practical, in-the-trenches experience other people on the board don't have. So you can't resign." Hiss decided instead to recuse himself where necessary.

Quint had interned for Mitchell right out of college, went to Boston and became an editor for the *Christian Science Monitor*, then went to law school. She had her own recognition story about Mitchell, a time when she saw him years later at LaGuardia Airport, introduced herself by name, and he replied, "Colleen, how are you doing? Have you gone to law school?" She said, "I couldn't believe he recognized me after a four-month internship." Quint was not a universally popular choice, according to Barbara Keefe. "It was probably a decision that was not well understood, because there were a lot of people who'd been involved," and they thought one of them would be chosen. "In hindsight, it was the best selection he could have made," Keefe said, and compared Quint's selection to Joe Brennan's choice of Mitchell over Ken Curtis for the Senate. "She's brilliant, has some very good instincts, is a superb writer, and just as tenacious as anyone you'd want to meet." Quint's first task was to reach out to high schools to convince them the scholarship program had expanded, and it made sense to apply even if a student there had been chosen previously; they no longer had to wait their turn. She also set up a leadership weekend for new scholars, often held at a remote or wilderness location. Quint served until 2011, when she was succeeded by Meg Baxter.

Mitchell's niece Mary Mitchell Friedman wasn't the first chair of the Mitchell Institute board, but she served longer in that role than anyone else. When she talks about its work, she sometimes mentions her uncle's experience in his summer job on the Colby College grounds crew, and his father telling him, "George, look around you—this is the only way you'll ever set foot on the Colby campus." When Mitchell went to Bowdoin, she said, "It was probably a case of leaving town a little bit, but not going too far, and taking the scholarships that were offered to him."

Mitchell plainly considered himself fortunate to have gone to an elite school and, she said, "He wanted to encourage a group of kids to pursue a college education who maybe hadn't thought about doing it before." As things developed, "We give them a check, but then we offer them a huge array of programming options. We offer mentoring, we offer leadership weekends, we are in constant touch with them so they'll do organized community service events . . . and we have a 95 percent retention rate with our scholars, which is extraordinary. The average statewide is 60 percent." She said it's important to look beyond Maine. "I echo his feelings in that regard," she said. "Education is the key for our citizens. Without it, we can't compete globally. . . . Our leaders have to come from an educated pool of people if we're going to be able to grasp the global issues and the local issues equally well." Chairing the board, she said, "is by far and away the best thing I've ever done."

THERE HAVE BEEN MORE THAN 2,400 MITCHELL scholars to date, and at least two current scholars speak at the annual dinner. Bill Hiss remembers one of the first, Lien Le, a Vietnamese refugee who had come to Portland through a Catholic Charities relief program. She was the oldest of five children, her father had died, and while helping raise her siblings she became the valedictorian at Portland High School, graduated with honors from Bates, received a medical degree from Brown, and then joined the faculty at Dartmouth. Few elite schools would have looked at Lien before she became a Mitchell scholar, Hiss said, because she had only a 400 verbal score on the SAT. "She's our poster child for those you don't want to miss because of their SAT scores. . . . The woman with a 400 verbal has been appointed to the faculty of the Dartmouth Medical School."

Terry Bagley of Centerville, a small village in Washington County, was forty-nine, and had been a computer specialist, real estate agent, and waitress when she received one of the nontraditional scholarships. "Nothing ever clicked," she told a reporter. She enrolled at the University of Maine at Machias to study biology, and said of the scholarship program, "It gives you a feeling that you're not alone, and you have a support system," calling it "one of the best-kept secrets in Maine." A speaker at the 2014 Mitchell Institute dinner talked about becoming homeless as she left behind a drug-addicted parent, then having teachers at Bangor High School willing to pay for her college applications and drive her to appointments.

Though it is by far Mitchell's most ambitious effort, the Mitchell Institute is not his only scholarship program. An exchange program between the Maine Community College System and University of Maine System, and Ireland's Department of Education & Science, has since 1999 allowed two university students and two community college students annually to attend public colleges and universities in Ireland as George Mitchell Peace Scholars.

Mitchell chose family members to lead his educational program in its early years, but the twenty-four-member board of directors has shifted to include many professionals, including CEOs, attorneys, physicians, and professors. Estelle Lavoie and Mary McAleney are still on the board; Hiss, Keefe, Pachios, and several family members have shifted to the advisory board. Heather Mitchell is a relatively recent addition to the board of directors. Its new chairman, the first nonfamily member to hold the post, is David Johnson, who came to Mitchell's Senate office in 1980, and has played many roles for him since then. Johnson, who now lives in Portland, decided to move to Maine with his wife to raise their children. He joined the board in 2008, and was mildly surprised, but pleased, when Mary Mitchell Friedman decided to step down and Mitchell asked him to become chair.

Dan Wathen, the former Maine chief justice who represented Freddie Vahlsing alongside Mitchell in the 1960s, said the Mitchell Institute "is probably the best use campaign contributions have ever been put to, and will have a more lasting effect than anything else." Sandy Maisel, the government professor, said, "We've had a lot of Mitchell scholars at Colby. They think he walks on water, and so do I." Bill Hiss regularly attends the annual brunch that Mitchell hosts to honor all the new scholars, now nearly 160. Mitchell always includes a version of his growing-up story, including the Lebanese immigrant community, the dedication of his parents to their children's education, and the encouragement of Elvira Whitten. "There'll be hundreds of people in the room," Hiss said, "and each Mitchell scholar will come and have their picture taken with the senator. I say to the parents at these gatherings, clean off your mantelpiece—you have a picture of Senator Mitchell with your kid, as a new Mitchell scholar."

When Mitchell spoke at the 2014 dinner in South Portland, he first told two of his favorite funny stories, "which I do when I get emotional." He joked about how his invitations to the dinner sometimes prompt recipients to say, "It's very expensive to be your friend," and then settled into his reflections. Of the scholarship program, he said, "We have to make this opportunity available to every child in Maine." As he looked around the room, he saw "mirror images of myself when I was their age." When he left the Senate and thought about a legacy, what became the Mitchell Institute was his first and only choice, he said. "I can help these kids," he said he told himself. "I must help these kids. I have an obligation." And though he said the program "was a huge and perhaps financially ambitious" undertaking, he never doubted it would succeed. "I've never done anything more meaningful in my life."

There are fewer buildings and places than one might expect named for George Mitchell. There's the George J. Mitchell School that serves all the elementary students of Waterville, and the post office at the north end of town. There is the George J. Mitchell Field in Harpswell, and a few others. Mitchell's demeanor is not that of a military hero, or a president. The Mitchell Special Collections at the Bowdoin College library are tucked away discreetly on the fourth floor, overlooking the quad. When he was designing his educational foundation, however, he decided to name it for himself. It is likely to be his monument.

AFTERWORD

From the time George Mitchell first sought elective office to the moment he retired from politics was just twenty years, and he was sixty years old when he decided to leave the Senate. Public service, however, was the essence of his professional life, and almost all the multifarious tasks he has undertaken are related, in his own mind, to service. His niece, Mary Mitchell Friedman, said, "I have met in the course of my lifetime a great number of political figures, so-called celebrities . . . and I have never met a man who has a deeper sense of what it means to serve the people of his state and his country. I think that has defined his life."

Portland attorney Norman Reef, father of legislative aide Grace Reef, knew Mitchell from his days as a defense attorney, then prosecutor. Reef realized some of his own clients chose him because they thought it might get Mitchell to ease off in his prosecutions, but said, "He never bent for anyone, or showed personal favor." It was a trait Reef saw carrying over to Mitchell's Senate career. "There never was, and there never will be, another politician like George."

Mitchell sometimes couches his overarching belief in the value of education, and providing opportunity to every child, in explicitly moral terms. Children who grow up without parents, or those without skills or employment, "can cause violence and divisions that not only ruin lives but undermine our future prosperity," he says in *Not for America Alone*. Hard work is a virtue—"I believe that the values of discipline, self-control, delayed gratification, and the work ethic are central to achievement in human life," but there must be more— "values grounded in the broader value of individual liberty and other American ideals." Without public morality, even hard work "can as easily produce a disciplined and successful criminal as they can a law-abiding citizen."

For Mitchell, working together in pursuit of a common goal is as essential as individual achievement. When he allowed another senator to take precedence on an important amendment, or describes one of his own legislative monuments as a "minor bill," he isn't engaging in false humility, but practicing his belief that giving credit is more important than taking it. He often observed of the Senate, "It's amazing how much you can accomplish if you don't try to take all the credit." His legislative aides were surprised by how often he publicly noted their contributions. Harold Pachios was astonished that Mitchell credited him with the key idea for his Iran-Contra speech. Deference was there from the beginning, as Mitchell always showed to Joe Brennan, the governor who made his Senate career possible. Like any legislator, Mitchell endured failure, but his signal successes were achieved in large part because he saw himself not primarily as actor, but as agent.

His Senate colleague Alan Simpson, who called him a "citizen politician," sometimes shifted from his trademark humor to eloquence when speaking of Mitchell. "His roots went deep into his own heritage. . . . He didn't come up with a silver spoon, he came up with a piece of cast iron in his teeth. And he was strong, he was annealed by the hammer and the forge, and there's a strength to him, an inner strength, which is quite unique and startling. And that's why the Irish troubles finally yielded to him, the baseball thing, his work on drugs and steroids. Whatever criticisms came from that all just fell away, because it was George Mitchell who did it."

Bill Cohen, who served with Mitchell during his entire Senate career, said Mitchell's ability to gain agreement was based on his patience and his willingness to let all sides be heard. Mitchell often succeeded, Cohen said, because "his logic is disarming." Fellow Republicans would tell Cohen, "He sounds so damn reasonable." Cohen, younger than Mitchell, isn't sure when either of them will retire. Cohen said that, after a lifetime in bakeries, "My father said he would never retire, and he died at work at age eighty-six. He was making dough. That would be my good fortune if I could continue."

Mitchell's departure from the Senate, though not intended that way, has increased his stature. Of all the national political figures prominent in the 1980s and '90s—George Bush, Bill Clinton, Newt Gingrich, Bob Dole, Jim Wright, Tom Foley—he was the only one not to suffer political defeat or scandal, the only one to leave office with his reputation fully intact. Tony Buxton observed, "There are very few people who have achieved high public office in the United States who did anything significant after they left it. George Mitchell has. Jimmy

Carter has. It's not a big list. . . . In George's case, it's not celebrity, it is dedication to achieving certain change, and it is an absence of ego."

In another unusual distinction for a former politician, Mitchell became a character in a novel, Irish writer Colum McCann's *Transatlantic*, published in 2013. The portrait of Mitchell vies with historical figures, the two British aviators who flew the Atlantic in 1919, before Charles Lindbergh, and abolitionist Frederick Douglass, who visited Dublin in 1845 and 1846. Perhaps for that reason the depiction of Mitchell seems attenuated. A more telling appreciation for what Mitchell achieved in Ireland is contained in lines from a 2015 short story by Colm Toibin: "One day you ask me if I hate the British, and I say that I do not. All that is over now. It is easy to be Irish these days."

While Mitchell has left politics, and perhaps diplomacy as well, he has become an observer of international affairs, drawing on both of those experiences. In contrast to those who see a chaotic present, followed by American decline, he reasons his way to a different conclusion. In 1997, at the end of *Not for America Alone*, he predicted that "our greatest years lie ahead of us, in the twenty-first century, a century I predict will be described by future historians as the American Century."

More recently, he expanded on the theme. "People talk about turbulence in the world today," he said, but he believes this century will be far more peaceful than its predecessor. "In the twentieth century, in just the two world wars, seventy-eight million people died. In terms of the world population, the scale of destruction was enormous. Today, a dozen people are killed in a bomb blast and it's worldwide news. The single most important reason for that is the military and economic dominance the United States has achieved. There is no one country, or feasible group of countries, that could challenge us in a conventional military sense. . . . They can threaten our leadership, but they don't challenge our dominance." American dominance, however, is a double-edged sword, he said. "One of the burdens under which we suffer is the belief that we can somehow control events around the world. We can influence events, but nobody can control them. It's a fantasy to think that we can and should."

The need for American leadership will not diminish, he said, observing that the world's population is anticipated to grow from seven billion to nine-and-a-half billion by 2050, and most of the growth will take place in the Muslim world, which already accounts for one in five humans. "All these intersecting and overlapping conflicts will continue. There is going to be turbulence." China and India—potential successors now that Russia and Japan face aging and declining populations—"suffer from burdens far greater than ours," he said. "Both face epidemic corruption. China has no established rule of law, which is so essential to economic progress and the whole concept of innovation." India, he said, "has a terribly corrupt, slow-moving bureaucracy with a huge population in rural areas that is lacking in education, skills, and health care."

The US political system, Mitchell acknowledges, is also showing signs of stress, though he believes the Republican Party "is making a mistake by co-opting the tea party's full program, not just their slogans." He points out that Republican hostility to immigration began with ballot questions in California. In a single generation, it turned a reliably Republican state that had produced Richard Nixon and Ronald Reagan into an overwhelmingly Democratic one. "It's not only wrong politically, it's inconsistent with the whole history of the United States," he said. "We've always had eruptions of what we call the know-nothings, and it tends to happen at times of economic stress. When our economy turns around, when growth returns and jobs come back, it just dissipates."

One issue where the United States cannot act alone is climate, Mitchell said. "It looms so large because it is beyond our individual ability to resolve. We haven't shown the leadership that's needed." With that large exception, "It's essential that we figure out how to solve our own problems."

ACKNOWLEDGMENTS

A book such as this one is written by one author, but it is also the work of many hands, and there are contributions to its narrative and interpretations that go beyond any formal acknowledgement. I list here some of those who helped; George Mitchell is a subject who draws people in and encourages cooperation, of which I am the beneficiary.

Senator Mitchell himself has been unfailingly helpful and attentive to all my requests. It cannot be easy to have someone delving into one's personal and public life, and he has borne it with his usual good grace and courtesy.

The Mitchell oral histories at Bowdoin College, and their counterparts, the Muskie archives at Bates College, comprise an enormously rich and detailed account of the political landscape surrounding these two senators from Maine. They are a boon to anyone who writes about this period.

The capable staff of the George J. Mitchell Department of Special Collections & Archives at Bowdoin College provided prompt and thorough assistance whenever needed, and I especially thank Curator Caroline Moseley and former Director Richard Lindemann.

Senator Mitchell's large and now far-flung Senate staff answered many questions and queries. Those I particularly relied on include Bob Carolla, Mike Hastings, Kate Kimball, Mary McAleney, Jeff Peterson, Grace Reef, Sarah Sewall, and Chris Williams.

Don Nicoll, Ed Muskie's chief of staff, provided perspective on the early Senate years. He undoubtedly knows and remembers more about Muskie's career than any other living person. Maine historian Earle Shettleworth made many helpful suggestions.

ACKNOWLEDGMENTS

The staff at Down East Books has been patient and accommodating to a first-time author, and the contributions of my editor, Michael Steere, and copy editor, Melissa Hayes, deserve special note.

There were several early and attentive readers of the manuscript, who helped shape and improve it. They include John Allard, Wesley McNair, Frank O'Hara, and my brothers, Alan Rooks and Byron Rooks.

I was assisted in my research by a grant from the Maine Arts Commission, an independent state agency supported by the National Endowment for the Arts.

Finally, I acknowledge the literally unquantifiable contributions to this book by my wife, Janine Bonk. Without her support, it could not have been written.

BIBLIOGRAPHY

BOOKS BY GEORGE J. MITCHELL

Men of Zeal: A Candid Inside Story of the Iran-Contra Hearings (with William S. Cohen), New York: Viking, 1988

World on Fire: Saving an Endangered Earth, New York: Charles Scribner's Sons, 1991

Not for America Alone: The Triumph of Democracy and the Fall of Communism, New York: Kodansha International, 1997

Making Peace, New York: Alfred A. Knopf, 1999

The Negotiator: A Memoir, New York: Simon & Schuster, 2015

BOOKS

Allen, Tom, *Dangerous Convictions: What's Really Wrong with the U.S. Congress*, New York: Oxford University Press, 2013

Asbell, Bernard, *The Senate Nobody Knows*, Garden City, New York: Doubleday & Company, 1978

Coffin, Frank M., *The Ways of a Judge: Reflections from the Federal Appellate Bench*, Boston: Houghton Mifflin Company, 1980

Cohen, Richard E., *Washington at Work: Back Rooms and Clean Air*, New York: Macmillan Publishing Company, 1992

Johnson, Haynes and David S. Broder, *The System: The American Way of Politics at the Breaking Point*, Boston: Little, Brown and Company, 1996

Johnson, Willis, *The Year of the Longley*, Stonington, Maine: Penobscot Bay Press, 1978

Lipez, Kermit, *Kenneth Curtis of Maine: Profile of a Governor*, Brunswick, Maine: Harpswell Press, 1974

Lippman, Theo, Jr. and Donald C. Hansen, *Muskie*, New York: W.W. Norton & Company, 1971

McCann, Colum, *TransAtlantic: A Novel*, New York: Random House, 2013

Nevin, David, *Muskie of Maine*, New York: Random House, 1972

Witherell, James L., *Ed Muskie: Made in Maine, 1914–1960*, Thomaston, Maine: Tilbury House, Publishers, 2014

INTERVIEWS

Interviews by the Author

Severin Beliveau, Augusta, Maine, October 6, 2014

Larry Benoit, Cape Elizabeth, Maine, October 8, 2014

Berl Bernhard, October 15, 2014

Berl Bernhard, Washington, D.C., November 19, 2014

Leon Billings, Portland, Maine, November 15, 2014

Tony Buxton, Augusta, Maine, November 13, 2014

Tony Buxton, February 26, 2015

Joe Brennan, Portland, Maine, October 29, 2014

Bob Carolla, June 22, 2015

Nancy and Bruce Chandler, Kennebunk, Maine, October 24, 2014

Bill Cohen, October 28, 2014

Ken Curtis, December 19, 2014

Bob Dole, February 10, 2015

David Flanagan, Hallowell, Maine, March 31, 2014

Mike Hastings, Orono, Maine, November 5, 2014

Anita Jensen, Gaithersburg, Maryland, November 19, 2014

David Johnson, Portland, Maine, October 29, 2014

Jamie Kaplan, Brunswick, Maine, October 27, 2014

Kate Kimball, June 8, 2015

Angus King, Brunswick, Maine, November 4, 2014

Kermit Lipez, Portland, Maine, December 9, 2014

Clyde MacDonald, Bangor, Maine, November 5, 2014

Mary McAleney, Freeport, Maine, September 19, 2014

George Mitchell, South Portland, Maine, August 25, 2001

George Mitchell, South Portland, Maine, October 13, 2001

George Mitchell, Seal Harbor, Maine, August 26, 2014

George Mitchell, December 15, 2014

Janet Mitchell and Mary Mitchell Friedman, Waterville, Maine, April 29, 2014

John "Swisher" Mitchell, Waterville, Maine, April 8, 2014

Paul Mitchell and Barbara Atkins, Waterville, Maine, March 25, 2014

Don Nicoll, Portland, Maine, March 13, 2014

Don Nicoll, Portland, Maine, July 16, 2014

Don Nicoll, Portland, Maine, December 9, 2014

Harold Pachios, Portland, Maine, May 6, 2014

Jeff Peterson, Washington, D.C., November 19, 2014

Martha Pope, Washington, D.C., November 20, 2014

Grace Reef and Sandy Brown, Washington, D.C., November 18, 2014

Bob Rozen, Washington, D.C., November 18, 2014

Sarah Sewall, January 2, 2015

Earle Shettleworth, Augusta, Maine, March 3, 2014

Mark Shields, Portland, Maine, November 15, 2014

Chris Williams, Washington, D.C., November 20, 2014

George J. Mitchell Department of Special Collections & Archives, Bowdoin College Library, Brunswick, Maine

George J. Mitchell Oral History Project

Timothy Agnew, Interview by Mike Hastings, April 14, 2009

Thomas "Tom" H. Allen, Interview by Andrea L'Hommedieu, August 28, 2009

Richard "Rich" A. Arenberg, Interview by Brien Williams, December 19, 2008

Barbara Atkins and Janet Mitchell, Interview by Andrea L'Hommedieu, July 14, 2008

Michael "Mike" Aube, Interview by Mike Hastings, June 20, 2009

John E. Baldacci, Interview by Andrea L'Hommedieu, February 24, 2010

Donna L. Beck, Interview by Andrea L'Hommedieu, March 22, 2010

Severin Beliveau, Interview by Mike Hastings, September 5, 2008

Robert "Larry" L. Benoit, Interview by Mike Hastings, July 29, 2008

Berl Bernhard, Interview by Brien Williams, February 9, 2009

Thomas "Tom" Bertocci, Interview by Mike Hastings, November 8, 2008

Jesse "Jeff" F. Bingaman, Interview by Brien Williams, September 18, 2009

Edward "Ed" M. Bonney, Interview by Andrea L'Hommedieu, April 29, 2010

William "Bill" W. Bradley, Interview by Brien Williams, July 17, 2009

John B. Breaux, Interview by Brien Williams, January 28, 2010

Joe and Connie Brennan, Interview by Andrea L'Hommedieu, October 24, 2009

Marjorie M. Bride, Interview by Mike Hastings, July 24, 2009

Paul P. Brountas, Interview by Mike Hastings, February 20, 2009

Paul P. Brountas, Interview by Andrea L'Hommedieu, April 12, 2010

Dale L. Bumpers, Interview by Brien Williams, March 5, 2009

Sheila P. Burke, Interview by Brien Williams, May 6, 2009

Anthony "Tony" W. Buxton, Interview by Andrea L'Hommedieu, December 17, 2009

Robert "Bob" J. Carolla, Interview by Brien Williams, March 25, 2009

Robert "Bob" J. Carolla, Interview by Brien Williams, April 30, 2009

James "Jim" W. Case, Interview by Andrea L'Hommedieu, August, 19, 2008

Nancy and Bruce Chandler, Interview by Andrea L'Hommedieu, February 24, 2010

William "Bill" S. Cohen, Interview by Brien Williams, March 12, 2009

Kenneth "Ken" M. Cole III , Interview by Mike Hastings, May 8, 2009

Kent Conrad, Interview by Diane Dewhirst, February 27, 2009

Walter E. Corey III, Interview by Andrea L'Hommedieu, May 18, 2010

Carole S. Cory, Interview by Brien Williams, October 26, 2009

Deborah "Deb" Cotter, Interview by Brien Williams, November 9, 2009

Kelly T. Currie, Interview by Brien Williams, April 22, 2010

Kenneth "Ken" M. Curtis, Interview by Andrea L'Hommedieu, April 9, 2010

Eliot R. Cutler, Interview by Mike Hastings, September 11, 2009

Thomas "Tom" A. Daffron, Interview by Brien Williams, October 5, 2009

Thomas "Tom" A. Daschle, Interview by Brien Williams, April 20, 2009

Lula J. Davis, Interview by Brien Williams, August 17, 2009

Harold J. Decker, Interview by Brien Williams, May 4, 2010

Dennis W. DeConcini, Interview by Brien Williams, September 16, 2009

Diane Dewhirst, Interview by Mike Hastings, February 17, 2010

Diane Dewhirst, Interview by Mike Hastings, May 17, 2010

John N. and Marcia L. Diamond, Interview by Mike Hastings, October 6, 2008

Robert "Bob" J. Dole, Interview by Brien Williams, September 22, 2009

Robert "Bob" J. Dunfey, Sr., Interview by Andrea L'Hommedieu, February 5, 2010

David F. Durenberger, Interview by Brien Williams, October 28, 2009

David F. Emery, Interview by Mike Hastings, December 18, 2009

David T. Flanagan, Interview by Mike Hastings, April 22, 2009

William "Bill" E. Frenzel, Interview by Brien Williams, April 13, 2009

Mary Mitchell Friedman and Harold J. Friedman, Interview by Andrea L'Hommedieu, September 8, 2008

Thomas "Tom" D. Gallagher, Interview by Brien Williams, April 29, 2009

Richard "Dick" A. Gephardt, Interview by Diane Dewhurst, March 17, 2010

Daniel "Bob" Robert Graham, Interview by Brien Williams, December 4, 2009

Patrick J. Griffin, Interview by Brien Williams, May 7, 2009

Floyd L. Harding, Interview by Mike Hastings, September 27, 2008

W. "Steve" Stephen Hart, Interview by Brien Williams, December 11, 2008

Michael "Mike" M. Hastings, Interview by Andrea L'Hommedieu, January 21, 2009

Michael "Mike" M. Hastings, Anita Jensen, Estelle Lavoie, Mary E. McAleney, Interview by Andrea L'Hommedieu, July 21, 2008

Robert "Hap" Hazzard, Interview by Andrea L'Hommedieu, August 31, 2009

Merton "Mert" G. Henry, Interview by Andrea L'Hommedieu, September 4, 2008

Lauren G. Higgins, Interview by Brien Williams, June 4, 2009

Horace "Hoddy" A. Hildreth, Jr., Interview by Mike Hastings, April 3, 2009

John L. Hilley, Interview by Brien Williams, May 11, 2009

William "Bill" C. Hiss, Interview by Andrea L'Hommedieu, March 20, 2008

Frederic "Fred" C. Hof, Interview by Brien Williams, March 24, 2009

Ernest "Fritz" F. Hollings, Interview by Andrea L'Hommedieu, June 20, 2012

Kelly R. Horwitz, Interview by Andrea L'Hommedieu, May 20, 2009

Patrick E. Hunt, Interview by Mike Hastings, September 27, 2008

Scott F. Hutchinson, Interview by Andrea L'Hommedieu, October 7, 2009

Harold M. Ickes, Interview by Diane Dewhirst, March 27, 2009

George Isaacson and Margaret McGaughey, Interview by Andrea L'Hommedieu, March 15, 2010

Anthony "Tony" Jabar, Sr., Interview by Andrea L'Hommedieu, March 27, 2008

Christopher "Chris" C. Jennings, Interview by Diane Dewhirst, May 27, 2009

Anita Jensen, Interview by Diane Dewhirst, February 17, 2009

David E. Johnson, Interview by Andrea L'Hommedieu, April 28, 2009

J. Bennett Johnston, Interview by Brien Williams, July 13, 2009

James "Jamie" E. Kaplan, Interview by Andrea L'Hommedieu, April 29, 2008

Barbara Keefe, Interview by Andrea L'Hommedieu, August 26, 2009

Joseph "Bob" Robert Kerrey, Interview by Brien Williams, June 11, 2009

Brian J. Kilroy, Interview by Andrea L'Hommedieu, November 19, 2009

Kate Kimball, Interview by Brien Williams, November 13, 2009

Angus S. King, Interview by Andrea L'Hommedieu, November 3, 2009

Edward "Ed" L. King, Interview by Brien Williams, November 16, 2009

Charles L. Kinney, Interview by Diane Dewhirst, July 27, 2009

Ralph "Ike" I. Lancaster, Jr., Interview by Mike Hastings, May 9, 2009

Estelle A. Lavoie, Interview by Andrea L'Hommedieu, June 9, 2008

Patrick J. Leahy, Interview by Brien Williams, March 18, 2010

Shepard "Shep" Lee, Interview by Andrea L'Hommedieu, March 20, 2008

David Lemoine, Interview by Mike Hastings, August 5, 2008

Robert "Bob" O. Lenna, Interview by Andrea L'Hommedieu, September 14, 2009

Carl M. Levin, Interview by Brien Williams, January 25, 2010

Kermit V. Lipez, Interview by Mike Hastings, November 20, 2009

Lee E. Lockwood, Interview by Brien Williams, December 8, 2008

Susan W. Longley, Interview by Andrea L'Hommedieu, March 23, 2010

Najeeb "Naj" S. Lotfey, Interview by Andrea L'Hommedieu, September 24, 2009

Clyde MacDonald, Interview by Mike Hastings, May 23, 2008

Clyde MacDonald, Interview by Mike Hastings, June 12, 2008

L. Sandy Maisel, Interview by Mike Hastings, March 15, 2010

Paul P. Maroon, Interview by Andrea L'Hommedieu, March 31, 2010

John L. Martin, Interview by Mike Hastings, October 7, 2009

Mary E. McAleney, Interview by Andrea L'Hommedieu, May 1, 2008

Brendan G. Melley, Interview by Brien Williams, December 10, 2009

Charles "Charlie" J. Micoleau, Interview by Andrea L'Hommedieu, October 9, 2008

Barbara A. Mikulski, Interview by Brien Williams, May 4, 2010

George J. Mitchell, Interview by Andrea L'Hommedieu and Mike Hastings, August 19, 2008

George J. Mitchell, Interview by Andrea L'Hommedieu and Mike Hastings, September 11, 2008

George J. Mitchell, Interview by Andrea L'Hommedieu, December 20, 2010

George J. Mitchell, Interview by Andrea L'Hommedieu, March 21, 2011

George J. Mitchell, Interview by Andrea L'Hommedieu, May 10, 2011

George J. Mitchell, Interview by Andrea L'Hommedieu, June 6, 2011

George J. Mitchell, Shep Lee and Harold Pachios, Interview by Mike Hastings and Andrea L'Hommedieu, September 11, 2009

Heather M. Mitchell, Interview by Brien Williams, February 5, 2010

Heather M. Mitchell, Interview by Brien Williams, March 2, 2010

James "Jim" Mitchell, Interview by Andrea L'Hommedieu, December 7, 2009

Janet F. Mitchell and Barbara M. Atkins, Interview by Andrea L'Hommedieu, July 14, 2008

John "Swisher" and Prin Mitchell, Interview by Andrea L'Hommedieu, April 24, 2008

Paul J. Mitchell, Interview by Mike Hastings, July 31, 2008

Gary S. Myrick, Interview by Brien Williams, June 3, 2010

Thomas "Tom" J. Nale, Interview by Mike Hastings, October 16, 2009

David H. Nexon, Interview by Brien Williams, September 18, 2009

Donald "Don" E. Nicoll, Interview by Andrea L'Hommedieu, April 9, 2008

Brett O'Brien, Interview by Diane Dewhirst, November 24, 2009

Jane F. O'Connor, Interview by Brien Williams, May 20, 2010

H. "Tim" Timothy O'Neil, by Mike Hastings, June 26, 2009

Paul and Germaine Orloff, Interview by Andrea L'Hommedieu, April 9, 2009

Harold "Hal" Pachios, Interview by Andrea L'Hommedieu, May 12, 2008

Robert "Bob" W. Packwood, Interview by Brien Williams, June 18, 2009

Jeffrey "Jeff" W. Peterson, Interview by Brien Williams, February 7, 2009

Gerald "Gerry" F. Petrucelli, Interview by Mike Hastings, July 26, 2009

Laurence "Larry" E. Pope, Interview by Andrea L'Hommedieu, May 14, 2008

Martha Pope, Martin "Marty" P. Paone, C. "Abby" Abbott Saffold, Interview by Diane Dewhirst, May 26, 2009

Martha Pope and David Pozorski, Interview by Brien Williams, November 30, 2009

Jeffrey "Jeff" W. and Mary A. Porter, Interview by Andrea L'Hommedieu, June 25, 2009

Christian "Chris" P. Potholm, Interview by Andrea L'Hommedieu, August 12, 2009

Colleen Quint, Interview by Andre L'Hommedieu, March 6, 2008

Grace Reef, Interview by Diane Dewhirst, March 26, 2009

Norman "Norm" S. Reef, Interview by Mike Hastings, April 3, 2009

Harry M. Reid, Interview by Brien Williams, July 24, 2010

Charles "Chuck" S. Robb, Interview by Brien Williams, August 4, 2009

John "Jay" D. Rockefeller, Interview by Brien Williams, April 16, 2010
Robert "Bob" M. Rozen, Interview by Diane Dewhirst, October 9, 2009
Robert "Bob" M. Rozen, Interview by Diane Dewhirst, November 20, 2009
Warren S. Rudman, Interview by Brien Williams, June 2, 2010
Patricia "Pat" A. Sarcone, Interview by Brien Williams, September 11, 2009
James "Jim" R. Sasser, Interview by Diane Dewhirst, April 27, 2010
Allan "Bud" H. Selig, Interview by Andrea L'Hommedieu, June 4, 2010
Sarah B. Sewall, Interview by Mike Hastings, April 24, 2009
Sam and Carol Shapiro, Interview by Andrea L'Hommedieu, September 11, 2009
Audrey Sheppard, Interview by Brien Williams, May 8, 2009
Paula D. Silsby, Interview by Mike Hastings, June 10, 2009
Alan K. Simpson, Interview by Brien Williams, November 11, 2009
Charlene Sturbitts, Interview by Brien Williams, June 16, 2009
Sharon Sudbay, Interview by Mike Hastings, January 10, 2009
Steven S. Symms, Interview by Brien Williams, August 11, 2009
Ann P. Tartre, Interview by Andrea L'Hommedieu, September 11, 2009
Barbara M. Trafton, Interview by Andrea L'Hommedieu, May 7, 2008
Robert "Bob" S. Tyrer, Interview by Brien Williams, March 12, 2009
Barry L. Valentine, Interview by Andrea L'Hommedieu, August 11, 2008
Deborah "Debbie" B. Ward, Interview by Andrea L'Hommedieu, February 5, 2010
John W. Warner, Interview by Brien Williams, March 31, 2009
Daniel "Dan" E. Wathen, Interview by Andrea L'Hommedieu, September 29, 2009
Gordon L. Weil, Interview by Andrea L'Hommedieu, August 17, 2009
Fred Wertheimer, Interview by Diane Dewhirst, July 10, 2009
Christine G. Williams, Interview by Brien Williams, November 21, 2008
L. Joe Wishcamper, Interview by Mike Hastings, July 10, 2009
Harris L. Wofford, Interview by Brien Williams, June 12, 2009

Archives and Special Collections Library, Bates College, Lewiston, Maine

Edmund S. Muskie Oral History Collection

Tom Allen, Interview by Don Nicoll, February 2, 2004
Barbara (Mitchell) Atkins, Interview by Mike Richard, August 13, 1999
Howard H. Baker, Interview by Don Nicoll, February 28, 2001
John Baldacci, Interview by Andrea L'Hommedieu, August 1, 2007
Severin Beliveau, Interview by Andrea L'Hommedieu, September 2, 1999
Berl Bernhard, Interview by Don Nicoll, April 30, 2002
Berl Bernhard, Interview by Don Nicoll, September 17, 2002
Berl Bernhard, Interview by Don Nicoll, January 28, 2003

Leon Billings, Interview by Henry Sirgo, July 9, 1998

Leon Billings, Interview by Don Nicoll, November 29, 2001

Leon Billings, Interview by Don Nicoll, May 1, 2002

Leon Billings, Interview by Don Nicoll, September 16, 2002

Leon Billings, Interview by Don Nicoll, January 27, 2003

Leon Billings, Interview by Don Nicoll, October 23, 2003

Leon Billings, Interview by Don Nicoll, November 13, 2003

Leon Billings, Interview by Don Nicoll, April 15, 2004

Frank Morey Coffin, Interview by Don Nicoll, Stuart O'Brien and Rob Chavira, July 21, 1998

Frank Morey Coffin, Edmund S. Muskie, Shep Lee, Don Nicoll, Interview by Chris Beam, August 6, 1991

Frank Morey Coffin and Don Nicoll, Interview by Erin Griffiths and Chris Beam, November 20, 1996

Eliot Cutler, Interview by Andrea L'Hommedieu, April 12, 2002

Eliot Cutler, Interview by Andrea L'Hommedieu, May 24, 2002

Eliot Cutler, Interview by Andrea L'Hommedieu, June 27, 2003

John Day, Interview by Andrea L'Hommedieu, August 18, 2000

Don Hansen, Interview by Andrea L'Hommedieu, September 20, 2000

Anita Jensen, Interview by Don Nicoll, May 2, 2002

Kermit Lipez, Interview by Andrea L'Hommedieu, September 20, 2001

George Mitchell, Interview by Don Nicoll, May 2, 2002

George Mitchell, Interview by Don Nicoll, August 9, 2002

George Mitchell, Interview by Don Nicoll, September 19, 2002

Edmund S. Muskie, Interview by Jim Ross, August 14, 1985

Edmund S. Muskie, Interview by Chris Beam, September 3, 1991

Edmund S. Muskie, Interview by Don Larrabee, November 28, 1995

Don Nicoll, Interview by Chris Beam, November 13, 1991

Don Nicoll, Interview by Henry Sirgo, July 7, 1998

Robert S. Strauss, Interview by Don Nicoll, January 29, 2003

Charlene Sturbitts, Interview by Don Nicoll, September 18, 2002

Daniel E. Wathen, Interview by Jeremy Robitaille, July 23, 2001

Jim Wright, Interview by Henry Sirgo, April 10, 1998

FILM / VIDEO

Interview with George Mitchell by Charlie Rose, PBS, May 26, 2011

George J. Mitchell at the Maine Irish Heritage Center, Portland, Maine, 2012 Claddagh Award Recipient

George Mitchell: My Journey's End, Michael Fanning, Belfast, Northern Ireland: Picture House, BBC, 2012.

ARTICLES AND REPORTS

By the Author

"The Domino Effect: Democrats Still Struggling after Mitchell's Departure," *Maine Times*, Portland, Maine, September 14, 1995

"Is There Hope for Politics? George Mitchell Abroad and at Home," *Maine Times*, Hallowell, Maine, September 10, 1998

"George Mitchell Still Holds Out Hope for Middle East Peace," *Sun Journal*, Lewiston, Maine, May 27, 2012

John Aloysius Farrell, "Integrity for Sale? George Mitchell's Post-Senate Career, from Northern Ireland to Big Tobacco," *Boston Globe Magazine,* March 3, 2002

Joel K. Goldstein, "Campaigning for America: Edmund Muskie's 1968 Vice Presidential Campaign," *New England Journal of Political Science*, Spring 2010, pp. 153–174

The Maine Action Plan, Secretary of State Kenneth M. Curtis, Augusta, Maine, October 1966

Maine Political Handbook, 1966, Maine Democratic Party, Lewiston, Maine

Maine Political Handbook, 1968, Maine Democratic Party, Lewiston, Maine

George J. Mitchell, "The Liberal Arts and the Constitution," *Kentucky Review*, Spring 1989

Report of the Congressional Committees Investigating the Iran-Contra Affair, with Supplemental, Minority and Additional Views. Daniel K. Inouye, Chairman, Senate Select Committee, and Lee H. Hamilton, Chairman, House Select Committee, November 17, 1987

Report of the Sharm el-Sheikh Fact-Finding Committee, Suleyman Demirel, Thorbjoern Ragland, George J. Mitchell, Chairman, Warren B. Rudman, Javier Solana, April 30, 2001

Senator Ed Muskie Testimonial Dinner, 10 Years of Public Service, Portland, Maine, April 29, 1964

"Temper and Temperament in an Admirable Man: A Tempered Conversation," by Senator Edmund S. Muskie's Administrative Assistants (Don Nicoll, John McEvoy, Maynard Toll, Charles Micoleau, Leon Billings), September 2013

NEWSPAPERS

Bangor Daily News, Bangor, Maine

Kennebec Journal, Augusta, Maine

Maine Sunday Telegram, Portland, Maine

Maine Times, Topsham, Maine

New York Times, New York, N.Y.

Portland Press Herald, Portland, Maine

Sun Journal, Lewiston, Maine
Times Record, Brunswick, Maine
Washington Post, Washington, D.C.

DOCUMENTS

George J. Mitchell Department of Special Collections & Archives, Bowdoin College Library, Brunswick, Maine

George J. Mitchell Papers, 1948–2012

Baseball Reports
Foreign Affairs
Governor's Race 1974
Health Care
Muskie 1972 Campaign
Personal Correspondence
Private Papers
Senate Campaign 1982
Senate Campaign 1988
Speeches
State and National Democratic Committees
Taxes and Budget
U.S. Attorney and U.S. District Court Judge

INDEX

Aaron, Hank, 499

Abbas, Mahmoud, 466, 467, 469–72

Abbas, Mohammed (Abu Abbas), 452

abortion, 173–74, 181, 229

Abrahamson, Albert "Jim," 52

Acadia National Park, 399, 400

acid rain: Canada and, 302; Clean Air Act provisions for, 302, 315; Emery and, 172; Mitchell, George, and, 149, 166, 171–72, 294, 301, 302, 305, 307, 315

Adams, Gerry, 434, 435, 438, 439, 444–46, 449

Advisory Committee on Student Financial Assistance, 522

Affordable Care Act, 355, 360, 364, 367, 373, 374

Afghanistan invasion, 487

AFL-CIO, 44, 148, 265, 287, 398

Agency for Health Care Research and Quality, 374

Agnew, Spiro, 86, 213

Agnew, Tim, 250, 523

agricultural issues, 391

Ahern, Bertie, 443, 447

AIPAC. See American Israel Public Affairs Committee

Airline (Route 9), 56, 243

air traffic controllers strike, 397

Albright, Madeleine, 440

Alderdice, John, 438

Allagash Wilderness waterway, 156

Allen, Tom, 55, 85, 117, 402, 413, 520

American Israel Public Affairs Committee (AIPAC), 452, 453

American Legion, 29, 254

American Red Cross: Liberty Fund, 489, 491, 492, 494; Mitchell, George, and, 489, 492–94; September 11 attacks and, 489–94

Americans with Disabilities Act, 259

American University, Beirut, 202, 346

Americare, 355

Amtrak, 394–96, 398

Andrews, Mark, 199

Andrews, Tom, 422

Andrews Air Force Base, 283

Angelone, Joe, 126, 162, 510

Anglo-Irish Agreement, 429–30, 433

antiwar protesters, 80–81, 138

appellate judges, 135

ARA. See Area Redevelopment Administration

Arafat, Yasser, 451–53, 456, 457, 460, 465, 467, 472
Area Redevelopment Administration (ARA), 70
Arenberg, Rich, 194–95, 204–5, 218, 230, 232, 234, 257, 376
Armey, Dick, 477
Armitage, Richard, 454, 459, 477
arms control, 172, 323, 324, 325. *See also* nuclear freeze
arms for hostages sales, 201–3, 206, 207, 210, 214–15
Army Intelligence: Berlin assignment, 27–30; School, 26–27
Aroostook sugar beet project, 69–72
Atkins, Barbara, 20, 110, 520–21
Atkins, Eddie, 20, 110
Attica State Prison, 88
Aube, Mike, 107, 108, 110, 111, 496
Auerbach, Red, 509
Augusta, Maine, 43, 46, 79, 113, 120, 176, 178, 192, 221, 302, 353, 376, 427
Austin, Phyllis, 118

Bagley, Terry, 527
Bailey, Dennis, 176
Baird, Ken, 52–53, 67
Baker, Howard, 172, 198, 294, 307, 412, 425
Baker, James, 328, 335, 345, 452, 463
Baldacci, John, 171, 182, 422, 521
Ball, William, 387–88
Bangor, Maine, 380
Bangor Daily News, 71, 113, 119, 134, 144, 159, 167, 181, 382
Bangor High School, 217, 523, 527
Barak, Ehud, 453, 456, 460, 462, 466, 467
Barnes, Michael, 198, 215
baseball: Boston Red Sox, 495–500, 505; drug-testing, 504, 506, 507, 508;

Mitchell, George, and, 407, 495–509, 512; Mitchell, Paul, and, 495; MLB, 407, 485, 498–504; Players Association, 506, 513; players' union strike of 1994-1995, 499, 500, 501, 502; Senators and, 497; World Series, 497, 498, 499, 502, 503
baseball commissioner, MLB: Blue Ribbon Panel on Baseball Economics, 502–4; Bush, George W., and, 501; Mitchell, George, as possibility for, 407, 498, 500–501; overview, 498–99; Selig as, 499, 500, 501, 502, 504–5, 508
baseball steroid use: Mitchell, George, report on, 503–9, 512; problem of, 504–5
base closing commission, 386, 422
basketball: Mitchell, George, and, 16, 25, 155, 169, 217, 406, 509; Mitchell, John "Swisher," and, 8, 19, 22, 155, 495, 515; Mitchell, Paul, and, 495
Bates College, 36, 59, 522, 526
Bath Iron Works (BIW), 177, 179, 323, 384–86
Baucus, Max, 230–31, 242, 306-8
Baxter, Meg, 526
Bayh, Birch, 91, 159, 423
Beck, Donna, 189, 191
Beirut, Lebanon, 202, 326, 346, 454
Beliveau, Severin, 68, 78–79, 80, 96, 102, 106, 136, 145; as lobbyist, 241, 477
Benoit, Larry, 166, 168, 174, 226, 228, 237, 393, 409, 413, 422, 426
Bentsen, Lloyd, 154, 195, 196, 197, 248, 278, 287, 297–98, 368, 394; as Treasury Secretary, 361
Berlin, Germany, 473; Army Intelligence assignment, 27–30; visit to, 29–30, 335
Berlin Wall, 27, 29, 327, 334

Bernhard, Berl, 81, 83, 88, 143, 144, 157, 467, 480, 492, 500; Muskie presidential campaign (1972) and, 89–93, 96–99, 103, 409, 427; at Verner Liipfert, 474–77

Bernstein, Carl, 95, 96

Bertocci, Tom, 217

Bicentennial Lighthouse Fund, 400

Biden, Joe, 248, 314, 465, 470

Billings, Leon, 55, 57, 142–43, 145, 146, 150

Bill of Rights, 255

Bingaman, Jeff, 233

Bishop, Neil, 43, 49, 85

BIW. *See* Bath Iron Works

Bkassine, Lebanon, 8, 21

Blair, Tony, 442, 443, 447, 448

Blakmun, Harry, 408

Blue Ribbon Panel on Baseball Economics (Blue Ribbon Commission), 502–4

board memberships, 481–85

Bobker, Lee, 166, 178, 226

Boland Amendment, 201, 206

Bonds, Barry, 504, 508

Bonney, Ed, 61, 78, 80–81, 136

Booth, Philip, 177–78

Boren, David, 203, 361, 414, 415, 418

Boston Celtics, 509

Boston Globe Magazine, 479

Boston Red Sox, 495–500, 505

Bowdoin College, 1, 8, 15, 16, 22–24, 30, 497, 518, 526; Hawthorne-Longfellow Library, 25; Mitchell Special Collections, 528; ROTC program, 26

Bowen, Otis, 359

BP Deepwater Horizon blowout, 300

Bradley, Bill, 154–55, 202, 203, 230, 231, 332; tax reform and, 272, 273, 285

Brady, Nicholas, 280, 281

Brady Bill, 382–83

Brandeis, Louis, 218

Brann, Louis, 35

Brannigan, Jim, 128, 130

Breaux, John, 200, 231, 232, 241, 286, 364–65, 411, 511

Brennan, Joe, 68–69, 76, 124, 137, 165, 166, 171, 182; governor's campaigns of, 107–10, 112–13, 126–27, 381–82; as Maine governor, 65, 138, 143–49, 156; Mitchell's appointment to Senate by, 29, 68, 144–50, 158, 163, 515, 530

Brewster, Ralph Owen, 36, 213

Breyer, Stephen, 408

Bride, Marjorie, 512

Bridges, Styles, 31

Brinkley, Douglas, 481

British-Irish diplomacy: Anglo-Irish Agreement, 429–30, 433; Mitchell, George, and, 430, 431. *See also* North Ireland peace talks

Broder, David, 95, 96, 180; *The System* of, 357, 361, 365, 368, 370, 419

Broderick, Faye, 121

Brody, Rick, 81–82

Brountas, Paul, 25

Brown, Ron, 511

Brown, Sandy, 389, 392, 395

Brunelle, Jim, 106

Brunswick, Maine, 24

Brunswick Naval Air Station, 384, 388

Bruton, John, 430, 442–43

Bryan, Richard, 278

Buchanan, Pat, 98, 285

Buckley, "Fat Jack," 99

Buckley v. Valeo, 183, 414

Buckner, Bill, 497

budget, federal: balance budget amendment, 269–70; Bush, George H. W., and, 276, 280–85, 288; Clinton, Bill, and, 288–91; cuts to domestic programs, 269, 274; Mitchell, George, and, 224, 247, 253, 265, 269–71, 276, 278, 280–86, 288–91; 1990 agreement, 284–86, 288; Paygo, 285, 286, 287; Reagan and, 177, 265, 268–71. *See also* Senate Budget Committee

budget deficit: Dole and, 270–71; Gramm-Rudman budget act and, 280; Mitchell, George, and, 224, 247, 253, 265, 269–71, 276, 278, 280, 282, 288, 289; of Reagan, 265, 268–71, 277; recession of 1990-1991 and, 288; reduction, 280, 282, 284, 288, 289; Social Security surpluses used for reduction of, 286, 288; under various presidents, 270

Bumpers, Dale, 230, 233, 249, 322, 342

Burdick, Quentin, 319

Burke, Sheila, 240–41, 245, 373

Burns, William, 464

Bush, Barbara, 317

Bush, George H. W., 178, 199, 204, 215, 216, 229; campaign finance and, 415; China and, 329–32; Clean Air Act and, 306, 307, 311–17, 320; climate change and, 320; Defense Secretary nominations of, 259–60; environmental legislation and, 306, 307, 311–18, 320; federal budget and, 276, 280–85, 288; health care legislation and, 357–58; Israel, 452–53; at Malta Summit, 334; Mitchell, George, and, 246, 247, 251, 256, 258–61, 276–86, 306, 307, 311–18, 320, 328–33, 339–43, 346, 357–58, 423, 452, 488; Noriega and, 329; nuclear testing freeze and, 325; Pan Am Flight 103 explosion and, 487–88; Persian Gulf War and, 260, 284, 339–43, 459; Social Security and, 286–87; Supreme Court nominations

of, 258–59, 261; taxation and, 276–85, 288

Bush, George W., 133; Afghanistan invasion and, 487; baseball commissioner and, 501; Bush-Gore presidential election, 204, 456; Iraq War and, 487; Israeli-Palestinian negotiations and, 454, 459–60, 464–65, 466; Mitchell, George, and, 454, 459–60, 464–65, 501; September 11 attacks and, 487; Sharm el-Sheikh Fact Finding Committee and, 454, 459–60, 464

Bush-Gore presidential election, 204, 456

Bush v. Gore, 204

Buxton, Tony, 128, 134, 135, 162, 239–40, 402, 409, 426, 530–31; as Mitchell's governor's campaign manager, 32, 108, 110–12, 115, 116, 119, 124, 401, 476

Byrd, Robert, 154, 164, 231, 393, 425; Clean Air Act and, 305, 306, 312–14, 316; health care legislation and, 361; Iran-Contra scandal and, 202–5; Mitchell, George, and, 155, 192–95, 197, 202–5, 221, 230, 234, 235, 245, 246, 248–51, 305, 312–14, 326, 412; overview, 192–93; as Senate Majority Leader, 220–21, 230, 232–35, 239, 245–46, 248–51, 414

Byrd Amendment, 313–14, 316

Califano, Joseph, 64

Callan, Jane, 52

Cambodia, 344–45

campaign finance: Bush, George H. W., and, 415; Clinton, Bill, and, 415–16; Common Cause and, 258, 414–15; disclosure, 225; Federal Election Campaign Act of 1974, 414; McCain-Feingold Act, 257, 417, 418;

Mitchell, George, and, 110, 117, 183–84, 185, 225, 228, 257, 414–18; public, 228, 257, 414–18; soft money, 415, 417, 418; Supreme Court and, 414, 418. *See also* fundraising; political action committees

Camp David, 340, 453, 462, 463, 467

Canada: acid rain and, 302; climate change and, 320; health care, 356, 358; Olympics corrupt selection process and, 512–13

"Canuck letter," 94, 95, 96

cap and trade system, 311–12

capital gains tax, 272–73, 276–80, 284

capital punishment, 383

Caribou-Speckled Mountain Wilderness, 379

Carolla, Bob, 189–91, 348, 380, 385, 386–88, 390, 391, 397, 398, 422–23, 426; on Pan Am Flight 103 explosion, 487–88

Carter, Gene, 318

Carter, Jimmy, 121, 143, 158, 202, 261, 530–31

Case, Jim, 150, 151, 153, 157, 193, 194, 267, 376

Castro, Fidel, 201

Catastrophic Health Care law, 358–59

Catholicism: of Mitchell, George, 173; of Muskie, Ed, 44

CBO. *See* Congressional Budget Office

Central Intelligence Agency (CIA), 159, 202, 206, 215, 329, 488

Central Maine Power (CMP), 14, 22

CFCs. *See* chlorofluorocarbons

Chafee, John, 131, 154, 182, 272, 279, 352; environmental legislation and, 295–98, 300, 307, 310; health care legislation and, 363–66, 371

Chamberlain, Joshua, 74, 224

Chamber of Commerce, 363

Chandler, Bruce, 31, 67, 111, 119, 424

Chandler, Nancy, 31, 101, 111–12, 424

Chavez, Linda, 198

Cheney, Dick, 204, 206, 211, 214, 216; as Defense Secretary, 260; as vice president, 459

Chicago Seven trial, 138

Chicago White Sox, 498, 499

China: Bush, George H. W., and, 329–32; Mitchell, George, and, 329–32; Tiananmen Square, 329–31; trade with, 330, 331

chlorofluorocarbons (CFCs), 303, 315

Christianity, 222–23

Christian Science Monitor, 357, 525

Christopher, Warren, 143, 439–40, 470

Church, Frank, 159, 322

Churchill, Winston, 148

Chute, David, 133

CIA. *See* Central Intelligence Agency

citizenship, naturalization ceremonies, 128, 140

Citizens United v. Federal Election Commission, 418

Clarke, John, 505

Clauson, Clinton "Doc," 49

Clawson, Ken, 95

Claytor, Graham, 395, 396

Clean Air Act, 319; acid rain provisions, 302, 315; Bush, George H. W., and, 306, 307, 311–17, 320; Byrd Amendment, 313–14, 316; Byrd and, 305, 306, 312–14, 316; cap and trade system in, 311–12; climate change and, 317, 320; coal interests and, 294, 301, 305, 307, 311–13; Daschle amendment on ethanol, 314–15; environmental groups and, 309–11; EPA and, 380–81; Maine and emissions standards of, 380–82; Mitchell, George, and, 6, 60, 64, 244, 256, 293, 299, 301, 302, 304–17, 380–82; motor source reductions

in, 308–9, 313, 315; Muskie, Ed,
and, 5, 60, 142, 293, 309, 317;
non-attainment areas in, 308, 315;
Obama and, 308–9, 318; presidential
enforcement of, 317–18
clean air hearings, 304, 305
Clean Elections Act, 183
Clean Water Act, 176, 293, 319;
Mitchell, George, and, 6, 64, 295–98;
Muskie, Ed, and, 5, 9, 294–95
clean water bills, presidential vetoes of,
298
Clemens, Roger, 504
Clifford, Clark, 89–90
climate change, 320, 321, 532; Bush,
George H. W., and, 320; Canada and,
320; Clean Air Act and, 317, 320
Clinton, Bill, 480; campaign finance
and, 415–16; Congress and, 262;
economic legislation, 360; federal
budget and, 288–91; health care
legislation and, 359–74, 404, 408;
Israeli-Palestinian negotiations and,
453–56, 459, 460, 464; Mitchell,
George, and, 124, 259, 261–62, 288–
91, 331, 359–63, 367, 370, 372, 404,
408, 412–13, 423, 430, 431, 440,
453, 456, 460, 520; NAFTA and,
391; North Ireland and, 430, 431,
434, 440, 445, 447, 448; reelection in
1996 of, 427, 440; Sharm el-Sheikh
Fact Finding Committee and, 453–56,
459, 460; Social Security and, 289;
stimulus bill of, 262, 289; taxation
and, 288–89
Clinton, Hillary, 434, 440; health care
legislation and, 361–62, 370–71;
Israeli-Palestinian negotiations and,
465, 470; Mitchell, George, and, 465,
470
CMP. See Central Maine Power
Coates, Dan, 475

CODEL. See congressional delegation
Coelho, Tony, 197, 257
Coffin, Frank, 47, 49–50, 122, 137, 184;
as judge, 45, 129, 141, 147; Maine
Democratic Party and, 34–35, 38–44,
73, 79, 136; The Ways of a Judge of,
135
Coffin, Ruth, 38
Cohen, Bill, 144, 285, 378; defense issues
and, 384–85, 387–88; as Defense
Secretary, 408, 440; Emery and, 177,
179–80; insurance reform and, 358;
Iran-Contra scandal and, 202–10, 216–
19, 223; Maine Republican Party and,
223; as Maine Senator, 126, 154, 155,
178, 187, 202–10, 216–19, 260, 261,
408; Men of Zeal of, 202, 203, 206–10,
218–19, 223; Mitchell, George, and,
121, 126, 154, 155, 179–80, 202–4,
206–10, 217–19, 223, 253, 358, 379,
384–85, 387–88, 423, 530; retirement
from Senate, 408; Wyman and, 223
Cohen, Richard E., 312, 315, 317
Colby College, 5, 10, 15, 19, 26, 518,
526, 527
Cole, Ken, 134, 170
College of the Atlantic, 303, 465
Collins, Susan, 381, 402
Committee to Re-Elect the President
(CREP), 90, 94, 95, 97, 98, 99, 114
Common Cause, 258, 414–15
Concourse, Waterville, 11, 20
Congressional Budget Office (CBO),
277, 278, 280
congressional delegation (CODEL), 237,
332, 335
Congressional Quarterly, 280, 287
Congressional Record, 267, 273
Conley, Gerry, 65, 145
Connally, John, 100
Connolly, Tom, 401
Conrad, Kent, 199, 200, 252, 290, 361

Constitution, 255; original intent theory, 136

"The Constitution and the Liberal Arts" (Mitchell), 216

Contract with America, 270, 419–21

Contras, 201, 202, 206, 211, 215, 328, 329. *See also* Iran-Contra scandal

Corey, Walter, 125–26, 162

Cory, Carole, 188–89, 438

Cory, Gayle, 145, 151, 187–89, 242–43, 324, 380, 402, 438, 511

Cotter, Deb, 240

Cox, Archibald, 258

Cox, Peter, 181

Cranston, Alan, 159, 178, 196, 257

CREP. *See* Committee to Re-Elect the President

cribbage, 516

crime bill (1990), 383

Cross, Burton, 39, 43, 44

Crowe, William, 340

C-SPAN, 273

Culver, John, 159

Cummock, Victoria, 487, 488

Currie, Kelly, 263, 376, 435, 440, 441, 447–48, 454

Curtis, Ken, 42, 50, 71, 103, 106, 118–20, 125, 144, 146, 183–84; as governor of Maine, 73–76, 78, 85, 105, 107, 108, 110, 114, 115, 143, 160, 161; Senate campaign of 1982 and, 159, 160–61

Cutler, Eliot, 89, 98, 121, 124, 134, 152, 153, 402, 511

Daffron, Tom, 180, 217, 314

Danforth, John, 274

Danzig, Richard, 388

Darman, Dick, 279, 281

Daschle, Tom, 198, 200, 231, 236, 249, 377, 412, 421, 475, 487; Clean Air Act ethanol amendment of, 314–15;

Democratic Policy Committee and, 248, 250

Davis, Marvin, 91

Davis, Wayne, 395–96

Day, John, 71, 144, 159, 160, 176, 177, 180–81

de Chastelain, John, 434, 435

Decker, Harold, 489–94

"Declaration of Conscience" (Smith, Margaret), 36, 212

DeConcini, Dennis, 153, 199, 200, 245, 249, 250, 332; as one of Keating Five, 257–58

Defense Department (Department of Defense; DoD), 172

defense issues: Cohen, Bill, and, 384–85, 387–88; Maine and, 384–90; Mitchell, George, and, 166, 172, 179, 227, 384–90; Reagan's defense buildup, 166, 170, 172, 227, 269, 322–23, 384, 385

Defense Secretary: Bush, George H. W., nominations for, 259–60; Cheney as, 260; Cohen, Bill, as, 408, 440; Weinberger as, 215, 216

defense spending, 422; Mitchell, George, and, 166, 172, 179, 227, 386–90; reductions, 386–89. *See also* defense issues

Delahanty, Tom, 40, 46, 133, 137, 176

DeLay, Tom, 386

DeLogu, Orlando, 118

DeMars, Bruce, 387–88

Demirel, Suleyman, 453

Democratic Caucus, 272; Mitchell, George, and, 248, 250, 262; Senate Majority Leader and, 248

Democratic Conference, 248, 249, 250

Democratic Leadership Council (DLC), 246, 254, 366

Democratic National Committee (DNC), 38, 78, 80, 93, 100–103, 106

Democratic National Convention (1968), 71; antiwar protesters at, 80–81, 138; Mitchell, George, at, 80–81; Muskie at, 77, 80–81

Democratic Party, 87; as majority party after 1964 election, 65–66; opposition to Mitchell, George, 383; Vietnam War and, 76. *See also* Maine Democratic Party; *specific topics*

Democratic Policy Committee (DPC), 243, 276; Daschle and, 248, 250; Mitchell, George, and, 248, 250, 251; Sewall, Sarah, at, 327; staff, 251

Democratic Senatorial Campaign Committee (DSCC): Johnson, David, and, 196–97; Mitchell, George, as chair of, 195–200, 220, 230, 231; 1986 election and, 196–200

Democratic Steering Committee, 249, 250

Democratic Unionist Party (DUP), 436, 449

Democrats: spending priorities of, 253. *See also specific topics*

Department of Agriculture, 390

Department of Energy, 379

Department of Housing and Urban Development (HUD), 274; Section 8 program, 275

Department of Justice, Antitrust Division, 32–33

de Valera, Eamon, 433, 443

Dewhirst, Diane, 188, 197, 221–22, 237, 240, 244–45, 252, 300, 304–5, 329, 330, 332, 351

Diamond, John, 171

Dickey-Lincoln project, 155, 156

DiMaggio, Joe, 496

Dingell, John, 308, 316

Disney, Roy, 482–85

Disney Entertainment, 407, 481–86

"Dissent on the Kiddie Porn Trial" (Chute), 133

Dixon, Alan, 389

DLA Piper, 478, 481, 514

DLC. *See* Democratic Leadership Council

DNC. *See* Democratic National Committee

Dodd, Chris, 236, 361, 421

Dodd, Thomas, 90, 260

Dole, Bob, 164, 178, 195, 199, 221, 342, 425; budget deficit and, 270–71; health care legislation and, 357, 359, 363, 365, 366, 371, 372–73; Iran-Contra scandal and, 203, 204; Mitchell, George, and, 200, 239–41, 245, 247, 251, 252, 255, 256, 270, 335, 346, 363, 371–73, 423, 468, 474–75, 488; on partisanship, 256; on Senate Finance Committee, 239, 241, 268, 270; as Senate Majority Leader, 271, 273, 420–21; as Senate Minority Leader, 200, 239–41, 258, 288; at Verner Liipfert, 475

Dolloff, Maynard, 49, 121

Dome of the Rock, 458

Donovan, John, 54

Douglass, Frederick, 531

Dowd, John, 505

Downeaster, 392, 396, 398

DPC. *See* Democratic Policy Committee

DSCC. *See* Democratic Senatorial Campaign Committee

Dubinin, Yuri, 335, 336

Dubord, Dick, 58

Dubord, Harold, 36, 40, 58

Dukakis, Michael, 25, 229, 254

Dunfey, Bob, 38

DUP. *See* Democratic Unionist Party

Durenberger, David, 203, 258, 307, 316, 364, 372

Eagleton, Tom, 200

early years, of George Mitchell: baseball in, 495–96; basketball in, 16, 25, 169,

406; birth of, 5, 7, 8; childhood health, 11; growing up in Waterville, 7–23; schooling, 15–16, 19, 22–23, 519

Earth in the Balance (Gore), 313, 321

East Jerusalem, 469, 470

economic issues: Blue Ribbon Panel on Baseball Economics, 502–4; Clinton, Bill, and economic legislation, 360; Mitchell, George, on, 265–66, 276; North Ireland-US economic conference, 431–33. *See also* budget, federal; finance; taxation; *specific economic issues*

Educare Center, 521

Eisenhower, Dwight, 35, 238, 514

Eisner, Michael, 481–86

Elizabeth, Queen, 246

Emery, David, 120, 124, 136; abortion and, 173, 174; acid rain and, 172; Cohen, Bill, and, 177, 179–80; debates with Mitchell, George, 178, 179; endorsements of, 181; nuclear freeze and, 172–73; Senate campaign of 1982, 159–62, 166, 168–83; Social Security and, 173; veterans affairs and, 174–75; Whatever Race and, 176

environmental groups, 479; Clean Air Act and, 309–11

environmental legislation: Bush, George H. W., and, 306, 307, 311–18, 320; Chafee and, 295–98, 300, 307, 310; Mitchell, George, and, 149, 172, 293–320; Muskie, Ed, and, 5, 9, 49, 60, 64, 118, 142, 149, 156, 171, 292–95; Nixon and, 293; Reagan and, 294, 295, 296, 298, 302–3, 305, 306. *See also* Senate Environment and Public Works Committee; *specific environmental legislation*

Environmental Protection Agency (EPA), 293, 295, 297, 303, 304, 315; Clean Air Act and, 380–81

EPW. *See* Senate Environment and Public Works Committee

Ervine, David, 444, 445

Erwin, Jim, 85, 108, 114–17, 120

ESPN, 483, 504

European Union (EU), 453. *See also* Sharm el-Sheikh Fact Finding Committee

evangelical right, 223

Evans and Novak, 93, 99

Exon, James, 325, 370, 407

Exxon Valdez, 299, 300

FAME. *See* Finance Authority of Maine

farm bill, 390

Farrell, John Aloysius, 479

Fatah, 466, 467

Fayyad, Salam, 472

FDA. *See* Food and Drug Administration

federal budget. *See* budget, federal

Federal Election Campaign Act of 1974, 414

Federal Facility Compliance Act, 318

federal judge, George Mitchell as, 135–41, 144–48, 517

Federal Nursing Home Reform Act, 351–52, 359

Federle, Mary, 192

Fed Ex, 482, 486

Fehr, Don, 506, 513

Feingold, Russ, 361

Feinstein, Dianne, 422

Fenway Park, 495, 496, 497, 498

Fianna Fail, 433–34, 443

filibusters: army cot room for, 165; LBJ and Rule 22, 48; Mitchell, George, and, 164–65, 421; Republican use of, 421; rules changes, 164

finance: Mitchell, George, on federal finances, 265–66. *See also* budget, federal; campaign finance; Senate Finance Committee

Finance Authority of Maine (FAME), 523
Finance health care subcommittee: health
    care legislation and, 350–52, 356,
    365, 372; Mitchell, George, and,
    350–54, 365
Fine Gael, 433, 434
First Amendment, 255
First Circuit Court of Appeals, 34, 50,
    55, 130, 134, 141, 147
Fisher, Dean, 39
fish inspection bill, 390–91
Fitzgerald, Buzz, 188, 385
FitzGerald, Garret, 430, 433, 434
flag-burning, 254–55
Flanagan, David, 156, 157
Foley, Tom, 244, 254, 281–82, 289,
    359, 373, 415, 416
Food and Drug Administration (FDA),
    391, 480, 489, 490
Ford, Gerald, 116–17
Ford, Wendell, 195, 196, 268
Fowler, Wyche, 232, 281
Freeh, Louis, 514
French, Dwight, 162
Frenzel, Bill, 283, 284
Friedman, Harold, 138–39, 497
Front Street, Waterville, 5, 9, 10, 17, 83,
    111, 516
Frost, Jack, 161–62
Fulbright, J. William, 322
Fullam, Paul, 40–42, 44
fundraising: by Mitchell, George, 169–
    70, 185, 220, 224, 225, 227, 228. See
    also campaign finance; Keating Five;
    political action committees

Gallagher, Claire, 450
Gallagher, Tom, 150, 267, 268, 270–71
Gallen, Hugh, 101
Gardner, John, 414–15
Gates Foundation, 524
Gaza, 451, 453, 455–56, 466, 467, 470

GE. See General Electric
Gejdenson, Sam, 418
General Electric (GE), 479–80
George J. Mitchell Field, 390, 528
George J. Mitchell School, 521, 528
George Mitchell Peace Scholars, 527
Georgetown University Law School,
    28–32
Gephardt, Dick, 244, 262, 281–83, 359,
    373, 377, 416, 417, 423, 427, 487
Giamatti, Bart, 499
Giambi, Jason, 507
Gignoux, Edward, 129–30, 132, 138
Gingrich, Newt, 252, 257, 282–84,
    419–21
Ginsburg, Ruth Bader, 408
Glenn, John, 235, 257, 361
global warming. See climate change
Gold, Stanley, 482–85
Goldwater, Barry, 50
Good Friday Agreement, 445–49. See
    also North Ireland peace accord
Goodwin, Richard, 84, 86, 87, 152, 212
Gorbachev, Mikhail, 246, 329; Mitchell,
    George, and, 323, 332–39; nuclear
    testing freeze and, 325; Reagan and,
    323. See also Soviet Union
Gore, Al, 313, 321, 341, 342, 440; Bush-
    Gore presidential election, 204, 456
graduation speeches, of Mitchell, George:
    basic text of, 518; Maine, 517–19;
    University of Maine School of Law,
    517
Graham, Bob, 198, 200, 251, 253, 308,
    411
Gramm, Phil, 279
Gramm-Rudman budget act, 280
Gray, Boyden, 307
Gray, Jane, 10, 37. See also Muskie, Jane
Gray Cary, 478
Great Depression, 7, 338
Great Society, 64

Greenspan, Alan, 277
Greider, William, 270
Greve, Frank, 419
Griffin, Patrick, 155, 193, 202, 230, 233, 262, 371, 431
Guilford Transportation, 396, 397–98
Gulf War. *See* Persian Gulf War
gun legislation: assault weapons ban, 422; Mitchell, George, and, 382–83

Haggett, Bill, 179, 384–85
Hall, Fawn, 215, 218
Hamas, 466–67
Hamilton, Lee, 204, 209, 489
Hand, Lloyd, 474
Hansen, James, 321
Haram esh-Sharif visit, 458
Harding, Floyd, 66, 118, 163
Harkin, Tom, 313
Harriman, Averell, 39, 86, 89, 90, 96
Harrington, John, 498
"Harry and Louise" ads, 369–70
Hart, Gary, 200, 218, 487
Hart, Phil, 47
Hart, Steve, 190, 191, 379–80, 386, 391, 410
Harvard University, 518
Hasenfus, Eugene, 201
Haskell, Robert, 45–46
Hastert, Dennis, 487
Hastings, Mike, 152, 154, 161, 181, 186–89, 324, 387, 402–3
Hatfield, Mark, 325
Hathaway, William "Bill," 60, 73, 77, 105, 120, 136, 142, 144, 145, 379
Hathaway Shirt, 10
Hazzard, Robert "Hap," 25
Head of Falls, Waterville, 5, 10, 11, 12
HealthAmerica, S. 1227, 355–58
health care, Canadian, 356, 358
health care legislation: Affordable Care Act, 355, 360, 364, 367, 373, 374; bipartisan caucus on, 363–64, 366–67; Bush, George H. W., and, 357–58; Byrd and, 361; Chafee and, 363–66, 371; Clinton, Bill, and, 359–74, 404, 408; Clinton, Hillary, and, 361–62, 370–71; Dole and, 357, 359, 363, 365, 366, 371, 372–73; employer mandate in, 364, 370; Finance health care subcommittee and, 350–52, 356, 365, 372; "Harry and Louise" ads about, 369–70; Health Security Act, 363; HEL and, 353, 365, 366; Heritage Foundation and, 363, 364; House of Representatives and, 373; individual mandate in, 364; Kennedy, Ted, and, 355, 356, 357, 358, 365–70; Mitchell, George, and, 354–67, 369–74, 404, 408, 420; Moynihan and, 360, 361, 364, 367–70, 372, 373; Republicans and, 355–57, 359, 363–66, 369–73; Senate Finance Committee, 353, 356, 361, 362, 364, 365, 367, 369, 371, 372, 374; single-payer, 356, 358, 361; *The System* on Clinton, 357, 361, 365, 370, 419; universal coverage in, 353, 357, 363–65, 370; White House Task Force on Health Care Policy, 361–63, 366; Williams, Christine, and, 350–59, 362, 364, 369, 371, 372, 373, 374, 400, 420, 497. *See also* nursing home legislation
Health Security Act, 363
Healy, Bernadine, 489–93
Heath, Sally, 31. *See also* Mitchell, Sally
Heflin, Howell, 208, 232, 411
Heinz, John, 311, 354
HEL. *See* Senate Health, Education and Labor Committee
Helms, Jesse, 174, 328
Henry, John, 498
Henry, Merton, 52, 53, 58, 67, 69, 72, 85, 120, 121, 138, 147, 183

Heritage Foundation, 363, 364
Higgins, Lauren, 191–92, 212, 250
Hildreth, Hoddie, 150
Hildreth, Horace, 37, 49
Hill, Anita, 259, 261
Hilley, John, 243, 248, 262, 275–76, 278, 289–90
Hiss, Bill, 378, 522–28
Hof, Fred, 454, 456, 459–61, 468
Hoffman, Julius, 138
Holkeri, Harri, 435
Hollings, Ernest "Fritz," 61, 248, 280
Hollingsworth & Whitney mill, 5, 17
Horwitz, Kelly, 189–90, 377, 380, 389
House Armed Services Committee, 384
House of Representatives, 238; Gingrich as Speaker of, 419–21; health care legislation and, 373; House Bank scandal, 421
House select committee, on Iran-Contra, 203, 204
housing: affordable, 274–75; HUD, 274, 275; Low Income Housing Credit, 275
HUD. *See* Department of Housing and Urban Development
Hughes, Harold, 93, 243
Hume, John, 434, 445, 447, 449
Humphrey, Hubert: Muskie, Ed, and, 48, 58, 72, 77, 78, 80–81, 83–84, 91, 97; presidential campaign of, 58, 77, 78, 80–84; Vietnam War and, 82
Hunt, Patrick, 130
Hussein, Saddam, 215, 260, 283, 339, 341. *See also* Iran-Iraq war; Persian Gulf War
Hutchinson, Scott, 108, 111, 162, 169, 170, 220, 413
Hybl, Bill, 512, 513

Ickes, Harold, 369–71
Iger, Bob, 485, 486

Indian Land Claims Act, 144, 156–57
Indian Land Claims case, 138, 144
Indyk, Martin, 460
Inhofe, James, 321
Inouye, Daniel, 202, 203, 205, 206, 208, 209, 221, 230–36
Intermodal Surface Transportation Efficiency Act (ISTEA), 392, 394, 396
internationalism, 338
International Olympic Committee (IOC), 512–14
International Paper strike, 398
IOC. *See* International Olympic Committee
IRA. *See* Irish Republican Army
Iran, 472
Iran-Contra scandal: arms-for-hostages sales and, 201–3, 206, 207, 210, 214–15; Cohen, Bill, and, 202–10, 216–19, 223; covert activities and, 206, 207, 210, 216; hearings, 204–14, 217, 218, 219; House select committee on, 203; Iran-Iraq war and, 207; Mitchell, George, and, 201–14, 216–20, 223–25, 230, 530; overview, 201–2; Reagan and, 201–3, 205, 206, 210, 214–16, 225; Senate Intelligence Committee and, 202, 203, 205; Senate select committee on, 202–9, 215–16; speech to North by Mitchell, George, 212–14, 219; Tower Commission on, 202, 203, 205, 225
Iran-Iraq war, 207, 326
Iraq: Iraq War (2003), 487; Persian Gulf War, 260, 284, 321, 339–43
Ireland. *See* North Ireland; Republic of Ireland
Irish Republican Army (IRA), 430, 431, 434, 435, 441, 444, 445, 449
Isaacson, George, 130, 133–34

Israel, 322; Bush, George H. W., and, 452–53; Haram esh-Sharif visit and, 458; Mitchell, George, and, 451–53; Palestinians and, 451–54, 466–67, 473; PLO and, 451–53; Six Day War, 451; UN and, 451–52

Israeli-Palestinian negotiations: Bush, George W., and, 454, 459–60, 464–65, 466; Clinton, Bill, 453–56, 459, 460, 464; Clinton, Hillary, and, 465, 470; Obama, Barack, and, 130, 465–70; US and, 452–67. *See also* Sharm el-Sheikh Fact Finding Committee

ISTEA. *See* Intermodal Surface Transportation Efficiency Act

Ivory Coast slave labor, 479

Jabar, John, 33, 51, 52
Jabar, Tony, 12, 15, 17
Jackson, Henry "Scoop," 94, 97, 169
Jackson Laboratories, 400
Jacobs, Charlie, 151–52, 162, 163, 186
Jagland, Thorbjørn, 453, 461, 462
Jefferson, Thomas, 136
Jeffords, Jim, 261, 391
Jennings, Chris, 356, 360–61, 371
Jensen, Anita, 343, 377; Mitchell, George, and, 57, 152–53, 157, 166, 189–91, 193, 227, 242, 243, 331, 344, 410, 413, 518
Jensen Baird (law firm), 52, 53, 65, 67, 126, 136, 138, 474
Johnson, David, 230, 267; DSCC and, 196–97; Mitchell, George, and, 150–53, 155, 157, 163, 170, 173, 177, 179, 180, 183, 194, 196, 220, 379, 520, 527
Johnson, Frank, 137
Johnson, Haynes, 357, 361, 365, 368, 370, 419
Johnson, Lula, 191, 253

Johnson, Lyndon Baines (LBJ): filibuster and Rule 22, 48; Great Society of, 64; Muskie, Ed, and, 47–48, 50, 64, 65, 72, 91; as Senate Majority Leader, 47–48, 236, 238–39, 252; Vietnam War and, 76–77, 82
Johnston, Bennett, 195, 196, 261, 385, 386, 511; in race for Senate Majority Leader, 221, 230–36
Jones, Woody, 116, 162
Jordan, 471
Jordanians, 458
Jordan Pond House, 400–401
judicial activism, 136–37

Kaplan, Jamie, 205, 206, 208, 209, 211–12, 215–17, 509, 511
Kassebaum, Nancy, 179, 260
Kean, Tom, 489
Keating, Charles, 257
Keating Five, 257–59, 280. *See also* S&L crisis
Keefe, Barbara, 167, 228, 524, 525
Kelley, Peter, 107, 109, 113
Kelly, Gerry, 441
Kennebec Journal, 221–22, 382–83
Kennebec River, 5, 6, 7, 9, 176
Kennedy, John F., 50, 112, 236
Kennedy, Robert "Bobby," 65, 75, 77, 78
Kennedy, Ted, 86, 137, 165, 231, 248, 485, 511; health care legislation and, 355, 356, 357, 358, 365–70; Senate committee work of, 249
Kerrey, Bob, 248, 251, 252–53, 285, 289, 290, 342, 366–67, 407, 411, 425
Kerry, John, 98, 308, 313, 349
Khmer Rouge, 344
Khomenei, Ayatollah, 201, 202
Kilroy, Brian, 52
Kilroy, Francis, 52

Kilroy, Jane Callan, 52
Kilroy, Michael Joseph, 13–14. *See also*
    Mitchell, George John, Sr. "Jiddoo"
Kimball, Kate, 303–5, 308, 309, 311,
    312, 315–19, 321
King, Angus, 50, 60, 121, 381–82, 401,
    402, 427–28
King, Ed, 251, 327, 328, 329, 330, 341,
    408, 431, 470
King, Martin Luther, 344
King Court, 7
Kinney, Charles, 155, 248, 249, 251,
    313
Kinnock, Neil, 442
Kissinger, Henry, 487, 488, 489
Kochanovsky, Moshe, 457
Kohl, Herbert, 500
Ku Klux Klan, 36, 192
Kuwait, 260, 283, 284, 321, 339–43
Kyl, John, 257
Kyros, Peter, 72, 73, 87, 105–6, 120,
    166

labor-management relations, 44, 397–99
LaFountain, Lloyd, 107, 109, 113
Lake, Tony, 89, 431
Lancaster, Ralph, 134, 140
Landers, Ann, 476
Landis, Kenesaw Mountain, 498, 500,
    505
Langhart, Janice, 408
Lautenberg, Frank, 273, 290, 313
Lavoie, Estelle, 186, 242, 252, 287–88,
    350, 399, 521, 527
lawyer, George Mitchell as, 104, 123,
    125, 494, 529; as assistant county
    attorney for Maine, 68–69, 71–72;
    chocolate manufacturers labeling
    case, 479; conflicts and dilemmas of,
    478–81; DLA Piper and, 478, 481,
    514; GE and, 479; at Georgetown
    University Law School, 28–32; Jensen

Baird and, 52, 53, 65, 67, 126, 136,
    138, 474; as mega-lawyer, 477; Piper
    Rudnick and, 477–78; Preti Flaherty
    and, 476–77; tobacco industry and,
    480–81; Verner Liipfert and, 474–77.
    See also federal judge, George Mitchell
    as; US attorney for Maine, George
    Mitchell as
LBJ. *See* Johnson, Lyndon Baines
Le, Lien, 526–27
Leahy, Patrick, 230, 232, 250, 252, 384
Lebanese community, Waterville, 5, 8,
    11, 12, 14, 15, 17, 468
Lebanon, 451, 466; Beirut, 202, 326,
    346, 454; Bkassine, 8, 21; Mitchell,
    George, as Senator, and, 345–47
Lee, Shep, 54, 83, 126, 146, 512
legal discrimination, 133–34
Lemieux, Lionel, 43, 44
Lemoine, David, 168
Lenna, Bob, 115–16, 119, 161
Levin, Carl, 154, 194, 250, 260, 342,
    420
Levin, Richard, 502
Levine, Julius, 67–68
Lewiston, Maine, 38, 39, 44, 75, 79,
    114, 119, 120, 181, 186, 228, 243,
    375
Liberty Fund, 489, 491, 492, 494
Lieberman, Joe, 277
Liman, Arthur, 207
Lipez, Kermit, 55, 73, 118, 121, 123,
    124, 143, 144, 152, 162, 510–11
Lithuania, 335, 336
Lockwood, Lee, 378
Loeb, William, 94, 95
Long, Russell, 191, 200, 270
Longley, Jim, 114–15, 117–21, 156, 187,
    228
Longley, Susan, 187, 190
long-term care, 352–53. *See also* nursing
    home legislation

Loring Air Force Base, 384, 387, 389, 422

Lotfey, Najeeb, 167, 237, 478

Lott, Trent, 420, 487

Low Income Housing Credit, 275

MacBride Principles, 430, 437

MacDonald, Clyde, 109, 111, 119, 147, 171, 172, 380, 382, 391

MacDonald, Paul, 127

MacLachlan, Heather, 405–7. *See also* Mitchell, Heather

Magaziner, Ira, 361, 362, 370

Magnuson, Warren, 142

Maine: agricultural issues, 391; Aroostook sugar beet project, 69–72; Clean Air Act emission standards and, 380–82; defense issues and, 384–90; graduation speeches of Mitchell, George, 517–19; labor-management relations, 397–99; Massachusetts and, 401; Mitchell, George, as Senator, and, 375–403, 412, 422; nursing home legislation, 352–53; scholarship funds of Mitchell, George, 519–28; transportation issues, 392–98. *See also specific Maine topics*

Maine Action Plan, 74, 75

Maine Christian Civic League, 222–23, 225

Maine Community Foundation, 520

Maine Democratic Party, 49; Coffin, Frank, and, 34–35, 38–44, 73, 79, 136; Mitchell, George, and, 72–79, 104–5, 136, 146, 176, 401–2; Muskie, Ed, and, 34–48, 50, 72–73, 79, 136; 1968 state convention, 71, 76–78; 1982 state convention speech by Mitchell, George, 176; state Senate 1982 sweeping victory, 182

Maine Democratic State Committee, 383

Maine governors: Brennan, 65, 138, 143–46, 156, 515; Curtis, 73–76,

78, 85, 105, 107, 108, 110, 114, 115, 143, 160, 161; Mitchell's 1974 governor's campaign, 31, 32, 104–24; Muskie, Ed, 34, 39, 40–47, 292. *See also specific Maine governors*

Maine Long Term Care Association, 352

Maine Management and Cost Survey, 115

Maine press: Mitchell, George, and, 244–45, 382–83. *See also specific Maine newspapers*

Maine Republican Party, 35–37, 41, 43–47, 53, 79, 114, 223

Maine Sports Hall of Fame, 496

Maine Sunday Telegram, 119, 175, 423

Maine Young Democrats, 107, 117

Maisel, Sandy, 105, 111, 120, 183, 468, 527

Major, John, 247, 430, 435, 436, 441, 442

Major League Baseball (MLB), 407, 485, 498–504

Major League Baseball commissioner. *See* baseball commissioner, MLB

Making Peace (Mitchell), 18, 410, 433, 442, 450

Makinson, Larry, 481

Malta Summit, 334

Manatt, Charles, 101

Mandela, Nelson, 343–44, 445

Mansfield, Mike, 48, 65, 84, 92, 194, 239, 246

Mansfield Room, 404, 409, 410, 422

Maroon, Paul, 14, 17

Marshall, John, 136

Marshall, Thurgood, 259, 261

Martin, John, 65, 79, 85, 145

Martin, Lynn, 227

Marx, Karl, 338

Massachusetts, and Maine, 401

Matthews, Eddie, 499

Maynard, Thomas, 104–5

McAleney, Mary, 396, 527; Mitchell, George, and, 168, 176, 183, 186, 188, 229, 242, 243, 353, 376, 391–92, 425, 521; on Mitchell, Sally, 237

McCain, John, 240, 257, 505

McCain-Feingold Act, 257, 417, 418

McCann, Colum, 450, 531

McCarthy, Eugene, 47, 86, 99

McCarthy, Joseph, 35–36, 40, 212–14

McCartney, Bob, 444

McEvoy, John, 62, 93, 267

McGaughey, Margaret, 38, 128–31, 133, 135

McGovern, George, 92, 93–95, 97, 98, 100, 105, 159

McGovern Commission, 93, 100, 109

McGuinness, Martin, 438, 444, 449

McIntire, Clifford, 58–59, 73

McKelvey, Charles "Smooth', 28

McKernan, John, 221, 352, 381, 430

McLaughlin, David, 492

McMahon, Dick, 40, 41, 56

McPherson, Harry, 90, 474, 481

Medicaid, 353, 355, 370

Medical Outcomes Research Act, 374

Medicare legislation, 358–59

Meese, Ed, 204, 215

Melley, Brendan, 454, 455, 458, 461, 462

Menard, Kevin, 132, 133

Men of Zeal (Cohen and Mitchell), 202, 203, 206–10, 218–19, 223

Merrill, Phil, 144, 146

Metzenbaum, Howard, 186, 240

Michel, Bob, 282

Micmac tribe, 354

Micoleau, Charlie, 73, 75–77, 84, 85, 91, 102, 115, 118, 135

Middle East, and George Mitchell, 451

Middle East envoy, George Mitchell as: for Bush, George W., 454, 459–60, 464–65; Clinton, Hillary, and, 465; 470; for Clinton, Bill, 453, 456, 460; features leading to position as, 347; for Obama, 130, 465–72; Sharm el-Sheikh Fact Finding Committee and, 453–64; State Department and, 431, 466

Mikulski, Barbara, 109, 198, 215, 218, 251, 353, 407, 411

Millennium Vodka, 476

Mills, Peter, 127, 129–30

Milwaukee Braves, 499

Milwaukee Brewers, 499

Minow, Nell, 485

Mitchell, Andrea (daughter), 32, 104, 237

Mitchell, Andrew MacLachlan (son), 439, 446

Mitchell, Barbara (sister), 8, 9, 10, 12, 16, 110; Mitchell, George, and, 20–21, 495, 509–10, 515, 520–21. *See also* Atkins, Barbara

Mitchell, Claire (daughter), 450

Mitchell, Edward (brother), 8

Mitchell, George John, Jr.: board memberships of, 481–85; book reading of, 16, 124, 263; career overview, 474; dating of, 25–26; friends of, 125–26; on international affairs, 531; leadership of, 2–3; life after retirement from office, 474, 530; presidential aspirations, 31, 426–28; public and personal style of, 123–24, 347–48; public service of, 529; stature after leaving Senate, 530–31. *See also specific topics*

Mitchell, George John, Sr. "Jiddoo" (father), 8–10, 21–22, 26, 62, 495; early years, 13–15

Mitchell, Heather (wife), 375, 438, 450, 465, 527; North Ireland peace talks and, 439. *See also* MacLachlan, Heather

Mitchell, Janet (Robbie's wife), 8, 9, 12, 16–19, 162, 237, 409, 438, 511

Mitchell, Jim (nephew), 12, 110, 401, 422

Mitchell, John (father's father), 14

Mitchell, John "Swisher" (brother), 120, 182, 413, 424; basketball and, 8, 19, 22, 155, 495, 515; early years, 8, 9, 12, 19, 495

Mitchell, Libby, 167, 402

Mitchell, Mary (father's mother), 14

Mitchell, Mary (mother), 6, 8, 11–13, 21, 68, 83, 111, 345, 346

Mitchell, Paul (brother), 20, 52; baseball and, 495; basketball and, 495; Mitchell, George, and, 7, 9, 11, 19, 147, 495, 496, 516, 521

Mitchell, Robert "Robbie" (brother), 157, 409, 516; business career, 18; death, 18, 438; early years, 8, 9, 16–19; tennis and, 17, 511

Mitchell, Sally Heath (wife): death of, 237; divorce from Mitchell, George, 237; Mitchell, George, meeting, 31, 104; Mitchell's politics and, 31–32, 111–12, 120, 147, 161, 183, 185, 237

Mitchell, Yvette, 20

Mitchell Amendment, 272–73, 279

Mitchell family, 83; early years, 5, 8–13, 15–22

Mitchell Friedman, Mary (niece), 83, 139, 497, 515, 526, 527, 529

Mitchell Institute, 378, 497, 515; scholarship fund, 523–28

Mitchell Principles, 437–38, 444, 445

Mitchell scholars, 522, 526–28

Mitchell Special Collections, Bowdoin, 528

MLB. *See* Major League Baseball

Model Cities Act, 20, 49, 53, 64–65

Mondale, Walter, 98, 268, 273

Monks, Robert A. G., 105, 126

Morning Sentinel, 164, 175

Mount Desert Island, 399–400

Mowlam, Marjorie "Mo," 443–44

Moynihan, Daniel, 175–76, 286, 287, 297–98; health care legislation and, 360, 361, 364, 367–70, 372, 373

Mudd, Roger, 101

Mulroney, Brian, 320

Murray, Steve, 139

Muskie, Ed: Aroostook sugar beet project and, 69–71; back pain of, 38, 61; broken back of, 37–38; Catholicism of, 44; "The Challenge of Liberal Consensus" speech, 89; Clean Air Act and, 5, 60, 142, 293, 309, 317; Clean Water Act and, 5, 9, 294–95; common themes of Mitchell, George, and, 63; death of, 438; at Democratic National Convention (1968), 77, 80–81; in DNC, 38; driving trips with, 54–57; environmental legislation and, 5, 9, 49, 60, 64, 118, 142, 149, 156, 171, 292–95; EPW and, 49, 142, 172, 292–94; Humphrey and, 48, 58, 72, 77, 78, 80–81, 83–84, 91, 97; LBJ and, 47–48, 50, 64, 65, 72, 91; legislation management by, 64; as liberal, 63, 253; Maine Democratic Party and, 34–48, 50, 72–73, 79, 136; Maine governorship campaign of, 40–44; in Maine legislature, 36–37; Maine Republican Party and, 44–47; as Maine's governor, 34, 39, 44–47, 292; as mentor to Mitchell, George, 5, 26, 64; Mitchell, George, and 1970 Senate reelection campaign of, 85, 87–88, 212; Mitchell, George, and 1972 presidential campaign of, 84, 88, 91–98, 154; Mitchell, George, and vice presidential campaign of, 77–78, 80–83; Mitchell, George, as federal judge and, 135, 137; Mitchell, George, as Senator and, 292, 293, 517; Mitchell, George, Senate campaign of 1982 and, 181–82; Mitchell, George, Senate reelection campaign of 1988 and, 224–25; Mitchell's appointment to Senate seat of, 29, 68, 144–50, 158, 163, 515, 530; Mitchell working for, 33–34, 51–61, 65–66, 68, 107, 158; Model Cities Program and, 20, 64–65; National Governors Association speech, 88–89; newspapers and candidacies of, 167; Nicoll and, 33, 35, 38–40, 42, 45, 51–54, 57–62, 64, 81, 84, 85, 92, 93, 98, 293, 294; as Office of Price Stabilization state director, 37; Pachios working for, 82–83; pain medication taken by, 61; presidential campaign (1972), 51, 55, 58, 60, 61, 81, 84, 88–100, 103, 154, 166, 427; Prestile Stream and, 71; as Secretary of State, 143, 145, 474; Senate Budget Committee and, 267; Senate committees and, 47–49, 153–54; Senate Public Works Committee and, 49, 292; Senate reelection campaign (1970), 84–88, 212–14; Senate reelection campaign (1976), 84, 85, 126, 142; as Senator, 47–66, 69–71, 84–88, 142–44, 152, 153, 474; shyness of, 62–63; staff of Senator, 152, 153, 155, 186, 188–89; televised address on 1970 election eve, 86–87, 212–14; temper of, 60–62; urban renewal and, 64–65; vice presidential campaign (1968), 25, 77–78, 80–84; Vietnam War and, 91, 92; Watergate and, 98–99; in Waterville, 10

Muskie, Irene, 60
Muskie, Jane, 10, 37, 55, 56, 61, 64, 83, 95
Muskie, Stephen (father of Ed Muskie), 36, 62, 82
Muskie, Stephen (son of Ed Muskie), 37
Myrick, Gary, 376, 413

NAFTA. See North American Free Trade Agreement
Nale, Thomas, 19
Nastase, Ilie, 405
National Collegiate Athletic Association (NCAA), 514–15
National Conservative Political Action Committee (NCPAC), 158–59
National Estuaries Program, 297
National Institutes of Health (NIH), 490
National Marine Fisheries Service, 390
National Organization for Women (NOW), 128
National Security Commission report, 487
naturalization ceremonies, 128, 140
Natural Resources Council of Maine, 303
Natural Resources Defense Council (NRDC), 310
NCAA. See National Collegiate Athletic Association
NCPAC. See National Conservative Political Action Committee
The Negotiator (Mitchell), 146, 219
Nelson, Ben, 374
Nelson, Gaylord, 301
Netanyahu, Benjamin, 467, 469–71
New Deal, 9, 22, 246, 266, 338, 419, 420
New York, 375
New York Times, 88, 137, 273, 290–91, 310, 449, 485, 508
New York Yankees, 496, 498, 502
Nexon, David, 356, 365–68, 370, 373

Nicaragua, 201, 202, 206, 210, 215, 328, 329. *See also* Iran-Contra scandal

Nicoll, Don, 36, 121, 141, 425; Muskie, Ed, and, *33*, 35, 38–40, 42, 45, 51–54, 57–62, 64, 81, 84, 85, 92, 93, 98, 293, 294

Niebuhr, Reinhold, 224

Nields, John, 208–9

NIH. *See* National Institutes of Health

Nixon, Richard, 50, 65, 202, 488; environmental legislation and, 293; Ford pardon of, 116–17; presidential campaign (1968), 81, 82, 84, 86, 87; presidential reelection campaign (1972), 91, 92, 94–95, 97–100, 114. *See also* Committee to Re-Elect the President; Watergate

Nobel Peace Prize, 445, 460

Noriega, Manuel, 328–29

North, Oliver, 201–2, 205–19, 225

North American Free Trade Agreement (NAFTA), 391

North American Wetlands Conservation Act, 318

North Ireland: Clinton, Bill, and, 430, 431, 434, 440, 445, 447, 448; economic conference with US, 431–33; Mitchell, George, and, 429–33, 449–50, 473; United Kingdom and, 429–30; US and, 430–49

North Ireland peace accord: as Good Friday Agreement, 445–49; Mitchell, George, and, 247, 430, 445–50, 468–69; tests of, 448–49

North Ireland peace talks: Mitchell, George, and, 430–43, 445–50, 468–69; Mitchell Principles in, 437–38, 444, 445; overview, 430–48; Pope, Martha, and, 435, 439–42, 444, 448

Not for America Alone (Mitchell), 10, 21, 338–39, 419–20, 529, 531

NOW. *See* National Organization for Women

nuclear freeze: Bush, George H. W., and nuclear testing freeze, 325; Emery and, 172–73; Gorbachev and nuclear testing freeze, 325; Mitchell, George, and, 171, 172–73, 322, 323, 325; Reagan and, 172, 323, 325. *See also* arms control

Nuclear Non-Proliferation Treaty, 323, 325

nuclear waste site, 379, 380

Nunn, Sam, 248, 260, 326

nursing home legislation: Federal Nursing Home Reform Act, 351–52, 359; in Maine, 352–53; Mitchell, George, and, 351–53; Spousal Impoverishment Act, 353

Obama, Barack, 373, 374; Clean Air Act and, 308–9, 318; Israeli-Palestinian negotiations and, 130, 465–70; Mitchell, George, as Middle East envoy for, 130, 465–72. *See also* Affordable Care Act

O'Brien, Brett, 347, 377, 386, 388

O'Brien, Larry, 64, 76, 102

obscenity laws, 132–33

O'Connor, Jane, 192

O'Donnell, Larry, 368

Office of Management and Budget (OMB), 270, 365

Office of Price Stabilization (OPS), 37, 38

oil spill prevention legislation, 299–301

oil tanker disasters, 299, 300

Oliver, Jim, 40, 43, 44, 50

Olmert, Ehud, 467, 469, 471

Olympics: Canada and corrupt selection process for, 512–13; Mitchell, George, report on scandal, 512, 513–14; Salt Lake City selection scandal, 512, 513–14

OMB. *See* Office of Management and Budget

O'Neil, Tim, 221, 511

OPS. *See* Office of Price Stabilization

Orloff, Germaine, 25, 26

Orloff, Paul, 16–18

Ortega, Daniel, 201

Oslo Accords, 453, 454, 460, 463

Otten, Les, 498

Oxford University, 520

ozone, 303, 305, 308, 315, 317, 381

Ozone Transport Zone, 381

PA. *See* Palestinian National Authority

Pachios, Harold "Hal," 71, 105, 136, 148, 150, 157, 170–71, 426–27, 477, 520; advice to Mitchell about Iran-Contra hearings, 209–10, 530; as friend to Mitchell, George, 31–32, 123, 125, 126, 250, 285, 383; Muskie, Ed, and, 82–83; at Preti Flaherty, 78, 139, 476; tennis and, 125, 510

Packwood, Bob, 154, 181, 245, 246, 254, 255, 260, 261, 373; on Senate Finance Committee, 271–72, 279, 414; tax reform and, 271–72

PACs. *See* political action committees

Paigen, Ken, 400

Paisley, Ian, 429, 434–36, 438, 441, 443–45, 449

Palestine Liberation Organization (PLO), 456, 466; Israel and, 451–53; Mitchell, George, and, 451, 452; UN and, 451. *See also* Israeli-Palestinian negotiations

Palestinian National Authority (PA), 453, 455, 466. *See also* Sharm el-Sheikh Fact Finding Committee

Palestinians, 472; Israel and, 451–54, 466–67, 473. *See also* Israeli-Palestinian negotiations

Panama crisis, 328–29

Pan Am Flight 103 explosion, 487–88

partisanship: Dole on, 256; of Mitchell, George, 255–57; partisanship wars climaxing in 1994, 257

Passamaquoddy Tribe, 144, 354

PATCO. *See* Professional Air Traffic Controllers Organization

Paterno, Joe, 514

Paulson, Greg, 351

Paygo, 285, 286, 287

Payne, Frederick, 36, 47, 52, 127, 129

Pearson, Mike, 182

Pease, Violet, 115

Pease Air Force Base, 387, 389

Pell, Claiborne, 327, 431

Pelosi, Nancy, 330

Penn State, and Sandusky sexual abuse scandal, 514

Penobscot Tribe, 144, 354

Pentagon, 53, 178, 340, 386, 490, 491

Pepper, John, 354, 486

Pepper Commission, 354, 364

Percy, Charles, 180, 322

Peres, Shimon, 460, 461

performance-enhancing drugs (steroids): in sports, 508–9. *See also* baseball steroid use

Perot, Ross, 415

Perry, William, 439

Persian Gulf War, 260, 284, 321, 339–43, 459

Peterson, Jeff, 295–99, 304, 318–19, 373, 410

Petrucelli, Gerry, 132, 135–36, 159

Picker, Arnold, 90

Pickup, Jim, 454, 492

Pierce, Samuel, 274

Piper Rudnick, 477–78

Pledge of Allegiance, 227

Plimpton, Lisa, 524

PLO. *See* Palestine Liberation Organization

Podesta, Tony, 89, 93
Poindexter, John, 205, 216
Point 10, 74–75
political action committees (PACs), 418; *Buckley v. Valeo* and, 414; Mitchell, George, and, 228, 414; NCPAC, 158–59; reform of, 414–17
Pope, Larry, 454, 457–59, 460, 464
Pope, Martha, 241, 314; Mitchell, George, and, 204, 217, 231, 235, 242, 243, 253, 276, 418, 422, 435, 439, 441–42, 448; North Ireland peace talks and, 435, 439–42, 444, 448
Popov, Gavril, 337
Porter, Jeff, 190, 191, 192, 227, 375, 500
Portland, Maine, 34, 52, 64, 68, 161, 299; debate in, 178, 179; Head Light lighthouse, 400; Jensen Baird in, 53, 67, 474; Mitchell, George, and, 104, 107, 110, 115, 122, 125, 126, 128–30, 134, 138, 150, 162, 178–79, 181, 182, 186, 187, 226, 377, 395, 399, 474, 476, 478, 509, 510, 515, 519, 521, 528; Model Cities program, 20, 120; Portland–South Portland bridge, 289, 393; Preti Flaherty in, 476; South Portland, 104, 122, 162, 186, 237, 289, 509, 515, 528; trains in, 394, 396, 397
Portland Press Herald, 68, 175, 310, 412
Portsmouth Naval Shipyard, 323, 384, 387–88
Potholm, Chris, 223, 228
Powell, Colin, 342, 459–60, 464
Pozorski, David, 431–33, 435, 436, 443, 445
Pratt & Whitney aircraft engine plant, 384
presidential aspirations, 31
Presque Isle, Maine, 66, 117, 377
Prestile Stream, 70–71

Preti Flaherty, 108, 125, 132; Mitchell, George, at, 476–77; Pachios at, 78, 139, 476
Primakov, Yevgeny, 334, 335
Professional Air Traffic Controllers Organization (PATCO), 397
Proxmire, William, 178
Pryor, David, 356, 360–61

Quayle, Dan, 317
Queens University, Belfast, 449, 466, 498
Quinn, Tom, 106
Quint, Colleen, 522, 525–26

Rabin, Yitzhak, 453, 460
Rath, Tom, 409
Reagan, Ronald, 87, 158, 159, 161, 221, 365; arms control and, 172, 323, 324; budget deficit of, 265, 268–71, 277; defense buildup of, 166, 170, 172, 227, 269, 322–23, 384, 385; environmental legislation and, 294, 295, 296, 298, 302–3, 305, 306; federal budget of, 177, 265, 268–71; Gorbachev and, 323; Iran-Contra scandal and, 201–3, 205, 206, 210, 214–16, 225; Iran-Iraq war and, 207, 326; labor-management relations and, 397–98; Medicare legislation and, 359; Mitchell, George, and, 166, 172, 173, 178, 224, 266–71, 294, 295, 298, 302–3, 305, 306, 322–24, 326–27, 392; nuclear freeze and, 172, 323, 325; reelection of, 195, 269; Social Security cuts and, 166, 168, 173, 267; Soviet Union and, 323; taxation and, 265, 267–70, 278; transportation issues and, 392, 397; War Powers Act and, 326–27
Red Cross. *See* American Red Cross
Red Sox. *See* Boston Red Sox

Reed, John, 49, 50, 70, 75, 76, 121
Reef, Grace, 273, 392–94, 396, 410, 529
Reef, Norman, 529
Reid, Harry, 200, 231, 252, 261
Reid, James, 129
Republican National Committee (RNC), 102
Republican Party, 87; tea party and, 532. *See also* Maine Republican Party; *specific topics*
Republicans: filibuster use by, 421; health care legislation and, 355–57, 359, 363–66, 369–73; Senate Majority Leader Mitchell and, 253; spending priorities of, 253. *See also specific topics*
Republican Senatorial Campaign Committee, 181, 220, 225
Republic of Ireland: George Mitchell Peace Scholars in, 527; partition of, 429, 433; United Kingdom and, 429–30, 433. *See also* British-Irish diplomacy; North Ireland peace accord
Reuther, Walter, 365
Reynolds, Paul, 382
Rhodes, Cecil, 520
Rhodes Scholarships, 520
Richards, Ann, 475
Richardson, Harry, 108, 114, 115, 120
Ridge, Steve, 130, 137
Riegle, Don, 248, 257
RNC. *See* Republican National Committee
Robb, Charles "Chuck," 200, 217, 233, 248, 253, 341–42
Rockefeller, Jay, 248, 262, 342, 356, 362, 372, 374, 497
Rockefeller, Nelson, 88
Roe v. Wade, 173, 223
Rolde, Neil, 114, 354
Romania, 405

Roosevelt, Franklin Delano, 7, 10, 22, 35, 266, 338–39, 420
Roosevelt, Theodore, 514
Rostenkowski, Dan, 359
Royal Ulster Constabulary (RUC), 430
Rozen, Bob, 268–75, 277–79, 281, 283, 284, 313, 373, 417, 418
Rubin, Robert, 331
Ruby, Donald, 129
RUC. *See* Royal Ulster Constabulary
Ruckelshaus, William, 303, 304
Rudman, Warren, 204, 208, 216, 253, 411–12, 487; Sharm el-Sheikh Fact Finding Committee and, 453–57
Rumford, Maine, 26, 36, 41, 56, 62
Russell, Richard, 236, 238
Russell Office Building, 190, 208
Russert, Tim, 369
Ruth, Babe, 498, 499
Ryan, Timothy, 259

Saad, Mintaha, 8, 12, 21. *See also* Mitchell, Mary
Saco Defense, 384
S&L. *See* savings and loan
S&L crisis, 257, 259, 280. *See also* Keating Five
Salt Lake City Olympics selection scandal, 512, 513–14
Sandinistas, 201, 206, 210, 328. *See also* Iran-Contra scandal
Sandusky, Jerry, 514
Sanford, Terry, 258
Sarbanes, Paul, 208, 230, 248–49
Sarcone, Pat, 243–44
Sasser, Jim, 236, 250, 284, 336; Mitchell, George, and, 102, 195–97, 230, 233, 240, 248, 276, 282–83, 289, 329, 411; Senate Budget Committee and, 240, 275–76, 281, 287
satellite communication, 33

savings and loan (S&L), 257; bailout, 259, 280. *See also* S&L crisis
Sawyer, Herb, 69
Schilling, Curt, 508
scholarship funds, of Mitchell, George, 519–28
Scott Paper Co., 5, 519
Scowcroft, Brent, 345
SDLP. *See* Social Democratic and Labour Party
Sebasticook River, 6
Second Intifada, 454
Secord, Richard, 215
Secretary of State: Mitchell, George, as potential, 439–40; Muskie, Ed, as, 143, 145, 474. *See also specific Secretaries of State*
Securities and Exchange Commission, 293
Selig, Bud, 499, 500, 501, 502, 504–5, 508
Senate, 185, 238; courting of Senators in leadership races, 232; deputy president pro tempore, 204, 231; president pro tempore, 204, 231; television and, 221
Senate Appropriations Committee, 221, 230, 233
Senate Armed Services Committee, 260, 384
Senate Banking Committee, 153, 178
Senate Budget Committee, 275, 278; Mitchell, George, and, 150, 267, 268; Muskie, Ed, as chairman of, 63, 107, 143, 267; Sasser and, 240, 275–76, 281
Senate committees, 1; Kennedy, Ted, and, 249; Mitchell, George, and chairs of, 248; Mitchell, George, on, 153; Muskie, Ed, and, 47–49, 153; weekly prayer breakfast for chairmen

of, 194. *See also specific Senate committees*
Senate Democratic Conference. *See* Democratic Conference
Senate Democratic Policy Committee. *See* Democratic Policy Committee
Senate Democratic Steering Committee. *See* Democratic Steering Committee
Senate Environment and Public Works Committee (EPW), 303; Mitchell, George, and, 153, 172, 193, 292, 294–96, 298, 301, 304, 306–9, 319, 321, 392, 394; Muskie, Ed, and, 49, 142, 172, 292–94
Senate Ethics Committee, 189; Keating Five and, 257, 258
Senate Finance Committee, 287; Dole on, 239, 241, 268, 270; health care legislation and, 353, 356, 361, 362, 364, 365, 367, 369, 371, 372, 374; health care subcommittee, 350–54, 356, 365, 372; Mitchell, George, and, 150, 153–54, 185–86, 193, 239, 241, 266–68, 271, 272, 292, 319, 350; Packwood and, 271–72, 279, 414
Senate Foreign Relations Committee, 322, 327
Senate Health, Education and Labor Committee (HEL), 353, 365, 366
Senate Intelligence Committee, 236, 242, 326; Iran-Contra scandal and, 202, 203, 205
Senate Judiciary Committee, 136, 259
Senate Majority Leader, 265; Byrd as, 220–21, 230, 232–35, 239, 245–46, 248–51, 414; Democratic Caucus and, 248; Dole as, 271, 273, 420–21; LBJ as, 47–48, 236, 238–39, 252; race for 1988, 220–21, 230–37
Senate Majority Leader, George Mitchell as, 238, 322, 368; agricultural issues

and, 391; AIPAC and, 452, 453; Berlin visit of, 29–30, 335; Bush, George H. W., and, 246, 247, 251, 256, 258–61, 276–86, 306, 307, 311–17, 328–33, 339–43, 346, 357–58, 423, 452, 488; capital punishment and, 383; China and, 329–32; Clinton, Bill, and, 124, 259, 261–62, 288–91, 331, 359–63, 367, 370, 372, 404, 408, 412–13, 423; crime bill and, 383; debating skills of, 252–53; decisiveness of, 256; Democratic Caucus and, 248, 250, 262; Democratic Conference and, 249, 250; Democratic opposition to, 383; Democratic Policy Committee and, 250, 251; Democratic Steering Committee and, 250; duties, 328; effectiveness of, 257; on flag-burning, 254–55; foreign policy and, 327–47; Gorbachev and, 323, 332–39; Keating Five and, 257, 258, 259, 280; leadership style of, 248, 250–53; Maine and, 375–77, 422; Mandela and, 343–44; NAFTA and, 391; news media and, 244–45; 1988 race for, 220–21, 230–37; Pan Am Flight 103 explosion and, 488; partisanship of, 255–57, 411; Persian Gulf War and, 260, 284, 339–43; persuasion of, 249; PLO and, 451, 452; policy objectives, 246–47; Republicans and, 253; retirement from Senate, 372, 377, 404–5, 407–13, 418, 422–27, 482, 530; Senate committee chairs and, 248; Senate opposition to, 328; Senate rules and, 247, 251–52; single life of, 262–63; skill in removing obstacles, 248; Soviet Union and, 246, 323, 332–39; staff of, 241–44, 283, 347–48, 375–78, 409–10; trade and, 330, 331; tributes to retiring,

422–26. *See also* Senator, George Mitchell as

Senate Minority Leader, Dole as, 200, 239–41, 258, 288

Senate Public Works Committee, 49, 188, 292. *See also* Senate Environment and Public Works Committee

Senate rules: on amendments, 247; on debate, 247; Mitchell, George, and, 247, 251–52; on presidential nomination holds, 247. *See also* filibusters

Senate select committee, on Iran-Contra, 202–9, 215–16

Senate Veterans Affairs Committee, 29, 153, 174, 175

Senator, George Mitchell as, 529; abortion and, 173–74, 181, 229; acid rain and, 149, 166, 171–72, 294, 301, 302, 305, 307, 315; affordable housing and, 274–75; aid to constituents, 380; appointment to Muskie's seat, 29, 68, 144–50, 158, 163, 515, 530; Arenberg and, 194–95, 204–5, 218, 230, 232, 257, 376; arms control and, 172, 323, 324, 325; budget deficit and, 224, 247, 253, 265, 269–71, 276, 278, 280, 282, 288, 289; Byrd and, 155, 192–95, 197, 202–5, 221, 230, 234, 235, 245, 246, 248–51, 305, 312–14, 326, 412; campaign brochure and slogan, 224; campaign finance and, 183–84, 185, 225, 228, 257, 414–18; campaign of 1982, 71, 157–85, 220; campaigns, 29; campaign staff for, 167, 171; as centrist or liberal, 253–54; Clean Air Act and, 6, 60, 64, 244, 256, 293, 299, 301, 302, 304–18, 320, 380–82; Clean Water Act and, 6, 64, 295–98; climate change and, 320, 321;

constituents of, 377–80; cool persona with staff, 347–48; correspondence of, 378–79; cot story of, 164–65, 245; cow jokes of, 163–64; debates with Emery, 178, 179; debates with Wyman, 228; decision-making of, 194–95; defense issues and, 166, 172, 179, 227, 384–90; defense spending and, 166, 172, 179, 227, 386–90; departure from Senate, 351; as deputy president pro tempore, 204, 231; Dewhirst and, 188, 197, 221–22, 237, 240, 244–45, 252, 300, 304–5, 329, 330, 332, 351; Dole and, 200, 239–41, 245, 247, 251, 252, 255, 256, 270, 335, 346, 363, 371–73, 423, 474–75, 488; as DSCC chair, 195–200, 220, 230, 231; early days as, 149–57, 164–65; economic issues and, 265–66, 276; electronic political database of, 168; endorsements of, 181; environmental legislation and, 149, 172, 293–320; EPW and, 153, 172, 292, 294–96, 298, 301, 304, 306–9, 319, 321, 392, 394; federal budget and, 224, 247, 253, 265, 269–71, 276, 278, 280–86, 288–91; federal finances and, 265–66; field hearings in Maine, 379–80; filibusters and, 164–65, 421; Finance health care subcommittee and, 350–54, 365; fish inspection bill of, 390–91; foreign policy and, 322–47; fundraising, 169–70, 185, 220, 224, 225, 227, 228; graduation speeches of, 517–19; gun legislation and, 382–83; health care legislation and, 354–67, 369–74, 404, 408, 420; Iran-Contra scandal and, 201–14, 216–20, 223–25, 230, 530; Israel and, 451–53; Jensen and, 57, 152–53, 157, 166, 189–91, 193, 227, 242, 243, 331, 344, 410, 413,

518; Johnson, David, and, 150–53, 155, 157, 163, 170, 173, 177, 179, 180, 183, 194, 196, 220, 379, 520; labor-management relations and, 397–98; Lebanon and, 345–47; Maine and, 375–403, 412, 422; Maine and legislation of, 380–82; Maine press and, 244–45, 382–83; McAleney and, 168, 176, 183, 186, 188, 229, 242, 243, 353, 376, 391–92, 425; Middle East and, 451; Muskie, Ed, and, 292, 293, 517; Muskie, Ed, and 1982 campaign of, 181–82; Muskie, Ed, and 1988 reelection campaign of, 224–25; newspapers and Senate campaign of, 167–68; 1986 election and, 196–200; nuclear freeze and, 171, 172–73, 322, 323, 325; nursing home legislation and, 351–53; oil spill prevention legislation and, 299–301; PACs and, 228, 414; personal habits of, 157; political ads for, 166–67; polling on, 225–26, 228; Reagan and, 166, 172, 173, 178, 224, 266–71, 294, 295, 298, 302–3, 305, 306, 322–24, 326–27, 392; reelection campaign (1988), 220–29; religion story of, 165; salaries of staff, 191–92; on Senate Banking Committee, 153, 178; Senate Budget Committee and, 150, 267, 268; on Senate committees, 153; Senate Democratic friends of, 248–49; Senate Finance Committee and, 150, 153–54, 185–86, 193, 239, 241, 266–68, 271, 272, 292, 319, 350; on Senate Veterans Affairs Committee, 29, 153, 174, 175; Sewall, Sarah, and, 187, 221–22, 324–28, 331, 333–35, 341–43, 345, 347–49, 430, 452, 520; Social Security and, 166, 168, 171, 173, 185–86, 266–68, 287, 289; Southern senators and, 232; spending

priorities, 173, 253; staffers from
Maine, 375–77; staff of, 150–55, 186–
92, 269, 273, 309, 343–44, 347–48,
375–80, 426; storytelling and humor
of, 163; taxation and, 226, 265, 268,
270–86, 288–89; tax reform and,
271–75; town hall meeting of, 378;
transportation issues and, 392–98;
UN and, 451–52; veterans affairs and,
29, 153, 174–75; view of government,
224; visitors from Maine and, 377–78;
War Powers Act reform legislation
and, 326–27; women on staff of, 188–
90. *See also* Senate Majority Leader,
George Mitchell as
SEOG. *See* Supplemental Educational
Opportunity Grant
September 11 attacks: American Red
Cross and, 489–94; Bush, George
W., and, 487; commission on, 487,
488–89; Mitchell, George, and, 477,
486–89, 492–94
Sewall, Joe, 119, 146, 162, 182
Sewall, Loyall, 187, 221–22, 324, 348
Sewall, Sarah, 337, 340, 344, 386;
Mitchell, George, and, 187, 221–22,
324–28, 331, 333–35, 341–43, 345,
347–49, 387, 430, 452, 520
Shapiro, Sam, 501
Sharm el-Sheikh Fact Finding
Committee: Bush, George W., and,
454, 459–60, 464; Clinton, Bill,
and, 453–56, 459, 460; Mitchell,
George, and, 453–64; report, 461–64;
Rudman and, 453–57; staff, 454, 461
Sharon, Ariel, 454, 457, 460, 461, 463,
466, 467
Shelby, Richard, 261
Sheppard, Audrey, 196, 197
Sherlock, Pat, 121–22
Shields, Mark, 88, 100, 244
Shiro, Ted, 509

Shrum, Bob, 89
Shultz, George, 215
Sierra Club, 310
Sigma Nu, 24
Silsby, Paula, 128, 129, 130, 133,
140–41, 186
Simon, Paul, 322
Simpson, Alan, 154, 199, 236, 255–56,
285, 305–7, 310, 316, 342, 412, 420,
425, 530
Sinn Fein, 434–36, 438, 441, 443–45,
448, 449
Six Day War, 451
Smith, Fred, 482
Smith, George, 174–75, 176, 179, 183
Smith, Margaret Chase, 35–36, 40, 44,
105, 129, 142, 145, 238, 379, 402–3;
"Declaration of Conscience" speech,
212–14
Snowe, Olympia, 133, 159, 160, 177,
183, 187, 221, 373, 422, 522
Social Democratic and Labour Party
(SDLP), 434, 445, 449
Social Security: Bush, George H. W.,
and, 286–87; changes to payroll
withholding for, 286–87; Clinton, Bill,
and, 289; cost-of-living adjustments,
289; Emery and, 173; Mitchell,
George, and, 166, 168, 171, 173,
185–86, 266–68, 287, 289; Reagan
and cuts to, 166, 168, 173, 267;
surpluses used for deficit reduction,
286, 288; surpluses used for spending,
286–88; Trust Fund, 288
Solana, Javier, 453, 457
Sontag, Frederick, 118
Souter, David, 204, 259, 409
South Africa, 343–44
Soviet Union: Mitchell, George, and,
246, 323, 332–39; Reagan and, 323.
See also Gorbachev, Mikhail
Spahn, Warren, 499

Speedy Trial Act, 139

Spence, Gusty, 444

Spitzer, Eliot, 492–93

sports: cribbage, 516; Maine Sports Hall of Fame, 496; Mitchell, George, competitiveness in, 509; NCAA and Mitchell, George, 514–15; Penn State and Sandusky sexual abuse scandal, 514; performance-enhancing drugs in, 508–9; "Teddy" award for Mitchell, George, 514–15. *See also* baseball; basketball; Olympics; tennis

Spousal Impoverishment Act, 353

Spring, Dick, 430–31, 442

Squier, Bob, 225–26

Stafford, Robert, 149, 182

Stangeland, Arlan, 298

Stark, Pete, 352

State Department, 35, 431, 466

Stemberg, Tom, 482

Stennis, John, 221, 230, 231

Stern, Ed, 424

Stern, Jason, 424–25

Stern, Marshall, 424–25

steroid use. *See* baseball steroid use

Stevens, John Paul, 254

Stevens, Ronnie, 496

Stevens, Ted, 390, 412

Stewart, Joe, 231

St. Joseph Maronite School, 15

St. Joseph's Church, 11, 21

Stockman, David, 270, 365

Strauss, Robert, 100–103

Sturbitts, Charlene, 149, 188, 190, 293–94, 301–4, 368, 407, 420

Sullivan, Brendan, 208, 209, 212

Sunrise at Campobello, 266

Sununu, John, 259, 261, 281, 282, 284, 306, 314, 426, 488

Superfund, 304

Supplemental Educational Opportunity Grant (SEOG), 522

Supreme Court: *Buckley v. Valeo*, 183, 414; Bush, George H. W., nominations to, 258–59, 261; *Bush v. Gore*, 204; campaign finance and, 414, 418; *Citizens United v. Federal Election Commission*, 418; on flag-burning, 254, 255; Mitchell, George, refusal of nomination to, 408–9; *Roe v. Wade*, 173, 223; Thomas, Clarence, nomination to, 258–59, 261

Symms, Steve, 256, 260, 279, 316, 319, 322, 394, 425

Syria, 346

The System (Broder and Johnson), 357, 361, 365, 368, 370, 419

Taft, Robert, 238

Talmadge, Maine, 229

Tartre, Ann, 243, 302

taxation: Bush, George H. W., and, 276–85, 288; capital gains tax, 272–73, 276–80, 284; Clinton, Bill, and, 288–89; Mitchell, George, and, 226, 265, 268, 270–86, 288–89; Reagan and, 265, 267–70, 278

tax reform: affordable housing and, 274–75; Bradley and, 272, 273, 285; flat tax, 271; Mitchell, George, and, 271–75; Mitchell Amendment, 272–73, 279; Packwood and, 271–72

Taylor, Elizabeth, 165

Taylor, John, 436

"Teddy" award, 514–15

Temple Mount, 463

tennis: MacLachlan and, 405, 406; Mitchell, George, and, 21, 125–26, 150–51, 405–6, 509–12; Mitchell, Robert, and, 17, 511; Pachios and, 125, 510; US Open tournament, 405

terrorism: National Security Commission report on, 487; Pan Am Flight 103

explosion, 487–88; September 11
attacks, 477, 486–94

Thadani, Ramesh, 490–91

Thatcher, Margaret, 429, 430, 434, 442

Thomas, Clarence, 258–59, 261

Thomas, Frank, 506, 507, 508

Thomas, Lee, 304

Thurmond, Strom, 136

Tiananmen Square, 329–31

Tierney, Jim, 480

Tirac, Ion, 405

tobacco industry, 480–81

Toibin, Colm, 531

Toll, Maynard, 152

Topsham-Brunswick Bypass, 393

Tower, John, 65, 202, 259–60, 388

Tower Commission, 202, 203, 205, 225

trade: cap and trade system, 311–12;
with China, 330, 331; Mitchell,
George, and, 330, 331; NAFTA, 391

Trafton, Barbara, 167, 170, 253

train issues, 394–98

Trainriders/Northeast, 395, 397

Transatlantic (McCann), 531

transportation issues, 392–98

Travelers Insurance, 30, 32

Trible, Paul, 178

Trimble, David, 429, 434–36, 444–46,
449

Trout, Mike, 508

Truman, Harry, 37, 213–14, 232, 236

Tsongas, Paul, 194–95

Tupper, Stan, 74

Tureen, Tom, 138

Turner, Jesse, 346

Tyrer, Bob, 162, 180, 217, 378–79, 408,
425

Ulster Unionist Party (UUP), 436, 444,
449

Umphrey, Lee, 431, 432, 440

UN. *See* United Nations

Union Leader, 94, 95, 96

United Kingdom: North Ireland and,
429–30; Republic of Ireland and,
429–30, 433; US-British extradition
treaty, 430. *See also* British-Irish
diplomacy; North Ireland peace talks

United Nations (UN): General Assembly,
451, 452; Israel and, 451–52; Mitchell,
George, and, 451–52; PLO and, 451

United States (US): current international
affairs and, 531; Israeli-Palestinian
negotiations and, 452–67; Mitchell,
George, on political system of, 532;
North Ireland and, 430–49; US-
British extradition treaty, 430. *See also*
specific US topics

University of Bologna, 518

University of Maine: aspirations
conference, 519; Mitchell Scholars at,
522; School of Law graduation speech
by Mitchell, George, 517; System,
521, 527

University of Rhode Island, 19, 495

University of Southern California (USC),
482

urban renewal, 20, 64–65

US. *See* United States

US attorney for Maine, George Mitchell
as, 103, 127, 135, 136, 139, 140;
antiques burglary ring case, 131; drug
cases, 131–32; legal discrimination
and, 133–34; obscenity cases,
132–33; phone answering of, 130,
131; remarks at swearing in, 128; self-
promotion distaste of, 134; staff of,
128–29

USC. *See* University of Southern
California

US Olympic Committee (USOC), 512,
513–14

U.S. v. Menard, 132

UUP. *See* Ulster Unionist Party

Vahlsing, Freddie, 66, 69–72, 527

Valentine, Barry, 113

Vance, Cyrus, 90, 143

Vermont, 391

Verner Liipfert, 474–77

Verrill Dana, 32, 129

veterans affairs: Emery and, 174–75; Mitchell, George, and, 29, 153, 174–75; Senate Veterans Affairs Committee, 29, 153, 174, 175

Veterans of Foreign Wars (VFW), 174–75

Vietnam War, 76–77, 82, 92, 104–5, 344, 414

Vincent, Fay, 499

Violette, Elmer, 145

V. Lance Tarrance & Associates, 159

Volcker, Paul, 502

Waldorf Astoria Hotel, 261, 454, 455

Wallace, George, 96, 97, 98, 137

Walsh, Lawrence, 206, 216

Warner, John, 165, 217, 245, 316, 342, 394, 468

War Powers Act, 246, 325–27

Washington at Work (Cohen, Richard), 312

Washington Post, 82, 95, 147, 207, 244, 289, 314, 449, 467, 469, 485, 502, 508

Watergate, 90, 94, 98–100, 102–3, 114, 116–18, 414

Water Quality Act of 1987, 298

Waterville, Maine: Concourse, 11, 20; Educare Center, 521; Front Street, 5, 9, 10, 17, 83, 111, 516; growing up in, 7–23; Head of Falls, 5, 10, 11, 12; Lebanese community, 5, 8, 11, 12, 14, 15, 17, 468; Muskie, Ed, in, 10; urban renewal in, 20

Waterville Boys Club, 5, 10, 16, 18

Waterville High School, 10, 15

Waterville Rotary Club, 161

Wathen, Dan, 72, 127, 135, 140, 527

Waxman, Henry, 308, 352

The Ways of a Judge (Coffin), 135

Webster, William, 511

Weil, Gordon, 147, 389, 390, 427

Weinberger, Caspar, 215, 216

Wellersdieck, Beryl, 25–26

Wells, Frank, 482

Wellstone, Paul, 343

Werner, Tom, 498

Wertheimer, Fred, 414–18, 481

West Bank, 451, 453, 466, 467, 471–73

Westwood, Jean, 100–101

White, Byron, 408

White, Wallace, 238

White House Task Force on Health Care Policy, 361–63, 366

Whittemore, Dick, 19, 515

Whitten, Elvira, 15–16, 520, 521, 528

Will, George, 502

Williams, Christine "Chris," 376, 409–10; health care legislation and, 350–59, 362, 364, 369, 371, 372, 374, 400, 420, 497

Williams, Karen, 188

Williams, Ted, 496, 504

Wilson, Woodrow, 238

Winslow paper mill, 519

Wishcamper, Joe, 275

Wofford, Harris, 194, 354, 368, 411, 422, 468

Wolfe, Sidney, 358

Woodward, Bob, 95, 96

Woodward, Tim, 205

World on Fire (Mitchell), 305, 306, 309, 320, 321

World Series, 497, 498, 499, 502, 503

World Trade Center, 486, 490

Wright, Jim, 189, 257

Wyman, Jasper "Jack," 222–23, 225–29

Yakovlev, Aleksandr, 335, 336
Yang Ye, 330
Yawkey, Jean, 497
Yawkey, Tom, 497

Yawkey Charitable Trust, 497–98
Yeltsin, Boris, 336–37

Ziffren, Paul, 169